Enhancing the Scholarship of Teaching and Learning in Online Learning Environments

Regina Rahimi
Georgia Southern University, USA

Lina Soares
Georgia Southern University, USA

IGI Global
Scientific Publishing
Publishing Tomorrow's Research Today

Vice President of Editorial	Melissa Wagner
Managing Editor of Acquisitions	Mikaela Felty
Managing Editor of Book Development	Jocelynn Hessler
Production Manager	Mike Brehm
Cover Design	Phillip Shickler

Published in the United States of America by
IGI Global Scientific Publishing
701 East Chocolate Avenue
Hershey, PA, 17033, USA
Tel: 717-533-8845
Fax: 717-533-8661
Website: https://www.igi-global.com E-mail: cust@igi-global.com

Library of Congress Cataloging-in-Publication Data

Names: Rahimi, Regina, 1971- editor. | Soares, Lina Bell, editor.
Title: Enhancing the scholarship of teaching and learning in online learning environments / Edited by Regina Rahimi, Lina Soares.
Description: Hershey, PA : IGI Global Scientific Publishing, [2025] | Includes bibliographical references and index. | Summary: "This edited volume will highlight SoTL (Scholarship of Teaching and Learning) projects related to teaching and learning within online educational spaces"-- Provided by publisher.
Identifiers: LCCN 2024055673 (print) | LCCN 2024055674 (ebook) | ISBN 9798369375952 (hardcover) | ISBN 9798369375969 (paperback) | ISBN 9798369375976 (ebook)
Subjects: LCSH: Web-based instruction. | Transformative learning. | Learning and scholarship. | Education--Computer-assisted instruction.
Classification: LCC LB1028.57 .E54 2025 (print) | LCC LB1028.57 (ebook) | DDC 371.33/44678--dc23/eng/20250116
LC record available at https://lccn.loc.gov/2024055673
LC ebook record available at https://lccn.loc.gov/2024055674

British Cataloguing in Publication Data
A Cataloguing in Publication record for this book is available from the British Library.

Table of Contents

Preface xiii

Acknowledgement xix

Chapter 1
Advancing Pedagogical Excellence: Strategies for Enhancing SoTL in Digital Classrooms 1
Semiu Olawale Makinde, Al-Hikmah University, Ilorin, Nigeria

Chapter 2
Transforming Pedagogy: Best Practices for SoTL in Online Learning Environments 21
Muhammad Usman Tariq, Abu Dhabi University, UAE & University College Cork, Ireland

Chapter 3
Leveraging a Scholarship of Teaching and Learning Values Framework to Build Online Faculty Learning Communities 47
Alesia Mickle Moldavan, Georgia Southern University, USA
Kevin J. Reagan, Georgia Southern University, USA
Diana Botnaru, Georgia Southern University, USA
Anna C. Brady, Georgia Southern University, USA
Bailey Nafziger, Georgia Southern University, USA
Jackie Mesenbrink-Sainz, Georgia Southern University, USA

Chapter 4
Engaging in SoTL Through Faculty Learning Communities: Implementing "Small Teaching Practices" to Improve Graduate Online Courses 75
Regina Rahimi, Georgia Southern University, USA
Lina Bell Soares, Georgia Southern University, USA

Chapter 5
Professional Development Focused on Teaching and Learning in Online Environments 95
R. Velmurugan, Karpagam Academy of Higher Education, India
J. Sudarvel, Karpagam Academy of Higher Education, India
R. Bhuvaneswari, Dr. Mahalingam College of Engineering and Technology, Pollachi, India
Ravi Thirumalaisamy, Modern College of Business and Science, Oman

Chapter 6
A Higher Education Scholarship of Teaching and Learning Online Community of Practice 119
Sue A. Sharpe, Australian National University, Australia
Jennifer Z. Sun, University of Sydney, Australia
Trisha L. Poole, University of Southern Queensland, Australia
Phuc Diem Le, RMIT Vietnam, Vietnam
Melissa J. Saligari, University of Melbourne, Australia
Deb K. Clarke, Charles Sturt University, Australia

Chapter 7
Building Community and Engagement in Online Nursing Education: Strategies and Challenges 151
Tiago Manuel Horta Reis da Silva, King's College London, UK

Chapter 8
Interactive Activity Communications That Support Course Implementation and Instructional Engagement: Creating Digital Spaces in Distance Education 177
Janice Newsum, University of Houston-Clear Lake, USA
Sharon K. Andrews, University of Houston-Clear Lake, USA
Caroline M. Crawford, University of Houston-Clear Lake, USA

Chapter 9
Elaborative Encoding as a Teaching Tool in Online Learning Environments: Making It Meaningful Makes It Memorable 227
Alyson Froehlich, University of Utah, USA

Chapter 10
E-Teaching via an Online Flipped Class on Facebook Group: During COVID-19 Pandemic and Beyond 263
Faiza Benaicha, GSLSD Research Lab, Abdelhamid Ibn Badis University, Algeria
Rafik El Amine Ghobrini, DSPM Research Lab, Abdelhamid Ibn Badis University, Algeria
Khadidja Boudour, DSPM Research Lab, Abdelhamid Ibn Badis University, Algeria
Abed Hamadouch, DSPM Research Lab, Abdelhamid Ibn Badis University, Algeria

Chapter 11
Connecting Adult Learners: The Role of Communication Tools in an Adv MPH Online 295
Jonathan Zaccarini, Mailman School of Public Health, Columbia University, USA
Roxanne Russell, Mailman School of Public Health, Columbia University, USA

Chapter 12
Revolutionizing Community Engagement and Impact With AI 323
Margaret S. Sass, Boise State University, USA
Brian Martin, Boise State University, USA

Chapter 13
Nurturing a Socio-Emotionally Engaged Learner in Higher Education Online Setting: Rapid Literature Review 353
Nymisha Yadati, Christ University, India
Benny Thomas, Christ University, India
Santhosh Kareepadath Rajan, Christ University, India

Compilation of References 375

About the Contributors 439

Index 447

Detailed Table of Contents

Preface xiii

Acknowledgement xix

Chapter 1
Advancing Pedagogical Excellence: Strategies for Enhancing SoTL in Digital Classrooms 1
Semiu Olawale Makinde, Al-Hikmah University, Ilorin, Nigeria

This chapter explores strategic initiatives to advance the Scholarship of Teaching and Learning (SoTL) in digital classrooms, with a focus on promoting pedagogical excellence. It offers educators practical, evidence-based strategies to enhance teaching effectiveness, boost student engagement, and improve learning outcomes in online environments. Drawing on recent research, case studies, and best practices, the chapter provides a roadmap for educators navigating the complexities of digital teaching. It emphasizes the importance of using digital tools and pedagogical innovations to foster interactive and inclusive learning experiences. The chapter also highlights the role of reflective teaching practices and continuous professional development in refining instructional methods. Offering a comprehensive guide to both theory and practice, it equips educators with essential tools to succeed in the evolving digital education landscape, ultimately enhancing student achievement and success.

Chapter 2
Transforming Pedagogy: Best Practices for SoTL in Online Learning Environments 21
Muhammad Usman Tariq, Abu Dhabi University, UAE & University College Cork, Ireland

The improvement of educational practices in virtual spaces is the focus of this chapter's exploration of the Scholarship of Teaching and Learning (SoTL). It offers a thorough introduction to SoTL highlighting its significance in the context of online learning for both teachers and students. Exploring cutting-edge techniques that enhance student engagement and learning outcomes the chapter explores best practices for successful online teaching backed by research and case studies. In addition, the chapter looks at how online educators should always be improving their professional development and how to use professional learning communities (PLCs) to promote collaboration. It also discusses the value of having students participate in SoTL projects and the advantages of having learners involved in these endeavours. Common issues that educators run into when conducting SoTL online are covered along with workable fixes and effective case studies.

Chapter 3
Leveraging a Scholarship of Teaching and Learning Values Framework to Build Online Faculty Learning Communities 47
Alesia Mickle Moldavan, Georgia Southern University, USA
Kevin J. Reagan, Georgia Southern University, USA
Diana Botnaru, Georgia Southern University, USA
Anna C. Brady, Georgia Southern University, USA
Bailey Nafziger, Georgia Southern University, USA
Jackie Mesenbrink-Sainz, Georgia Southern University, USA

Scholarship of Teaching and Learning (SoTL) enhances teaching practices and improves student learning outcomes while fostering a culture of continuous professional development and reflective practice (Felten, 2013; Hutchings et al., 2011; Trigwell et al., 2000). Faculty Learning Communities (FLCs) serve as dynamic hubs for collaborative exchange, enabling faculty to engage with SoTL principles, share diverse perspectives, and develop innovative teaching strategies that benefit learners (Cox, 2004). This chapter examines an online SoTL FLC at a multi-campus institution as a case study to propose a SoTL Values Framework to guide best practices in online professional development. The framework is built on four key values: inclusivity, collaboration, scholarly approach, and reflectiveness, each aligned with unique opportunities offered by the online environment. By drawing on SoTL literature and reflecting on the experiences within this online SoTL FLC, the chapter offers insights to inform future online SoTL initiatives fostering sustained growth in SoTL practices.

Chapter 4
Engaging in SoTL Through Faculty Learning Communities: Implementing "Small Teaching Practices" to Improve Graduate Online Courses...................... 75
Regina Rahimi, Georgia Southern University, USA
Lina Bell Soares, Georgia Southern University, USA

In the spirit of the scope of this book, this chapter highlights the potential impact collaborative faculty work can have on course design and pedagogy for online graduate students. The chapter describes the development and implementation of a faculty learning community (FLC) engaged in discussions centered on "small teaching practices" and the knowledge gleaned from the collaborative experience that will inform our practice. Emphasizing collaborative faculty engagement, our Scholarship of Teaching and Learning (SoTL) project has sought to strengthen our online graduate students' learning experiences and support their learning needs.

Chapter 5
Professional Development Focused on Teaching and Learning in Online Environments 95
R. Velmurugan, Karpagam Academy of Higher Education, India
J. Sudarvel, Karpagam Academy of Higher Education, India
R. Bhuvaneswari, Dr. Mahalingam College of Engineering and Technology, Pollachi, India
Ravi Thirumalaisamy, Modern College of Business and Science, Oman

Professional development focused on teaching and learning in online environments is crucial in equipping educators with essential skills for digital education. This abstract explores the significance of ongoing training in mastering technological tools, addressing unique challenges of online teaching, incorporating best practices, and fostering reflective practice. Mishra and Koehler's TPACK framework guides educators in integrating technology effectively, while Guskey emphasizes support for maintaining engagement and academic integrity. Darling-Hammond advocates for personalized learning experiences, and Wenger highlights the role of communities of practice in fostering collaboration. Effective professional development ensures educators deliver high-quality education, enhancing student learning outcomes in virtual settings.

Chapter 6
A Higher Education Scholarship of Teaching and Learning Online Community of Practice 119
Sue A. Sharpe, Australian National University, Australia
Jennifer Z. Sun, University of Sydney, Australia
Trisha L. Poole, University of Southern Queensland, Australia
Phuc Diem Le, RMIT Vietnam, Vietnam
Melissa J. Saligari, University of Melbourne, Australia
Deb K. Clarke, Charles Sturt University, Australia

To improve global rankings, increase student numbers and enhance the quality of teaching and learning, Australian Higher Education institutions have increased emphasis on faculty to engage in the scholarship of teaching and learning (SoTL). However, there is an absence of SoTL capacity-building opportunities to support those with limited knowledge of, and engagement with SoTL. This lack of support has broad implications for scholars' identity, professional confidence and capacity to undertake SoTL. Using collective autoethnography, the chapter showcases the experiences of eight scholars who participated in a two-year SoTL online community of practice, aimed at building SoTL capacity. Results indicated increased confidence, refashioned scholarly identity, institutional recognition of SoTL and leadership skills, and heightened professional self-worth. The chapter yields key messages for those mentoring SoTL scholars, and those adopting a community of practice approach to professional learning. More pointedly, the chapter provides recommendations for institutional policy and practice.

Chapter 7
Building Community and Engagement in Online Nursing Education: Strategies and Challenges 151
Tiago Manuel Horta Reis da Silva, King's College London, UK

In the digital era, online nursing education offers unprecedented opportunities for flexible learning, yet fostering a sense of community and engagement remains a challenge. This chapter explores the strategies to build robust communities in online nursing programs, focusing on creating emotional connections, active participation, and collaborative learning. Emotional Intelligence (EI) is emphasised as a crucial skill for both educators and students in fostering a supportive online environment. The integration of essential nursing topics such as chronic and acute conditions, into the online curriculum presents unique pedagogical opportunities and challenges. The chapter also examines the role of online education in advancing Sustainable Development Goals (SDGs), particularly those related to health and well-being. Finally, it highlights best practices in online teaching that support the development of emotional resilience, holistic care approaches, and interdisciplinary collaboration, all while preparing nursing professionals for the complexities of modern healthcare.

Chapter 8
Interactive Activity Communications That Support Course Implementation and Instructional Engagement: Creating Digital Spaces in Distance Education 177
Janice Newsum, University of Houston-Clear Lake, USA
Sharon K. Andrews, University of Houston-Clear Lake, USA
Caroline M. Crawford, University of Houston-Clear Lake, USA

Three participants come together in a multiple case study approach, to analyze learner-focused and instructor-focused interactive activities within distance learning environments. Instructors and learners are considered from an instructor perspective, reflecting upon specific experiences, implementing and facilitation communication dynamics in distance education courses, from a learner experience and an instructional facilitator experience. Equally impactful is the consideration towards the extent that distance education has changed during the participant's careers as embedded in the higher education field. Additionally, consideration towards generative artificial intelligence, large language models as considerations towards machine learning, and simulations, are considered as current and future considerations within distance education course implementation and instructional facilitation efforts. Emphasized are significant gaps in practice and gaps in the literature.

Chapter 9
Elaborative Encoding as a Teaching Tool in Online Learning Environments: Making It Meaningful Makes It Memorable 227
Alyson Froehlich, University of Utah, USA

This chapter surveys elaborative encoding as a tool for enhancing learning in online environments. By connecting to-be-learned information to learners' pre-existing knowledge, elaborative encoding facilitates deeper understanding and better retention of materials ranging from simple to complex. Research on elaborative encoding has explored various methods applicable to online learning environments; five will be examined here: elaborative interrogation, self-explanation, use of the self-reference effect, use of analogies, and etymological elaboration. The chapter shares practical ideas to encourage elaborative encoding in learners, considering both synchronous and asynchronous elements. The goal is to equip instructors with effective techniques to foster meaningful and memorable learning in their online learning environments.

Chapter 10
E-Teaching via an Online Flipped Class on Facebook Group: During COVID-19 Pandemic and Beyond 263
Faiza Benaicha, GSLSD Research Lab, Abdelhamid Ibn Badis University, Algeria
Rafik El Amine Ghobrini, DSPM Research Lab, Abdelhamid Ibn Badis University, Algeria
Khadidja Boudour, DSPM Research Lab, Abdelhamid Ibn Badis University, Algeria
Abed Hamadouch, DSPM Research Lab, Abdelhamid Ibn Badis University, Algeria

Amidst the global pandemic of Covid-19, the shift towards online learning has become inevitable for students, especially for those who will sit for the Baccalaureate exam -secondary school graduation exam. To address this, a web-designed research method was opted for to develop an online flipped virtual classroom that can enhance secondary school students' engagement and provide them with the adequate assistance needed to prepare for this crucial exam. The web-driven solution was refined in every iteration through the continuous feedback of 52 students from 8 different provinces in Algeria. By the end, 25 secondary school teachers were invited to the Facebook group to share their perspectives on this web-enhanced online method of teaching and validate the framework through a self-reported questionnaire. The findings report an approved framework of how to practically leverage the flipped model in an online-only setting along with the implications it holds on a local and global scale.

Chapter 11
Connecting Adult Learners: The Role of Communication Tools in an Adv MPH Online 295
Jonathan Zaccarini, Mailman School of Public Health, Columbia University, USA
Roxanne Russell, Mailman School of Public Health, Columbia University, USA

Higher education institutions need to adapt to new technology and new student demographics; however, this requires careful consideration of communication tools among adult learners. The main focus of this chapter is to examine the need for communication tools, along with asynchronous and synchronous learning activities, and how they contribute to peer social presence amongst adult learners within an online graduate public health program. Student experiences with using Yellowdig and Zoom will be discussed, using data from a survey focus group. Results show that these adult learners were able to perceive impressions of each other and build a community while completing the first year of their graduate program. This chapter extends the findings on student perceptions of technology facilitated social presence within text-centered environments; however, additional research is needed using larger student samples within online graduate public health programs.

Chapter 12
Revolutionizing Community Engagement and Impact With AI 323
Margaret S. Sass, Boise State University, USA
Brian Martin, Boise State University, USA

The evolution of artificial intelligence (AI) has profoundly impacted education, particularly in service-learning (SL) and community-based learning (CBL). This chapter explores how AI enhances these pedagogical approaches by enabling educators to design innovative, community-based assignments and projects. It highlights AI's role in addressing equity and access challenges, encouraging engagement, and supporting personalized learning experiences for diverse student populations. The chapter discusses how AI tools assist in curriculum development, real-world problem-solving, and stakeholder collaboration while emphasizing the importance of ethical considerations in AI integration. Grounded in the Scholarship of Teaching and Learning (SoTL), this work underscores AI's potential to transform experiential education, advancing both student success and meaningful community impact.

Chapter 13
Nurturing a Socio-Emotionally Engaged Learner in Higher Education Online Setting: Rapid Literature Review 353
Nymisha Yadati, Christ University, India
Benny Thomas, Christ University, India
Santhosh Kareepadath Rajan, Christ University, India

Given the growth of online learning courses in higher education, there is a need to understand the role of Social-Emotional Learning (SEL) in online learning spaces to ensure holistic development. This rapid literature review aims to identify factors influencing SEL among higher education students in online space. PRISMA method of screening was adopted to conduct this review. Four databases were systematically searched and, 23 studies were selected. The findings highlighted the importance of five factors contributing to nurturing a socio-emotionally engaged learner in an online higher education setting: student-centric pedagogy, online instructional tools, online instructors' proficiency, ensuring a safe learning environment, and online SEL workshops. Research on online SEL is developing and needs a clearer structure. Integration of scholarship of teaching-learning with online SEL can provide directions for further exploration into content knowledge, pedagogical knowledge and building a mutually engaged online learning space focusing on students' social-emotional well-being.

Compilation of References 375

About the Contributors 439

Index 447

Preface

In recent years, the Scholarship of Teaching and Learning (SoTL) has emerged as a transformative force in education, offering educators and researchers invaluable insights into effective teaching practices and learner engagement. The rapid expansion of online learning environments has further amplified the need to explore how SoTL principles can be applied in virtual spaces. *Enhancing the Scholarship of Teaching and Learning in Online Learning Environments* aims to address this critical need by presenting a collection of innovative and thought-provoking projects that examine teaching and learning within online educational spaces.

This volume brings together a diverse range of perspectives and methodologies, showcasing how instructors and learners engage in the study of teaching and learning in virtual environments. By highlighting the work of scholars actively engaged in SoTL, we hope to provide a resource that not only demonstrates effective practices but also inspires further exploration and application in online learning settings.

We are pleased to present chapters that represent a variety of disciplines, demonstrating the interdisciplinary nature of SoTL. The approaches detailed within this text reflect the creativity and dedication of educators who are passionate about advancing teaching and learning practices in the digital age. From fostering meaningful learner engagement to addressing challenges unique to online education, these contributions offer practical insights and strategies that educators can adapt and implement in their own contexts.

We envision this book as a valuable resource for educators, researchers, and professional learning communities seeking to enhance their understanding of teaching and learning in online environments. Whether you are new to SoTL or a seasoned practitioner, the perspectives and findings presented here will provide inspiration and practical guidance for improving educational experiences in virtual spaces.

We extend our deepest gratitude to the contributors for their scholarly efforts and innovative ideas. Their work not only enriches the field of SoTL but also underscores the importance of continuous learning and adaptation in an ever-evolving educational landscape.

We invite you, the reader, to delve into these chapters with an open mind and a curiosity to explore the possibilities that SoTL offers in online learning environments. May this volume serve as a catalyst for reflection, dialogue, and innovation in your own teaching and learning practices.

ORGANIZATION OF THE BOOK

Chapter 1: Advancing Pedagogical Excellence: Strategies for Enhancing SoTL in Digital Classrooms

In this chapter, educators are provided with a strategic roadmap to enhance the Scholarship of Teaching and Learning (SoTL) within digital classrooms, emphasizing pedagogical excellence. Through evidence-based strategies, the chapter explores ways to boost teaching effectiveness, increase student engagement, and improve learning outcomes. Leveraging recent research, case studies, and best practices, it advocates for interactive and inclusive learning experiences supported by digital tools and innovative pedagogies. Reflective teaching practices and continuous professional development are highlighted as key components for evolving instructional methods. This comprehensive guide equips educators to navigate and excel in the rapidly changing digital education landscape, fostering greater student success and achievement.

Chapter 2: Transforming Pedagogy: Best Practices for SoTL in Online Learning Environments

This chapter examines how the Scholarship of Teaching and Learning (SoTL) can drive the improvement of online educational practices. By delving into cutting-edge techniques and research-backed strategies, it highlights approaches to enhance student engagement and learning outcomes in virtual environments. The chapter underscores the significance of continuous professional development and the value of Professional Learning Communities (PLCs) for collaborative growth. Additionally, it explores the benefits of involving students in SoTL projects and addresses common challenges faced by educators, offering practical solutions and successful case studies to inspire transformative pedagogy in online learning.

Chapter 3: Leveraging a Scholarship of Teaching and Learning Values Framework to Build Online Faculty Learning Communities

Focusing on faculty development, this chapter introduces a SoTL Values Framework to guide best practices in online Faculty Learning Communities (FLCs). Drawing on the experiences of an online SoTL FLC at a multi-campus institution, it identifies four core values: inclusivity, collaboration, scholarly approach, and reflectiveness. Through these principles, educators can foster professional growth and innovation in teaching practices. By integrating insights from SoTL literature and practical reflections, the chapter provides a blueprint for future initiatives that build and sustain SoTL capacity, enhancing both faculty collaboration and student learning outcomes in online environments.

Chapter 4: Engaging in SoTL through Faculty Learning Communities: Implementing "Small Teaching Practices" to Improve Graduate Online Courses

This chapter illustrates the collaborative potential of Faculty Learning Communities (FLCs) in refining online graduate courses. By focusing on "small teaching practices," the chapter highlights how these targeted strategies, combined with faculty discussions and shared experiences, can enhance course design and pedagogy. It underscores the transformative power of SoTL projects in supporting graduate students' learning needs and improving their overall educational experience, advocating for collaborative approaches to foster meaningful, student-centered teaching innovations.

Chapter 5: Professional Development Focused on Teaching and Learning in Online Environments

This chapter emphasizes the critical role of professional development in equipping educators to thrive in digital teaching environments. Grounded in theoretical frameworks such as TPACK and supported by experts like Guskey and Darling-Hammond, it explores strategies for mastering technological tools, addressing online teaching challenges, and fostering reflective practices. Communities of practice are presented as vital for collaboration, ensuring educators can deliver high-quality education. By integrating personalized learning approaches and best practices, the chapter underscores the transformative potential of professional development for enhancing student outcomes in online learning.

Chapter 6: A Higher Education Scholarship of Teaching and Learning Online Community of Practice

Through the lens of collective autoethnography, this chapter explores the impact of an online SoTL Community of Practice (CoP) on eight scholars at Australian higher education institutions. It highlights the challenges of limited SoTL capacity-building opportunities and showcases how participation in the CoP bolstered scholarly identity, confidence, and professional skills. By detailing the transformative outcomes for participants, including institutional recognition and leadership development, the chapter provides actionable recommendations for mentors and institutions aiming to adopt a CoP approach to SoTL capacity building and professional learning.

Chapter 7: Building Community and Engagement in Online Nursing Education: Strategies and Challenges

This chapter addresses the challenges of fostering community and engagement in online nursing education. It highlights strategies that emphasize emotional intelligence, active participation, and collaborative learning to create supportive digital spaces. By integrating essential nursing topics with innovative pedagogical approaches, the chapter aligns online education with Sustainable Development Goals (SDGs), particularly those focused on health and well-being. Best practices for nurturing emotional resilience, holistic care, and interdisciplinary collaboration are presented, equipping nursing educators to prepare students for the demands of modern healthcare.

Chapter 8: Interactive Activity Communications that Support Course Implementation and Instructional Engagement: Creating Digital Spaces in Distance Education

Using a multiple case study approach, this chapter examines the role of interactive activities in distance education. By reflecting on the experiences of instructors and learners, it identifies key communication dynamics that support engagement and course implementation. The chapter also explores the transformative potential of generative AI and machine learning in future distance education practices. Addressing gaps in both literature and practice, it provides actionable insights for designing effective digital spaces that enhance learning and teaching experiences.

Chapter 9: Elaborative Encoding as a Teaching Tool in Online Learning Environments: Making It Meaningful Makes It Memorable

This chapter delves into the cognitive strategy of elaborative encoding, highlighting its potential to deepen understanding and improve knowledge retention in online environments. By exploring five specific methods—elaborative interrogation, self-explanation, self-reference effect, analogies, and etymological elaboration—the chapter offers practical techniques for fostering meaningful learning. With applications for both synchronous and asynchronous learning, it equips instructors to create impactful educational experiences that resonate with online learners.

Chapter 10: E-Teaching Via an Online Flipped Class on Facebook Group During Covid-19 Pandemic and Beyond

This chapter presents a case study of an innovative online flipped classroom model developed for Algerian secondary school students during the Covid-19 pandemic. Utilizing a Facebook group as the platform, the approach was refined through student feedback and validated by teachers. The findings outline a practical framework for leveraging the flipped model in online settings, emphasizing its implications for enhancing engagement and academic preparation on both local and global scales.

Chapter 11: Connecting Adult Learners: The Role of Communication Tools in an Adv MPH Online

Focusing on adult learners in a Master of Public Health (MPH) program, this chapter investigates the role of communication tools in fostering peer social presence. Using platforms like Yellowdig and Zoom, the study highlights how asynchronous and synchronous activities contribute to community building and student engagement. The chapter provides insights into the effective use of technology to enhance social interactions and collaborative learning among graduate students, while advocating for further research on larger cohorts.

Chapter 12: Revolutionizing Community Engagement and Impact with AI

This chapter explores the transformative role of artificial intelligence (AI) in enhancing service-learning (SL) and community-based learning (CBL). It discusses AI's capacity to address equity challenges, support personalized learning, and foster meaningful community impact through innovative curriculum design. Grounded in

SoTL principles, the chapter emphasizes ethical considerations in AI integration and showcases its potential to revolutionize experiential education, advancing student success and societal benefits.

Chapter 13: Nurturing a Socio-emotionally Engaged Learner in Higher Education Online Setting: Rapid Literature Review

This chapter conducts a rapid literature review on Social-Emotional Learning (SEL) in online higher education environments, emphasizing its importance for holistic student development. By identifying factors that influence SEL, it provides a foundation for creating inclusive and supportive digital spaces that prioritize socio-emotional engagement. This exploration underscores the need for SEL integration in online learning to enhance both academic and personal growth.

CONCLUSION

As editors of this volume, we have sought to bring together a diverse array of voices and perspectives to illuminate the transformative potential of the Scholarship of Teaching and Learning (SoTL) in digital classrooms. Each chapter in this collection demonstrates the innovative strategies, evidence-based practices, and collaborative frameworks that empower educators to meet the challenges of modern online education. From fostering socio-emotional connections to leveraging advanced technologies like artificial intelligence, the contributions herein illustrate the dynamic interplay of pedagogy, technology, and community in enhancing teaching and learning outcomes.

We hope this book serves as a catalyst for further exploration and inspires educators, researchers, and policymakers to embrace the opportunities that SoTL offers for professional growth and student success in the digital age. As the landscape of education continues to evolve, it is our shared responsibility to create learning environments that are inclusive, engaging, and transformative. It is our belief that the insights presented here will contribute meaningfully to this ongoing endeavor, equipping educators with the tools to innovate and thrive in an ever-changing educational world.

Acknowledgement

We wish to acknowledge our Editorial Review Board members who served as chapter reviewers for this text.

Yasar Bodur
Shelli-Casler Failing
Kip Sorgen
Deloris Liston
Amee Adkins
Ming Fang He
Antonio Gutierez de Blume
Juli Mcbrayer
Alisa Leckie
Cynthia Bolton-Gary
Dan Calhoun
Rachael Smith
Alesia Moldavan
Devon Jernigan
John Hobe

Chapter 1
Advancing Pedagogical Excellence:
Strategies for Enhancing SoTL in Digital Classrooms

Semiu Olawale Makinde
https://orcid.org/0000-0001-5456-3464
Al-Hikmah University, Ilorin, Nigeria

ABSTRACT

This chapter explores strategic initiatives to advance the Scholarship of Teaching and Learning (SoTL) in digital classrooms, with a focus on promoting pedagogical excellence. It offers educators practical, evidence-based strategies to enhance teaching effectiveness, boost student engagement, and improve learning outcomes in online environments. Drawing on recent research, case studies, and best practices, the chapter provides a roadmap for educators navigating the complexities of digital teaching. It emphasizes the importance of using digital tools and pedagogical innovations to foster interactive and inclusive learning experiences. The chapter also highlights the role of reflective teaching practices and continuous professional development in refining instructional methods. Offering a comprehensive guide to both theory and practice, it equips educators with essential tools to succeed in the evolving digital education landscape, ultimately enhancing student achievement and success.

DOI: 10.4018/979-8-3693-7595-2.ch001

INTRODUCTION

In today's fast-paced world of technological change, the landscape of teaching and learning is shifting dramatically. Digital tools and platforms have become integral to educational environments, presenting both challenges and opportunities for educators and students. With the rise of digital classrooms, the demand for innovative pedagogical approaches that foster active learning, student engagement, and retention has become increasingly important. At the forefront of this transformation is the Scholarship of Teaching and Learning (SoTL), a reflective and research-based approach that focuses on improving educational practices through evidence-driven inquiry. SoTL, building upon Boyer's (1990) foundational work on the scholarship of teaching, encourages educators to systematically examine and refine their teaching methods to enhance student learning outcomes.

In digital learning environments, SoTL takes on an even greater significance as it offers a structured framework to help educators navigate the unique challenges of online education. These digital settings differ from traditional classrooms in various ways, particularly in how students interact, how content is delivered, and how learning is assessed. Digital education often demands new teaching strategies that cater to the diverse needs of students while utilizing technology to promote collaboration and engagement (Koehler et al., 2013). Through the adoption of SoTL practices, educators can evaluate the effectiveness of digital tools and teaching techniques, ensuring they are aligned with sound educational principles while addressing the evolving needs of learners in virtual environments.

A core aspect of SoTL is its emphasis on continuous improvement. Through ongoing reflection, educators can determine what works effectively in digital classrooms and what areas need further development. This often involves gathering and analyzing data on student performance, participation, and satisfaction, which can be used to inform future teaching decisions (Felten, 2013). In online environments, learning analytics play a crucial role in SoTL, enabling educators to monitor student progress, identify areas where students may be struggling, and tailor instruction to improve learning outcomes (Yang et al., 2024). Incorporating data-driven approaches into teaching practice is essential for advancing both teaching and learning in digital settings. Moreover, SoTL fosters collaboration among educators, helping to build a culture of shared learning and innovation. The digital classroom offers unique opportunities for educators to collaborate beyond geographical boundaries, participating in professional learning communities that facilitate the sharing of effective teaching practices (Bates, 2019). These communities create a platform for the exchange of ideas, strategies, and research, allowing educators to collectively address the challenges of digital teaching while contributing to the advancement of online education.

As the presence of digital education continues to grow, SoTL will remain a key factor in helping educators achieve pedagogical excellence. This chapter explores the strategies for strengthening SoTL in digital classrooms, focusing on the importance of reflective practice, data-driven decision-making, and collaborative inquiry. By embracing these strategies, educators can not only enhance their own teaching methods but also contribute to the ongoing conversation about the future of education in the digital age.

FOUNDATION

This chapter showcases multiple effective pedagogical strategies to enhance online learning via the Scholarship of Teaching and Learning (SoTL) in digital classrooms. The literature was sourced from a range of reputable academic databases, including Scopus, Web of Science, Google Scholar, and ResearchGate. To ensure a comprehensive exploration of the topic, the review incorporated a variety of academic materials, such as peer-reviewed journal articles, conference proceedings, books, book chapters, and expert reports. These sources were selected based on their relevance to SoTL, online education, and pedagogical strategies for digital learning environments. The analysis was structured around four key areas.

First, the significance of SoTL in improving teaching and learning in digital classrooms was explored. This included examining how SoTL promotes reflective and evidence-based teaching practices, allowing educators to continuously assess and refine their teaching methods. This section focused on the importance of SoTL in fostering continuous professional development and creating a framework for systematic inquiry into online teaching effectiveness.

Second, the chapter investigated the role of technology in supporting active learning and student engagement in digital classrooms. The literature on various digital tools, including Learning Management Systems (LMS) like Moodle and Canvas, interactive platforms, multimedia resources, and gamification strategies, was reviewed. The analysis also examined how these technologies facilitate active learning by offering students interactive and personalized learning experiences that are adequate for different learners of diverse learning styles and preferences.

Third, inclusive course design strategies were investigated, with particular attention on Universal Design for Learning (UDL). Designing online courses that effectively serve learners from diverse backgrounds and with varying abilities is crucial for ensuring equitable access to education. By implementing the core principles of Universal Design for Learning (UDL) which include offering multiple means of engagement, representation, and action/expression, educators can create digital learning environments that are both accessible and adaptable to individual learner needs. These principles play a crucial role in fostering accessible and adaptable digital learning environments.

Finally, the chapter explored the application of data analytics in online education. Studies on the use of learning analytics to track student progress, engagement, and performance were analyzed to understand how data-driven insights can inform instructional decisions and improve learning outcomes. The role of predictive analytics in identifying at-risk students and enabling timely interventions was also examined, offering strategies for improving student retention and success in digital settings.

This review provided a thorough and nuanced understanding of the challenges and opportunities presented by digital learning environments. By synthesizing insights from SoTL, technology integration, inclusive design, and data analytics, the chapter offers evidence-based strategies for enhancing teaching effectiveness and student learning outcomes in online education.

UNDERSTANDING SOTL IN DIGITAL CLASSROOMS

Definition and Significance of SoTL

SoTL is a systematic and reflective process focused on evaluating and improving teaching practices to enhance learning outcomes. It originates from Boyer's (1990) idea of scholarly teaching - SoTL encourages educators to investigate teaching methods through research and evidence, focusing on how best to support student learning in various settings. Within digital classrooms, SoTL provides a framework for evaluating and refining instructional strategies, helping educators adapt to technological changes and the diverse needs of online learners.

SoTL's importance lies in its role in promoting continuous growth and innovation in education. By engaging in SoTL, teachers adopt an investigative mindset, using research and reflection to identify and implement the most effective strategies for fostering student success. This approach leads to better engagement, higher student achievement, and more effective learning environments (Collins, 2023). In digital education, where the dynamics of teaching and learning differ greatly from traditional methods, SoTL plays a crucial role in addressing these unique challenges while maximizing the benefits of technology-enhanced learning.

The Unique Challenges and Opportunities in Digital Teaching and Learning

Digital classrooms bring about distinct challenges that require tailored strategies to ensure success for both instructors and students. A significant challenge is the absence of in-person interaction, which can make it difficult to build strong connections between educators and learners. Furthermore, online students may face difficulties with self-discipline, motivation, and maintaining engagement due to the independent nature of digital learning environments (Khumalo, 2024). Technical issues, such as unstable internet access and unfamiliarity with digital tools, can further complicate the online learning experience.

Despite these challenges, digital classrooms also provide unique advantages that traditional learning environments may lack. For example, online platforms allow for flexible learning schedules, enabling students to access course materials when it suits them. This flexibility supports inclusivity, catering to various learning preferences and personal circumstances (Yılmaz & Malone, 2020). Additionally, the use of digital tools opens up opportunities for innovative teaching methods like personalized learning, gamification, and multimedia resources, which can greatly boost student engagement and overall learning outcomes.

SoTL offers a structured approach for educators to systematically address these challenges and capitalize on the opportunities in digital education. By incorporating SoTL practices, educators can develop research-driven strategies that improve their online teaching techniques and promote better student results. For instance, teachers can study the effects of specific digital tools or pedagogical approaches in virtual settings, contributing to the growing body of knowledge on effective online education practices.

The Role of SoTL in Enhancing Online Education Quality

SoTL plays a pivotal role in improving the quality of online education by encouraging educators to continuously evaluate and enhance their teaching methods using empirical data. Through SoTL, instructors engage in a cycle of inquiry, experimentation, and reflection, which enables them to identify effective teaching strategies and improve student learning outcomes. This scholarly process ensures that teaching approaches remain relevant, responsive to change, and grounded in research (Fanghanel et al., 2016). In the fast-evolving context of digital classrooms, where new technologies and tools emerge frequently, SoTL offers a structured way for educators to assess the effectiveness of these innovations. By applying SoTL principals and teachers can evaluate how well online platforms and technologies support student learning and pinpoint areas that require improvement. This not only improves the quality of individual courses but also contributes to the broader understanding of best practices in online education.

In summary, SoTL provides a robust framework for educators who aim to enhance teaching and learning in digital classrooms. By fostering a culture of inquiry and continuous reflection, SoTL equips educators to overcome the specific challenges of online education while leveraging its opportunities to improve student learning outcomes.

EFFECTIVE STRATEGIES FOR ADVANCING PEDAGOGICAL EXCELLENCE

Integrating Technology to Support Active Learning and Engagement

The incorporation of technology into education has fundamentally changed traditional learning environments, creating new opportunities to promote active learning and student engagement. Active learning is an instructional approach where students actively participate in their own learning process, leading to improved comprehension and retention of information (Freeman et al., 2014). Technology significantly facilitates active learning by offering interactive tools like quizzes, discussion boards, simulations, and collaborative platforms is essential for effective technology integration. A primary approach to achieving this is through Learning Management Systems (LMS), which enable students to engage with course content at their own pace while enabling engaging activities such as peer collaboration and instant feedback (Mayer, 2020). Instructors can leverage digital tools to cultivate environments that encourage exploration, experimentation, and reflection. For instance, the use of multimedia resources, like videos and simulations, can enhance the learning experience by making complex concepts more relatable and engaging. Moreover, gamification—where elements of games are incorporated into the learning process—can greatly boost student motivation and engagement. Tools such as Kahoot and Quizlet introduce competitive and reward-based features into learning, keeping students engaged and active throughout their courses.

Designing Interactive and Inclusive Online Courses

The success of an online course is primarily influenced by its design, which must aim to engage and include all students. An inclusive design ensures that learners from diverse backgrounds and with varying abilities can fully participate in the learning experience. The Individuals with Disabilities Education Act (IDEA, 2004) expanded the concept of Universal Design (UD) to educational environments, leading to the development of Universal Design for Learning (UDL). According to Centre for Applied Special Technology ([CAST], 2021) in 2020, UDL is founded on three core principles: providing multiple means of engagement, presenting information in different ways, and offering various options for action and expression. These principles align with the brain's unique learning networks (CAST, 2021). UDL is often applied to online course design to accommodate a range of learning styles and needs. By promoting flexibility in how students access materials, engage with content, and demonstrate their understanding, UDL ensures that no learner is left behind (Rosa Plata, 2020).

Interactive online courses frequently feature discussion forums, live sessions, group work, and peer reviews to encourage collaboration and foster a sense of community. These components help mitigate the feelings of isolation that can accompany online learning, prompting students to take an active role in their education. Additionally, adaptive learning technologies—platforms that personalize content based on individual learner performance—enhance interaction by providing tailored support to meet each student's unique needs (Beetham & Sharpe, 2013). Furthermore, accessibility tools such as screen readers, captioning services, and alternative text descriptions for images make course materials more inclusive for students with disabilities. The use of varied multimedia formats and flexible assessment methods ensures that all learners can engage with the content in ways that align with their abilities and preferences.

Utilizing Data Analytics to Inform Teaching Practices and Improve Student Outcomes

Data analytics has become an essential tool for enhancing teaching effectiveness by offering key insights into student behavior, performance, and engagement can be gained through learning analytics. Educators can collect and analyze data on how students interact with course content, track their progress, and identify patterns that highlight areas where they may be struggling. This evidence-based approach enables timely interventions, allowing instructors to deliver targeted support and resources aimed at improving student outcomes (Yang et al., 2024).

For instance, educators can leverage data analytics to track student involvement in online discussions, evaluate the frequency and duration of logins to the course platform, and monitor assignment and assessment completion rates. These insights empower instructors to modify their teaching strategies, provide additional resources when necessary, and tailor the learning experience to meet the individual needs of students. Additionally, predictive analytics can identify students who may be at risk of falling behind, enabling instructors to take proactive steps and offer assistance before problems escalate. This method fosters a more responsive learning environment, where student success is actively promoted through data-driven teaching practices (Yang et al., 2024).

INNOVATIVE TEACHING TECHNIQUES AND APPROACHES

Flipped Classrooms and Blended Learning Models

The flipped classroom model has become increasingly popular as an effective educational strategy that alters the conventional learning sequence. In this approach, direct instruction—often delivered via lectures or presentations—is moved outside the classroom, usually through pre-recorded videos or reading materials. This allows students to learn at their own pace. Consequently, classroom time is dedicated to interactive, hands-on activities that encourage deeper comprehension, critical thinking, and problem-solving skills (Makinde, 2023). By coming to class prepared, students can participate in more engaging, student-centered learning experiences.

Blended learning models merge online education with face-to-face instruction, resulting in a flexible and dynamic learning environment. These models integrate digital tools with traditional teaching methods, providing students with the advantages of both self-directed online learning and collaborative, instructor-led sessions in a classroom setting (Palmerola, 2024). Blended learning facilitates differentiated instruction, enabling students to revisit online resources, receive immediate feedback through digital quizzes, and engage in discussions that extend beyond the physical classroom.

Both the flipped classroom and blended learning approaches enhance student engagement, create personalized learning opportunities, and offer greater flexibility. These methods accommodate various learning styles and allow instructors to use class time more effectively for practical activities that reinforce the material.

Gamification and Game-Based Learning in Online Settings

Gamification and game-based learning are innovative strategies that leverage the motivational aspects of games to enhance student engagement and improve educational outcomes. Gamification refers to the integration of game elements—such as points, badges, and leaderboards—into non-game educational activities, making learning more enjoyable and interactive (Deterding et al., 2011). In contrast, game-based learning involves using actual games as part of the educational process, allowing students to learn through game mechanics like challenges, quests, and problem-solving scenarios.

In online learning environments, gamification can be implemented on digital platforms where students earn rewards for completing assignments, engaging in discussions, or mastering concepts. This not only boosts motivation but also fosters a sense of accomplishment and competition, driving higher levels of engagement. Game-based learning, utilizing interactive simulations or educational games, allows students to explore concepts in a low-stakes, immersive setting. For example, tools like Classcraft or Minecraft Education enable educators to create game-based experiences that align with curriculum goals while promoting creativity and collaboration.

Research indicates that gamification and game-based learning can enhance cognitive skills, increase retention, and improve student attitudes towards learning (Hassan, 2024). These strategies make learning more dynamic, particularly in online environments where maintaining student engagement can often be challenging.

Collaborative and Social Learning through Digital Platforms

Collaborative and social learning emphasizes the importance of interaction, communication, and shared experiences in the learning process. In digital classrooms, these concepts are facilitated through various online platforms that enable students to work together, share ideas, and construct knowledge collectively. Tools such as discussion forums, wikis, and collaborative software like Google Docs or Microsoft Teams foster peer interaction and group collaboration, which are essential components of a constructivist learning environment (Vygotsky, 1978).

Social learning platforms such as Edmodo or Slack enable students to engage in real-time discussions, share resources, and work together on group projects, thereby extending learning beyond the boundaries of the physical classroom. These platforms support a more interactive, student-centered approach, where learners are encouraged to co-create knowledge and reflect on their understanding through dialogue and collaboration.

The use of social media platforms like Twitter or private Facebook groups in education can also promote informal learning, where students can engage in discussions, ask questions, and share insights with both peers and instructors. Such platforms encourage a community of practice where learning is continuous, collective, and driven by the exchange of knowledge among participants (Mehdizadeh et al., 2024).

By leveraging collaborative and social learning tools, educators can create a more inclusive and participatory learning environment that fosters deeper understanding and peer support. These approaches are particularly beneficial in online and blended learning settings, where physical separation can be mitigated by robust, interactive digital engagement.

ASSESSMENT AND EVALUATION IN ONLINE LEARNING

Effective Online Assessment Strategies

In online learning environments, assessment plays a crucial role in evaluating student progress and understanding, while also guiding instructional decisions. To be effective, online assessment strategies must align with learning objectives and provide diverse opportunities for students to showcase their knowledge and skills. Quizzes and tests are common assessment methods, offering immediate feedback and the potential for automation in large-scale evaluations (Zhan et al., 2024). However, moving beyond traditional exams, authentic assessments—such as projects, case studies, and simulations—are increasingly encouraged, as they replicate real-world applications and promote deeper learning (Donnelly & Kennelly, 2024).

Authentic assessments in online settings can take various forms, including problem-based learning tasks or portfolio submissions, where students compile and reflect on their work over time. These approaches foster critical thinking and allow students to demonstrate their learning in more dynamic and personalized ways. Additionally, peer assessment, facilitated through digital platforms, encourages engagement and accountability by enabling students to review and critique each other's work, benefiting both the reviewer and the reviewed (Kerman et al., 2024). To further enhance the effectiveness of online assessments, instructors should consider integrating adaptive assessment tools that adjust the difficulty of questions based on student performance, creating a more tailored evaluation experience. These tools not only assess current understanding but also help identify learning gaps and areas needing improvement.

FORMATIVE AND SUMMATIVE ASSESSMENT TECHNIQUES

Formative assessments are ongoing, low-stakes evaluations designed to monitor student learning throughout a course. These assessments provide timely feedback, enabling both students and instructors to assess learning progress and make necessary adjustments. Examples of formative assessments in online learning include short quizzes, contributions to discussion boards, and reflective journals, which provide insights into student comprehension without the pressure of high-stakes grading (Birgin & Yılmaz, 2023).

In contrast, summative assessments evaluate student learning at the conclusion of an instructional unit, often through high-stakes exams, final projects, or cumulative assignments. These assessments are crucial for determining whether students have met the course's learning outcomes. In online contexts, summative assessments can include digital exams, capstone projects, or comprehensive essays that synthesize course material (Abd Halim et al., 2024). With tools such as plagiarism detection and timed exams available on online platforms, summative assessments can be effectively managed while ensuring academic integrity.

Combining formative and summative assessment techniques within an online course enhances the overall evaluation process by providing multiple opportunities for students to receive feedback and improve. This balanced approach fosters consistent engagement and ensures that final evaluations reflect ongoing learning rather than isolated testing events.

Using Feedback to Enhance Student Learning and Course Design

Feedback is a vital aspect of the learning process, particularly in online environments where direct interaction between students and instructors may be limited. Effective feedback is timely, specific, and actionable, guiding students on how to enhance their work and deepen their understanding of the subject matter. Research indicates that feedback is most effective when it is formative, given throughout the learning process rather than solely at the end (Wu & Schunn, 2023).

In online settings, instructors can employ a range of digital tools to provide feedback, such as written comments, audio responses, and video annotations. Platforms like Moodle or Canvas allow instructors to leave detailed comments directly on student submissions or in discussion forums, fostering an ongoing dialogue about learning progress. Peer feedback also adds value, allowing students to engage in critical reflection and collaborative learning (Carless & Boud, 2018).

Moreover, feedback not only aids students but also informs course design and instructional strategies. By analyzing trends in student performance and feedback, instructors can pinpoint areas of the course that may require revision. For instance, if many students struggle with a specific concept or task, it may indicate the need for clearer material or additional resources. Continuous improvement based on feedback data ensures that courses remain relevant and effective in addressing students' learning needs.

PROFESSIONAL DEVELOPMENT FOR ONLINE EDUCATORS

Building a Community of Practice among Online Educators

A community of practice (CoP) for online educators encourages collaboration, sharing of knowledge, and professional development. These CoPs consist of professionals united by a common goal to enhance their skills and expertise through regular interaction (Bicchi, 2024). For online educators, such communities offer vital support as they face the challenges associated with digital teaching. Being part of a CoP enables educators to exchange best practices, explore pedagogical strategies, and collaboratively address issues related to online instruction. Platforms like Twitter, LinkedIn, and specialized forums (such as The Chronicle of Higher Education or Educause) provide spaces for educators to engage in meaningful discussions, share resources, and keep up with the latest trends in educational technology. Those involved in these communities are better prepared to embrace new teaching methodologies, enhance their digital skills, and devise innovative solutions suited to online learning environments (Anderson, 2024). CoPs also encourage reflective practice, enabling educators to critically evaluate their teaching methods, share their experiences, and learn from their peers. This collaborative process of knowledge-building fosters continuous improvement and professional growth, which is essential for delivering high-quality online education.

Continuous Professional Development and Lifelong Learning

In the fast-changing realm of online education, ongoing professional development (CPD) is crucial for educators to remain updated on technological advancements and pedagogical innovations. CPD consists of continuous training and education aimed at enhancing an educator's skills, knowledge, and competencies over time (Kennedy, 2005). For those teaching online, CPD programs often emphasize integrating digital tools, understanding online student engagement, and applying evidence-based instructional design practices.

Lifelong learning is an important component of CPD, highlighting the necessity for educators to continually develop their professional skills. Many universities and educational institutions offer formal training programs, such as certifications in online teaching or educational technology, to facilitate this development. Organizations like the Online Learning Consortium (OLC) and Quality Matters (QM) provide webinars, workshops, and certification programs designed to enhance the quality of online education (Anderson & Rivera Vargas, 2020).

By participating in lifelong learning, educators not only advance their own teaching capabilities but also contribute to the overall enhancement of online education by staying informed about emerging trends and methodologies. This commitment to ongoing education ensures that educators are equipped to utilize the latest technologies effectively and address the diverse needs of their students.

Resources and Support for Enhancing Teaching Skills in Digital Environments

Teaching in digital environments necessitates a unique skill set that differs from those required in traditional classrooms. To aid online educators in developing these skills, a wide range of resources and tools are available. Many institutions provide internal resources, such as instructional design teams that work with educators to create effective online courses, and teaching and learning centers that offer training in areas like learning management systems (LMS) and universal design for learning (UDL) principles (Bates, 2019).

Online educators can also take advantage of external resources, including professional development courses, online tutorials, and open educational resources (OERs). For instance, MOOCs (Massive Open Online Courses) from platforms like Coursera, edX, and FutureLearn allow educators to improve their skills in instructional design, digital assessment, and student engagement. These resources are often flexible, enabling educators to learn at their own pace, fitting their schedules. Additionally, peer mentoring and coaching programs are increasingly recognized as effective strategies for professional growth in digital teaching environments. Through mentoring, less experienced educators can gain valuable insights from seasoned professionals, while coaching programs provide personalized feedback focused on enhancing teaching practices (Palmerola, 2024). These initiatives support individual development and foster a culture of continuous learning within educational institutions.

In conclusion, professional development for online educators is multifaceted, incorporating participation in communities of practice, continuous learning through formal and informal avenues, and access to a variety of resources aimed at enhancing teaching skills. By engaging in these activities, online educators can stay updated with technological advancements, refine their teaching methodologies, and ultimately create more engaging and effective online learning experiences.

CASE STUDIES AND BEST PRACTICES

Real-World Examples of Successful Online Teaching and Learning Initiatives

Real-world case studies give important intuition into the successful implementation of online teaching and learning strategies. For instance, the University of Central Florida (UCF) has effectively utilized blended learning and online courses. This approach combines traditional face-to-face learning with comprehensive digital components, offering flexibility while engaging students through technology (Dziuban et al., 2018). As a result, UCF has seen improved student retention rates, higher satisfaction levels, and enhanced learning outcomes compared to conventional courses.

Another notable case study is Harvard University's transition to online formats during the COVID-19 pandemic. The institution used platforms like Zoom and Canvas to maintain high-quality instruction. Faculty members adapted their teaching methods to include breakout rooms, interactive polls, and virtual office hours, ensuring continuous support for students (Chandra, 2021). This shift not only maintained learning continuity but also demonstrated how well-structured online programs can meet diverse student needs while preserving academic rigor.

CONCLUSION

The Scholarship of Teaching and Learning (SoTL) in digital classrooms provides a comprehensive framework for enhancing online education through reflective practices, evidence-based methods, and ongoing improvement. As digital learning environments continue to evolve, educators must navigate the distinct challenges and opportunities that technology presents. SoTL is instrumental in this process, fostering a deeper understanding of how to assess and improve teaching effectiveness in online contexts.

To advance pedagogical excellence, effective strategies such as technology integration to encourage active learning, inclusive online courses design, and the application of data analytics to guide instructional practices. These approaches empower educators to create engaging and accessible digital learning experiences while continually improving student outcomes.

Innovative teaching techniques, such as flipped classrooms, gamification, and collaborative learning, introduce new dimensions to online education. These methods not only enhance student engagement but also encourage critical thinking and social interaction, essential elements of a holistic educational experience.

Assessing and evaluating student performance in online learning necessitates a careful balance between formative and summative assessment methods, with a strong focus on providing meaningful feedback. Supported by digital tools, these strategies enable educators to effectively monitor student progress and tailor their teaching to meet individual needs.

Ongoing professional development for online educators is crucial for upholding high standards in digital education. Building communities of practice, participating in continuous professional development opportunities, and accessing resources tailored for digital teaching equip educators to stay abreast of technological advancements and pedagogical innovations.

Finally, case studies and best practices showcase the real-world implementation of these strategies, providing valuable insights from seasoned educators. Successful online learning initiatives, alongside the lessons learned, underscore the significance of adaptability, collaboration, and a commitment to excellence in creating impactful digital classrooms. Through these efforts, educators can cultivate an environment that promotes both teaching excellence and student success.

This chapter contributes to the existing literature on SoTL by providing a focused exploration of strategies and practices specifically tailored for digital classrooms. It offers valuable insights and practical guidance for educators at all levels, supporting their efforts to achieve pedagogical excellence and enhance student learning outcomes in online education.

REFERENCES

Abd Halim, H., Hamzah, M. I., & Zulkifli, H. (2024). A systematic review on the formative assessment practice in teaching and learning in secondary school. *International Journal of Evaluation & Research in Education*, 13(2), 1173–1183. DOI: 10.11591/ijere.v13i2.26187

Anderson, O. (2024). *Professional learning communities as transformative spaces for the advancement of social and emotional learning in schools* (Doctoral dissertation, California State University, Stanislaus https://scholarworks.calstate.edu/concern/theses/ng451r36t,)

Anderson, T., & Rivera Vargas, P. (2020). A critical look at educational technology from a distance education perspective. *Digital Education Review*, 2020(37), 208–229. DOI: 10.1344/der.2020.37.208-229

Bates, A. W. (2020, December 16). A review of online learning in 2020. *Online Learning and Distance Education Resources*. https://www.tonybates.ca/2020/12/16/a-review-of-online-learning-in-2020

Beetham, H., & Sharpe, R. (Eds.). (2019). *Rethinking pedagogy for a digital age: Principles and practices of design* (3rd ed.). Routledge., DOI: 10.4324/9781351252805

Bicchi, F. (2024). Cultivating communities of practice: From institutions to practices. *Global Studies Quarterly*, 4(1), 1–10. DOI: 10.1093/isagsq/ksad076

Birgin, O., & Yılmaz, M. (2023). Development and validation of a scale to assess the frequency of using classroom assessment tools and methods for mathematics teachers. *IJERI: International Journal of Educational Research and Innovation*, (20), 1–20. DOI: 10.46661/ijeri.8075

Boyer, E. L. (1990). *Scholarship reconsidered: Priorities of the professoriate*. Princeton University Press.

Carless, D., & Boud, D. (2018). The development of student feedback literacy: Enabling uptake of feedback. *Assessment & Evaluation in Higher Education*, 43(8), 1315–1325. DOI: 10.1080/02602938.2018.1463354

Centre for Applied Special Technology. ([CAST], 2021). Universal design for learning guidelines version 2.2. https://www.cast.org/impact/universal-design-for-learning-udl

Chandra, Y. (2021). Online education during COVID-19: perception of academic stress and emotional intelligence coping strategies among college students. *Asian education and development studies, 10*(2), 229-238.

Collins, A. (2023). *Examining teachers' perceptions of preparedness to teach in low-income schools upon completing a Master of Arts in teaching degree*. [Doctoral dissertation, National Louis University https://digitalcommons.nl.edu/diss/723/,]

Deterding, S., Dixon, D., Khaled, R., & Nacke, L. (2011). From game design elements to gamefulness: Defining "gamification." *Proceedings of the 15th International Academic MindTrek Conference: Envisioning Future Media Environments*, 9–15. DOI: 10.1145/2181037.2181040

Donnelly, R., & Kennelly, I. (2024). A framework-based cross-institutional CPD for academic staff in Gen-AI literacy, critical inquiry, and authentic assessment. In *Effective Practices in AI Literacy Education: Case Studies and Reflections* (pp. 51-59). Emerald Publishing Limited. DOI: 10.1108/978-1-83608-852-320241006

Dziuban, C., Graham, C. R., Moskal, P. D., Norberg, A., & Sicilia, N. (2018). Blended learning: The new normal and emerging technologies. *International Journal of Educational Technology in Higher Education*, 15(1), 1–16. DOI: 10.1186/s41239-017-0087-5

Fanghanel, J., Pritchard, J., Potter, J., & Wisker, G. (2016). *Defining and supporting the scholarship of teaching and learning (SoTL): A sector-wide study*. Higher Education Academy.

Felten, P. (2013). Principles of good practice in SoTL. *Teaching & Learning Inquiry*, 1(1), 121–125. DOI: 10.20343/teachlearninqu.1.1.121

Freeman, S., Eddy, S. L., McDonough, M., Smith, M. K., Okoroafor, N., Jordt, H., & Wenderoth, M. P. (2014). Active learning increases student performance in science, engineering, and mathematics. *Proceedings of the National Academy of Sciences of the United States of America*, 111(23), 8410–8415. DOI: 10.1073/pnas.1319030111 PMID: 24821756

Hassan, L. (2024). Gamification. A conceptual critique to move forwards. *Gamevironments*, (20), 88–113.

Kennedy, A. (2005). Models of continuing professional development: A framework for analysis. *Journal of In-service Education*, 31(2), 235–250. DOI: 10.1080/13674580500200277

Kerman, N. T., Banihashem, S. K., Karami, M., Er, E., Van Ginkel, S., & Noroozi, O. (2024). Online peer feedback in higher education: A synthesis of the literature. *Education and Information Technologies*, 29(1), 763–813. DOI: 10.1007/s10639-023-12273-8

Khumalo, N. (2024). Online learning changed the learning motivation: Challenges of the higher education students. In *Accessibility of Digital Higher Education in the Global South* (pp. 20–38). IGI Global.

Koehler, M. J., Mishra, P., & Cain, W. (2013). What is technological pedagogical content knowledge (TPACK)? *Journal of Education*, 193(3), 13–19. DOI: 10.1177/002205741319300303

Makinde, S. O. (2023). Effects of a developed flipped classroom package on senior secondary school students' performance in mathematics in Lagos, Nigeria. *The Journal of Educational Research*, 13(2), 115–116. DOI: 10.51474/jer.v13i2.718

Mayer, R. E. (2020). Designing multimedia instruction in anatomy: An evidence-based approach. *Clinical Anatomy (New York, N.Y.)*, 33(1), 2–11. DOI: 10.1002/ca.23265 PMID: 30144175

Mehdizadeh, M., Pourhaji, M., & Derakhshan, A. (2024). Evolution of communities of practice, realignment of possible selves, and repositionings in EFL teacher professional identity development: A longitudinal case study. *Language Learning Journal*, 52(3), 336–348. DOI: 10.1080/09571736.2022.2163685

Palmerola, E. D. (2024). Clarification evaluation of e-learning implementation: A developmental research design. *American Journal of Education and Technology*, 3(2), 119–127. DOI: 10.54536/ajet.v3i2.2890

Plata, M. R. (2020). *Applying the universal design for learning in higher education; A guide for increased learning in the classroom.* [Thesis, University of Oklahoma, https://shareok.org/items/381c2efa-8538-4594-b7eb-ddb20a5fe824].

Vygotsky, L. S. (1978). *Mind in society: The development of higher psychological processes*. Harvard University Press.

Wu, Y., & Schunn, C. D. (2023). Passive, active, and constructive engagement with peer feedback: A revised model of learning from peer feedback. *Contemporary Educational Psychology*, 73, 102160. DOI: 10.1016/j.cedpsych.2023.102160

Yang, C. C., Wu, J. Y., & Ogata, H. (2024). Learning analytics dashboard-based self-regulated learning approach for enhancing students' e-book-based blended learning. *Education and Information Technologies*, •••, 1–22. DOI: 10.1007/s10639-024-12913-7

Yılmaz, Ö., & Malone, K. L. (2020). Preservice teacher's perceptions about the use of blended learning in a science education methods course. *Smart Learning Environments*, 7(1), 18. DOI: 10.1186/s40561-020-00126-7

Zhan, Y., Sun, D., Kong, H. M., & Zeng, Y. (2024). Primary school teachers' classroom-based e-assessment practices: Insights from the theory of planned behaviour. *British Journal of Educational Technology*, 55(6), 2740–2759. DOI: 10.1111/bjet.13478

Chapter 2
Transforming Pedagogy:
Best Practices for SoTL in Online Learning Environments

Muhammad Usman Tariq
https://orcid.org/0000-0002-7605-3040
Abu Dhabi University, UAE & University College Cork, Ireland

ABSTRACT

The improvement of educational practices in virtual spaces is the focus of this chapter's exploration of the Scholarship of Teaching and Learning (SoTL). It offers a thorough introduction to SoTL highlighting its significance in the context of online learning for both teachers and students. Exploring cutting-edge techniques that enhance student engagement and learning outcomes the chapter explores best practices for successful online teaching backed by research and case studies. In addition, the chapter looks at how online educators should always be improving their professional development and how to use professional learning communities (PLCs) to promote collaboration. It also discusses the value of having students participate in SoTL projects and the advantages of having learners involved in these endeavours. Common issues that educators run into when conducting SoTL online are covered along with workable fixes and effective case studies.

INTRODUCTION

The Scholarship of Teaching and Learning (SoTL) has become an essential foundation for improving teaching methods via the incorporation of academic research into the process of teaching and learning. SoTL, which is defined as a methodical analysis of teaching and learning practices, helps teachers to evaluate their pedagogical strategies, collect information on student learning, and make well-informed decisions

DOI: 10.4018/979-8-3693-7595-2.ch002

that promote better learning outcomes. With the use of this academic approach, teachers may investigate a wide range of facets of their teaching techniques, including technology integration, student involvement, curriculum creation, and assessment tactics. SoTL fosters a culture of continuous improvement throughout educational institutions in addition to enhancing the performance of individual teachers by placing a high priority on evidence-based approaches (Fukuzawa & Rawle, 2020). The need of SoTL has become more apparent in recent years in online learning settings, which have grown exponentially as a result of global events like the COVID-19 epidemic and technical improvements. The transition to online learning has put established pedagogical approaches to the test and called for a reassessment of how instruction takes place in virtual environments. A strong foundation for comprehending and improving online teaching is offered by SoTL, which helps instructors navigate this constantly changing environment. In order to enhance student learning, encourage engagement, and solve the particular difficulties of virtual classrooms, instructors must employ SoTL in online learning settings. Under the SoTL paradigm, for example, research might reveal best practices for online discussion forums, emphasizing the ways in which prompts, and timely response can promote student involvement and deeper learning (Botes & Botha, 2021).

Furthermore, SoTL gives teachers the instruments they need to evaluate the effectiveness of their online instruction. Understanding how students engage with peers and course material in virtual environments requires a self-reflective approach. By using SoTL, teachers may collect information using a variety of techniques, including surveys, student evaluations, and reflective diaries, to examine how their pedagogical decisions are affecting the performance of their students. In an online course, for instance, a teacher may use the flipped classroom approach, in which students participate in group projects during synchronous meetings and review lecture materials at home. Through an analysis of student performance and feedback, the instructor may ascertain the efficacy of this strategy and implement any required modifications to improve learning outcomes (Eady et al., 2021).

This chapter's goals and objectives are to examine effective strategies for integrating SoTL in virtual learning environments, with a focus on the value of evidence-based pedagogy in promoting successful teaching and learning. The objective of this chapter is to furnish instructors with pragmatic approaches for incorporating SoTL ideas into their virtual classes, hence augmenting student involvement and academic achievements. It will also provide several instances of effective SoTL efforts in online learning environments, demonstrating how teachers have innovated their teaching strategies by utilizing research and reflective practices. Important subjects covered in this chapter include the function of evaluation in SoTL, the value of community and teamwork in online learning, and methods for creating a welcoming and encouraging online learning environment (Gansemer-Topf et al., 2021). The importance of assessment as a key element of the teaching and learning process is one important feature of SoTL. Assessment is essential for directing student learning and influencing instructional decisions in online learning settings. Teachers can obtain important information about the development and comprehension of their students by using formative and summative assessment techniques. For example, using online tests and reflective diaries enables teachers to keep an eye on students' progress in real time and provide prompt feedback that may be used to improve education in the future. Peer evaluations also stimulate students to interact critically with the work of their classmates, which fosters group learning and a more thorough comprehension of the material (Botes & Botha, 2021; Tariq, 2024a).

The chapter will also look at how crucial it is for educators using SoTL to create a community of practice. Collaboration and relationships are crucial since online learning settings may frequently seem alienating for both teachers and students. In their pursuit of SoTL, educators may assist one another by fostering communication and shared learning opportunities. For instance, an online faculty learning community can get together on a regular basis to talk about their research projects, exchange findings, and work together to create creative lesson plans. This collaborative approach improves individual teaching methods while also fostering an academic culture inside the organization (Eady et al., 2021). This chapter will cover tactics for fostering an inclusive and encouraging online learning environment in addition to educator cooperation. An essential component of good pedagogy is inclusivity, and SoTL offers insightful information on how to meet the requirements of a wide range of students in online courses. Teachers can use SOTL research to comprehend the distinct difficulties encountered by different student demographics, including minority students and those with impairments (Gansemer-Topf et al., 2021). For example, including Universal Design for Learning (UDL) principles into course design guarantees equal access to learning resources and engagement opportunities for all students. Teachers may establish an online learning environment that is more inclusive and supports the achievement of all students by considering and modifying their methods through the lens of service-learning (Cruz & Ngoenha, 2021). Another important factor to consider while discussing SoTL and online learning is the incorporation of technology. Teachers need to be up to date on the newest developments in digital technologies and how they affect instruction and learning. A framework for analyzing how technology might improve teaching methods is offered by SoTL. Learning management system (LMS) adoption, for instance, can simplify course administration and improve communication between teachers and students. Educators must, however, also evaluate these technologies' efficacy and influence on student learning. In order to make sure that technology improves rather than diminishes the learning process, educators may engage in continuous

SoTL research to determine the best technological tools and tactics for their unique educational environments (Tariq, 2025a).

The final section of the chapter will cover SoTL's potential future paths in online learning settings. Teachers need to be flexible and receptive to new methods and ideas as online learning develops. These changes will be greatly aided by SoTL, which will give teachers a framework for critically analyzing their instruction and enhancing it over time. Teachers may successfully negotiate the difficulties of remote learning and eventually improve their students' educational experiences by adopting a culture of research and inquiry (Botes & Botha, 2021). Thus, the goal of this chapter is to emphasize the value of the Scholarship of Teaching and Learning in online learning settings by providing educators with useful tactics and real-world examples to improve their instruction. Through the use of SoTL, teachers may evaluate student learning results, conduct systematic investigations into their educational strategies, and promote a continuous improvement culture within their organizations. The insights obtained by SoTL will be crucial in changing pedagogy and guaranteeing that every student has the chance to succeed in their learning pursuits as online education grows (Tariq, 2024b).

BACKGROUND

The origins of SoTL may be found in higher education's emphasis on evaluation of student learning as a crucial element of good instruction in the late 20th century. At first, SoTL was restricted to conventional classroom settings, but as technology developed and online learning environments proliferated, SoTL's reach expanded. Teachers began investigating how traditional pedagogical techniques may be modified for virtual environments as a result of the internet's and digital technologies' emergence in education, which presented both new opportunities and problems for teaching and learning. For instance, studies on the effectiveness of online discussion forums in promoting student engagement and learning started in the early 2000s. The significance of SoTL in comprehending the distinct dynamics of online education is becoming increasingly apparent, as seen by this historical context (Botes & Botha, 2021). A number of noteworthy advancements have resulted from the development of SoTL in online learning. Teachers started utilizing a variety of digital technologies to improve their instruction and evaluate students' performance as online learning gained popularity. By integrating learning management systems (LMS) like Blackboard and Canvas, instructors were able to design online courses that were organized and could support evaluation, communication, and teamwork (Cruz et al., 2024). These platforms also made it possible to gather information on student performance and engagement, which teachers could then use to improve their methods of instruction. For both teachers and students, there are several advantages to using SoTL in online learning. Participating in SoTL promotes a culture of professional development and ongoing growth for educators. Through methodical inquiry into their methods, instructors can find useful tactics that improve student learning and help them adjust to the rapidly changing online education environment. For instance, after reviewing formative assessment data, a teacher may find that a specific idea is difficult for some pupils. This realization may lead a teacher to adjust their teaching strategies, such as adding multimedia materials or rewriting tasks to encourage deeper comprehension (Botes & Botha, 2021). Furthermore, SoTL promotes cooperation among instructors, which strengthens the feeling of community and shared learning. Teachers may exchange best practices, do group data analysis, and create cutting-edge lesson plans that will help their students through cooperative SoTL projects (Cruz & Grodziak, 2021). To improve their methods and raise student engagement, a multidisciplinary team of educators may, for example, investigate the efficacy of project-based learning in virtual environments. They would then share their experiences and results (Bunnell et al., 2024). In virtual environments, SoTL can make learning more effective and enjoyable for students. Students gain from a learning environment that respects their opinions and adjusts to meet their needs when teachers actively use SoTL concepts into their instruction. An increase in student motivation and achievement may result from this response. Teachers can modify their pedagogical approaches to better suit the requirements and preferences of their students by implementing regular feedback loops in their courses, wherein students offer feedback on their learning and reflect on the contents they have studied (Baker et al., 2024). Furthermore, SoTL's emphasis on evidence-based methods guarantees that students are participating in pertinent and meaningful learning activities. Educators may develop assessments and activities that effectively evaluate student comprehension and are in line with learning objectives when they use data and research to influence their teaching. For example, students who received quick feedback on their performance were more likely to retain material and show improved learning outcomes, according to research looking at the use of online quizzes as formative assessments. Students may take charge of their own learning since the assessment and learning objectives are in line, which promotes a better comprehension of the subject matter (Cruz & Grodziak, 2021; Tariq, 2024c).

RESEARCH ON BEST PRACTICES IN ONLINE TEACHING

With online education becoming more and more common, current research on best practices in online teaching has become a crucial field of study. Understanding what makes for good online education becomes crucial as educators and organizations move toward virtual learning settings. According to recent research, effective online teaching practices depend on a number of important elements, such as the presence of the teacher, the design of the course, student participation, and evaluation techniques. According to studies, for example, students are far more engaged and satisfied when there is a strong teacher presence, which is demonstrated by prompt communication and active participation in discussions. This presence boosts motivation and academic performance in addition to creating a sense of community among students (Harvey & Jones, 2021). Effective course design is another essential component of successful online teaching, in addition to teacher presence. Studies highlight the significance of well-defined learning goals, well-structured course materials, and a variety of teaching approaches to accommodate different learning preferences. For instance, 2009 research by Bernard et al. showed that learning results are enhanced in well-designed online courses that use multimedia materials like movies and interactive exercises. These design components make studying more interesting and aid students in better understanding difficult ideas. Incorporating cooperative learning activities, such group projects or peer evaluations, also motivates students to interact with one another and creates a feeling of community inside the virtual classroom (Cook, 2020).

The use of best practices in online education is demonstrated by a number of accomplished SoTL projects, which also highlight the beneficial effects of these practices on student learning. A university that used the peer-led team learning (PLTL) paradigm in an online chemistry course was the subject of one noteworthy case study. Peer leaders led online conversations and assisted their classmates in problem-solving sessions as part of this initiative, which focused on student cooperation. When compared to typical online formats, the results showed a considerable boost in both student performance and retention rates. The collaborative element of the course was cited by students as the reason for their success, as they expressed feeling more involved and encouraged in their learning. This case study demonstrates how cutting-edge teaching techniques may effectively raise student success in virtual learning environments (Baker, Hornsby, & Turner, 2024). The application of gamification to online courses to raise student interest and engagement was the subject of another case study. In this project, teachers combined features of a game, including leaderboards, badges, and point systems, with an online learning environment (How, 2020). According to research findings, students who took part in the gamified course shown greater enthusiasm and engagement than students who took a conventional online course. The gamified method enhanced learning outcomes and completion rates by appealing to students' innate motivations through aspects of competition and accomplishment. This example shows how creative teaching strategies may provide an engaging and dynamic virtual classroom (Bunnell et al., 2024; Tariq, 2024d).

Because of the constant need to improve student engagement and learning in online education, innovative teaching approaches are evolving. One such approach is the flipped classroom model, which flips the conventional teaching paradigm by employing in-person class time for active learning activities and online delivery of instructional information. Studies have indicated that this method promotes deeper learning since it allows students to interact with the content before synchronous meetings. Students who used the flipped classroom model showed enhanced critical thinking abilities and better academic achievement, according to research looking at the approach's efficacy in an online environment. A technique that reverses typical teaching methods is the flipped classroom approach, which uses in-person class time for active learning activities and online delivery of educational information. Because students have the chance to interact with the content prior to synchronous meetings, research indicates that this technique promotes deeper learning. Students who engaged in this paradigm showed enhanced critical thinking abilities and superior academic achievement, according to research looking at the efficacy of the flipped classroom in an online environment. The emphasis on active learning has grown, which motivates students to take charge of their education and increases student engagement (Baker et al., 2024). Personalized learning pathways are also becoming more and more popular in online education. This method customizes educational opportunities to meet the requirements, interests, and advancement of each unique learner. Personalized learning has been linked to increased student success and satisfaction, according to recent studies. One online platform that used adaptive learning technology, for example, let students go through the course content at their own speed and got customized feedback according to how well they did. Pupils in this individualized setting expressed feeling more in control of their education, which boosted their motivation and produced better academic results (Bunnell et al., 2024).

PROFESSIONAL DEVELOPMENT IN ONLINE TEACHING AND LEARNING

In the quickly changing educational environment of today, it is more crucial than ever for online educators to engage in ongoing professional development. In order to effectively engage their students, educators need to remain up to speed on the newest tools, pedagogical practices, and research results as online teaching and learning technology continue to evolve. The success and contentment of students are directly impacted by this continuous learning process, which also improves the teaching skills of instructors. A dynamic and successful online learning experience is mostly dependent on highly qualified instructors, particularly in a virtual setting where contact and engagement can occasionally be difficult to achieve. For example, a teacher who has taken part in professional development centred on active learning tactics is probably going to be more skilled at applying these practices in their online courses, which will improve student engagement and results (Anselmo et al., 2022). Some techniques need to be implemented in order to guarantee the efficacy of professional development for online instructors. First, educators' learning experiences may be greatly improved by adding collaborative learning opportunities to professional development programs. Through involvement in collaborative workshops or training sessions, educators may exchange their experiences, obstacles, and accomplishments with fellow professionals. This cooperative method encourages the sharing of creative teaching techniques while also building a feeling of community among educators. For instance, a virtual workshop that enables teachers to create online course materials in small groups might encourage the exchange of various viewpoints and resources, which will ultimately improve the calibre of the teachers' instruction.

Using blended learning models, which integrate in-person and online training, is another successful tactic for professional growth in virtual environments. This method makes it easier for teachers to comprehend and use efficient online teaching practices by allowing them to reap the benefits of both face-to-face and virtual learning. For example, a blended learning program may consist of an introductory in-person training on best practices for online teaching, followed by a series of online courses that allow teachers to advance their knowledge and abilities. In addition to meeting the needs of different learning styles, this format offers teachers continuous assistance and tools to help them improve or switch to online instruction (Cleary et al., 2022). Case studies of professional development initiatives that emphasize the Scholarship of Teaching and Learning (SoTL) offer insightful analyses of effective strategies. A major university's initiative to improve faculty involvement with SoTL in online education serves as one illustration. A number of seminars and online courses were made available by the initiative to assist teachers in creating research projects that were connected to their online teaching strategies. It was urged of participants to work in interdisciplinary teams and disseminate their research through publications and presentations. Along with enhancing faculty members' comprehension of SoTL, the initiative promoted more cooperation and creative teaching methods throughout the university. Teachers who took part expressed greater confidence in their abilities to evaluate their own success as teachers and make data-driven adjustments to their online curricula (Tariq, 2025b).

A community college that established an extensive professional development program for its online professors was the subject of another interesting case study. The institution created a year-long program that incorporated peer observation, online workshops, and mentorship opportunities after seeing the need for ongoing assistance and development. Teachers were matched with seasoned mentors who offered advice and criticism on their methods for teaching online. Faculty members claimed to feel more competent of putting new teaching tactics into practice and more supported as a consequence. Student satisfaction and retention rates increased significantly as a result of the program, indicating the benefits of continued professional development for both teachers and students (Cleary et al., 2022). Moreover, improving learning outcomes has been demonstrated to be a successful consequence of using technology into professional development programs for online instructors. For example, professional development courses hosted on learning management systems (LMS) enable teachers to work together on projects, participate in conversations, and access materials whenever it's convenient for them. One institution used its learning management system (LMS) to build a collection of online teaching best practices, complete with discussion boards, video lectures, and carefully chosen articles on efficient online pedagogy. These materials would be available to faculty members as required, encouraging a culture of lifelong learning. This freedom encouraged teachers to take charge of their professional development and enabled them to improve their teaching techniques (Anselmo et al., 2022; Tariq, 2025c).

BUILDING PROFESSIONAL LEARNING COMMUNITIES ONLINE

Through encouraging collaboration, reflection, and shared practice among educators, professional learning communities (PLCs) play a critical role in enhancing the Scholarship of Teaching and Learning (SoTL). These communities offer a flexible yet organized setting where teachers may exchange research findings, have meaningful conversations about their methods, and work together to solve issues related to online learning. PLCs are fundamental to the dynamic world of online learning because they foster a culture of support and ongoing development. Teachers are urged to investigate cutting-edge teaching techniques, consider their own methods, and assess how their methods affect the learning results of their students as they participate in Professional Learning Communities (PLCs) (Cleaver et al. 2020) In order to facilitate cooperation and participation in virtual learning communities, a number of strategies can be used. Setting up explicit objectives and participation expectations is a basic tactic. Members can better link their conversations and efforts with the larger goal of developing SoTL by clearly defining the PLC's objectives. For example, by exchanging best practices and examining input from students, a PLC may concentrate on raising the level of student involvement in online courses. Members may be kept responsible and encouraged by setting quantifiable goals, which will drive them to actively participate in the community's conversations and projects (Cleary et al., 2022).

Using a variety of communication technologies that promote connection, and engagement is another successful strategy for encouraging cooperation. Online PLCs may create a dynamic learning environment by utilizing platforms like video conferencing, discussion forums, and collaborative document editing tools. One way to promote a feeling of community and camaraderie is by adopting a platform like Zoom for frequent virtual meetings, which enables members to interact in real time. Asynchronous discussion boards also accommodate various schedules and time zones by allowing users to exchange ideas, pose queries, and offer responses whenever it's convenient for them. This adaptability promotes engagement from a greater variety of instructors, fostering a diversity of experiences and viewpoints (Cleaver et al., 2020). Including organized exercises in virtual PLC sessions can help improve participation and teamwork. In "lesson study" sessions, for example, teachers could work together to plan, carry out, and evaluate a particular lesson or teaching technique. Members may improve their methods and learn from each other's experiences by watching one another teach and giving helpful criticism. This cooperative research fosters a sense of responsibility and dedication to enhancing student learning outcomes in addition to deepening awareness of successful teaching techniques (Anselmo et al., 2022).

Collaborating among educators has been a powerful force in the progress of SoTL, as seen by successful online PLCs. The "Online Teaching Community," which was founded by a group of universities, is one such example. This PLC is dedicated to exchanging best practices in online teaching and learning, giving teachers a forum to talk about difficulties, acknowledge accomplishments, and work together to investigate novel ideas. Members of the community may interact intimately with the ideas of SoTL through the frequent webinars, discussion forums, and cooperative projects that are hosted by the community. Participants have therefore reported better student outcomes and increased teaching efficacy, demonstrating the influence of collaborative learning on professional development (Cleaver et al., 2020). The Teaching Online Collaborative, another effective virtual professional learning community, unites instructors from different universities to concentrate on certain topics associated with virtual learning. Members of this PLC are encouraged to do action research to investigate the efficacy of various teaching pedagogies and techniques in their online courses. Members add to the expanding body of information regarding online teaching strategies and their effects on student learning by sharing their research and experiences. Because of this PLC's collaborative culture, thorough resource guides and toolkits have been developed, giving teachers useful tips for improving their online instruction (How, 2020).

Furthermore, one PLC that concentrates on incorporating SoTL into online instruction is the SoTL Collaborative. In addition to encouraging members to share research results pertaining to teaching and learning, this community places a strong emphasis on the value of evidence-based approaches. Collaborative research projects involving participants delve into several facets of virtual education, including instructional design, student involvement, and evaluation methodologies. The SoTL Collaborative has advanced knowledge in the field of online education by encouraging a culture of inquiry and reflection. It has also motivated members to implement practices that are informed by research and improve student learning (Supple & Cronin, 2023).

Online PLCs have also been crucial in helping to address the issues presented by the COVID-19 epidemic, in addition to these successful cases. Many teachers discovered that they had to quickly switch to teaching online, frequently without any assistance or preparation. As a result, a large number of PLCs with a shared emphasis on techniques, materials, and firsthand knowledge of remote teaching were formed. These networks helped educators who were dealing with similar issues communicate with one another so they could work together to find answers and exchange best practices. For example, the Emergency Remote Teaching Community gave teachers a forum to share lesson plans, exchange experiences, and get guidance from other teachers. In addition to assisting educators with the shift, this cooperative effort advanced the discussion on efficient online teaching techniques (Cook, 2020). One cannot emphasize how important online PLCs are to improving SoTL. These communities enable educators to participate in reflective practice and ongoing growth by giving them a collaborative and encouraging atmosphere. Establishing clear objectives, making use of a variety of communication technologies, and implementing planned activities are just a few of the collaboration-fostering strategies that are necessary to create a stimulating online learning environment. Online PLCs have the ability to improve teaching methods and student learning outcomes by contributing to the area of education. This is demonstrated by the successful instances of online PLCs (Supple & Cronin, 2023). Professional learning communities will play a crucial role in encouraging an environment of inquiry and continual improvement as educators continue to negotiate the challenges of online learning, which will eventually benefit both educators and students (Anselmo et al., 2022).

ENGAGING LEARNERS IN THE STUDY OF TEACHING AND LEARNING

Incorporating students into the study of teaching and learning (SoTL) is a crucial tactic that enhances the educational process and fosters a more profound comprehension of it. Teachers may create a more inclusive and collaborative learning environment where students take an active role in their own education by incorporating them in SoTL initiatives. Students that participate in this activity can offer insightful contributions, improve their critical thinking abilities, and forge closer bonds with the material. Although there are several approaches to getting students involved in SoTL initiatives, all of them aim to provide students the power to actively shape the educational process (Tan & Chen, 2020). Adding student input and experiences into the design and delivery of courses is an effective way to include students in stakeholder learning. In order to get feedback from students on what they think is working and what needs to be changed in the course, educators might promote their participation in reflective activities including focus groups, questionnaires, and reflective diaries. Students in an online graduate program course, for example, could participate in weekly conversations regarding the efficacy of particular teaching tactics, such group projects or the usage of multimedia content. Teachers may gather extensive data on student learning experiences by offering structured feedback opportunities. This data can then be utilized to improve teaching strategies and increase the efficacy of the course (Swaminathan & Mulvihill, 2022).

Including students in the planning and execution of research projects with an educational component is an additional strategy. This can take the shape of student-led SoTL projects, in which students are given the freedom to look into certain facets of their education, such how well-different assessment techniques work or how peer cooperation affects learning results. Students enrolled in an online course, for instance, may collaborate to create research that looks at the connection between student participation and asynchronous discussion boards. Students who take charge of their research not only help to further SoTL but also acquire important research skills that they may use in other academic or professional settings (Supple et al., 2017). Engaging students in SoTL is made especially successful by collaborative learning settings, where teachers and students co-create knowledge. Students are seen as collaborators in the learning process in these settings, and their contributions are valued equally with those of the teachers. Offering students the chance to co-author research papers or discuss their findings at academic conferences is one way to encourage this kind of cooperation. To produce a study on the effects of employing virtual reality in online learning environments, for example, a group of students enrolled in an online course on educational technology may collaborate with their teacher. Students that participate in this way improve their academic performance as well as feel prouder of their contributions to the field and a sense of ownership (Maurer, 2022). Students that participate in SoTL get great benefits for the larger educational community as well as for themselves. Students who take part in SoTL projects get a greater knowledge of pedagogical concepts and are better able to critically reflect on their learning experiences. Students become more skilled at controlling their academic progress and acquire understanding of how various instructional styles affect their learning via active participation in research and reflection. Through encouraging students to actively shape their educational experience, this reflective technique helps them develop the sense of accountability and independence necessary for lifelong learning (Supple et al., 2017).

Teachers get important insights into the student experience via including students in SoTL. Students' distinct viewpoints and ideas can assist teachers in identifying areas for development and putting more successful teaching techniques into practice. The results of student-led SoTL projects may be used by educators to guide their instruction and make data-driven decisions, which further helps to close the knowledge gap between theory and practice. In the end, this cooperative approach results in better instructional strategies and higher learning objectives for every student (Tan & Chen, 2020). The benefits of student involvement in the study of teaching and learning are demonstrated by case studies of student-led SoTL projects in online courses. A group of undergraduate students taking an online psychology course was the subject of one such case study. Under the direction of their instructor, these students carried out a study to find out how well different online learning resources, such interactive tests and video lectures, affected students' understanding and recall. Through self-reflection and peer data collection, the students were able to acquire important knowledge about the advantages and drawbacks of various teaching strategies. Following the presentation of their findings at a regional teaching and learning conference, educators and students had the chance to talk about the research's implications for online course design (Maurer, 2022).

In an online business management course, students were charged with examining the influence of peer evaluation on group project outcomes. This is another instance of how students were involved in SoTL. Based on group performance and student satisfaction, the students created research that compared two distinct feedback models: anonymous peer feedback and instructor-led feedback. They then assessed the data. Through this effort, the students were able to provide suggestions on how to improve group work in subsequent iterations of the course and had a greater knowledge of the value of constructive feedback in collaborative learning environments. Through a webinar, the study's findings were presented to the larger online learning community, and the students had the opportunity to debate and reflect on their experiences as SoTL researchers (Openo, 2024). In a third case study, instructors and students in an online teacher preparation program worked together to examine the function of gamification in virtual learning settings. The students were especially curious to find out how features of game-based learning, including leaderboards and point systems, affected student engagement and motivation. Students gathered information about how various gamification techniques affected their own learning experiences by creating surveys and interviewing classmates. In order to improve student engagement, the project's findings were utilized to revamp the course for next cohorts. A stronger focus was placed on integrating game-based aspects (Sienkewicz, 2021). These case studies highlight the importance of student-led SoTL efforts in online courses and show how including students in the study of teaching and learning may result in significant enhancements to the educational process as a whole as well as the learning environment. Teachers who include students in SoTL actively cultivate a culture of cooperation and ongoing development that is advantageous to both teachers and students (Swaminathan & Mulvihill, 2022).

CHALLENGES AND SOLUTIONS IN ONLINE SOTL PROJECTS

Because of the intricacies of virtual instruction and the inherent distinctions between in-person and virtual learning contexts, conducting SoTL studies in online settings poses special challenges for educators. These difficulties may make it more difficult to conduct useful research and develop online teaching techniques. However, many of these challenges may be effectively overcome with careful preparation and workable solutions, resulting in a SoTL process that is more significant and effective. The absence of direct, in-person engagement between educators and students while conducting SoTL in online contexts is one of the most frequent problems they encounter. In conventional educational environments, educators frequently depend on casual, impromptu exchanges with pupils to assess their comprehension and involvement. But with online classes, these real-time indicators are absent, so it's challenging for teachers to gauge how well their students are understanding the subject. For example, teachers could find it difficult to get students to provide thoughtful comments during asynchronous online forums or lecture recordings. The capacity to gather rich, qualitative data—which is necessary for SoTL projects meant to enhance teaching practices—may be impacted by this separation (Sienkewicz, 2021).

Teachers may address this issue by putting techniques into place that promote more thoughtful and engaged student engagement in the virtual classroom. A good way to replicate the immediacy of in-person interactions is to incorporate real-time interactive features into synchronous meetings, including live polls, quizzes, or breakout room conversations. For instance, during a live lecture in an online biology course, the instructor may utilize polling software to get immediate feedback from the class on how well they understood a particular idea. This information may then be used to inform future SoTL research. Furthermore, students may contribute more in-depth and reflective insights into their learning experiences through asynchronous activities like discussion forums or reflective journaling, which can give educators the qualitative information they need to carry out their SoTL projects successfully (Plews & Ngoenha, 2020). Ensuring student involvement and participation presents a significant problem while doing SoTL online. Students sometimes have more control over their study schedules in online classes, which may cause them to become disengaged or participate irregularly. The efficacy of SoTL initiatives, particularly those that depend on continuous communication with students over a semester, may be hampered by this lack of persistent participation. For example, if students don't regularly engage in group projects, research looking at the effects of peer-to-peer cooperation in an online course may not succeed (Maurer, 2022).

To solve this issue, educators should utilize tactics that promote persistent engagement by making online learning environments more dynamic and individualized. Creating assignments that prioritize peer cooperation and active learning is one way to address this. Since students are held responsible to their peers, employing project-based learning, for example, where they collaborate in groups to address real-world challenges, can promote more constant engagement. Personalized learning pathways can also boost motivation and engagement as they give students some control over the subjects and tasks they choose to study. The effectiveness of this strategy was shown in a case study of an online history course where students were allowed to choose from a list of project subjects. The teacher discovered that pupils were more committed to their work, which improved the calibre of the information gathered for the SoTL project (Swaminathan & Mulvihill, 2022). Another major obstacle in online SoTL programs is data collecting and analysis. In contrast to conventional classroom settings, where data may be obtained by surveys, interviews, or observations, data collection in online contexts necessitates the use of digital technologies, which some instructors may find daunting or unfamiliar. Furthermore, evaluating the massive volume of data produced in online courses—from forum postings to quiz results—can be quite difficult, particularly for instructors with no background in data analytics (Plews & Ngoenha, 2020).

Educators can employ digital tools that are easy to use and particularly made for gathering and analysing data in online learning settings to help overcome these challenges. Analytics tools are frequently included in learning management systems (LMS) like Canvas or Blackboard, enabling teachers to monitor assessment results, completion rates, and student participation. For SoTL initiatives, these data points can offer insightful information without requiring a high level of technical knowledge. Additionally, low-cost or free technologies like SurveyMonkey and Google Forms may make getting student input easier, and programs like NVivo or ATLAS.ti can help with qualitative data analysis. (Pechenkina, 2020). For example, in a SoTL project investigating student satisfaction in an online business course, the teacher may monitor discussion forum activity using LMS analytics and conduct surveys to obtain more input. By using these technologies, the teacher may concentrate on analyzing the data to enhance their pedagogical approaches and expedite the process of gathering data. Despite these difficulties, a number of SoTL initiatives in online learning have overcome barriers by using workable solutions. One noteworthy case study included an online nursing school that used virtual simulations to increase student participation. The first issue was a deficiency in participation in conventional discussion-based tasks, which resulted in a gap between the application of theory and reality. In response, the teachers devised virtual simulations that allowed students to hone their clinical judgment abilities in a secure setting. Along with raising student engagement, this invention produced extensive data on how students really used their information. The educators were successful in breaking through the engagement barrier and producing significant results for their SoTL study by modifying their approaches and utilizing technology to create more engaged learning experiences (Tierney et al., 2020).

An additional case study from an online language learning course demonstrates how using LMS technologies already in place helped to overcome technical difficulties in data collecting. In order to assess how well peer feedback improves language ability, the teacher first had trouble gathering reliable and thorough data from asynchronous discussion boards. The teacher collected the required data in an effective manner by tracking word counts, reaction rates, and interaction patterns using the built-in analytics of the LMS. The teacher then enhanced this by adding a brief online poll to find out how the students felt about the peer review procedure. These modifications simplified the data collecting procedure and offered lucid insights into the ways in which peer feedback impacted learning objectives (Pechenkina, 2020).

FUTURE DIRECTIONS FOR SOTL IN ONLINE LEARNING

Emerging trends and new technology that influence teaching methods and learning objectives will propel a considerable evolution in the SoTL in online learning settings. The future of SoTL promises to explore unexplored territory and present new opportunities for educators and scholars alike, as online education continues to grow and diversify. These new paths will probably expand on what's already been done while welcoming the creative, collaborative, and learner-focused opportunities that come with virtual learning environments (Swaminathan & Mulvihill, 2022). The use of artificial intelligence (AI) and data analytics into online education is one of the most noteworthy new trends in SoTL. Adaptive learning platforms and intelligent tutoring systems are two examples of AI-driven solutions that are revolutionizing how students engage with course content. By customizing the material and pacing to meet each student's unique requirements and providing personalized feedback and support in real-time, these technologies personalize the educational experience. These AI systems have the capacity to produce enormous volumes of data about student behaviour, engagement, and learning outcomes in the context of SoTL, giving teachers access to rich datasets for analysis. Educators may gain a more nuanced picture of what works in various situations by utilizing AI to more precisely quantify the efficacy of interventions and teaching tactics in online courses (Maurer, 2022).

In order to enhance instructional design, a future SoTL research may examine, for instance, the effects of adaptive learning platforms on student accomplishment and retention in extensive online courses, utilizing data provided by artificial intelligence. The growing emphasis on social and collaborative learning is another trend influencing the direction of SoTL in online education. Although the apparent lack of connection in traditional online learning settings has frequently been criticized, new technology and pedagogical techniques are creating virtual places that are more dynamic and socially engaged. Collaborative, experiential learning is made possible by technologies such as virtual reality (VR), augmented reality (AR), and immersive simulations, which were formerly hard to duplicate in an online environment. These resources can be especially useful in fields where hands-on, experiential learning is crucial, including the arts, engineering, and healthcare (Pechenkina, 2020). In the future, a SoTL research may, for example, look into how critical thinking and teamwork are enhanced by VR-based simulations in an online medical training program. This would provide insights into the potential of immersive technology to improve social and cognitive learning outcomes (Tierney et al, 2020).

It is also expected that the future of SoTL will emphasize accessibility and inclusion as online learning becomes more and more common. Reaching a wide community of learners who would encounter obstacles to traditional in-person education, such as geographic location, disability, or employment responsibilities, is one of the benefits of online education (Manokore & McRae, 2021). However, ensuring that online courses are really inclusive involves continual study into best practices for building accessible learning environments. Future SoTL studies may investigate how various technologies, and instructional practices might help students with a range of requirements. For example, they could look at making digital content more accessible or using AI to give students with disabilities individualized support. An investigation of the effects of text-to-speech technology and captioning tools on the academic performance and participation of students with hearing impairments in online courses, for instance, might be the subject of a SoTL research (Swaminathan & Mulvihill, 2022). Predictions on the growth of SoTL practices in virtual learning environments point to the increasing importance of multidisciplinary and cross-institutional collaboration as a major development. Geographical barriers to education are being broken down by online learning, which gives researchers and educators from many institutions and areas additional chances to work together on SoTL initiatives (Tierney et al., 2020).

Richer, more thorough research that explore the junction of pedagogy, technology, and topic understanding may result from this multidisciplinary approach. In a future SoTL program, for example, educators from many disciplines may work together on a large-scale research study that looks at how virtual laboratories affect students' learning in a variety of STEM professions. These collaborative SoTL projects can provide findings that are more broadly relevant and generalizable across a variety of educational situations by combining resources and expertise (Waller & Prosser, 2023). The growing significance of students as knowledge co-creators is another important forecast for the future of SoTL. In the past, SoTL has mostly concentrated on the viewpoint of the instructor, using students as the study subjects. But with online learning, the move to learner-centred pedagogy is promoting a more collaborative approach in which students actively participate in the research process (Manarin et al., 2021). Students may play increasingly significant roles in future SoTL initiatives, contributing to the design of research studies, offering suggestions for improving course layout, and even carrying out independent study on learning processes. This change to student-led research is consistent with the larger trend of democratizing education and giving students the freedom to direct their own learning. A future study on support of learning (SoTL) may, for instance, look at how better learning outcomes and increased student satisfaction result from incorporating students in the creation and assessment of online assessments (Pechenkina, 2020).

There are a ton of opportunities for more study and development in SoTL, especially as new technologies keep coming out and online education gets more advanced. Investigating how online learning settings might promote higher-order thinking abilities like critical thinking, problem-solving, and creativity is one interesting topic for future study. Although the traditional focus of online courses has been on acquiring fundamental information, there is increasing interest in the application of digital technologies and pedagogies to foster the development of more advanced cognitive skills. Inquiry-based learning and problem-based learning's capacity to develop critical thinking in online courses may be the subject of a future SoTL study. Data analytics and qualitative feedback might be used to evaluate the effects of these strategies (Swaminathan & Mulvihill, 2022; Tan & Chen, 2020).

CONCLUSION

The chapter has looked at the many facets of online education's Scholarship of Teaching and Learning (SoTL), highlighting how it may change both teachers and students. We looked at the foundational ideas of SoTL, its historical development, and its numerous advantages in the context of online learning environments during the conversation. In addition to highlighting the incorporation of creative approaches, professional development tactics, and best practices, there were also successful case studies of SoTL initiatives that showed how SoTL may really improve educational outcomes. This chapter presented a thorough strategy for improving online teaching and learning via the lens of SoTL, including everything from the difficulties faced by educators to the answers offered by cooperation and technology. The significance of constantly changing teaching techniques and strategies in virtual learning environments is one of the main lessons learned. The chapter emphasizes how important it is for teachers to use SoTL in order to evaluate the efficacy of their instructional tactics, reflect on their own teaching practices, and ultimately enhance the learning outcomes of their students. By embracing SoTL, educators may move beyond traditional teaching methods and add evidence-based, learner-centred techniques that are more suited to the challenges of online education. For instance, educators have shown via best practice research that peer-to-peer interactions and collaborative projects are examples of active learning tactics that greatly improve student engagement and retention in online courses (Waller & Prosser, 2023).

Future instructional design might be influenced by these SoTL-gave insights to emphasize student learning and create a more engaging and encouraging online community. The necessity of professional development for educators was again emphasized in this chapter, especially with regard to online teaching and learning. For educators to keep up to date on the latest pedagogical ideas, tools, and techniques, ongoing professional development is crucial as technology advances and educational practices change. Examples of SoTL-focused professional development initiatives include seminars, online courses, and learning communities. These initiatives demonstrate how educators may work together, exchange knowledge, and acquire new skills in order to enhance their instruction. By encouraging a culture of continual development, these possibilities not only support individual progress but also enhance the standard of online education as a whole. Teachers who take part in SoTL-focused professional development programs, for example, frequently report feeling more confident in their ability to teach and having a better grasp of how to modify their approaches to suit the requirements of different types of learners in online contexts.

The chapter's discussion on professional learning communities' (PLCs) contribution to the advancement of SoTL in online education is also very important. These communities give educators a place to work together, exchange best practices, and take part in cooperative research initiatives that advance the field of educational research. Together, educators can better address the issues posed by online learning and create creative solutions that improve instruction. The chapter's case studies of prosperous online PLCs highlight the importance of these communities for promoting cooperation and producing fresh perspectives on efficient teaching methods. In one instance, instructors from several universities worked together on a SoTL study that investigated how asynchronous conversations affected students' participation in online courses. Their research provided useful answers for other educators dealing with comparable issues, and it also added to the corpus of knowledge on online pedagogy. Their results not only influenced their own teaching techniques. Regarding student involvement, the chapter stressed how crucial it is to include students in SoTL initiatives. Involving students in the study of teaching and learning not only gives them the confidence to take an active role in their education but also offers educators insightful information that they can use to enhance their methods. Education professionals may gain a deeper understanding of the requirements, preferences, and difficulties encountered by students in virtual learning settings by embracing student input and supporting student-led research projects. The potential for students to make a significant contribution to the advancement of online education is demonstrated by the examples of student-led SoTL projects, such as the establishment of peer mentorship programs and student-driven research on course design. These programs not only improve the educational experience for kids, but they also instil a feeling of accountability and ownership, which makes the student body more involved and driven.

Although there are numerous advantages to SoTL in online learning, the chapter also discussed the difficulties that instructors may have when working on SoTL projects in virtual settings. Common problems including time restraints, technology obstacles, and hurdles in gauging the effectiveness of instructional interventions were explored, along with workable ways to get beyond them. For instance, educators have discovered that using technology to gather and examine data on student performance and engagement can assist in resolving the difficulty associated with monitoring the efficacy of online teaching tactics. Furthermore, participating in PLCs and working with colleagues can offer resources and support to educators who might be feeling overburdened by the obligations of performing SoTL research on top of their teaching duties. The case studies that show how SoTL issues may be successfully resolved provide educators with real-world examples of how to overcome these obstacles and keep refining their methods of instruction. The chapter concludes by highlighting the revolutionary potential of SoTL in online learning.

Educators may improve student learning outcomes, their own teaching methods, and the continuous development of successful online pedagogies by adopting SoTL. Since rising developments like artificial intelligence (AI), data analytics, and collaborative technologies present new avenues for study and innovation, the future of SoTL in virtual learning environments is quite promising. As online education continues to develop and change (**see Appendix A for Key Terms & Definitions**), SoTL will play a critical part in determining the future of teaching and learning, providing educators with the tools and insights they need to create more engaging, inclusive, and successful learning experiences (Waller & Prosser, 2023).

REFERENCES

Anselmo, L., Wright, A., & Stepanchuk, A. (2022). Advancing the scholarship of teaching and learning in large enrolment courses: Lessons learned from an online community of practice. *Imagining SoTL*, 2(2), 52–62. DOI: 10.29173/isotl613

Baker, N., Hornsby, D. J., & Turner, N. K. (n.d.). The importance of online, open, and equitable education during the global pandemic. *Online, Open, and Equitable Education, 1*.

Bernard, R., Abrami, P. C., Lou, Y., Borokhovski, E., Wade, A., Wozney, L., Wallet, P. A., Fiset, M., & Huang, B. (2009). How does distance education compare with classroom instruction? A meta-analysis of the empirical literature. *Review of Educational Research*, 74(3), 379–439. DOI: 10.3102/00346543074003379

Botes, K., & Botha, A. J. (2021). Experiential e-learning: A creative prospect for education in the built environment? In advances in web-based learning–ICWL 2021: 20th International Conference, ICWL 2021, Macau, China, November 13–14, 2021, Proceedings (pp. 102-114). *Springer International Publishing*. DOI: 10.1007/978-3-030-90785-3_9

Bunnell, S. L., Chick, N., Hamilton, M., Leoni, A. S., & Woolmer, C. (2024). Generations of SoTL scholars: Transferable lessons and new possibilities. *Transformative Dialogues: Teaching and Learning Journal*, 17(1), 24–40.

Cleary, K., Loton, D., & Samarawickrema, G. (2022). Activating SoTL partnerships and ethical processes: A model to capture pedagogical innovation. In *Ethics and the Scholarship of Teaching and Learning* (pp. 79–94). Springer International Publishing., DOI: 10.1007/978-3-031-11810-4_6

Cleaver, E., Mclinden, M., Lintern, M., & Birch, A. (2020). The enquiring university: The scholarship of teaching and learning as a foundation for strategic educational transformation. In *Evidence-Based Faculty Development Through the Scholarship of Teaching and Learning (SoTL)* (pp. 20–41). IGI Global., DOI: 10.4018/978-1-7998-2212-7.ch002

Cook, S. C. (2020). Emerging response-abilities: A reflection on the 2019 SoTL in the South conference. *Scholarship of Teaching and Learning in the South*, 4(1), 69–85. DOI: 10.36615/sotls.v4i1.135

Cruz, L., Leoni, A. S., & Mojarad, S. N. (2024). Meaning and manifesto: Embracing transdisciplinarity in SoTL. *Transformative Dialogues: Teaching and Learning Journal*, 17(1), 1–13.

Cruz, L. E., & Grodziak, E. M. (2021). SoTL under stress: Rethinking teaching and learning scholarship during a global pandemic. *Teaching & Learning Inquiry*, 9(1), 3–13. DOI: 10.20343/teachlearninqu.9.1.2

Eady, M. J., Abrahamson, E., Green, C. A., Arcellana-Panlilio, M., Hatfield, L., & Namaste, N. (2021). Re-positioning SoTL toward the T-shaped community. *Teaching & Learning Inquiry*, 9(1), 262–278. DOI: 10.20343/teachlearninqu.9.1.18

Fukuzawa, S., Ashbourne, D., & Rawle, F. (2020). Overcoming challenges to impactful SoTL. In *Evidence-Based Faculty Development Through the Scholarship of Teaching and Learning (SoTL)* (pp. 366–387). IGI Global., DOI: 10.4018/978-1-7998-2212-7.ch019

Gansemer-Topf, A., Webb, A., Kensington-Miller, B., Maheux-Pelletier, G., Lewis, H., Luu, J., & Hofmann, A. (2021). Navigating the chaos: The value of SoTL during times of uncertainty. *Transformative Dialogues: Teaching and Learning Journal, 14*(2).

Harvey, M., & Jones, S. (2021). Enabling leadership capacity for higher education scholarship in learning and teaching (SoTL) through action research. *Educational Action Research*, 29(2), 173–190. DOI: 10.1080/09650792.2020.1803941

How, Z. J. (2020). A systematic review of scholarship of teaching and learning research in higher education institutes from 2014–2019. In *Transforming teaching and learning in higher education: A chronicle of research and development in a Singaporean Context* (pp. 11–43). Springer Singapore., DOI: 10.1007/978-981-15-4980-9_2

Khosa, N. G. (2022). A review of literature on the effective pedagogy strategies for online teaching and learning in higher education institutions: Lessons from the COVID-19 pandemic. *European Journal of Education*, 5(1), 43–55. DOI: 10.26417/738tqq65

Manarin, K., Adams, C., Fendler, R., Marsh, H., Pohl, E., Porath, S., & Thomas, A. (2021). Examining the focus of SoTL literature—Teaching and learning? *Teaching & Learning Inquiry*, 9(1), 349–364. DOI: 10.20343/teachlearninqu.9.1.23

Manokore, V., & McRae, D. (2021). Revolutionizing learning environments with guerrilla pedagogy in large classes. *Journal of Practical Nurse Education and Practice*, 1(1). Advance online publication. DOI: 10.29173/jpnep7

Maurer, T. W. (2022). Leveraging SoTL to improve teaching and learning during the COVID-19 pandemic. *International Journal for the Scholarship of Teaching and Learning*, 16(1), 3. DOI: 10.20429/ijsotl.2022.160103

Openo, J. (2024). The right relationship between teaching and educational technology: How Ursula Franklin's technology as practice can guide SoTL. *The Canadian Journal for the Scholarship of Teaching and Learning*, 15(1). Advance online publication. DOI: 10.5206/cjsotlrcacea.2024.1.15640

Pechenkina, E. (2020). Chasing impact: The tale of three SoTL studies. *Teaching & Learning Inquiry*, 8(1), 91–107. DOI: 10.20343/teachlearninqu.8.1.7

Plews, R. C., & Ngoenha, M. L. (2020). At the crossroads of transformative learning and SoTL: The flipped classroom in teacher education. In *Evidence-Based Faculty Development Through the Scholarship of Teaching and Learning (SoTL)* (pp. 201–220). IGI Global., DOI: 10.4018/978-1-7998-2212-7.ch011

Sienkewicz, J. A. (2021). Guest editor introduction: Cultivating our field through SoTL practice: Teaching and learning the art history of the United States. *Art History Pedagogy & Practice*, 6(1), 1.

Supple, B., & Cronin, J. G. (2023). A pedagogy of slow: Integrating experiences of physical and virtual gallery spaces to foster critical engagement in SoTL. *Teaching & Learning Inquiry*, 11, 11. DOI: 10.20343/teachlearninqu.11.2

Supple, B., Fennell, C., & McCarthy, M. (n.d.). Reviewing reflective teaching portfolios about online learning: What are they telling us? *Transforming Patterns through the Scholarship of Teaching and Learning, 13*, 245.

Swaminathan, R., & Mulvihill, T. (2022). Synergistic pedagogies in virtual spaces: Preparing social justice educational researchers through SoTL. In *Teaching and Learning for Social Justice and Equity in Higher Education: Virtual Settings* (pp. 85-105). Springer International Publishing. https://doi.org/DOI: 10.1007/978-3-030-86683-6_5

Tan, S. C., & Chen, S. H. A. (2020). *Transforming teaching and learning in higher education*. Springer Singapore., DOI: 10.1007/978-981-15-4980-9

Tariq, M. U. (2024a). Generative AI in curriculum development in higher education. In Fields, Z. (Ed.), *Impacts of generative AI on creativity in higher education* (pp. 227–258). IGI Global., DOI: 10.4018/979-8-3693-2418-9.ch009

Tariq, M. U. (2024b). Harnessing persuasive technologies for enhanced learner engagement and motivation. In M. Sanmugam, D. Lim, N. Mohd Barkhaya, W. Wan Yahaya, & Z. Khlaif (Eds.), *Power of persuasive educational technologies in enhancing learning* (pp. 30-62). IGI Global. https://doi.org/DOI: 10.4018/979-8-3693-6397-3.ch002

Tariq, M. U. (2024c). Navigating the personalization pathway: Implementing adaptive learning technologies in higher education. In Minh Tung, T. (Ed.), *Adaptive learning technologies for higher education* (pp. 265–291). IGI Global., DOI: 10.4018/979-8-3693-3641-0.ch012

Tariq, M. U. (2024d). AI-powered language translation for multilingual classrooms. In Doshi, R., Dadhich, M., Poddar, S., & Hiran, K. (Eds.), *Integrating generative AI in education to achieve sustainable development goals* (pp. 29–46). IGI Global., DOI: 10.4018/979-8-3693-2440-0.ch002

Tariq, M. U. (2025a). *AI-driven learning and engagement in higher education.* IGI Global., DOI: 10.4018/979-8-3693-4074-5

Tariq, M. U. (2025b). Navigating bias and fairness in digital AI systems. In Bhattacharya, P., Hassan, A., Liu, H., & Bhushan, B. (Eds.), *Ethical dimensions of AI development* (pp. 127–156). IGI Global., DOI: 10.4018/979-8-3693-4147-6.ch006

Tariq, M. U., & Sergio, R. P. (2025c). Innovative assessment techniques in physical education: Exploring technology-enhanced and student-centered models for holistic student development. In Garcia, M. (Ed.), *Global innovations in physical education and health* (pp. 85–112). IGI Global., DOI: 10.4018/979-8-3693-3952-7.ch004

Tierney, A. M., Aidulis, D., Park, J., & Clark, K. (2020). Supporting SoTL development through communities of practice. *Teaching & Learning Inquiry*, 8(2), 32–52. DOI: 10.20343/teachlearninqu.8.2.4

Waller, K. L., & Prosser, M. (2023). The rapidly changing teaching and research landscape: The future of SoTL and the teaching-research nexus. In *The educational turn: Rethinking the scholarship of teaching and learning in higher education* (pp. 27–41). Springer Nature Singapore., DOI: 10.1007/978-981-19-8951-3_3

KEY TERMS AND DEFINITIONS

SoTL: The Scholarship of Teaching and Learning (SoTL) is the systematic study of teaching methods and student learning to improve educational practices.

Online Learning: A mode of education where instructional content is delivered via the internet, allowing for remote access to learning materials and activities.

Student Engagement: The level of interest, participation, and interaction that students exhibit in their learning processes and activities.

Professional Development: Continuous learning opportunities aimed at improving the skills and knowledge of educators to enhance teaching effectiveness.

Virtual Classrooms: Digital platforms where educators and students interact in real time or asynchronously to facilitate learning.

Assessment: The process of evaluating student performance and understanding through various tools, including tests, projects, and reflective activities.

Chapter 3
Leveraging a Scholarship of Teaching and Learning Values Framework to Build Online Faculty Learning Communities

Alesia Mickle Moldavan
https://orcid.org/0000-0001-7946-9028
Georgia Southern University, USA

Anna C. Brady
https://orcid.org/0000-0003-1361-2412
Georgia Southern University, USA

Kevin J. Reagan
Georgia Southern University, USA

Bailey Nafziger
https://orcid.org/0000-0001-5525-7039
Georgia Southern University, USA

Diana Botnaru
Georgia Southern University, USA

Jackie Mesenbrink-Sainz
Georgia Southern University, USA

ABSTRACT

Scholarship of Teaching and Learning (SoTL) enhances teaching practices and improves student learning outcomes while fostering a culture of continuous professional development and reflective practice (Felten, 2013; Hutchings et al., 2011; Trigwell et al., 2000). Faculty Learning Communities (FLCs) serve as dynamic hubs for collaborative exchange, enabling faculty to engage with SoTL principles, share diverse perspectives, and develop innovative teaching strategies that benefit learners (Cox, 2004). This chapter examines an online SoTL FLC at a multi-campus institution as a case study to propose a SoTL Values Framework to guide best practices in online professional development. The framework is built on four key values: inclusivity,

DOI: 10.4018/979-8-3693-7595-2.ch003

collaboration, scholarly approach, and reflectiveness, each aligned with unique opportunities offered by the online environment. By drawing on SoTL literature and reflecting on the experiences within this online SoTL FLC, the chapter offers insights to inform future online SoTL initiatives fostering sustained growth in SoTL practices.

INTRODUCTION

Engaging in the Scholarship of Teaching and Learning (SoTL) offers numerous benefits, including enhancing teaching practices and improving student learning outcomes (Hutchings et al., 2011; Trigwell et al., 2000). Additionally, SoTL facilitates a culture of continuous professional development and reflective practices that encourage college instructors and staff to critically evaluate and refine their teaching strategies (Felten, 2013). By publicly disseminating evidence-based pedagogical insights, SoTL fuels the collective knowledge of scholarly communities, offering rich opportunities for learning and collaboration. Faculty Learning Communities (FLCs) play a vital role in this process, serving as dynamic hubs where colleagues can engage with SoTL, exchange diverse ideas, and cultivate innovative teaching practices that benefit all learners across a variety of disciplines (Cox, 2004). Leveraging SoTL within these communities elevates individual teaching and creates spaces for sustained growth and pedagogical excellence.

This chapter uses a multi-campus institution's online SoTL FLC as a case study to propose a SoTL Values Framework to guide best practices in online professional development for faculty. The framework centers on four SoTL values aligned with the online environment: 1) inclusivity, 2) collaboration, 3) scholarly approach, and 4) reflectiveness. By drawing on SoTL literature and examining the practices within our online SoTL FLC, we aim to offer a SoTL Values Framework that can inform online SoTL professional development initiatives—thus addressing the International Society for the Scholarship of Teaching and Learnings (ISSOTL)'s Grand Challenge #5 "the practice, use, and growth of SoTL" (Scharff et al., 2023, para. 1).

In the following sections, we provide an in-depth description of the online SoTL FLC that served as the foundation for this case study, exploring its unique context and challenges in the online environment. We showcase the four key values integral to SoTL and illustrate how online SoTL FLCs can powerfully cultivate these principles. Building on our experiences, we also identify opportunities for growth to improve SoTL faculty development opportunities within online environments. Through these insights, we hope to share our strategies and inspire others to create thriving online communities where faculty engage in meaningful dialogue that transforms teaching and learning and promotes SoTL research.

CONTEXT

Teaching and learning are inherently shaped by the environments and contexts in which they occur, including institutional cultures and geographical differences. Therefore, recognizing the unique context of our online SoTL FLC is critical to upholding the core principles of "good practice in SoTL," as Felten (2013) outlined. These principles emphasize student learning, contextual grounding, methodological rigor, partnerships with students, and public sharing. In the following sections, we explore the evolution and current context of our SoTL FLC. This overview directly informs the specific values that we argue are essential to developing an effective online SoTL FLC. While we have opted to use first-person language, not all authors of this chapter were involved in every iteration of the SoTL FLC's development, but our collective insights shape the narrative.

Foundation and Evolution

The Faculty Center at Georgia Southern University launched an FLC program in 2007, initially supporting several FLCs on faculty-selected topics. Notably, the 2007-2008 FLC on SoTL developed the foundation for a university-wide initiative, "SoTL at Georgia Southern" (Botnaru et al., 2022), seeking to recognize, sustain, expand, and promote SoTL research. Since then, the Faculty Center has continually supported the annual international *SoTL Commons Conference*, the peer-reviewed *International Journal for the Scholarship of Teaching and Learning*, and FLCs focusing on SoTL. Through these efforts, faculty across the university have been educated on the principles and practices of SoTL, cultivating a robust culture that emphasizes the value and impact of conducting SoTL research. This focus underscores the importance of institutional support in advancing SoTL research and building a scholarly teaching community.

Scope and Resources

Initially, all FLCs were provided with modest budgets to support their activities. However, these allocations ceased due to budgetary constraints. Nevertheless, the SoTL FLC remained the only active community due to faculty initiative and dedication (Maurer et al., 2010). Its goal was to engage faculty new to SoTL by introducing them to the relevant approaches and theories while equipping them with the skills necessary to continue their engagement in SoTL (Georgia Southern Faculty Center, n.d.). Initially, all FLC meetings were conducted in person. However, two significant events led to a transition to an online format. First, the 2018 institutional merger added two additional campuses approximately 50 miles apart, creating logistical challenges for cross-campus inclusivity for in-person professional development events. Second, the COVID-19 lockdown in spring 2020 necessitated a shift to online professional development. During this period, however, faculty members were overwhelmed by the demands of remote teaching, resulting in limited engagement with the SoTL FLC. The SoTL FLC was relaunched in 2022 as a fully online community, providing an accessible platform for faculty across all campuses to participate in professional development and collaboration.

Organization of the Online Faculty Learning Community

To understand the guiding SoTL principles and develop our project, we used Bishop-Clark and Dietz-Uhler's (2012) book, *Engaging in the Scholarship of Teaching and Learning: A Guide to the Process, and How to Develop a Project from Start to Finish*. In the early iterations of the SoTL FLC, we conducted a book study where members read and discussed the text while being encouraged to develop individual SoTL projects. However, few faculty members completed their planned SoTL projects after participating in a SoTL FLC. In response, we revised the goal of the SoTL FLCs in 2022 to "practice SoTL" by "doing" SoTL through collaborative efforts, emphasizing developing, designing, and implementing one SoTL project for the entire group. This approach aligns with Fanghanel's (2013) assertion that "inquiry into practice through SoTL is the only way for academics to understand practice" (p. 62).

The new approach also prompted us to rethink how we scheduled the online SoTL FLC. Prior to 2022, SoTL FLCs started in the fall semester and continued into spring. In 2022, we transitioned to a calendar year schedule, using the spring semester (i.e., January – May) to learn about SoTL, develop a research idea, and consult relevant literature. The summer semester (i.e., May – July) was designated for finalizing the project and submitting an Institutional Review Board (IRB) application, while the fall semester (i.e., August – December) focused on data collection. To facilitate the spring tasks, we established synchronous online meetings on a day and time prior to the advertising of the SoTL FLC. This allowed faculty to sign up based on their existing schedules and ensured consistent attendance.

The Faculty Center supported the recruitment and scheduling efforts and integrated the SoTL FLC into our centralized faculty development accounts, allowing us to easily access our participation records in professional development events. During the spring semester, we met synchronously on Zoom. During the summer and fall semesters, the SoTL FLC primarily operated asynchronously via Google Drive, with occasional synchronous meetings on Zoom, as needed. The calendar year approach proved beneficial in allowing more time to finalize the project (using the summer semester) and aligned with the faculty annual review schedule.

The SoTL FLC attracts diverse members from various roles across the university, representing different colleges and campuses. Moreover, members possess a wide range of prior experience with SoTL scholarship. Generally, there is a consistent pattern in the representation of colleges year after year, likely due to varying levels of acknowledgment and support for SoTL research at the college level. For example, some colleges explicitly recognize SoTL as a valid form of scholarship in their tenure and promotion criteria, while others do not. Although the SoTL FLC has no authority to alter such criteria, FLCs can contribute to developing a community culture that values, supports, and advocates for SoTL research.

2023 SoTL Faculty Learning Community

The organization and flow of the 2023 SoTL FLC aligned with the description of the SoTL FLCs outlined in the previous section. Our group exhibited diverse experiences with SoTL research; among our seven members (plus two co-facilitators), four were new to SoTL and undertaking a SoTL project for the first time. Additionally, the 2023 SoTL FLC included representatives from seven departments across four colleges, namely the College of Education, the Waters College of Health Professions, the College of Arts and Humanities, and the Jiann-Ping Hsu College of Public Health, as well as the University Libraries. This breadth of representation encompassed various disciplines, including educational psychology, teacher education, human anatomy and physiology, library and information studies, art history, biology, and health administration.

Bringing together faculty from diverse backgrounds to tackle shared interests and potential research questions was a significant achievement afforded by the online environment. Each member contributed unique disciplinary expertise, research methodologies, and writing styles, which added complexity to a shared research project. However, as SoTL research thrives on integrating varied scholarly insights, our SoTL FLC found strength in our differences. Through collaborative discussions, we recognized that our diverse voices and perspectives enriched our collective endeavor. In our pursuit of a common research goal, we honored individual contributions while embracing the richness of our diversity. This process reaffirmed the importance of SoTL principles: every discipline has a seat and a voice at the table (Felten, 2013). Consequently, the SoTL Values Framework we developed articulates the voices, perspectives, and perceptions of our faculty's collective experience, united in enhancing our teaching through systematic investigation of students' learning experiences.

Our 2023 SoTL FLC identified topics of interest, including sense of belonging, artificial intelligence, and online learning. This led to a research project examining the influence of a learning management system tool (i.e., intelligent agents in D2L) on online students' sense of belonging, academic engagement, and performance (Brady et al., 2024). Utilizing a quasi-experimental approach, we collected quantitative and qualitative data to address our research questions, directly informed by the experiences and interests of our group members.

While this chapter uses our 2023 SoTL FLC as a case study to inform the development of the SoTL Values Framework, the significance of context in SoTL research cannot be overstated. Context shapes every aspect of teaching and learning, and by recognizing and incorporating specific contextual factors, we can foster more effective, inclusive, and responsive learning environments. In the following sections, we share four key values that emerged from our experience, offering insights into how they guided the creation of the SoTL Values Framework. These values provide essential context-specific considerations for the design, implementation, and sustainability of SoTL initiatives and offer valuable lessons that can contribute to the success of online SoTL efforts in other institutions.

VALUE 1: INCLUSIVITY

Inclusivity is a cornerstone of SoTL, often referred to as a "big tent" where scholars from all disciplines are welcomed (Huber & Hutchings, 2005, p. 30). We argue that this first value in the SoTL Values Framework is paramount to the prosperity of online SoTL FLCs, as it ensures that diverse perspectives are represented and that no voices are obfuscated or wholly neglected. Without inclusivity, essential insights could be missed, and the richness of transdisciplinary collaboration would be diminished. In an online SoTL FLC environment, inclusivity allows scholars from various fields, such as art history and biology, to come together and share pedagogical practices that might otherwise never permeate their usual fields. This cross-pollination of ideas, when encouraged through recruitment messages emphasizing that everyone is welcomed, fosters innovation and supports a goal that SoTL-minded faculty share: improved teaching and student learning outcomes. Thus, inclusivity is vital in environments, especially online ones, where vastly different disciplines converge to achieve a common goal.

Transdisciplinary Approach

One aspect of inclusivity is the presence of different disciplines in SoTL work. SoTL flourishes when transdisciplinary collaboration is embraced, creating a space where faculty from different academic disciplines "rise above disciplinary boundaries… for exchanging ideas, fostering insights, and generating new ways of knowing about what happens within and among a wide (and ever-expanding) range of university classrooms" (Cruz et al., 2024, p. 1). This approach leverages the diverse academic discourses and research paradigms that each discipline brings, enabling deeper inquiry and the dissemination of innovative knowledge in teaching and learning (Bunnell et al., 2024; Chick, 2015; McCarthy, 2024; McSweeney et al., 2023).

A transdisciplinary SoTL community offers a variety of research methodologies, allowing for a robust and comprehensive investigation into complex educational challenges. For instance, transdisciplinary teams with expertise in educational technology and instructional design, higher education policy and administration, public health, and economics could be well-positioned to support SoTL research by addressing complex challenges like those posed by COVID-19. Such teams can explore the impact of the pandemic on remote instruction, rising tuition costs, and broader socioeconomic challenges students face. Their combined expertise allows for a comprehensive investigation into digital learning environments and effective engagement strategies for faculty while also considering the well-being implications of isolated learning, financial pressures, and student retention. By examining how these factors intersect, the team can uncover actionable insights to support research on teaching and learning, ultimately enhancing student success and academic resilience. Although this example of a transdisciplinary team does not represent our SoTL FLC, the shared goal of continuously reflecting on faculty representation and encouraging greater participation from various disciplines demonstrates a beneficial outcome. By leveraging transdisciplinary teams' diverse perspectives and expertise, complex problem-solving and information exchange in such groups can advance SoTL research (Gómez-García et al., 2022; Marg & Theiler, 2023).

Online SoTL FLCs as a Method of Bolstering Inclusivity

The online format of our SoTL FLC enabled the inclusion of scholars from diverse disciplines across Georgia Southern University's multiple campuses, fostering a transdisciplinary team that strengthened our SoTL research in several significant ways. First, while identifying a particular topic and formulating research questions, we were able to discuss cross-cutting trends and challenges permeating various disciplines. This ensured that our project had broad applicability and strong relevance across various fields. Second, when designing our data collection and analysis plans, we elevated research methodologies from all disciplines, leading to a mixed-methods approach incorporating quantitative (i.e., Likert-scale questionnaires) and qualitative (i.e., open-ended items) data. Third, the diverse expertise within our team allowed us to divide research tasks strategically. For instance, we leveraged the expertise of those more experienced in textual and creative analysis to provide insight into the study's discussion and conclusion. Fourth, due to the siloed nature of disciplinary-specific work, the SoTL FLC helped build valuable connections among faculty members who may not have otherwise collaborated. The online format provided a platform for faculty to engage with one another and establish meaningful relationships, fostering a sense of belonging and collegiality. This demonstrates how online environments can effectively create opportunities for forming transdisciplinary teams, encouraging collaboration across diverse academic fields.

Opportunities for Growth

Creating inclusive environments is not a static endeavor, for it requires continuous growth and adaptability. In our SoTL FLC, the group's success was measured by its collective evolution. Together, we achieved several milestones, such as completing a manuscript, submitting to multiple conferences, and contributing to a book chapter. These achievements were made possible through adaptations that facilitated mutual learning and collaboration, where each member's development strengthened the group's overall success. While the project experienced fluctuations, we persisted as a team, leveraging our diverse backgrounds, experiences, and voices to overcome challenges and accomplish more collectively than we could individually.

Conducting FLCs online offers additional opportunities for inclusivity that previous FLCs had not fully explored at our university. While our SoTL FLC brought together faculty with varied experiences, all members were from the same institution. Expanding future FLCs to include faculty from other institutions would introduce even more diverse perspectives, enriching SoTL work. In face-to-face formats, multi-institution collaborations can be expensive and travel-intensive. Online formats significantly lower these barriers, as seen in the example of International Writing Groups sponsored by ISSOTL or the MegaSoTL projects (Nasrollahian Mojarad & Cruz, 2022). In addition to including even more transdisciplinary teams, multi-institution collaborations have the added benefit of allowing researchers to examine whether particular phenomena are specific to a single university or pervasive across universities. This may lead to stronger, more generalizable recommendations about teaching and learning.

Furthermore, while our SoTL FLC primarily consisted of faculty who currently teach or are expected to teach undergraduate or graduate courses, including perspectives from additional higher education practitioners and students could enhance SoTL projects. Faculty may not wholly understand the student experience, which could be enriched by the insights of staff members who work directly with students, like academic advisors, university housing staff, or students themselves, that might allow for a more holistic perspective on student learning. Felton (2013) notes that collaboration between students and faculty emphasizes a shared commitment to learning. Furthermore, online environments make this type of inclusion possible.

Finally, a pattern emerged across different iterations of the university's SoTL FLCs: certain colleges were consistently represented, while others were not. This representation and lack of representation likely reflect the varying levels of support for SoTL research across departments and colleges, with some disciplines more actively engaged in SoTL work than others. Addressing this gap by advocating for SoTL research in underrepresented disciplines remains a critical goal, as it would bring new perspectives to FLCs and further enrich the SoTL community.

VALUE 2: COLLABORATION

Collaboration is another central aspect of SoTL research and represents the second key value in the SoTL Values Framework. Collaboration is characterized by fostering an environment of collegiality, mentorship, mutual support, and shared expertise among faculty (Cox, 2004; Cruz et al., 2023). The notion that collaboration among diverse researchers is imperative to SoTL is evident in the field's vast body of literature. When looking at how SoTL defines and values collaboration, one might begin with Felten's (2013) article, "Principles of Good SoTL." The concept of "collaborative" appears in the article and describes how "good SoTL" is done in partnership with students. Furthermore, Felten (2013) notes how faculty often practice SoTL "with colleagues in ad hoc professional development settings" and that diversity working in such settings "has allowed SoTL to develop and grow widely in the US and across the world" (p. 121). Harnessing the diversity of perspectives and expertise that strengthens SoTL projects in professional settings would be profoundly challenging without a collaborative nature. The SoTL FLC at hand leveraged a myriad of collaboration tools exemplifying characteristics of Felten's (2013) "good SoTL," thereby providing a foundational model for other online FLCs.

Online FLCs as a Method of Bolstering Collaboration

The SoTL FLC benefited from virtual collaboration, given that Georgia Southern University has faculty and staff in Statesboro, Savannah (Armstrong Campus), and Hinesville (Liberty Campus). Because the campuses are approximately an hour from each other, the faculty and staff are accustomed to leveraging virtual collaboration tools. Accordingly, the SoTL FLC was able to integrate existing virtual collaboration practices into its workflows. Examples include Zoom, Google Docs, Google Sheets, and Zotero. These tools allowed faculty members to contribute meaningfully to the project. Moreover, the virtual collaboration tools diminished the reliance on synchronous meetings since information could be conveyed asynchronously, freeing up each faculty member's time. This section outlines how the various collaboration tools were used, allowing or inspiring SoTL-minded communities to adopt or adapt our practices.

Like many institutions, our university adopted Zoom as its virtual meeting platform. As a multi-campus institution, Zoom was crucial in ensuring all SoTL community members could meet consistently, regardless of campus location or availability. If someone had to miss a meeting due to a conflict, Zoom's recording capabilities ensured that community members could catch up on action items and deadlines. Furthermore, Zoom's accessibility features (i.e., Zoom accessibility link) ensured that any members with disabilities could fully participate, with accessibility features including captions and audio transcripts. Ultimately, despite the institution consisting of multiple campuses, Zoom enabled the community to participate in a SoTL project, uniting members who might otherwise never work together, given their distance and departmental differences.

The structure of our SoTL FLC meetings emphasized collaboration. The first meeting was used for community-building activities. Using Google Docs as an asynchronous collaboration tool, group members were asked to find and share a research article from *The International Journal of Scholarship of Teaching and Learning*. Additionally, we compiled a shared document with our college affiliations, experiences and interests in SoTL, and classes taught. We used the asynchronous space to learn each other's strengths and identify similar research interests to guide our collective research endeavor. For example, we had a collaborative "Tasks and Responsibilities" file where everyone could sign up for specific tasks. Every meeting had an agenda, and the SoTL FLC facilitators kept the group on track as we progressed through the steps.

Our SoTL FLC enhanced its effectiveness by leveraging online collaboration platforms, enabling all members to contribute to our data-driven SoTL project. Throughout the first semester, we held seven synchronous meetings via Zoom. At the same time, Google Drive housed asynchronous work and served as a centralized repository for all of our SoTL FLC-related documents. These formats and digital tools fostered a truly collaborative environment, eliminating concerns over transportation or scheduling conflicts with on-campus priorities. Moreover, each participant could use the repository to support subsequent SoTL projects.

Google Drive was organized to curate resources needed for each research project step, with files structured into folders reflecting the steps outlined in Bishop-Clark and Dietz-Uhler's (2012) book. These folders included: "Introduction," "Generating the Research Idea/Literature Review," "Designing the Project," "IRB Application," "Data Collection and Analysis," and "Making It Public." For example, the "IRB Application" folder contained our CITI certificates, while the "Making it Public" folder was used to develop multiple conference proposals and the final manuscript.

Specifically, the asynchronous "Tasks and Responsibilities" file reflects SoTL values outlined in Howard et al. (2023). By providing an opportunity for people to sign up for tasks directly related to their skills or disciplinary strengths, the learning community ensured no single academic perspective or agenda dominated the study or community, keeping the focus on the shared goal of inquiring into best practices for facilitating belonging and engagement in online courses. Many tasks allowed two (or more) people to sign up, meaning those unfamiliar with a given task could learn from a more experienced faculty member. For instance, if someone inexperienced in quantitative research analysis and methods wanted to gain experience in quantitative methods, they could sign up for that part of the task, noting to the senior researcher that they signed up to gain more experience.

Allowing each member to sign up for a particular task also addressed a growing concern regarding SoTL and collaboration: the role of the arts and humanities in SoTL (see, e.g., Copland, 2023; Jaber et al., 2024; Potter & Wuetherick, 2015). Though this scholarly paradigm is too vast to be fully discussed in this chapter, noting how people with a background in arts and humanities research methods were able to contribute to the project is worthwhile. Leveraging their expertise in textual and visual analytical skills, the group members representing the University Libraries and the College of Arts and Humanities were able to provide rhetorical guidance in the composition process, facilitate literature reviews, manage citations, and edit for clarity and accuracy. Indeed, these tasks are essential to any study, regardless of whether someone has a background in the arts or humanities. However, faculty in the arts and humanities are uniquely equipped to lead such efforts, given their specialized training. While the social science approach to SoTL may be unfamiliar to some in the arts and humanities, recognizing such faculty contributions in explicit ways can articulate and acknowledge the vital role faculty play in SoTL research. Moreover, leveraging the strengths of individuals from these fields reinforces the principle that SoTL is most effective when researchers are empowered to contribute from their areas of expertise. Ultimately, SoTL is a scholarly endeavor that invites collaboration across disciplines to improve teaching practices and enhance student learning outcomes.

Opportunities for Growth

The goals of our SoTL FLC meetings tended to center on decision-making and discussion. The tasks members signed up to complete, such as drafting the IRB or preparing the data for analysis, tended to occur outside the scheduled meeting times. While this approach was effective, there were times when members became busy, and the project completion slowed. One way to circumvent this challenge in the future is to schedule virtual, synchronous times to complete SoTL tasks. As an example, writing accountability groups that provide blocked time to write independently or with colleagues can serve as one way to encourage team members to accomplish tasks. These groups are highly adaptable in their frequency and format. For instance, Zoom can be used to offer writing group breakout rooms or whole group writing sprints with set blocks of time. Thus, these groups can be modified to fit the particular needs of a project and its members needs.

As described in prior sections, members of the SoTL FLC signed up for tasks given their skill sets. Thus, different sections of the ultimate manuscript were drafted by different team members. This allowed all members to engage in the project in ways that aligned with their strengths. However, this collaboration also necessitated a final step in drafting the manuscript: ensuring the voice was consistent throughout the draft. This added challenge may mean collaborative FLCs should allow time to ensure voice consistency. Including a task checking for voice consistency may be an effective task for members to sign up for.

VALUE 3: SCHOLARLY APPROACH

Academics sometimes find themselves at a crossroads, diverging in two directions between teaching and research. The field of SoTL provides an opportunity for academics to merge their fields and open the doors of their private classroom practices to the public eye. The shift from scholarly teaching (Shulman, 2004) to SoTL research requires academics to ground their teaching in research, develop research questions related to student learning, employ methodological structures to collect credible data, and publish results for the broader community's benefit (Boyer, 1990; Felton, 2013). High-quality SoTL research "begins with what the teacher knows" (Boyer, 1990, p. 23) with the end goal of helping SoTL scholars improve their teaching practices based on published empirical or reflective data (Shulman, 2000). Wherever SoTL is placed within academic visions and missions, it must always include a scholarly approach, the third value in the SoTL Values Framework. Therefore, for our SoTL FLC to "do" SoTL, we collaboratively designed a research project that celebrated the diversity of strengths within our online SoTL FLC and led to a methodologically sound empirical research publication.

Online FLCs as a Method of Bolstering a Scholarly Approach

Our SoTL FLC began with an introduction to the field of SoTL, fostering a shared goal among all group members: to collaboratively undertake a SoTL project. Establishing this common objective was crucial for the success of our SoTL FLC. Following virtual, synchronous community-building activities designed to explore

SoTL, uncover individual interests, and highlight research strengths, we engaged in a structured brainstorming session to determine the focus of our research project. The most time-intensive and significant part of this process involved discussing our shared challenges in the classroom and collaboratively generating a list of potential research topics. This deliberate effort ensured that we reached a consensus on a topic of mutual interest and crafted research questions that aligned with our collective goals.

We narrowed our focus to two topics: one focused on student engagement and a sense of belonging, and the second focused on Artificial Intelligence (AI). Given the novelty of AI tools and our institution's record-setting enrollment trends, our SoTL FLC members sought methods to efficiently increase student engagement, sense of belonging, and academic performance in an online environment. After agreeing on a topic, a librarian within the FLC generated a spreadsheet shared with all group members and filed it into the "Literature Review" folder within the SoTL FLC's shared Google Drive folder. The librarian's role was instrumental in streamlining the literature review process for our group by using generated keywords and pulling resources our university's library had access to. Within the spreadsheet, our SoTL FLC divided SoTL and other germane peer-reviewed journals between members to investigate and review current literature on related topics. All members could review current literature asynchronously and note key ideas on the shared spreadsheet. It proved to be an effective technique for identifying gaps in the literature.

While we identified many previous studies focused on understanding student engagement and belonging, there was an apparent lack of research exploring how AI could support student engagement and belonging. As more students use AI, we wondered how to harness this tool to help us improve student learning. As a D2L institution, we can access an Intelligent Agent (IA) tool, which analyzes class lists based on predefined criteria, generates reports, and schedules personalized emails for those meeting specific conditions (Shepard, 2024). Our research questions focused on investigating if the use of IA in large-enrollment, online asynchronous classes can improve student engagement and sense of belonging (see Brady et al., 2024) and aligned with ISSOTL's Grand Challenge #2: "How to encourage students to be engaged in learning" (Scharff et al., 2023, para. 1).

An adequate methodology with systematic data collection is required for work to be considered "good SoTL" (Felten, 2013). After asynchronously researching and synchronously crafting our research questions, we settled on a mixed-methods quasi-experimental methodology to enhance the study's depth, breadth, and applicability. The mixed-methods methodology allowed our SoTL FLC to leverage the knowledge and research skills within our group. Led by our group's quantitative researcher, we asynchronously searched for previously validated instruments and adapted them to our use. Surveys composed of Likert-scale and short-answers were administered to student participants (n=235) across intervention and control groups at the beginning and end of the semester. The SoTL FLC divided the project's completion into smaller work groups based on each faculty member's assets and interests. The quantitative group conducted statistics to examine the influence of IA agents on students' self-reported belonging, self-reported engagement, and course performance, while the qualitative group conducted a thematic analysis to explore the student participants' perceptions of a sense of belonging in the course. Each group reported findings while assigned members generated cross-connections between the statistical trends and qualitative themes. The multi-faceted analysis was possible due to the collaborative efforts and iterative process where findings from one method informed the other, enhancing the overall robustness of the study's findings. While the data analysis portion did require more frequent synchronous meetings between qualitative teams, quantitative teams, writing teams, and a whole group, the flexibility of the online nature of the SoTL FLC allowed for more flexible work time due to not having to travel between campuses or buildings. Additionally, this tactic allowed for a rapid turnaround of conference proposals and a manuscript draft.

Within our SoTL FLC, the collaborative and diverse assets of the team members allowed us all to move past *scholarly teaching* (i.e., using literature to inform teaching practices) to *SoTL* work (i.e., publications and presentations, both empirically and reflective; Kern et al., 2015). Thus far, our SoTL FLC collaboration has led to three presentations, one paper, this book chapter, and established professional relationships for members to break out and pursue other research agendas that align with the goals of SoTL. Our research-focused collaboration has positively advanced students' learning due to faculty members' teaching because of the systematical and methodological collection and dissemination of data in both SoTL and disciplinary-specific literature. Our online SoTL FLC honors the diversity of the field (Felton, 2013) by fostering communication between faculty members across campuses and colleges. Additionally, it serves as a model for other SoTL FLCs to formally recognize the significant intellectual work behind teaching practices that impact student learning occurring in individual classes through peer-reviewed outlets.

Opportunities for Growth

To ensure that findings from a study are being interpreted accurately, all researchers must develop a clear understanding of the findings. In cases where researchers may not have prior experience conducting and interpreting a particular type of analysis, this interpretation may be more challenging. This is particularly imperative when conducting mixed-method research, where the findings from one set of analyses may be used to guide and inform a second set of analyses. In SoTL FLCs, where a large team collaborates, all members may benefit from a meeting where the analyses and results are discussed in detail to ensure that all members understand the findings. An online format benefits this meeting by allowing researchers to easily share their screens to display figures, tables, and data reflecting the findings. Interpretation of findings is critical when the members of the research team who conduct analyses and draft the discussion differ from the researchers who write the discussion section. As the goal of the discussion is to provide readers with a clear interpretation of results with a connection to practice, misunderstanding the results can be a hurdle.

In some ways, disseminating SoTL research can be more challenging than identifying outlets for disciplinary research. When publishing SoTL research, researchers may need to choose between general SoTL journals and journals focused on teaching and learning in a particular subdiscipline. Some SoTL journals do not have an impact factor, which can disadvantage faculty whose promotion and tenure guidelines require specific metrics. One way to address this challenge is to discuss the audience for a particular study and identify the journal at the beginning of the research process (Cruz, 2023).

VALUE 4: REFLECTIVENESS

Reflection plays a pivotal role in enhancing the effectiveness of SoTL research, which is why it is noted as the fourth key value in the SoTL Values Framework. The process of reflection allows individuals to critically evaluate their experiences, examining their emotions, thoughts, and practices to identify areas for growth and innovation. Engaging in reflection within a SoTL FLC setting encourages individuals to scrutinize their teaching approaches and uncover potential blind spots (Brookfield, 1995). This reflective practice, which is foundational to SoTL research, facilitates both individual and collective learning, supporting the development of authentic teaching and learning practices (Zizka, 2020); thus, we recognize reflectiveness as an approach that exemplifies "good SoTL" (Felten, 2013).

Through reflective practice, individuals can move beyond a simple recounting of events (i.e., a surface-level analysis) to one that is a deeper reflection. When engaged in deeper reflection, one can critically examine their underlying assumptions and their work's broader societal, political, and ethical implications. Cranton (2011) emphasizes that this form of reflection extends into critical reflection, where "learning about teaching is to learn about supporting students' learning of the discipline in the best way possible" (p. 81). In critically examining specific actions, one must assess the impact of those actions and evaluate whether they align with their intended outcomes. It is equally important to recognize that the impact may differ based on individuals' diverse backgrounds and experiences, and these varying perspectives are often the catalyst for meaningful reflection.

Consider, for example, a college instructor reflecting on a lesson. The instructor might reflect on how they felt implementing the lesson, how students responded, and what activities were effective in relation to the lesson's purpose. If the instructor wished to engage further in critical reflection, they might question why a particular teaching method was used over another and why the method may have been more effective with some students than others. Students' assets, prior knowledge, and background, including social and cultural factors (e.g., race, gender, socioeconomic status), can be considered in how such factors influence the outcomes. Thus, reflection can extend from a focused personal improvement perspective to a more critical one involving the analysis of broader contexts, assumptions, and systemic factors (Cranton, 2011). Furthermore, reflection can provoke collective reflection across a group, providing individuals with opportunities to build meaning-making and clarity through the lens of varying perspectives. The group can support one another in helping individuals understand their identities in relation to their work. Being transparent in one's positionality and identity in SoTL research can assist others in making connections to their contexts.

Online FLCs as a Method of Bolstering Reflection

In our SoTL FLC, leveraging online tools such as Zoom and Google Drive aided our reflective processes. For instance, during one of our initial online meetings, we reflected on our individual practices and our observed needs to improve student outcomes. We also reflected on the context of our practice, access to conduct an intervention in that setting, and how others in the group could support the planning and implementation of the intervention. After sharing our project ideas, we found student engagement and a sense of belonging as shared interests, particularly in large online asynchronous courses. While there exists literature identifying a strong connection between student success and a sense of belonging to academic success (Chen et al., 2021; Lei & Yin, 2020), we also saw the need to develop a deeper understanding of what tools and strategies could be used to support engagement and a sense of belonging in online asynchronous courses. Considering what online asynchronous teaching and learning looks like, we examined the potential for an IA communication tool, as previously described, to support students in a required class for health majors that typically enrolls 150 students per section, without support from teaching assistants, and is delivered in an asynchronous format. This setting became the focus of our SoTL FLC's project.

While engaged in the research process, we used the online nature of our SoTL FLC to seamlessly integrate reflection into our shared repository. For example, the structured folders in our Google Drive organized the materials related to the various research processes of literature review, data collection, and data analysis.

Additionally, reflection notes or researcher memos accompanied them. The open nature of such documents provided accessibility to others who might not have been part of that particular stage to learn of others' reflections and offer feedback. For those engaged in that stage, individuals could revisit their work, using their reflective notes to jump back into the project and use the feedback of others to challenge their thinking. Thus, our Google Drive provided a space for us to reflect individually and collectively as the project progressed.

We also made use of Zoom as another platform for collective reflection. Since our SoTL FLC benefited greatly from the diverse expertise of its members, each contributing their strengths in unique ways to analyze our research findings, Zoom allowed our SoTL FLC to engage in meaningful discussions about how each person or small group contributed their specialized knowledge to different aspects of the project. The recording capabilities and saved transcripts provided by Zoom were particularly valuable in guiding our reflections and facilitating the write-up of our research report. Members could view and refer to the Zoom recordings while working on the results and discussion.

By reviewing Zoom recordings and transcripts, group members could better understand the steps and reasoning behind each group's analysis, enabling collective brainstorming on the overall findings and their implications. The seamless access to shared folders, reflection notes, recordings, and transcripts fostered a continuous flow of communication and collaboration, ensuring that all FLC members remained connected and engaged throughout the research process. Moreover, our findings highlighted that IAs are relatively easy to implement, require minimal training, and can be customized to meet the expectations of the course, instructor, and students—insights that were directly informed by the collaborative and reflective nature of our online SoTL FLC environment.

Opportunities for Growth

The ultimate purpose of facilitating a SoTL FLC is to help faculty new to SoTL learn about SoTL and develop the research skills necessary to design, implement, and disseminate a SoTL project. We feel that our approach to "learn by doing" allows members to gain a deeper understanding of each step in conducting SoTL research in a supportive environment. As described in prior sections, our SoTL FLC included regular synchronous meetings during study design. As tasks were assigned and data collection was underway, we moved to primarily working asynchronously. While this approach was beneficial for members to complete research-related tasks amidst busy schedules, moving to asynchronous meetings may take time away from group reflections, which could feed into future projects. In future iterations of SoTL FLCs, it may be beneficial to integrate reflection opportunities as the research project is coming to a close. This reflection could focus on encouraging researchers to consider their growth in knowledge and skills, set goals for future SoTL work, and explore potential new collaborations that team members can work on together.

Reflections from the Collaborators

Each member found the online nature of the SoTL FLC to be intriguing. In the following sections, we share what brought us to the SoTL FLC, how it served us, and how the online setting benefited our participation and contributions. We organized the reflections into two groups, one consisting of more experienced, veteran SoTL scholars and one with emerging SoTL scholars who were new to SoTL. The structure of the organization for veteran and emerging SoTL scholars helps to compare similarities across the group members while also providing insights into how the online nature transformed their associated experience levels.

Veteran SoTL Scholars

Three group members self-identified as veteran SoTL scholars, given their prior experience engaging with SoTL research: Diana Botnaru, Anna C. Brady, and Kevin J. Reagan. While at various points in their career, the three group members saw value in FLCs that shared a common interest, especially ones that offered collaboration through online modalities. Their experiences learning about SoTL and mentoring others in SoTL are shared to highlight their continued commitment to promoting SoTL FLCs to build transdisciplinary teams invested in such SoTL research.

Diana Botnaru

I appreciated the online format of the FLC. Online settings can be a significant advantage for faculty who find in-person interactions exhausting. The flexibility of an online format, especially when it incorporates both synchronous and asynchronous elements, creates a balanced way to engage in a collaborative project when the group has a common goal.

As a facilitator, when mentoring faculty new to SoTL, I always strive to support their autonomy and competence and build a sense of ownership. In my opinion, the online format, with its blend of asynchronous flexibility and synchronous support, provided an ideal environment to achieve these goals. Faculty could choose when and how to engage with the project, discussions, and tasks. For instance, asynchronous content enabled the SoTL FLC members to work at their own pace, giving them control over their schedules and reducing the pressure of attending live sessions. At the same time, synchronous meetings provided opportunities for real-time interaction while still allowing faculty to opt in according to their comfort level. The

Google Drive folders kept our tasks organized and allowed each member to revisit the material at their own pace. Most importantly, they could use the material as a scaffolding for future SoTL projects. For example, over the years, I had many faculty overwhelmed by the idea of applying for IRB approval for a SoTL project. However, having a draft of the IRB submission made subsequent projects much more manageable. Additionally, facilitators and other team members often offer timely feedback, guidance, and support in synchronous sessions. Both online modalities can reinforce confidence in faculty members' ability to conduct a SoTL project. Finally, giving faculty the autonomy to decide how to engage with the project, select the aspects they wish to focus on, and determine how to collaborate with peers in group work enhances their sense of ownership and fosters an environment where all members are fully invested in the project's success. I find it rewarding to see the group progress through the steps, learn from each other, and, most importantly, create a supportive community.

Anna C. Brady

My introduction to SoTL occurred during graduate school while working with the University Center of the Advancement of Teaching (now called the Drake Institute) at The Ohio State University. While at Ohio State, I had the opportunity to collaborate with biologists to conduct a SoTL study focused on metacognition and time management. This experience taught me many benefits of working on a transdisciplinary team. When I joined the College of Education at Georgia Southern University in 2021, I immediately opted to join one of the SoTL FLCs. My primary purpose in participating in the SoTL FLC was to network with faculty members across campuses. I wanted to connect with other people interested in research that had strong practical implications for their classrooms. A huge bonus of this FLC was that it occurred virtually! This allowed me to connect with faculty members across campuses to begin building a network at the university. In turn, these connections have led to additional research projects and opportunities.

Kevin J. Reagan

I stumbled into SoTL early in my academic career, which some find odd because I am a librarian. Many often question why I am involved in SoTL when I tell people I am a librarian. The perplexity continues even when I relate that I am an instruction librarian. After all, my teaching typically takes the form of a one-shot session, whereby a faculty member invites me into their room to teach or demonstrate a database or library resource. Usually, faculty refer to what I do as a "library presentation," but that is not accurate. Instead, what I do, which SoTL has helped me realize, is teaching more than presenting. I am allotted, at best, 75 minutes to cover information literacy concepts while introducing students to who I am, giving them a general overview of the library, and explaining why they are having a "library presentation."

Nonetheless, being involved in SoTL has allowed me to better understand how to evaluate and improve my teaching, even for library one-shots. Because I only get 50 to 75 minutes with students (at best), I must make every second count, quite literally. SoTL has given me the professional resources, network, and knowledge to ensure that every second of my time with students is meaningful, ensuring that I make a lasting impact on how they understand and use the library and its myriad resources.

Emerging SoTL Scholars

While learning from veteran SoTL perspectives can provide insights into the long-term advantages professionally and personally, three group members contributed their unique perspectives on what drew them into the SoTL FLC. Alesia Mickle Moldavan, Bailey Nafziger, and Jackie Mesenbrink-Sainz share how the SoTL FLC supported their first encounters with SoTL research and how it related to their professional goals. The online nature of the SoTL FLC fostered a collaborative network to meet other colleagues and develop transdisciplinary partnerships.

Alesia Mickle Moldavan

Since starting a faculty position in 2018, my first encounter with SoTL work occurred five years later during my first year in the College of Education at Georgia Southern University. I learned about the university's FLCs, particularly the SoTL FLC, which aimed to foster a multi-campus community while promoting innovative research in one's pedagogical practice. The online format of the FLC especially appealed to me, given that my primary campus is located over 50 miles from the other campus. Using online synchronous meetings and asynchronous tools allowed me to network and collaborate with colleagues, providing opportunities I might not have had with in-person meetings alone. During our synchronous meetings, we often reflected on the various demands at the college, department, and course levels, which made it difficult for many to find time to meet, let alone travel to the other campus. I felt fortunate to establish supportive, transdisciplinary relationships with colleagues, which enriched my understanding of SoTL. Given the online format, I felt included when designing, implementing, and analyzing data for our SoTL project. I could contribute my research expertise while miles away to enhance the study. The meeting platform allowed us to check in as a larger group before breaking into smaller groups to work on assigned tasks. These breakout sessions often used the platform's features to effectively structure our meetings. Additionally, the online resources provided a space for group members to track progress at individual and group levels. This transparent approach allowed us to balance respecting each other's work while ensuring alignment on big-picture goals.

Meeting my collaborators for the first time at an in-person conference and reporting on our work felt surprisingly natural, as our online interactions had already fostered a strong sense of connection. Although we had not physically met, I felt like I knew my collaborators on a deeper level, one focused more on expertise rather than their accessibility. This reminded me of how collaborative SoTL work can be conducted digitally without the constraints of physical presence. You do not need to study your practice independently. In fact, you can use digital tools to invite others into your classroom, opening doors for more diverse participation and the exchange of innovative ideas, even when applied in different contexts. You also do not need to do the work in your setting to see the benefits of an intervention. Likewise, you can learn from other's work and see what strategies can be applied to your context. For a new SoTL researcher, this experience highlighted how online SoTL FLCs can build a sustainable support network, encouraging collaboration in an inclusive environment. The flexibility of online SoTL FLCs allows colleagues to transcend the limitations of in-person accessibility, experiment with new ideas, and work more productively while fostering a sense of belonging and shared purpose.

Bailey Nafziger

After spending a decade as a public educator in 2nd-8th grade, evaluating and improving teaching within my classroom was not new to me. However, as a new faculty member in higher education, making my iterative improvements public was new. Not only was it new, but it was also mandatory for tenure and promotion. I first learned about the SoTL FLC during a faculty development day sponsored by our university's Faculty Center. That day, I signed up before their presentation was finished. I was grateful for a professional development opportunity I knew would lead to a publication. While collaborating as a SoTL FLC member, I gained more than one publication. First, there was an inherent sense of belonging beginning the first meeting. I met colleagues across colleges and campuses within our large institution in our first synchronous Zoom meeting. I learned about my newly introduced colleagues' research, including how to work with mixed methods studies, librarians, and researchers in the arts. Each of us had strengths, and they were all valued within our learning community. Secondly, I was pleasantly surprised at how the large group of individual researchers with individual interests collaborated to achieve one shared goal. I believe this was only possible due to the online nature of our collaboration.

Before the first meeting, a Google Drive folder was shared that had been well organized. It was easy to orient myself with agendas, brainstorming documents, and data before and during the process. Synchronous Zoom meetings allowed me to participate, even when attending conferences out of town. Asynchronous tasks allowed me to "pull my weight" when scholarship, service, and teaching obligations were heaviest in the semester. Lastly, joining the online SoTL FLC provided me with more than one peer-reviewed product. We have collaborated with a research manuscript, this book chapter, and multiple presentations. I am thankful that our university and college values SoTL work. It has allowed me to focus on my strengths and interests while expanding my research network.

Jackie Mesenbrink-Sainz

As a new member of SoTL, I was uncertain about what to expect. My previous knowledge of SoTL work was limited, and although it was briefly mentioned in public health, it often felt like a secondary topic compared to our primary research. This group has enabled me to connect with diverse disciplines and individuals I might not have encountered otherwise. As a faculty member not based on the main campus and primarily teaching online, I sometimes felt isolated. I also lack extensive experience and am still navigating the expectations of the tenure track. Additionally, my program has recently transitioned from one college to another within the university, adding to a sense of instability. In this context, the group has provided a sense of stability and a supportive space to ask questions and discuss various topics. From our initial project formation to producing a chapter and presenting at multiple conferences, this group has demonstrated remarkable perseverance to keep going for new challenges. It has shown me that collaboration can lighten our workload and inspire creativity. We have been able to exchange ideas and engage in tangential discussions that have sparked additional initiatives within my college and with colleagues beyond our group. Most importantly, this experience has highlighted the value of asking for help. I often struggle to seek assistance, especially in online formats where I prefer to solve problems independently. However, this group encouraged me to embrace my strengths while addressing areas for improvement and feeling more comfortable asking for support. SoTL groups are something I recommend to new faculty members to connect through multiple disciplines and come together to inspire creativity.

CONCLUSION

SoTL emphasizes research-driven practices and the importance of making research on teaching and learning publicly available (Boyer, 1990). As Spake and Salem (2005) state, SoTL is "public, open to critique and evaluation, and in a form others can build on" (p. 5). This chapter exemplifies these principles by exploring the benefits and challenges of an online SoTL FLC as a professional development opportunity. By examining SoTL literature and detailing our SoTL FLC's processes, we sought to demonstrate how online communities can effectively embody SoTL principles and offer a SoTL Values Framework for others. Online SoTL FLCs provide a unique and invaluable space for fostering inclusivity, collaboration, scholarship, and reflection. The online format enhances accessibility by removing geographic and time barriers, enabling broader participation from faculty across institutions and disciplines. It promotes inclusivity by accommodating varied schedules and preferences, ensuring diverse voices and expertise can contribute toward a common goal of advancing teaching and learning. Collaboration is also strengthened through online platforms and digital tools that support both real-time and asynchronous exchange of resources, research findings, and feedback. Additionally, the online format offers opportunities for sustained scholarship and reflection through shared access to repositories and resources that can inform and guide future SoTL projects. We close the chapter reflecting on Felten and Chick's (2018) view of SoTL as a transformative process (Fanghanel, 2013), posing the questions: Can a SoTL FLC be facilitated online? Can our experience inform others? How can our expertise drive future growth and learning in SoTL?

REFERENCES

Bishop-Clark, C., & Dietz-Uhler, B. (2012). *Engaging in the scholarship of teaching and learning: A guide to the process, and how to develop a project from start to finish*. Routledge.

Botnaru, D., Maurer, T. W., & Langdon, J. (2022). SoTL at Georgia Southern: Perceptions, engagement and impact. *International Journal for the Scholarship of Teaching and Learning*, 16(1), 1–15. DOI: 10.20429/ijsotl.2022.160104

Boyer, E. L. (1990). *Scholarship reconsidered: Priorities of the professoriate*. Carnegie Foundation for the Advancement of Teaching. https://eric.ed.gov/?id=ed326149

Brady, A. C., Botnaru, D., Alt, K., Carroll, G. D., Moldavan, A. M., Mesenbrink-Sainz, J., Nafziger, B., Reagan, K. J., & Rich, L. E. (2024). Understanding the influence of intelligent agents on students' sense of classroom belonging, engagement, and academic performance in online classes. *American Journal of Distance Education*, 1–17. Advance online publication. DOI: 10.1080/08923647.2024.2430766

Brookfield, S. D. (1995). *Becoming a critically reflective teacher*. JosseyBass.

Bunnell, S. L., Chick, N., Hamilton, M., Leoni, A. S., & Woolmer, C. (2024). Generations of SoTL scholars: Transferable lessons and new possibilities. *Transformative Dialogues: Teaching and Learning Journal, 17*(1), 25–40. DOI: 10.26209/td2024vol17iss11801

Chen, S., Binning, K. R., Manke, K. J., Brady, S. T., McGreevy, E. M., Betancur, L., & Kaufmann, N. (2021). Am I a science person? A strong science identity bolsters minority students' sense of belonging and performance in college. *Personality and Social Psychology Bulletin*, 47(4), 593–606.

Chick, N. L. (2014). 'Methodologically sound' under the 'big tent': An ongoing conversation. *International Journal for the Scholarship of Teaching and Learning*, 8(2), 1–15. DOI: 10.20429/ijsotl.2014.080201

Chick, N. L. (2015). Holding it up to the light: Looking at learning through the lenses of the arts and humanities. *The Canadian Journal for the Scholarship of Teaching and Learning*, 6(2), 1–7. DOI: 10.5206/cjsotl-rcacea.2015.2.3

Copland, S. (2023). A case study on the value of humanities-based analysis, modes of presentation, and study designs for SoTL: Close reading students' pre-surveys on gender-inclusive language. *Teaching & Learning Inquiry*, 11. Advance online publication. DOI: 10.20343/teachlearninqu.11.34

Cox, M. (2004). Introduction to faculty learning communities. *New Directions for Teaching and Learning*, 97(97), 5–23. DOI: 10.1002/tl.129

Cranton, P. (2011). A transformative perspective on the Scholarship of Teaching and Learning. *Higher Education Research & Development*, 30(1), 75–86. DOI: 10.1080/07294360.2011.536974

Cruz, L. (2023). *Finding your audience: A workshop on publishing your SoTL project* [Workshop]. SoTL Commons Conference, Savannah, Georgia.

Cruz, L., Grodziak, E., Botnaru, D., Walker, D., Maurer, T., Altany, A., Abraham-Settles, B., Amos, M., Bunch-Crump, K., Cook, A., Eisenreich, H., Gregory, D., Howell, M., James, I., Landge, S., Lynes, J., Pompey, J., Shapiro, B., Smith, A., & Zhang, Y. (2023). The hospitality of the Commons: A collaborative reflection on a SOTL conference. *International Journal for the Scholarship of Teaching and Learning*, 17(2), 1–10. DOI: 10.20429/ijsotl.2023.17207

Cruz, L., Santucci Leoni, A., & Nasrollahian Mojarad, S. (2024). Meaning and manifesto: Embracing transdisciplinarity in SoTL. *Transformative Dialogues: Teaching and Learning Journal, 17*(1), 1–13. https://doi.org/DOI: 10.26209/TD-2024VOL17ISS11836

Fanghanel, J. (2013). Going public with pedagogical inquiries: SoTL as a methodology for faculty professional development. *Teaching & Learning Inquiry*, 1(1), 59–70. DOI: 10.20343/teachlearninqu.1.1.59

Felton, P. (2013). Principles of good practice in SoTL. *Teaching & Learning Inquiry*, 1(1), 121–125. DOI: 10.20343/teachlearninqu.1.1.121

Felton, P., & Chick, N. (2018). Is SoTL a signature pedagogy of educational development? *To Improve the Academy*, 37(1), 4–16. DOI: 10.1002/tia2.20077

Georgia Southern Faculty Center. (n.d.). *SoTL learning community.* Georgia Southern University. https://www.georgiasouthern.edu/academics/sotlgsu/

Gómez-García, G., Ramos-Navas-Parejo, M., de la Cruz-Campos, J. C., & Rodríguez-Jiménez, C. (2022). Impact of COVID-19 on university students: An analysis of its influence on psychological and academic factors. *International Journal of Environmental Research and Public Health*, 19(16), 10433. DOI: 10.3390/ijerph191610433 PMID: 36012067

Howard, B., Ilyashenko, N., & Jacobs, L. (2023). Cross-cultural collaboration through virtual teaming in higher education. *Perspectives in Education*, 41(1), 74–87. DOI: 10.38140/pie.v41i1.6319

Huber, M. T., & Hutchings, P. (2005). *The advancement of learning: Building the teaching commons*. Jossey-Bass.

Hutchings, P., Huber, M. T., & Ciccone, A. (2011). *The scholarship of teaching and learning reconsidered: Institutional integration and impact*. Jossey-Bass/Wiley.

Jaber, L., Stirbys, C., & Saint-Cyr, C. (2024). Decolonizing the higher education curriculum: An evaluation of incorporating indigenous ways of knowing and pedagogy. *The Canadian Journal for the Scholarship of Teaching and Learning*, 15(1), 6. Advance online publication. DOI: 10.5206/cjsotlrcacea.2024.1.14796

Kern, B., Mettetal, G., Dixson, M., & Morgan, R. K. (2015). The role of SoTL in the academy: Upon the 25th anniversary of Boyer's scholarship reconsidered. *The Journal of Scholarship of Teaching and Learning*, 15(3), 1–14. DOI: 10.14434/josotl.v15i3.13623

Kreber, C. (2006). Developing the scholarship of teaching through transformative learning. *The Journal of Scholarship of Teaching and Learning*, 6(1), 88–109.

Lei, S., & Yin, D. (2020). Curricular and departmental characteristics influencing satisfaction, retention and success of undergraduate students: A review of literature. *College Student Journal*, 54(3), 357–363.

Marg, O., & Theiler, L. (2023). Effects of transdisciplinary research on scientific knowledge and reflexivity. *Research Evaluation*, 32(4), 635–647. DOI: 10.1093/reseval/rvad033

Maurer, T., Sturges, D., Shankar, P., Allen, D., & Akbarova, S. (2010). A faculty learning community on the scholarship of teaching & learning: A case study. *International Journal for the Scholarship of Teaching and Learning*, 4(2), 1–7. DOI: 10.20429/ijsotl.2010.040208

McCarthy, M. (2024). Building transdisciplinary SoTL: Creating a culture and language of listening and learning for understanding. *Transformative Dialogues: Teaching and Learning Journal, 17*(1), 101–113. DOI: 10.26209/td2024vol17iss11810

McKinney, K. (2007). *Enhancing learning through the scholarship of teaching and learning: The challenges and joys of juggling*. Anker Publishing.

McSweeney, J., & Schnurr, M. (2023). Can SoTL generate high quality research while maintaining its commitment to inclusivity? *International Journal for the Scholarship of Teaching and Learning*, 17(1), 1–15. DOI: 10.20429/ijsotl.2023.17104

Nasrollahian Mojarad, S., & Cruz, L., (2022). MegaSoTL: Supporting pedagogical research across multiple institutions. *To Improve the Academy: A Journal of Educational Development, 41*(1), 78–95. DOI: 10.3998/tia.470

Potter, M. K., & Wuetherick, B. (2015). Who is represented in the teaching commons?: SoTL through the lenses of the arts and humanities. *The Canadian Journal for the Scholarship of Teaching and Learning*, 6(2), 2. Advance online publication. DOI: 10.5206/cjsotl-rcacea.2015.2.2

Scharff, L., Capocchiano, H., Chick, N., Eady, M., Friberg, J., Gregory, D., Loy, K., & Maurer, T. (2023). Grand challenges for SoTL. *International Society for the Scholarship of Teaching and Learning*. https://issotl.com/grand-challenges-for-sotl/

Shepard, K. (2024, April 15-16). *Support online student engagement using intelligent agents* [session presentation]. University Systems of Georgia Teaching and Learning Conference, Athens, Georgia. https://virtual.oxfordabstracts.com/#/event/5034/submission/205

Shulman, L. S. (2004). *The wisdom of practice: Essays on teaching, learning, and learning to teach.* Jossey-Bass.

Spake, E., & Salem, A. (2005). Setting the stage: The scholarship of teaching and learning. *Journal, Physical Therapy Education*, 19(3), 5–13. DOI: 10.1097/00001416-200510000-00003

Trigwell, K., Martin, E., Benjamin, J., & Prosser, M. (2000). Scholarship of teaching: A model. *Higher Education Research & Development*, 19(2), 155–168. DOI: 10.1080/072943600445628

Zizka, L. (2020). Reflections and SoTL: Putting reflection (back) on faculty radar. In Plews, R., & Amos, M. (Eds.), *Evidence-based faculty development through the scholarship of teaching and learning (SoTL)* (pp. 96–120). IGI Global., DOI: 10.4018/978-1-7998-2212-7.ch006

Chapter 4
Engaging in SoTL Through Faculty Learning Communities: Implementing "Small Teaching Practices" to Improve Graduate Online Courses

Regina Rahimi
Georgia Southern University, USA

Lina Bell Soares
Georgia Southern University, USA

ABSTRACT

In the spirit of the scope of this book, this chapter highlights the potential impact collaborative faculty work can have on course design and pedagogy for online graduate students. The chapter describes the development and implementation of a faculty learning community (FLC) engaged in discussions centered on "small teaching practices" and the knowledge gleaned from the collaborative experience that will inform our practice. Emphasizing collaborative faculty engagement, our Scholarship of Teaching and Learning (SoTL) project has sought to strengthen our online graduate students' learning experiences and support their learning needs.

INTRODUCTION

As Shulman (2011) offered,

DOI: 10.4018/979-8-3693-7595-2.ch004

SOTL is an area of scholarship that does not solve problems once and for all. The challenges of teaching and learning are persistent. They mutate and grow as new disciplines are invented, new challenges of practice emerge and new generations of both students and faculty come to inhabit and define our classrooms and institutions. (p. 6)

As professors who teach an online graduate program, we could not agree more with Shulman's (2011) words. We have firsthand experience with a multiplicity of challenges brought to the educational arena, and our graduate online program is no exception. Due to an ever-increasing online student enrollment fueled by the Coronavirus (COVID-19) pandemic in March 2020, we are continually faced with the issue of student readiness, student retention, and student success. At the same time, we recognize that high quality online programs are reliant on instructors who understand effective course design and instruction that facilitates positive student performance outcomes (Rapanta et al., 2021). This in turn means that we must be adequately prepared for the virtual learning environment.

To improve our courses and the experiences of our graduate students in the online higher education program, we determined that a formalized collaboration among our program faculty could serve to strengthen our practice and address concerns with student performance. As a result, we created a faculty learning community (FLC), designed to examine theory and the literature, to expand our practice more thoroughly, and as Shulman (1998) endorsed, to share the experiences of our collaboration with the scholarship community. Therefore, it follows that we conceptualize the scholarship of teaching and learning as a channel between theory and praxis. More specifically, we endorse the premise that the scholarship of teaching and learning is about improving our pedagogical content knowledge in the courses we teach to improve student learning via evidence-based approaches (Shulman, 1986, 1987).

BACKGROUND

In preparation and to begin our project, we planned three phases. The goal for the first phase was: 1) to engage in the study of best practices for online graduate courses and 2) to share through collaborative discussion and reflection our insights from reading "small teaching practices" coined by James Lang (Darby & Lang, 2019; Lang, 2016) related to improving the teaching and learning experience. Thus, the first phase chronicled and highlighted our discussions of the readings and the knowledge gained through collaboration. Through shared discussions, we discovered ourselves as collaborative problem-solvers, reflective practitioners, and course and program strategists (Authors, under review).

As a direct outcome from our collaborative discussion, the second phase delved into an individual examination and ongoing research of a "small teaching practice" that we each chose to focus on for implementation in our spring course/courses. From our collective conversations, professional development reading, and reflection, the contents of this chapter examine the second phase of the project and highlights specific new approaches for our courses and program, focusing on our respective course experiences and goals for addressing these new approaches.

The final phase of this project will be the actual implementation of that "small teaching practice" and a subsequent investigation into its success in supporting student learning and enhancing our graduate student experience. We are motivated by four overarching goals for the completion of this project: 1) to implement best-practices within our designated online graduate classes utilizing a "small teaching practice" (Darby & Lang, 2019; Lang, 2016), 2) to determine the effectiveness of the "small teaching practices," 3) to share our experiences with the respective teaching practice with others and the larger community through scholarly presentations and publications, and 4) to contribute to the quality of online graduate programs at our institution and within the field through this collaborative project.

It is worthy to note the backdrop to this chapter is a specific graduate program - the Education Specialist (Ed.S.) in Teaching and Learning program. It is a fully online program that offers an advanced degree between the master's and doctoral levels. Specifically, our program is designed to include opportunities for graduate students who seek to be accomplished in their practice, both within the profession and the larger community, to develop and implement classroom or school-based projects for school and student improvement, and design inclusive classroom and school practices that support P-12 student learning. Our graduate program is one of several educational specialist programs in our College of Education (COE) at a mid-size university located in the Southeastern part of the United States. Since the fall of 2017, we have witnessed the growth in graduate student enrollment of 189%, distinguishing the program as the largest specialist program in the COE. Given this increase, we have also been faced with numerous challenges, such as larger class sizes and an array of levels of student preparation for the rigors of graduate school. Our development of our FLC was a direct response to these challenges.

In this chapter, we will share how we determined the "small teaching practice" we plan to incorporate into our online courses, a description of the particular approach grounded in research and theory, and our plans for implementation of this approach in upcoming offerings. We hope by sharing our experience, particularly within the context of this text, that others may consider developing a FLC in their SoTL work to address common challenges faced in their own academic programs.

LEARNING FROM EACH OTHER

During the first phase of our project, the two faculty online instructors featured in this chapter, engaged in collective readings of two texts: *Small teaching online: Applying learning science to online classes* (Darby & Lang, 2019) and *Small teaching: Everyday lessons from the science of learning* (Lang, 2016). Due to our particular focus, the texts chosen for our FLC center on the notion that small changes in pedagogical approaches can have meaningful impact on the learning experiences of students. These are both practical and powerful texts for supporting this idea. As the basis of our FLC, each faculty member respectively and alternately assigned specific readings and general discussion questions.

During our monthly meetings, we discussed the assigned readings and shared our experiences with our own teaching practices. Since we teach in the same academic program, we share many students and are privy to the overall curriculum offered. This made our discussions particularly helpful in addressing program and course challenges. Since our meetings were held virtually, our recorded sessions were used to help us determine three themes that underscore the power of this FLC: the collaborative efforts to problem-solve; reliance on reflective practice, and the use of our collective and individual experience to work towards developing specific strategies to enhance the overall learning experience for our students. The outcome was for each of us to identify areas that we hoped to improve upon in our courses and narrow those down to one particular "small teaching practice" that we wanted to address specifically in future semesters. As members of this FLC, Lina selected student engagement as her "small teaching practice" to address and Regina identified implementation of predictive strategies as a tenet of universal design for learning (UDL). What follows is a discussion to share our respective experiences in the FLC and our "small teaching practice" goals. We also specifically address how we hope to incorporate those practices into our designated courses.

LINA

As a professor with over 15 years' experience of teaching online, I have tried to stay abreast of the current online learner management system offered through my university. Each of my courses are asynchronous with two to three synchronous class meetings held each semester. Like others, I have found that the nature of asynchronous instruction offers my students the convenience they enjoy and flexibility (Kossen & Ooi, 2021). Flexibility is achieved because my graduate students do not have to worry about keeping up with the traditional lecture style. Instead, they are able to work independently at their own pace and to engage in self-directed learning

(Al Rawashdeh et al., 2021). Further, asynchronous instruction permits my students the time needed to view instructional notes, instructional videos and supplementary materials, and assignment examples more than once. It is a method that appeals to some of the students who are reluctant to engage in real-time discussions.

The instructional design for each of my online courses entails a series of modules to organize the course content. Subsequently, each module builds upon the previous module, such as building blocks or schemata (Piaget, 1936). This intentional structure allows my students to acquire new schemata by tapping into prior learning. My graduate students can expect each course to begin with a *Start Here Module* that houses crucial files such as the course syllabus, schedule, major assignments and assessments, and stellar examples of the major assignments from former students. Moreover, the *Start Here Module* includes my welcome message, a video that presents an overview of the course, and my personal and course expectations.

Following the *Start Here Module*, the learning modules are numbered and designated by topic title. The learning modules begin with an *Overview* file to address the topic to be studied, student learning objectives, and the tasks to be completed. The *Overview* file is followed by assignment files, rubrics, supplementary resources, and instructional videos. Additionally, I incorporate a variety of learning activities ranging from participation in study groups and the discussion board to multiple writing activities, as well as the creation of multimedia projects. My purpose in doing so is to appeal to my students' diverse learning styles. However, I am reminded that experts have found that the effectiveness of an online course relies on an instructor's understanding and ability to foster student engagement through active learning, and this underscores the significance of technology integration to initiate student engagement (Kamya & Otim, 2019; Wilkie et al., 2018).

THE IMPORTANCE OF STUDENT ENGAGEMENT

Engagement can be defined as one's active involvement in learning the course content (Kuh, 2009) and from a review of the literature, research has shown that engaging students to be active learners is a crucial factor for online education (Bendelier et al., 2020; Rajabalee et al., 2020; Zheng et al., 2021). Bollinger and Halupa (2018) posit that active engagement in an online course can be a positive influence on students' academic performance. Research has further shown that when students are actively engaged in learning, they have positive feelings of self-efficacy (Bond & Bendelier, 2019; Honicke & Broadbent, 2016; Jung & Lee, 2018), and personal satisfaction (Bendelier et al., 2020). Additionally, research has shown that when students are motivated, they are more inclined to actively engage, and they are more likely to persevere in an online learning environment. Subsequently, students who demonstrate strong motivation and persistence correlate with higher rates of course completion, graduation, and positive student performance outcomes (Bollinger & Halupa, 2018; Kuzminykh et al., 2021). Mumma and Kalam (2021) offer that active learning plays a prominent role in enhancing student participation and engagement in an online learning setting.

Based on the research findings on collaborative learning (Means et al., 2009; Yunus et al., 2021), student engagement as a "small teaching practice" in this chapter draws upon Garrison et al.'s (2000) Community of Inquiry (CoI) Model, and Shea et al.'s (2012) updated version of the CoI Model. Garrison et al.'s (2000) widely established CoI framework is based on the assumption that meaningful learning occurs in an online learning environment due to the interactions of the members in a learning community, understood to include the instructor and the students. The framework further assumes that three forms of presence (teaching, social, and cognitive presence) work together in an online learning community and are necessary for learning to occur. According to Anderson et al. (2001), teaching presence is characterized as the presence of the instructor, through direct instruction or in the role as a facilitator. Teaching presence further includes the instructor's presence manifested through instructional design and course organization that facilitates online learners' social and cognitive processes; processes that influence positive student performance outcomes. Garrison et al. (2000) offered that social presence is characterized by online students' ability to communicate and interact with the instructor and with their peers in an online learning environment. Social presence enables students to experience an online environment as if they were in real time. Cognitive presence is characterized by the construction of knowledge as students engage with the instructor, course material, and discussion forums (Garrison et al., 2000). The presence requires sustained communication and active participation in an online learning environment.

Whiteside et al. (2017) pointed out that social presence is critical in an online learning. Social presence allows students to actively engage and in doing so, students develop a greater sense of community (Lowenthal & Dunlap, 2020). When online students are not afforded opportunities to actively participate as a learning community, Luo et al. (2022) explicated that students feel isolated and academic performance suffers. Subsequently, it is the recognition that online students need to feel a part of a community that I have endorsed a fourth form of presence as an addition to the CoI framework.

Through a series of quantitative factor analyses, learner presence is a construct developed by Shea et al. (2012) to account for online learner agency. While learner presence has not been widely accepted, learner presence is characterized by online learners' attitudes and behaviors that are indicative of the self-regulated and self-directed online learners who possess the attributes to apply those behaviors in an online collaborative learning environment. Shea et al. (2012, p. 90) offers:

> *We suggest that the name 'learning presence' integrates with the other forms of presence in the CoI framework and reflects the proactive stance adopted by students who marshal thoughts, emotions, motivations, behaviors and strategies in the service of successful online learning. Learning presence thus indicates the exercise of agency and control rather than compliance and passivity and more fully articulates popular beliefs about the importance of self-direction in online environments.*

Given that our Ed.S. program has grown exponentially, I agree with Shea et al. (2012) that it is important for course instructors to consider the role that self-regulation plays and serves as a basis for learner presence in an online learning environment.

ADDRESSING STUDENT ENGAGEMENT AS A "SMALL TEACHING PRACTICE"

Recognizing that student engagement is critical for positive student outcomes in an online learning environment, one of the take-aways from our FLC was the criticality of collaborative or teamwork activities to enhance student engagement. My commitment stems from a mind-set that engagement equates to active participation, active learning; hence, my intention is to implement three collaborative learning experiences for my online graduate students as they finalize their capstone projects. The three collaborative learning experiences will be: 1) peer review partners on the capstone project – the Problem of Practice, 2) a team-based live presentation on the program's capstone project, 3) team-based reflections on the capstone project presentation using the same presentation teams.

The capstone project that provides the basis for my graduate students' collaborative learning experiences is a major thesis that is developed in three required Ed.S. program courses and finalized in the third course. To elaborate, our Ed.S. students undertake capstone projects to improve practice by solving problems and contributing to improved curriculum and instructional performance. To do this, they inquire into and analyze the nature and dimensions of a problem and establish that there is a difference between the present and the ideal state. The students then build a case for improvements and make persuasive recommendations for action. Once students identify their problem of practice, the form of disciplined inquiry translates into an instructional development plan of improvement targets (goals) and finalized in a substantial thesis.

Peer Review Partners

With the focus on the capstone thesis, the first collaborative experience is to engage my students in the peer review process. Using our LMS platform, I will meet with my students in a synchronous class meeting to introduce the process, materials, and significance for peer review. It is important for my graduate students to experience peer review because the process provides them the opportunity to learn from each other by offering their peer partner suggestions to improve their work and simultaneously, to discover areas in their own papers that need to be strengthened. Due to the nature that my graduate students are online learners, I will assign peer partners, establish the timeline for the review process, and develop guiding questions for each partner to use as a peer review form. As one who evaluates graduate students' writing on a weekly basis, I believe it is also important to share essential elements of an effective review. As Van Popta et al. (2017) offered, peer review engages students in the "cognitive processes to evaluate, suggest, and explain" needed improvements to be made (p. 32). From this perspective, I will discuss the merits of constructive and positive feedback and point out it is necessary to be specific and highlight confusing sentences, phrases, and paragraphs that require more clarification.

Team-based Live Presentation

The second active learning experience will consist of a team-based presentation. Specifically, each member will present a 10-minute discussion on their capstone thesis in a Zoom meeting. The purpose is to permit my online graduate students to share the culmination of their academic work in an interactive virtual environment and to showcase their knowledge on the problem they have identified in their practice. It is a time for my graduate students to engage. According to Henrikson (2020), online instructors should structure their courses to provide opportunities that encourage student engagement, and such opportunities include group projects, presentations, and group discussions. As the instructor, I will facilitate by assigning the collaborative teams, determine the presentation timeline, and develop a power point as a presentation resource my graduate students can use during the Zoom meeting. The power point and instructions for my students will consist of several slides to feature:

1. Introduction

    An introduction of the Problem of Practice that includes the reason for selecting it and a general reason of its significance that impacts student achievement.
2. National Issue

The national issue, federal law, or federal policy that created the problem of practice.

3. Research

   A discussion of the findings from the literature by offering how the literature pertains to the topic and lays the foundation to support the problem you have identified that needs improvement. Highlight four to five research articles to share.

4. Student Performance Outcomes

   Discuss the four student performance outcomes that you will address that provide the evidentiary data that a problem does exist for your students.

5. Professional Goals

   Discuss the four professional goals you will implement to address the targeted student performance outcomes and how your professional goals will ultimately improve the problem of practice.

Team-based Reflections

The third collaborative learning experience is reflection. Reflection has been a hallmark in teacher education for decades. The seminal work by Dewey (1933) endorsed reflection, emphasizing that reflection involves the process of critical analysis on one's instruction as a necessary method to inform one's practice. However, collaborative reflection has recently garnered attention due to the significance of social interaction in a collaborative community (Li et al., 2020). As a team, it is important for my graduate students to share what they have learned from the team-based presentation and what modifications would be made, both individually and collectively.

In a synchronous class meeting, I will explain to my graduate students the expectations for the collaborative reflection. Drawing upon Think-Pair-Share (Lyman, 1981), the strategy will be modified to accommodate a Think-Group-Share. First, each member of the group thinks and responds individually to the following questions:

1. What were my strengths in presenting my capstone thesis?
2. What were areas to improve in my presentation?
3. What did I learn from the presentation experience?
4. What changes would we make to the collaborative presentation?

Next, the individual members share their thoughts with their group members and the group will then present their reflections using one of the following methods:

1. Create an audio and video-recorded power point presentation to address the four questions and share the power point on our discussion forum.
2. Present a Zoom discussion as you address the four questions. Record the Zoom discussion and share the link to our discussion forum.
3. Create a Microsoft Word document to feature each team member's individual responses to the four questions and a collective response to question #4. Share the document on our discussion forum.

As I stop to reflect on my collaborative work in our FLC, it is fair to say that my commitment to implement student engagement as a "small teaching practice" is due to the heightened interest from our discussions related to Lang's (2016) and Darby and Lang's (2019) texts. My commitment to provide my online graduate students the opportunities for productive collaborative learning activities is further reinforced by my understanding of social presence and its importance as an online course designer. I agree with Henrikson (2020) that it is my responsibility to structurally design my courses to promote group collaboration. Additionally, I find that my role as an online instructor is to facilitate the opportunity for my graduate students to actively engage and in doing so, it is my hope that my students will develop a greater sense of community (Lowenthal & Dunlap, 2020).

REGINA

As long as 15 years ago, and in the face of a decline in student enrollment in our graduate programs, our faculty decided to transition our education graduate programs from face-to-face offerings to exclusively hybrid (a blend of on campus and online) and online only. Our graduate programs, which largely serve working teachers, could better accommodate teachers' needs and were more able to reach our populations of rural students who found it difficult to come to campus after their teaching day ended if offered in online formats. At this time, online learning was a newly evolving experience and many sought to distinguish it from its early predecessor distance learning (Kuzminykh, et al., 2021). Our university worked to provide voluntary professional development specifically on online learning, and I was a faculty member that took advantage of this training. One of the largest emphases in this particular training was on the importance of accommodating diverse needs of students in the course, referenced as Universal Design for Learning (UDL). As a faculty member in the COE for numerous years, I was familiar with UDL as a concept to support diverse learners and sought to incorporate those practices both within my face-to-face courses, but also worked to encourage our future teachers to embrace the tenets of this design. However, I had no real experience with how

UDL would translate into online courses. The training was quite informative, and I recall learning very practical ideas for incorporating practices for accommodating all students in the online setting. I was able to initially develop courses that addressed UDL in a comprehensive manner. However, to be honest, over the course of many years and through changes in programs, courses and even university structures, I lost some of the insight into UDL practice. Sure, I have remained committed to developing quality online courses for my students, but I have not remained as faithful to the principles of UDL as I had in the past.

It was through our discussions related to Lang's (2016) and Darby and Lang's (2019) texts, that I was sharply reminded of my derelict efforts in this regard. As a result, I renewed my commitment to focus on UDL, and this project is allowing me that space to improve. Since UDL is multi-faceted, I have decided to specifically focus on ways in which I can encourage prediction, previewing, and anticipation within my courses as a learning strategy. Methods related to predictive strategies can be an integral aspect of the UDL approach, and I am hoping will yield benefits for student success. My renewed commitment to designing course structures attainable for all students is a direct result of my experience with this FLC.

PREDICTIVE STRATEGIES

As Lang (2016) points out in his text, predictive activities can be implemented as "small teaching practices" and can help students recognize gaps in their understanding of material and can lead to a desire to connect and/or "repair" their knowledge while interacting with course material. Through our engagement with both course texts and in our discussions in the FLC, I was reminded of the importance of tapping into students' prior knowledge and allowing them to bring up organized schemata prior to engaging in course topics. Aligned with the principles of UDL, predictive learning practices specifically address designs for multiple means of engagement, representation, and action and expression, as outlined by the Center for Applied Technology (CAST). Predictive strategies provide learners with opportunities to "address bias and distractions, clarify meaning and purpose of goals, recognize expectations, connect prior knowledge to new learning, and anticipate and plan for challenges" (CAST, 2024, p. 8).

As a strategy, prediction has been found to boost learners' surprise about unexpected answers, which can lead to heightened interest and better retention of information (Brod, 2021; Mera et al., 2022). Prediction has been used in reading instruction for years and has been thought of as an effective means of connecting readers' prior knowledge to the anticipated text (Beers, 2015) which aids in comprehension and understanding. Activating prior knowledge increases the likelihood of one learning and retaining information (Wade & Kidd, 2019). I am hoping through consciously and deliberately integrated course activities related to prediction, previewing and anticipation I can enhance students' learning experience and create more opportunities for all students to critically interact with and reflect on course material, as aligned with the tenets of UDL.

ADDRESSING PREDICTIVE STRATEGIES AS A "SMALL TEACHING PRACTICE"

As a direct outcome of the FLC experience, I plan to implement various strategies related to prediction in my online graduate courses. To begin, and in the spirit of "small teaching practices" outlined by Lang (2016), I will be working to integrate these practices into one of the three courses I will be teaching in an upcoming semester. To provide context for this course, it is a course that consists of two major papers (one to be turned in a mid-point in the semester and the second at the conclusion of the semester). For these papers, the students are allowed to select their own topics, related to the course theme, goals, and expected outcomes. The course also consists of weekly modules that encompass readings, links and videos for students to peruse, and then a required written response and discussion post or related response. The modules encourage students to critically engage in diverse perspectives on course topics and respond in a variety of ways. I perceive that within these weekly modules the strategies of prediction will likely best serve students. There are three particular predictive strategies that I hope to incorporate: anticipation guides, KWL(Q), and the use of pretests. I will be putting effort into their design and ensuring there are diverse ways in which students can respond to these.

Anticipation Guides

Anticipation guides are a useful too with the general purpose of activating students' prior knowledge and piquing curiosity about a topic. Largely regarded as an effective reading comprehension strategy (Merkely, 1997), there are a range of ways anticipation guides can be presented in both print and non-print media (Head & Readence, 1986). They are extremely versatile and can be used with a range of disciplines and topics including controversial statements to arouse curiosity (Head & Readence, 1986). Anticipation guides are typically presented as general statements related to the upcoming reading or other material that requires the respondent to tap into their prior knowledge in order to answer the anticipation statements (Dufflemer, 1994). One common form of anticipation guides asks the participant to respond with *Agree/Disagree* to explicit statements. The process provides students with opportunities to begin thinking about the topic and predicting what will be found from the reading. I plan to incorporate this strategy as an introduction to weekly modules.

Example Statements from an Anticipation Guide

The McKinney-Vento Act addresses school lunch requirements. Agree/Disagree

The McKinney-Vento Act does not provide access to healthcare. Agree/Disagree

Legislation is needed to recommend class size. Agree/Disagree

KWLKWL was originally created by Donna Ogle in 1986. KWL is an acronym for "Know," "Want-to-Know," and "Learned." This strategy has been expanded in recent years to KWLHQ, with the H representing "How did we find this out?" and Q representing the "Questions that remain" for the learner. While often presented as a graphic organizer with three distinct columns, it serves as an easy organizational tool that sets the purpose for reading. Found to be an effective tool in reading comprehension (Riswanto, et al., 2014), it can also be useful as a predictive strategy through tapping into students' prior knowledge by first eliciting what students already know (K) about the upcoming topic and helping them gain interest in the topic through exploring what they want to know(K)For the purpose of examination of the prediction as a learning strategy, I will be focusing primarily on the initial aspect of this strategic tool. I plan to integrate this strategy into the weekly course modules as well.

Example Topic: Supporting Students with Disabilities

Table 1. Predictive aspect of strategy

K (what do you currently know about this topic?)	W (what do you want to know about this topic?)	L (what have you learned about through the module?)	H Extended Version (how did you learn this?)	Q Extended Version (What questions were generated or remain for you?)

Pretests

I hope to incorporate a pretest or "test your knowledge" at the conclusion of one module and prior to the next. This would be a non-graded assessment designed to have the students anticipate the next week's lesson and begin to build connections between modules. Students' responses to this mini pretest would allow me to anticipate any misconceptions regarding the next week's module and build the following lesson to more deliberately tailoring it for students' needs and interests related to the topic.

Through the use of these predictive strategies, I am hoping to tap into students' prior knowledge, help them tap into and further organize schema related to course material, and to develop more meaningful learning experiences for my online students, directly aligning with the principals of Universal Design for Learning.

NEXT STEPS

When looking back to our commitment to improve our online graduate students' learning experiences, we are reminded of the significant challenges that acted as the impetus for the inception of our FLC. The rapid advancements in technology, coupled with the substantial increase in student enrollment in our Ed.S. program, resulted in a realization that changes needed to be made to address our students' needs. These signaled changes that would accommodate the diversity of our graduate students who enjoy the convenience and flexibility of online learning, but also changes that would also be beneficial for the varied array of readiness skills our students possess. As instructors involved in the scholarship of teaching and learning, we understand that the first changes to be made begin with us. As a result, it is fortuitous that the significant challenges we have faced in our Ed.S. program have alternatively presented new opportunities; opportunities for us to retool our pedagogical practices and course learning activities to support our students who seek to be "specialists" in their schools.

According to Happel and Song (2020), faculty learning communities provide a space for faculty who wish to improve the teaching and learning experiences for their students. From this perspective, we would be remiss without emphasizing that the formation of our FLC provided the context for our plans to implement the "small teaching practices" presented in our chapter. We are excited about implementing these practices and examining their effectiveness for our students. We are hoping to see tangible gains in our students' performance through course grades, but we are also hoping to qualitatively measure the impact of these course adjustments through surveying students' perceptions of these practices.

The formation of this FLC, the meaningful collegial discourse that has ensued, and the subsequent research into best practices has served to reinvigorate our professional outlook. We plan to sustain this FLC through seeking new texts to jointly study and continue to find new strategies and ideas to implement in our courses. As we commit to this professional practice, we will also be looking to build this FLC, potentially adding faculty from other programs within our college and instructors from other disciplines.

Like the other chapters found in this text, we recognize and understand the fertility that online spaces can provide for developing teaching practices and developing our scholarship in teaching and learning.

REFERENCES

Anderson, T., Liam, R., Garrison, D. R., & Archer, W. (2001). Assessing teaching presence in a computer conferencing context. *Online Learning : the Official Journal of the Online Learning Consortium*, 5(2), 1–17. DOI: 10.24059/olj.v5i2.1875

Beers, K. (2015). *When kids can't read-what teachers can do: A guide for teachers*. Pearson Education.

Bendelier, S., Bond, M., Buntins, K., Zawacki-Richter, O., & Kerres, M. (2020). Facilitating student engagement through educational technology in higher education: A systematic review in the field of arts and humanities. *Australasian Journal of Educational Technology*, 36(4), 126–150. DOI: 10.14742/ajet.5477

Brod, G. (2021). Prediction as a learning strategy. *Psychonomic Bulletin & Review*, 28(6), 1839–1847. DOI: 10.3758/s13423-021-01904-1 PMID: 33768503

CAST. (2024). *Universal design for learning guidelines version 3.0*. https://udlguidelines.cast.org

Darby, F., & Lang, J. (2019). *Small teaching online: Applying learning science to online classes*. Jossey-Bass.

Dewey, J. (1933). *How we think: A restatement of the relation of reflective thinking to the educative process*. Heath.

Dufflemeyer, F. (1994). Effective anticipation guide statements for learning from ex. *Journal of Reading*, 37(6), 452.

Garrison, D. R., Anderson, T., & Archer, W. (2000). Critical inquiry in a text-based environment: Computer conferencing in higher education. *The Internet and Higher Education*, 2(2), 87–105.

Head, M. H., & Readence, J. E. (1986). Anticipation guides: Meaning through prediction. In Dishner, E. R., Bean, T. W., Readence, J. E., & Moore, D. W. (Eds.), *Reading in the content areas* (2nd ed., pp. 229–234). Kendall/Hunt.

Henrikson, R. (2020). Using online lectures to promote engagement: Recognizing the self-directed learner as critical for practical inquiry. *Journal of Open, Flexible &. Distance Learning : for Educators, Trainers, and Leaders*, 24(1), 17–32.

Kamya, M., & Otim, S. (2019). Integration of technology-enabled learning at higher education in developing countries: A case of Uganda Management Institute (UMI) [Paper presentation]. Pan-Commonwealth Forum, Scotland.

Kuh, G. D. (2009). What student affairs professionals need to know about student engagement. *Journal of College Student Development*, 50(6), 683–706. DOI: 10.1353/csd.0.0099

Kuzminykh, I., Ghita, B., & Xiao, H. (2021, August). The relationship between student engagement and academic performance in online education. In *2021 5th International Conference on E-Society, E-Education and E-Technology* (pp. 97-101). DOI: 10.1145/3485768.3485796

Lang, J. M. (2016). *Small teaching: Everyday lessons from the science of learning*. Jossey-Bass.

Li, Y., Li, X., Su, Y., Peng, Y., & Hu, H. (2020). Exploring the role of EFL learners' online self-regulation profiles in their social regulation of learning in wiki-supported collaborative reading activities. *Journal of Computers in Education*, 7(4), 575–595. DOI: 10.1007/s40692-020-00168-3

Luo, N., Li, H., Zhao, L., Wu, Z., & Zhang, J. (2022). Promoting student engagement in online learning through harmonious classroom environment. *The Asia-Pacific Education Researcher*, 31(5), 541–551. DOI: 10.1007/s40299-021-00606-5

Lyman, F. (1981). The responsive classroom discussion: The inclusion of all students. In A. Anderson (Ed.), *Mainstreaming digest* (pp. 109-113), University of Maryland College of Education.

Means, B., Toyama, Y., Murphy, R., Bakia, M., & Jones, K. (2010). *Evaluation of Evidence-based practices in online learning: A meta-analysis and review of online learning studies*. U.S. Department of Education.

Mera, Y., Rodriguez, G., & Marin-Garcia, E. (2022). Unraveling the benefits of experiencing errors during learning: Definition, modulating factors, and explanatory theories. *Psychonomic Bulletin & Review*, 29(3), 753–765. DOI: 10.3758/s13423-021-02022-8 PMID: 34820785

Merkley, D. J. (1997). Modified anticipation guide. *The Reading Teacher*, 50(4), 365–368.

Munna, A. S., & Kalam, M. A. (2021). Impact of active learning strategy on the student engagement. *GNOSI: An Interdisciplinary Journal of Human and Theory Praxis*, 4, 96–114.

Ogle, D. (1986). K-W-L: A teaching model that develops active reading of expository text. *The Reading Teacher*, 39(6), 564–570. DOI: 10.1598/RT.39.6.11

Piaget, J. (1936). *Origins of intelligence in the child*. Routledge & Kegan Paul.

Rajabalee, B. Y., Santally, M. I., & Rennie, F. (2020). A study of the relationship between students' engagement and their academic performances in an eLearning environment. *E-Learning and Digital Media*, 17(1), 1–20. DOI: 10.1177/2042753019882567

Rapanta, C., Botturi, L., Goodyear, P., Guàrdia, L., & Koole, M. (2021). Balancing technology, pedagogy and the new normal: Post-pandemic challenges for higher education. *Postdigital Science and Education*, 3(3), 715–742. DOI: 10.1007/s42438-021-00249-1

Shea, P., & Bidjerano, T. (2010). Learning presence: Towards a theory of self-efficacy, self-regulation, and the development of a communities of inquiry in online and blended learning environments. *Computers & Education*, 55(4), 1721–1731. DOI: 10.1016/j.compedu.2010.07.017

Shea, P., Hayes, S., Smith, S. U., Vickers, J., Bidjerano, T., Pickett, A., Gozza-Cohen, M., Wilde, J., & Jian, S. (2012). Learning presence: Additional research on a new conceptual element within the Community of Inquiry (CoI) framework. *The Internet and Higher Education*, 15(2), 89–95. DOI: 10.1016/j.iheduc.2011.08.002

Shea, P., Hayes, S., Uzuner Smith, S., Vickers, J., Bidjerano, T., Gozza-Cohen, M., Jian, S.-B., Pickett, A., Wilde, J., & Tseng, C. H. (2013). Online learner self-regulation: Learning presence viewed through quantitative content-and social network analysis. *International Review of Research in Open and Distance Learning*, 14(3), 427–461. DOI: 10.19173/irrodl.v14i3.1466

Shulman, L. (2011). Feature essays: The scholarship of teaching and learning: A personal account and reflection. *International Journal for the Scholarship of Teaching and Learning*, 5(1), 30. Advance online publication. DOI: 10.20429/ijsotl.2011.050130

Shulman, L. S. (1986). Those who understand: Knowledge growth in teaching. *Educational Researcher*, 15(2), 4–14. DOI: 10.3102/0013189X015002004

Shulman, L. S. (1987). Knowledge and teaching: Foundations of the new reform. *Harvard Educational Review*, 57(1), 1–23. DOI: 10.17763/haer.57.1.j463w79r56455411

Shulman, L. S. (1998). *Teaching and teacher education among the professions. 38th Charles W. Hunt Memorial Lecture*. AACTE Publications.

Van Popta, E., Kral, M., Camp, G., Martens, R. L., & Simons, P. R. J. (2017). Exploring the value of peer feedback in online learning for the provider. *Educational Research Review*, 20, 24–34. DOI: 10.1016/j.edurev.2016.10.003

Wade, S., & Kidd, C. (2019). The role of prior knowledge and curiosity in learning. *Psychonomic Bulletin & Review*, 26(4), 1377–1387. DOI: 10.3758/s13423-019-01598-6

Wade, S., & Kidd, C. (2019). The role of prior knowledge and curiosity in learning. *Psychonomic Bulletin & Review*, 26, 1377–1387.

Yunus, M., Setyosari, P., Utaya, S., & Kuswandi, D. (2021). The influence of online project collaborative learning and achievement motivation on problem-solving ability. *European Journal of Educational Research*, 10(2), 813–823. DOI: 10.12973/eu-jer.10.2.813

Zheng, M., Bender, D., & Lyon, C. (2021). Online elarning during COVID-19 produced equivalent or better student course performance as compared with pre-pandemic: Empirical evidence from a school-wide comparative study. *BMC Medical Education*, 21(1), 495. DOI: 10.1186/s12909-021-02909-z PMID: 34530828

Chapter 5
Professional Development Focused on Teaching and Learning in Online Environments

R. Velmurugan
https://orcid.org/0000-0002-7925-9757
Karpagam Academy of Higher Education, India

J. Sudarvel
https://orcid.org/0000-0001-6656-1992
Karpagam Academy of Higher Education, India

R. Bhuvaneswari
https://orcid.org/0009-0003-9396-6129
Dr. Mahalingam College of Engineering and Technology, Pollachi, India

Ravi Thirumalaisamy
https://orcid.org/0000-0002-5954-5940
Modern College of Business and Science, Oman

ABSTRACT

Professional development focused on teaching and learning in online environments is crucial in equipping educators with essential skills for digital education. This abstract explores the significance of ongoing training in mastering technological tools, addressing unique challenges of online teaching, incorporating best practices, and fostering reflective practice. Mishra and Koehler's TPACK framework guides educators in integrating technology effectively, while Guskey emphasizes support for maintaining engagement and academic integrity. Darling-Hammond advocates for

DOI: 10.4018/979-8-3693-7595-2.ch005

personalized learning experiences, and Wenger highlights the role of communities of practice in fostering collaboration. Effective professional development ensures educators deliver high-quality education, enhancing student learning outcomes in virtual settings.

INTRODUCTION

The digital revolution has irrevocably altered the landscape of education, as evidenced by the increasing popularity of online courses and virtual learning environments (VLEs) alongside traditional classrooms (Graham et al., 2001). This paradigm shift necessitates a parallel evolution in professional development (PD) for educators. The traditional skillset honed for face-to-face teaching needs to be augmented with competencies specific to the virtual realm. This essay delves into the key elements of effective PD for online teaching, acknowledging the distinct challenges and opportunities that digital education presents. One of the fundamental pillars of successful online PD is the development of strong technological fluency. Mastering the Learning Management System (LMS) – the software platform used to deliver and manage online courses – is paramount. Educators need to be adept at navigating the LMS interface, utilizing its functionalities as described by Bates (2019) to create engaging content, administer assessments, and facilitate online discussions. Furthermore, familiarity with a range of educational technology (EdTech) tools like video conferencing platforms, collaborative whiteboards, and online polling software empowers teachers to create interactive and dynamic learning experiences, as advocated by Rosenberg (2001).

Beyond technical proficiency, fostering an engaging online presence is crucial. Effective online educators cultivate a sense of community within the VLE, a concept explored by Rovai (2004). Techniques for fostering this online camaraderie include incorporating icebreaker activities, promoting discussions through forums and chat tools, and providing personalized feedback. Developing clear communication strategies specifically tailored to the virtual environment is equally important. This includes crafting concise and well-structured written instructions, and utilizing audio and video effectively for lectures and presentations, as suggested by Moore (1997) in his theory of transactional distance. Articulating expectations explicitly and establishing consistent communication protocols helps students navigate the online learning environment smoothly. Assessment practices in online learning require careful consideration. PD programs should equip educators with the skills to design and implement online assessments that accurately gauge student learning, as emphasized by Bangert et al. (2000). This encompasses exploring various online assessment tools, crafting effective test items suited to the virtual format, and addressing issues of academic integrity in online testing. Additionally, providing ongoing formative assessment through quizzes, polls, and peer feedback allows for continuous monitoring of student progress and enables timely adjustments to learning activities, a concept championed by Wiliam and Black (1998) in their work on formative assessment.

Catering to the diverse needs of online learners is another critical facet of PD for online teaching. Developing an understanding of various learning styles, as identified by Howard Gardner (1983) in his theory of multiple intelligences, and incorporating strategies for differentiation is essential for ensuring an inclusive learning environment. PD programs can equip educators with techniques for scaffolding instruction for students who may require additional support, while also providing opportunities for advanced learners to delve deeper into the subject matter. Fostering a culture of inclusivity in online learning also involves ensuring accessibility – making sure course materials and activities are adaptable for students with disabilities, as mandated by the Americans with Disabilities Act (1990). The unique challenges of online learning necessitate specific pedagogical approaches. PD programs should equip educators with strategies to address issues like student engagement and motivation in the virtual environment. Techniques for fostering active participation can include incorporating collaborative activities, gamification elements (Kapp, 2012), and regular opportunities for students to interact with the instructor and their peers. Furthermore, cultivating self-directed learning skills in students empowers them to take ownership of their learning journey in the asynchronous nature of online courses, a concept explored by Garrison (1997) in his theory of community of inquiry.

However, the digital classroom is not without its benefits. PD programs should highlight the opportunities afforded by online learning. The asynchronous nature of online courses allows for greater flexibility for students, particularly those juggling work or family commitments, as confirmed by Phipps and Merrill (2000) in their research. Furthermore, online platforms offer access to a wider range of resources and learning materials than might be available in a traditional classroom setting. Educators can leverage these advantages by incorporating multimedia elements such as video lectures, simulations, and interactive learning modules into their online courses. In conclusion, the proliferation of online learning environments necessitates a comprehensive approach to professional development for educators. Effective PD programs equip teachers with the technical skills, pedagogical strategies, and online communication skills required to create engaging and effective learning experiences in the virtual realm. By acknowledging the unique challenges and opportunities presented by digital education, we can empower educators to thrive in this evolving landscape and ensure all students have access to high-quality learning experiences, regardless of their location. This reimagined approach to PD paves the way for a future where online learning is not just a viable alternative, but a powerful tool for fostering deeper engagement and broader educational access.

THE EVOLUTION OF ONLINE LEARNING

Online learning has undergone a metamorphosis, blossoming from rudimentary correspondence courses to intricate, interactive platforms. These platforms now facilitate real-time collaboration and multimedia engagement, fostering a dynamic learning experience far removed from the static mail packets of the past. This evolution can be attributed, in part, to the relentless march of technological advancements. However, a significant catalyst for this rapid transformation was the unforeseen global crisis – the COVID-19 pandemic.

The pandemic's grip on the world forced educational institutions across the globe to scramble for remote learning solutions. This unprecedented situation thrust educators, many with limited prior experience in online teaching, into the unfamiliar territory of virtual classrooms. Suddenly, the responsibility of delivering effective instruction shifted from the physical space of a traditional classroom to the digital realm, demanding a new set of skills and pedagogical approaches (Bates, 2023).

This rapid shift exposed a critical gap in many educators' professional development toolkits. The skillset honed for face-to-face instruction, as described by Garrison (2016) in his work on communities of inquiry, proved insufficient for the online environment. Educators unfamiliar with the intricacies of Learning Management Systems (LMS) found themselves struggling to navigate the technical aspects of online course creation and management (Anderson, 2011). Furthermore, fostering a sense of community and maintaining student engagement within the virtual sphere presented a distinct challenge compared to the traditional classroom setting (Rovai, 2004).

However, this period of upheaval also presented a unique opportunity for innovation. Educational institutions, recognizing the urgency of the situation, invested heavily in professional development programs specifically designed to equip educators with the necessary skills for online teaching (Cavanaugh et al., 2020). These programs focused on developing technological fluency, exploring the functionalities of LMS platforms, and integrating interactive tools for enhanced student engagement (Yildirim & Chandra, 2013). Additionally, fostering a sense of community online through forums, discussions, and collaborative activities became a central theme in these PD programs.

The large-scale adoption of online learning during the pandemic, while driven by necessity, has paved the way for a future where online and traditional learning methods can coexist and complement each other. This blended learning approach, as explored by Graham et al. (2001), offers greater flexibility for students and allows educators to leverage the strengths of both physical and virtual classrooms. As online learning platforms continue to evolve and educators become more adept at navigating them, this approach has the potential to revolutionize education, making it more accessible and engaging for learners of all backgrounds.

KEY COMPETENCIES FOR ONLINE EDUCATORS

The rise of online learning environments has fundamentally altered the educational landscape. Traditional brick-and-mortar classrooms now share space with virtual learning platforms, demanding a parallel evolution in professional development (PD) for educators. The skillset honed for face-to-face instruction is no longer sufficient. Effective online teaching requires a multifaceted repertoire that equips educators to navigate the complexities and capitalize on the opportunities of the digital classroom.

1. Technological Proficiency

The landscape of education has undeniably shifted, demanding educators to become adept at using a diverse range of digital tools and platforms. This goes beyond basic computer literacy; educators must be architects, crafting engaging and effective learning experiences with the digital building blocks available. A core skill in this digital toolkit is mastery of Learning Management Systems (LMS). Pawan Singh (2018) emphasizes the power of LMS platforms to streamline classroom management, allowing for efficient distribution of materials, submission of assignments, and communication with students. Popular LMS options like Canvas or Moodle offer a robust foundation for organizing the virtual classroom.

Beyond organization, educators must leverage the power of video conferencing software to foster a sense of community and interaction, especially in remote learning environments. According to a study by Bates (2019), video conferencing tools like Zoom or Google Meet can create a more engaging learning experience, allowing for real-time discussions and fostering a sense of connection between students and educators. However, the true power of digital tools lies in their pedagogical applications. Moving beyond rote memorization, collaborative tools like discussion boards (as advocated by Garrison & Anderson, 2006) and digital whiteboards can transform classrooms into vibrant learning communities. Discussion boards allow for asynchronous communication and reflection, while digital whiteboards, as highlighted by Friesen (2020), enable real-time collaboration and brainstorming sessions, fostering critical thinking and problem-solving skills.

Effective professional development programs must address both the technical aspects of these tools and their pedagogical applications. Training should not just focus on how to use a specific platform, but also equip educators with the knowledge of how these tools can be used to create differentiated learning experiences that cater to diverse student needs. This aligns with the work of Mishra & Koehler (2006), who emphasize the importance of Technological Pedagogical and Content Knowledge (TPACK) for effective technology integration in the classroom. Thus, educators today must be well-versed in the language of digital tools. By mastering Learning Management Systems, video conferencing software, and collaborative tools, educators can craft engaging and effective learning experiences that cater to the needs of the modern student. However, simply knowing how to use these tools is not enough. Educators must also be equipped with the pedagogical knowledge to leverage the tools' potential and create a dynamic learning environment that fosters collaboration, critical thinking, and a love of learning.

2. Instructional Design

Effective online teaching requires a significant departure from traditional classroom methods. Unlike the fixed schedule and face-to-face interactions of a physical space, online learning demands flexibility and active student participation. Educators must become architects, crafting engaging and interactive content that caters to diverse learning styles and can be delivered asynchronously or synchronously. This new blueprint for online learning prioritizes active learning over passive lectures. Weller (2010) advocates for incorporating activities that spark curiosity and go beyond rote memorization, such as online quizzes with immediate feedback, collaborative problem-solving exercises using virtual whiteboards, and gamified learning experiences that reward progress and mastery. These activities not only maintain engagement but also foster critical thinking skills and a deeper understanding of the subject matter.

The flexibility of online learning allows for the inclusion of asynchronous activities, which students can complete at their own pace. Salmon (2009) proposes the use of online discussion forums with clear guidelines to encourage thoughtful discourse and peer-to-peer learning. Asynchronous discussions enable students to reflect on their responses and engage in meaningful dialogue with their peers, fostering a deeper understanding of the content. Additionally, educators can incorporate multimedia resources, such as recorded lectures, podcasts, and interactive simulations, to cater to different learning styles and provide a rich, varied learning experience.

While asynchronous activities offer flexibility, synchronous learning is crucial for real-time interaction and community building. Video conferencing software, such as Zoom or Microsoft Teams, can facilitate live discussions, virtual office hours, and group projects. Salmon (2009) emphasizes the importance of establishing a sense of community in online courses. Group projects facilitated through video conferencing or collaborative writing exercises using shared documents can promote collaborative learning and build a sense of belonging among students. These synchronous sessions provide opportunities for immediate feedback, clarification of doubts, and the development of interpersonal skills.

Online platforms can be powerful tools for fostering a sense of community that transcends physical limitations. By designing activities that require collaboration and critical thinking, educators can create a dynamic learning environment. For example, group projects can be managed through collaborative platforms like Google Docs or Microsoft OneDrive, allowing students to work together on documents in real-time. Discussion forums, with well-structured prompts, can encourage students to engage in critical analysis and exchange ideas, thereby enhancing their critical thinking abilities. By embracing these design principles, online courses can become vibrant, interactive ecosystems that foster not just knowledge acquisition, but also critical thinking, collaboration skills, and a passion for learning. Insights from Weller (2010) and Salmon (2009) highlight the importance of active learning, community building, and the effective use of digital tools in online education, ensuring that online learning is not only flexible and accessible but also engaging and effective in promoting deep learning and student success.

3. Digital Pedagogy

Understanding how to teach effectively in an online environment is crucial for modern educators. This involves mastering techniques such as flipped classrooms, blended learning, and the use of multimedia resources. Additionally, educators must be adept at facilitating discussions and providing feedback in a virtual setting to ensure that students remain engaged and motivated. The flipped classroom model, popularized by Bergmann and Sams (2012), reverses the traditional learning structure by having students first engage with new material at home, typically through video lectures, and then using class time for hands-on activities and discussions. In an online environment, this model can be particularly effective. Educators can create video lectures or curate existing resources for students to review asynchronously. Class time, conducted through video conferencing platforms, can then be dedicated to deeper exploration of the material, problem-solving sessions, and collaborative projects. This approach not only promotes active learning but also allows students to engage with the content at their own pace, enhancing understanding and retention.

Blended learning, which combines online and face-to-face instruction, offers a flexible approach that can cater to diverse learning needs. According to Garrison and Vaughan (2008), blended learning integrates the best aspects of both online and traditional classroom experiences. In a fully online setting, this can be achieved by blending synchronous sessions with asynchronous activities. Synchronous sessions, held via platforms like Zoom or Microsoft Teams, can provide real-time interaction and immediate feedback, fostering a sense of community. Asynchronous components, such as discussion forums, quizzes, and self-paced learning modules, allow students to engage with the material at their convenience, promoting a more personalized learning experience.

The use of multimedia resources is essential for creating engaging and dynamic online courses. Mayer (2009) emphasizes the importance of multimedia learning, which involves using text, images, audio, and video to enhance understanding and retention. Educators can incorporate a variety of multimedia elements, such as interactive simulations, video demonstrations, and podcasts, to cater to different learning styles and make the content more accessible. These resources not only make the learning experience more enjoyable but also help to clarify complex concepts and provide multiple avenues for students to engage with the material. Effective facilitation of discussions and provision of feedback are critical for maintaining student engagement and motivation in an online environment. Salmon (2009) highlights the importance of e-moderating, where educators guide and support online discussions to ensure meaningful interaction. Clear guidelines and structured prompts can help facilitate thoughtful discourse in discussion forums. Additionally, regular and timely feedback is crucial for student success. According to Hattie and Timperley (2007), feedback that is specific, actionable, and focused on the learning process can significantly enhance student achievement. In an online setting, educators can use a combination of written comments, audio feedback, and video messages to provide personalized and constructive feedback. By mastering these techniques and tools, educators can ensure that their students remain motivated and engaged, receiving a high-quality education regardless of their physical location.

4. Assessment and Feedback

Online assessments present unique challenges, such as ensuring academic integrity and providing timely, meaningful feedback. To address these issues effectively, professional development (PD) for educators must cover a range of assessment strategies, including quizzes, exams, project-based assessments, and peer reviews, and how to implement them successfully in an online environment. One of the primary concerns with online assessments is maintaining academic integrity. According to Olt (2002), online assessments are prone to higher risks of cheating due to the lack of physical supervision. To mitigate these risks, PD programs should introduce educators to various proctoring tools and techniques. For instance, software like Respondus LockDown Browser and ProctorU can help monitor student activities during exams, reducing the likelihood of dishonest behavior. Additionally, designing assessments that require higher-order thinking skills and personalized responses can make it more difficult for students to engage in academic dishonesty. Educators can also use question banks to generate random questions for each student, thereby minimizing the chances of collusion.

Providing timely and meaningful feedback is another crucial aspect of online assessments. Hattie and Timperley (2007) emphasize that feedback is one of the most powerful influences on student achievement. In an online setting, feedback needs to be more deliberate and structured. PD programs should train educators on how to use digital tools to provide various forms of feedback, such as written comments, audio recordings, or video messages. Tools like Turnitin's Feedback Studio or Google Classroom's comment feature can facilitate detailed, constructive feedback that helps students understand their strengths and areas for improvement. Timely feedback is essential to keep students engaged and motivated; hence, educators must be adept at managing their time and using automated feedback mechanisms for objective assessments like quizzes. PD should also cover a range of assessment strategies beyond traditional quizzes and exams. Project-based assessments are particularly effective in online learning environments as they encourage active learning and practical application of knowledge. According to Bell (2010), project-based learning (PBL) fosters collaboration, critical thinking, and problem-solving skills. Educators should be trained on how to design and manage online PBL tasks, ensuring clear guidelines, appropriate scaffolding, and the use of collaborative tools like Google Docs or Trello for project management. Furthermore, incorporating peer reviews can enhance the assessment process by promoting reflective learning and critical evaluation skills among students. Educators should learn how to structure peer review activities, using platforms like Peergrade or Moodle, to ensure fairness and consistency in peer evaluations.

Lastly, PD should emphasize the importance of formative assessments. Nicol and Macfarlane-Dick (2006) highlight that formative assessments are vital for continuous learning and improvement. Online quizzes, polls, and interactive activities using tools like Kahoot! or Socrative can provide immediate insights into student understanding, allowing educators to adjust their teaching strategies in real-time. Regular formative assessments keep students engaged and provide ongoing feedback, helping them to stay on track with their learning goals. Thus, effective online assessments require comprehensive PD programs that address the unique challenges of the digital learning environment. By equipping educators with strategies to ensure academic integrity, provide timely and meaningful feedback, and implement a variety of assessment methods, we can enhance the quality and effectiveness of online education. Insights from Olt (2002), Hattie and Timperley (2007), Bell (2010), and

Nicol and Macfarlane-Dick (2006) underscore the importance of well-rounded PD programs in preparing educators to navigate the complexities of online assessments.

CHALLENGES IN PROFESSIONAL DEVELOPMENT FOR ONLINE TEACHING

While the need for professional development (PD) in online teaching is evident, several challenges must be addressed to ensure its effectiveness. One of the primary challenges is the varying levels of technological proficiency among educators. Not all teachers are equally comfortable with digital tools and platforms, which can hinder the adoption of online teaching methods. As Borko (2004) points out, PD programs must be tailored to meet the diverse needs of educators, offering differentiated training that ranges from basic technological skills to advanced instructional strategies. Another significant challenge is the resistance to change. Many educators have spent years, if not decades, perfecting their in-person teaching techniques and may be reluctant to alter their approach. Ertmer (2005) emphasizes that overcoming this resistance requires PD programs to highlight the benefits of online teaching, providing concrete examples of its effectiveness and success stories from peers who have made the transition smoothly. Additionally, fostering a growth mindset, as suggested by Dweck (2006), can help educators embrace the challenges of learning new technologies and pedagogical approaches.

Time constraints also pose a challenge. Educators are often overwhelmed with their existing responsibilities, leaving little time for engaging in PD activities. According to Darling-Hammond et al. (2017), successful PD programs must be flexible and convenient, integrating seamlessly into teachers' schedules. This can be achieved by offering asynchronous learning modules, online workshops, and virtual communities of practice, allowing educators to participate at their own pace and convenience. Furthermore, the rapid pace of technological advancements means that PD programs must be continuously updated to stay relevant. Educators need ongoing support and access to the latest tools and best practices. As noted by Mishra and Koehler (2006), the Technological Pedagogical Content Knowledge (TPACK) framework emphasizes the need for integrating technology, pedagogy, and content knowledge. PD programs should, therefore, provide sustained support, including follow-up sessions, mentorship, and access to a repository of resources that educators can refer to as they adapt to new technologies and methodologies.

Finally, measuring the impact of PD programs on teaching practices and student outcomes is crucial. Guskey (2002) argues that effective PD should result in tangible improvements in both teaching and learning. Therefore, PD programs must include mechanisms for evaluating their effectiveness, such as pre- and post-training assessments, feedback surveys, and ongoing monitoring of educators' progress. By addressing these challenges, PD programs can better support educators in navigating the complexities of online teaching, ultimately enhancing the quality of education provided to students.

In conclusion, while the need for professional development in online teaching is clear, addressing challenges such as varying technological proficiency, resistance to change, time constraints, the pace of technological advancements, and measuring impact is essential. By tailoring PD programs to meet these challenges, providing ongoing support, and ensuring flexibility and relevance, educators can be better equipped to deliver high-quality online education. Insights from Borko (2004), Ertmer (2005), Dweck (2006), Darling-Hammond et al. (2017), Mishra and Koehler (2006), and Guskey (2002) underscore the importance of a well-rounded and responsive approach to professional development in the evolving landscape of online education.

1. Access and Equity

Not all educators have equal access to professional development opportunities, which can significantly impact their ability to enhance their teaching practices. To address this disparity, institutions must take proactive measures to ensure that all staff, regardless of their location or resources, can participate in training programs. This commitment involves providing financial support, flexible scheduling options, and access to necessary technology. Financial support plays a crucial role in enabling educators to engage fully in professional development. According to Darling-Hammond et al. (2017), financial constraints are a significant barrier for many teachers, especially those working in under-resourced schools or regions. Institutions can alleviate this burden by offering grants, scholarships, or stipends to cover the costs associated with attending workshops, conferences, or online courses. By removing financial barriers, educators can focus on their professional growth without worrying about affordability.

Flexible scheduling is another essential consideration for ensuring equitable access to PD opportunities. Many educators face demanding schedules filled with teaching responsibilities, meetings, and other obligations. Offering flexible PD options, such as asynchronous online modules or weekend workshops, allows educators to participate in professional development at times that are convenient and manageable. This approach not only accommodates varying workloads but also respects the diverse personal commitments that educators balance alongside their professional roles. Access to necessary technology is fundamental in today's digital age, particularly for online professional development initiatives. As highlighted by Mishra and Koehler (2006), the Technological Pedagogical Content Knowledge (TPACK) framework emphasizes the integration of technology into teaching practices. Institutions should ensure that educators have access to reliable internet connections, computers, and software tools required for participating in virtual training sessions or accessing online resources. Additionally, providing training on how to effectively utilize these technologies enhances educators' confidence and competence in integrating digital tools into their teaching.

Moreover, geographical location can pose a challenge for educators in rural or remote areas who may have limited access to face-to-face PD opportunities. Lee et al. (2021) discuss the importance of equity in educational access, advocating for inclusive strategies that reach all educators, regardless of their geographic location. Institutions can address this issue by offering virtual PD sessions, webinars, or video conferences that allow educators from diverse locations to participate without the need for extensive travel. Thus, ensuring equal access to professional development opportunities is essential for fostering continuous growth and improvement among educators. By providing financial support, flexible scheduling options, and access to necessary technology, institutions can empower all educators to participate fully in PD activities. Insights from Darling-Hammond et al. (2017), Mishra and Koehler (2006), and Lee et al. (2021) underscore the importance of equitable access to PD in supporting educators' professional development and enhancing educational outcomes for all students.

2. Resistance to Change

Addressing educators' resistance to adopting new teaching methods and technologies is crucial for the successful implementation of professional development (PD) programs in educational settings. Resistance can stem from various factors, including familiarity with traditional teaching methods, concerns about technology integration, and perceived challenges in adapting to new instructional approaches. Effective PD programs must therefore incorporate strategies to mitigate this resistance, highlight the benefits of online learning, and provide ongoing support to educators throughout the transition. One of the primary reasons educators may resist adopting new teaching methods is their deep-rooted familiarity and comfort with traditional approaches. As Ertmer (2005) discusses, teachers often develop pedagogical beliefs and practices over years of experience, making it challenging to embrace unfamiliar methodologies. To address this, PD programs should emphasize the incremental benefits of online learning, such as enhanced student engagement, personalized learning experiences, and broader access to educational resources.

By illustrating how these benefits align with educators' goals of improving student outcomes, resistance can gradually be overcome.

Another significant concern for educators is the integration of technology into their teaching practices. Mishra and Koehler (2006) propose the Technological Pedagogical Content Knowledge (TPACK) framework, which emphasizes the need for educators to balance technological proficiency with pedagogical and content knowledge. PD programs should provide training that not only enhances educators' technical skills but also demonstrates how technology can amplify their teaching effectiveness. Hands-on workshops, online tutorials, and peer mentoring can help educators gain confidence in using digital tools and understanding their instructional impact. Moreover, addressing resistance requires ongoing support and mentorship throughout the transition to new teaching methods. Guskey (2002) emphasizes the importance of sustained professional development that includes follow-up sessions, coaching, and collaborative learning communities. These opportunities allow educators to reflect on their experiences, troubleshoot challenges, and share successful strategies with their peers. By fostering a supportive environment, PD programs can nurture a culture of continuous improvement and innovation in teaching practices.

Furthermore, PD programs should provide concrete examples and case studies that showcase successful implementations of online learning. Darling-Hammond et al. (2017) suggest that illustrating real-world examples of how online teaching has positively impacted student engagement and learning outcomes can effectively persuade educators of its value. By highlighting success stories and demonstrating tangible results, PD facilitators can inspire confidence and motivation among educators to explore and integrate new teaching methods and technologies. Thus, addressing educators' resistance to adopting new teaching methods and technologies requires a multifaceted approach that combines persuasion, training, support, and evidence-based examples. Insights from Ertmer (2005), Mishra and Koehler (2006), Guskey (2002), and Darling-Hammond et al. (2017) underscore the importance of tailored strategies that respect educators' existing practices while encouraging innovation and adaptation to meet the evolving needs of modern education. By effectively addressing resistance, PD programs can empower educators to embrace change and enhance their teaching practices for the benefit of student learning.

3. Sustainability

Continuous professional development (CPD) is indispensable in the dynamic realm of online education, where technological advancements and evolving pedagogical approaches continually reshape teaching practices. Institutions play a pivotal role in fostering a culture of lifelong learning among educators by establishing robust and adaptive training programs. Central to effective CPD is the integration of the latest technologies into educational practices. As noted by Mishra and Koehler (2006), the Technological Pedagogical Content Knowledge (TPACK) framework underscores the importance of educators mastering the intersection of technology, pedagogy, and content knowledge. CPD programs should thus focus on equipping educators with practical skills in utilizing diverse digital tools, such as Learning Management Systems (LMS), interactive multimedia resources, and collaborative platforms. Hands-on workshops and online modules can empower educators to confidently integrate these technologies into their teaching, enhancing engagement and learning outcomes for students.

Moreover, CPD must address evolving pedagogical strategies that cater to diverse learning needs and preferences. Darling-Hammond et al. (2017) advocate for personalized professional development that aligns with educators' instructional goals and challenges them to innovate in their teaching practices. This approach encourages educators to explore flipped classrooms, blended learning models, and adaptive learning technologies that promote active student participation and deeper conceptual understanding. Furthermore, the rapid pace of change in educational technology necessitates continuous updates and refinements to CPD offerings. Guskey (2002) emphasizes the need for ongoing support and follow-up sessions to reinforce learning and address emerging challenges. Virtual communities of practice, where educators can share insights and best practices, offer a collaborative space for professional growth and problem-solving.

Institutions must also consider the scalability and accessibility of CPD initiatives to accommodate educators across diverse settings and roles. Lee et al. (2021) stress the importance of inclusive PD strategies that reach educators in rural or underserved areas through online platforms and virtual conferences. By providing flexible scheduling options and ensuring equitable access to resources, institutions can empower all educators to participate actively in CPD activities, fostering a culture of continuous improvement and innovation in online education. Thus, continuous professional development in online education is essential for empowering educators to adapt to evolving technological landscapes and pedagogical paradigms. Mishra and Koehler (2006), Darling-Hammond et al. (2017), Guskey (2002), and Lee et al. (2021) underscore the importance of tailored, accessible, and ongoing CPD programs that equip educators with the skills and knowledge needed to excel in digital learning environments.

BEST PRACTICES IN PROFESSIONAL DEVELOPMENT FOR ONLINE TEACHING

1. Needs Assessment

Expanding on the importance of conducting a thorough needs assessment in professional development programs for educators is crucial for ensuring their effectiveness and relevance. According to Guskey (2002), a needs assessment is the foundational step in designing professional development initiatives that truly meet the requirements of educators. It involves systematically identifying the current skills, knowledge gaps, and instructional challenges faced by teachers in their respective contexts. By conducting a needs assessment, institutions can tailor their training programs to address specific areas where educators require support the most. For instance, Mishra and Koehler (2006) emphasize the Technological Pedagogical Content Knowledge (TPACK) framework, which highlights the integration of technology, pedagogy, and content knowledge. A needs assessment guided by TPACK principles would identify whether educators lack technological proficiency, struggle with effective instructional strategies in online environments, or need support in adapting curriculum content for digital platforms.

Moreover, Darling-Hammond et al. (2017) stress the importance of personalized professional development that respects educators' individual needs and challenges. A needs assessment enables PD facilitators to gather insights directly from educators about their preferences, learning styles, and professional goals. This information can inform the design of training sessions that are engaging, relevant, and directly applicable to educators' daily teaching practices. Additionally, Lee et al. (2021) highlight the role of needs assessments in promoting equity in professional development. By understanding the unique challenges faced by educators in different geographic locations or educational settings, institutions can develop inclusive training strategies. This might include offering flexible scheduling options, providing resources in multiple formats, or leveraging online platforms to ensure accessibility for all participants. Thus, a thorough needs assessment forms the cornerstone of effective professional development programs for educators. By identifying specific skills and knowledge gaps, institutions can design targeted training that enhances educators' competencies, fosters innovation in teaching practices, and ultimately improves student learning outcomes.

2. Blended Learning Approach

Conducting a thorough needs assessment is foundational to designing professional development programs that effectively support educators in their evolving roles. Guskey (2002) stresses the significance of this initial step, highlighting that a needs assessment allows institutions to systematically identify the specific skills gaps, knowledge deficits, and instructional challenges faced by educators. This process ensures that the training provided is targeted and directly addresses the real needs of participants, rather than offering generic or irrelevant content.

Mishra and Koehler (2006) introduce the Technological Pedagogical Content Knowledge (TPACK) framework, which emphasizes the integration of technology, pedagogy, and content knowledge. Incorporating TPACK principles into a needs assessment enables facilitators to discern whether educators lack proficiency in leveraging technology for teaching, struggle with adapting instructional strategies to online environments, or require support in aligning curriculum content with digital platforms. By aligning professional development initiatives with the specific demands identified through a TPACK-informed needs assessment, institutions can ensure that educators receive training that enhances their effectiveness in using technology to facilitate learning.

Furthermore, Darling-Hammond et al. (2017) advocate for personalized professional development that respects educators' individual contexts and challenges. A needs assessment guided by principles of personalized learning enables facilitators to gather insights directly from educators regarding their preferences, learning styles, and professional goals. This information empowers PD designers to tailor training sessions that are engaging, relevant, and immediately applicable to educators' instructional practices, thereby maximizing the impact of professional development efforts on student learning outcomes.

3. Collaborative Learning

Encouraging collaboration among educators is pivotal for enhancing the professional development experience, fostering a supportive and dynamic learning environment. Peer mentoring, as advocated by Vygotsky (1978), involves experienced educators guiding their peers through reflective discussions, sharing insights, and offering practical advice. This approach not only promotes mutual learning but also builds a sense of community and camaraderie among colleagues. Collaborative projects, as discussed by Fullan (1993), provide educators with opportunities to work together on common goals or challenges. By collaborating on curriculum development, assessment strategies, or innovative teaching methods, educators can leverage collective expertise and creativity to achieve shared objectives. This collaborative effort not only enhances professional growth but also cultivates a culture of teamwork and innovation within educational institutions.

Discussion groups, facilitated by experts or experienced educators, offer structured forums for sharing experiences and best practices. According to Wenger (1998), communities of practice foster collaborative learning by encouraging active participation, knowledge sharing, and collective problem-solving. Educators can engage in discussions on emerging trends, pedagogical innovations, or challenges in implementing new technologies, gaining valuable insights and strategies from their peers. Moreover, collaborative approaches in professional development align with the principles of social constructivism, where learning occurs through social interaction and collaboration (Vygotsky, 1978). By encouraging educators to collaborate, institutions not only promote continuous learning and professional growth but also empower educators to adapt to changing educational landscapes effectively. Thus, fostering collaboration among educators through peer mentoring, collaborative projects, and discussion groups enriches the professional development experience. Drawing on insights from Vygotsky (1978), Fullan (1993), and Wenger (1998), these collaborative approaches not only enhance knowledge sharing and innovation but also contribute to a supportive and vibrant professional learning community within educational settings.

4. Practical Application

Training programs in education are most effective when they integrate opportunities for educators to apply newly acquired knowledge and skills in real-world contexts. This experiential learning approach not only reinforces theoretical concepts but also cultivates practical expertise through hands-on application. Designing and delivering online lessons is a cornerstone of experiential learning in educational training. According to Mishra and Koehler (2006), educators benefit greatly from actively creating and implementing digital content, as it allows them to directly apply pedagogical theories and technological tools in a simulated classroom environment. By engaging in this process, educators can experiment with different instructional strategies, multimedia resources, and interactive activities, thereby gaining insights into their effectiveness and relevance for diverse student needs.

Moreover, receiving constructive feedback from peers and trainers plays a crucial role in enhancing learning outcomes. Feedback, as highlighted by Hattie and Timperley (2007), should be specific, actionable, and focused on the learning process. Peer feedback fosters a collaborative learning environment where educators can exchange ideas, share best practices, and refine their teaching approaches based on collective insights and observations. Trainers, equipped with expertise in pedagogy and technology integration, provide valuable guidance and suggestions to help educators improve their instructional practices and address any challenges encountered during their online lesson delivery. Reflecting on experiences is another essential component of experiential learning in professional development. Darling-Hammond et al. (2017) emphasize the importance of educators critically analyzing their teaching experiences to identify strengths, areas for improvement, and lessons learned. Reflection encourages educators to refine their instructional strategies, adapt to evolving educational contexts, and continuously enhance their professional practice. Thus, integrating opportunities for educators to design and deliver online lessons, receive feedback from peers and trainers, and reflect on their experiences enriches training programs by promoting active learning, collaboration, and continuous improvement. Insights from Mishra and Koehler (2006), Hattie and Timperley (2007), and Darling-Hammond et al. (2017) underscore the value of experiential learning in preparing educators to effectively navigate the complexities of modern teaching environments.

5. Supportive Community

Establishing a supportive community of practice is instrumental in fostering continuous learning and professional growth among educators. According to Wenger (1998), communities of practice are groups of people who share a passion for a domain of knowledge or practice and interact regularly to learn from each other. In the context of education, these communities provide a space where educators can exchange ideas, share experiences, and collaborate on solutions to common challenges in online teaching. One of the key benefits of a community of practice is its role in providing ongoing support. Educators often face complex issues in their teaching practices, from integrating new technologies to adapting instructional strategies for diverse student needs. By participating in a community of practice, educators can seek advice from peers who have encountered similar challenges, tap into collective expertise, and receive constructive feedback on their approaches. This collaborative environment not only enhances problem-solving skills but also builds a sense of camaraderie and mutual support among members.

Moreover, communities of practice facilitate continuous learning by keeping educators informed about developments in online teaching. As technology evolves and pedagogical trends shift, staying updated with current practices and research is essential for effective teaching. Wenger (1998) emphasizes that communities of practice provide a platform for discussing emerging trends, sharing best practices, and exploring innovative approaches to enhance teaching effectiveness. Through webinars, online forums, and collaborative projects, educators can engage in professional dialogue and access valuable resources that support their professional development journey. Furthermore, a community of practice encourages reflective practice, as advocated by Darling-Hammond et al. (2017). Educators can reflect on their teaching experiences, evaluate the impact of their instructional decisions, and refine their approaches based on insights gained from community interactions. This reflective cycle promotes continuous improvement and empowers educators to adapt to the evolving demands of online education effectively. Thus, establishing a supportive community of practice plays a vital role in nurturing continuous learning, fostering collaboration, and enhancing professional growth among educators in online teaching. Wenger (1998) and Darling-Hammond et al. (2017) underscore the importance of these communities in providing ongoing support, promoting reflective practice, and keeping educators engaged with advancements in educational practices and technologies.

CONCLUSION

Professional development tailored to teaching and learning in online environments is becoming increasingly essential as education embraces digital transformation. In the digital age, educators must possess specific competencies to effectively engage students in virtual settings, overcome challenges inherent in online teaching, and integrate best practices to optimize learning outcomes. This essay explores how ongoing professional development can equip educators with these essential skills and knowledge.

Firstly, effective online teaching requires educators to master technological tools and platforms while maintaining pedagogical rigor. Mishra and Koehler (2006) introduced the Technological Pedagogical Content Knowledge (TPACK) framework, emphasizing the intersection of technology, pedagogy, and content knowledge. Educators need training that not only enhances their technical proficiency but also equips them with strategies to integrate technology meaningfully into their teaching practices. Professional development programs should offer hands-on workshops and simulations where educators can experiment with various digital tools such as Learning Management Systems (LMS), multimedia resources, and interactive applications. By gaining practical experience, educators can develop confidence in using these tools to create engaging online learning experiences that cater to diverse student needs.

Moreover, addressing the unique challenges of online teaching is crucial in professional development. Educators often face issues such as maintaining student engagement, ensuring equitable access to resources, and promoting academic integrity in digital assessments. Guskey (2002) highlights the importance of ongoing support and follow-up sessions to address these challenges effectively. Professional development workshops can provide strategies for designing interactive content, facilitating online discussions, and using data-driven insights to personalize learning experiences. Furthermore, educators can benefit from training on effective communication in virtual environments, managing time effectively in asynchronous and synchronous settings, and leveraging collaborative tools to foster student collaboration and interaction.

Incorporating best practices in online teaching is another key focus of professional development initiatives. Darling-Hammond et al. (2017) advocate for personalized learning experiences that align with educators' professional goals and instructional contexts. Professional development programs should encourage educators to explore flipped classroom models, blended learning approaches, and adaptive learning technologies. These strategies not only enhance instructional flexibility but also promote active learning and deeper conceptual understanding among students. By sharing success stories and case studies of effective online teaching implementations, professional development facilitators can inspire educators to innovate and adapt their teaching practices to meet the evolving needs of digital learners.

Furthermore, continuous improvement in online teaching requires educators to engage in reflective practice. Vygotsky (1978) emphasized the role of peer mentoring and collaborative reflection in professional growth. Establishing communities of practice, as discussed by Wenger (1998), provides a supportive environment where educators can share experiences, seek feedback, and collaborate on solutions to common challenges. Through these communities, educators can refine their instructional strategies, exchange best practices, and stay abreast of emerging trends in educational technology.

In conclusion, ongoing professional development focused on teaching and learning in online environments is essential for preparing educators to thrive in the digital age. Mishra and Koehler (2006), Guskey (2002), Darling-Hammond et al. (2017), and Wenger (1998) provide valuable insights into the competencies, challenges, and best practices that should inform professional development initiatives. By equipping educators with the skills to integrate technology effectively, overcome online teaching challenges, incorporate best practices, and engage in reflective practice, institutions can ensure that their educators deliver high-quality education and enhance student learning outcomes in virtual settings.

REFERENCES

Americans with Disabilities Act of 1990, Pub. L. 101-336, 104 Stat. 327 (1990).

Anderson, T. (2011). The MOOC revolution: The promise and the problem. *Educational Researcher*, 40(4), 16–24.

Bangert, D., Blakeslee, T., & Burns, J. (2000). Evaluating online learning: The need to go beyond student satisfaction. *American Journal of Distance Education*, 14(3), 10–25.

Bates, T. (2019). Teaching in a digital age: Guidelines for designing teaching and learning. BCcampus Open Education.

Bates, T. (2023). Teaching in a digital age: Guidelines for designing teaching and learning. BCcampus Open Education.

Bergmann, J., & Sams, A. (2012). *Flip Your Classroom: Reach Every Student in Every Class Every Day*. International Society for Technology in Education.

Bonwell, C. C., & Eison, J. A. (1991). ASHE-ERIC Higher Education Report: Vol. 1. *Active Learning: Creating Excitement in the Classroom*. George Washington University.

Borko, H. (2004). Professional Development and Teacher Learning: Mapping the Terrain. *Educational Researcher*, 33(8), 3–15. DOI: 10.3102/0013189X033008003

Cavanaugh, C., Dawson, K., & Bali, M. (2020). Teacher professional development and online learning during COVID-19: Emergency response and lasting change. *Educational Researcher*, 49(8), 650–658.

Darling-Hammond, L., Hyler, M. E., & Gardner, M. (2017). *Effective Teacher Professional Development*. Learning Policy Institute. DOI: 10.54300/122.311

Dweck, C. S. (2006). *Mindset: The New Psychology of Success*. Random House.

Ertmer, P. A. (2005). Teacher Pedagogical Beliefs: The Final Frontier in Our Quest for Technology Integration? *Educational Technology Research and Development*, 53(4), 25–39. DOI: 10.1007/BF02504683

Friesen, S. (2020). The Flipped Classroom with Digital Whiteboards [TechTrends]. *Enhancing Student Engagement and Learning.*, 64(2), 182–192.

Fullan, M. (1993). *Change Forces: Probing the Depths of Educational Reform*. Falmer Press.

Gardner, H. (1983). *Frames of mind: The theory of multiple intelligences.* Basic Books.

Garrison, D. R. (1997). *Distance education and critical theory.* Falmer Press.

Garrison, D. R. (2016). E-learning in the 21st century: A community of inquiry approach. Routledge.

Garrison, D. R., & Anderson, T. (2006). E-learning in the 21st century: A framework for the research agenda. *The Internet and Higher Education*, 9(2), 1–17. DOI: 10.1016/j.iheduc.2005.11.001

Garrison, D. R., Anderson, T., & Archer, W. (2000). Critical Inquiry in a Text-Based Environment: Computer Conferencing in Higher Education. *The Internet and Higher Education*, 2(2-3), 87–105. DOI: 10.1016/S1096-7516(00)00016-6

Garrison, D. R., & Vaughan, N. D. (2008). *Blended Learning in Higher Education: Framework, Principles, and Guidelines.* Jossey-Bass.

Graham, C. R., Manheim, J. B., & McLaughlin, M. W. (2001). Teachers' professional development in a blended learning environment. *Journal of Technology and Teacher Education*, 9(1), 49–65.

Guskey, T. R. (2002). Professional Development and Teacher Change. *Teachers and Teaching*, 8(3), 381–391. DOI: 10.1080/135406002100000512

Hattie, J., & Timperley, H. (2007). The Power of Feedback. *Review of Educational Research*, 77(1), 81–112. DOI: 10.3102/003465430298487

Hrastinski, S. (2008). Asynchronous and Synchronous E-Learning. *EDUCAUSE Quarterly*, 31(4), 51–55.

Kapp, K. M. (2012). *The gamification of learning and instruction: Game-based methods for improving performance.* Pfeiffer Publishing.

Lee, C., Nguyen, H., & Seel, N. M. (Eds.). (2021). *Equity and Quality in Digital Learning: Realizing the Promise in Remote and Hybrid Environments.* Routledge.

Lee, J., Bae, S. J., & Lee, K. M. (2021). The role of online platforms in professional development for teachers: A systematic review. *Computers & Education*, 166, 104181.

Lee, J. S., Srinivasan, S., Trail, T., Lewis, D., & Lopez, S. (2021). Examining the impact of professional development on early childhood educators' self-efficacy and practices. *Journal of Research in Childhood Education*, 35(1), 124–139.

Mayer, R. E. (2009). *Multimedia Learning* (2nd ed.). Cambridge University Press. DOI: 10.1017/CBO9780511811678

McBrien, J. L., Jones, P., & Cheng, R. (2009). Virtual Spaces: Employing a Synchronous Online Classroom to Facilitate Student Engagement in Online Learning. *International Review of Research in Open and Distance Learning*, 10(3). Advance online publication. DOI: 10.19173/irrodl.v10i3.605

Mishra, P., & Koehler, M. J. (2006). Technological pedagogical content knowledge: A framework for teacher knowledge. *Teachers College Record*, 108(6), 1017–1054. DOI: 10.1111/j.1467-9620.2006.00684.x

Mishra, P., & Koehler, M. J. (2006). Technological pedagogical content knowledge: Learning to teach with technology. *Journal of Research on Technology in Education*, 38(4), 375–400.

Moore, M. G. (1997). *Distance education: Theory and practice*. Wadsworth Publishing Company.

Moore, M. G., & Kearsley, G. (2011). *Distance Education: A Systems View of Online Learning* (3rd ed.). Wadsworth.

Phipps, R., & Merrill, M. D. (2000). What makes learning technologies effective? *Journal of Interactive Learning Research*, 11(2), 117–144.

Rosenberg, M. B. (2001). *E-learning: Strategies for delivering knowledge in the digital age*. Macmillan Publishers Limited.

Rovai, A. P. (2004). Building learning communities in online classrooms: A conversation map approach. [JETDE]. *Journal of Educational Technology Development and Exchange*, 1(1), 1–16.

Salmon, G. (2009). *E-moderating: The Key to Teaching and Learning Online* (2nd ed.). Routledge.

Singh, P. (2018). Learning Management Systems: Benefits and Challenges. [Journal of Educational Technology Development and Exchange (JETDE)], 11(2), 121-132.

Vygotsky, L. S. (1978). *Mind in Society: The Development of Higher Psychological Processes*. Harvard University Press.

Weller, M. (2010). *The Digital Scholar: How Technology Is Transforming Scholarly Practice*. Bloomsbury Academic.

Wenger, E. (1998). *Communities of Practice: Learning, Meaning, and Identity*. Cambridge University Press. Wenger's work emphasizes the role of communities of practice in facilitating learning and knowledge sharing among professionals. DOI: 10.1017/CBO9780511803932

Wiliam, D., & Black, P. (1998). Meaningful assessment in classroom education. *Schooling for Tomorrow*, 1(1), 31–52.

Yildirim, S., & Chandra, Y. (2013). University students' perceptions of online interactive activities in web-based learning environments: A case study. [JETDE]. *Journal of Educational Technology Development and Exchange*, 6(2), 111–129.

Chapter 6
A Higher Education Scholarship of Teaching and Learning Online Community of Practice

Sue A. Sharpe
https://orcid.org/0009-0003-1571-0064
Australian National University, Australia

Jennifer Z. Sun
https://orcid.org/0000-0002-5066-0205
University of Sydney, Australia

Trisha L. Poole
https://orcid.org/0000-0002-5336-6669
University of Southern Queensland, Australia

Phuc Diem Le
https://orcid.org/0000-0001-9705-8599
RMIT Vietnam, Vietnam

Melissa J. Saligari
https://orcid.org/0000-0001-7608-8975
University of Melbourne, Australia

Deb K. Clarke
https://orcid.org/0000-0001-5369-6556
Charles Sturt University, Australia

ABSTRACT

To improve global rankings, increase student numbers and enhance the quality of teaching and learning, Australian Higher Education institutions have increased emphasis on faculty to engage in the scholarship of teaching and learning (SoTL). However, there is an absence of SoTL capacity-building opportunities to support those with limited knowledge of, and engagement with SoTL. This lack of support has broad implications for scholars' identity, professional confidence and capacity to undertake SoTL. Using collective autoethnography, the chapter showcases the experiences of eight scholars who participated in a two-year SoTL online community of practice, aimed at building SoTL capacity. Results indicated increased confidence,

DOI: 10.4018/979-8-3693-7595-2.ch006

refashioned scholarly identity, institutional recognition of SoTL and leadership skills, and heightened professional self-worth. The chapter yields key messages for those mentoring SoTL scholars, and those adopting a community of practice approach to professional learning. More pointedly, the chapter provides recommendations for institutional policy and practice.

INTRODUCTION

This chapter showcases the processes, benefits, and outcomes of a two-year, synchronous online Scholarship of Teaching and Learning (SoTL) mentoring initiative. The aims of the initiative were to raise awareness of the value of and enhance members' capacity to engage in SoTL. Members met online fortnightly to initially explore the Higher Education Research and Development Society of Australasia (HERDSA) SoTL resource: five sequentially scaffolded online modules with embedded readings and learning activities. The meetings were facilitated by an experienced SoTL scholar who adopted the tenets of a community of practice (CoP) (Lave & Wenger, 1991) in the design and functioning of meetings.

Eight geographically dispersed members employed in learning and teaching roles, from varying higher education institutions, shared their scholarly journey in the CoP. To function effectively, a range of technologies were used allowing real-time group conversation and collaboration as well as supporting asynchronous planning and reading tasks (Corcoran & Duane, 2017).

The CoP members used collaborative autoethnography (Bochner & Ellis, 2022), sharing their SoTL stories to create the data for this chapter. These data were analysed thematically (Yin, 2015) and triangulated with Lave and Wenger's (1991) communities of practice (CoPs) characteristics, as well as literature on scholarly identity and transition (Gardner & Wiley, 2016; Hathaway et al., 2018; Kolomitro et al., 2017; Simmons et al., 2013; Supramaniam et al., 2020). The results are presented thematically using extracts from each member's autoethnographic 'story'.

The chapter highlights (a) the professional and personal outcomes for the members and (b) the conditions conducive to the sustainability and efficacy of an online SoTL CoP. The results revealed that members reported an enhanced understanding of the nature and purpose of SoTL, legitimising its place in relation to their own teaching and, once disseminated, as a contribution to the academy: a pursuit they now viewed as worthy of serious academic attention. Furthermore, the members identified that their engagement in the SoTL CoP resulted in an emerging sense of scholarly identity, together with a heightened self-confidence in pursuing SoTL. The CoP had allowed them 'permission to thrive' in the institutional jigsaw of the academy. Many voiced feeling a level of relief as their CoP engagement empowered them to now inhabit the SoTL space in their own institutions and beyond. In addition, their stories revealed a recognition of their increased ability to value-add in scholarly conversations and successfully apply for promotional positions aligned with scholarship and quality teaching. Tangible outcomes included refereed abstracts, presentations at learning and teaching conferences, peer-reviewed manuscripts, and selection for learning and teaching leadership positions.

This chapter illustrates key messages for three groups of scholars: those transitioning from discipline-based research to SoTL, those working in the third space, and early-career academics. The study on which this chapter draws also explored how the mentoring environment acted as a relational and pedagogical space for building members' SoTL capacity and assisted in (re)fashioning their professional identity to one that values the integrity and worth of SoTL. The chapter further evidences the importance of sustained, facilitated engagement in a safe learning context in a community of practice that assisted these members to re-emerge as confident, capable SoTL scholars who are subsequently leading SoTL activities in their own institutions.

STATE OF PLAY: BACKGROUND AND CONTEXT

The Australian government is employing policy strategies to improve the quality of teaching in higher education institutions. One aspect of this policy agenda, the Higher Education Standards Framework (Tertiary Education Quality and Standards Agency [TEQSA], 2022), called for higher education scholars to ensure currency of discipline and pedagogical knowledge through engagement in scholarship. TEQSA's *Guidance Note: Scholarship* (2022) refined the definition of scholarship as "those activities concerned with gaining new or improved understanding, appreciation and insights into a field of knowledge, and engaging with and keeping up to date with advances in the field" (para. 1).

With this growing emphasis on and need for compliance for scholarship, higher education institutions have increased their emphasis on investigating the quality of teaching and pedagogical innovation. This shift is part of a broader transformation in the higher education landscape, where institutions strive to improve student outcomes that contribute to universities gaining a competitive edge in global rankings. These shifts underscore the increasing need for scholars to engage in SoTL and subsequently contribute to enhancing the overall educational experience for students.

THE PROBLEM

As illustrated by the inclusion of SoTL into TEQSA guidance documents, workload models, academic promotion frameworks, and position descriptions (Miller-Young & Chick, 2024; TEQSA, 2022), there is an increased focus on and institutional requirement to engage in SoTL. At the same time, there is an identified absence of SoTL capacity-building opportunities for those in academic, professional, and third-space roles (How, 2020; Miller-Young & Chick, 2024; Smith & Walker, 2021). This deficiency of SoTL support in higher education institutions, and the sector itself, has several implications. Firstly, much SoTL work has become box-ticking and compliance-related rather than *true* SoTL aimed at developing capacity and investigating one's own teaching and learning practice (How, 2020). Secondly, the lack of avenues for professional learning and lack of confidence has disrupted scholars' professional identity (Miller-Young & Chick, 2024), and this has resulted in scholars questioning who they are, where they fit, and where they should place themselves both within the higher education sector and in relationship to SoTL. Lastly, scholars' minimal understanding of the different voice and investigative approaches to SoTL is recognised as impacting their confidence, sense of scholarly worth, and subsequently, their SoTL engagement. Addressing these issues was the impetus for the initiation of the SoTL CoP described in this chapter.

LITERATURE

The increased emphasis on SoTL in higher education highlights the value of scholars in all roles (Eady et al., 2021; Miller-Young & Chick, 2024; TEQSA, 2022) and illustrates the overt need to provide systematic capacity-building for those aligned with informing the quality of teaching and learning in higher education. The relationship between undertaking SoTL and its impact on those new to the academy, discipline scholars transitioning to SoTL, and third space practitioners is explored.

Newcomers to SoTL

SoTL is a young and changing field that actively invites new scholars (Chick et al., 2019) and considers SoTL expertise to be continually developing (Poole & Chick, 2016). Recent growth in SoTL has thus been accompanied by a rise in the number of those engaging in SoTL (Frake-Mistak et al., 2023). Those new to SoTL come from a broad range of backgrounds including academics, professional staff, and students (Chick et al., 2019). Uniquely, almost all SoTL practitioners come as novices to the space (Chick et al., 2023). As described by Abbot (2024), almost all those new to SoTL feel marginalised in some way.

SoTL Transitions: Discipline Academics

SoTL helps to meet the competing demands to both publish and focus on teaching (Liston & Rahimi, 2017b), supporting career progression, particularly for education-focussed academics. However, the disciplines can be seen as academic societies with their own way of thinking and behaving that can be threatened by the interdisciplinary nature of SoTL, particularly as it tries to embed itself within those disciplines (Simmons et al., 2013). SoTL is often devalued by disciplines and creates discomfort as academics actively navigate tensions between the two (Simmons et al., 2013). SoTL's investigative characteristics (as qualitative research, small participant numbers) may result in academics being sidelined in their discipline (Chick et al., 2023), finding themselves isolated (Meijerman et al., 2023), and experiencing barriers to career progression. Discipline academics who engage with SoTL create the risk of being seen as novices as they learn new methods and literature (Chick et al., 2023; Healey et al., 2016). Even those from similar fields may experience this struggle with insecurity, imposter syndrome, doubt, and fear (Simmons et al., 2013). A disciplinary identity may result in an academic questioning their SoTL identity (Chick et al., 2023).

Veles and Carter (2016, p. 520) define the higher education 'third space' as one where professional and academic staff work collaboratively on complex projects. Staff within the third space sit 'between' both spaces, crossing the boundary between professional and academic (Ryttberg, 2022) and collaborating on specific projects (Veles & Carter, 2016). Third space practitioners are more specifically known as academic developers, learning designers, education designers, employability and student support staff, and library services staff. These staff work both centrally in institutional teaching and learning centres (T&LCs) and peripherally embedded with faculty.

While vulnerability is needed to learn and improve in teaching and learning, being vulnerable or making mistakes in academic spaces can have negative consequences, creating a risk that is often avoided (Pleschová et al., 2021). The vulnerability and difficulty of SoTL identity development are amplified for those still developing their discipline identity as new academics (Simmons et al., 2013).

SoTL Transitions: Third Space Practitioners

SoTL has helped change T&LCs into places to share ideas and spread interest in teaching and learning (Liston & Rahimi, 2017a). In turn, teaching and learning centres provide a legitimised and strategically supported home for SoTL (Frake-Mistak et al., 2023), positioning the staff in these centres as knowledgeable in SoTL; however, this is not always the case.

Third space practitioners such as academic developers contribute to evidence-based learning, support academics to make meaningful innovations, and create a culture that propagates deeper transformations (Pleschová et al., 2021). To do this, they need a diverse range of skills involving charting their own route to "demonstrate and develop [their] skills, manage colleagues' perceptions and align to institutional goals" (Smith et al., 2021, pp. 506-507). Many third space practitioners use professional development to gain legitimacy and clarify their career options separate to the needs of their institutions (Moran & Misra, 2018). Engagement in SoTL is important as it raises their professionalism, credibility, expertise, and effectiveness when working in these collaborative spaces with academics.

Third space practitioners in T&LCs experience barriers to developing SoTL capacity. While many would like to conduct SoTL research, not all have support or time provided by their institutions (McClurg et al., 2019). Those without a research degree or minimal research experience lack the confidence to explore SoTL, concerned that they will appear like a novice or feel their scholarship is irrelevant or insufficiently rigorous (Chick et al., 2023).

SCHOLARLY IDENTITY

Academic or scholarly identity refers to the meaning a person attaches to the roles and tasks required within a specific institution and context (Simmons et al., 2013). However, identity is dynamic and contextual, allowing us to hold multiple identities with which we identify at different times (Simmons et al., 2013). Significant vulnerability, anxiety, and excitement are involved in the development of a scholarly identity (Kamler & Thomson, 2014). SoTL identity construction perhaps involves these feelings even more so, as it involves active "deconstruction" of our personal practices, moving outside a sphere of expertise, and working in a space that is often actively devalued by academia (Simmons et al., 2013, p. 11). In SoTL, many practitioners are developing their identities as SoTL scholars at the same time as they are writing and publishing about SoTL (Healey et al., 2019). Feelings of failure, not belonging, and performance anxiety have the capacity to limit success, impact, and development of a scholarly identity (Chick et al., 2023). Those who already feel 'othered' in the workplace, such as third space practitioners or education-focused academics, may be particularly susceptible (Chick et al., 2023). A workplace alongside colleagues may not provide an effective environment for this identity work. Informal conversations outside of formal academic and administrative spaces can better support the risk-taking required for learning and change (Pleschová et al., 2021). Purposeful reflection, engagement in communities of practice or group-based reading and discussion may support successful identity (re)development and transition to the third space (Aguilar & Rütti-Joy, 2023).

COMMUNITIES OF PRACTICE: ADDRESSING BARRIERS TO ENGAGEMENT IN SOTL

Approaches to minimising barriers to engaging in SoTL include networking and support via conferences and events, providing mentorship with experienced SoTL practitioners, and supporting participation in communities of practice (CoPs) (Meijerman et al., 2023).

The term 'Community of Practice' was first coined by Lave and Wenger (1991), referring to groups of practitioners who have a "shared domain of interest" (i.e., a passion or concern). In order to pursue their interest and enhance their competence in their shared domain, they engage in regular joint activities like discussing and sharing information and developing a shared repertoire of resources (Wenger-Trayner & Wenger-Trayner, 2015). CoPs have been established in higher education for various reasons, including supporting initiatives, mentoring individuals, and collaborating on solving problems (Kenney et al., 2013). Originally, CoPs were spontaneously emerging groups (Goodyear & Casey, 2015); however, nowadays, organisations and institutions often initiate CoPs to support and promote learning and knowledge sharing among their staff (Bourhis & Dube, 2005). CoPs facilitate socially situated and practice-based learning, challenging the cognitivist theory of learning that assumes learning is an individual process of knowledge acquisition taking place within the learner's mind (Omidvar & Kislov, 2014).

SoTL provides the potential to establish commonality within previously separate learning communities (Liston & Rahimi, 2017a). It specifically positions itself as a space for cross-disciplinary communication (Simmons et al., 2013). SoTL often features collaborations where members have different experiences and knowledge (within and outside the disciplines) that combine to form extensive "collective expertise" (Poole & Chick, 2016, p. 2). This type of collaborative knowledge and development lends itself well to communities of practice (CoPs). CoPs have often been used effectively for professional development (González et al., 2024). Those who engage in SoTL are 'transformed' into scholars (Liston & Rahimi, 2017b, p.

328), helping to further establish the identities of third space and new staff. CoP participation supports this process (Meijerman et al., 2023). As members engage in a CoP, an identity change occurs where members begin to become one (Kamler & Thomson, 2014). As the CoP progresses, members may gradually become confident and increase their autonomy (Camarao & Din, 2023). SoTL has the potential to be transformative for teachers and learners (Liston & Rahimi, 2017a). To support pedagogical transformation, CoPs need to have cross-disciplinary members with established trust and caring, a supportive space, and an co-creation approach (González et al., 2024; Pleschová et al., 2021). For example, Camarao and Din (2023) describe the psychological safety of their CoP as allowing members to share mistakes and challenges, and in turn, this sharing strengthened the sense of safety week-by-week.

CoPs decrease the isolation and fear felt by many new to SoTL (Meijerman et al., 2023). In a community, the boundaries between the roles of teacher and learner are indistinct; in SoTL communities, everyone is a learner, teacher, and researcher (Liston & Rahimi, 2017a). With their experience-based social approach, CoPs allow members to develop mutual respect and reciprocity, creating the safety needed for members to display vulnerability and take risks, and to reflect and address uncertainty (González et al., 2024). Identities are formed in CoPs through the shared participation and outputs of the group, and the stories that CoPs tell about themselves (Kamler & Thomson, 2014).

The barriers to engaging in SoTL have wide-ranging impacts for new scholars, third space practitioners, and discipline academics. These barriers have the capacity to impact the growth and development of scholars individually and the field of SoTL more generally (Chick et al., 2023). Support is needed to address each of these barriers to SoTL, including isolation, boundary-crossing from disciplines, lack of knowledge, and challenges to professional identity (Meijerman et al., 2023). SoTL CoPs have the potential to support diverse groups of scholars to develop their identity and scholarship, creating impact and advancing the field.

Online Community of Practice

With the advent of Web 2.0 technologies, an increasing number of online CoPs have been established for individuals in geographically dispersed areas (Pan et al., 2015). It is important to note, however, that while there seems to be a consensus on the definition of online CoPs, in practice, a wide range of activities have been labelled as online CoPs. Many discussion forums, blogs, and informal video conferences claim to be online CoPs, leading some researchers to consider the term academically ambiguous (Kellam, 2023). Some online CoPs are considered parts of knowledge management systems (e.g., those in Alali et al., 2016) with a heavy emphasis on using these online CoPs for storing and sharing information. These complexities, combined with the lack of consensus on the indicators of success of a CoP (Bourhis & Dubé, 2010), have posed challenges to identifying factors affecting their effectiveness.

Some researchers (García-Monge et al., 2019; Peeters & Pretorius, 2020) believe that building and maintaining an online CoP requires a balance between the creation and enhancement of knowledge, access to it, and the maintenance of a community where members feel a sense of belonging, share a group identity, and are willing to interact and contribute. If these elements are lacking, members may feel disconnected, lose momentum, and become disengaged in the online community (García-Monge et al., 2019; Howard & McKeown, 2011).

In their systematic review, Hernández-Soto et al. (2021) found that willingness to interact and contribute through knowledge sharing in online CoPs relies on personal factors (personal beliefs, expertise, and need for affiliation), interpersonal factors (interpersonal trust, social ties, and expertise), contextual factors (contextual domain, culture, and support), and technological factors (technological quality, support, and ease of use). Among these factors, the role of leadership is particularly important in building trust and connections within the community. Effective leadership can encourage and increase member commitment, ensuring the group makes progress (Barnett et al., 2014), acting as sources of support and assistance for members (Retna & Tee, 2011), serving as centres of specialised tacit knowledge for the community, facilitating discussions, and keeping community activities engaging and vibrant (Bourhis & Dube, 2005).

There is also some evidence (Bourhis & Dube, 2005; Mason et al., 2008) highlighting the advantages of traditional face-to-face interactions in contrast to online channels and platforms for building relationships and trust among a CoP's members. In online CoPs, opportunities for additional live interactions and face-to-face meetings at strategic times are considered extremely important. These interactions help establish members' commitment to the CoP, which in turn leads to more effective online interactions (Bourhis & Dube, 2005).

METHODOLOGY

Data Collection and Analysis

The data collection used collaborative autoethnography (Bochner & Ellis, 2022) to deeply investigate the lived experiences and professional perspectives of the eight members of the SoTL CoP (who are also the researchers). Chang (2008) asserts that autoethnography "transcends mere narration of self to engage in cultural analysis and interpretation" (p. 43). We adopted autoethnography as we were reflecting on how we understood ourselves in the 'practice of SoTL', within the cultural space of higher education. The members' autoethnographies were also guided by Rolfe et al.'s (2010) reflective model of *What? So What? Now What?* In an online meeting, members brainstormed a set of questions under each of the reflective frames (What? So What? Now What?). For example, in the *What?* frame, these questions were generated: *Why did I join the CoP? What expectations did I have of CoP members and the facilitator?* These questions acted as generative prompts for members to write their stories of their two-year SoTL CoP experiences. The members' stories were written as informal observations and reflections of thoughts, feelings, and actions (Bochner & Ellis, 1996). Each member shared their story during a subsequent online meeting.

The stories were thematically analysed using Yin's (2015) five phase analysis cycle: (i) compile data, (ii) disassemble data, (iii) reassemble data, (iv) interpret data, and (v) conclude. Rolfe et al.'s (2010) generative questions were also used in the analysis to identify themes. Online CoP meetings were dedicated to collectively analysing each member's story, as well as identifying specific extracts that would most poignantly illustrate the agreed themes.

RESULTS

The resultant themes are clustered into three groups:

1. **What**, which describes the members' expectations, reasons for joining, and the gaps they hoped to fill.
2. **So what**, which addresses members' experiences and the reality of the CoP and its practices.
3. **Now what**, which identifies the outcomes and unfolding impact.

Each section gave rise to two major themes, professional and personal, with resulting sub-themes as illustrated in Table 1. Though some sub-themes appear to repeat, their content differs according to their grouping.

Table 1. Themes and subthemes from the collective autoethnographic narratives

	Professional Themes			Personal Themes		
What	**Theme 1: Professional expectations and gaps**			**Theme 2: Personal expectations and gaps**		
	1a: Layers of support for different roles	1b: Improving knowledge, skill and practice	1c: Professional connections and networking	2a: Looking for understanding, belonging and support	2b: Identity development	2c: Addressing imposter syndrome and lack of confidence
So What	**Theme 3: Professional experiences and practices**			**Theme 4: Personal experiences and practices**		
	3a: The CoP Structure: Schedule and Logistics	3b: Improving knowledge, skill and practice	3c: Diversity	4a: Finding understanding and belonging	4b: Providing a safe space to be vulnerable	4c: Confidence-building
Now What		**Theme 5: Professional outcomes and impacts**		**Theme 6: Personal outcomes and impacts**		
		5a: Improving knowledge, skill and practice	5b: Impact on career progression, leadership and mentorship capacity	6a: Finding understanding and belonging	6b: Identity development	

Members who joined the CoP were driven by a desire for support beyond their own institutions (1a), were eager to enhance their knowledge in SoTL (1b), and were motivated to expand their professional networks (1c). They sought engagement with supportive individuals and a sense of belonging (2a), hoping the CoP would help them build their skills (1b), boost their confidence in their roles (2c), and facilitate their identity development (2b).

Throughout their engagement with the CoP, members found that the CoP had a supportive structure that prioritised relationship building. The structure provided flexibility and time for members to get to know each other and take ownership of the space they collectively created (3a). As members built shared understanding and trust, they became each other's supporters (4a), and the CoP became a safe space in which to engage (4b). As the relationship within the CoP grew stronger, members shared and supported each other in developing their knowledge and practices (3b), and they benefited from being part of a diverse group (3c). Throughout their engagement in the CoP, members' personal and professional identities were nourished, boosting their confidence in working in SoTL. The improved clarity around SoTL and their roles helped to shape members' professional identities (6b) and led to career advancement (5b), such as promotions or transitioning into new roles.

WHAT?

Theme 1: Professional Expectations and Gaps

Though themes 1 and 2 primarily identified intrinsic reasons for joining the CoP, both professional and personal, it should be acknowledged that a significant unstated underlying external factor also drove participation. The regulator TEQSA (and consequently each institution) has driven academic and third space practitioners in higher education to engage in and evidence scholarship (TEQSA, 2022).

Theme 1a: Layers of support for different roles. To explain their impetus to join the CoP, the members cited several reasons related to their institution. Some mentioned a lack of explicit expectations and clear definitions of responsibilities concerning their involvement in SoTL: "a lot of the things were not clearly stated or defined" (Laura) or there was a "lack of clear research expectations" (Diana). One member felt that their efforts were not valued by their institutions and peers, noting, "I do not feel that what I was doing was valued by my school and my colleagues" (Julia). The issue was coupled with the lack of support for staff to first understand what SoTL entailed or how to engage in it. This lack of support included insufficient mentoring and/or inadequate time allocation. Julia wrote that she had "limited support to understand the Scholarship of Teaching and Learning (SoTL) in my discipline" and that she "struggled to differentiate SoTL from good teaching practices and scholarly teaching - terms I was unfamiliar with at the time". Bella felt completely isolated: "I didn't have a [SoTL] support network".

Even when there were clear expectations, a lack of support remained. Diana stated that there was "insufficient support for SoTL, despite the expectation for its implementation" and "the absence of a structured forum for discussing or receiving feedback on research within my broader Learning and Teaching unit at work".

Laura also mentioned the lack of a well-defined career and growth path for her education-focused roles: "There wasn't a well-defined career trajectory to follow for roles I was in, or a clearly structured career progress framework specifically for teaching specialists".

Theme 1b: Improving knowledge, skills, and practice. The next reason for joining the CoP, cited by most members, was to improve their knowledge and/or capability in undertaking SoTL, including conducting education-based research. For example, Emily stated her "motivation for joining this non-discipline-specific CoP was to broaden my understanding of SoTL, to gain a clearer picture of what SoTL entailed, and to feel more equipped to conduct SoTL research".

Julia believed an improved capability in SoTL could help her better navigate her role in the future: "My primary goal for attending the workshop was to learn more about education-related research and explore how I could progress in my role". Other members also highlighted specific areas of benefit they hoped to gain from the CoP. These included enhancing their competence in reviewing and self-reviewing scholarly works, giving and receiving feedback, and obtaining feedback on current projects.

Theme 1c: Professional connections and networking. CoP members also sought professional connections and networking. This theme was specifically professional, distinct from theme 2a, looking for understanding, belonging, and support. This was expressed most clearly by Diana: "one crucial form of support discussed was the chance to share our own research projects and seek feedback from other CoP members". Members aimed to reduce professional isolation ("I was the only EF academic", Julia), find role commonality, create networks outside of the university ("I was hoping that the SoTL CoP would be able to provide a network that I didn't have within my university", Bella; "what I needed at that time was a connection outside my institution", Agatha), and fill gaps that were not being met within their own institution.

While most CoP members cited personal and intrinsic motivation as the driving force behind their decisions to participate, two members added the encouragement and urging from their seniors (either manager or mentor) as reasons for involvement. Diana also mentioned the experimental mindset as a prompting factor for her to join the CoP:

> *As someone unfamiliar with CoPs, I had doubts about what to expect. Furthermore, I questioned the sustainability of such an initiative ... With a hint of scepticism, I ... [adopted] an experimental mindset fuelled by the notion that it couldn't hurt to try.*

Theme 2: Personal Expectations and Gaps

Theme 2a: Looking for understanding, belonging, and support. CoP members also sought to meet a range of personal needs and gaps. Several identified a search for understanding, belonging or support. This was seen as separate from the professional need for development support, mentoring or collegial connection. Instead, this was a personal need for acknowledgement and validation. Members were also looking for "their people" who could relate to their struggles, something they often expressed as absent in their current work contexts. For example, Bella stated that "I didn't have a support network that I could talk to and bounce ideas from", and Julia echoed this with "I want to find my people and have someone to acknowledge what I am doing is important and meaningful". Agatha also felt similarly in her institution: "What I needed at that time was a connection outside my institution.... I felt isolated from colleagues at other institutions".

Theme 2b: Identity development. Given the lack of consistent understanding of SoTL at a broad level, those who worked in SoTL areas were anecdotally often unsure of what was expected of them or how to begin working on SoTL. They were also uncertain about their career trajectory. This uncertainty was often compounded by their location in the 'third space', as education designers, academic developers, education-focused academics, and other intersecting roles that are poorly defined and consist of aspects of both traditional academic and professional roles.

Members of the CoP expressed a need to develop an understanding of who they were professionally, both within their institution and the broader higher education landscape. Several had recently undergone significant role changes, and their professional self-concept had not yet changed to accommodate this. For example, Laura was "looking for a proper identity for myself professionally at the university and also in the broader teaching and learning community", whereas Stephanie considered herself "an experienced educator, however I had only dabbled in SoTL and education research". Other members had also experienced significant professional identity challenges and changes, such as Agatha, who stated, "My professional identity was in a time of enormous change as a new third space professional". Emily had "recently pivoted to an education-focused role". In addition, Bella was conflicted, "My role as a third space academic did not support my feeling of a strong professional identity", and Julia was uncertain, "I joined the Community of Practice (CoP) during a time of uncertainty about whether to pursue a career trajectory in an education-focused (EF) role".

The autoethnographic reflections on this theme were retrospective. While the initial discussions in the CoP did not focus on professional identity development, it became a central topic as members recognised their shared experiences in the third space and became more familiar with the relevant literature. The conversations then shifted explicitly toward developing professional identity and its implications. This theme was closely connected to belonging (theme 2a) and lack of confidence (theme 2c). As professional identities were constructed and reconstructed, so too was a sense of belonging to the group and having confidence in the knowledge underlying their professional identity. While separate, each of these personal needs was interconnected. Illustrating this theme of identity development is a quote from Bella: "I was neither a "real" academic nor a professional staff member" and "I was looking for my tribe ... who could ... support me in exploring my professional identity".

Theme 2c: Addressing imposter syndrome and lack of confidence. Many members also expressed a lack of confidence as SoTL scholars, feeling like an imposter or fraud. For example, Agatha stated, "Back then, my confidence was low", and Bella reiterated this with "I felt like an imposter in the SoTL field".

While members hoped to build capacity, they separately wished to increase their confidence and resolve their concerns about exposure. Doing this involved some apparent contradiction: they simultaneously wanted to participate to develop their confidence while not wanting to demonstrate their lack of knowledge and skill to other members. In this way, Bella "hoped that by strengthening [her] SoTL understanding and practice, it would help [her] feel like a more legitimate academic". Emily stated, "My confidence in sharing and contributing about SoTL was limited and I worried my questions would seem out of place or "silly" in this new interdisciplinary setting". Agatha was even more concerned: "I didn't want everyone to know how many gaps I had in my knowledge", and Julia was "a bit anxious about that because [she] was unsure if [she] was using the correct terminology or methodologies in SoTL".

As described later, this issue was somewhat resolved by developing trust and a mutually safe space.

SO WHAT?

Theme 3: Professional Experiences and Practices

Theme 3a: The CoP structure: Schedule and logistics. The community of practice works best when it has a structure but also provides the flexibility for the members to improvise as different needs arise. This involves intentionally scheduling multiple meeting streams to cater for the collective availability of the members and considering the group size to ensure it is not overwhelmingly large, thus allowing effective engagement opportunities for each member. This framework ensures the CoP does not leave anyone behind. Agatha noted this flexibility as follows:

> *We determined our own best availability and preferences for frequency, increasing the sense of ownership over the CoP. The split between two times ... initially functioned as a support, keeping the number of people smaller and consistent enough to assist with rapport-building.*

Members found that regular online meetings with a small cohort of the same people helped to build relationships and connections because they had more time to share. Across the two sessions the CoP offered, the facilitator took on the role of bridging communication by sharing the discussion from one meeting with the other. This was achieved through in-meeting discussions, meeting recaps, and follow-up emails after meetings. In addition, the meetings were recorded and were available in the CoP's shared online folder, thereby improving the visibility of the discussions members had over time. Using a combination of a shared online drive and online meeting space provided greater flexibility, visibility, and inclusion within the CoP.

In addition to structural flexibility, the CoP also offered content flexibility. Discussions were tailored to individual needs, allowing them to address challenges that members were currently facing. Agatha noted this most emphatically:

Sometimes ... the session would change entirely ..., as we responded to a query in depth or needed something different that day. The flexibility meant that we 'got what we needed' each week. ...there was still a flexibly structured capacity-building process despite each detour.

Agatha also noted that the facilitator supported the members' increasing capacity and independence in a flexible and responsive manner.

The facilitator set the standard for being genuine, responding openly without judgement, and supporting others. Her straightforward approach helped us to make knowledge and capacity gains. I felt safe within the space she created. She was very flexible.... Her approach was to respond to the needs of the group.

The facilitator's approach was directly connected in the autoethnographic narratives with the CoP subthemes, such as confidence-building, identity development, safety, and belonging.

Theme 3b: Improving knowledge, skill and practice. It might be questioned how much professional development could be gained from participating in a CoP when there was so much flexibility, and it focused on fostering relationships rather than a clear agenda on knowledge building. Certainly, the knowledge-building may not be an immediate outcome after just a few meetings, but over time, it is surprising how much members have learned from each conversation and how far they have travelled on this journey. Stephanie highlighted this when she reflected on her improved practice: "I felt comfortable mentoring and encouraging junior academics. I also believe that it helped me mentor early career researchers in education focussed roles". For some members, it was upon reflection that they realised there had been significant development in their SoTL knowledge and skills through these conversations. For example, Emily reflected that:

We established a culture of mutual support and continuous learning that encouraged each of us to step out of our comfort zones... Each question, each discussion, opened new doors of understanding and confidence, not just for me but for all of us.

This development was rooted in the flexibility of members guiding their own conversations, which made the learning journey tailored to each member's needs. Diana commented on this, saying, "The diverse topics discussed ... have enriched my knowledge base, proving invaluable for my role as an educational developer". Agatha also identified her professional development: "The facilitator helped us to reflect on our practice of teaching, then engage with some of the literature ..., then encouraged us gradually to share about teaching at my first conference presentation, a roundtable". Sharing knowledge and collectively navigating the learning process had become essential components of capacity building in the CoP, which Agatha reflected clearly on:

> *The facilitator didn't immediately provide answers but encouraged us all to give feedback and ask questions, and we became more competent in making judgments of our own work as we reviewed others. My feedback literacy was expanded in this new context, and I became more knowledgeable and capable by supporting others in the CoP.*

Theme 3c: Diversity. Although not intentionally designed, the CoP members have seen significant benefits in having a group with diverse characteristics. Diversity presented itself as different roles (e.g., education-focused academic, academic developer) and classifications (academic, professional), as well as levels of seniority, years of experience, physical location, institutions of origin, and cultural background. The variation in members' backgrounds provided opportunities to learn from different perspectives and appreciate the context that each member brought, which provided a richer context for the discussion. Julia recognised the benefits of this diversity: "The diversity of our group consists of members from various areas, roles, and institutions, which significantly enriches our collective perspective". Emily noted that the diversity did not mean that commonalities could not be found, "We were a group from diverse disciplines, yet we shared a common goal". Laura stated: "We share similar questions in the broader university context, although we were all at different stages of a career from different disciplines and institutes".

The diversity provided some members with a strong sense of belonging. This sense of belonging is reflected in Stephanie's comment: "The group is so diverse in age, ethnicity, discipline, institution, and experience, that I immediately felt as though I belonged". However, another member found the diversity challenging but still recognised the benefits of the support from the CoP, stating:

> *I found myself even more quiet in this diverse CoP environment, where the majority came from different cultural backgrounds ... which was different from my own... Although I still grapple with navigating cultural diversity within the group at times, particularly when certain cultures seem to exert more influence than others, I'm grateful for the real connections I've forged, knowing that I can rely on these individuals for support and guidance in various aspects of my profession.*

Due to the various levels of seniority, there were instances where members and their direct supervisors were both part of the group. This did not appear to impact impressions of safety in the group in this instance.

Theme 4: Personal Experiences and Practices

Theme 4a: Finding understanding and belonging. As members spent more time together in conversation, they developed a deeper understanding of and connection to each other. Over time, members came to realise that it was acceptable when they were unable to contribute or attend every single meeting if "life [got] in the way" (Julia). This approach contrasts with the typical expectations in a workplace, especially for key members. The sense of flexibility was not an immediate outcome of participating in the CoP, but rather it was gained through consistent effort in building relationships with all members. After about a year, members began to feel comfortable enough to be flexible without feeling the need to apologise for missing a deadline or a task. This created a supportive 'village' where members could rely on each other without fear of judgement. Bella and Julia both voiced this sense of comfort as follows:

> *I feel like I can come as I am – we have a motto of "come as you are" so that there is less pressure on what we have achieved between meetings, and this is very supportive, particularly when I don't feel as supported in my institution at times. (Bella)*
>
> *There is homework for every week that aims to get everyone building up their understanding of SoTL, but there is no judgment if life gets in the way, and you show up with no preparation... We are not rushed into solving anything within an hour of chat. (Julia)*

Theme 4b: Providing a safe space to be vulnerable. Working in a higher education context often creates assumptions about people being the experts in their role. It can be emotionally difficult for people to share their challenges and weaknesses without making themselves feel unprofessional or lacking in their role. At the start of the CoP, the facilitator provided space and opportunities for people to share their own challenges and to take time to acknowledge that we are not experts in SoTL. Bella wrote, "The CoP is a very safe place – a place where I can be me and be vulnerable. There are no [institutional expectations], so I am free to show these weaknesses and vulnerabilities". This honest conversation gradually helped members to build trust, a shared understanding, and a sense of belonging. As the members started to build relational safety, the CoP became a safe space to be vulnerable: that openness kept attracting the regular members to the meetings and made the CoP more sustainable. Agatha noted that she "realised this was a safe space to ask the 'obvious' questions and admit things you didn't know.... As members grew to know each other, they incrementally shared more, allowing themselves to be vulnerable, just as I did." Julia wrote that these were the reasons why she continued to attend:

There was no judgement, and the feedback was always positive. This is very assuring for someone new to SoTL to build up their confidence in what they are working on. ...This approach to retaining group members through creating a supportive space and fostering mutual trust without adding pressure, to me, has been the key reason that drives the sustainability of the CoP.

Theme 4c: Confidence-building. Despite the possibility of last-minute changes in the meeting theme, which was collectively decided by the attending members, the purpose of the CoP meetings did not divert from core discussions of SoTL. SoTL is a complex area that involves academic development, identity development, capacity building, and the human experiences associated with all these activities. The CoP members acknowledged the importance of addressing these experiences and, through these discussions, felt they could become more well-rounded and experienced. Tailoring the conversation to their own learning journey within a very supportive community of peers increased their confidence. This is exemplified through Agatha and Bella's reflective responses.

The autonomy to guide our own priorities and scaffolded our ability to support each other to solve our own problems. We have gradually become more confident at providing input into others' work and reviewing our own with a critical eye. (Agatha)

I felt validated in the time that I had spent participating in the CoP and that there was real value in the work that I was doing .... I am feeling more confident in being positioned as a "SoTL expert" in my institution .... This experience gave me confidence that I can do SoTL and support others to do SoTL within my institution. (Bella)

NOW WHAT?

Theme 5: Professional Outcomes and Impact

Theme 5a: Improving knowledge, skill, and practice. All CoP members reflected on their improved knowledge, skills, and practice that originated from active participation. Members identified that while some capacity building was overt, other aspects of skill development became clear after reflecting on the journey. For example, Julia reflected that, "only when I looked back did I realise that I'd built up my capacity without knowing it". CoP members also found that their knowledge grew over time, with Diana reflecting that "most importantly a deeper understanding of SoTL and the challenges surrounding its implementation and development". Emily voiced that "over time, my capacity to contribute, share feedback, and engage in meaningful dialogue grew exponentially".

Members further reflected that these increases in knowledge and skills have supported and impacted their professional roles and identity. Diana has "enriched [her] knowledge base, proving invaluable for [her] role as an educational developer" and noted that "these skills and knowledge can really help [us] to improve [our] professionalism, credibility, and effectiveness".

Members described how the CoP directly led to outputs such as a joint roundtable abstract, co-facilitation of a special interest group, and other new personal and professional skills. However, specific mention was made of the capacity-building nature of the CoP, which led to members' independent growth and development. Emily reflected that "this transformation was mirrored in tangible achievements: awards for my teaching initiatives, publications that expanded on the innovative pedagogies we discussed in the CoP, and even a significant promotion that acknowledged my growing expertise in the field of education". Laura also increased her professional visibility and she "[will be] presenting at the International Consortium of Educational Development conference this year". In her reflection, Diana stated that "[the CoP has] equipped me with important skills, such as managing a roundtable and writing autoethnographic papers". Agatha also identified improved knowledge, skills, and practice:

> *[During my CoP membership] I have collaboratively written my first ethics application and parts of my first SoTL paper; have given my first conference presentation and subsequently submitted abstracts for two more – stepping up from roundtable to showcase and independently writing the latter.*

One CoP member described the authentic CoP context as immediately preparing members to support others, which was reflected in members' subsequent career development. Stephanie also noted that she "felt comfortable mentoring and encouraging junior academics". The improved knowledge, skills, and practice have led to further tangible outcomes in career progression, leadership, and mentorship capacity.

Theme 5b: Impact on career progression, leadership, and mentorship capacity. Members' growth in confidence was obvious to the extent that they now engaged increasingly in leadership and mentorship activities, and they began evidencing them more intentionally. Subsequently, some members applied for more senior roles, and the CoP had a positive impact on their career progression. For example, Julia reflected that "since I was able to build my confidence throughout this journey with the CoP and I've been able to learn more about SoTL, I have moved to a new institution with a better role". Diana also noted that "some members effortlessly stepped into leadership roles". Other members had more subtle yet overwhelmingly positive impacts on their career progression, leadership, and mentorship capacity. For example, Bella gained confidence that "I can do SoTL and support others to do

SoTL within my institution". Similarly, Agatha had a newfound understanding of her capacity: "Not only did I know more, but I recognised what I knew, and I became sure of the value I could add both in the CoP and at work". Julia also experienced similar impacts on her capacity: "I have been able to take more and more leadership roles, put my hands up for education-related development, and share my thoughts in the working groups in relation to how our institution could improve its policy". These impacts relate to the further development of members' professional identity (Theme 6b).

Theme 6: Personal Outcomes and Impact

Theme 6a: Finding understanding and belonging. A foundational reason for members joining the CoP was that they were seeking understanding and belonging. Most members began to feel like they belonged to a 'village' that understood what they were experiencing in the diverse contexts in which they worked: they connected with each other on a deeper level. Laura reflected that "this is a group I feel connected with", and Bella stated, "The CoP has become more than a normal CoP – it is my tribe of colleagues who understand me and my situation". In doing so, the core members of the CoP were further solidified, and this connection with each other was evident in the regular discussions and communication. The "culture of mutual support and continuous learning" (Emily) was evident in the "collaborative, cooperative, and inclusive" structure (Emily) that the CoP evolved into and continues to maintain. Julia wrote, "This approach to retaining group members through creating a supportive space and fostering mutual trust without adding pressure, to me, has been the key reason that drives the sustainability of the CoP". Diana also reflected that the sense of belonging, and connection have broader impacts on her work: "I'm grateful for the real connections I've forged, knowing that I can rely on these individuals for support and guidance in various aspects of my profession".

When members found this connection through the online CoP space, it was clear that the group was cohesive and had a common purpose, which is a foundation of successful CoPs. Emily reflected on this connection and success: "It was about all of us, together, creating a space where everyone felt valued and heard".

It should be noted that not all members felt the same sense of belonging in the CoP; as Diana commented, "So I actually have kept asking myself, 'Do I belong, do I not belong here?', 'Should I come back, should I not?'" This was only recently acknowledged when Diana felt safe enough to write and share this with others. She also mentioned that "the CoP stories [of other members] all have happy endings, but for me, I don't feel the same way" and "I feel like I'm watching a Hollywood movie, and sometimes I'm part of it and sometimes I'm not". While these reflections indicate that Diana was uncertain at times, she continued to participate and build a sense of safety (theme 4b) and belonging.

Theme 6b: Identity development. Through sharing common experiences and understandings of SoTL, the CoP "culture of mutual support and continuous learning" (Emily) extended to positively impact professional identity. This impact was evident through CoP members identifying that they felt more confident in their contexts and careers. Bella identified a change in her professional identity: "My professional identity has been solidified more. I am feeling more confident in being positioned as a 'SoTL expert' in my institution". Agatha echoed a similar experience: "Within the CoP, I developed an understanding of myself as a third space professional … gained a sense of where I want to take my career". Diana wrote about how her understanding of her professional identity supported her work with others: "This realisation has not only fostered my empathy, knowing that many lecturers and educational developers face similar hurdles, but has also made me feel I have to try harder for my professional identity". As a result of these professional identity changes, many CoP members had further positive impacts on their professional lives, particularly in career progression, leadership, and mentorship capacity (theme 5b).

DISCUSSION

This collaborative autoethnography documented a longitudinal SoTL CoP, providing insights into the structure, processes, and outcomes of a two-year synchronous online SoTL mentoring initiative. Participation in the CoP had both personal and professional impacts. Personally, members built confidence, developed their professional identity, and found understanding and belonging within the group. It was clear the members' enhanced personal capacity supported and led to professional impacts of improved knowledge, skill, and practice. The improved capacity of the members resulted in a marked impact on career progression, leadership, and mentorship capacity. Members' narratives documented the processes of professional identity development, illustrating how participation in a CoP can reshape scholarly identities and enhance confidence in engaging with SoTL. These outcomes highlight the need for structured SoTL capacity building in the absence of a whole-of-institution or sector approach to supporting and nurturing SoTL capacity.

While a CoP has a shared purpose (learning, knowledge sharing, or practice improvement) within a common area of interest (Wenger-Trayner, 2015), the third element is community. It takes time to build relationships, develop trust, and address the relational aspects that a community requires. It is suggested by the autoethnographic narratives that the focus on 'community' should come before 'practice'.

It was suggested by members that the focus on the group relationality and its process, rather than the products of the CoP, were what supported its success. This included flexibility in time (two meeting options) and participation ("come as you are", Bella), with adaptive mentorship that changed according to members' needs. Relational building was prioritised in the initial stages, which aided membership retention and fostered stronger connections, common practices, and interest. This focus on relationships resulted in the efficacy and longevity of the CoP. As bonds strengthened, members provided increasing professional and personal support to each other.

The processes of relationship-building and knowledge-building were not linear. For a CoP to be sustained, it is crucial to strike a balance between the creation and enhancement of knowledge, including access to it, and the maintenance of a community where members feel a sense of belonging and share a group identity (García-Monge et al., 2019; Peeters, & Pretorius, 2020). It is suggested that relationship building should be prioritised, particularly in an online CoP comprising practitioners who lack confidence in SoTL. The members attribute this lack of confidence to the perceived inadequate support, uncertainty about their professional identity, or unclear pathways for career progression.

Once relationships were initially established, members naturally progressed with professional development, concurrently strengthening their connections with other CoP members. At times when an output became the priority (such as co-writing a paper), the CoP became transactional, and members began to withdraw. The 'core' of what members gained from the CoP was lost. At that point, the relational aspect was redefined, and the CoP was reinvigorated.

Members of the CoP also recognised that face-to-face meetings significantly shifted how they perceived and engaged with the CoP. Face-to-face meetings assisted members in feeling better connected. This feeling was particularly true for the members who felt unsure about their sense of belonging. For example, Diana reflected:

> *Meeting almost everyone in person, engaging in quick chit-chat between sessions, working together on the preparation for our shared session, and doing quick goodbyes after the event - all these experiences contributed to a deeper understanding of each individual. It suddenly felt more real. Certain members showed a different energy compared to our online interactions, allowing me to understand them better. This newfound familiarity made it easier for me to connect and open up to others within the group. Since then, my enthusiasm for contributing to discussions has grown.*

This result ties well with previous studies wherein Bourhis and Dube (2005) and Mason et al. (2008) reported the advantages of face-to-face interactions for building relationships and trust among a CoP's members compared to online meetings. In online CoPs, opportunities for additional synchronous interactions and face-to-face meetings at important times should be available because they can establish members' commitment and sense of belonging, which in turn leads to more effective online interactions (Bourhis & Dube, 2005). In this case, the members convened offline to prepare and present their roundtable session at the HERDSA 2023 conference, approximately one year after the start of their online CoP. This timing was significant and strategic, as it marked their first collaborative effort to produce a tangible outcome. The task was notably challenging, necessitating a high level of trust among members to successfully execute the session.

It was also found that the role of the facilitator is particularly important for the growth and sustainability of this CoP. This finding aligns with previous studies, which have reported that effective leadership can help build trust and connections among members by encouraging and increasing member commitment and ensuring the group makes progress (Barnett et al., 2014). Facilitators can act as sources of support and assistance for members (Retna & Tee, 2011), serve as centres of specialised tacit knowledge for the community, and facilitate discussions, keeping community activities engaging and vibrant (Bourhis & Dube, 2005). In this context, the facilitator is a senior scholar, who is devoted to supporting less experienced professionals to develop their capability in SoTL. She has contributed to the growth of the CoP in various ways, as reported in the literature, and her contribution has been well acknowledged by the members as one of the motivations behind their ongoing engagement and commitment to the community.

LIMITATIONS

One of the limitations of this study is that the 'what' and 'so what' sections of the narratives provided by the online CoP members were predominantly retrospective. These sections were written more than one year after the actual experiences. Retrospective data have certain disadvantages, as highlighted in the literature (e.g., Gearing et al., 2006; Müggenburg, 2021), including issues with the accuracy of the data due to the subjects' limited ability to remember and recall events. Schacter (1999) identified three reasons for the inability to recall: transience (forgetting), lack of focus, and blocking. The second reason, lack of focus, is often attributed to a lack of motivation. However, this is not applicable in our study, as all the online CoP members were highly motivated to recall their experiences and meeting recordings were available for review.

Another limitation of this study is that while it follows the journey of an online CoP that has been in operation for almost three years at the time of publication, this timeframe might not capture the entire life cycle of an online CoP. According to Wenger et al. (2002), there are five stages in the life cycle of a CoP: (a) potential,

(b) coalescing, (c) maturing, (d) stewardship, and (e) transformation. This online CoP appears not to have reached the transformation stage yet, thus not completing its life cycle. Therefore, a longitudinal approach in future studies could provide a more comprehensive understanding of an online CoP and the elements that contribute to its sustainability and growth.

Additionally, this study focuses on a single online CoP with a small Australasian membership (one member is based in Vietnam, within an Australian university) in the context of tertiary education. It follows a specific leadership model, where a senior member facilitates and leads the team. Due to these characteristics, the findings may not be easily generalisable to other contexts.

RECOMMENDATIONS

The chapter findings point to the need for the following:

1. ***Institutional Support Structures***: Institutions should establish formalised support structures that recognise and incentivise SoTL engagement. This includes dedicated funding for research, teaching relief, and professional development opportunities tailored to SoTL practitioners.
2. ***Professional Development Pathways***: Develop clear pathways for professional development in SoTL, catering to the needs of early career academics, discipline scholars transitioning to SoTL, and third space practitioners. This can be achieved through mentorship programs, workshops, and collaborative projects within CoPs.
3. ***Integration of Technology***: Embrace innovative technologies to enhance collaboration and knowledge sharing within SoTL CoPs. Platforms for online collaboration, digital resources repositories, and online training modules can facilitate broader participation and engagement.
4. ***Cross-Institutional Collaboration***: Foster partnerships between institutions to create regional or national networks of SoTL CoPs. This collaboration can facilitate the exchange of ideas, resources, and best practices, enhancing the impact of SoTL initiatives on a broader scale.
5. ***Promotion of Reflective Practice***: Encourage reflective practice as a core component of SoTL. Facilitate regular opportunities for members to reflect on their teaching practices, experiment with new pedagogies, and document their findings in a structured manner.

These recommendations lend themselves to further investigation through engaging in the scholarship of teaching that influences institutional policy and practice.

REFERENCES

Abbot, S. (2024). SoTL citizen: A memoir of home and exile in the scholarship of teaching and learning. In Miller-Young, J., & Chick, N. L. (Eds.), *Becoming a SoTL scholar* (pp. 36–51)., DOI: 10.36284/celelon.oa6.3

Aguilar, J. M., & Rütti-Joy, O. (2023). Language teaching in the 'third space': Identity trajectories and professional development needs. *Language Teaching Research Quarterly*, 33, 99–114. DOI: 10.32038/ltrq.2023.33.05

Alali, H., Salim, J., Zwayda, Y., & Alsewi, S. M. (2016). Knowledge sharing success model of virtual communities of practice in healthcare sector. In Lee, I. (Ed.), *Encyclopedia of e-commerce development, implementation, and management* (pp. 272–284). IGI Global., DOI: 10.4018/978-1-4666-9787-4.ch021

Barnett, S., Jones, S. C., Caton, T., Iverson, D., Bennett, S., & Robinson, L. (2014). Implementing a virtual community of practice for family physician training: A mixed-methods case study. *Journal of Medical Internet Research*, 16(3), e83–e83. DOI: 10.2196/jmir.3083 PMID: 24622292

Bochner, A. P., & Ellis, C. (2022). Why autoethnography? *Social Work & Social Sciences Review*, 23(2), 8–18. DOI: 10.1921/swssr.v23i2.2027

Bourhis, A., & Duba, L. (2005). The success of virtual communities of practice: The leadership factor. *Electronic Journal of Knowledge Management*, 3(1), 23–34. https://academic-publishing.org/index.php/ejkm/article/view/719

Camarao, J., & Din, C. (2023). "A group of people to lean on and learn from": Graduate teaching assistant experiences in a pedagogy-focused community of practice. *Teaching & Learning Inquiry*, 11. Advance online publication. DOI: 10.20343/teachlearninqu.11.11

Chang, H. (2008). *Autoethnography as method*. Left Coast Press.

Chick, N., Nowell, L., & Lenart, B. (2019). The scholarship of teaching and learning: A scoping review protocol. *Teaching & Learning Inquiry*, 7(2), 186–19. DOI: 10.20343/teachlearninqu.7.2.12

Chick, N. L., Cruz, L., Friberg, J. C., & Steiner, H. H. (2023). Making space for failure in the scholarship of teaching and learning: A blueprint. *Teaching & Learning Inquiry*, 11. Advance online publication. DOI: 10.20343/teachlearninqu.11.36

Corcoran, N., & Duane, A. (2017). Using enterprise social networks as a knowledge management tool in higher education. *VINE Journal of Information and Knowledge Management Systems*, 47(4), 555–570. DOI: 10.1108/VJIKMS-12-2016-0073

Eady, M. J., Abrahamson, E., Green, C. A., Arcellana-Panlilio, M., Hatfield, L., & Namaste, N. (2021). Re-positioning SoTL toward the T-shaped Community. *Teaching & Learning Inquiry*, 9(1), 262–278. DOI: 10.20343/teachlearninqu.9.1.18

Frake-Mistak, M., Friberg, J., & Hamilton, M. (2023). Reimagining the 4M framework in educational development for SoTL. *Teaching & Learning Inquiry*, 1. Advance online publication. DOI: 10.20343/teachlearninqu.11.14

García-Monge, A., González-Calvo, G., & Bores-García, D. (2019). "I like the idea but...": The gap in participation in a virtual community of practice for analysing physical education. *Open Learning*, 34(3), 257–272. DOI: 10.1080/02680513.2018.1505486

Gardner, A., & Willey, K. (2016). Academic identity reconstruction: The transition of engineering academics to engineering education researchers. *Studies in Higher Education*. Advance online publication. DOI: 10.1080/03075079.2016.1162779

Gearing, R. E., Mian, I. A., Barber, J., & Ickowicz, A. (2006). A methodology for conducting retrospective chart review research in child and adolescent psychiatry. *Journal of the Canadian Academy of Child and Adolescent Psychiatry = Journal de l'Académie Canadienne de Psychiatrie de l'Enfant et de l'Adolescent*, 15(3), 126–134. https://psycnet.apa.org/record/2006-12856-002 PMID: 18392182

González, G., Azucena, M., Mandeville, C., Edwards, F., & Rice, P. (2024). Innovating interdisciplinarity in higher education: Exploring the impact of a grassroots community of practice. *Teaching & Learning Inquiry*, 12, 1–17. DOI: 10.20343/teachlearninqu.12.11

Goodyear, V. A., Casey, A., & Kirk, D. (2014). Tweet me, message me, like me: Using social media to facilitate pedagogical change within an emerging community of practice. *Sport Education and Society*, 19(7), 927–943. DOI: 10.1080/13573322.2013.858624

Hathaway, T. (2018). Negotiating transitions in academic identity: Teacher or researcher? In Hosein, A., Rao, N., Yeh, C. S.-H., & Kinchin, I. M. (Eds.), *Academics' international teaching journeys: Personal narratives of transitions in higher education* (pp. 93–108). Bloomsbury Academic.

Healey, M., Flint, A., & Harrington, K. (2016). Students as partners: Reflections on a conceptual model. *Teaching & Learning Inquiry*, 4(2), 1–13. DOI: 10.20343/teachlearninqu.4.2.3

Healey, M., Matthews, K. E., & Cook-Sather, A. (2019). Writing scholarship of teaching and learning articles for peer-reviewed journals. *Teaching & Learning Inquiry*, 7(2), 28–50. DOI: 10.20343/teachlearninqu.7.2.3

Hernández-Soto, R., Gutiérrez-Ortega, M., & Rubia-Avi, B. (2021). Key factors in knowledge sharing behavior in virtual communities of practice: A systematic review. *Education in the Knowledge Society*, 22, 1–14. DOI: 10.14201/eks.22715

How, Z. J. (2020). A systematic review of scholarship of teaching and learning research in higher education institutes from 2014–2019. In Tan, S. C., & Chen, S. H. A. (Eds.), *Transforming teaching and learning in higher education: A chronicle of research and development in a Singaporean context* (pp. 11–43). Springer., DOI: 10.1007/978-981-15-4980-9_2

Howard, S., & McKeown, J. (2011) Online practice & offline roles: A cultural view of teachers' low engagement in online communities. American Educational Research Association. https://hdl.handle.net/10779/uow.27697410.v1

Kamler, B., & Thomson, P. (2014). *Helping doctoral students write: Pedagogies for supervision* (2nd ed.). Taylor & Francis Group., DOI: 10.4324/9781315813639

Kellam, H., Cook, C., Smith, D. L., & Haight, P. (2023). The virtual community of practice facilitation model: A conceptual framework for healthcare professional education. *International Journal of Technology and Human Interaction*, 19(1), 1–14. DOI: 10.4018/IJTHI.328578

Kenney, J., Kumar, S., & Hart, M. (2013). More than a social network: Facebook as a catalyst for an online educational community of practice. *International Journal of Social Media and Interactive Learning Environments*, 1(4), 355–369. DOI: 10.1504/IJSMILE.2013.057467

Kolomitro, K., Laverty, C., & Stockley, D. (2017). Sparking SoTL: Triggers and stories from one institution. *The Canadian Journal for the Scholarship of Teaching and Learning*, 9(1). Advance online publication. DOI: 10.5206/cjsotl-rcacea.2018.1.10

Lave, J., & Wenger, E. (1991). *Situated learning: Legitimate peripheral participation*. Cambridge University Press., DOI: 10.1017/CBO9780511815355

Liston, D. D., & Rahimi, R. (2017a). Introduction: Unlocking SoTL's potential for transformative education. In Liston, D. D., & Rahimi, R. (Eds.), *Promoting social justice through the scholarship of teaching and learning* (pp. xi–xxx). Indiana University Press., DOI: 10.2307/j.ctt2005zc2.3

Liston, D. D., & Rahimi, R. (2017b). SoTL: Next steps toward social justice. In Liston, D. D., & Rahimi, R. (Eds.), *Promoting social justice through the scholarship of teaching and learning* (pp. 328–332). Indiana University Press., DOI: 10.2307/j.ctt2005zc2.22

Mason, C., Castleman, T., & Parker, C. M. (2008). Socio-technical factors influencing channel use for knowledge-sharing in regional SME networks. *International Journal of Knowledge Management Studies*, 2(3), 303–319. DOI: 10.1504/IJKMS.2008.018794

McClurg, C., MacMillan, M., & Chick, N. (2019). Visions of the possible: Engaging with librarians in SoTL. *Teaching & Learning Inquiry*, 7(2), 3–13. DOI: 10.20343/teachlearninqu.7.2.1

Meijerman, I., Kirschner, F., & Prins, F. (2023). Experiences with supporting teachers with scholarship of teaching and learning at a research-intensive university: Lessons learned. *Teaching & Learning Inquiry*, 11. Advance online publication. DOI: 10.20343/teachlearninqu.11.27

Miller-Young, J., & Chick, N. L. (Eds.). (2024). *Becoming a SoTL scholar*. Elon University Center for Engaged Learning., DOI: 10.36284/celelon.oa6

Moran, E., & Misra, D. (2018). Professional doctorates: A pathway to legitimacy for non-academic HE professionals? *London Review of Education*, 16(1), 75–89. DOI: 10.18546/LRE.16.1.08

Müggenburg, H. (2021). Beyond the limits of memory? The reliability of retrospective data in travel research. *Transportation Research Part A, Policy and Practice*, 145, 302–318. DOI: 10.1016/j.tra.2021.01.010

Omidvar, O., & Kislov, R. (2014). The evolution of the communities of practice approach: Toward knowledgeability in a landscape of practice—An interview with Etienne Wenger-Trayner. *Journal of Management Inquiry*, 23(3), 266–275. DOI: 10.1177/1056492613505908

Pan, Y., Xu, Y., Wang, X., Zhang, C., Ling, H., & Lin, J. (2015). Integrating social networking support for dyadic knowledge exchange: A study in a virtual community of practice. *Information & Management*, 52(1), 61–70. DOI: 10.1016/j.im.2014.10.001

Peeters, W., & Pretorius, M. (2020). Facebook or fail-book: Exploring "community" in a virtual community of practice. *ReCALL*, 32(3), 291–306. DOI: 10.1017/S0958344020000099

Pleschová, G., Roxå, T., Thomson, K. E., & Felten, P. (2021). Conversations that make meaningful change in teaching, teachers, and academic development. *The International Journal for Academic Development*, 26(3), 201–209. https://doi.org/https://doi.org/10.1080/1360144X.2021.1958446. DOI: 10.1080/1360144X.2021.1958446

Poole, G., & Chick, N. L. (2016). On the nature of expertise in SoTL. *Teaching & Learning Inquiry*, 4(2). Advance online publication. https://doi.org/https://doi.org/10.20343/teachlearninqu.4.2.1. DOI: 10.20343/teachlearninqu.4.2.1

Retna, K. S., & Tee Ng, P. (2011). Communities of practice: Dynamics and success factors. *Leadership and Organization Development Journal*, 32(1), 41–59. DOI: 10.1108/01437731111099274

Rolfe, G., Jasper, M., & Freshwater, D. (2010). *Critical reflection in practice: Generating knowledge for practice*. Palgrave Macmillian.

Ryttberg, M. (2022). Legitimacy dynamics of professional support staff at higher education institutions. *Higher Education Policy*, 35(1), 218–233. DOI: 10.1057/s41307-020-00206-w

Schacter, D. L. (1999). The seven sins of memory: Insights from psychology and cognitive neuroscience. *The American Psychologist*, 54(3), 182–203. DOI: 10.1037/0003-066X.54.3.182 PMID: 10199218

Simmons, N., Abrahamson, E., Deshler, J., Kensington-Miller, B., Manarin, K., Morón-García, S., Oliver, C., & Renc-Roe, J. (2013). Conflicts and configurations in a liminal space: SoTL scholars' identity development. *Teaching & Learning Inquiry*, 1(2), 9–21. DOI: 10.20343/teachlearninqu.1.2.9

Simmons, N., Scharff, L., Eady, M., & Gregory, D. (2021). SoTL in the margins: Teaching-focused role case studies. *Teaching & Learning Inquiry*, 9(1), 61–78. DOI: 10.20343/teachlearninqu.9.1.6

Smith, C., Holden, M., Yu, E., & Hanlon, P. (2021). 'So what do you do?': Third space professionals navigating a Canadian university context. *Journal of Higher Education Policy and Management*, 43(5), 505–519. DOI: 10.1080/1360080X.2021.1884513

Smith, S., & Walker, D. (2021). Scholarship and academic capitals: The boundaried nature of education-focused career tracks. *Teaching in Higher Education*. Advance online publication. DOI: 10.1080/13562517.2021.1965570

Supramaniam, K., Razak, M. I. M., & Arumugam, N. (2020). Changing identities in community of practice: Expert teachers to novice researchers. *Asian Journal of University Education*, 16(2), 59–68. DOI: 10.24191/ajue.v16i2.10297

Tertiary Education Quality and Standards Agency (TEQSA). (2022). *Guidance Note: Scholarship* (Version 3.0). https://www.teqsa.gov.au/guides-resources/resources/guidance-notes/guidance-note-scholarship

Veles, N., & Carter, M.-A. (2016). Imagining a future: Changing the landscape for third space professionals in Australian higher education institutions. *Journal of Higher Education Policy and Management*, 38(5), 519–533. DOI: 10.1080/1360080X.2016.1196938

Watts, L. (2015). An autoethnographic exploration of learning and teaching reflective practice. *Social Work Education*, 34(4), 363–376. DOI: 10.1080/02615479.2015.1016903

Wenger, E. (1998). *Communities of practice: Learning, meaning, and identity*. Cambridge University Press., DOI: 10.1017/CBO9780511803932

Wenger, E., McDermott, R., & Snyder, W. (2002). *Cultivating communities of practice: A guide to managing knowledge*. Harvard Business School Press.

Wenger-Trayner, B. (2015). *Communities of practice: A brief overview of the concept and its uses*. 08 Brief introduction to communities of practice (wenger-trayner.com)

Yin, R. K. (2015). *Qualitative research from start to finish*. Guilford Publications.

KEY TERMS AND DEFINITIONS

Collaborative Autoethnography: This is a qualitative research method that combines collaborative, autobiographical, and ethnographical approaches. It involves self-reflection and writing to explore personal experiences and connect them to wider cultural, political, and social meanings and understandings. In our case, it is a cooperative and synergistic approach to investigating the personal experiences of the online community of practice.

Higher Education Standards Framework (HESF): This framework is a set of standards that the Tertiary Education Quality and Standards Agency (TEQSA) uses to regulate Australian higher education providers and courses, including requirements for scholarship and teaching quality. It is a comprehensive framework with seven domains that ensures institutions meet certain quality and performance benchmarks. The HESF helps maintain high standards in higher education, ensuring that students receive quality education and support.

Online Community of Practice: An online community of practice is a group of people who share a common interest or profession and engage in collective learning through regular interactions with a shared purpose. The majority of interactions occur in online spaces, such as synchronous online meetings, asynchronous learning activities, asynchronous document collaborations, and regular engagement in online spaces. In our context, it refers to an online group of scholars collaborating online to enhance their SoTL practices.

Scholarly Identity: This describes how individuals perceive themselves as scholars within their professional context. It involves the roles, tasks, and self-concept related to their academic, professional, and teaching responsibilities. In our context, 'scholarly identity' is distinct from discipline academic or other work role identity.

Scholarship of Teaching and Learning: This refers to the systematic study of teaching and learning practices and processes. It involves researching and reflecting on teaching practices to improve educational outcomes and sharing findings with the academic community.

Special Interest Group (SIG): A special interest group (SIG) is typically a smaller group within a larger organisation that shares an interest in and goal of developing a specific area of learning, teaching, knowledge, and practice through networking and information sharing. It differs from a community of practice (CoP) because CoPs tend to have more active participation and focus on continuous learning and professional development through regular interaction, collaboration, and practice sharing.

Third Space Practitioner: These practitioners work at the intersection of academic and professional roles in higher education. They often include role titles such as academic developers, learning designers, educational technologists, librarians, student success advisors, and other staff who facilitate teaching and learning.

Chapter 7
Building Community and Engagement in Online Nursing Education:
Strategies and Challenges

Tiago Manuel Horta Reis da Silva
https://orcid.org/0000-0001-5220-1718
King's College London, UK

ABSTRACT

In the digital era, online nursing education offers unprecedented opportunities for flexible learning, yet fostering a sense of community and engagement remains a challenge. This chapter explores the strategies to build robust communities in online nursing programs, focusing on creating emotional connections, active participation, and collaborative learning. Emotional Intelligence (EI) is emphasised as a crucial skill for both educators and students in fostering a supportive online environment. The integration of essential nursing topics such as chronic and acute conditions, into the online curriculum presents unique pedagogical opportunities and challenges. The chapter also examines the role of online education in advancing Sustainable Development Goals (SDGs), particularly those related to health and well-being. Finally, it highlights best practices in online teaching that support the development of emotional resilience, holistic care approaches, and interdisciplinary collaboration, all while preparing nursing professionals for the complexities of modern healthcare.

DOI: 10.4018/979-8-3693-7595-2.ch007

INTRODUCTION

The transition from traditional in-person nursing education to online platforms has been a complex and multifaceted process, particularly accelerated by the COVID-19 pandemic. This shift has presented both significant challenges and opportunities for educators and learners alike (Reis da Silva and Mitchell, 2024a). As nursing programs adapt to digital environments, the importance of fostering a sense of community and engagement among students cannot be overstated (Reis da Silva and Mitchell, 2024a). This chapter explores the theoretical and practical aspects of building community in online nursing education, drawing from current research, teaching methodologies, and best practices to address the specific needs of nursing students and educators in this evolving educational landscape.

One of the primary challenges faced by nursing educators during the transition to online learning has been maintaining student motivation and engagement (Reis da Silva and Mitchell, 2024a). The concept of "emergency remote education" emerged as a response to the abrupt shift from traditional methods to online platforms, highlighting the necessity for educators to adapt quickly to new teaching modalities while still delivering quality education (İnangil et al., 2022). Research indicates that the effectiveness of online education can be significantly enhanced through innovative teaching strategies such as gamification and animation, which have been shown to improve student engagement and learning outcomes (İnangil et al., 2022). Furthermore, the integration of collaborative tools and communication platforms is essential for creating an interactive learning environment that fosters a sense of community among nursing students (Kosteniuk et al., 2019).

The unique nature of nursing education, which traditionally relies heavily on hands-on practice and clinical experience, poses additional challenges in an online format. The shift to online learning has necessitated the development of alternative methods to deliver practical skills training effectively (Reis da Silva and Mitchell, 2024a). Studies have shown that online simulations and virtual clinical experiences can provide valuable opportunities for nursing students to practice their skills in a safe and controlled environment (Kim, 2024). For instance, the use of standardised patient simulations in online modules has been found to enhance learning outcomes for nursing students, particularly in complex clinical scenarios such as heart failure management (Silva et al., 2021). These innovative approaches not only help bridge the gap created by the lack of in-person clinical experiences but also promote collaboration and peer learning among students (Xing et al., 2018).

Moreover, the psychological impact of the transition to online learning cannot be overlooked. Research has indicated that nursing students experience heightened levels of stress and anxiety during this period, which can adversely affect their academic performance and overall well-being (Çelik et al., 2022). It is crucial for educators to recognize these challenges and implement supportive measures to help students navigate the emotional and psychological demands of online learning. Strategies such as providing mental health resources, fostering open communication, and creating a supportive online community can significantly alleviate stress and enhance student resilience (Galanis, 2024). Additionally, incorporating metacognitive strategies into the curriculum can empower students to take charge of their learning, thereby improving their self-directed learning readiness and overall performance (Kim, 2024).

The effectiveness of online nursing education also hinges on the educators' ability to adapt their teaching methodologies to suit the digital environment. Research highlights the importance of utilizing a blended learning approach that combines online and face-to-face interactions to maximize learning outcomes (Siah et al., 2020). This hybrid model not only facilitates the transfer of knowledge but also allows for the development of critical thinking and problem-solving skills essential for nursing practice (Siah et al., 2020). Furthermore, the implementation of structured training programs for nurse educators can enhance their proficiency in online teaching, ultimately benefiting student learning experiences (Stanley & Martin, 2019).

As nursing education continues to evolve, the integration of technology into the curriculum will play a pivotal role in shaping the future of nursing practice (Fitzpatrick et al., 2023; Cowley et al., 2023). The use of mobile applications and online platforms for continuous education has been shown to improve nurses' knowledge and skills, particularly in specialized areas such as infection prevention and control (Hamid, 2024). Additionally, the incorporation of e-learning modules into nursing curricula can facilitate ongoing professional development, ensuring that nurses remain competent and up-to-date with current practices (Lhbibani et al., 2022).

Building a sense of community in online nursing education is essential for fostering collaboration and peer support among students. The Community of Inquiry (CoI) framework provides a valuable theoretical foundation for promoting social presence, cognitive presence, and teaching presence in online learning environments (Padilla, 2023). By creating opportunities for students to engage in meaningful discussions, collaborate on projects, and provide peer feedback, educators can cultivate a supportive online community that enhances the overall learning experience (Siah et al., 2020). Furthermore, leveraging social media and online forums can facilitate informal interactions among students, further strengthening their sense of belonging and community (Xing et al., 2018).

This chapter is organised into eight interconnected sections, each addressing critical aspects of online nursing education. It begins with an Introduction that contextualises the growing relevance of online learning in nursing education, emphasising the need for innovation in fostering engagement and emotional intelligence. The second section, Emotional Intelligence in Online Nursing Education, explores how virtual environments can nurture EI among nursing students to enhance their interpersonal and professional skills. The third section, Nursing Curriculum: Key Areas for Online Learning, identifies essential content areas and pedagogical adjustments suited for digital platforms. Next, Engagement Strategies in Online Learning delves into techniques for cultivating active student participation and a sense of community. The fifth section, Advancing the Sustainable Development Goals (SDGs) through Online Nursing Education, examines how online nursing programs can align with global sustainability priorities. Challenges in Building Community and Engagement addresses barriers to fostering meaningful connections and collaborative learning in virtual spaces. The penultimate section, Future Research and Call for Action, highlights emerging gaps and opportunities for scholarly inquiry and practical implementation. The chapter concludes by synthesising these insights and reinforcing the transformative potential of online nursing education.

EMOTIONAL INTELLIGENCE IN ONLINE NURSING EDUCATION

Emotional Intelligence (EI) is increasingly recognised as a vital component in online nursing education, particularly in fostering community and engagement among students (da Silva, 2022). In virtual classrooms, where non-verbal cues are often absent, the ability to recognise, understand, and manage emotions becomes essential for both educators and learners (Reis da Silva, 2024a).

High levels of EI among educators can create a more empathetic and supportive environment, which is crucial for helping students navigate the unique challenges posed by online learning, such as feelings of isolation, burnout, and the lack of face-to-face interactions (Ainiyah et al., 2021; Aljarboa et al., 2022; Reis da Silva, 2024b). Research has shown that educators who exhibit strong emotional intelligence are better equipped to engage with their students, fostering an atmosphere of trust and collaboration (Reis da Silva, 2024b; Reis da Silva, 2024c; Reis da Silva, 2024d). This is particularly important in nursing education, where the emotional demands of the profession necessitate a high level of interpersonal skills. For instance, Çam & Büyükbayram's study (2015) highlights that training programs aimed at enhancing emotional intelligence skills can significantly improve resilience among nurses, thereby enhancing their ability to cope with the stresses of both education and practice. Furthermore, the ability to empathise with students' experiences can lead to more effective teaching strategies that address their emotional and academic needs (Chikobvu & Harunavamwe, 2022).

Integrating EI into the online nursing curriculum can be achieved through various strategies. One effective approach is the implementation of active listening techniques in discussion forums and video sessions (Ainiyah et al., 2021; Aljarboa et al., 2022). This not only encourages open communication but also allows educators to better understand the emotional states of their students, facilitating a more responsive teaching approach (Ainiyah et al., 2021; Aljarboa et al., 2022). Additionally, providing opportunities for reflective practice through journaling and peer feedback can help students explore their emotional responses to case studies and clinical scenarios, thus enhancing their emotional awareness and resilience (Ainiyah et al., 2021).

Mindful communication is another critical strategy for integrating EI into online nursing education. Training both educators and students in mindful communication can reduce misunderstandings and foster a sense of belonging within the online learning environment. This is particularly pertinent in nursing, where effective communication is essential for patient care and collaboration among healthcare teams (Ainiyah et al., 2021; Aljarboa et al., 2022). By cultivating an environment where emotional expression is encouraged and valued, nursing programs can significantly enhance student engagement and satisfaction.

The development of emotional intelligence in nursing students not only bolsters their personal resilience but also equips them with the interpersonal skills necessary for effective patient care (Reis da Silva, 2024b). This is especially crucial in emotionally demanding areas such as palliative care and oncology, where nurses must navigate complex emotional landscapes while providing compassionate care (Ainiyah et al., 2021; Aljarboa et al., 2022; Reis da Silva, 2024e). Studies have indicated that nursing students with higher levels of emotional intelligence tend to exhibit better coping strategies and lower levels of stress, which can lead to improved academic performance and clinical outcomes (Ainiyah et al., 2021).

Moreover, emotional intelligence has been linked to improved critical thinking skills and decision-making abilities in nursing students. For example, a study found that emotional intelligence training significantly enhanced the critical thinking skills and self-esteem of nursing students, suggesting that EI is not only beneficial for personal development but also for professional competencies (Ahmed et al., 2023). This is particularly relevant in the context of online education, where students may face unique challenges that require adaptive problem-solving and critical thinking skills. In addition to enhancing individual competencies, fostering emotional intelligence within nursing education can contribute to building a cohesive community among students. When students feel understood and supported, they are more likely to engage actively in their learning and collaborate with peers. This sense of community is essential for creating a positive online learning environment that encourages participation and knowledge sharing (Ainiyah et al., 2021; Aljarboa et al., 2022).

Furthermore, the role of emotional intelligence in nursing education extends beyond the classroom. As future healthcare providers, nursing students must be equipped with the skills to manage their emotions and those of their patients effectively. Research has shown that nurses with high emotional intelligence are better able to provide emotional support to patients and their families, leading to improved patient satisfaction and outcomes (Aljarboa et al., 2022). This underscores the importance of integrating emotional intelligence training into nursing curricula to prepare students for the emotional demands of their profession (Reis da Silva, 2024f; Reis da Silva, 2024g).

NURSING CURRICULUM: KEY AREAS FOR ONLINE LEARNING

The integration of key areas such as chronic conditions, palliative care, falls prevention, and acute care into online nursing education is essential for preparing future nurses to meet the complex needs of patients (Reis da Silva, 2024f). Each of these areas presents unique challenges and opportunities for curriculum development that can be effectively addressed through online learning methodologies.

Chronic Conditions

Online nursing education provides a robust platform for delivering content related to chronic disease management, including conditions such as diabetes, hypertension, heart failure, and chronic kidney disease (Reis da Silva, 2024h). The use of multimedia tools, case-based learning, and virtual simulations allows nursing students to engage with patient scenarios that reflect the complexities of real-world healthcare settings (Reis da Silva and Mitchell, 2024a). For instance, Kang et al. (2022) emphasise the importance of developing a curriculum that aligns with international nursing standards, which includes comprehensive training on chronic disease management. Also, Reis da Silva and Mitchell (2024b) highlight the importance to include service users to provide a more realistic experience in simulation. This approach not only enhances students' clinical competencies but also prepares them to address the needs of an ageing population increasingly affected by long-term conditions (Ji et al., 2021; Reis da Silva, 2024i; Reis da Silva, 2024j).

The inclusion of chronic disease management in the nursing curriculum is critical, as it equips students with the knowledge and skills necessary to provide effective care for patients with chronic illnesses. Ji et al. (2021) highlights the significance of integrating patient safety topics into nursing education, which is particularly relevant when managing chronic conditions that require ongoing monitoring and intervention. By utilising virtual simulations, and include service-users, students can practice making clinical decisions in a controlled environment, thereby enhancing their confidence and competence in managing chronic diseases (Reis da Silva and Mitchell, 2024a; Reis da Silva and Mitchell, 2024b).

Palliative Care and Oncology

Teaching palliative care and oncology in an online setting necessitates a sensitive approach that combines theoretical knowledge with emotional support (Reis da Silva, 2024e; Reis da Silva, 2024j). The use of case studies, video testimonies from patients and families, and virtual role-play can foster empathy and provide students with insights into the holistic nature of care for terminally ill patients (Reis da Silva and Mitchell, 2024a). Weaver et al. (2019) demonstrates that integrating educational sessions based on established palliative care curricula can significantly improve nursing students' knowledge of end-of-life care concepts. This is particularly important in preparing nurses to provide compassionate care in emotionally charged situations.

Furthermore, the integration of emotional intelligence training is crucial in these areas, as it helps students develop resilience and the ability to provide compassionate care remotely (Reis da Silva, 2024b; Reis da Silva, 2024c). Emotional intelligence not only enhances interpersonal skills but also prepares nursing students to handle the emotional complexities associated with palliative care and oncology (Weaver et al., 2019). By incorporating reflective practices and peer feedback into the curriculum, educators can create a supportive learning environment that encourages students to explore their emotional responses to challenging clinical scenarios.

Falls Prevention

Falls prevention is a critical component of nursing education, especially concerning older adults who are at a higher risk of falls (Reis da Silva, 2023a; Reis da Silva, 2023b). Online courses can leverage interactive tools, videos, and virtual assessments to teach students how to assess and mitigate fall risks in various settings (Reis da Silva and Mitchell, 2024a). Research by Isangula et al. (2023) emphasizes the importance of improving nursing education curricula to strengthen nurse-client relationships, which is vital for effective falls prevention strategies. Through collaborative online projects, students can work in groups to design comprehensive care plans that address falls prevention, thereby enhancing their understanding of interdisciplinary approaches (Isangula et al., 2023).

Moreover, the use of simulation-based learning can be particularly effective in teaching falls prevention strategies (Horta Reis da Silva, 2022). Reis da Silva (2024k) highlight the benefits of using patient simulations to promote best practices in fall prevention and post-fall assessment, indicating that such methods can significantly enhance nursing students' preparedness for real-world scenarios. By engaging in role-playing exercises and case studies, students can develop critical thinking skills and learn to apply evidence-based interventions in fall prevention (Reis da Silva and Mitchell, 2024a).

Acute Care: Dehydration and Nutrition

Acute care, including the management of dehydration and nutrition, can be effectively taught online through case-based learning and virtual simulations (Reis da Silva, 2024l; Reis da Silva, 2024m). These strategies allow students to make clinical decisions in a controlled environment, offering immediate feedback and opportunities for self-assessment. Research indicates that discussions on clinical decision-making and patient safety can be enriched through peer interaction and reflective practice in online forums. This collaborative approach not only enhances learning outcomes but also fosters a sense of community among nursing students (Reis da Silva and Mitchell, 2024a).

The management of dehydration and nutrition is particularly relevant in acute care settings, where timely and effective interventions are critical (Reis da Silva, 2024l; Reis da Silva, 2024m). Studies have shown that nursing students who engage in simulation-based learning demonstrate improved knowledge and skills in managing acute conditions (Reis da Silva and Mitchell, 2024a). By incorporating real-life scenarios into the curriculum, educators can prepare students to respond effectively to the complexities of patient care in acute settings (Reis da Silva and Mitchell, 2024b).

ENGAGEMENT STRATEGIES IN ONLINE LEARNING

Engagement strategies in online nursing education are essential for fostering a sense of community and enhancing student learning experiences (Mukattil, 2024). As nursing programs increasingly transition to online platforms, it is crucial to implement effective strategies that promote collaboration, critical thinking, and instructor presence (Mukattil, 2024). This section discusses three key engagement strategies: collaborative learning, virtual simulation and case-based learning, and instructor presence and interaction.

Collaborative Learning

Creating collaborative learning opportunities in online nursing education is vital for fostering a sense of community among students. Techniques such as group projects, peer-review assignments, and discussion forums can help build connections among students. Research indicates that collaborative learning not only enhances academic performance but also improves interpersonal skills, which are crucial in nursing practice (Mukattil, 2024). For instance, Mukattil (2024) emphasizes the importance of innovative approaches in nursing education, such as collaborative projects that allow students to engage with their peers and share diverse perspectives. Additionally, the use of social media and online study groups can offer informal support networks, encouraging students to remain engaged with the content and each other (Reis da Silva and Mitchell, 2024a). Studies have shown that social media platforms can facilitate communication and collaboration among nursing students, leading to increased motivation and a sense of belonging (Cant et al., 2022). By creating opportunities for students to interact outside of formal learning environments, educators can enhance student engagement and foster a supportive community.

Virtual Simulation and Case-Based Learning

Virtual simulations and case-based learning provide an immersive experience that enhances critical thinking and decision-making skills (Reis da Silva and Mitchell, 2024a). In an online environment, virtual simulations can be adapted to replicate various clinical scenarios, from acute care to community health interventions. Cant et al. (2022) highlight the effectiveness of virtual simulations in nursing education, noting that they allow students to develop essential skills such as communication and patient-centred care in a safe and controlled environment. This method helps bridge the gap between theory and practice, ensuring that students are well-prepared for clinical placements. Moreover, the integration of case-based learning into the curriculum allows students to apply theoretical knowledge to real-world situations (Cant et al., 2022). Jeon (2024) emphasizes that simulation-based education provides valuable rehearsal opportunities for teamwork and communication, which are critical in nursing practice.

By engaging in case studies and virtual simulations, students can enhance their clinical judgment and decision-making abilities, ultimately improving patient care outcomes (Reis da Silva and Mitchell, 2024a). The use of virtual simulations has gained particular importance during the COVID-19 pandemic, as traditional clinical placements were disrupted (Jeon, 2024). Research indicates that virtual simulations can effectively replace a portion of clinical hours, allowing nursing students to continue their education without compromising the quality of their training (Rossler et al., 2019). This adaptability is crucial for maintaining the integrity of nursing education in challenging circumstances.

Instructor Presence and Interaction

Instructor presence in online courses plays a pivotal role in student engagement. Regular interactions through video lectures, personalised feedback, and live discussion sessions help humanise the online experience and keep students motivated (Barbosa, 2023). Studies have shown that a strong instructor presence can significantly enhance student satisfaction and learning outcomes in online nursing education (Barbosa, 2023). For example, Barbosa (2023) discusses how the combination of virtual simulations and instructor-led discussions can improve students' skills performance and confidence in patient care.

Instructors should also foster a culture of open communication, where students feel comfortable sharing their thoughts, concerns, and feedback on the learning process (Barbosa, 2023). This approach not only encourages student participation but also helps identify areas for improvement in the curriculum. Research by Ahmed et al. (2022) indicates that effective communication between instructors and students is essential for building trust and promoting a positive learning environment. Furthermore, the integration of debriefing sessions after virtual simulations can enhance the learning experience by allowing students to reflect on their performance and receive constructive feedback from instructors and peers (Jan, 2023). This reflective practice is crucial for developing critical thinking skills and promoting continuous improvement in nursing education (Ahmed et al., 2022; Jan, 2023).

ADVANCING THE SUSTAINABLE DEVELOPMENT GOALS (SDGS) THROUGH ONLINE NURSING EDUCATION

Online nursing education plays a pivotal role in advancing the Sustainable Development Goals (SDGs), particularly Goal 3: Good Health and Well-Being. By providing accessible and flexible learning opportunities, online education ensures that nurses are well-prepared to address health disparities, manage chronic conditions, and deliver care in underserved regions (da Silva and Rodrigues, 2023; Reis da Silva, 2024n; Reis da Silva, 2024o). This chapter explores how online nursing education contributes to various SDGs, emphasizing its impact on health outcomes, lifelong learning, and the integration of critical health topics into nursing curricula.

Contribution to Goal 3: Good Health and Well-Being

The primary focus of online nursing education aligns closely with SDG 3, which aims to ensure healthy lives and promote well-being for all at all ages (da Silva and Rodrigues, 2023). Online programs facilitate the training of nurses who can effectively manage chronic diseases such as diabetes, hypertension, and heart failure, which are increasingly prevalent in ageing populations (Hawkins, 2024).

The flexibility of online education allows nurses to acquire essential skills and knowledge at their own pace, making it easier for them to balance their studies with professional responsibilities. This is particularly important in regions where healthcare access is limited, as online education can help bridge the gap in nursing workforce shortages (Hueske et al., 2021). Moreover, online nursing education supports the development of competencies necessary for addressing health disparities. By incorporating topics such as palliative care, falls prevention, loneliness and social isolation, elder abuse, pharmacokinetics and medicine management, and acute care into the curriculum, nursing programs ensure that graduates are equipped to meet the immediate and long-term healthcare needs of diverse populations (Fields et al., 2021; Reis da Silva, 2024p; Reis da Silva, 2024q, Reis da Silva, 2024r). This focus on comprehensive care aligns with global health priorities and contributes to improved health outcomes.

Support for Goal 4: Quality Education

In addition to promoting health and well-being, online nursing education significantly contributes to SDG 4, which emphasises the importance of inclusive and equitable quality education and promotes lifelong learning opportunities for all (Reis da Silva and Mitchell, 2024a). The integration of online learning platforms allows practicing nurses to engage in continuous professional development, ensuring that they remain current with evolving healthcare practices and technologies (Rosa et al., 2021). This is particularly relevant in the context of rapid advancements in medical knowledge and technology, which necessitate ongoing education for healthcare professionals.

Furthermore, online nursing education fosters a culture of lifelong learning by providing various resources and opportunities for skill enhancement. For instance, the use of open educational resources (OER) can facilitate access to high-quality educational materials, thereby promoting equitable learning opportunities (Ossiannilsson, 2023). By leveraging technology, nursing programs can reach a broader audience, including those in remote or underserved areas, thereby contributing to the overall goal of quality education for all (Rosa et al., 2021).

Addressing Global Health Priorities

The integration of critical health topics into online nursing curricula is essential for preparing nurses to address global health challenges (Hawkins, 2024). Topics such as chronic disease management, palliative care, and mental health are increasingly relevant in today's healthcare landscape.

Online education allows for the dissemination of best practices and evidence-based approaches across borders, contributing to improved health outcomes on a global scale (Osingada & Porta, 2020). By equipping nursing students with the knowledge and skills necessary to address these pressing health issues, online education plays a vital role in advancing the SDGs (Hawkins, 2024). For example, the COVID-19 pandemic has highlighted the importance of palliative care and mental health support in nursing practice.

Online nursing education programs that incorporate these topics can better prepare nurses to provide compassionate care in times of crisis (Hawkins, 2024). Additionally, the emphasis on falls prevention and acute care in nursing curricula ensures that graduates are equipped to manage the complexities of patient care effectively (Osingada & Porta, 2020).

Facilitating Global Collaboration

Online nursing education also facilitates global collaboration among healthcare professionals, which is essential for achieving the SDGs (Abodunrin, 2023). By connecting nursing students and educators from different regions, online programs promote the exchange of ideas, experiences, and best practices. This collaborative approach can lead to innovative solutions for addressing health disparities and improving healthcare delivery (Fields et al., 2021). For instance, international partnerships between nursing schools can enhance the quality of education and provide students with diverse perspectives on healthcare challenges.

Moreover, the use of technology in online nursing education enables the sharing of resources and expertise across borders (Abodunrin, 2023). This is particularly important in addressing global health emergencies, where timely access to information and training can make a significant difference in patient outcomes (Abodunrin, 2023). By fostering a culture of collaboration and knowledge sharing, online nursing education contributes to the collective effort to achieve the SDGs (Hawkins, 2024).

CHALLENGES IN BUILDING COMMUNITY AND ENGAGEMENT

Building community and engagement in online nursing education presents several challenges that require careful consideration and strategic approaches. Among these challenges, technological barriers, student engagement and retention, and assessment and feedback mechanisms are particularly significant (Kim-Godwin et al., 2022). This section explores these challenges in detail, highlighting their implications for nursing education and suggesting potential strategies for overcoming them.

Technological Barriers

One of the primary challenges in online nursing education is the accessibility and usability of technology (Kim-Godwin et al., 2022). Many students and educators face difficulties related to internet connectivity, unfamiliarity with learning management systems (LMS), and the lack of necessary hardware or software. Research indicates that inadequate access to technology can hinder the learning experience and create disparities among students (Kim-Godwin et al., 2022). For instance, Kim-Godwin et al. (2022) emphasise that students often encounter challenges with narrative pedagogy in online learning due to technological limitations, which can impede their ability to engage fully with the curriculum.

Addressing these technological barriers requires institutional support, including comprehensive training for both faculty and students. Institutions must invest in resources that enhance technological accessibility, such as providing laptops or tablets to students in need and ensuring reliable internet connectivity (Barbosa, 2023). Additionally, training programs that familiarise educators and students with the LMS can help mitigate feelings of frustration and enhance the overall learning experience (Langan et al., 2022). By creating a supportive technological environment, nursing programs can foster greater engagement and community among students.

Student Engagement and Retention

Maintaining student engagement in an online environment is another significant challenge, as the lack of physical interaction can lead to feelings of isolation and disengagement (Rembish et al., 2022). Studies have shown that students in online nursing programs often report lower levels of motivation and engagement compared to their peers in traditional classroom settings (Xing et al., 2018). To combat this issue, educators must be proactive in employing a variety of teaching methods that promote interaction and collaboration (Xing et al., 2018).

Techniques such as interactive content, group discussions, and multimedia resources can help keep students motivated and involved in their learning (Rembish et al., 2022). Furthermore, providing opportunities for informal social interaction can help reduce feelings of isolation. Creating virtual study groups or discussion forums where students can connect outside of formal coursework can foster a sense of community and belonging (Wea, 2022). Additionally, incorporating elements of gamification into the curriculum can enhance student engagement by making learning more enjoyable and interactive (Lhbibani et al., 2022). By prioritising student engagement, nursing programs can improve retention rates and create a more vibrant online learning community (Xing et al., 2018).

Assessment and Feedback

Online assessment presents unique challenges, particularly in ensuring that evaluations are fair, transparent, and effective in measuring student competencies. Traditional assessment methods may not translate well to online formats, leading to concerns about academic integrity and the validity of evaluations (Huang & Fang, 2023). Creative approaches such as peer assessments, formative quizzes, and reflective assignments can help address some of these challenges while ensuring that students receive timely, constructive feedback (Nurse-Clarke & Sockol, 2022). For example, peer assessments can encourage collaboration and critical thinking, allowing students to learn from one another while also developing their evaluative skills (Molato & Sehularo, 2022). Additionally, incorporating formative assessments throughout the course can provide students with ongoing feedback, helping them identify areas for improvement before final evaluations (Cho et al., 2022). By adopting innovative assessment strategies, nursing educators can enhance the learning experience and ensure that students are adequately prepared for clinical practice.

FUTURE RESEARCH AND CALL FOR ACTION

As online nursing education continues to evolve, it is imperative to identify and address the challenges that hinder its effectiveness. Future research should focus on several key areas to enhance the quality of online nursing education and ensure that it meets the needs of both students and educators. This section outlines potential research directions and calls for action to improve online nursing education.

Investigating Technological Barriers

Research should explore the specific technological barriers faced by nursing students and educators in online learning environments (Reis da Silva and Mitchell, 2024a). Studies such as those by Molato and Sehularo (2022) highlight the necessity of adequate resources for students to access online education effectively. Future investigations could assess the impact of internet connectivity, access to devices, and familiarity with learning management systems on student engagement and learning outcomes. By identifying these barriers, institutions can develop targeted interventions to support students and educators, ensuring equitable access to online nursing education (Molato and Sehularo, 2022).

Enhancing Student Engagement Strategies

Understanding how to maintain student engagement in online nursing education is crucial for improving retention rates (Kim-Godwin et al., 2022). Future research should examine the effectiveness of various engagement strategies, such as collaborative learning, interactive content, and informal social interactions, as suggested by Kim-Godwin et al. (2022). Additionally, studies should investigate the role of emotional intelligence in fostering a supportive online community. By exploring these dimensions, educators can develop evidence-based practices that enhance student motivation and involvement in their learning (Kim-Godwin et al., 2022).

Assessing Innovative Assessment Methods

The challenges associated with online assessment necessitate further research into innovative evaluation methods (Cho et al., 2022). As highlighted by Cho et al. (2022), online education can positively impact nursing students' knowledge and skills. Future studies should explore the effectiveness of peer assessments, formative quizzes, and reflective assignments in measuring student competencies and providing timely feedback. Additionally, research should focus on developing standardized assessment tools that ensure fairness and transparency in online evaluations (Cho et al., 2022).

Addressing Mental Health and Well-Being

The transition to online learning has been associated with increased stress and anxiety among nursing students, as noted in various studies (Huang & Fang, 2023; Çelik et al., 2022). Future research should investigate the mental health implications of online nursing education and identify strategies to support students' emotional well-being (Huang & Fang, 2023; Çelik et al., 2022). This could include exploring the effectiveness of counselling services, peer support groups, and wellness programs in mitigating the psychological challenges faced by nursing students during their online education (Huang & Fang, 2023; Çelik et al., 2022).

Developing Faculty Training Programs

To enhance the quality of online nursing education, it is essential to invest in faculty training programs that equip educators with the necessary skills and confidence to teach effectively in virtual environments (Stanley & Martin, 2019). Research by Stanley and Martin (2019) emphasizes the importance of structured training for online nurse educators. Future studies should evaluate the impact of professional development initiatives on faculty performance and student outcomes, ultimately leading to improved online teaching practices (Stanley & Martin, 2019).

CONCLUSION

The transformation from traditional in-person nursing education to online platforms presents both challenges and opportunities for educators and learners. By embracing innovative teaching methodologies, fostering a sense of community, and providing adequate support for students, nursing programs can effectively navigate this transition and enhance the quality of education delivered to future healthcare professionals. As the landscape of nursing education continues to evolve, it is imperative for educators to remain adaptable and responsive to the changing needs of their students, ensuring that they are well-prepared to meet the demands of the healthcare environment.

Emotional intelligence plays a crucial role in building community and engagement in online nursing education. By fostering an environment that prioritises emotional awareness and communication, educators can enhance student resilience and interpersonal skills, ultimately leading to better patient care. As nursing education continues to evolve in the digital age, the integration of emotional intelligence into the curriculum will be essential for preparing competent and compassionate healthcare professionals.

The integration of key areas such as chronic conditions, palliative care, falls prevention, and acute care into online nursing education is essential for preparing competent and compassionate healthcare professionals. By leveraging innovative teaching strategies, including multimedia tools, case-based learning, and virtual simulations, nursing programs can effectively address the unique challenges posed by these critical areas of practice. As the landscape of nursing education continues to evolve, it is imperative for educators to remain adaptable and responsive to the changing needs of their students and the healthcare environment.

Engagement strategies such as collaborative learning, virtual simulation and case-based learning, and instructor presence and interaction are essential for fostering a sense of community and enhancing student learning experiences in online nursing education. By implementing these strategies, nursing programs can effectively prepare students for the complexities of clinical practice while promoting a supportive and engaging learning environment. As the landscape of nursing education continues to evolve, it is imperative for educators to remain adaptable and responsive to the changing needs of their students.

Online nursing education plays a crucial role in advancing the Sustainable Development Goals, particularly in promoting good health and well-being (SDG 3) and ensuring quality education (SDG 4). By providing accessible and flexible learning opportunities, online programs prepare nurses to address health disparities, manage chronic conditions, and deliver compassionate care in diverse settings. The integration of critical health topics into nursing curricula and the facilitation of global collaboration further enhance the impact of online education on health outcomes worldwide. As the healthcare landscape continues to evolve, the importance of online nursing education in achieving the SDGs will only grow.

Building community and engagement in online nursing education is fraught with challenges, including technological barriers, student engagement and retention issues, and the complexities of online assessment. Addressing these challenges requires a multifaceted approach that includes institutional support, innovative teaching strategies, and creative assessment methods. By prioritising these areas, nursing programs can foster a more inclusive and engaging online learning environment that prepares students for the demands of the nursing profession.

Key Messages

Building community and engagement in online nursing education requires a multifaceted approach that combines emotional intelligence, effective curriculum design, and innovative teaching strategies. By addressing the challenges of online learning and leveraging its strengths, nursing educators can create dynamic, supportive environments that prepare students for the complexities of modern healthcare. As online education continues to evolve, it will play an increasingly important role in advancing global health priorities and equipping nursing professionals with the skills they need to provide compassionate, high-quality care.

Call for Action

In light of the challenges and opportunities presented by online nursing education, it is crucial for educational institutions, policymakers, and nursing organizations to collaborate in advancing this field. Key actions include:

1. Investing in Technology: Institutions should prioritise investments in technology infrastructure to ensure that all students have access to the necessary resources for online learning.
2. Implementing Comprehensive Training: Faculty development programs must be established to equip educators with the skills needed to navigate online teaching effectively and engage students in meaningful ways.
3. Fostering Research Collaborations: Collaborative research efforts should be encouraged to explore innovative practices in online nursing education, focusing on student engagement, assessment methods, and mental health support.
4. Creating Supportive Policies: Policymakers should develop guidelines and standards for online nursing education that promote quality, equity, and accessibility, ensuring that all nursing students receive a high-quality education regardless of their circumstances.
5. Encouraging Lifelong Learning: Nursing organisations should promote continuous professional development opportunities for practicing nurses to enhance their skills and adapt to the evolving healthcare landscape.

By addressing these areas and taking decisive action, the nursing education community can enhance the effectiveness of online learning, ultimately improving the quality of care provided by future nursing professionals.

REFERENCES

Abodunrin, O., Olagunju, M. T., Alade, O. T., & Foláyan, M. O. (2023). Relationships between oral health and the sustainable development goals: A scoping review. *Biomed*, 3(4), 460–470. DOI: 10.3390/biomed3040037

Ahmed, N., Adam, S. M. A., & Mohamed, R. M. H. (2023). Effect of emotional intelligence training program on critical thinking skills and self-esteem of nurse students. *JPTCP*, 30(5), 548–561. DOI: 10.47750/jptcp.2023.30.05.055

Ahmed, S., Mohammed, H., Ayed, M., El-Ghadban, F., & Amin, F. (2022). Effect of simulation-based education on nurses' performance and satisfaction regarding peripherally inserted central catheters at neonatal intensive care unit. *Tanta Scientific Nursing Journal*, 26(3), 252–269. DOI: 10.21608/tsnj.2022.254429

Ainiyah, N., Zahroh, C., Khamida, K., Budury, S., Nurjanah, S., Hasina, S., & Wardhany, S. E. (2021). Emotional intelligence and self-efficacy as predictor factors of student resilience in online learning during pandemic era. *Open Access Macedonian Journal of Medical Sciences*, 9(T5), 40–43. DOI: 10.3889/oamjms.2021.7854

Aljarboa, B., An, E., Dator, W., Alshammari, S., Mostoles, R., Uy, M., & Gonzales, A. (2022). Resilience and emotional intelligence of staff nurses during the covid-19 pandemic. *Health Care*, 10(11), 2120. DOI: 10.3390/healthcare10112120 PMID: 36360460

Barbosa, A. (2023). Graduating nurses in the time of covid-19. *Open Journal of Nursing*, 13(10), 641–663. DOI: 10.4236/ojn.2023.1310042

Çam, O., & Büyükbayram, A. (2015). The results of nurses' increasing emotional intelligence and resilience. *Journal of Psychiatric Nursing/Psikiyatri Hemsireleri Dernegi, 6*(3) 130-136 DOI: 10.5505/phd.2015.96729

Cant, R., Ryan, C., & Kelly, M. (2022). Use and effectiveness of virtual simulations in nursing student education. *Computers, Informatics, Nursing*, 41(1), 31–38. DOI: 10.1097/CIN.0000000000000932 PMID: 35926237

Çelik, M. Y., Öztürk, E., Karasu, F., & Elmaoğlu, E. The Stress Dimension of Online Education in Nursing Students During The Covid-19 Process: A University Example. Sağlık Akademisi Kastamonu, 7(Covid-19 Ek Sayısı), 65-77.

Chikobvu, P., & Harunavamwe, M. (2022). The role of emotional intelligence and work engagement on nurses' resilience in public hospitals. *SA Journal of Human Resource Management*, 20, 259–268. DOI: 10.4102/sajhrm.v20i0.1690

Cho, D., Lee, W., Kim, S., & Choi, S. (2022). Effect of online education on the knowledge on, attitudes towards, and skills in patient safety for nursing students in Korea: A mixed-methods study. *Journal of Educational Evaluation for Health Professions*, 19, 14. DOI: 10.3352/jeehp.2022.19.14 PMID: 35918141

Cowley, S. A., Tzouvara, V., & Horta Reis da Silva, T. (2023). Public Health: healthy ageing and well-being. In *Redfern's Nursing Older People*. Fifth edition. Editors: Ross, Harris, Fitzpatrick and Abley. Elsevier.

da Silva, T. H. R. (2022). Emotional awareness and emotional intelligence. *British Journal of Community Nursing*, 27(12), 573–574. DOI: 10.12968/bjcn.2022.27.12.573 PMID: 36519463

da Silva, T. H. R., & Rodrigues, E. C. P. (2023). Body Image Related Discrimination. In Leal Filho, W., Azul, A. M., Brandli, L., Lange Salvia, A., Özuyar, P. G., & Wall, T. (Eds.), *Reduced Inequalities. Encyclopedia of the UN Sustainable Development Goals*. Springer., DOI: 10.1007/978-3-319-71060-0_61-1

Fields, L., Perkiss, S., Dean, B., & Moroney, T. (2021). Nursing and the sustainable development goals: A scoping review. *Journal of Nursing Scholarship*, 53(5), 568–577. DOI: 10.1111/jnu.12675 PMID: 34056841

Fitzpatrick, J. M., Bianchi, L. A., Hayes, N., Da Silva, T., & Harris, R. (2023). Professional development and career planning for nurses working in care homes for older people: A scoping review. *International Journal of Older People Nursing*, 18(1), e12519. DOI: 10.1111/opn.12519 PMID: 36441621

Galanis, P., Katsiroumpa, A., Moisoglou, I., Nikiforou, A., Kothonas, K., Athanasopoulou, K., & Panagiotopoulos, E. (2024). Effectiveness of an e-learning activity regarding research methodology and fragility fractures in a sample of nurses: Evidence from Greece. https://doi.org/DOI: 10.21203/rs.3.rs-3975218/v1

Hamid, F. (2024). Effect of massive online courses on improving nurses' performance regarding infection prevention measures. *Zagazig Nursing Journal*, 20(1), 40–60. DOI: 10.21608/znj.2024.335085

Hawkins, J. E., Chiu, P., Mumba, M. N., Gray, S. E., & Hawkins, R. J. (2024). Nurses' Knowledge and Attitudes Regarding the Sustainable Development Goals: A Global Study. *The American Journal of Nursing*, 124(7), 18–27. DOI: 10.1097/01.NAJ.0001025184.93381.68 PMID: 38837235

Horta Reis Da Silva, T. (2022). Falls - prevention, assessment and management. In Curr, S., & Fordham-Clarke, C. (Eds.), *Clinical Skills at Glance* (pp. 130–131). Wiley. [56]

Huang, H., & Fang, Y. (2023). Stress and coping strategies of online nursing practicum courses for Taiwanese nursing students during the covid-19 pandemic: A qualitative study. *Health Care*, 11(14), 2053. DOI: 10.3390/healthcare11142053 PMID: 37510494

Hueske, A., Pontoppidan, C., & Iosif-Lazar, L. (2021). Sustainable development in higher education in Nordic countries: Exploring e-learning mechanisms and SDG coverage in MOOCS. *International Journal of Sustainability in Higher Education*, 23(1), 196–211. DOI: 10.1108/IJSHE-07-2020-0276

İnangil, D., Dinçer, B., & Kabuk, A. (2022). Effectiveness of the use of animation and gamification in online distance education during pandemic. *Computers, Informatics, Nursing*, 40(5), 335–340. DOI: 10.1097/CIN.0000000000000902 PMID: 35266898

Isangula, K., Pallangyo, E., & Ndirangu-Mugo, E. (2023). Improving nursing education curriculum as a tool for strengthening the nurse–client relationships in maternal and child healthcare: Insights from a human-centered design study in rural Tanzania. *Frontiers in Public Health*, 11, 1072721. Advance online publication. DOI: 10.3389/fpubh.2023.1072721 PMID: 36817890

Jan, N. (2023). A literature review of simulation-based training for nurses in India. *International Journal of Advance Research in Nursing*, 6(2), 46–48. DOI: 10.33545/nursing.2023.v6.i2.A.340

Jeon, H. (2024). The impact of virtual simulation in capstone design: Enhancing communication, critical thinking, and team efficacy. *Asia-Pacific Journal of Convergent Research Interchange*, 10(2), 709–719. DOI: 10.47116/apjcri.2024.02.54

Ji, Y., Lee, H., Lee, T., Choi, M., Lee, H., Kim, S., Do, H. K., Kim, S., Chu, S. H., Park, J., Kim, Y. M., & Park, T. (2021). Developing an integrated curriculum for patient safety in an undergraduate nursing program: A case study. *BMC Nursing*, 20(1), 172. Advance online publication. DOI: 10.1186/s12912-021-00694-0 PMID: 34535121

Kang, Y., Yang, I., Lee, E., & Bang, C. (2022). Development of international nursing standard–based curriculum for north Korean nurses. *International Nursing Review*, 69(4), 503–513. DOI: 10.1111/inr.12761 PMID: 35775835

Kim, S. (2024). The effect of metacognition and self-directed learning readiness on learning performance of nursing students in online practice classes during the covid-19 pandemic period. *Nursing Open*, 11(1), e2093. Advance online publication. DOI: 10.1002/nop2.2093 PMID: 38268284

Kim-Godwin, Y., Matthias, A., & Dieckman, L. (2022). Graduate nurse educator students' perceptions of the use of narrative pedagogy in online learning: A pilot study. *Nursing Education Perspectives*, 44(4), 241–243. DOI: 10.1097/01.NEP.0000000000001053 PMID: 36731071

Kosteniuk, J., Stewart, N., Wilson, E., Penz, K., Martin-Misener, R., Morgan, D., Karunanayake, C., & MacLeod, M. (2019). Communication tools and sources of education and information: A national survey of rural and remote nurses. *Journal of the Medical Library Association: JMLA*, 107(4). Advance online publication. DOI: 10.5195/jmla.2019.632 PMID: 31607811

Langan, L., Halligan, P., Frazer, K., Darley, A., Goodman, L., & Redmond, C. (2022). Inclusive pedagogy in online simulation-based learning in undergraduate nursing education: A scoping review protocol. *HRB Open Research*, 5(39), 538–554. DOI: 10.12688/hrbopenres.13557.2 PMID: 37224309

Lhbibani, A., Daaif, J., Lotfi, S., Tridane, M., & Belaaouad, S. (2022). Effect of online training in the continuing education of nurses in hospitals in the casablanca-settat region. *The Open Nursing Journal*, 16(1), e187443462208100. Advance online publication. DOI: 10.2174/18744346-v16-e2208100

Molato, B., & Sehularo, L. (2022). Recommendations for online learning challenges in nursing education during the covid-19 pandemic. *Curationis*, 45(1). Advance online publication. DOI: 10.4102/curationis.v45i1.2360 PMID: 36331216

Mukattil, N., & Pangandaman, H. (2024). Barriers and strategies in the implementation of virtual learning modalities amid covid-19 among students in nursing schools at Sulu province, Philippines. *Critical Medical and Surgical Nursing Journal*, 13(1), 20–25. DOI: 10.20473/cmsnj.v13i1.51366

Nurse-Clarke, N., & Sockol, L. (2022). An exploration of resiliency among nurse educators during the covid-19 pandemic. *Nursing Education Perspectives*, 43(5), 283–286. DOI: 10.1097/01.NEP.0000000000001014 PMID: 35947139

Osingada, C., & Porta, C. (2020). Nursing and sustainable development goals (SDGS) in a covid-19 world: The state of the science and a call for nursing to lead. *Public Health Nursing (Boston, Mass.)*, 37(5), 799–805. DOI: 10.1111/phn.12776 PMID: 32716089

Ossiannilsson, E. (2023). Open educational resources (OER) and some of the United Nations Sustainable Development Goals. *International Journal of Information and Learning Technology*, 40(5), 548–561. DOI: 10.1108/IJILT-01-2023-0002

Padilla, B. (2023). Using the community of inquiry as a framework to promote online teaching and learning in advanced practice nursing education. *Journal of the American Association of Nurse Practitioners*, 35(9), 575–581. DOI: 10.1097/JXX.0000000000000909 PMID: 37410024

Reis da Silva, T. H. (2023a). Falls assessment and prevention in the nursing home and community. *British Journal of Community Nursing*, 28(2), 68–72. DOI: 10.12968/bjcn.2023.28.2.68 PMID: 36735363

Reis da Silva, T. H. (2023b). Ageing in place: Ageing at home and in the community. *British Journal of Community Nursing*, 28(5), 213–214. DOI: 10.12968/bjcn.2023.28.5.213 PMID: 37130715

Reis da Silva, T. H. (2024a). Chapter 7 – Emotional Intelligence in Higher Education: Humanising Technology for Holistic Student Development. In Tikadar, S.; Liu, H.; Bhattacharya, P.; Bhattacharya, S. *Humanizing Technology With Emotional Intelligence*. Pp. 145-168. IGI Global. DOI: 10.4018/979-8-3693-7011-7.ch007

Reis da Silva, T. H. (2024b). The Value of Emotional Intelligence in Midwifery: Enhancing Care and Outcomes for Mothers and Infants through Sustainable Development Goals and Leadership. *Journal of Womens Healthcare & Midwifery Research, 3*(4), 1-6. SRC/JWHMR-133. Link: https://www.onlinescientificresearch.com/articles/the-value-of-emotional-intelligence-in-midwifery-enhancing-care-and-outcomes-for-mothers-and-infants-through-sustainable-developme.pdf

Reis da Silva, T. H. (2024c). Chapter 8 – Emotional Intelligence in Teaching Geriatric Nursing: Humanising Technology for Compassionate Care in Higher Education. In Tikadar, S.; Liu, H.; Bhattacharya, P.; Bhattacharya, S. *Humanizing Technology With Emotional Intelligence*. Pp. 145-168. IGI Global. DOI: 10.4018/979-8-3693-7011-7.ch008

Reis da Silva, T. H. (2024d). Chapter 12 – Emotional Intelligence in Integrative Medicine: Enhancing Patient-Centred Care Through Humanised Technology. In Tikadar, S.; Liu, H.; Bhattacharya, P.; Bhattacharya, S. *Humanizing Technology With Emotional Intelligence*. Pp. 145-168. IGI Global. DOI: 10.4018/979-8-3693-7011-7.ch012

Reis da Silva, T. H (2024e). Oncology and Cancer Medicine: Understanding the complexities in Older Patients. *Biomed J Sci & Tech Res 55*(3)-2024. DOI: DOI: 10.26717/BJSTR.2024.55.008720

Reis da Silva, T. H. (2024f). Chapter 11 - Integrating business essentials into Gerontological Nursing: Enhancing Care for Older Adults in Diverse Settings. In Sedky, A. *Resiliency Strategies for Long-Term Business Success*. Pp. 283-316. IGI Global. DOI: DOI: 10.4018/979-8-3693-9168-6.ch011

Reis da Silva, T. H. (2024g). Chapter 6 – Navigating Healthcare Complexity: Integrating Business Fundamentals into Nursing Leadership. In Sedky, A. *Resiliency Strategies for Long-Term Business Success*. Pp. 145-168. IGI Global. DOI: 10.4018/979-8-3693-9168-6.ch006

Reis da Silva, T. H. (2024h). Chronic kidney disease in older adults: Nursing implications for community nurses. *Journal of Kidney Care*, 9(4), 174–179. DOI: 10.12968/jokc.2024.9.4.174

Reis da Silva, T. H. (2024i). The Evolution of Nursing for Older Adult: A Historical Perspective. *Associative J Health Sci*. 3(3). AJHS. 000561. 2024. DOI: . Link: https://crimsonpublishers.com/ajhs/pdf/AJHS.000561.pdfDOI: 10.31031/AJHS.2024.03.000561

Reis da Silva, T. H. (2024j). Death and its significance in Nursing Practice. *Palliative Medicine & Care International Journal*, 4(3), 1–7.

Reis da Silva, T. H. (2024k). Falls prevention in older people and the role of nursing. *British Journal of Community Nursing*, 29(7), 335–339. DOI: 10.12968/bjcn.2024.0005 PMID: 38963269

Reis da Silva, T. H. (2024l) Understanding body fluid balance, dehydration and intravenous fluid therapy. *Emergency Nurse*. *32*(4) doi:DOI: 10.7748/en.2024.e2201

Reis da Silva, T. H. (2024m). Can supplementing vitamin B12 improve mental health outcomes?: a literature review. *British Journal of Community Nursing, 29*(3), 137–146. https://doi.org/DOI: 10.12968/bjcn.2024.29.3.137

Reis da Silva, T. (2024n). Advancing Gender Equity In Nursing Care For Older Adults: A Pathway To Achieving The United Nations Sustainable Development Goals. *J Comm Med and Pub Health Rep*, 5(12). Advance online publication. DOI: 10.38207/JCMPHR/2024/JUL051201105

Reis da Silva, T. (2024o). Gender Equity In Healthcare: Integrating Emotional Intelligence To Achieve The United Nations Sustainable Development Goals. *J Comm Med and Pub Health Rep*, 5(12). Advance online publication. DOI: 10.38207/JCMPHR/2024/JUL051202106

Reis da Silva, T. H. (2024p). Loneliness in older adults. *British Journal of Community Nursing*, 29(2), 60–66. DOI: 10.12968/bjcn.2024.29.2.60 PMID: 38300245

Reis da Silva, , T. H. (2024q). Prevalence of elder abuse: A narrative review. *British Journal of Community Nursing*, 29(9), 442–446. DOI: 10.12968/bjcn.2024.0004 PMID: 39240800

Reis da Silva, T. H. (2024r). Pharmacokinetics in older people: An overview of prescribing practice. *Journal of Prescribing Practice*, 6(9), 374–381. DOI: 10.12968/jprp.2024.6.9.374

Reis da Silva, T. H., & Mitchell, A. (2024a). Integrating Digital Transformation in Nursing Education: Best Practices and Challenges in Curriculum Development. In Lytras, M., Serban, A. C., Alkhaldi, A., Malik, S., & Aldosemani, T. (Eds.), *Digital Transformation in Higher Education, Part B Cases, Examples and Good Practices*. Emerald Publishing Limited.

Reis Da Silva, T. H., & Mitchell, A. (2024b). Simulation in nursing: The importance of involving service users. *British Journal of Nursing (Mark Allen Publishing)*, 33(5), 262–265. DOI: 10.12968/bjon.2024.33.5.262 PMID: 38446515

Rembish, M., Snyder, M., Sarage, D., Spadafora, N., & Alexander, I. (2022). Transforming clinical education during a global pandemic: Building new approaches to clinical education. *Nursing Education Perspectives*, 43(5), 325–327. DOI: 10.1097/01.NEP.0000000000001018 PMID: 35947103

Rosa, W., Burnett, C., Butler, C., Rolle, P., Salvage, J., Wignall, A., & Mason, D. (2021). The ICN global nursing leadership institute: Integrating the SDGs into leadership and policy development. *The American Journal of Nursing*, 121(12), 54–58. DOI: 10.1097/01.NAJ.0000803204.19511.8a PMID: 34792506

Rossler, K., Sankaranarayanan, G., & Duvall, A. (2019). Acquisition of fire safety knowledge and skills with virtual reality simulation. *Nurse Educator*, 44(2), 88–92. DOI: 10.1097/NNE.0000000000000551 PMID: 29847356

Siah, C., Lim, F., Lau, S., & Tam, W. (2020). The use of the community of inquiry survey in blended learning pedagogy for a clinical skill-based module. *Journal of Clinical Nursing*, 30(3-4), 454–465. DOI: 10.1111/jocn.15556 PMID: 33174239

Silva, S., Gates, M., & Waczek, A. (2021). Utilization of an online education module and standardized patient simulation experience to improve nursing student learning outcomes with heart failure patients. *Nursing Education Perspectives*, 43(3), 178–180. DOI: 10.1097/01.NEP.0000000000000782 PMID: 33660684

Stanley, M., & Martin, C. (2019). Training model for online nurse educators. *Journal of Nursing Education and Practice*, 9(6), 82. DOI: 10.5430/jnep.v9n6p82

Wea, L. (2022). Effect of the standard operating procedure box method to increase self-confidence and basic nursing skills of nursing students during the covid-19 pandemic. *Gaceta Medica de Caracas*, 130(Supl. 5), S1101–S1107. DOI: 10.47307/GMC.2022.130.s5.33

Weaver, M., Jenkins, R., Wichman, C., Robinson, J., Potthoff, M., Menicucci, T., & Vail, C. (2019). Sowing across a state: Development and delivery of a grassroots pediatric palliative care nursing curriculum. *Journal of Palliative Care*, 36(1), 22–28. DOI: 10.1177/0825859719889700 PMID: 31771423

Xing, W., Ao, L., Xiao, H., Cheng, L., Liang, Y., & Wang, J. (2018). Nurses' attitudes toward, and needs for online learning: Differences between rural and urban hospitals in shanghai, east China. *International Journal of Environmental Research and Public Health*, 15(7), 1495. DOI: 10.3390/ijerph15071495 PMID: 30011965

Chapter 8

Interactive Activity Communications That Support Course Implementation and Instructional Engagement:

Creating Digital Spaces in Distance Education

Janice Newsum
https://orcid.org/0009-0001-4222-5043
University of Houston-Clear Lake, USA

Sharon K. Andrews
University of Houston-Clear Lake, USA

Caroline M. Crawford
University of Houston-Clear Lake, USA

ABSTRACT

Three participants come together in a multiple case study approach, to analyze learner-focused and instructor-focused interactive activities within distance learning environments. Instructors and learners are considered from an instructor perspective, reflecting upon specific experiences, implementing and facilitation communication dynamics in distance education courses, from a learner experience and an instruc-

DOI: 10.4018/979-8-3693-7595-2.ch008

tional facilitator experience. Equally impactful is the consideration towards the extent that distance education has changed during the participant's careers as embedded in the higher education field. Additionally, consideration towards generative artificial intelligence, large language models as considerations towards machine learning, and simulations, are considered as current and future considerations within distance education course implementation and instructional facilitation efforts. Emphasized are significant gaps in practice and gaps in the literature.

INTERACTIVE COMMUNICATIONS IN DIGITAL LEARNING ENVIRONMENTS

The latest technology trends directly impact the ever-evolving digital learning landscape is continuously impacted by newly introduced as well as touted technology trends that support and guide the process associated with course implementation and instructional facilitation. Through this understanding, the learning management system environment (LMS) within which structured learning experiences are engaged, has evolved into an impactfully controlled environment within which course design is structured as an underlying philosophical understanding associated with course design and development; however, the LMS is equally impactful around course implementation and instructional facilitation within distance education environments.

A recognition of the Scholarship of Teaching and Learning (SoTL) is imperative within this discussion, due to the recognition that SoTL is an inherent concern within the learning that occurs within digital spaces. The more recent work in the field (Cruz, 2024; McDonald III et al., 2024; Smith & Walker, 2024; Wald & Harland, 2024) is bound within the work of Bishop-Clark and Dietz-Uhler (2012), Bishop-Clark et al. (2023), Fanghanel (2013), and Hutchings et al. (2011), emphasizing the framing of scholarship within the frames of the teaching and learning process, no matter whether within the more traditional learning environments or distance education environments of digital spaces.

How a course is designed directly impacts a course delivery, recognizing course implementation as well as instructional facilitation as guided by the LMS structure. Efforts associated with motivational theory that includes self-efficacy (Schunk & DiBenedetto, 2016, 2021; Schunk & Usher, 2011) and self-regulation (Pintrich, 1999; Schunk & Zimmerman, 2008) are impactful, as well as a recognition of the strengths associated with basic understandings associated with the instructional design process (Nilson & Goodson, 2021; Rao, 2021; Straub & Rummel, 2020). Yet, with the introduction of the more recent generative artificial intelligence (AI) tools with a nod to large language models (LLMs), as well as an overarching effort to embrace machine learning (ML) considerations that also include associated supports, yield a consideration towards course implementation and instructional facilitation.

The engagement of generative AI tools and LLMs within the learning process has been a looping style of understanding, wherein the speed through which AI has evolved within digital spaces has enhanced concerns related to the integration of ML as formal and informal supports for the learning expectations that occur within digital spaces. Learners implement AI as ways through which to develop an understanding of the subject matter, as well as to guide their own learning efforts; however, AI retains the initial knowledge that may be incorrect or even evolve inappropriate or associated mistakes within the prompt results. As such, the learner's analytic ability must be in top form so as to successfully address mistakes and incorrect information within the results presented.

Equally, the integration of AI results into products must be appropriately cited, due to the recognition that all AI results are associated with someone else's work; recognizing this, plagiarism remains a concern. Yet as the development process loops into the next advancements, the learning process and associated assessments must evolve past rote memorization and response or even written documentation of learning, and into an evolved action-oriented usage of the knowledge that reflects creative and novel presentations of learning outcomes.

The efficient acceleration of process and product directly impacts the learning process, as the nuanced approach and guiding efforts associated with generative AI, LLMs, and ML, implement a differentiated layer of course experience and, therefore, ways through which the instructor engages with the learner and may facilitate the course experience. The consideration brought forward highlights concerns related to the serious ethical considerations, curious to what end are resources integrated and implemented as learner support and instructional synchronous versus asynchronous engagement occurring.

The simultaneous evolution or regression of learning within digital spaces is not occurring within a silo, as all forms of formal and informal learning processes are impacted by the quest for learner experience and attainment of competencies as well as capabilities. Intriguing is to probe to what extent might AI, including AI-enriched simulations, revolutionize digital spaces for learning engagement. Examining to what extent, to what outcome, might communication dynamics through interactive activities lead towards a support of course implementation and instructional facilitation within distance education environments is a worthy and perplexing curiosity. A focus upon creating digital spaces for learning engagement introduces the questions associated with the instructional viability of generative AI, LLMs, and ML supports as well as enhancements.

Recognizing the developing engagement of AI, LLMs, and ML supports throughout learning environments, the question arises as concerns to the potential impact upon the learning environment, cognitive engagement, as well as learner self-efficacy associated with the knowledge learning as results in competencies and potential capabilities. A perplexing review associated with how the learning process engagement with AI might, LLMs, and ML supports, engage with learners and the need for interactive activities that occur within learning environments offers an opportunity to examine opportunities within this realm. Specifically, the focus of this discussion is upon interactive activities that occur within digital spaces that are embedded within learning engagement opportunities.

The Scholarship of Teaching and Learning (SoTL) within this discussion, emphasizes the real world recognition and reflection of experts within their own areas of specialization, bridging subject matter expertise with the analytic reflections associated with the teaching and learning process. As suggested by Shulman (2023), "Truth and its consequences in teacher education form a web of interconnected relationships that align our attentions with our intentions" (p. 149), urging the deeply personal engagement as an instructional facilitator who engages deeply in the teaching and learning process. Indeed, as Shulman (2002) suggests:

> *What kind of research on teaching is of most worth? To what extent should researchers in this field be conducting highly functional investigations that attempt to identify the key elements of accomplished teaching or the most important components of teacher preparation programs or experiences? Should we be asking whether teacher education programs significantly improve the likelihood that someone will teach effectively? Should we instead be conducting inquiries that explore the rich complexities of teaching, learning, schooling, and development and the contexts that support them? What genres of research are worth undertaking? (p. 248)*

This chapter focuses upon this inquiry and associated exploration of the personalized analysis of academics who strengthen their own understandings, talents, and tools associated with the teaching and learning process. Additionally, this self-examination supports and enhances the SoTL through the personalized experiences and associated narratives that emerge from the participants' own words.

The interrelated understanding associated with course implementation and instructional facilitation within distance education environments directly emphasizes the creation of digital spaces for learning engagement. Communication dynamics that engage through an understanding of interactive activities may further support this understanding of support and engagement. Indeed, supporting course implementation and instructional facilitation within distance education environments note a continuously evolving as well as devolving understanding of digital spaces.

Moore's work (1989) was the first to highlight the importance associated with the interactive activities that occur within learning environments. Specifically associated with the learner's interactions with course content, with the course instructor, as well as with other learners. This experience occurred within a face-to-face learning environment, as the internet and associated world wide web were not yet available to a wider audience. Yet Moore's (1989) emphasis upon learner interactive activities and learner engagement within the learning experience were vital and considered impactful towards future discussions around interactive activities within different learning environments.

Hillman et al. (1994) was the next to publish a discussion associated with interactive activities, supporting the burgeoning recognition of distance learning engagement through the digital environment, by emphasizing the learner's interactions with the learning environment interface. This was an important enhancement to occur within the discussion associated with interactive activities within learning environments, due to the recognition of the potential within screen-engaged learning opportunities. Burnham and Walden (1997) followed to bring forward an additional form of interactivity, especially within distance learning experiences. The focus on social learning emphasized the learner's community within which the learner experienced information and framed understandings associated with new learning experiences and information engagement within the wider mapping of informational understanding within short-term and long-term memory.

Crawford (2001) enhanced the discussion associated with interactive activities within learning environments, specifically focused upon the distance learning environment, with the introduction of the learner's critically reflective efforts as internal "self" experiences and understandings of the new knowledge and integration into short-term and long-term memory. Equally impactful was Crawford's (2001) move from learner-focused to a recognition of the impact of the instructor's efforts and interactive activity engagement within distance education learning environments, through the introduction of the instructor's interactive activities with the community, the content, the interface, as well as the instructor's critically reflective and critically analytic understandings of "self" (Crawford, 2001, 2003) within distance education learning environments.

Crawford enhanced the already considerable work associated with interactive activities within the learning environment, when Crawford et al. (2021) embraces the learner's as well as the instructor's engagement with the Web of Things within distance education's experiential understanding associated with the encompassing of the world wide web into everyday learning experiences that emphasize the integration of computer devices and computer software systems that are able to interface with learners as well as instructors, through fully communicative engagement and efforts. Crawford et al. (2021) also introduced the interactive activity conception that instructors also bring forward an impact within the learning environment, through the instructor's interactions and either proactive or passive engagement with instructor colleagues within and throughout the learning environment. The interactive activities may be perceived as occurring within traditional face-to-face learning environments, but within the effort towards creating digital spaces within distance education, the focus of this manuscript is upon distance education learning environments and the interactive activity communications that occur so as to support course implementation and instructional engagement.

Through the lens of interactive activities, three higher education professionals considered the communication dynamics towards learning engagement within digital spaces. A multiple inquiry self-study approach was implemented. The reflective queries sought an understanding of the current recognition of generative artificial intelligence (AI) and large language models (LLMs), through a potential association with machine learning (ML), as well as current feasibility of learning management system environments (LMS) and associated impacts upon the associated implementation of digital spaces with equally viable instructional facilitation for learning engagement.

FRAMING THE MULTIPLE INQUIRY STUDY APPROACH

The implementation of a multiple inquiry self-study approach to a deeper metaphoric dive into better understanding philosophies, lived experiences, and developing perceptions associated with communication dynamics that support course implementation and instructional facilitation within distance education environments is important, through the lens of interactive activities within the creation of digital spaces for learning engagement. Two guiding queries supported the consideration and engagement of each participant:

How many years have you taught/instructed/facilitated within learning management system (LMS) environments (WebCT, Moodle, BlackBoard, Canvas, etc.)?

What has been your experience, implementing and facilitating communication dynamics within distance education LMSs?

Four additional guiding queries engaged the participants:

- Please reflect upon your own specific experiences, implementing and facilitating communication dynamics in distance education LMSs. Describe the *learner experience.*
- Please reflect upon your own specific experiences, implementing and facilitating communication dynamics in distance education LMSs. Describe the *instructional facilitator experience.*

- What do you perceive as the changing viewpoints regarding distance education environments, viewed through the academic journey associated with teaching, instructing, and facilitating, within learning management systems (LMSs)?
- What is your current opinion of artificial intelligence (generative AI), large language models (LLMs), machine learning (ML), and simulations, and the potential impact upon communication dynamics within distance education environments?

Participant Descriptive Information and Understandings

Three participants engaged in this multiple inquiry self-study approach to a deeper understanding associated with interactive activity communication dynamics that support creating digital spaces for learning engagement, within course implementation and instructional facilitation within distance education environments. Each case was chosen as worthy of inclusion within this qualitative approach towards more fully understanding the current understanding and potential impact of AI, LLM, ML, and simulations, upon the creation of digital interactive activities and approaches towards communications that specifically support distance education course implementation and instructional engagement. Each participant brought forward extensive experience from an instructional understanding, and specifically within a distance education learning environment, through their personally articulated experiences and understandings.

Of the participants, one is an associate professor and two are full professors within the university level of experience and engagement. The participants each bring extensive instructional experience, with two of the participants having decades of elementary and secondary K-12 classroom teaching and professional staff experience, while the participants as a cumulative statement bring forward almost seventy years of higher education's university experience and instructional expertise. With a multitude of kudos and awards between the participants, it is worthy of note that one participant received the student alumni's outstanding professor award; this highly impressive award was achieved through distance education learner experiences and never previously engaging the learner nominees in face-to-face instructional engagement.

Recognizing the expertise and extensive experiences of the three participants included in this multiple inquiry self-study approach, it was deemed an acceptable approach through which to bring forward a depth and breadth of critically considered and cumulatively reflective understandings associated with the focused interactive activity communications that support course implementation and instructional engagement within the focus upon creating viable digital spaces within distance education environments.

Participant One Philosophy and Experience

I am viewed as a superior academic professional with extensive distance education course design, development, and implementation experience. I have created content for implementation within distance education learning management systems (LMSs) for well over fifteen years of my professional career. During this period, I have progressed forward through my academic career, to achieve full professor in a program that has earned prestigious national recognition as a quality program in my area of specialization.

My experience associated with designing and creating digital spaces for learning engagement, specifically within learning management system environments, is well established. My experience reflects that I have taught graduate classes within various LMS environments for more than 15 years. Blackboard and Canvas are the two most recent LMS environments I have used. On a superficial level, communication dynamics is supported very similarly within Blackboard and Canvas. Meaning, if I follow a simplified course structure where students are guided in step-by-step linear fashion then there is not a clear advantage to course design and delivery between these two LMA. However, there is a clear advantage to using BlackBoard to create a hierarchical and cyclical course structure that results in a more in-depth, effective, and context reflective navigation design that mirrors the data flow and control flow needed to convey technical software processes as is fundamental to teaching system design, architecture, system modeling and testing.

Trying to use Canvas to support this type of more complex course materials has proved cumbersome. Basically, when moving my course to canvas from blackboard my course structure had to be flattened and much of the inherent dynamics of material presentation lost, while implementing a different navigation route through the subject matter. The previous and next buttons that are auto added onto each file imposes a control flow restriction that does not make sense in every course design, but this feature is core and must be either worked around or students instructed to ignore in the cases of a course design whose flow is not linear.

Also, Canvas imposes a standard set of top-level navigation choices rather than providing for the building of customized navigation, as can be done in BlackBoard. This is another example of the flattening of course design and delivery dynamics. Additionally, the removal of the simple course level ability to color the navigation and background area in a Canvas course is a drawback. In Blackboard, I used a color scheme for the background of all pages in a course instance. When teaching two or more courses at a time, this feature allows me and my students to know instantly what course is being viewed. This reduces the error of loading files into the wrong course as all courses have a unique look and feel. In contrast, within Canvas all standard course sections of Announcements, Assignments, Modules, etc., are composed of the same type, same font, same background color, and all navigation sections are a subset of a limited defined set.

Customization is not provided except within the pages feature. This may simplify the Canvas environment to reduce the ability to customize the look and feel of a course, but it does not improve the effectiveness of the course dynamics as color alone can convey fundamental conceptual models held by a user or course facilitator. All of these issues affect the communication dynamics of a course, though not to an unacceptable extent, but certainly at the level of annoyance that has to be worked around either through increased verbal and written instructions or course design. In general, when switching from BlackBoard to Canvas, the linear navigation Canvas imposes upon the implementation and delivery of complex concepts had to be circumvented in less than ideal ways to deliver the natural non-linear dynamics of the course topics.

Participant Two Philosophy and Experience

I bring forward extensive professional experience within the K-12 classroom teaching and teacher leadership roles, with equally impressive experience within the higher education environment at the graduate level of engagement.

While my years teaching/instructing using BlackBoard is approximately seven years, I used other LMS platforms while working in K-12 public education. By the time I left K-12 public education, school districts were utilizing such LMS platforms as Schoology, Google Classroom, and Canvas. More and more K-12 students were learning in virtual space, with educators serving as curators of content and instructional facilitators. For a period of time, flipped classrooms were in vogue, with many K-12 educators assigning work to be done outside of the classroom while in class time was spent engaging in other activities.

As a graduate student, I was introduced to BlackBoard for a master's level degree program. While the program was synchronous with regularly scheduled class times, assignments were completed via independent readings, viewings, and asynchronous discussions. In higher education, teaching with LMSs has been exclusively with BlackBoard and recently with Canvas. While my use of Canvas has been less than a full calendar year, I have six years using BlackBoard since becoming a fulltime faculty member in higher education.

My initial introduction to machine facilitated learning was as a "learner" rather than as "instructor." The K-12 public school district in which I was employed implemented educator professional development using Moodle. These were self-paced learning modules, an approach currently used for university mandated training for both faculty and students. Personally, I find communication dynamics in distance education using an LMS is difficult. Students frequently overthink the assignment or focus on "what the professor wants" rather than on the expected learning. Printed instructions are better facilitated with a rubric, but they can still be misinterpreted or misunderstood.

The program in which I work is asynchronous and requires at least one or two virtual class meetings in an attempt to clarify instructions and expectations. Most of the standard communication methods, discussion boards, emails, assignment feedback, announcements, prove less than ideal compared to the traditional communication in a face-to-face situation where students and faculty are able to take advantage of facial cues, body language, social behaviors, to produce the social interaction as envisioned by Vygotsky (1978) and Vygotsky and Cole (1978).

Participant Three Philosophy and Experience

I have gained extensive experience within many realms of the teaching and learning milieu, from K-12 classroom teacher to business and industry trainer, innumerable professional development presentations associated with different professional organizations as well as academic conference presentations, as well as well over a quarter of a century as a university faculty member who has earned an outstanding professor award from the students. I have been creating online learning supports and instructional guidance many years prior to a recognition of the concept of distance learning, much less the creation of the conception associated with learning management system environments. As a round number, I have been creating online learning supports and instructional guidance for over thirty years. However, specifically related to the query associated with the years within which I have taught, instructed, and facilitated within learning management system environments; the response would be at least twenty-five years of experience.

Within the first year of my accepting a faculty position, my program of study led the way in designing, developing, and implementing online courses within the WebCT LMS. The university shifted LMSs from WebCT to BlackBoard, and recently shifted LMSs to Canvas. Meanwhile, in the midst of the university's push towards online course creation and offering, I continue to enjoy instructing face to face courses, during the time in which the state's oversight committee and the university administration did not conceive of a blended, hybrid, or flipped classroom environment consideration. During these years, I created blended, or hybrid learning and flipped classroom, support resources external to the university-mandated LMS. Specifically, because blended, hybrid, and flipped course experiences were fully developed courses within a regular web site environment. As the state oversight committee and the university recognized the potential strength associated with a blended, hybrid, or flipped course learning enhancement consideration, slowly catching up with what the faculty were already implementing, I would slowly move my previously designed and tested courses into the university LMS environment.

My experience associated with implementing and facilitating communication dynamics within distance education LMSs may be described as extensive. An initial journey into cognitive dissonance and cognitive comfortability within the shift into an online learning environment in the very early days of distance learning understandings, the field was in the midst of touting the focused efforts around the instructional design process. I perceived that a realized *if we build it they will come* erroneous mentality, usually reflecting the design of online courses that metaphorically *included everything and the kitchen sink* mentality that erroneously and foolishly designed courses that were overwhelming from a cognitive standpoint.

During this time, a research colleague and I were intrigued by the integration of graphic semiotic supports within the distance education learning environment. How would graphic signs, symbols, and forms of metaphoric representations of information support Vygotsky's (1978) conception of conceptual frameworks of understanding as well as aligning prior knowledge, working knowledge, and supports for new knowledge acquisition. The innovators who were still standing on the *if we build it they will come* metaphoric soapbox were actively engaged in deriding my semiotic work; however, this worked formed the basis of future endeavors and understandings associated with cognitive supports and perhaps an expanded consideration around social learning affirmations and indications as bound and embedded within distance education environments that found themselves created within LMSs.

Yet, it's equally important and impactful, to recognize that the vast majority of the citizenry were using dial-up internet, so the speed associated with online learning efforts were a major hurdle to overcome. The majority of the courses in LMSs were text-based and uninspiring, with the majority of graphic integration reflecting non-instructional additions with the instructional designer, graphic artist, and instructor's mentality being *because I can*. This appeared to reflect a desire to engage with the online learners and create a more attractive LMS-based learning environment; yet instead of developing a viably engaging course experience, the cognitive dissonance and download time due to the unimportant addition of cute graphics merely added an additional layer of angst and frustration to the learner's already unstable levels of motivation.

During these early periods of distance learning implementation, I printed out several aspects of the course that included the course syllabus, and also burned CDs or DVDs depending upon the size of the instructional materials to share with the learners, and then sent these packets of resources to each learner through postal mail. These efforts were created during my own time, and many times purchased through my own monetary resources, towards an attempt to support a positive learning experience. I was creating resources such as documents, videos, audio files, and additional resources that were meant to enhance the learner's instructional experience as well as motivational engagement within the course experience, but the issues around internet speed and dial-up issues mandated a way to work around the initial foray into distance learning endeavors while equally attempting to support successful learner experiences.

To more directly respond to my experiences associated with implementing and facilitating communication dynamics within distance education LMSs, the majority of efforts and experiences have been focused upon *working around* the mandated LMS tools and philosophically designed and controlling structures that seem to embed a profound sense of power and control over the learning that may occur within the LMS.

COMMUNICATION DYNAMICS: LEARNER EXPERIENCE

Participant One: Learner Experience Ruminations

This participant engaged in a discussion associated with the seven learner-focused experiences associated with communication dynamics.

Learner-Content

Within the LMS system, the learner is supported in interaction with the content depending on the feature of assignment design, course navigation, course discussion and peer feedback. The learner, through assigned tasks in the class, must make use of both synchronous and asynchronous communication tools. Within Canvas and BlackBoard, the synchronous communication tool I use the most is Zoom. Zoom can be used adjacent to the LMS or within the LMS. Students attend zoom session for lecture, demonstrations, guest speakers, and assignment feedback. Zoom is also used by the students to give in class required presentations, and Zoom is also used for office hours and for discussions regarding project or assignments or grading questions. Teams is another heavily used tool that I have used for student meetings. Asynchronous tools include discussion boards with collaboration areas that allow for file sharing and editing about groups of students and of course email as well as canvas announcements.

Learner-Interface

The interface of the Canvas LMS is extremely simple and therefore easily used and understood by any student. The interface to the course I present to the learner is typically centered around phases in the software life cycle and the order of presentation is dependent if course is designed for a planned development process model (like Waterfall) or incremental process model (Agile for example). For example, in my architecture course, the architectural concepts that are relevant to phases of the planned development process model, are presented followed by design phase concepts that require architectural considerations, and so one through testing and maintenance.

Each of these concept topics will involve watching videos, reading assigned papers and PowerPoint slides, and attending the Zoom session for live discussion. After such preparatory work, assignments are given to exercise concepts related to the topic. In BlackBoard, these topics were presented as a set of hyperlinked html files which allowed students to move freely between the various elements of each topic and the different units as needed to prepare and formulate a solution to an assigned project, essay, test, quiz, or software specific knowledge application task. In Canvas, these topics were turned into modules which have an imposed linear order. In Blackboard, the order was not imposed, and the html hyperlinked interface could be used to move through the course via a set of assigned topics depending on the phases of the lifecycle being emphasized.

Learner-Instructor

The communication dynamics between the instructor and the student within the Canvas LMS and Blackboard LMS both support and enable communication with discussion groups, discussion areas, class announcements and display of task deadlines. In addition, in class synchronous communication is best supported and heavily enhanced by regular synchronous Zoom sessions which can be held within the LMS or in conjunction with.

My course is designed so that students must access, read, and absorb the notes, reviews, lectures, and videos in order to understand the basic knowledge and then synthesize and apply this knowledge by performing the assignments. As the instructor, my role is to provide the information in several different communication styles and with multiple different viewpoints with different mediums of delivery. Examples of different viewpoints include my viewpoint as a subject expert, videos, and papers that express other known experts' viewpoints of the same topic. I make it a point to provide different mediums of expression of these viewpoints such a textual as in narrative writings, graphical as in html pages with graphics that contain hyperlinked explanations as well as automation of animation that illustrates the process control and process steps including inputs and outputs that the learners need to understand.

Learner-Learner

Peer feedback is a feature of Canvas that directly supports communication dynamics from student to student. Assignments can be designated as requiring peer feedback and the peers assigned by the instructor or randomly assigned by Canvas. This feature can increase communication and engagement among the students. Utilizing group discussion as an integral part of the course can increase the dynamics of engagement also. If the group discussion is centered around the tasks required of a semester long group software development project, as mine typically are, the group discussion becomes a major driving force in communication dynamics. Some students will lean heavily on other group members, basically not contributing, and if so, this is easy to track and identify in the group discussion area, as well as with use of the Canvas New Analytics feature.

Most of my courses are designed so that students can take the course and learn the material without a lot of interaction with other students. There is of course the usual exception of group assignments and group discussion and peer feedback, that I provide for supports student's efforts at working with other students in the class. I vary the number and depth of group assignments from semester to semester, as well as the number and depth of required group discussion and peer feedback. In project classes, group projects are the main emphasis and students must primarily work together to specify, design, and implement a software project. In such classes, group work can be both rewarding and frustrating depending on the group makeup. Students who are non-contributing to the group become a stress factor for the group and students typically will report such behavior. There is typically one student in each class that starts the class with this behavior. In most cases this student's behavior is remedied once they realize their grade is negatively affected by this.

Learner-Self

Ideally, the course material should be designed in such a way that learners can navigate the topics as the course designer intended and with clear directions and ample resources provided. The bulk of the learning materials provided should be readily and easily available. In my courses, learners are provided within Canvas the necessary background reading materials and videos, as well as question and answers files that surround each course topic which are framed to ask important questions regarding the topic and provide multiple depth levels of answers that address the questions. Also, topic reviews are provided, as well as PowerPoint slides that were used in lecture and recording videos that explain and demonstrate the various course topics. These are designed with the intent of the single student reviewing these files and videos in preparation for project assignments, quizzes, course discussions, and presentations.

The course is designed so that a learner can hopefully find a mode of instruction most suited to the type of learning they find most beneficial. For example, if a student's learning styles responds well to multiple explanations of the same concept from different viewpoints and in different mediums then that is available. If the student finds attending a zoom session and bringing a set of questions to ask of the instruction and engage in a discussion with the instructor and or the class, that is an option as Question-and-Answer Zoom sessions are held for each online class. Additionally, a set of self-check quizzes are provided for students to take up to three times each to test themselves on their understand of very base fundamental concepts.

Learner-Community

In support of a community of learners, the Canvas LMS has features built in that allow for access to the university library and as well as a *Commons* area where course models in various topics have been posted by instructors and made freely available. My course design addresses all learners in my class as a community of learners most directly in student required topic presentations. In many of my classes the course design involves assigning each student a unique topic in the class. Each student must study that topic and understand the basics of the topic, its intersection with the class objectives, why the topic is important to the course, advantages, and disadvantages relative to the topic and other fundamental understandings important to the topic. The topic assigned will be fairy fine grained to allow for all such ideas to be ascertained in a relatively short amount of time (four weeks for example) and can be presented in about 20 to 25 minutes in an oral presentation.

The goal is for the student to present the topic to the class and be able to answer questions I may pose to the student during the presentation. It is in effect a mini oral exam. This type of exercise has proven to hone the student's motivation for preparation, knowledge acquisition, and study skills. Also, during the presentation, I will not only question the student but correct any misunderstanding or misstatements and give advice on what the student needed to include or should have left out or should clarify and expand.

This activity lets the other students in the class have a dynamic view of a detailed discussion of the topic. Other students learn from the interaction as much as the presenter. This is most effective, but it is quite exhausting for both the student presenter and the instructor. It requires a lot of class time so is only feasible in classes of about 15 or less which fortunately is a typical graduate class size in my program.

Learner-Web of Things

In my classes, students utilize all freely available open-source software tools to assist with class assignments. Most of my classes require the specification, design and coding of a software product that may interact with web-based tools or cloud-based servers or databases. Essentially class activity involves the design of tools others will utilize in the Web of Things.

In my course design, I have access to freely available tools the students may find helpful in both the course itself as well as outside of the course. Tools such as web site generators, word processors, spreadsheets, wikis, software measurement tools, and software analysis tools. Also, some course designs will require students to find available software tools and use these tools and compare and analyze such tools. Assignments to analyze AI tools is an example of some of the most current ones I have incorporated into the course design of some of my courses.

Participant Two: Learner Experience Ruminations

This participant engaged in a discussion associated with the seven learner-focused experiences associated with communication dynamics.

Learner-Content

Vygotsky (1978) and Vygotsky and Cole (1978) perceived learning as socially mediated, which begs to question if social interactions extend beyond person to person to machine to person interactions more prevalent in modern society. Although Vannevar Bush (1945, 2021) brilliantly suggested the concept of an information society in which the collective knowledge, the collective memory, would be housed in an easily accessible environment, it is hardly likely that 20th century educational thought leaders could have envisioned the technological advances of the 21st century that so fundamentally changed the learning landscape facilitated by artificial intelligence, large language models, and machine learning.

With the dawn of the internet and the proliferation of computers in education settings, the more traditional methods (Sharma, 2017) of sharing learning content were replaced by machine facilitated instruction. Successful engagement with learner content using an LMS requires learner stamina as readers, good comprehension, and self-directed independence as learners.

Learner-Interface

Accessibility is perhaps the most important element of an LMS. The user experience is greatly augmented by an interface that is easy to navigate and available and optimized for both computers and mobile devices. Students' usability of an LMS can more than likely be correlated to the ease of use.

The transition from the long-used BlackBoard to Canvas resulted in some angst for both faculty and students. The expectations that Canvas offered features similar to the very familiar BlackBoard, were not adequately met. For example, although available within Canvas, Zoom does not allow students to create meeting invites. Google documents do not function well within Canvas and require a download to access. These nuances of using a new LMS have a learning curve that varies from individual to individual.

Learner-Instructor

The primary role of the instruction in distance learning is to help develop community within the course. When students feel isolated in online courses, it is important to attempt to increase participation with others in the course. Personally, creating a community has proven difficult for me as an instructor. I recognize that my learning style is more individualistic. Group assignments have not proven to be successful and while students have the same assignments, they approach the assignments differently.

Learner-Learner

Students frequently create their own learning network with each other. Students communicate through the email system within the LMS and communicate via the discussion forums within the courses. My experience has been that the dialogue (via discussion forums) seldom extends beyond the required minimum two responses to classmates.

The graduate level students that I work with are all fully employed people with families and other responsibilities. They are not the traditional students, which impacts their ability to interact with each other. In terms of adult learning, distance learning is convenient and allows for the continuation of employment opportunities while upgrading academic credentials.

Learner-Self

The implementation of LMSs allows students to take ownership of their own learning. Self-responsibility for improving skills, obtaining new knowledge, securing additional credentials, is easily facilitated by computer-based systems. I have emphasized to my students that while online/distance education offers greater flexibility, it also requires self-discipline and independence.

More time may be required to complete a distance course because of the requirements to read more, research, and actively engage in online discussions. Using project-based learning, connects students to more authentic problems and application driven learning.

Learner-Community

One of the statements I try to reinforce with students is that the instructor is not the only source of information. To encourage students to actively participate with their classmates, they are sometimes directed to ask a classmate before asking the instructor. In general, however, students seem to be frustrated by this approach and I find it ineffective for the most part. Distance education has the benefit of removing constraints of time and place. Distance learners are able to generate defined virtual communities.

Learner-Web of Things

Recently, I asked my daughter a question to which she responded, “I don’t know. You have a tiny computer in your hand. Ask it.” It was at this point that I realized every students’ capability to answer any question, learn new knowledge, and assess information anywhere, anytime. Students have multiple devices, mobile phones, laptops/tablets, e-readers, gaming devices, all of which operate remotely and fairly seamlessly.

Participant Three: Learner Experience Ruminations

This participant engaged in a discussion associated with the seven learner-focused experiences associated with communication dynamics.

Learner-Content

Communication dynamics within distance education environments begin with the learner interface, but quickly shifts to the importance and impactful flow of work associated with the quality of the instructional content. Understanding this, the learner experience associated with the course content that is integrated into the distance education course must ensure an ease of use, and removing the potentially embedded LMS issues that have the potential to cause content issues as well as learner access concerns.

Associated with designing courses, the content takes central focus, with significant time and effort focused upon laying out a flow of content presentation that is equal and paralleled within each course unit of instruction's focus. Everything associated with content must be easily and simply accessible, with the specific intent towards an assurance that the learner's learning, unlearning, and relearning efforts are not impeded by content access issues as well as content ease of understanding.

Learner-Interface

The interface of the distance education course is imperative and is one of the initial aspects of impact upon the learner's motivation as well as conceptualized understanding of the learning experience. Information must be simplistically presented to the learner, easily accessible, and an assurance that important information is not hidden behind several levels of access and puzzling forays that might be considered similar to an *Alice in Wonderland* (Carroll, 1897) journey down a rabbit hole that wastes time, effort, cognitive energy, and learner motivation.

As a simplistic consideration around the madness associate with the Alice in Wonderland journey down the rabbit hole, Callen (2012) suggests that the story reflects the ability of Alice to develop a sense of *becoming* into her own sense of self and stability, communicated through a well described understanding that, "Madness is very much nonsense, or perhaps it is un-nonsense—in any case, Alice in Wonderland is not a story of Alice's finding her way back home as it is of her becoming a 'self' through being with madness" (p. 120).

If one might consider a distance education LMS and the equally impactful course interface decisions to reflect the learning journey inherent within an online course experience, the learner's parallel with Alice's journey emphasizes the nuanced ability to maneuver through the LMS and associated online course design, towards achieving a viable learning experience and associated sense of learned "self." The distance education interface is directly impactful to the learner success associated with learning, directly impacted by the LMS decisions and equally impactful course design decisions.

Learner-Instructor

I am continuously amazed by the horror stories that I hear from students who have taken distance education courses. This statement is not a university-specific statement but, instead, a global phenomenon wherein the learners share narratives around positive experiences, negative experiences, threatening experiences, and even wildly ridiculous and unbelievable stories about what occurs within distance education courses.

These statements might not be as impactful, if I did not make these statements within the focused response associated with the learner's experiences with the distance education facilitative instructor. The professionalism, the dispositional acuity, the stability, and forthright clarity of the facilitative instructor is directly aligned and impactfully associated with the learner's success throughout the course learning journey. Yet, the horrific stories that I continuously hear form learners about missing instructors, vacuous instructors, instructors who are more interested in demeaning the learners than in supporting the learner's understanding and instructional access. As well as innumerable additional areas of concern, are continuous and have not lessened or weakened in ferocity as distance education has developed from an initial foray into a curious new realm of opportunity that is unknown, and uncomfortable.

Further it is curiously parallel to the concept of the *wild west* of learning opportunity, into a well-established and funded recognition of a *next step* area of growth within all realms of teaching, learning, and talent development. The instructor remains a centric and impactful figure within the learning process. This may be, perhaps partially, due to the efforts to closely align distance education with traditional physical classroom environments.

However, the reality is that the instructor is the subject matter expert in the learning environment and endeavors to guide the learners towards attaining learning objectives, that may include articulated competencies and forward-leaning capabilities. The importance and impact of the facilitative instructor within distance education experiences *sets the tone* of the course experience, creates the potential for a community culture, and equally creates a level of quality expectation and work requirement that is embedded within the style, flow, and engagement of the instructor within the distance education course experience.

Learner-Learner

Learner engagement within a distance education environment supports the conception that the learners are not floating somewhere out in the ether, the nether regions of distance education learning efforts. I have taken mandatory course-based training events that were so lonely, so unmotivating, and so unengaging, that the growing desperation to feel as if someone else was also experiencing the anxiety-laden angst of a low-quality and exceedingly boring online course, that there was a desperate need to find someone with whom to commiserate. At least within mind-numbing *butt in the seat* courses, learners could roll their eyes in communal anguish, but the digital ethers of distance learning do not easily allow for learners to make connections and easily create a community of support and potential mutual suffering.

Having experienced these types of weak distance education learning experiences, I was desperate in my attempts to create a supportive, viable community environment in courses that I designed and instructed. I carefully designed team experiences into my courses, so that the learners would develop a sense of community, of responsibility to their colleagues, that I equally desired to develop into a form of learner motivation and self-regulation so as to support a successful course experience. The concept of creating learner engagement and connections with other learners was an important element that was designed into courses as a formal expectation; however, equally considered were the extension into informal learner engagements and a desire to hopefully create relational interactions and relationships that would sustain the course experience and perhaps extend beyond the end of the course timeline.

Learner-Self

I perceive the concept of learner-self to reflect a critically analytic, reflective, and ruminating understanding that the learner journeys through during which new learning and new understandings may occur. The learner needs time to consider and reflect upon new knowledge, new information. Equally, the learner needs time to consider how the new knowledge fits into prior knowledge and understandings, within Vygotsky's (1978) conceptual frameworks of understanding, that are equally supported through the social learning engagement with others associated with the learning process.

Designing the expectation for the learner to reflect upon the new knowledge, to work with the new knowledge so as to develop a sense of expanded understanding and working engagement so as to support not only cognitive approaches to learning but also the potential for *muscle memory* that may be cognitive in nature but may equally be real world design and development of viable deliverable products that support a recognition of competency achievement and that is focused upon the learner's understanding of self as well as self-efficacy.

Learner-Community

The learner's integration and embedding within the larger distance education community is one way through which to consider the learner-community interactive activity engagement; however, this type of interactive activity equally suggests and reflects upon the concept of learning in landscapes of practice (Wenger, 1998; Wenger-Trayner, et al., 2014; Wenger-Trayner & Wenger-Trayner, 2015, 2020) that are far beyond the metaphoric four walls of a course learning experience and evolves into the learner's natural community that may include family, friends, co-workers, supervisors, and even expand into other course learning experiences and other facilitative instructors.

The ability of the learner to expand their learning into a larger realm and gently test their new knowledge and understandings is important and impactful to my own course design as well as expectation that the course information and associated experience remains useful and is retained as viable to the learner far beyond and long after the distance education learning experience has been forgotten.

Learner-Web of Things

Learners are consistently pulling together old information, new information, research efforts, interactions with other learners and subject matter experts, and innumerable other and associated resources so as to embrace the concept of learning within the digital age. Especially within a distance education learning environment, the importance and impactfulness associated with resourcefulness is brought forward, supporting the concept associated with the interconnectedness of information and resources. This is the concept undergirding the Web of Things (WoT) within the distance education learning environment.

How do learners pull together information and resources, towards creating new understandings, new applications of ideas and information, in new and potentially creative ways? The creativity embedded within professional knowledge, understandings, and experiences, is a perfect melting pot within which learners have an opportunity to embrace the WoT concept and create something that has never before been conceived, within the supportive structure of a relevant and hopefully well-designed distance education instructional experience.

COMMUNICATION DYNAMICS: FACILITATOR EXPERIENCE

Participant One: Facilitator Experience Ruminations

This participant engaged in a discussion associated with the six facilitator-focused experiences associated with communication dynamics.

Instructor-Community

My experience with facilitation of improved communication dynamics among instructors as a community of facilitators of online course design within an LMS have centered around the recognition of course design as the application domain and the design of course materials as the products in that domain that (Andrews, 2021c). As noted by Andrews (2021c),

Recognizing online course development as a domain and the course itself as a product, the RDM-OC is a risk-driven process that guides development of a course that promotes good course design by capturing heuristics from a community of practitioners. Collaboration between novice and expert practitioners can further shape the model's knowledge base over time. The model's process steps guide knowledge base creation and use of the knowledge captured to create products. The model serves as a framework and focus for collaboration during the elicitation of an expert's course development knowledge. The collaboration activities are focused by the structures defined by the model which drive documentation of expert heuristics within a knowledge base. (p. 146)

The RDM-OC model (Andrews, 20021c) builds upon previous work associated with the risks and requirements identified for the product (Andrews & Sheppard, 2020) and forms a framework that enables the theories of good course design to be explicitly captured and subsequently updated, expanded, or revised. The model provides for reuse of course design knowledge within a given domain enabling formal collaboration within a community of practitioners.

My online courses are designed for my use only and are not shared purposely by myself with the community of other instructors at large. Nor are my course materials placed in public sites for download. However, students are known to download course materials and distribute them. With the use of AI, I believe students will be feeding all course materials into the AI tool sites to that most of the hard designed course materials will be used without attribution.

Instructor-Content

My experience with online course creation has taken place over 20 years and predates any LMS system. My online courses design from the mid-1990s were housed simply as websites and were quite extensive, colorful, and engaging with built in web-page animations that illustrated the various software life cycle models. Online testing support and Online group discussion were added in late 1990s with the transition to Blackboard LMS. During this transition to Blackboard, the content was modified to conform to multiple modes of instruction and the interaction between instructional designers and instructors increased as courses progressed to fully online within an LMS (Andrews, 2021b).

The evolution of distance of education in my Software Engineering Graduate program and its relationship to the content that was produced for the various modes of instruction have been detailed in Andrews (2021b). Essentially the delivery modes, and the corresponding content type required, started in 1995 with 2-way satellite, 100% synchronous delivery, to Web Supported 10% synchronous deliver, to 100% Online 100% Asynchronous to today's mix of delivery modes as 100% Online or <50% online or >50% online with a blend of synchronous and asynchronous is all classes.

My online courses are all designed so that I can change the course easily from semester to semester in terms of the topics to be included, the types of assignments, the number and types of quizzes and the types of projects. For example, I have developed for each course an extensive database of quiz questions for a fine-grained set of topics contained in each course. Each topic is contained in a quiz data base in BlackBoard, and in Question Banks for each topic in Canvas. Each topic contains between 30 – 60 questions with half essay and half of multiple choice. From this database a quiz in any course can be quickly created for a topic or set of topics. This is one of the more efficient aspects of my course design. The assignments are not as modular and cannot be generated from a set of topics but instead, be hand designed or reused. I typically do not reuse assignments or quizzes unless several years have passed in between uses.

Instructor-Interface

The communication dynamics of Interfacing with an LMS is impacted by both the features of the LMS as well as the instructor's beliefs regarding what impacts the instructional success of the learner as well as beliefs regarding the instructional success of the learning environment (Andrews et. al., 2021c). For most, these beliefs formed from years of design, delivering and teaching within online, blended and face to face environments where instructors build conceptual models around how an instructor instructs, how an instructor believes other people learn, and how an instructor believes a subject is best taught (Andrews et.al., 2021c). In support of these beliefs an LMS needs to have features to:

- support tasks that implement the conceptual model of how one instructs;
- support tasks the instructor needs to both design and deliver effectively to allow students to learn; and
- provide for reasonable navigation and tools to support the instructors conceptual model of creating and supports class tasks that will result in the subject's topics being well taught.

The interface in my course design is centered around a central content document which is an html document that links all topics to all content related to that topic.

In addition to this, I provide a set of weekly assignments, quizzes, discussion boards, peer reviews and at times special presentation assignments. The navigation through the material from the content html allows the user to move freely from topic to topic as required in order to accomplish the assignments. In effect the content html removes the linear restriction of moving module to module that canvas imposes. Canvas modules include assignment instructions, presentation instructions, and support files for assignments and course tasks.

Instructor-Self

As instructor, my job is to guide the students to and through the set of topics and necessary topic details student must learn to meet the course objectives. The course materials I create deliver these topic details. It is my job to design a course that illustrates and explains the most important concepts needed to apply the skills learned. The selection of topics and the depth of them, what to include and what to leave out is most important. Too many details confuse where not enough detail is insufficient. Knowing what is most important about a topic is the hallmark of good instruction and of an effective course. All class assignments and activity must center and reflect this guiding principle. I don't find that an LMS in and of itself has any noticeable effect on improving my ability to design a course or to improve my conceptual models of what is needed to present concepts in a course. It is a tool to house and deliver but I have found no real inspiration or insight from the tool itself. However, I did find Zoom to inspire new communication dynamics for online learners that were a great improvement over having an online class without a reliable tool to support a synchronous communication component.

In my experience, an online class requires some synchronous aspects for true engagement. But, inspiration for the classroom, such as how to improve the creativity and innovation of engineers and how to inject such knowledge comes not from an LMS, but from research. My classes have been inspired to include research into class projects drawing upon work by Andrews' (2021a) Innovation Process for Problem Conceptualization and work in defining methods for attacking architectural erosion (Andrews & Sheppard, 2020).

Instructor-Web of Things

As instructor I do at times make use of freely available open-source software to assign to students to study or modify or analyze. The communication dynamics of an LMS does not hinder or help me as an instructor in creating courses for students that involve creating products or using problems that involve or interact with the so called "Web of Things."

However, projects in my classes spin off from, as well as directly analyze and create web tools, that support my research projects within the world of human trafficking prevention and detection (Andrews & Crawford, 2022) as well as women in e-sports (Andrews & Crawford, 2021), and the exploration of Fiero and flow in online gaming (Andrews et.al., 2020). The LMS houses the resources the students need to perform these project spin offs and provides the collaboration tools needed such as discussion boards, peer reviews, and file sharing.

Instructor-Instructor Colleagues

Canvas does enable a robust file copying and sharing facility that allows an instructor to easily and quickly copy any part of an existing course to another course. This includes sharing across different instructor's courses which could better enable team teaching. I have not participated in team teaching a lecture course with a colleague, but this is the most prominent example of direct colleague course interaction I can think of. I have given thought to participating in such an endeavor, but it presents a reimbursement entanglement at my university such that I have not been willing to negotiate. I have had discussion regarding how such a course would be structured and I believe if not careful with topic distribution it could be more confusing to the students than helpful. Though I do think the instructors would enjoy the endeavor. However, if the course were a seminar or project style course, I think team teaching could be easily implemented and two or more instructors could be quite engaging and helpful to students.

Participant Two: Facilitator Experience Ruminations

This participant engaged in a discussion associated with each of the six facilitator-focused experiences associated with communication dynamics.

Instructor-Community

I have not experienced an extensive instructor-community in the facilitation of distance education. Much of that may be because we work in isolation and have limited personal contact with the majority of the faculty. With the exception of service activities, there are minimal opportunities for personal interactions with other faculty, especially with faculty outside of the department and program. The once monthly meetings are not conducive to personal interactions.

Instructor-Content

While my great desire is to rework the content of the courses, time and other duties hinder accomplishing that work. Content is updated to be as current as possible and responsive to changing politics and social conditions that impact the work of school librarians. Technological changes are so rapid that it is barely humanly possible to remain in front of the changes.

Instructor-Interface

My experience with the instructor interface of the predominate LMSs has been limited by the platforms themselves. Canvas is especially limited in the options to change colors, fonts, or add images. Having only used Canvas for two semesters, I really have not fully explored the features that will most appropriately enhance the look and feel of the LMS.

Instructor-Self

While some would argue that imposter syndrome is not real, there are times that I feel truly out of place. I acknowledge my shortcomings and personal challenges. At the same time, it seems impossible to work on needed changes because there is always a "new" task to be completed in a short time. Toward that end, however, I proactively accepted a developmental leave, with the goal to organize, revamp, and re-energize.

Instructor-Web of Things

Personally, while I rarely engage with multiple devices, limiting most of my connectivity to a laptop and mobile phone, I am aware that the Web of Things creates an ecosystem of connected technology that makes it possible to even have a "smart" car!

Instructor-Instructor Colleagues

For the most part, my use of the LMS has been on my own. With BlackBoard, there was an attempt to standardize the navigation within the courses. There has been less effort with Canvas.

Participant Three: Facilitator Experience Ruminations

This participant engaged in a discussion associated with the six facilitator-focused experiences associated with communication dynamics.

Instructor-Community

My programmatic environment within which the distance education coursework is embedded, and within a larger organizational environment, is directly impacted. This impact may be a potentially supportive environment within which I can thrive and enhance the instructional success of the learners. However, equally impactful to my support structure and the environment within which the distance education environment metaphorically lives, are negative impacts upon my facilitative efforts within distance education coursework.

Within difficult work environments that may be described as toxic organizations or within which academic mobbing situations arise, the direct impact upon me cannot be easily disregarded or dismissed. Yet, what is academic mobbing? To better understand the direct impact upon myself by the community within which I work occurs, Khoo (2010) offers a well-developed description of the experience:

> *Academic mobbing is a non-violent, sophisticated, 'ganging up' behaviour adopted by academicians to "wear and tear" a colleague down emotionally through unjustified accusation, humiliation, general harassment and emotional abuse. These are directed at the target under a veil of lies and justifications so that they are 'hidden' to others and difficult to prove. Bullies use mobbing activities to hide their own weaknesses and incompetence. Targets selected are often intelligent, innovative high achievers, with good integrity and principles. Mobbing activities appear trivial and innocuous on its own but the frequency*

and pattern of their occurrence over long period of time indicates an aggressive manipulation to 'eliminate' the target. (p. 61)

This type of work environment, work community, takes an emotional and physical toll on myself as the distance education instructor. This directly impacts the development of a strong learning community within the online learning environments, while equally impacting myself as the facilitative instructor. My experiences, well described by Crawford (2023), reflect that:

Instead of finding joy in my job, I began to feel like a cornered animal due to the academic mobbing, manipulations and threats, gaslighting by bullies as well as institutions, the sense of moral injury that occurs within the bounds of institutional betrayal, disinformation that consistently impeded my work efforts, and the impossibility of truthful reconciliation between what is occurring and the humanist reality of quality, productivity, and professional impact. Even the well-meaning sharing of different yet aligned syndromes, such as recognition of tall poppy syndrome, the Procrustean effect, the Dunning Kruger effect, and so many others, did not help move through the trauma of the continuous and impactful experiences. (p. 8)

The discussion around other forms of community engagement is equally impactful upon the distance education environment.

One strengthening and positive impact upon the distance learning environment is the introduction of guest discussants who are embedded in the field of study, in the real world, and who are invited into the distance education environment to discuss the real-world experience associated with the course subject matter. This is an impactful exercise wherein professionals working in the field are invited into the course experience to engage with the learners. This community engagement offers the learners access to opportunities that are comfortable as well as thoughtfully reflective, sharing not only a perspective of the professional field-embedded work environment, while equally engaging the learners in a recognition that the coursework learning and associated experiences are supportive and closely align with the professional expectations that are current and worthy of acknowledgement.

These opportunities more fully develop a recognition of the course experience impact upon learners who may not have previously taken the course experience as a serious representation of real-world professional expectations. I have found the embedding and engagement of the professional community within distance education coursework to be a game-changing reality, that may be deemed to be positively impactful for learners.

Instructor-Content

My engagement with course content is a vitally important aspect of distance education course design, redesign, and continuous improvement expectations. The difficulty associated with ensuring that the course resources are continuously available, that hyperlinked resources remain viable, the course flow of work and course assignments continue to align with appropriate competencies and capabilities that have been articulated in the field, are all continuous efforts. Each time a new resource is integrated into the course experience, the course redesign must be considered, along with an assurance that all resources and linked information remains accessible.

No matter my efforts prior to the beginning of each course experience, no matter the time and effort associated with an assurance that all course materials are accessible, there continues to be at least one issue each semester, in at least one course. The time and effort embedded within the continuous course stability, course enhancements, and potential course redesign are not fully understood by the organization. This means that the time and effort involved in maintaining a quality course environment, and associated course experience within a distance education environment, is under-acknowledged and lacking in understanding by the administrative leadership who are charged with evaluating my quality. This annual review experience tends to ignore these significant efforts on the part of distance education instructors, demeaning the quality of time and effort that strong instructors attempt to focus upon and with which the instructors continuously engage towards an assurance of learner experience and learner success.

Instructor-Interface

The distance education interface is very much controlled by the organization's chosen LMS, directly impacting the course design and flow of work that is capable within the learning environment. As an instructor who desires to create course experiences that are positively impactful to the learners, I find that I spend significant time and effort attempting to understand the LMS environment. This is important, because the intent is not only to understand the LMS environment within which I desire to design distance education courses; but instead, my efforts are more so focused upon attempting to understand the LMS, so that I can design workarounds to address the impediments and poor design that have been experienced within so many LMSs.

Would it be easier and a better use of time, merely to design a course that works within the LMS? Yes, absolutely. But, after recognizing and acknowledging this reality, the inherent quality of the learner's course experience and the desire to enhance the learner's knowledge acquisition so as to embed real world understandings that will enhance the learner's experience and recognition in the professional world, are worthy recognitions that support the use of time and effort by myself as the instructor. This quality endeavor may not be easily recognized nor acknowledged by the organization, but the focus upon student success and the learner's professional journey is, sometimes, reward enough.

Instructor-Self

I have many opportunities to critically analyze and reflect upon what is working well, what is not working well, and differentiated yet significant impacts upon the learner's progression through the distance education experience. This critically reflective time, within which I analyze their pedagogical, andragogical, and heutagogical styles of learning engagement within a facilitative coursework experience, directly support and potentially impact my perception of self. This sympathetic recognition of the reflective efforts and understandings of strengths, weaknesses, opportunities to strengthen my own professional understandings as well as engagements, is a time honored and impactfully continuous journey. The self-efficacy and self-regulatory supports are equally important within a distance education environment, as for the learners.

Instructor-Web of Things

I am in a continuous search for appropriate resources, new information, ways through which the learners can more successfully work with the subject matter, as well as supporting a differentiated approach to the learner's experience within the distance education course experience. The Web of Things (WoT) supports the ability to engage with resources, framing the integration of useful and available resources that have the potential to be designed into the distance education environment. Equally, this is impactful towards ensuring a level of intellectual property and ethics associated with the WoT resources integrated into a course experience.

Instructor-Instructor Colleagues

As an instructor, I find that I learn so much from distance education learner colleagues, as well as instructor colleagues who are impressive facilitative instructors and creative professionals. I learn from instructor colleagues, within my university as well as from distance education instructors from the global stage. As a cyclical support, I find that I equally enjoy sharing and supporting my own learned understandings, tips, and tricks, with other instructor colleagues. The symbiotic professional relationships that naturally arise from a sense of collegial survival, leads to opportunities to learn from each other and thrive within distance education instructional spaces.

CHANGING DISTANCE EDUCATION ENVIRONMENT VIEWPOINTS

Participant One: Perceived Changing Viewpoints

I believe online education should be an aspect of any degree. For graduate programs this aspect should be at least 50%. For undergraduate programs I believe at least 20% of the course work should be online. Between an experienced online instructor, a good LMS system and the use of Zoom or other synchronous meeting tool, it is simply much more practical and effective to reduce the amount of physical on campus time and its associated travel requirements.

AI has not been integrated into my course design except as a class project topic whereby I assign students to analyze, compare and asses current AI Tools and their implementation methods. I have yet to find a need or good reason to use current flawed AI tools to grade, detect cheating, or create my lectures. Software included with Blackboard (Safe Assign) and Canvas to detect cheating is minimally useful. If future plagiarism or other AI tools built into Canvas prove to be correct and reliable then I would test them and consider how I might use them to improve aspects of my course.

Participant Two: Perceived Changing Viewpoints

When distance education first began, it was maligned by "brick and mortar" institutions. I was personally reproached by an academic library director because my MLIS was obtained through a fully online degree program. She very proudly informed me that she "would never hire a person who had gotten a library degree online." At the time, I was merely looking for a way to get a degree that did not require travel to classes, was more favorable to full time employment, and could be accomplished with the least disruption to my family and parenting responsibilities. I was already employed full time as a school librarian and at the time had no interest in seeking other employment. During the 15 years between getting my MLIS and beginning my PhD journey, both public and institutional perceptions of distance education became more positive. Of course, with the COVID19 pandemic, distance education became mainstream.

While my initial view of distance education was driven by the element of convenience, I have come to understand that this type of learning is not for all students. Additionally, in some ways, the learning can be superficial surface learning. Moving students to more critical, higher order thinking can be a challenge. Some of the students I encounter lack the in-depth self-discipline, strong reading skills, effective communication skills in writing, and critical thinking that characterize life-long learners.

Participant Three: Perceived Changing Viewpoints

I enjoy the opportunity to delve deeper into distance education environments, as the years pass. With a personality that is naturally shy and introverted, the opportunity to reach out through a distance and equally supportive is the ability to walk away from the technology in order to take care of myself emotionally, physically, and intellectually, aligns well with my own personality and style. Yet I can understand the learners when they communicate that distance education learning environments are not yet fully viable. The sense of community, the sense of engagement within the larger learning environmental structure, has not yet been well designed within the LMS environment. This may come in time, but currently I find that this next-level of course enhancement remains an illusion and this illusory effort must be proactively designed into the course by the course designer.

In my courses, the course designer is also the facilitative instructor so I have a comfortability with the concept of layering enhancements in an attempt to personalize and more fully engage learners in the flow of learning as well as within the learning community. Even though the past thirty years of distance education efforts have been fruitful due to the growth of the concept from nothingness and moving into a more viable consideration within an organizational structure, the reality is that distance education environments still have a long way to go before being truly viable and worthy of quality recognition. With the COVID-19 pandemic lockdowns that occurred on the global stage, the significant growth of distance education was jump-started and has become a more serious discussion within K-12 and higher education organizations, as well as within business and industry, medical education, and military education, with equal consideration within for-profit and non-profit organizations.

COMMUNICATION DYNAMIC IMPACTS BY AI, LLM, ML, AND SIMULATIONS

Participant One: Communication Dynamic Impacts

This participant engaged in a discussion associated with a snapshot understanding, the participant's current opinion, of generative artificial intelligence (generative AI), large language models (LLMs) as considerations towards machine learning (ML), and simulations.

The communication dynamics are currently negatively affected by my student's rudimentary and unskilled use of current generative AI. The weaker students try to use it to answer homework questions or tests but the answers they submit utilizing such are typically off base or do not directly address the issues required. In other words, so far it is not proving beneficial to use to respond to my assignments or quizzes which require graduate level work. Current generative AI tools are simply a tool and as such is only as good as the understanding of the job the tool is to perform from the person using it.

The use of AI as a vehicle for the student to study and compare software tools in terms of its limitations and strengths, what it can and cannot do well, is a worthy exercise of benefit to graduate software students. Students need to study such tools to be aware of the implementation methods employed and the extent to which each tool is effective. Learning to perform such an analysis and comparison assessment is a highly effective learning activity. The viability of each AI tool resides in the correctness of the large language model it is based upon as well as the correctness of the domain analysis and domain knowledge behind the model. The larger the domain the less likely the model will be correct. The direct use of current AI tools in a graduate software engineering class has little to no benefit as the class requires skills that are very hard to capture and automate in solving novel software problems. AI tools can be of benefit for the generation and reuse of well-known solution to common coding solution to known problems. Such can be used to free the software developer to concentrate on hard to solve novel aspects of system design problems.

Participant Two: Communication Dynamic Impacts

This participant engaged in a discussion associated with a snapshot understanding, the participant's current opinion, of generative artificial intelligence (generative AI), large language models (LLMs) as considerations towards machine learning (ML), and simulations.

The impact of the rapidly evolving technologies of artificial intelligence, machine learning, and simulations are already having a significant impact on distance education. As with any new technology, proper use lags behind creation. Relative to K-12 educators, the nature of these technologies will fundamentally change pedagogy, requiring the development of new assignments to foster creativity, promote ethical use, and ensure cultural relevance. Each of these technologies has the potential for significant positive change in educational practices.

Participant Three: Communication Dynamic Impacts

This participant engaged in a discussion associated with a snapshot understanding, the participant's current opinion, of generative artificial intelligence (generative AI), large language models (LLMs) as considerations towards machine learning (ML), and simulations.

This is a difficult topic through which to fully respond, because I tend to move beyond the marketing and touting of the shiny new toy and progress more swiftly into a so what attitude associated with questioning the viability, the stability, and the worthiness of the tool, to ease the flow of learning without extensive back-end efforts and an egregious learning curve. From this perspective, from this lens, I am currently waiting on the metaphoric sidelines. The different generative AI resources that I've had the opportunity to evaluate have flaws in usability and user experience needs. From an ethical perspective, intellectual property and copyright concerns seem to be continuously ignored or under-considered in the race to create the next big thing. This perception is equally viable, when considering LLMs, ML, and even simulations.

There are some outstanding first step products that demonstrate a potential to develop into future successes, supporting a potential positive growth. Equally, I perceive that there are many processes and flows of work that could be eased by fewer physical hands in the work; this emphasizes an opportunity to integrate AI, MLs, and simulations, as potentially viable resources to ease the workflow. Yet, user experience and stability of resources, including a significant nod towards cybersecurity, must be central topics that remain not only centered and centric to the mission, but equally with ethical considerations associated with an assurance of personal privacy, protection from overstepping boundaries of constitutional rights and obligations, as well as equally considered assurances associated with the viability of product capability and future enhancement growth, that is stable enough to grow upon a strong undergirding structure. There are significant potentials herein, but the desire for a quick buck and moving a shiny new toy to the marketplace must be reconsidered and refocused towards the standard of quality and ethical usage of resources that emphasize intellectual property rights as well as constitutional rights that will not be infringed upon.

THEMATIC FINDINGS

The quality of participant engagement with the different prompts supported a depth and breadth analysis of the data sets, resulting in seven themes: visual acuity; digital spaces; motivation and self-regulation design; quality of course information design and instructor intellectual property; instructional facilitator impact; larger organizational impact; and, impact of generative AI upon learning process.

Visual Acuity

The first theme articulated is an understanding of the impact of visual acuity upon the learner experience throughout the course environment. Participant One reflected that, "I used a color scheme for the background of all pages in a course instance", as well as emphasizing a Canvas interface recognition that, "Customization is not provided except within the pages feature". Further, "All of these issues affect the communication dynamics of a course, though not to an unacceptable extent, but certainly at the level of annoyance that has to be worked around either through increased verbal and written instructions or course design" (Participant One). Visual acuity is recognized as having a direct concern and impact upon the learner by the recognition that:

> *"To more directly respond to my experiences associated with implementing and facilitating communication dynamics within distance education LMSs, the majority of efforts and experiences have been focused upon working around the mandated LMS tools and philosophically designed and controlling structures that seem to embed a profound sense of power and control over the learning that may occur within the LMS." (Participant Three)*

Visual acuity is an environmental impact upon the initial organizational design and learner space and place success.

Digital Spaces

The second theme articulated is digital spaces. Participant Three noted that, "Online learning experience at the beginning of the online course design effort was "a realized *if we build it they will come* erroneous mentality, usually reflecting the design of online courses that metaphorically *included everything and the kitchen sink* mentality that erroneously and foolishly designed courses that were overwhelming from a cognitive standpoint." The initial foray into online digital spaces for learning may have emphasized a narrower recognition and reality, associated with the learning environment. This progressed towards a deeper understanding of the learning process, such as "My initial introduction to machine facilitated learning was as a 'learner' rather than as 'instructor'" (Participant Two), with an understanding that:

> *"Most of the standard communication methods, discussion boards, emails, assignment feedback, announcements, prove less than ideal compared to the traditional communication in a face-to-face situation where students and faculty are able to take advantage of facial cues, body language, social behaviors, to produce the social interaction as envisioned by Vygotsky." (Participant Two)*

Yet consideration towards digital spaces that, "Ideally, the course material should be designed in such a way that learners can navigate the topics as the course designer intended and with clear directions and ample resources provided. The bulk of the learning materials provided should be readily and easily available" (Participant One), urges a real world, balanced approach to understanding:

> *"While my initial view of distance education was driven by the element of convenience, I have come to understand that this type of learning is not for all students. Additionally, in some ways, the learning can be superficial surface learning. Moving students to more critical, higher order thinking can be a challenge. Some of the students I encounter lack the in-depth self-discipline, strong reading skills, effective communication skills in writing, and critical thinking that characterize life-long learners." (Participant Two)*

Digital spaces are imperative and the development of this environmental impact is recognized as being of emphatic importance.

Motivation and Self-Regulation

The third theme articulated is motivation and self-regulation design of online course digital spaces. Participant One suggested that, "Most of my courses are designed so that students can take the course and learn the material without a lot of interaction with other students. There is of course the usual exception of group assignments and group discussion and peer feedback, that I provide for supports student's efforts at working with other students in the class" continuing to reflect that, "The course is designed so that a learner can hopefully find a mode of instruction most suited to the type of learning they find most beneficial" (Participant One). Time allocation was recognized when stated that, "More time may be required to complete a distance course because of the requirements to read more, research, and actively engage in online discussions" (Participant Two). An intriguing metaphor associated with the learning environment is offered by Participant Three:

"If one might consider a distance education LMS and the equally impactful course interface decisions to reflect the learning journey inherent within an online course experience, the learner's parallel with Alice's journey emphasizes the nuanced ability to maneuver through the LMS and associated online course design, towards achieving a viable learning experience and associated sense of learned "self". The distance education interface is directly impactful to the learner success associated with learning, directly impacted by the LMS decisions and equally impactful course design decisions." (Participant Three)

Meanwhile, enhancements that are focused upon the learner's metacognitive analysis of their learning is supported as a motivational endeavor:

"Designing the expectation for the learner to reflect upon the new knowledge, to work with the new knowledge so as to develop a sense of expanded understanding and working engagement so as to support not only cognitive approaches to learning but also the potential for muscle memory that may be cognitive in nature but may equally be real world design and development of viable deliverable products that support a recognition of competency achievement and that is focused upon the learner's understanding of self as well as self-efficacy." (Participant Three)

Designing motivation and self-regulatory supports into the digital spaces offer supports to the success of the learner's experience as well as a focus upon attaining learning objectives.

Quality of Course Information Design and Instructor Intellectual Property

The fourth theme articulated is the quality of course information design that equally includes instructor intellectual property considerations. Strengths associated with the presentation of course materials is reflected by Participant Three:

"Communication dynamics within distance education environments begin with the learner interface, but quickly shifts to the importance and impactful flow of work associated with the quality of the instructional content. Understanding this, the learner experience associated with the course content that is integrated into the distance education course must ensure an ease of use, and removing the potentially embedded LMS issues that have the potential to cause content issues as well as learner access concerns." (Participant Three)

While necessary to the quality of the course information design, the instructor's intellectual property that evolves from not only instructional prowess but also research and creative activities as well as professional service efforts, results in the integration of an instructor's intellectual property and creative works:

"My online courses are designed for my use only and are not shared purposely by myself with the community of other instructors at large. Nor are my course materials placed in public sites for download. However, students are known to download course materials and distribute them. With the use of AI I believe students will be feeding all course materials into the AI tool sites to that most of the hard designed course materials will be used without attribution." (Participant One)

The symbiotic relationship between the quality of the course information design and the instructor's intellectual property supports this theme as vitally important within digital spaces of learning and associated experiential engagement.

Instructional Facilitator Impact

The fifth theme articulated is instructional facilitator impact. This appeared to be a primary focus by Participant Three, initially suggesting that:

"The instructor remains a centric and impactful figure within the learning process. This may be, perhaps partially, due to the efforts to closely align distance education with traditional physical classroom environments. However, the reality is that the instructor is the subject matter expert in the learning environment and endeavors to guide the learners towards attaining learning objectives, that may include articulated competencies and forward-leaning capabilities." (Participant Three)

While an equally balanced understanding is communicated as, "While my great desire is to rework the content of the courses, time and other duties hinder accomplishing that work. Content is updated to be as current as possible and responsive to changing politics and social conditions that impact the work of school librarians. Technological changes are so rapid that it is barely humanly possible to remain in front of the changes" (Participant Two). Equally noted is that:

"The time and effort embedded within the continuous course stability, course enhancements, and potential course redesign are not fully understood by the organization. This means that the time and effort involved in maintaining a quality course environment, and associated course experience within a distance education environment, is under-acknowledged and lacking in understanding by the administrative leadership who are charged with evaluating my quality." (Participant Three)

The course designer as well as course instructional facilitator, sometimes the same person, requires adequate time and effort towards an assurance of course quality.

Larger Organizational Impact

The sixth theme articulated is the larger organizational impact, by digital spaces and interactive activities that occur. Participant Three suggests a cyclical, symbiotic revelation between course experiences and the organization's experience:

"As a cyclical support, I find that I equally enjoy sharing and supporting my own learned understandings, tips, and tricks, with other instructor colleagues. The symbiotic professional relationships that naturally arise from a sense of collegial survival, leads to opportunities to learn from each other and thrive within distance education instructional spaces." (Participant Three)

Further, the fully developed digital learning space engagement as well as enhanced learning experience are realistic areas of consideration:

"Yet I can understand the learners when they communicate that distance education learning environments are not yet fully viable. The sense of community, the sense of engagement within the larger learning environmental structure, has not yet been well designed within the LMS environment. This may come in time, but currently I find that this next-level of course enhancement remains an illusion and this illusory effort must be proactively designed into the course by the course designer." (Participant Three)

How digital spaces are designed as continuously looping representations of distance learning experiences within the organization are directly aligned and impactful to the learner experience.

The Impact of Generative AI Upon the Learning Process

The seventh theme articulated is the insightful understandings associated with the impact of generative AI upon the learning process. As suggested by Participant One, "The viability of each AI tool resides in the correctness of the large language model it is based upon as well as the correctness of the domain analysis and domain knowledge behind the model. The larger the domain the less likely the model will be correct", while "The impact of the rapidly evolving technologies of artificial intelligence, machine learning, and simulations are already having a significant impact on distance education. As with any new technology, proper use lags behind creation" (Participant Two).

Additionally, "The different generative AI resources that I've had the opportunity to evaluate have flaws in usability and user experience needs. From an ethical perspective, intellectual property and copyright concerns seem to be continuously ignored or under-considered in the race to create *the next big thing*. This perception is equally viable, when considering LLMs, ML, and even simulations" (Participant Three). A well-enveloped recognition that generative AI is in its infancy, yet appears to evolve at a rapid speed that may not have been initially expected, suggests that digital spaces that are online learning environments require the space and ability to fully analyze the potential capabilities of generative AI, LLMs, ML, and simulations, in the potential to strengthen digital spaces as distance learning environments.

FUTURE RESEARCH DIRECTIONS

The clear inconsistencies in narratives and distance education experiences that the participants shared, must be more fully studied. Interactive activities within distance education environments are narrowly designed and defined; as such, the communication dynamics that support the course implementation and instructional facilitation within distance education environments are lacking. Not only lacking in capability, but equally lacking in research support. Additional, extensive research must occur so as to develop a baseline of understanding around the topic. The concept of creating digital spaces for learning engagement is equally lacking in research and associated understanding.

A question that naturally arises, refers to the expansive efforts towards designing and creating interactive activities within distance education environments, so as to support learning engagement, that is beyond the tools that are currently available and supports ease of user experience, within learning management systems (LMSs). The introduction of generative artificial intelligence (generative AI), large language models (LLMs) as considerations towards machine learning (ML), and simulations, offers the opportunity to significantly revise the current state of distance education communication dynamics, with consideration towards a game changing understanding of what is appropriate, worthy of inclusion, and supports the learning process through learner engagement.

An intriguing reality is developing, as regards implications of interactions with AI-augmented environments. One serious implication is the significant growth in cloud-based software and tools, that not only indicate cybersecurity concerns but there is a growing concern around the terms of use agreements that have been integrated into the terms of use and terms of service mandates that end-users must accept in order to use the development environment products. As AI-augmented development environment software has become a reality, there is the recognition amongst the creative communities that the terms of use and terms of service agreements have become more all-inclusive and a feeling of "Big Brother" control and ownership associated with someone else's intellectual property and proprietary information access may become a reality.

Currently, this is a significant maelstrom that has metaphorically blown up, around an industry standard software giant's new terms of service related to the cloud-based software development environments. Revisions to the mandatory-to-accept terms of use and terms of service agreement, the recognition that a perceived shift to a "Big Brother" sense of "you will own nothing and be happy" conception related to the software giant's ability to access and revise or use products stored within the cloud-based storage environment has become a reality. How is an account holder expected to work, when the product development and resources are held captive by the software giant's cloud-based storage?

These are equally impactful considerations when considering AI-driven and AI-augmented adaptive learning environments as well as immersive environments that reflect the manuscript's focus upon interactive activity communications that support course implementation and instructional engagement, with consideration towards creating digital spaces in distance education learning environments.

CONCLUSION

The interactive activities associated with communication dynamics are emphasized as opportunities to support course implementation and instructional facilitation within distance education environments. The ability to create digital spaces for learning engagement is currently in its infancy. The concept of student success and learner engagement are currently touted as necessary and viable, but the subsequent understandings associated with creating the resources and ease of work within distance education environments, specifically within learning management systems (LMSs) that focus upon the instructional design freedoms that are necessary and appropriate for course designers and course instructors to easily create, continue to be difficult to implement, layered approaches that are not necessarily easy to implement or available within different layers and levels of LMSs.

Recognizing this, the distance education course designers and facilitative instructors continue to focus upon creative ways to work around what is currently available. However, with the current, significant growth of generative artificial intelligence (generative AI), large language models (LLMs) as consideration towards machine learning (ML), and simulations that tout heightened quality and ease of creation, the quality of communication dynamics within distance education environments may be readying for a significant growth spurt. The desire is towards quality movement forward, with ethics, intellectual property, and constitutional rights as centric areas of emphasis.

In the world of the Scholarship of Teaching and Learning (SoTL), Schulman offers insightful recognitions, including his work related to better understanding diagnostic strategies and the teaching and learning process, noting that, "We had searched for a general method and the secrets of general expertise. Where we had sought the general, we found the particular. Where we had expected the universal, we discovered the specific" (p. v). Further, Shulman reflected upon his experiences, after specifically focusing upon the teaching and learning process, noting that:

What does someone need to know and be able to do to teach something he already understands to someone else who does not? Once again, I was working in a field that assumed the existence and central importance of universal principles of general pedagogy. Instead, we found that teaching and learning, like medical diagnosis, were domain specific. Yes, general methods did exist. But the same teacher who taught one subject well did not necessarily have the capacity to teach another well. Indeed, there were dramatic subject-specific differences in the pedagogical substance and method. (2023, p. vi)

Further reflecting upon investigations into the teaching and learning process, Shuman articulated that:

These studies required us to invent the concept of pedagogical content knowledge, the idea that teaching is itself domain and subject specific. Pedagogical content knowledge became an important idea in teacher education and eventually penetrated higher education circles. In retrospect, the concept of pedagogical content knowledge appears obvious, even inevitable. (2023, p. vi)

The strength of Shulman's work is clearly articulated in his efforts towards guiding the SoTL into not only generalizations of understanding but equally impactful are particularizations that may further enhance an understanding of the teaching and learning sciences, that may reflect not only science but equally impactful is the art and expertise.

Seek generalizations, relish them, challenge them, and take them as far as you can. Seek particularizations, collect them, explore them, and build local neighborhoods of understanding from them. And let those generalizations and particularizations interact and engage with each other, for only in that manner will our capacities for engaging in the practical work of teaching and learning flourish. (Schulman, 2023, ix)

It is through the engagement in analytic efforts of understanding, supporting generalizations as well as particularizations of subject specific as well as the larger umbrella of engagement, wherein SoTL will find its way forward. The understanding of interactive activity communications through which digital spaces that are currently reflected as distance education environments, support course implementation and instructional engagement.

REFERENCES

Andrews, S. (2021a). Innovation process for problem conceptualization. *International Journal of Software Innovation*, 9(3), 91–103. DOI: 10.4018/IJSI.2021070107

Andrews, S. (2021b). The evolution of elearning within a software engineering graduate program. In Crawford, C. M., & Simons, M. A. (Eds.), *Learning engagement in a transformative social learning environment* (pp. 244–262). IGI Global. DOI: 10.4018/978-1-7998-6956-6.ch012

Andrews, S. (2021c). A knowledge-based risk-driven model supporting collaborative online course creation. In L. M. Fraga, S. Hall, & K. Bottaro's (Eds.), *Shifting to online learning through faculty collaborative support* (pp. 142-162). IGI-Global. DOI: 10.4018/978-1-7998-6944-3.ch008

Andrews, S., Bradbury, R., & Crawford, C. (2020, January-March). Fiero and flow in online competitive gaming: The gaming engagement framework. *International Journal of Gaming and Computer-Mediated Simulations*, 12(1), 28–42. DOI: 10.4018/IJGCMS.2020010102

Andrews, S., & Crawford, C. (2021). Barriers, issues and similarities among women in esports and similar mixed gender sports: ascertaining common ground. In Andrews, S., & Crawford, C. M. (Eds.), *Handbook of research on pathways and opportunities into the business of esports* (pp. 25–46). IGI-Global., DOI: 10.4018/978-1-7998-7300-6.ch002

Andrews, S., Newsum, J., Crawford, C. M., & Moffett, N. L. (2021c). Sisyphus leans into the professoriate: faculty discuss career considerations and the academic landscape. In Moffett, N. L. (Ed.), *Navigating post-doctoral career placement, research, and professionalism* (pp. 185–226). IGI-Global., DOI: 10.4018/978-1-7998-5065-6.ch009

Andrews, S., & Sheppard, M. (2020). Architecture erosion: Impacts, causes, and management of issues. *International Journal of Computer Science and Security*, 14(2), 82–93.

Andrews, S. K., & Crawford, C. M. (2022). Synthesizing anti-human trafficking efforts: the paths already taken, amplifiers of risk, and the paths forward. In Andrews, S. K., & Crawford, C. M. (Eds.), *Paths to the prevention and detection of human trafficking* (pp. 1–23). IGI Global. DOI: 10.4018/978-1-6684-3926-5.ch001

Andrews, S. K., Lacher, L., & Dunnavant, T. (2021a). Additional elearning considerations around the instructor's philosophical belief systems: potential transformative impacts. In Crawford, C. M., & Simons, M. A. (Eds.), *eLearning engagement in a transformative social learning environment* (pp. 114–134). IGI Global. DOI: 10.4018/978-1-7998-6956-6.ch006

Andrews, S. K., Michael, T. B., William, M. A., Lacher, L. L., & Crawford, C. M. (2021b). Impact of esports upon higher education from a faculty perspective: transformational pathways and opportunities. In Andrews, S., & Crawford, C. M. (Eds.), *Handbook of research on pathways and opportunities into the business of esports* (pp. 149–178). IGI-Global., DOI: 10.4018/978-1-7998-7300-6.ch008

Bishop-Clark, C., & Dietz-Uhler, B. (2012). *Engaging in the scholarship of teaching and learning: A guide to the process, and how to develop a project from start to finish.* Stylus Publishing, LLC.

Bishop-Clark, C., Nelson, C. E., & Dietz-Uhler, B. (2023). *Engaging in the scholarship of teaching and learning: A guide to the process, and how to develop a project from start to finish.* Routledge.

Burnham, B., & Walden, B. (1997). Interactions in distance education: A report from the other side. In *Proceedings of the Adult Education Research Conference.* Oklahoma State University. http:// www.edst.educ.ubc.ca/aerc/1997/97burnham.html

Bush, V. (1945). *As we may think. The Atlantic.* Tribune Content Agency.

Bush, V. (2021). As we may think. In Lewis, H. R. (Ed.), *Ideas that created the future: Classic papers of computer science* (pp. 107–120). The MIT Press., DOI: 10.7551/mitpress/12274.003.0013

Callen, J. C. (2012). Impossible things: An investigation of madness as resistance in Tim Burton's *Alice in Wonderland.Administrative Theory & Praxis*, 34(1), 120–124. DOI: 10.2753/ATP1084-1806340108

Carroll, L. (1897). *Alice's adventures in wonderland.* Macmillan.

Crawford, C. M. (2001). Developing webs of significance through communications: Appropriate interactive activities for distributed learning environments. *Campus-Wide Information Systems*, 18(2), 68–72. DOI: 10.1108/10650740110386675

Crawford, C. M. (2003). Emerging learning environments: Enhancing the online community. *Academic Exchange Quarterly*, 7(4), 131–135.

Crawford, C. M. (2023). Now what?: A case study on the impact of nefarious Queen Bees. In Clarke, K. L., & Moffett, N. L. (Eds.), *Addressing the Queen Bee Syndrome in academia* (pp. 1–25). IGI Global., DOI: 10.4018/978-1-6684-7717-5.ch001

Crawford, C. M., Andrews, S., & Wallace, J. K. Y. (2021). Co-creative collegial communities of instructional engagement. *International Journal of Hyperconnectivity and the Internet of Things*, 5(2), 38–56. DOI: 10.4018/IJHIoT.2021070103

Cruz, L. (2024). Converging spaces? Re-imagining the scholarship of teaching and learning (SoTL) as the subject of transdisciplinary research. *Transformative Dialogues: Teaching and Learning Journal, 17*(1). DOI: 10.26209/td2024vol17iss11823

Fanghanel, J. (2013). Going public with pedagogical inquiries: SoTL as a methodology for faculty professional development. *Teaching & Learning Inquiry*, 1(1), 59–70. DOI: 10.20343/teachlearninqu.1.1.59

Hillman, D., Willis, D. J., & Gunawardena, C. (1994). Learner-interface interaction in distance education: An extension of contemporary models and strategies for practitioners. *American Journal of Distance Education*, 8(2), 30–42. DOI: 10.1080/08923649409526853

Hutchings, P., Huber, M. T., & Ciccone, A. (2011). *Scholarship of teaching and learning re-considered: Institutional integration and impact*. Jossey-Bass.

Khoo, S. (2010). Academic mobbing: Hidden health hazard at workplace. *Malaysian Family Physician : the Official Journal of the Academy of Family Physicians of Malaysia*, 5(2), 61–67. PMID: 25606190

LearnDash Collaborator. (2020). *How is AI being used in e-learning in 2020?*https://www.learndash.com/how-is-ai-being-used-in-e-learning-in-2020/

McDonald, B. D.III, Hatcher, W., Bacot, H., Evans, M. D., McCandless, S. A., McDougle, L. M., Young, S. L., Elliott, I. C., Emas, R., Lu, E. Y., Abbott, M. E., Bearfield, D. A., Berry-James, R. M., Blessett, B., Borry, E. L., Diamond, J., Franklin, A. L., Gaynor, T. S., Gong, T., & Zhang, Y. (2024). The scholarship of teaching and learning in public administration: An agenda for future research. *Journal of Public Affairs Education*, 30(1), 11–27. DOI: 10.1080/15236803.2023.2294654

Moore, M. (1989). Three types of interaction. *American Journal of Distance Education*, 3(2), 1–7. DOI: 10.1080/08923648909526659

Nilson, L. B., & Goodson, L. A. (2021). *Online teaching at its best: Merging instructional design with teaching and learning research*. John Wiley & Sons.

Online Education. (n.d.). *Artificial intelligence innovations in online learning*. https://www.onlineeducation.com/features/ai-in-distance-learning

Pintrich, P. R. (1999). The role of motivation in promoting and sustaining self-regulated learning. *International Journal of Educational Research*, 31(6), 459–470. DOI: 10.1016/S0883-0355(99)00015-4

Rao, K. (2021). Inclusive instructional design: Applying UDL to online learning. *The Journal of Applied Instructional Design*, 10(1), 1–10.

Schunk, D. H., & DiBenedetto, M. K. (2016). Self-efficacy theory in education. In Wentzel, K. R., & Miele, D. B. (Eds.), *Handbook of motivation at school* (pp. 34–54). Routledge.

Schunk, D. H., & DiBenedetto, M. K. (2021). Self-efficacy and human motivation. In Elliot, A. J. (Ed.), (pp. 153–179). Advances in motivation science. Elsevier Academic Press., DOI: 10.1016/bs.adms.2020.10.001

Schunk, D. H., & Usher, E. L. (2011). Assessing self-efficacy for self-regulated learning. In Zimmerman, B. J., & Schunk, D. H. (Eds.), *Handbook of self-regulation of learning and performance* (pp. 282–297). Taylor & Francis. DOI: 10.4324/9780203839010

Schunk, D. H., & Zimmerman, B. J. (Eds.). (2008). *Motivation and self-regulated learning: Theory, research, and applications*. Routledge.

Sharma, R. (2017). Computer-assisted learning – A study. *International Journal of Advanced Research in Education & Technology*, 4(3), 102–105.

Shulman, L. S. (2002, May/June). Truth and consequences? Inquiry and policy in research on teacher education. *Journal of Teacher Education*, 53(3), 248–253. DOI: 10.1177/0022487102053003009

Shulman, L. S. (2023). Foreword. In Huber, M. T., & Morreale, S. P. (Eds.), *Disciplinary styles in the scholarship of teaching and learning: Exploring common ground* (pp. v–ix). Taylor & Francis.

Shulman, L. S. (2023). Reprint: Truth and consequences? Inquiry and policy in research on teacher education. *Journal of Teacher Education*, 74(2), 144–148. DOI: 10.1177/00224871231161457

Shulman, L. S. (2023). Truth and consequences in teacher education. *Journal of Teacher Education*, 74(2), 149–150. DOI: 10.1177/00224871231160386

Smith, S., & Walker, D. (2024). Scholarship and teaching-focused roles: An exploratory study of academics' experiences and perceptions of support. *Innovations in Education and Teaching International*, 61(1), 193–204. DOI: 10.1080/14703297.2022.2132981

Straub, S., & Rummel, N. (2020). Promoting interaction in online distance education: Designing, implementing and supporting collaborative learning. *Information and Learning Science*, 121(5/6), 251–260. DOI: 10.1108/ILS-04-2020-0090

Vygotsky, L. S. (1962). *Thought and language*. MIT Press. DOI: 10.1037/11193-000

Vygotsky, L. S., & Cole, M. (1978). *Mind in society: Development of higher psychological processes*. Harvard University Press.

Wald, N., & Harland, T. (2024). Students as scholars and the scholarship of student learning. *Teaching in Higher Education*, 29(2), 442–453. DOI: 10.1080/13562517.2021.1989583

Wenger, E. (1998). *Communities of practice: Learning, meaning, and identity*. Cambridge University Press., DOI: 10.1017/CBO9780511803932

Wenger-Trayner, E., Fenton-O'Creevy, M., Hutchison, S., Kubiak, C., & Wenger-Trayner, B. (2014). *Learning in landscapes of practice: Boundaries, identity, and knowledgeability in practice-based learning*. Routledge., DOI: 10.4324/9781315777122

Wenger-Trayner, E., & Wenger-Trayner, B. (2015). Communities of practice: A brief introduction. https://wenger-trayner.com/introduction-to-communities-of-practice/

Wenger-Trayner, E., & Wenger-Trayner, B. (2020). *Learning to make a difference: Value creation in social learning spaces*. Cambridge University Press., DOI: 10.1017/9781108677431

KEY TERMS AND DEFINITIONS

Interactive Activity: Interactions that occur within a specific space may be informal, unanticipated, and unexpected, but within a learning environment these interactions are created as activities so that learners actively participate in the process so as to support social learning efforts.

Instructional Facilitation: A course learning experience normally includes a student and a teacher, with the teacher's label and role differentiated within distance education realms as a facilitative role that supports the instructional process and flow.

Distance Education: This is a learning process that is normally a formalized effort to teach information to people who want to learn, with the emphasis upon a physical distance between the student and the teacher.

Learning Management System: The software environment that supports the creation and security of a distance learning course environment.

Digital Spaces: These are online, digital environments within which people virtually come together for a task, for an experience, or for an event.

Learning Engagement: This is the effort to create an instructionally relevant flow of work for the student learner, although this may also include the instructional facilitator's engagement as a part of the learning process.

Course Design: The instructional design efforts of analysis, design, development, implementation, and evaluation, that are procedurally implemented so as to create a viable instructional product that is worthy of implementation within a learning environment.

Chapter 9

Elaborative Encoding as a Teaching Tool in Online Learning Environments:

Making It Meaningful Makes It Memorable

Alyson Froehlich
University of Utah, USA

ABSTRACT

This chapter surveys elaborative encoding as a tool for enhancing learning in online environments. By connecting to-be-learned information to learners' pre-existing knowledge, elaborative encoding facilitates deeper understanding and better retention of materials ranging from simple to complex. Research on elaborative encoding has explored various methods applicable to online learning environments; five will be examined here: elaborative interrogation, self-explanation, use of the self-reference effect, use of analogies, and etymological elaboration. The chapter shares practical ideas to encourage elaborative encoding in learners, considering both synchronous and asynchronous elements. The goal is to equip instructors with effective techniques to foster meaningful and memorable learning in their online learning environments.

DOI: 10.4018/979-8-3693-7595-2.ch009

INTRODUCTION

Figure 1. A cat with an unusual name

Note. You are more likely to remember the name of the cat in Figure 1 after hearing the story of how he got his name. Photo of cat by Nancy Ripley.

I would like to introduce you to a cat named Poin Nine (Figure 1). Now, Poin Nine has an unusual name- one that would typically be quite difficult to remember. However, let me tell you a short story about how this cat got his name, which may help you remember it.

Poin Nine belongs to a young girl. When the girl first got her new kitty, she told her mom she wanted to name the cat Poin Nine. The mom was confused by the unusual name but went along with it. Anyway, time went by, and one day the mom was listening to the radio. The radio station was 107.9, and eventually the little jingle for the station came on and sang *one o seven point nine* with a raised pitch on the sustained *point nine* like radio jingles often do. It was then at that moment the mom realized her daughter had named the cat after the jingle. The daughter had been hearing the point nine at the end of the jingle as *poin nine* and decided it was a good name for a cat.

Anyway, the point of this story is, by simply explaining how Poin Nine got his name, I got you to make connections between his name and some of your pre-existing knowledge- assuming you have heard of those radio station jingles or have simply had the experience of mishearing things. Because of this, you are much more likely to remember his name.

What Is the Point?

My hope for you, after reading this chapter, is for you to walk away with a general understanding of what elaborative encoding is, knowledge of a handful of methods and some considerations for each in applying them to online learning environments, and the confidence to try elaborative encoding enhancing approaches in your own teaching. You will also learn about processes involved in learning and memory, which is crucial for designing and implementing instructional strategies that align with how students learn best.

What Is Elaborative Encoding?

As you read the story about how Poin Nine the cat got his name, you engaged in something called elaborative encoding. Typically, when we think of what it means to elaborate, we think of things like adding detail, explaining, and describing. With regard to teaching and learning, elaboration does mean these things, but it is not only about providing *more* information. The key to using elaborative encoding as a teaching and learning tool is to help students make sense of new concepts and material in light of what they already know- to add detail, explain, and describe the new information by drawing upon students' pre-existing knowledge.

Elaborative encoding has been found to help students better understand what they are learning, to remember what they have learned, and to make more and better-quality inferences (i.e., to come to conclusions not explicitly provided in the learning content) (Chi et al., 1994; McDaniel & Donnelly, 1996). Not only does it support memory for facts (e.g., Chi et al., 1994; Vosniadou & Schommer, 1988; Woloshyn et al., 1992), but it is also a tool for increasing understanding of more complex learning materials, such as expository texts (e.g., Anderson & Reder, 1979; McNamara, 2004; Specht et al., 1999).

Elaborative encoding has most extensively been studied as a means for supporting the learning of conceptual knowledge (e.g., ideas, principles, objects), which will be the focus of this chapter. However, some elaborative encoding methods have also been found to be effective for procedural learning. We will look at examples in the "Asking Students to Explain" and the "Using Analogies" sections.

Before elaborating further on elaborative encoding, it may be helpful to take a step back and review background information on the learning and memory process, the structure of knowledge, and how the structure of knowledge supports learning.

What Is Encoding?

Encoding is the process by which newly presented information is translated into a format that the brain can understand. This is similar to how a computer encodes input into a recognizable code to process it. The idea of comparing human thinking to computer operations originated from seminal work by researchers like Miller (see Miller, 1994 for an update to his original work) and Atkinson and Shiffrin (as discussed in Malmberg et al., 2019). They likened human cognitive processes to the information processing of computers. Just as computers must encode data to use it, the human brain much encode information for it to become part of human memory.

One framework for thinking about how learning and memory work is to consider the three steps of encoding, storage, and retrieval (Savarimuthu & Ponniah, 2024). Elaborative encoding concerns that first step of getting information into memory. What makes it *elaborative* is that the encoded information is enhanced (i.e., elaborated on) with relevant detail drawn from pre-existing knowledge. As the new information is stored in memory, elaborative encoding supports greater connectivity and richness within the student's network of knowledge than it otherwise would have because those connections were fostered at encoding. As mentioned earlier, this enrichment supports understanding and memory (Anderson & Reder, 1979; Craik & Lockhart, 1972). Elaborative encoding also supports the retrieval step, or the act of accessing what has been stored in memory, and this will be described in greater detail shortly.

THE ROLES OF PRE-EXISTING KNOWLEDGE IN NEW LEARNING

Next let us consider the structure of knowledge, or how information is stored in memory. According to the highly influential spreading-activation theory of memory (Collins & Loftus, 1975; see Kumar, 2021 for a review), knowledge is organized and stored in memory as networks of interconnected nodes. Nodes represent individual concepts (or prepositions, Anderson, 1988), organized and stored in memory as networks of interconnected nodes. Nodes represent individual concepts (or prepositions, Anderson, 1988), and the nodes for semantically related concepts are more strongly connected than nodes for unrelated concepts. Further, when one node is activated (i.e., brought to mind or remembered), that activation can spread to other connected nodes, resulting in their activation. The extent of the spreading activation depends on the strength of the connections between the nodes, or how closely related their concepts are (i.e., how many properties they have in common, Collins & Loftus, 1975). In other words, bring one thing to mind, and without effort, you bring to mind other related knowledge.

Figure 2. Spreading activation within memory for knowledge

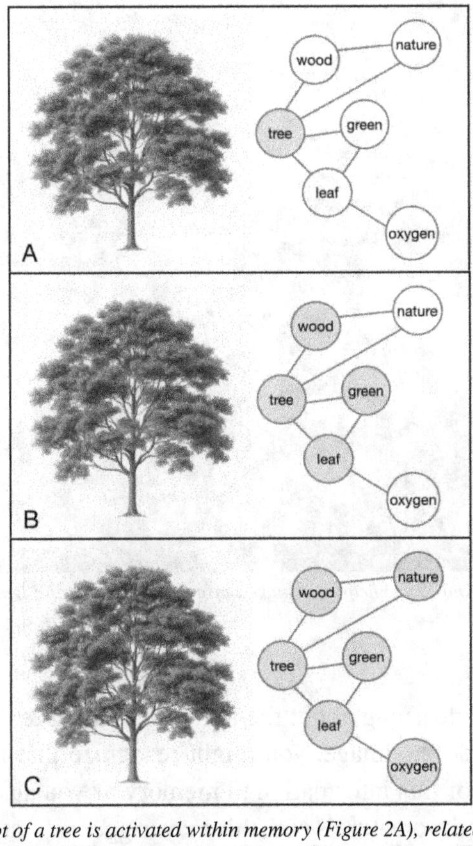

Note. When the concept of a tree is activated within memory (Figure 2A), related concepts may also become activated (Figure 2B), and this activation may continue to spread to some degree (Figure 2C).

Take for example Figure 2. If I ask you to think of a tree, not only do you activate what you know about trees in your relevant network of knowledge (Figure 2a), you also likely activate what you know about other related concepts, such as leaves and things that are green (Figure 2b). This activation may continue to spread, to a diminishing degree, to other more remote yet related concepts, such as nature and oxygen (Figure 2c). This sort of spreading activation allows for richer concept networks to be activated, even when only part of the network is triggered by encoding of new information. Spreading activation is believed to support many aspects of learning, including memory recall (Nelson et al., 2013), comprehension and making inferences (Collins & Loftus, 1975; Kintsch, 1988), divergent thinking and problem solving (Beaty et al., 2019), and creativity (Beaty et al., 2023).

Pre-Existing Knowledge and Comprehension

Figure 3. An unusual creature

Note. Your pre-existing knowledge helps you make sense of the creature in Figure 3. Image © 2013 Stelios Zacharias. Used with permission.

Let us say you are learning about the unfamiliar creature depicted in Figure 3. When you first encode the image, you might recognize that it has eyes and legs, triggering activation of this information in memory. If you also notice the fishtail-looking appendage at the creature's end, this may trigger activation of your concepts of fish or crustacean. The surrounding environment appears to consist of small rocks or sand, so encoding those features may lead to the activation of information about their typical size in relation to fish, leading you to conclude that this creature must be small. In this way, the activation of pre-existing knowledge can support inferences about and comprehension of new things to be learned. (Note that the creature in this image is not from the sea but rather the mountains of Greece. Regardless, recognizing the appendage at its end as being like a fishtail will lead to the activation of fish and fish-like concepts in pre-existing knowledge.)

Pre-Existing Knowledge and Memory

Pre-existing knowledge is not only helpful for comprehending new information; it can also help ensure the new information is more strongly rooted in memory (Anderson & Reder, 1979; Craik & Lockhart, 1972) and easier to retrieve later. Recall of learned content is more likely as the number of connections a new concept makes with other concepts already established in memory is increased (Anderson & Reder, 1979; Nelson et al., 2003). The analogy of a tree and its roots may be helpful. As a tree's root system beneath the ground becomes more extensive, it is less likely to topple over and become unearthed. It is a similar situation with a newly learned concept in memory. As the number of interconnections between new information and pre-existing knowledge increase, the to-be-learned concept will be more established and more resistant to forgetting.

The memory benefit that comes with newly learned information being interconnected with pre-existing knowledge may also result, in part, from ease of retrieval. Remembering is believed to be dependent on *retrieval cues* (Tulving, 1974; see Kumar, 2021 for a review). Retrieval cues are elements in the learning environment (words, images, objects, environmental context, mental states, etc.) that cause the target information to be activated. Further, according to the encoding specificity principle, retrieval cues are more effective if they closely match the conditions at the time of encoding (Roediger & Tekin, 2020; Tulving & Thomson, 1973). In other words, elements present in the learning context become retrieval cues to later access that learned information. By incorporating pre-existing knowledge at the time of encoding new information, that pre-existing knowledge becomes part of the interconnected network around the new information in memory.

Pre-existing Knowledge and How the Rich Get Richer

A study by Recht and Leslie (1988) provides a striking demonstration of the contribution that pre-existing knowledge can make to comprehension and memory. They assessed 7th and 8th grade students' memory and comprehension for a passage on baseball. Students had been previously assessed on a standardized reading comprehension test to organize them into low-ability and high-ability reader groups. Their pre-existing knowledge of baseball was also assessed. While high-ability readers outperformed their low-ability peers, pre-existing knowledge about baseball had much more of an influence on their memory scores for the baseball passage. In fact, low-ability readers with high pre-existing knowledge of baseball recalled more of the passage than the high-ability readers with low baseball pre-existing knowledge. This boost in memory was likely due to increased comprehension by the students who had more pre-existing knowledge of baseball; their knowledge helped them make sense of the events described in the passage (e.g., a double play), form a more connected and organized representation in memory, and then rely on it for better recall. In that sense, the rich get richer.

The point is not to imply that students are doomed if they do not have a certain degree of pre-existing knowledge related to the to-be-learned information. Elaborative encoding has also been shown to benefit students with little topic-specific pre-existing knowledge by making use of the general world knowledge they do have (Karpicke & Smith, 2012). What the Recht and Leslie (1988) study does illustrate is the key role of pre-existing knowledge in elaborative encoding.

WAYS TO PROMOTE ELABORATIVE ENCODING IN ONLINE LEARNING ENVIRONMENTS

There are many ways elaborative encoding can be used to support learning. In this next section, let us examine several that instructors can use in the online environment. We will look at both the benefits and some specific circumstances or limitations (referred to as Boundary Conditions below) to be considered when implementing each.

Asking Students to Explain

One way students may engage in elaborative encoding is by explaining the learning material, either during learning or shortly afterwards. This has been shown to benefit their memory for the material and ability to make inferences with it (Chi et al., 1994; McDaniel & Donnelly, 1996). Two noteworthy methods of prompting students to explain their learning are elaborative interrogation and self-explanation.

Elaborative Interrogation

Elaborative interrogation (McDaniel & Donnelly, 1996; Weinstein et al., 2019) involves prompting students to explain their understanding by answering *How?* and *Why?* questions about course concepts and content. In one example, after reading part of a passage from a textbook on digestion, Smith, Holliday, and Austin's (2010) participants were asked to respond to the question, *Saliva must mix with food to initiate digestion. Why is this true?* Participants who were asked to answer elaborative interrogation questions throughout the passage performed higher on a measure of comprehension than did participants who were simply asked to read the passage twice. This study posed questions about every 150 words, although many studies of elaborative interrogation prompt participants as frequently as following each sentence. A more dispersed approach of about every two pages was used by Callender and McDaniel (2007).

Self-Explanation

Another approach to encouraging students to explain their understanding is the method of self-explanation (Bisra et al., 2018; Chi et al., 1989). Self-explanation, like elaborative interrogation, involves prompts for students to explain their understanding during or following presentation of learning material, but the prompts are more often open-ended and intentional regarding connecting to-be-learned information with pre-existing knowledge. For example, Chi et al. (1994) presented participants with a chapter on the human circulatory system and prompted them to *explain what it means to you* following each sentence. Further guidance stated, *That is, what new information does each line provide for you, how does it relate to what you've already read, does it give you a new insight into your understanding of how the circulatory system works, or does it raise a question in your mind. Tell us whatever is going through your mind—even if it seems unimportant.* (Chi et al., 1994, p. 477). Participants who self-explained in this study, along with many others (see Bisra et al., 2018 for a meta-analysis), outperformed participants in a control condition on a range of question types addressing memory for facts to making inferences and applying what had been learned. Further, of the self-explainers in Chi et al. (1994) and other studies, those who provided more explanations outperformed those who provided fewer explanations.

More recently, Pi et al. (2022) demonstrated facilitated learning performance in an online environment by participants who were asked to type out their self-explanations after watching a video lecture (i.e., *You should type explanations about how the human immune system protects the human body to yourself after watching the video to ensure that you comprehend the lecture completely*). Participants in this self-explanation condition outperformed those in an instructional explanations condition that asked participants to *explain the content clearly and in sufficient detail* so that another fictional student *understands it without the use of additional materials.* In other words, self-explanation was more effective than explaining to another person.

Benefits of Asking Students to Explain

The self-explanation literature has demonstrated benefits not just for conceptual knowledge, as is the focus of the elaborative interrogation literature, but also for skills such as solving physics and math problems (Chi et al., 1989; Gjerde et al., 2022; Wong et al., 2002), which rely on both conceptual and procedural knowledge.

An added benefit of asking students to explain their understanding is that it may reveal to them gaps in their understanding (VanLehn et al., 1992), supporting metacognition. Students are notorious for being poor judges of how well they have comprehended newly presented information (Golke et al., 2022; Kruger & Dunning, 1999). Often it is not until students are asked to demonstrate what they have learned that gaps in understanding and missing connections are discovered.

It is believed that elaborative interrogation and self-explanation prompts are effective because they encourage students to go beyond recalling facts and to consider the relevance of those facts (Stein & Bransford, 1979). This extra effort requires students to draw upon related, pre-existing knowledge to answer the question, which in turn facilitates forming connections between it and the new information (McDaniel & Donnelly, 1996).

Boundary Conditions of Asking Students to Explain

In this next section we will explore important factors to consider when encouraging students to explain their understanding in online learning environments. These factors will help determine how effectively existing research can be applied in different online learning contexts.

For example, while the elaborative interrogation literature has focused heavily on learning from text-based materials, the self-explanation literature has been demonstrated both in text-based and a variety of multimedia-based materials, such as diagrams, animations, simulations, videos, computer games, and more (see Fiorella & Mayer, 2021; Wiley & Chi, 2014 for reviews). In other words, asking students to explain their understanding may lend itself well to the multimedia learning resources often used in online learning environments.

Another important factor to consider is the nature of the concepts or information being learned. Williams et al. (2013) suggested that self-explanation may support learning by encouraging students to make broad generalizations and identify patterns. However, this may come at the expense of recognizing exceptions to those general patterns. In their study, participants learned categories of objects and either self-explained or simply thought aloud. Those who self-explained were better at identifying patterns related to the categories but made more errors when categorizing exceptions. Thus, activities that prompt students to explain their understanding may be most effective for learning concepts and topics that do not heavily rely on recognizing exceptions.

Also to consider is that self-explanation prompts are not always open-ended. While early self-explanation research (Chi et al., 1994, for example) focused on open-ended prompts that did not direct participants to specific concepts or elements of a skill (e.g., *Explain what it means to you*), later research investigated more focused prompts (see Wylie & Chi, 2014). For example, Lin and Atkinson (2013) asked participants learning about the cardiovascular system, *Could you explain the function of blood in your own words?*. In another example, Rau et al. (2015) asked participants learning math concepts *How does the number line show the numerator of the fraction?*. While both open-ended and focused prompts can result in learning benefits, greater learning effects are generally found with focused over open-ended prompts (Wylie & Chi, 2014).

Finally, it may be most beneficial for students to concurrently explain their understanding as they consume the learning material, although this issue is still unsettled. While some limited research suggests that elaborative interrogation and self-explanation effects may become diminished the further distanced question prompts are from the learning content (Rubio et al., 2022; also see Dunlosky et al., 2013; McDaniel, 2023), research examining self-explanation immediately following learning has still found positive benefits (Berry, 1983; Zhu et al., 2024). So, it may be ideal to prompt students to explain concurrently as they study learning material, but benefits may still be found for explanations given following study.

Ideas for Utilizing Explanation in the Online Learning Environment

In this next section, let us look at some specific ways elaborative interrogation and self-explanation can be implemented in the online learning environment.

Create an Assignment Asking Students to Answer Explanatory Questions as They Read, Watch, or Listen to New Information

One method for asking students to explain their learning in an online environment that aligns most directly with what has been tested in the literature is to create an assignment that asks students to answer *How?*, *Why?*, and other self-explanation questions as they go through the learning material (e.g., readings, text-based or video-based lessons, etc.). This may be most easily accomplished by having students type or write their responses within a document as they study the relevant learning material.

Figure 4. An example of how students may be prompted to answer explanation questions concurrently with studying learning content in a learning management system

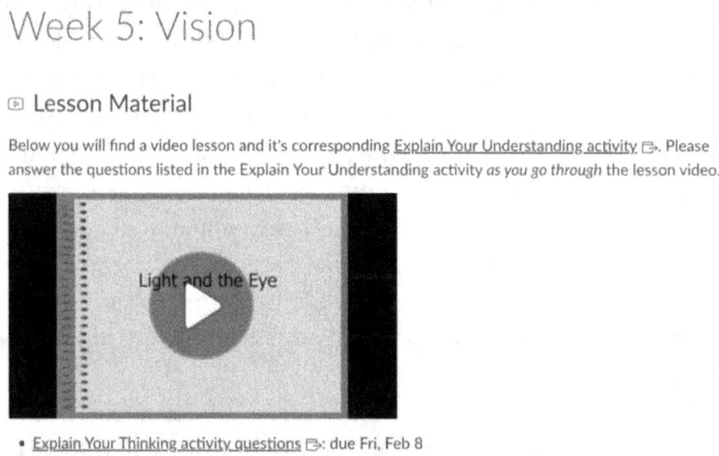

Note. To encourage students to complete an explanation questions assignment while studying learning content, place a link to the assignment and a note, next to the learning content in the learning management system, that explains that students should answer the questions as they review the material.

As mentioned above, it may be most advantageous for students to answer explanation questions concurrently with studying the learning material. To encourage students to do this, place next to the learning material within the learning management system either a link to the assignment or a note for students to answer the questions as they review the material (Figure 4). Alternatively, the learning material, or a link to the learning material, may be embedded directly within the assignment instructions (this may work within the quiz tool of the learning management system; Figure 5).

Figure 5. An example of how a learning management system's quiz tool may be used to prompt students to answer explanation questions concurrently with studying learning content

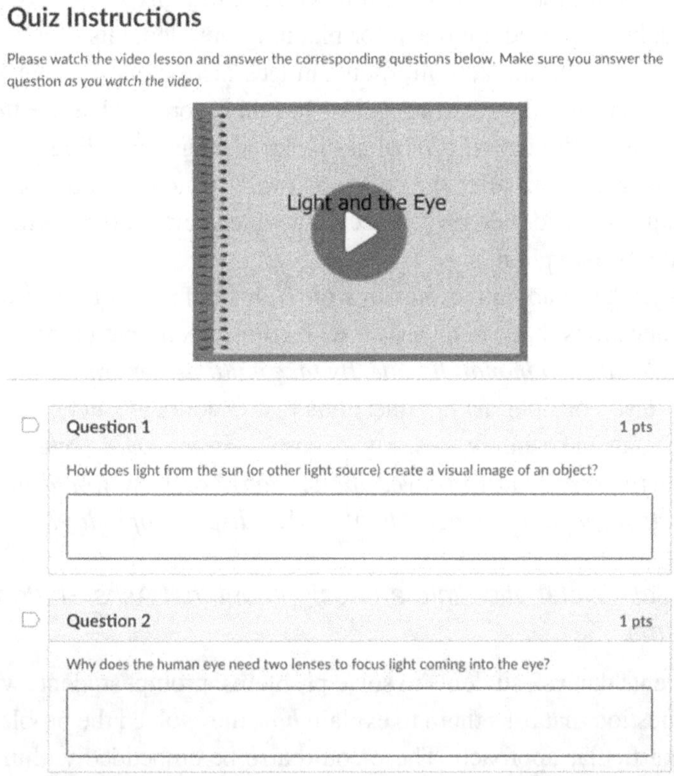

Note. A learning management system's quiz tool may be used to encourage students to answer explanation questions while studying learning content. Embed or link to the learning material within the instructions.

It may be helpful to indicate to students at which locations within the learning material each question should be answered. Indicators may be placed within the relevant locations of the learning material, so that students are prompted to answer a question as they read, watch, or listen. However, instructors without the ability to edit the learning material may find it easier to align questions with content within the assignment itself, perhaps giving page numbers, time indicators (for video or audio), or indicators based on headings or sections next to each question.

As mentioned above, research suggests that students may still benefit from answering explanatory questions following study of new information (see Bisra et al., 2018 for a meta-analysis). However, for optimal results, it may be better for the learning material to be accessible while students answer the explanation questions.

So, if question prompts are to be completed after studying an online reading, for example, be sure a link to the reading is available within the assignment instructions.

In settling on which questions to ask students, consider the learning goals (i.e., learning outcomes) for the course. Backwards course design (Wiggins & McTighe, 2005), the widely supported approach for planning out elements of a course such as assessments, content, and activities, encourages instructors to orient decisions of course design around the learning goals. In other words, what are the desired results of learning in the course? What skills, knowledge, or beliefs do you want students to walk away with after the course is over? Which facts or concepts help students get there? Consider this when deciding which parts of the learning content to prompt students to explain.

Additionally, when elaborative interrogation *How?* and *Why?* questions are posed, in addition to questions that can be answered by direct examination of the learning content (e.g., *Why does a monarch butterfly take multiple generations to complete a migration?*), also consider asking questions that encourage students to do some extra thinking and make inferences. For example, *How would (relevant person/ theory/ perspective) respond to (novel application)?* or *How would the original Gestalt theorists respond to the point light walker displays of today?*

Incorporate Self-Explanation into an Assignment that Asks Students to Solve Problems

In assignments that ask students to solve problems, prompt students with a self-explanation question that asks them to explain *how* they solved the problem or *why* they chose a particular approach. These could also be embedded within a quiz in the learning management system's quiz tool. Gjerde et al. (2022) found effective physics question prompts target procedural actions, goals, principles, and conditions of the problems.

Another option for embedding problems and self-explanation questions into a quiz is for the self-explanation questions to take the format of selection from a drop-down menu of choices. Studies have demonstrated self-explanation benefits when students select a prepared explanation from a drop-down list (see Wylie & Chi, 2014). For example, in a computer-based learning environment, Atkinson et al. (2003) presented participants with math probability problems to solve, and following the field for the participant's response was a drop-down menu for participants to select the relevant probably rule or principle being applied. Even just having leaners recognize and choose an explanation creates an opportunity for elaborative encoding.

Ask Students to Answer Explanatory Questions During a Video Conference Lesson

For synchronous video conference lessons (e.g., Zoom, Google Meet, Microsoft Teams, etc.), ask students to answer *How?*, *Why?*, and self-explanation questions following presentation of to-be-learned information. One option is to simply ask for volunteers to speak up and share an answer with the rest of the group, but that approach may only benefit the volunteers who speak up. Another option is to ask students to share their answers in the chat. A third option is to ask students to pair up in breakout rooms, if your video conferencing application allows for attendees to be sent to individual group spaces. In those breakout rooms, students could discuss the answer to the explanatory question together, and if desired, the answer could be discussed as a whole group after students return from their breakout rooms. While Novak et al. (2022) found similar learning gains between participants who answered explanatory questions with a partner and those who verbalized their answers independently, there may be added value in having students come together to discuss their answers as a whole class including the instructor.

Ask Students to Answer Explanatory Questions in a Discussion Board

Online discussion boards also offer opportunities for students to be prompted to explain their thinking. For example, Zheng et al. (2023) conducted a study where participants worked synchronously on a collaborative project through a discussion board. They received automated feedback on their postings from an AI-powered, knowledge graph-based tool, which prompted them to elaborate on their ideas and find connections between the knowledge presented and their pre-existing knowledge. This feedback led to better expansion of ideas and ultimate performance on the task than participants who did not receive the feedback prompting. While instructors may not have access to such a tool, they might consider doing their own prompting of students within the discussion.

Kwon et al. (2019) examined instructor prompting of students in an instructional design course to elaborate on their postings in asynchronous discussion boards that required the students to discuss case studies. The prompts resulted in a greater number of idea units expressed in response to peers' posts, and a greater number of response postings overall, than a control group not receiving the instructor prompt.

Relating to the Self (and Other Rich Networks)

As described earlier, students make sense of new information by using their existing networks of knowledge to interpret it. As those networks of relevant knowledge become richer with more and stronger concepts and connections, the comprehension and memory for the new information will become more potent.

If we consider a student's existing knowledge to be like glue for new learning because it helps the new learning to stick, then what students know specifically about themselves is like superglue for new learning. This is because knowledge about the self is considered to be richer than almost anything else a student knows (Rogers et al., 1977; Symons & Johnson, 1997). In fact, research has demonstrated that when new, to-be-learned information is related to the self, it is better remembered, referred to as the self-reference effect (Rogers et al., 1977; Symons & Johnson, 1997; see Liu et al., 2024, for a meta-analysis).

An early example of the self-reference effect is that provided by Rogers et al. (1977). They expanded on Craik and Tulving's (1975) classic experiments, which tested Craik and Lockhart's (1972) depth of processing theory. Craik and Tulving asked participants to make judgements about words using different encoding strategies that varied in the depth of processing (e.g., degree of meaningful or semantic thinking) required. For example, for the word *TABLE*, participants would be asked one of the following four questions in increasing order of required processing depth: *Is the word in capital letters?* (structural processing); *Does the word rhyme with WEIGHT?* (phonemic processing); *Is the word a type of fish?* (category processing); *Would the word fit the sentence: He met a ___ in the street?* (sentence processing). Results showed that as the depth of encoding increased, so did the likelihood that words would be remembered. In other words, the more participants considered the meaning of each of the words, the better they remembered those words. Rogers et al. (1977) expanded on these experiments by adding in a self-reference processing condition. For adjectives to be learned, participants were asked either a structural, phonemic, semantic (*Means same as (*possible synonym*)*, or self-reference (*Describes you?*) processing question. Recall of words was much greater for the self-reference processing questions than any of the others, including the semantic processing question.

In another demonstration of the self-reference effect, Serbun et al. (2011) displayed photographs of common, purchasable objects to participants, such as an ice cream cone or a camera. For each object, participants were asked one of three questions: *Is this an object <u>you</u> would buy sometime in the next year?*, *Is this an object <u>your mother</u> would buy sometime in the next year?*, or *Is this an object <u>Bill Clinton</u>* (former U.S. president) *would buy sometime in the next year?*. The intention was to ask participants to relate each object to three pre-existing knowledge networks of differing familiarity- the self being most familiar, the mother being a highly familiar other, and Bill Clinton being an unfamiliar but known other. Participants demonstrated better memory for objects that had been related to the self or the mother than objects that had been related to Bill Clinton. In another experiment, Serbun et al. (2011) repeated the conditions but asked whether each of a list of adjectives described the individual. Again, participants had better memory for adjectives related to the self than Bill Clinton, with adjectives related to the mother falling in the middle.

While studies demonstrating the self-reference effect generally require participants to make a judgement that elicits them to consider the learning material in relation to themselves and their lives, effects can be found incidentally, in the absence of a judgement (Kesebir & Oishi, 2010; Li et al., 2021; Turk et al., 2008). In other words, eliciting the self-reference effect does not always have to involve students answering questions. They may be able to hear an instructor make the association between themselves and the learning material (e.g., *your circulatory system* rather than *the circulatory system*), as discussed in the Ideas for Relating Material to the Self (and Other Rich Networks) in the Online Learning Environment section.

What all these findings suggest is that material related to the self is particularly privileged in memory, and the self-reference effect may be a function of degree of familiarity, or richness, of the associated network of pre-existing knowledge that new information is being related to. In other words, it is the superglue of elaborate encoding.

Boundary Conditions of the Self-Reference Effect

Klein (2012) has urged caution when interpreting studies that examine the self, which he argues is not a clearly defined construct and can involve different forms (e.g., episodic memories of one's life events, semantic knowledge of facts about one's life, the physical self/ one's own body, etc.). Therefore, the *self* that is examined in research may vary from study to study, confounding the interpretation of results. Klein (2012) argued that a potential explanation for discrepancies in the literature (see Symons & Johnson, 1997 for a review) is that most studies of the self-reference effect either examine knowledge about the self (semantic memory) or memories for personally experienced events from the participant's life (episodic memory). However, these are two different systems of memory and use different processes for supporting the self-reference effect (Klein et al., 1989). For example, asking a participant *Does this (to-be-remembered item) describe you?* guides them to consider what they know about themselves, or their semantic memory for themselves. On the other hand, asking a participant *Recall a time when (to-be-remembered item was experienced)* leads to them draw upon episodic memory for events. Klein (2012) points out that studies drawing on semantic knowledge about the self generally show stronger self-reference effects than those drawing on episodic memories from one's life, at least when comparisons are made to familiar others. Importantly, however, research drawing on participants' episodic memories has still found a self-reference effect (e.g., Kalenzaga et al., 2015; Klein et al., 1989). It may be that making connections between new material and what students know about themselves is a more potent tool for learning than is connecting to one's life memories, but both approaches have potential to benefit memory.

Finally, it is worth noting that the self-reference literature has overwhelmingly investigated effects on memory (i.e., being able to recognize or remember previously presented learning material) but less so on comprehension of the learning material. While memory for learning material is valuable in its own right and may, in turn, support higher levels of learning by reducing the cognitive load involved in holding that information in mind and working with it (see Sweller, 1988, for a description of cognitive load theory), at this time it is not possible to say that the self-reference effect supports forms of learning beyond memory for the learning material.

Ideas for Relating Material to the Self (and Other Rich Networks) in the Online Learning Environment

Next let us consider some ways instructors might encourage the self-reference effect in their online learning environments.

Prompt Students to Connect New Information to Their Lives

Whether in an assignment, a discussion prompt, the learning material (e.g., video or text-based lessons), or during a video conference lesson, ask students to consider a key concept in the context of their lives. Sometimes considering everyday life is relevant (which is mostly likely to draw from semantic memory), but it may be more applicable in some circumstances to ask students to recall how the concept has applied to a specific instance from their lives (which is mostly likely to draw from episodic memory).

For example, a discussion prompt for an online discussion board or for a video conference lesson could ask students to describe their own daily life experience with the concept (e.g., *How might your life have to change if you developed spatial hemineglect syndrome?* or *How do you decide whether a source of information is trustworthy?*). Or, the prompt could ask students to think of and share a time when they have observed a phenomenon they are learning about (e.g., *When have you found yourself succumbing to confirmation bias?* or *When have you based a decision on its environmental sustainability?*).

Prompt Students to Connect New Information to Other Well-Known Domains

Using a similar approach to the idea above, students could be asked to relate key concepts to other domains that are well-known. Considering the self-reference effect presumably gets its benefit from the self being so well-known to students and that relating learning material to well-known others (e.g., one's mother) may induce learning effects to a similar degree, it may be advantageous to relate important learning concepts to other domains the student is highly familiar with, such as pop-culture, personal interests, or other things students may have in common. A few examples might be *What sampling biases might we get if we were to conduct an experiment with students at the campus food court?*; *Can you think of any examples of natural selection in animals or plants that you see around your neighborhood?*, or *What similarities can you find between the events leading up to the American Revolution and any modern-day movements?*

Ask Students to Share Their Opinions

The self-reference effect may also be elicited when students share their opinions. For example, participants in Lawrence and Chai's (2021) study showed better memory for images of objects that they rated as liking or not liking than for images rated as living or not living. Consider whether the concept to be learned lends itself to forming an opinion. For example, some questions could start with *What do you think is the most significant factor contributing to…*, *Do you agree with the author's perspective…*, *Which (of the people being studied) do you relate to most?*, or even the tested *Do you like….*

Make the Lesson about Students' Selves and Their Lives

As we saw in the previous paragraphs, the self-reference effect can be elicited even without students making responses. That means it may be helpful, when possible, to incorporate into the lesson examples about and references to the students' selves, their lives, and other familiar domains. Rather than discussing *the* circulatory system, for example, refer to *students'* circulatory systems. In literature, ask students to consider how they feel when they face challenges, and how these emotions compare to those of the characters in the story. In physics, the principles of electricity and magnetism at work in students' smartphones can be discussed.

Using Analogies

Another method of elaborative encoding is to present new information and concepts with an analogy. For example, as mentioned previously, cognitive information processing has often been compared to the processing of a computer. A planetary analogy has been used to describe the structure of atoms. On a more modest level, electrical circuits have been compared to water flowing through pipes, cell membranes are like security gates at concerts, and gravity is like a magnet. Indeed, Gentner and Jeziorski (2012) accredited many major scientific discoveries to the use of analogies.

An analogy can be described as a comparison between two entities that maps systematic correspondences between their elements (Holyoak et al., 2024). The idea is that the better-known entity serves as a framework for which to make sense of the less-known entity being studied (Keefer & Landau, 2016). As with the other elaborative encoding methods mentioned earlier, analogy involves facilitating learning by supporting connections between what is known about that better-known entity and what is being learned.

Benefits of Using Analogies

Analogy has been found to support memory for facts (Halpern et al., 1990; Newby et al., 1995) and the ability to draw inferences (Donnelly & McDaniel, 1993; Halpern et al., 1990). Additionally, analogy is another elaborative encoding method that has been found to be helpful for procedural learning in addition to conceptual learning. For example, Hayes and Henk (1986) found analogy facilitated the learning of a knot-tying task, and Liao and Masters (2001) had participants use analogy for learning to hit a table tennis stroke.

Boundary Conditions of Using Analogies

One consideration to be made when using analogies to promote learning is the differential effects of near versus far analogies. Analogies can vary with respect to the degree of similarity between the to-be-learned entity and the better-known entity (Holyoak et al., 2024). Near analogies involve to-be-learned entities and better-known entities that are similar in function or concept and are typically drawn from the same domain of knowledge (e.g., *A chef is like an artist, crafting dishes with ingredients just as an artist combines elements of art to create a work.*). Far analogies tend to be drawn from semantically distant domains (e.g., *A struggling artist is like a seed trying to sprout through concrete.*). Holyoak et al. (2024) argued that while near analogies may be easier to apply, likely due to the causal relationships they have in common, far analogies may better facilitate creativity, perhaps by inducing a mind-set to focus on relationships over individual elements (Vendetti et al., 2014).

Another consideration with the use of analogies is that all too often analogies are not understood by students as intended. Niebert et al. (2012) argued that better analogies are those that students have embodied experience with and do not need extensive imaginative skills to understand. In other words, if the analogy depends on pre-existing knowledge that is limited for the student, the analogy may not help. For example, the analogy *balancing a chemical equation is like balancing a checkbook* might not be very effective analogy for most students today, considering checkbooks are not as commonly used as they once were.

Paris and Glynn (2003) found that *elaborate analogies*, those which provide more explicit mapping between components through verbal description and pictorial representation, supported better recall and inference-making than more simple analogies. The benefit that comes from elaborating on an analogy aligns with research by Holyoak and colleagues that demonstrated students do not always spontaneously notice the connections in an analogy and may need a hint (Gick & Holyoak, 1980, 1983; Holyoak & Koh, 1987).

Paris and Glynn's (2003) findings of enhanced learning from analogy when paired with an image also align with assertions from dual coding theory (Clark & Paivio, 1991). According to dual coding theory, information is better remembered when it is presented both verbally and non-verbally (most often in visual format). This is because it is believed that information can be encoded via at least two channels (verbal and non-verbal), and exceeding the processing capacity of one channel does not impact the processing capacity of the other channel. For example, lessons may be more effective if new concepts are both described (verbal channel) and presented with images (non-verbal channel) that illustrate that concepts. Dual processing channels are a key element of Mayer's cognitive theory of multimedia learning (Mayer, 2024).

Finally, users of analogy as an instructional tool should also be aware of the possibility that the analogy can influence what is inferred and applied to the target information by students in potentially unintended ways. For example, Thibodeau and Boroditsky (2011) provided participants with one of two short paragraphs concerning crime in a fictional city and subsequently asked them about approaches to be taken to address the crime. The paragraphs mostly presented statistics and were identical except for one word used as a metaphor for crime; in one paragraph crime was said to be a *beast* whereas in the other paragraph, crime was a virus. When crime was framed as a beast, participants were more likely to suggest law enforcement and punishment. When crime was framed as a virus, participants were more likely to suggest social reform. In other words, participants' suggestions differed to be in alignment with their likely pre-existing knowledge about beasts versus viruses.

Ideas for Using Analogies in the Online Learning Environment

This section is more along the lines of *tips* for using analogies than full ideas. In other words, let us look at ways to make analogy use more effective.

Make Analogies Relatable

Analogies can be shared in online lessons of any format- text, video, or video conference. When sharing an analogy, take care to make it relatable to your students. Consider the extent of students' experience with the intended better-known entity of the analogy, which they will need to draw from in order to make sense of the analogy. If it is difficult for students to imagine the details of that better-known entity, the analogy may not be effective.

Make Analogies Elaborate

Elaborate analogies were described by Paris and Glynn (2003) as having elaborated verbal explanations accompanied by representative pictures. When possible, explain the analogy to students in detail. Explicitly highlight the shared elements and the relationships that make the analogy. And consider adding in an illustrative picture or diagram that visually explains the analogy.

Consider Near or Far Analogies Depending on the Purpose

As discussed earlier, near analogies that make comparisons between more similar entities that share a domain may be easier for students to use. Consider these for particularly challenging concepts, at least initially. Far analogies that cross domains may provide a greater but perhaps desired challenge for students who have a sufficient baseline understanding of the concept.

Consider Using Analogies to Explain Procedural Skills

If your learning content involves motor skills, analogies may help. For example, within the hip-hop dance domain, popping could be described as like a quick electric shock where muscles contract and release rapidly to create sharp, jerky movements. For teaching how to play guitar, fingerpicking could be described as like plucking petals from a flower where each finger has a specific string to pluck, creating a delicate and precise sound. In rehabilitation therapy, performing range of motion exercises could be described as like oiling a rusty hinge where regular, gentle movements help keep the joints flexible and prevent stiffness.

Explaining the Etymology of Terms

Do you remember the name of the cat in Figure 1? His name was elaborated in the beginning of the chapter, which likely helped you to remember it despite it being an unusual name that might otherwise be difficult to recall. The cat's name was embedded within a story that explained its origins. While storytelling has been found to be a beneficial teaching and learning tool, for multiple potential underlying reasons

(Landrum et al., 2019), another mechanism likely benefitting your memory for the cat's name is that you learned about its origins (i.e., where the name came from).

Explaining the etymology (i.e., origin and background) of terms can support comprehension and memory for those terms and may even allow for inferences to be made about the characteristics of the concepts they represent. As with other forms of elaborative encoding, the student creates connections between the to-be-learned term and pre-existing knowledge related to the etymological content. For example, a new vegetable gardener may better understand and remember the name of the snow pea upon learning that it has high cold tolerance and can thrive in cooler, snowy environments. Further, inferences about its characteristics may be made even without being told them given pre-existing knowledge about snow and its implications for many vegetable plants (i.e., frost damage).

Boers et al. (2004) coined the term etymological elaboration to refer to this approach specifically with learning idioms within second language learning. Idioms are expressions with meanings that are different from the literal meaning of the words that make them up (e.g., bite the dust; out of the blue; talk someone's ear off; a sight for sore eyes). An example of elaborative encoding for an idiom might be for the idiom *jump on the bandwagon* to be explained as to *join others in doing something or supporting a cause that is fashionable or likely to be successful* (from *The Oxford Dictionary of Idioms, 4th edition*, by Ayto, 2020). Another example, provided to participants in Bagheri and Fazel (2010) for the idiom *to tie the knot*, was *Some marriage ceremonies tie together the wrists of the bride and the groom.*

Benefits of Explaining the Etymology of Terms

Pierson (1989) first reported, anecdotally, the value of incorporating etymology in the second language learning classroom, and much research has since corroborated its utility in students' comprehension and memory for foreign vocab words and expressions (Bagheri & Fazel, 2010; Baleghizadeh & Mohammad Bagheri, 2012; Boers, 2000; Boers et al., 2007; Zolfagharkhani & Ghorbani Moghadam, 2011).

While etymological elaboration has yet to be featured in the elaborative encoding literature, it is not a far stretch to consider this approach as being useful outside of the second-language learning domain, in the learning of terms, as is a need in just about any subject or discipline. It is considered an example of elaborative encoding here given the likely shared underlying mechanism of connecting new learning to pre-existing knowledge. Further, Boers et al. (2004, 2007) described etymological elaboration as being supported, in part, by levels of processing theory (Craik & Lockhart, 1972), a precursor theory to elaborative encoding theory.

And etymological elaboration findings do make sense in terms of Craik and Lockhart's (1972) levels of processing theory in that as a student's semantic and meaningful thinking about new information increases, the likelihood of it being later remembered also increases. For example, if you want to remember what a penumbral eclipse is, that may be more beneficial to consider that a penumbral eclipse is so named because it occurs when the moon passes only through the penumbra, or outer part, of the Earth's shadow than, say, trying to remember that the term starts with the letter *p*.

Boundary Conditions for Explaining the Etymology of Terms

Some research suggests combining etymological elaboration of idioms with the presentation of illustrative images may enhance the learning impact (Ghorbani, 2017; Golaghaei & Kakolian, 2015). This finding is similar to research mentioned earlier with analogy and the added benefit of images. Dual coding theory (Clark & Paivio, 1991), mentioned earlier, may help explain the consistent finding of enhancement of learning from verbal tasks with added images.

Another important consideration to be made here is that, unlike with many idioms, some terms have parts like prefixes that can provide clues to their meaning. For example, the prefix de- means *to reverse* or *to change*, which helps with comprehending words like declassify or decontaminate. The prefix auto- means *self* in words like autobiography or autograph. However, despite their common usage, it may still be worthwhile to highlight their meanings to students when relevant rather than relying on students to spontaneously process these meanings in understanding them.

An example comes from my Sensation and Perception Psychology course when students learn about color vision and the different types of cone cells in the back of the eye that contribute to color vision. Most humans have three cone types, or trichromacy. However, some people are missing or have a dysfunctional cone type, and they are said to have dichromacy, or only two functional cone types. They perceive fewer colors as a result. And finally, a small proportion of women have an extra cone type, or tetrachromacy, and they can perceive even more colors than can trichromats. Now, while the prefixes of *di-*, *tri-*, and *tetra-* (which have Greek origins indicating two, three, and four), when added to the base word *chromacy* (originating from the Greek word for color) provide helpful information about whether the term is referring to vision with two, three, or four cones, I find students do not always spontaneously notice this key to comprehension and memory for the terms, and often they will confuse trichromacy and tetrachromacy, for example. This is even though these prefixes are used across a variety of domains (e.g., dioxide, triangle, tricycle, tetrapod). However, once aware of the meaning of these prefixes, remembering them is a much easier task. It also allows students to infer the meaning of additional related words, such as pentachromacy (which describes some non-human animals, such as pigeons and butterflies).

Ideas for Using Etymological Encoding in the Online Learning Environment

Explain Terms and Phrases to Second Language Students

If you teach second language students, when terms or phrases such as idioms are more complex than their literal translation, consider elaborating on them to students. Add in an illustrative image if you are able for added benefit. This could be handled by some brief explanation within a text- or video-based lesson or during a video conference lesson early in the term, or it could be incorporated into an assignment.

Teach Students Common Parts of Terms that Reveal Their Meaning

For common parts of terms, such as prefixes, that appear across subject domains (e.g., *di-*, *tri-*, *tetra-*) or within domains (e.g., *geno-*, used in genetics; *sub-*, used in programming), it may be helpful to explicitly teach students their meanings. This may be best handled by some brief explanation within a text- or video-based lesson or during a video conference lesson early in the term.

Elaborate on the Meaningful Background of a Term

Some terms may not have common parts that indicate their meaning yet are still lendable to explanation. Poin Nine the cat's name is a great example of this. Another example is explaining the origins of the word *chlorophyll* to explain its meaning (*chloro* coming from the Greek word for *green*, and *phyll* from the Greek word for *leaf*).

FINALLY, COMBINE ELABORATIVE ENCODING WITH RETRIEVAL PRACTICE

We have examined a handful of methods for supporting learning and memory of new information through elaborative encoding: elaborative interrogation and self-explanation, relating to the self and other rich networks, using analogies, and etymological encoding. Retrieval practice is another well-supported learning approach with an extensive literature backing its effectiveness (see Roediger & Karpicke, 2006a for a review). It involves actively recalling information from memory, which has been shown to slow forgetting over time (Roediger & Karpicke, 2006b). In the classic experimental task, participants are given some material to study, such as a passage. In the experimental condition, participants are then asked to practice recalling what they remember from the material, often in the form of writing down everything that can be recalled. In the control condition, instead of a test of their memory, participants are simply given a second chance to study the learning material. It is generally found that participants who engage in retrieval practice better remember the learning material than those who restudy.

Retrieval practice in an online learning environment can take on many forms. Quizzes work well presumably because students try to remember what they have learned to answer the questions. Applications for online flashcards can be used by instructors to create flashcard sets, and some can even be embedded directly within a page of a learning management system for students to use. During synchronous video conference sessions, students can be asked to respond to retrieval practice questions using online polling software or even the video conferencing tool itself. See Millet et al. (2021) for additional examples.

In a review, McDaniel (2023) found that retrieval practice and elaborative encoding nicely complement each other as learning approaches and can be combined for an additive effect. It is believed that elaborative encoding enhances retrieval practice effects because it enriches the knowledge representation and, in turn, creates better retrieval cues. An important boundary condition for combining elaborative encoding and retrieval practice, however, is that the benefits are not quite the same when the two approaches are used simultaneously. It is therefore suggested that elaborative encoding should only be used during initial encoding and followed up with retrieval practice (Miyatsu & McDaniel, 2019; Karpicke & Smith, 2012).

BEFORE YOU GO

Part of the intention of this chapter has been to share some concrete ideas for implementing elaborative encoding in the online learning environment. However, the other part has been to highlight the general approach and benefit of connecting what students are learning to what they already know. Pre-existing knowledge plays a very important role in the learning process, and only a handful of the countless ways it can be utilized to give a boost to comprehension and memory for the learning content have been discussed here. As a scholar of teaching and learning, you are encouraged to continue to explore ways that new learning can be integrated with students' pre-existing knowledge in your own teaching and learning environments. Keep experimenting, keep connecting, and keep making it meaningful.

REFERENCES

Anderson, J. R. (1988). A spreading activation theory of memory. In Collins, A., & Smith, E. E. (Eds.), *Readings in cognitive science: A perspective from psychology and artificial intelligence* (pp. 137–154). Morgan Kaufmann Publishers, Inc., DOI: 10.1016/B978-1-4832-1446-7.50016-9

Anderson, J. R., & Reder, L. M. (1979). An elaborative processing explanation of depth of processing. In Cermak, L. S., & Craik, F. I. M. (Eds.), *Levels of processing in human memory* (pp. 385–403). Lawrence Erlbaum Associates., DOI: 10.4324/9781315796192

Atkinson, R. K., Renkl, A., & Merrill, M. M. (2003). Transitioning from studying examples to solving problems: Effects of self-explanation prompts and fading worked-out steps. *Journal of Educational Psychology*, 95(4), 774–783. DOI: 10.1037/0022-0663.95.4.774

Ayto, J. (2020). The Oxford dictionary of idioms (4th ed.). Oxford University Press eBooks. https://doi.org/DOI: 10.1093/acref/9780198845621.001.0001

Bagheri, M. S., & Fazel, I. (2010). Effects of etymological elaboration on the EFL students' comprehension and retention of idioms. *Journal of Pan-Pacific Association of Applied Linguistics*, 14(1), 45–55. https://files.eric.ed.gov/fulltext/EJ920503.pdf

Baleghizadeh, S., & Bagheri, M. I. M. (2012). The effect of etymology elaboration on EFL students' comprehension and retention of idioms. *3L: Language, linguistics, literature, 18*(1), 23-32. http://journalarticle.ukm.my/4061/

Beaty, R. E., Kenett, Y. N., & Hass, R. W. (2019). Fanning creative thought: Semantic richness impacts divergent thinking. *Proceedings of the Annual Meeting of the Cognitive Science Society, 41*, 126–131. https://escholarship.org/uc/item/40p1s98s

Beaty, R. E., Kenett, Y. N., Hass, R. W., & Schacter, D. L. (2023). Semantic memory and creativity: The costs and benefits of semantic memory structure in generating original ideas. *Thinking & Reasoning*, 29(2), 305–339. DOI: 10.1080/13546783.2022.2076742 PMID: 37113618

Berry, D. C. (1983). Metacognitive experience and transfer of logical reasoning. *The Quarterly Journal of Experimental Psychology. A, Human Experimental Psychology*, 35(1), 39–49. DOI: 10.1080/14640748308402115

Bisra, K., Liu, Q., Nesbit, J. C., Salimi, F., & Winne, P. H. (2018). Inducing self-explanation: A meta-analysis. *Educational Psychology Review*, 30(3), 703–725. DOI: 10.1007/s10648-018-9434-x

Boers, F. (2000). Metaphor awareness and vocabulary retention. *Applied Linguistics*, 21(4), 553–571. DOI: 10.1093/applin/21.4.553

Boers, F., Demecheleer, M., & Eyckmans, J. (2004). Etymological elaboration as a strategy for learning idioms. In *Language learning and language teaching* (pp. 53–78). John Benjamins Publishing Co., DOI: 10.1075/lllt.10.07boe

Boers, F., Eyckmans, J., & Stengers, H. (2007). Presenting figurative idioms with a touch of etymology: More than mere mnemonics? *Language Teaching Research*, 11(1), 43–62. DOI: 10.1177/1362168806072460

Callender, A. A., & McDaniel, M. A. (2007). The benefits of embedded question adjuncts for low and high structure builders. *Journal of Educational Psychology*, 99(2), 339–348. DOI: 10.1037/0022-0663.99.2.339

Chi, M. T., Bassok, M., Lewis, M. W., Reimann, P., & Glaser, R. (1989). Self-explanations: How students study and use examples in learning to solve problems. *Cognitive Science*, 13(2), 145–182. DOI: 10.1016/0364-0213(89)90002-5

Chi, M. T., De Leeuw, N., Chiu, M., & Lavancher, C. (1994). Eliciting self-explanations improves understanding. *Cognitive Science*, 18(3), 439–477. DOI: 10.1207/s15516709cog1803_3

Clark, J. M., & Paivio, A. (1991). Dual coding theory and education. *Educational Psychology Review*, 3(3), 149–210. DOI: 10.1007/BF01320076

Collins, A. M., & Loftus, E. F. (1975). A spreading-activation theory of semantic processing. *Psychological Review*, 82(6), 407–428. DOI: 10.1037/0033-295X.82.6.407

Craik, F. I., & Lockhart, R. S. (1972). Levels of processing: A framework for memory research. *Journal of Verbal Learning and Verbal Behavior*, 11(6), 671–684. DOI: 10.1016/S0022-5371(72)80001-X

Craik, F. I. M., & Tulving, E. (1975). Depth of processing and the retention of words in episodic memory. *Journal of Experimental Psychology. General*, 104(3), 268–294. DOI: 10.1037/0096-3445.104.3.268

Donnelly, C. M., & McDaniel, M. A. (1993). Use of analogy in learning scientific concepts. *Journal of Experimental Psychology. Learning, Memory, and Cognition*, 19(4), 975–987. DOI: 10.1037/0278-7393.19.4.975 PMID: 8345330

Dunlosky, J., Rawson, K. A., Marsh, E. J., Nathan, M. J., & Willingham, D. T. (2013). Improving students' learning with effective learning techniques: Promising directions from cognitive and educational psychology. *Psychological Science in the Public Interest*, 14(1), 4–58. DOI: 10.1177/1529100612453266 PMID: 26173288

Fiorella, L., & Mayer, R. E. (2021). The generative activity principle in multimedia learning. In Mayer, R. E., & Fiorella, L. (Eds.), *The Cambridge handbook of multimedia learning* (pp. 339–350). Cambridge University Press., DOI: 10.1017/9781108894333.036

Gentner, D., & Jeziorski, M. (2012). Historical shifts in the use of analogy in science. In Gholson, B., Shadish, W. R.Jr, Neimeyer, R. A., & Houts, A. C. (Eds.), *Psychology of science: Contributions to metascience* (pp. 296–325). Cambridge University Press., DOI: 10.1017/CBO9781139173667.016

Ghorbani, M. R. (2017). The synergistic effect of funny pictures and etymological elaboration on promoting EFL students' idiom retention and recall. *Journal of Language and Linguistic Studies*, 13(1), 146–155. https://files.eric.ed.gov/fulltext/EJ1140674.pdf

Gick, M. L., & Holyoak, K. J. (1980). Analogical problem solving. *Cognitive Psychology*, 12(3), 306–355. DOI: 10.1016/0010-0285(80)90013-4

Gick, M. L., & Holyoak, K. J. (1983). Schema induction and analogical transfer. *Cognitive Psychology*, 15(1), 1–38. DOI: 10.1016/0010-0285(83)90002-6

Gjerde, V., Paulsen, V. H., Holst, B., & Kolstø, S. D. (2022). Problem solving in basic physics: Effective self-explanations based on four elements with support from retrieval practice. *Physical Review. Physics Education Research*, 18(1), 010136. Advance online publication. DOI: 10.1103/PhysRevPhysEducRes.18.010136

Golaghaei, N., & Kakolian, S. (2015). The effect of visual and etymological treatments on learning decomposable idioms among EFL students. *International Journal of Applied Linguistics and English Literature*, 4(5), 72–81. DOI: 10.7575/aiac.ijalel.v.4n.5p.72

Golke, S., Steininger, T., & Wittwer, J. (2022). What makes students overestimate their text comprehension? The impact of student characteristics on judgment bias. *Educational Psychology Review*, 34(4), 2405–2450. DOI: 10.1007/s10648-022-09687-0

Halpern, D. F., Hansen, C., & Riefer, D. (1990). Analogies as an aid to understanding and memory. *Journal of Educational Psychology*, 82(2), 298–305. DOI: 10.1037/0022-0663.82.2.298

Hayes, D. A., & Henk, W. A. (1986). Understanding and remembering complex prose augmented by analogic and pictorial illustration. *Journal of Reading Behavior*, 18(1), 63–78. DOI: 10.1080/10862968609547556

Holyoak, K. J., Ichien, N., & Lu, H. (2024). Analogy and the generation of ideas. *Creativity Research Journal*, 36(3), 1–12. DOI: 10.1080/10400419.2023.2232673

Holyoak, K. J., & Koh, K. (1987). Surface and structural similarity in analogical transfer. *Memory & Cognition*, 15(4), 332–340. DOI: 10.3758/BF03197035 PMID: 3670053

Kalenzaga, S., Sperduti, M., Anssens, A., Martinelli, P., Devauchelle, A., Gallarda, T., Delhommeau, M., Lion, S., Amado, I., Krebs, M., Oppenheim, C., & Piolino, P. (2015). Episodic memory and self-reference via semantic autobiographical memory: Insights from an fMRI study in younger and older adults. *Frontiers in Behavioral Neuroscience*, 8. Advance online publication. DOI: 10.3389/fnbeh.2014.00449 PMID: 25628546

Karpicke, J. D., & Smith, M. A. (2012). Separate mnemonic effects of retrieval practice and elaborative encoding. *Journal of Memory and Language*, 67(1), 17–29. DOI: 10.1016/j.jml.2012.02.004

Keefer, L. A., & Landau, M. J. (2016). Metaphor and analogy in everyday problem solving. *Wiley Interdisciplinary Reviews: Cognitive Science*, 7(6), 394–405. DOI: 10.1002/wcs.1407 PMID: 27582354

Kesebir, S., & Oishi, S. (2010). A spontaneous self-reference effect in memory: Why some birthdays are harder to remember than others. *Psychological Science*, 21(10), 1525–1531. DOI: 10.1177/0956797610383436 PMID: 20855903

Kintsch, W. (1988). The role of knowledge in discourse comprehension: A construction-integration model. *Psychological Review*, 95(2), 163–182. DOI: 10.1037/0033-295X.95.2.163 PMID: 3375398

Klein, S. B. (2012). Self, memory, and the self-reference effect: An examination of conceptual and methodological issues. *Personality and Social Psychology Review*, 16(3), 283–300. DOI: 10.1177/1088868311434214 PMID: 22291045

Klein, S. B., Loftus, J., & Burton, H. A. (1989). Two self-reference effects: The importance of distinguishing between self-descriptiveness judgments and autobiographical retrieval in self-referent encoding. *Journal of Personality and Social Psychology*, 56(6), 853–865. DOI: 10.1037/0022-3514.56.6.853

Kruger, J., & Dunning, D. (1999). Unskilled and unaware of it: How difficulties in recognizing one's own incompetence lead to inflated self-assessments. *Journal of Personality and Social Psychology*, 77(6), 1121–1134. DOI: 10.1037/0022-3514.77.6.1121 PMID: 10626367

Kumar, A. A. (2021). Semantic memory: A review of methods, models, and current challenges. *Psychonomic Bulletin & Review*, 28(1), 40–80. DOI: 10.3758/s13423-020-01792-x PMID: 32885404

Kwon, K., Park, S. J., Shin, S., & Chang, C. Y. (2019). Effects of different types of instructor comments in online discussions. *Distance Education*, 40(2), 226–242. DOI: 10.1080/01587919.2019.1602469

Landrum, R. E., Brakke, K., & McCarthy, M. A. (2019). The pedagogical power of storytelling. *Scholarship of Teaching and Learning in Psychology*, 5(3), 247–253. DOI: 10.1037/stl0000152

Lawrence, R., & Chai, X. J. (2021). Self-referential encoding of source information in recollection memory. *PLoS One*, 16(4), e0248044. DOI: 10.1371/journal.pone.0248044 PMID: 33857141

Li, E., Xiao, F., Zou, T., & Guo, J. (2021). Positive emotion of self-referential contexts could facilitate adult's novel word learning: An fNIRS study. *Brain and Language*, 221, 104994. DOI: 10.1016/j.bandl.2021.104994 PMID: 34303109

Liao, C., & Masters, R. S. (2001). Analogy learning: A means to implicit motor learning. *Journal of Sports Sciences*, 19(5), 307–319. DOI: 10.1080/02640410152006081 PMID: 11354610

Lin, L., & Atkinson, R. K. (2013). Enhancing learning from different visualizations by self-explanation prompts. *Journal of Educational Computing Research*, 49(1), 83–110. DOI: 10.2190/EC.49.1.d

Liu, Z., Wen, J., Liu, Y., & Hu, C. (2024). The effectiveness of self: A meta-analysis of using self-referential encoding techniques in education. *The British Journal of Educational Psychology*, 94(1), 112–137. DOI: 10.1111/bjep.12636 PMID: 37722845

Malmberg, K. J., Raaijmakers, J. G. W., & Shiffrin, R. M. (2019). 50 years of research sparked by Atkinson and Shiffrin (1968). *Memory & Cognition*, 47(4), 561–574. DOI: 10.3758/s13421-019-00896-7 PMID: 30689198

Mayer, R. E. (2024). The past, present, and future of the cognitive theory of multimedia learning. *Educational Psychology Review*, 36(1), 8. Advance online publication. DOI: 10.1007/s10648-023-09842-1

McDaniel, M. A. (2023). Combining retrieval practice with elaborative encoding: Complementary or redundant? *Educational Psychology Review*, 35(3), 75. Advance online publication. DOI: 10.1007/s10648-023-09784-8

McDaniel, M. A., & Donnelly, C. M. (1996). Learning with analogy and elaborative interrogation. *Journal of Educational Psychology*, 88(3), 508–519. DOI: 10.1037/0022-0663.88.3.508

McNamara, D. S. (2004). SERT: Self-explanation reading training. *Discourse Processes*, 38(1), 1–30. DOI: 10.1207/s15326950dp3801_1

Miller, G. A. (1994). The magical number seven, plus or minus two: Some limits on our capacity for processing information. *Psychological Review*, 101(2), 343–352. DOI: 10.1037/0033-295X.101.2.343 PMID: 8022966

Millet, A., Turcotte, N., & Yan, S. (2021). Retrieval practice and online learning. In Hoffman, J., & Blessinger, P. (Eds.), *International perspectives in online instruction: Innovations in higher education teaching and learning* (Vol. 40, pp. 95–112). Emerald Publishing Limited., DOI: 10.1108/S2055-364120210000040007

Miyatsu, T., & McDaniel, M. A. (2019). Adding the keyword mnemonic to retrieval practice: A potent combination for foreign language vocabulary learning? *Memory & Cognition*, 47(7), 1328–1343. DOI: 10.3758/s13421-019-00936-2 PMID: 31077068

Nelson, D. L., Kitto, K., Galea, D., McEvoy, C. L., & Bruza, P. D. (2013). How activation, entanglement, and searching a semantic network contribute to event memory. *Memory & Cognition*, 41(6), 797–819. DOI: 10.3758/s13421-013-0312-y PMID: 23645391

Nelson, D. L., McEvoy, C. L., & Pointer, L. (2003). Spreading activation or spooky action at a distance? *Journal of Experimental Psychology. Learning, Memory, and Cognition*, 29(1), 42–52. DOI: 10.1037/0278-7393.29.1.42 PMID: 12549582

Newby, T. J., Ertmer, P. A., & Stepich, D. A. (1995). Instructional analogies and the learning of concepts. *Educational Technology Research and Development*, 43(1), 5–18. DOI: 10.1007/BF02300478

Niebert, K., Marsch, S., & Treagust, D. F. (2012). Understanding needs embodiment: A theory-guided reanalysis of the role of metaphors and analogies in understanding science. *Science Education*, 96(5), 849–877. DOI: 10.1002/sce.21026

Novak, R. T., Bailey, E. G., Blinsky, B. D., Soffe, B. W., Patterson, D., Ockey, J., & Jensen, J. L. (2022). Verbalized studying and elaborative interrogation in the virtual classroom: Students with social anxiety prefer working alone, but working with a peer does not hurt their learning. *Journal of Microbiology & Biology Education*, 23(1), e00232–e21. DOI: 10.1128/jmbe.00232-21 PMID: 35496708

Paris, N. A., & Glynn, S. M. (2003). Elaborate analogies in science text: Tools for enhancing preservice teachers' knowledge and attitudes. *Contemporary Educational Psychology*, 29(3), 230–247. DOI: 10.1016/S0361-476X(03)00033-X

Pi, Z., Zhang, Y., Shi, D., Guo, X., & Yang, J. (2022). Is self-explanation better than explaining to a fictitious student when learning from video lectures? *British Journal of Educational Technology*, 53(6), 2012–2028. DOI: 10.1111/bjet.13230

Pierson, H. D. (1989). Using etymology in the classroom. *ELT Journal*, 43(1), 57–63. DOI: 10.1093/elt/43.1.57

Rau, M. A., Aleven, V., & Rummel, N. (2014). Successful learning with multiple graphical representations and self-explanation prompts. *Journal of Educational Psychology*, 107(1), 30–46. DOI: 10.1037/a0037211

Recht, D. R., & Leslie, L. (1988). Effect of prior knowledge on good and poor readers' memory of text. *Journal of Educational Psychology*, 80(1), 16–20. DOI: 10.1037/0022-0663.80.1.16

Roediger, H. L.III, & Karpicke, J. D. (2006a). The power of testing memory: Basic research and implications for educational practice. *Perspectives on Psychological Science*, 1(3), 181–210. DOI: 10.1111/j.1745-6916.2006.00012.x PMID: 26151629

Roediger, H. L.III, & Karpicke, J. D. (2006b). Test-enhanced learning. *Psychological Science*, 17(3), 249–255. DOI: 10.1111/j.1467-9280.2006.01693.x PMID: 16507066

Roediger, H. L.III, & Tekin, E. (2020). Recognition memory: Tulving's contributions and some new findings. *Neuropsychologia*, 139, 107350. DOI: 10.1016/j.neuropsychologia.2020.107350 PMID: 31978402

Rogers, T. B., Kuiper, N. A., & Kirker, W. S. (1977). Self-reference and the encoding of personal information. *Journal of Personality and Social Psychology*, 35(9), 677–688. DOI: 10.1037/0022-3514.35.9.677 PMID: 909043

Rubio, A., Vidal-Abarca, E., & Serrano-Mendizábal, M. (2022). How to assist the students while learning from text? Effects of inserting adjunct questions on text processing. *Instructional Science*, 50(5), 749–770. DOI: 10.1007/s11251-022-09592-7

Savarimuthu, A., & Ponniah, R. J. (2024). Receive, retain and retrieve: Psychological and neurobiological perspectives on memory retrieval. *Integrative Psychological & Behavioral Science*, 58(1), 303–318. DOI: 10.1007/s12124-023-09752-5 PMID: 36738400

Serbun, S. J., Shih, J. Y., & Gutchess, A. H. (2011). Memory for details with self-referencing. *Memory (Hove, England)*, 19(8), 1004–1014. DOI: 10.1080/09658211.2011.626429 PMID: 22092106

Smith, B. L., Holliday, W. G., & Austin, H. W. (2010). Students' comprehension of science textbooks using a question-based reading strategy. *Journal of Research in Science Teaching*, 47(4), 363–379. DOI: 10.1002/tea.20378

Specht, J. A., Wood, E. J., Willoughby, T., & Boudreau, R. L. (1999). Evaluating the efficacy of elaborative strategies for remembering expository text. *The Alberta Journal of Educational Research*, 45(2), 170–183. https://www.proquest.com/scholarly-journals/evaluating-efficacy-elaborative-strategies/docview/228617178/se-2

Stein, B. S., & Bransford, J. D. (1979). Constraints on effective elaboration: Effects of precision and subject generation. *Journal of Verbal Learning and Verbal Behavior*, 18(6), 769–777. DOI: 10.1016/S0022-5371(79)90481-X

Sweller, J. (1988). Cognitive load during problem solving: Effects on learning. *Cognitive Science*, 12(2), 257–285. DOI: 10.1207/s15516709cog1202_4

Symons, C. S., & Johnson, B. T. (1997). The self-reference effect in memory: A meta-analysis. *Psychological Bulletin*, 121(3), 371–394. DOI: 10.1037/0033-2909.121.3.371 PMID: 9136641

Thibodeau, P. H., & Boroditsky, L. (2011). Metaphors we think with: The role of metaphor in reasoning. *PLoS One*, 6(2), e16782. DOI: 10.1371/journal.pone.0016782 PMID: 21373643

Tulving, E. (1974). Cue-dependent forgetting. *American Scientist*, 62(1), 74–82. https://psycnet.apa.org/record/1974-20253-001

Tulving, E., & Thomson, D. M. (1973). Encoding specificity and retrieval processes in episodic memory. *Psychological Review*, 80(5), 352–373. DOI: 10.1037/h0020071

Turk, D. J., Cunningham, S. J., & Macrae, C. N. (2008). Self-memory biases in explicit and incidental encoding of trait adjectives. *Consciousness and Cognition*, 17(3), 1040–1045. DOI: 10.1016/j.concog.2008.02.004 PMID: 18395467

VanLehn, K., Jones, R. M., & Chi, M. T. (1992). A model of the self-explanation effect. *Journal of the Learning Sciences*, 2(1), 1–59. DOI: 10.1207/s15327809jls0201_1

Vendetti, M. S., Wu, A., & Holyoak, K. J. (2014). Far-out thinking. *Psychological Science*, 25(4), 928–933. DOI: 10.1177/0956797613518079 PMID: 24463552

Vosniadou, S., & Schommer, M. (1988). Explanatory analogies can help children acquire information from expository text. *Journal of Educational Psychology*, 80(4), 524–536. DOI: 10.1037/0022-0663.80.4.524

Weinstein, Y., Sumeracki, M., & Caviglioli, O. (2019). *Understanding how we learn: A visual guide*. Routledge. https://eric.ed.gov/?id=ED591769

Wiggins, G., & McTighe, J. (2005). *Understanding by design* (2nd ed.). Association for Supervision and Curriculum Development ASCD.

Williams, J. J., Lombrozo, T., & Rehder, B. (2013b). The hazards of explanation: Overgeneralization in the face of exceptions. *Journal of Experimental Psychology. General*, 142(4), 1006–1014. DOI: 10.1037/a0030996 PMID: 23294346

Woloshyn, V. E., Pressley, M., & Schneider, W. (1992). Elaborative-interrogation and prior-knowledge effects on learning of facts. *Journal of Educational Psychology*, 84(1), 115–124. DOI: 10.1037/0022-0663.84.1.115

Wong, R. M., Lawson, M. J., & Keeves, J. (2002). The effects of self-explanation training on students' problem solving in high-school mathematics. *Learning and Instruction*, 12(2), 233–262. DOI: 10.1016/S0959-4752(01)00027-5

Wylie, R., & Chi, M. T. H. (2014). The self-explanation principle in multimedia learning. In Meyer, R. E. (Ed.), *The Cambridge Handbook of Multimedia Learning* (pp. 413–432)., DOI: 10.1017/CBO9781139547369.021

Zheng, L., Long, M., Chen, B., & Fan, Y. (2023). Promoting knowledge elaboration, socially shared regulation, and group performance in collaborative learning: An automated assessment and feedback approach based on knowledge graphs. *International Journal of Educational Technology in Higher Education*, 20(1), 46. Advance online publication. DOI: 10.1186/s41239-023-00415-4

Zhu, W., Wang, F., Mayer, R. E., & Liu, T. (2024). Effects of explaining a science lesson to others or to oneself: A cognitive neuroscience approach. *Learning and Instruction*, 91, 101897. DOI: 10.1016/j.learninstruc.2024.101897

Zolfagharkhani, M., & Ghorbani Moghadam, R. (2011). The effect of etymology instruction on vocabulary learning of upper-intermediate EFL Iranian students. *Canadian Social Science*, 7(6), 1–9. DOI: 10.3968/j.css.1923669720110706.180

KEY TERMS AND DEFINITIONS

Analogy: An analogy is a comparison between two entities that maps systematic correspondences between their elements. It serves as a framework to help students make sense of less-known entities by relating them to better-known entities. Analogy use is an elaborative encoding method.

Elaborative Encoding: Elaborative encoding is a teaching and learning tool that involves helping students make sense of new concepts and material by connecting them to their pre-existing knowledge. This process enhances the encoded information with relevant details, supporting better understanding, memory retention, and the ability to make inferences.

Elaborative Interrogation: Elaborative interrogation is an elaborative encoding method that involves prompting students to explain their understanding by answering *How?* and *Why?* questions about to-be-learned concepts and content.

Etymological Elaboration: Etymological elaboration involves explaining the origin and background of terms to students. By connecting new terms to their etymological roots, students can better understand and remember them. While this method is particularly useful for learning idioms and complex vocabulary in second language learning, it should be considered an elaborative encoding method to be applied to other subjects.

Self-Explanation: Self-explanation is an elaborative encoding method where students are prompted to explain their understanding of the learning material, either during or after its presentation.

Self-Reference Effect: The self-reference effect refers to the phenomenon where information related to the self is better remembered than information not related to the self. This effect is believed to occur because knowledge about the self is richer and more interconnected than other types of knowledge. Referring to students' selves is an elaborative encoding method.

Spreading Activation: Spreading activation refers to a theory of memory that suggests knowledge is organized in the brain as a network of interconnected nodes. When one node (representing a concept) is activated, this activation can spread to other connected nodes, resulting in their activation. The extent of this activation depends on the strength of the connections between the nodes, which is determined by how closely relate their concepts are.

Chapter 10

E-Teaching via an Online Flipped Class on Facebook Group: During COVID-19 Pandemic and Beyond

Faiza Benaicha
https://orcid.org/0000-0003-0692-029X
GSLSD Research Lab, Abdelhamid Ibn Badis University, Algeria

Rafik El Amine Ghobrini
https://orcid.org/0000-0003-4028-8793
DSPM Research Lab, Abdelhamid Ibn Badis University, Algeria

Khadidja Boudour
https://orcid.org/0009-0004-6119-6251
DSPM Research Lab, Abdelhamid Ibn Badis University, Algeria

Abed Hamadouch
https://orcid.org/0009-0006-6506-8315
DSPM Research Lab, Abdelhamid Ibn Badis University, Algeria

ABSTRACT

Amidst the global pandemic of Covid-19, the shift towards online learning has become inevitable for students, especially for those who will sit for the Baccalaureate exam -secondary school graduation exam. To address this, a web-designed research method was opted for to develop an online flipped virtual classroom that can enhance secondary school students' engagement and provide them with the adequate assistance needed to prepare for this crucial exam. The web-driven solution was refined

DOI: 10.4018/979-8-3693-7595-2.ch010

in every iteration through the continuous feedback of 52 students from 8 different provinces in Algeria. By the end, 25 secondary school teachers were invited to the Facebook group to share their perspectives on this web-enhanced online method of teaching and validate the framework through a self-reported questionnaire. The findings report an approved framework of how to practically leverage the flipped model in an online-only setting along with the implications it holds on a local and global scale.

INTRODUCTION

The outbreak of the virus led to a new way of life characterized by quarantine, social distancing, lockdown, health considerations and anxiety (Vaillancourt et al., 2021) particularly as the disease became highly contagious and no cure was initially available. For this reason, policymakers had to act quickly and efficiently to mitigate risks (Lancaster et al, 2020). It became clear that many countries were unprepared for this unprecedented outbreak, leading to critical instability across various sectors, including education (Munastiwi & Puryono, 2021). Students of all ages were forced to pursue their education online from home (Ghobrini et al., 2022), despite a shortage in ICT infrastructure in some developing countries (Orifamah, 2021). The burden primarily fell on teachers, who faced work overload (Hong et al., 2021), unfinished program, sanitary regulations (Valeeva & Kalimullin, 2021), unfamiliarity with e-learning tools (Octaberlina & Muslimin, 2020) and significant student concerns (Aslan, 2021) about their academic progress and degrees.

Fortunately, with the determination of teachers and collaboration of students (Gopinathan et al., 2022), many obstacles could be overcome. Despite the severity of the pandemic and the unavailability of some tech tools (Tadesse & Muluye, 2020), educational stakeholders managed to maintain a basic level of instruction at both school and university levels. In Algeria, for instance, university students continued their courses through the MOODLE platform during the COVID-19 pandemic (Elkateb, 2022). However, students' views and perceptions of e-learning varied significantly, with some Algerian university students preferring traditional learning over online alternatives due to various challenges (Chadli & Djaileb, 2023; Benadla & Hadji, 2021). Cohort studies report that teachers and students in Algerian universities show certain awareness about the necessity of implementing e-learning strategies and remain adaptable to ongoing global changes (Ghounane, 2022).

From a more context-specific standpoint, no official online learning pathway was mandated by the Algerian Ministry of Education, unlike at the university level. The only solution offered to secondary students was teacher-generated videos uploaded to YouTube, which many students were unaware of. Moreover, there was no direct contact between students and their respective teachers. As a result, both teachers and students turned to social media platforms, particularly Facebook (Ghobrini, 2020; Ghounane, 2020; Ghounane, 2021), where instructors - through trial and error - led initiatives to support students, particularly those preparing for the baccalaureate exam. Opting for social media rather than a formal educational platform may seem inadequate, but during that uncertain period, neither teachers nor students received any training on how to use these platforms. This lack of preparation made social media an ideal e-space, as online communities of students had already been formed there (Ghobrini et al., 2024).

During the first lockdown of the global pandemic, 80% of Algeria's population used Facebook (Social Media Stats Algeria, 2021). As a result, Facebook emerged as the primary online space connecting teachers and students, helping mitigate learning disruptions (Blizak et al., 2020; Ghounane, 2020). Studies consistently highlight students' preference for Facebook, prompting many teachers to adopt the platform to engage with their students. This is why, this research focuses on Facebook as the social outlet par excellence - chosen by teachers and students alike - (Haddad, 2020; Sahraoui & Chaibendraa, 2020) motivating the current study to explore the implementation of a flipped model in an online-only environment. The study adapts a traditional framework to this new context, aiming to develop a model that enriches the scholarship of teaching and learning (SoTL) -that no only seeks to apply research-based knowledge but to transform it according to new context (Boyer, 1990; Shulman, 2011) and that is exactly what this research is about - by offering practical guidance for instructors pursuing similar e-educational endeavours.

Building on this rationale, the current research aims to answer the following questions:

1. How can the flipped classroom model be effectively implemented in an online-only environment on social media - mainly on Facebook and supplementary tools (e.g., YouTube) to adequately prepare Algerian Baccalaureate exam students?
2. What are the key factors that contribute to the success of an online flipped classroom model particularly in terms of student motivation, interaction, and learning outcomes?

ONLINE LEARNING AND TEACHING SCHOLARSHIPS

While learning and teaching often occur in a physical environment, they can also take place in a virtual online setting where both processes of teaching and learning might occur in different places and times. Unlike the traditional mode of learning and teaching, e-learning and teaching can occur synchronously and/or asynchronously online, allowing the main actors - namely learners and teachers - to interact with content at their own pace (Berestok, 2021). In this context, the internet has become an essential tool that disseminates knowledge, without which distance learning and teaching would not be possible (Babu & Sridevi, 2018). Siemens 2002 defines e-learning as "the marriage of technology and education, and most often, the instructional designer's greatest role is that of "bridging" concepts between the two worlds" (p.1). Online education is also known as internet-based or web-based education, distance learning, digital learning or e-learning along with other terms and labels that serve the same objective. The latter is first and foremost centred on the learner, who consumes knowledge. According to Sadiku et al. (2018), the learner is the target objective of any learning experience, and the job of technology used is to keep him hooked. They claim that "online teaching and learning is designed to reach and engage the modern learner on one-to-one basis anywhere, anytime" (p.73). The shift to web-based learning is motivated by the fact that the internet offers a type of education that appeals to 21st-century learners and teachers who are born techno-driven creatures. Learners sought ways to overcome obstacles of accessibility and availability of knowledge in traditional in-person learning, whereas designers of online education made endeavours to provide up-to-date and efficient solutions to these constraints by offering remote learning experiences granted by technology. The dilemma occurs at the effectiveness in terms of engagement, retention and the overall academic performance (Navarro & McGrath, 2021).

The shift from traditional in-person education to web-based learning and teaching was incremental and it was done after a number of advents with occasional hybrid back-up from traditional education. However, the adoption of digital teaching and learning took place in a blink of an eye after the COVID-19 pandemic thanks to the full-fledged learning experience that technology could offer. This mode of instruction has been recognised as being "a catalyst to democratize access to education" (Navarro & McGrath, 2021, p. 496). Yet, distance online learning has proven its significance on different levels. Based on the model of Davis (1989) of perceived usefulness and ease of use and user acceptance, we can distinguish several qualities linked to online education:

1. Flexibility and autonomy of learning: Digital learning platforms, including learning management systems (LMS), allow teachers to create and design content based on the needs of learners as individuals or as groups along with increasing satisfaction and learning quality (Rabiman et al., 2020). Moreover, learners can consult courses made online by their respective instructors or public content at their own pace (Tallent-Runnels et al., 2006). Hence, with technology, instructors can offer personalised learning (Alamri et al., 2020) and cater to all types of learners and learning styles (Heitink et al., 2016).

2. Higher engagement rate: The digital environment of e-education is characterised by various stimuli that appeal to the digital learner, particularly in online collaboration, competition or even gamification (Hamari et al., 2014). It keeps users hooked to the digital content through different dynamics such as instant feedback, mastery-based protocol, rewards, achievement levels and so on (Dignan, 2011).

3. Academic performance: Technological-enabled education boosts engagement and motivation which can eventually improve academic performance (Fonseca, 2019; Tawafak et al., 2018; Tlhoaele et al., 2016) particularly in terms of self-regulation (Chung et al., 2022), knowledge retention, and critical thinking skills (Malik, 2023) despite the social and technical barriers (Mellati & Khademi, 2019).

4. Cost efficiency and time management: Online education can save tuition fees compared to on-campus education. Students can attend courses and get degrees through virtual classrooms, which saves time and money. As a matter of fact, technology has enabled free access to many resources. As argued by Bishop and Verleger (2013, p.1), "the technological movement has enabled the amplification and duplication of information at an extremely low-cost."

The transition to a technologically mediated mode of instruction has been widely accepted amongst learners and instructors alike since they look for flexibility and autonomy during their pursuit of knowledge. They look for valuable encyclopaedic content, which cannot be achieved unless access to internet is available.

EDUCATIONALIZING SOCIAL MEDIA

Facebook and YouTube

By and large, social media networks are occupying almost all aspects of personal, academic, and professional life despite ethical considerations. Networking platforms like Facebook, YouTube, Moodle, Zoom and WhatsApp have become the only bridge to education during the COVID-19 pandemic era (Shamsabadi et al., 2023). More particularly, studies report that platforms like Facebook and YouTube are the most frequently used social media sites by faculty staff because they are believed to be popular amongst young as well as adult learners who are fully immersed in their smart devices. Teachers design their online assignments and content accordingly (Moran et al., 2011). In the same vein, with the emergence of COVID-19 regulations, educationalizing social media has become a must-do rather than a can-do.

Undeniably, 21st-century students who are used to constant technological changes and trends did not object to the fact of integrating social media as the main means of instruction and the sole source of information during the pandemic lockdown. Furthermore, many assets are attributed to social media use in education. Chief among them is their crucial role in enhancing collaborative learning (Ford et al., 2011), peer interaction, teacher engagement, and knowledge-sharing behaviours, ultimately resulting in better academic performance (Ansari & Khan, 2020) in addition to socializing and community-building (Al-Bashabsheh & Pradhan, 2023). In fact, cohort research reported the utility and usefulness of Facebook as an online learning tool during the COVID-19 pandemic, since it connects them with their classmates and enables the discussion and sharing of academic content (Ulla & Perales, 2021).

Conversely, students and teachers encountered some limitations when enrolled in a Facebook online learning environment. These issues are often linked to internet connectivity, lack of family support, a noisy home environment, an increased number of assignments and the difficulty of understanding content in an asynchronous setting, along with the difficulty of gathering and organising a group chat learning session (Ulla & Perales, 2021). In addition, there was also a lack of clear policies and actions regarding distance learning, as well as an overload of information and limited methodological guidance for this new online academic approach (Shamsabadi et al., 2023).

Limitations

However, the proliferation of social media in education is not without consequences. Despite its usefulness, internet-based learning raises some concerns about integrity and privacy regarding social media (Moran et al., 2011) where students' social life and their academic pursuits have surprisingly merged, leading them to struggle to balance their needs and objectives and ultimately resulting in distractions (Al-Bashabsheh & Pradhan, 2023).

Eventually, social media platforms are an integral part of every digital individual's life; it would be utopian to avoid all distractions and notifications constantly appearing on smart screens. This attachment to the digital life can substantially affect learning due to the excessive and unwise use of social media Emerick et al. (2019). Further, being connected to these tempting and appealing social networks hinders users from pursuing their daily serious tasks and missions because their attention is diverted from the main goal to other stimuli (Koessmeier & Büttner, 2021).

Flipped Classroom in Online Education

Advocates of in-person learning and teaching sought ways to integrate technology into their educational practices through a variety of tools. Hence, the flipped classroom model emphasizes active learning during class, while students gain foundational knowledge on their own before attending in-person sessions (Long et al., 2016; Martinelli et al., 2018; Mortensen & Nicholson, 2015). This movement of bringing a change to educational practices is deeply ingrained into the principles of the scholarship of teaching and learning (SoTL) as it focuses on enhancing teaching and learning through educators' expertise, not only within their own courses but also in broader contexts, by leveraging their knowledge to improve educational practices (Bernstein, 2013). In essence, SoTL enables practitioners to take a more active role in sharing SoTL findings with colleagues, increasing the likelihood that these findings are applied or adjusted to fit their teaching, without requiring them to locate or interpret the research independently (Maurer, 2022). This shows how SoTL promotes generating and publicly disseminating evidence related to teaching and learning (McKinney, 2003) through different pathways including knowledge mobilization framework that fosters co-creation and dissemination (Maurer et al., 2021) in different educational endeavours particularly that of online flipped pedagogy.

In the same token, this flipped model is an innovative instructional approach that shifts lectures and teacher-led instruction to at-home or online settings, allowing in-class time to focus on interactive, student-cantered activities and hands-on practice (DeLozier & Rhodes, 2016; Hwang et al., 2015). According to Van Alten et al. (2019), the flipped classroom is a pedagogy that combines in-class instruction with online homework before in-person interaction. Moreover, this type of learning is akin to blended learning where students view the content before the scheduled class and prepare questions to be thoroughly discussed with the class instructor which is the investigation phase. As defined by Nwosisi et al. (2016, p. 348) flipped instruction or flipped classroom is "a form of blended learning in which students learn new content online usually at home, and what used to be homework (assigned problems) is now done in class with teachers offering more personalized guidance and interaction with students, instead of lecturing."

Arguably, much attention has been driven towards the flipped classroom, because not only is it innovative, collaborative and engaging but it also saves time and adds more value to class interaction. When students view core concepts of the content at home, they come to class with certain prerequisites on which they would build further knowledge and prepare questions for their instructors, and eventually, they will be able to invest face-to-face time in order to discuss, analyse problems and come up with solutions and conclusions (Van Alten et al., 2019). Unlike the "I do," "We do," and "You do" of the traditional teaching approaches, in the flipped classroom the process is reversed to "You do," "We do," and "I do" where the student starts the learning process beforehand through videos, PPT presentations and so forth. Very often students prefer flipped classes over in-class-only lectures (Bishop & Verleger, 2013). Further, Han (2022) argues that two fundamental elements contribute to positively shaping the academic upbringing of students namely educational technology and activity-based learning where the lesson starts technologically at home and class time is allocated to problem-solving and collaborative activities.

Flipped classrooms can be applied through different online tools amongst which we can distinguish social media being the most commonly used medium of interaction among students mainly (Collado-Valero, et al., 2021). Whether on Google Meet, Facebook, Telegram, or Instagram; learning can reach learners in their preferred zone and vice versa. This flipped model is not only applied in EFF but also applied across different disciplines most notably social sciences and humanities (e.g., Brooks, 2014; Kurtz et al., 2014), education (e.g., Fraga & Harmon, 2014; Vaughan, 2014), natural sciences (e.g., Ryan & Reid, 2015; Teo et al., 2014), engineering and technology (e.g., Amresh et al., 2013; Zappe et al., 2009), mathematics (e.g., Davies et al., 2013; Wilson, 2013), medical and health sciences (e.g., Pierce & Fox, 2012; Tune et al., 2013) and art (e.g., Enfeld, 2013). In a study conducted by Zhao and Yang (2023), it is argued that flipping an English as a Foreign Language (EFL) classroom through social media substantially improves the writing skills of EFL learners in addition to other assets attributed to the implementation of social media in the reverse classroom such as online group discussions and peer interaction, independent and responsible learning.

Despite the usefulness and the utility of social media networks in flipping the class, their drawbacks could impede the fulfilment of a desired academic outcome where learners and teachers would not benefit from the assets of social media if the latter is misused unreasonably. By the same token, Han (2022) points out the negative effects of social media use in the flipped environment, namely "academic dropouts, decreased class focus, cyber privacy harassment, internet addiction, inadequate information and violation of personal, legal or financial data" (p.5). Several challenges arise while flipping the classroom through social media. Therefore, the teacher should be well prepared to deliver off-class content that is clear, understandable and attractive to learners, because very often learners are faced with an overload of information in a lengthy pre-recorded video along with a bundle of assignments which puts more pressure on the cognition of learners. Additionally, the instructor's role in a flipped classroom is not limited to the physical classroom setting; they should be available to their learners before, during and after the class, which puts more responsibility and burden on his shoulders (Han, 2022).

THE E-EDUCATION CHALLENGES IN THE ALGERIAN EDUCATIONAL CONTEXT

Education has always gone through an evolutionary status where educators tried a variety of methods and approaches to transmit knowledge. The advent undertaken to try out these novelties does not go without challenges and obstacles, which urges teachers to seek other alternatives. Yet, the adoption of a particular approach does not diminish the qualities of the previous approaches but rather adds more assets to pre-existing gaps.

By far, the 2019 contagious crisis opened the door to the implementation of many online gateways to education, particularly in Algeria which is known to be amongst the countries that integrated ICTs in many aspects of life. In accordance with the Global Competitiveness Report of 2019 issued by the World Economic Forum on ICT adoption, Algeria ranked 97th globally (Bellatreche & Aloutti, 2020) showing its openness and readiness to face current challenges through online solutions. Hence, the COVID-19 pandemic was a blessing in disguise that paved the way for the implementation of online learning despite all the challenges and limitations.

As discussed earlier, the breakout of the COVID-19 pandemic imposed new regulations in the educational field, subsequently, Algerian universities abruptly adopted new e-learning platforms such as Moodle and other social media like Facebook. Surprisingly, teachers and students' perceptions and attitudes towards the decision varied widely. Some students have not welcomed the new online trend and showed reluctance towards the transition to an online mode of learning (Blizak, et al, 2020) despite the fact that they belong to the Z generation. As far as EFL is concerned, some students use L1 to interact with their teachers and peers because Facebook is already known to them as an informal setting, so they don't feel the need to communicate in English during an online lecture (Ghounane, 2021).

As a matter of fact, trying out a new educational approach like e-learning and teaching does not go without limitations mainly when the shift is sudden and without prior preparation. Algerian university students and teachers faced many challenges because they were not familiar with distance learning; hence, some Algerian students preferred a blend of online and traditional modes of learning (Elkateb, 2022), whereas others discarded the idea of studying exclusively online and favoured the conventional mode of learning through handouts (Guessabi, 2021).

There were other challenges associated with e-learning during the Coronavirus lockdown, mostly technical issues such as lack of digital infrastructure, technical issues with Moodle platform (Ghobrini et al., 2024), loads of disorganised lessons and assignments uploaded at once. These facts could be due to teachers who are digitally illiterate or lack training (Bellatreche & Aloutti, 2020). Moreover, some students had a slow flow of internet connection and sometimes no connection to the virtual world because they live in shadow rural areas (Elkateb, 2022). Shortage of internet connection is prevailing even though Algeria has made great improvement in integrating ICTs as part of the strategy towards the momentum of information and communication technology and reducing the digital divide (Bellatreche & Aloutti, 2020).

Eventually, all challenges experienced in hybrid instructional activities in a digital milieu during COVID-19 will be overcome provided that these challenges would be well transformed into opportunities. Considering learners' needs and motivations, teachers' continuous professional development (CPD), notably MOOC-based CPD (Massive Open Online Courses) can provide well-structured resources which, in turn, could bridge the gap towards the establishment of online learning programs in Algeria (Ghobrini et al., 2023).

METHODOLOGY

To conduct the study, a design-based research (DBR) method was opted for to develop and devise progressively and iteratively an e-flipped classroom model that could be leveraged, later on by other educators and instructors for similar educational purposes. In this sense, design-based research is a well-accepted paradigm of educational research as its contribution has been acknowledged in the field of education. As a matter of fact, it creates a productive link between educational theory and innovations in classroom practices (Penuel et al., 2011; Ryu, 2020). In the same line of thought, designed-based research is cyclical in nature, as feedback comes from data collected tools that inform the researcher to alter the existing solution with the aim to improve it and re-test it in the next iteration (Archer, 2019). In other terms, this reflective process on the teaching practice of each iteration guides the instructor to adjust the delivery method to better suit the online context we are operating. In a more practice-driven narrative, the basic process of DBR involves developing solutions, called "interventions" to problems. Then, the interventions are put to use to test how well they work. The iterations may then be adapted and re-tested to improve upon existing web-driven solutions as illustrated (Reeves, 2006) **(seeFigure 1)**. The main goal of this online SoTL initiative is to devise new up-to-date frameworks for conceptualizing online learning and teaching (Johnson et al., 2017). Specifically, this scholarship aims to: 1. develop and validate a web-based flipped classroom framework that leverages social media - mainly Facebook and supplementary tools (e.g., YouTube) - to enhance secondary school students' engagement and learning outcomes in an online-only environment, 2. identify the perceived benefits and challenges of using Facebook as the primary platform for conducting online flipped classes

Figure 1. Design-based research approach

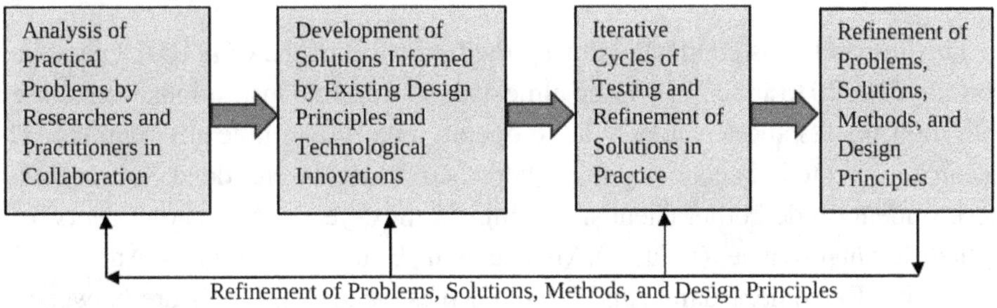

Source: Reeves (2006)

among Algerian secondary school students and teachers, 3. explore the implications of this web-based classroom framework using social media for optimizing online learning experiences and overcoming challenges associated with digital learning environments in Algeria. Along these lines, this research attempts to add to the existing body of literature in SoTL by attempting to re-configure the traditional concept of flipped class and adjust it in an online-only setting. SoTL is grounded in institutional, disciplinary, specific classroom, and cultural contexts (Hutchings & Huber, 2005) but it transcends into multi-disciplinary endeavours by transferring the acquired knowledge, often referred to as good practices, to other disciplines (Boyer, 1990). In fact, this research is based on the five SoTL principles (Felten, 2013): 1. investigating students' learning and trying to bring about solutions to enhance it, 2. being contextually grounded in a specific setting – in our case an online learning environment on social media, 3. employing sound research design – in our case DBR which is an effective research methodology that has the potential to bring about validated solutions to real-world academic challenges, 4. collaborating with learners which was the case as the final outcome was iteratively refined through students' continuous feedback and 5. sharing the findings publicly and this is what this book chapter is meant to do.

From another perspective, this method of research is similar to action research design, but they differ in the development and assessment process, as the final products need to be improved through the users' feedback - in our case the students - and experts in the domains - in our case the 25 secondary school instructors - that can validate the final outcome. Consequently, this aspect of collaboration is at the heart of the DBR-focused process (Denscombe, 2014) where all the participants' feedback was of utmost prominence in developing the web-based solution to an optimal stage (Ryu, 2020).

Context and Participants

This research was conducted during the first wave of the COVID-19 pandemic from April 2020 to June 2020 when almost all educational institutions were closed, obliging students and teachers alike to operate in a fully online environment. The researchers created a Facebook group where their students were added. Subsequently, these students added other friends, totalling 52 third-year secondary students from eight different provinces (wilayas): Mostaganem, Boumerdes, Algiers, Annaba, Sidi Bel Abbès, Relizane, Naama, and Oran. Of these students, 85.2% are between 17 and 19 years old, 11.1% are between 20 and 22, and 5.6% are over 23 years old. The students are from six different streams, namely: Technical Mathematics, Natural Sciences, Management and Economics, Mathematics, Literature and Philosophy, and Foreign Languages.

To validate the final web-based e-solution, 25 national secondary school teachers (males: 36% and females: 64%) from five different provinces, namely Mostaganem, Ain Temouchent, Chlef, Oran, and Tiaret, were involved. Of these teachers, 58% teach in urban areas and 42% teach in rural areas. Their teaching experiences vary: 32% stated that they are novices with 1 to 3 years of experience, 36% have between 4 and 8 years, and 32% have more than 9 years of teaching experience. Additionally, 88% of them have previously taught third-year secondary school students, which is a significant aspect as it lends more validity to the study.

Research Instruments

To complete this teacher-led research, three different data collection tools were utilized: online participant observation, student questionnaires, and teacher questionnaires. The first tool served to meticulously follow the step-by-step procedures undertaken in the Facebook group, where a considerable amount of student-student and student-teacher interactions were observed. It also helped the researchers trace the different stages and/or iterations of the research, during which the final web-oriented solution was progressively devised. The second tool was used to identify where students study, which stream they belong to, and their perspectives on this e-educational journey, including its pros and cons, as well as their suggestions on how to improve the overall e-teaching and learning process. The teachers were involved last to validate the end product through a self-reported questionnaire, which inquired about their teaching experiences and, most importantly, their assessments and standpoints regarding this entire socially-mediated instructional endeavour.

Research Procedure

Knowing the theory of flipped classrooms and adjusting it to a different online context is challenging. This research went through several iterations to properly apply the principles of flipped instruction. The first element was the online class in the Facebook group, and the second element was the type of communication, whether synchronous (in the Live meeting) or asynchronous (before or after the instantaneous meeting). With these elements, the adventure to reverse the classroom began. In the first iteration, students were given a simple assignment, and the solution would be discussed in the instant meeting. However, this assumed that some students already knew the lesson at hand, which was problematic for those who did not. Therefore, in the following iteration, grammatical tasks were given with a YouTube-based video of a grammatical lesson. Students were instructed to view the material and attempt to do the assignments alone, in pairs, or groups. Then, in the Live meeting, the instructor would address students' persisting gaps, followed by automatic quizzes to ensure full comprehension of the material. After a few iterations, the content posted in the group became chaotic. To address this in the final iterations, the content was structured using the "Guides"- a Facebook group feature- option which grouped the content into sections, helping students view the posted material in an organized manner - in this case, a mock back exam was assigned containing tasks related to text comprehension, grammar and writing. There were many iterations (**seeFigure 2).**Figure 2 showcases the three major iterations out of six that significantly assisted in developing the framework. Each iteration was drawn up after the end of the week and thus comprehended the pre-, during-, and post-meeting e-activities that were undertaken in this timeframe.

Figure 2. The major iterations of the study

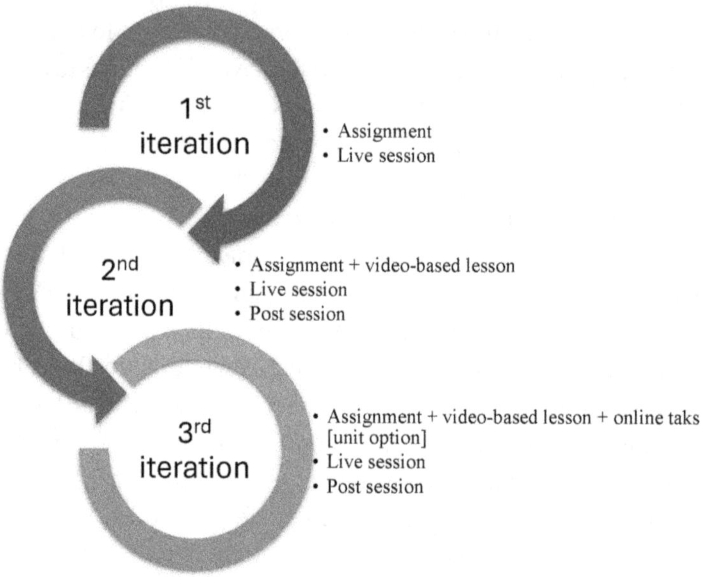

RESULTS AND DISCUSSION

After duly conducting this SoTL research endeavour, six elements rose into prominence notably, 1. online engagement, motivation and interaction, 2. self-paced learning and anonymity, 3. home-only e-education mindset and e-teacher's influence, 4. online collaboration and alternative/complementary platforms, 5. online distractions and limitations and finally, 6. the fruits of this research which is the framework and its implications.

Online Engagement, Motivation and Interaction

For starters, 71.15% of the students affirm that they like studying on Facebook. This finding was also reported by different studies (Ghobrini et al., 2024; Ghounane, 2021), which indicated that Facebook was the preferred e-space for conducting teaching-learning activities during the outbreak particularly in Algeria where 80% of the whole population was on this specific outlet (*Social Media Stats Algeria*, 2021). Additionally, students praised working on Facebook group by stating that it can not only "ease up the lessons," "understanding," and "expand our vocabulary background," but it also enables them to "exchange experiences," "work efficiently in collaboration with … peers," "ask … other members so as to get a detailed explanation of the answer" and "create a competitive and cooperative spirit." By the same token, the learners described learning in this socially-mediated sphere as "easy," "fun," "efficient," "helpful," "useful," "effortless," "fast," and even "relaxing." Another advantage is put forward by another student claiming that this tech-based mode of teaching helps them "… benefit from the wide range of students' ways of solving problems as they are from different parts of the country and thus discover new ideas." For these reasons, 100% of the students attest that this mode of online learning enhances both their motivation and engagement and these findings have been shed light on by Uçar and Goksel (2020) who assert that supplementary activities on Facebook play a crucial role in enhancing online EFL learners' motivation, engagement, and academic performance, fostering their persistence and dedication to achieving learning goals. Along these lines, after students prepare their pre-assigned task asynchronously, they would meet online via Facebook Live. Additionally, 88% of teachers found these e-meetings effective mainly because it is recorded (60%), the use of colloquial Algerian Arabic instead of the classical official Arabic (64%), and the use of colour when explaining on the online board (32%). For this reason, one teacher attests that "students feel more relaxed through it than in a classroom, and they feel excited and curious to listen and see their teacher explaining a lesson to them... it's a safe and encouraging environment for the learning process," and even suggest, "use it as an additional supportive method to the traditional one."

Self-Paced Learning and Anonymity

Another significant factor that was highlighted by some students is the self-paced mode of learning through the pre-recorded video-based lessons and recorded instantaneous meetings particularly for "slow learners" or for the ones who cannot attend the live meeting as mentioned by a participant, "If I am busy, unavailable or late I can always catch up" or "If I ever forget something (a part of the lesson) I can go back and review it." One student stressed that "If I do not understand, I re-watch the recording as much as I need until I understand." Another student adds that "I am very meticulous and don't like to miss anything that is why I must review it so as to grasp every aspect of the lesson." Moreover, one teacher attests that overall "slow learners and quick learners can adjust to their own pace of learning with the ability to fast forward or backwards in case they miss something." For this reason, 50% of students prefer to attend the meeting and have it saved for a later review, 28.85% prefer the recorded Live version, and 21.15% favour the e-meeting because, as claimed by a student, it allows us to "ask the teacher and get the corresponding answers." This means that during the online meeting, students can ask for clarification and thus obtain direct feedback which can help them clear out any ambiguity they might have about the task at hand. Parallel to this, almost half of the students (42, 30%) claim that they use an anonymous profile to tag along with the open class because of several reasons. One student said that he is "an introvert" which means that he is "not a social person." Another student alleged that "I join Facebook just to study and I don't interact or chat with other members." This signals that anonymity gives them a kind of comfort that they would not have if it were otherwise. One of the teachers clearly explains that:

> *Internet communication erases so many issues like shyness for some students since their identity is concealed. So, they can ask questions or make comments without feeling targeted by other classmates. These affective factors can hinder effective learning, and online learning is a good solution.*

This finding was equally emphasized in Ananyina's (2022) study as she contends that students who are used to digital tools bring their preference for anonymity into the virtual learning space, recognizing many advantages in remaining anonymous.

Home-Only E-Education Mindset and E-Teacher's Influence

In tandem with the benefits, self-paced learning in an online setting can yield a different perspective. The first is "no pressure" which means that students sit in the comfort of their homes and engage in the learning process. One student pointed out that "I can practice in an excellent and comfortable fashion as opposed to in class where all eyes are on me especially when I'm writing on the board." Another piece of the puzzle as one student mentioned is, "being in a room alone without clutter or disturbances is not like high school, where there are noisy classmates. On the contrary, you can study while drinking coffee - how can one not understand in such an environment?" What's more, this method "does not require much effort, especially because we can choose a suitable time for us to study, so the focus will increase significantly." In fact, one teacher noted that this is "new style of teaching … breaks down the boring routine" which shows that these technophile beings are very much into studying online. In other words, "it's an up-to-date method that matches students' lifestyle since they use internet and social media frequently," noted one of the teachers.

From another angle, the teacher-student rapport and the e-savoir-faire can play a crucial role in conducting an optimal e-teaching-learning experience. One student articulated that "having a highly-qualified teacher guide me and direct me to things that I cannot do on my own." "The teacher motivates us and gives us different pieces of information" and "… advice" so much so that "I feel that I am progressing" and "having fun" which made me "love the subject" and that is due to the teacher's "playful spirit and his method of teaching." These testimonials show how important the tutor-tutee relationship is and thus the necessity of creating a bond via targeted pedagogical strategies. This finding goes along the same vision as Glazier (2016) who reported that identifying a high-rapport relationship with the instructor is a crucial factor for student success and building rapport is a straightforward, instructor-led intervention that can greatly enhance online retention and grades. By contrast, some students feel that "the teacher is far" and hence prefer the face-to-face mode of teaching.

Online Collaboration and Alternative/Complementary Platforms

Operating in an online-only environment via social media, namely the Facebook group, enable students to "easily share ideas and information among students" and "know others' opinions" which helps in "consolidating information" mentioned some students. One student stated, "it helps students to exchange information and help each other overcome problems of understanding." This collaborative online spirit is integral in creating an e-community of peers where one can ask questions, share pedagogical materials and exchange ideas. The same findings have been uncovered in Selcuk and Jones's (2022) study which demonstrated that Turkish EFL students found that using Facebook groups for collaborative writing tasks was positive and comfortable, promotes an informal social connection, and creates a smart learning environment. All this collaborative work is taking place, first on the Facebook group, but also on YouTube to which 98,03% of the whole sample of students attested that watching the complementary YouTube videos shared before the online meeting helped them better grasp the grammatical lessons because they contain a "detailed explanation" of the lesson. A student mentioned that they were "short and they contain essential information" and another praised the "simplicity of lesson's presentation and method of delivering." In fact, all four videos are about seven minutes long so as not to lose the viewer's attention and give the students the main elements necessary for them to be able to fully understand the lesson. Specifically, 79,16% of all the teachers affirm that these YouTube videos are effective in revising grammatical lessons and 88% of them advise their students to watch these videos as supplementary materials for their grammatical lessons. A teacher noted that these videos "are an excellent way for learners to refresh their memory and correct possible wronged pre-established notions" as it "clarifies grammar lessons." Interestingly, one teacher remarked that it may fit "... to some types of learners' learning style" because "they grab the learner's attention, besides they are fun, motivating and often break from more traditional classroom activities." This finding is also discussed in Yu and Gao's study (2022) which focused solely on the effects of Video Length on a Flipped English Classroom and concluded that short videos (less than 5 minutes) and medium videos (10-20 minutes) greatly enhance English proficiency, student engagement, and satisfaction in flipped classrooms. Students highlighted that teachers utilize a range of online platforms for educational purposes, with the most prominent being YouTube (82.92%), Facebook (70.73%), Instagram (68.29%), Telegram (9.75%), and WhatsApp (2.43%). Likewise, students access both educational and non-educational platforms, such as YouTube (90.38%), Facebook (61.53%), Instagram (40.38%), Telegram (9.61%), Zoom (5.76%), WhatsApp (3.77%), and Google Meet (1.92%). This indicates that both teachers and students are leveraging diverse online platforms to support teaching and learning in virtual environments.

Online Distractions and Limitations

No one can deny the wide spectrum of advantages that this social-media-focused type of learning can offer students, but it is not without challenges and because of these distractions 73.08% of students declared that while studying online, they experienced a lack of concentration because of the manifold "distraction" online. For instance, pop-up phone notifications like receiving messages from other applications can disturb the students' learning process. That is why, some of them reported that, at times, they "can't focus" and thus "prefer face-to-face teaching" because it "is more efficient" vis-à-vis this aspect. Accordingly, 36,53% of the students communicated that these phone applications were a real distraction. Other students argue, that sometimes, unconsciously, "you can start browsing other applications" because after all these outlets "remain communication tools with others." Another factor that substantially affected the quality of online learning is the internet quality, particularly during online synchronous meetings. Indeed, 59,61% of the students confess that it did negatively influence the quality of their learning experience. This finding has been witnessed all around the world especially in developing countries (e.g. Adnan & Anwar, 2020; Chelghoum & Chelghoum, 2020; Efriana, 2021; Zermane & Aıtouche, 2020). Others reported that they were facing the screens so much that their eyes hurt. Moreover, because the number of students can be quite extensive online, the teacher cannot make sure that everyone is engaged and consequently, some students can be very passive in such online endeavours. In the same way, a student maintained that "this method helps the learners who master technology" which means that non-digitally fluent students can find difficulties taking part in such e-learning pursuits. This finding was showcased in Ghobrini's (2021) and Sarnou's (2020) studies.

FRAMEWORK AND ITS IMPLICATIONS

After conducting the experiment on the Facebook group and devising a web-based solution that ensured the successful implementation of the flipped class in an online-only environment through the use of pre-assigned researcher-created short YouTube videos to students and the Facebook "Guides" feature that organizes the content, teachers (84%) and students (98,07%) alike validate to a large extent this online pedagogical mode of instruction and subsequently shared the perspective on the advantages and disadvantages on such tech-based modality of instruction. The results of this research endeavour are encapsulated in Table 1 which constitutes a practical framework that teachers can leverage to launch an online-only learning journey. This framework consists of three stages; each associated with different modes of communication. First, the pre-online meeting is arguably the most time-consuming phase for the e-teacher, as it requires them to initially prepare the lesson in a video format and ensure it is accessible to students, either through a formal platform like Google Classroom or a socially mediated outlet like YouTube or Facebook. It is pivotal to establish an e-community where both students and teachers are present. Additionally, the e-instructor should accompany the video-based lesson with an assignment, allowing students to practice asynchronously at their own pace. Secondly, the Live online meeting should take place within the same e-platform or another, such as Zoom. In this virtual classroom, the instructor corrects tasks with students synchronously, identifies gaps in their understanding, and answers their questions. Clarifications should be simplified - in our case, the use of colloquial language greatly facilitated this process - to help students grasp the subject matter more thoroughly. The exchange of feedback between students and teachers can be highly productive, strengthening the rapport between both groups, especially when students receive personalized feedback particularly when they ask privately their questions via private text- or audio-based messages. Third, in the post-online meeting, the teacher can administer asynchronously instant quizzes to assess the students' grasp of the lesson. This formative assessment enables the instructor to gauge the students' progress while also offering students a chance for self-assessment. Additionally, students are encouraged to provide feedback on how the online learning process can be improved, sharing their insights on both the strengths and limitations of this e-learning model. This feedback loop helps the instructor continuously refine the process, addressing challenges and enhancing the overall e-teaching and learning experience.

Table 1. An E-flipped mode of instruction framework

Stages	Pre-live session	Live-session	Post-live session
(e)-activities	- Video format lesson - Practice task	- Completing the assignment - Teacher and students' interaction (feedback)	- Post assigment activities - Impoving the next session (feedback)
Mode of communication	Asychronous	Sychronous	Asychronous

Naturally, this model remains general and thus can be applied to different disciplines even the experimental and the hands-on ones. In the initial stage, the pre-Live session, instructors need to supply multi-media-based material for their students to acquire foundational knowledge and practice in virtual labs for instance, or simulators, they can send a video-format assignment to be discussed in the Live session where instructors can illustrate some Live practical experiments and, even invite students to perform similar tasks - this can be done through the use of virtual reality. The students can have real-time feedback from both their peers and their instructors. Then, the post-live session can be dedicated to an extension of the performed task or a re-submission to their assignment.

Ever-evolving E-Pedagogy and Continuous Professional Development Programs

One of the prominent challenges that teachers faced during this difficult period was their unpreparedness and limited savoir-faire in conducting a well-rounded online learning experience across different virtual platforms. However, with the adoption of such a framework, teachers and educators can operate in an only-from-home mode while still being able to deliver high-quality e-education to their students. The flipped model provides an opportunity for students to work at their own pace online, while instructors can maximize the effectiveness of online meetings. Since students are already familiar with the lesson - previously assigned to them - the interaction during the Live sessions can focus on specific aspects of the material. This dynamic benefits both teachers and students in that teachers save time by not having to re-explain the entire lesson, and students receive inquiry-based, personalized feedback on particular elements. Given these advantages, policymakers and educational leaders should integrate these guidelines and protocols into teachers' continuous professional development programs, thereby expanding the repertoire of teaching practices and ensuring the growth of the online teaching scholarship.

Scaling the E-Solution to other Levels and Specialties

Though the e-flipped mode of instruction was initially developed and used at the secondary level, it can also be applied in middle schools - where additional scaffolding is needed due to the students' young age, and at the university level, where students are more autonomous. This approach can prompt advanced learning strategies such as self-directed learning, collaborative and cooperative learning, and even project-based learning. The methodology remains the same across different educational levels, and the benefits it offers can be equally advantageous for both teachers and students. The system is easily replicable, which is crucial for instructors who may need to implement it in similar restricted environments. In other words, it is important to emphasize the universality of asynchronous preparation followed by synchronous explanation and elaboration. Furthermore, this framework is not limited to the EFL (English as a Foreign Language) context. Disciplines such as mathematics and natural sciences can also adopt the flipped classroom model with similar success. Of course, teachers will need training to effectively integrate such tech-based instructional modalities into their classrooms, but the simplicity of the system allows for rapid deployment in case of future emergencies, ensuring continuity in students' (e)-education.

CONCLUSION

In this scholarly research, a web-based solution was developed through multiple iterations, with the final product being approved by both students and teachers within the same context. This iterative process aligns with the core principles of SoTL that focus on continuous inquiry in teachers' practices to improve and enhance the quality of the learning process. The study also revealed key findings related to students' online engagement, motivation, and interaction in the targeted e-learning space where the teaching-learning process occurred reflecting the focus to which SoTL gives to students-centred learning. Positive feedback was particularly attributed to this modality of instruction, especially in the challenging COVID-19-driven context in which they were operating. Notably, the use of colloquial language instead of the official mainstream language distinguished this e-experience and, to some extent, enhanced students' engagement in their learning journey which shows the extent to which SoTL adapts to students' learning needs. Another significant point to consider is the self-paced nature of this instructional strategy, along with the option for students to choose whether or not to showcase their identity, a feature highlighted in the findings. The home-only learning mindset enabled students to participate comfortably online, and the teacher's ability to create an enjoyable, inclusive, and engaging environment not only fostered learning but also strengthened the bond between teacher and student. This clearly highlights how SoTL goes beyond structural practices and thus encompasses mastery of educational and behavioural practices to optimize not only students' education but the connection to them as well. Flexibility in using different online platforms to suit students' needs played a critical role in the success of this experiment. However, the research also highlighted challenges, particularly the online distractions that occasionally impacted the quality of the learning process. Overall, this framework provides teachers, educators, and policymakers with practical guidelines on how to harness its potential by effectively implementing an online flipped model in their respective educational institutions. This research adds to the existing literature in this niche of online SoTL and reaffirms that is field is ever-growing and constantly evolving.

REFERENCES

Adnan, M., & Anwar, K. (2020). Online learning amid the COVID-19 pandemic: Students' perspectives. *Journal of Pedagogical Sociology and Psychology, 2*(1), 45-51. https://www.doi.org/10.33902/JPSP. 2020261309

Al-Bashabsheh, M. W. T. F., & Pradhan, P. (2023). The importance of social media in education during COVID-19. [JARSSC]. *Journal of Advance Research in Science and Social Science*, 5(2), 1–13. DOI: 10.46523/jarssc.05.02.07

Alamri, H. A., Watson, S., & Watson, W. (2021). Learning technology models that support personalization within blended learning environments in higher education. *TechTrends*, 65(1), 62–78. DOI: 10.1007/s11528-020-00530-3

Amresh, A., Carberry, A. R., & Femiani, J. (2013, October). *Evaluating the effectiveness of flipped classrooms for teaching CS1. In 2013 IEEE Frontiers in Education Conference*. FIE., DOI: 10.1109/FIE.2013.6684923

Ananyina, A. (2022). Anonimity of learners in virtual learning environment. *Studia Humanitatis / Northern Humanitarian Studies, 3*, 71-76. .DOI: 10.15393/j12. art.2022.3881

Ansari, J., & Khan, N. (2020). Exploring the role of social media in collaborative learning the new domain of learning. *Smart Learning Environments*, 7(1), 9. Advance online publication. DOI: 10.1186/s40561-020-00118-7

Archer, E. (2019). Design research: Developing effective feedback interventions for school-based monitoring. *Research Methods in the Social Sciences*, 317, 317–336. Advance online publication. DOI: 10.18772/22019032750.25

Aslan, İ. (2021). Evaluating wellbeing and worries of university students during COVİD-19 pandemic. *Atatürk Üniversitesi Iktisadi Ve Idari Bilimler Dergisi, 35*(1), 245-261. https://dergipark.org.tr/en/download/article-file/1226893

Babu, G. S., & Sridevi, K. (2018). Importance of e-learning in higher education: A study. *International Journal of Research Culture Society*, 2(5), 84–88. https://www.academia.edu/36868903/IMPORTANCE_OF_E_LEARNING_IN_HIGHER_EDUCATION_A_STUDY

Bellatreche, R., & Alloti, L. (2020). E-learning challenges in higher education institutions: Algeria case study. , *11*(2), 264-276. Retrieved from https://www.asjp.cerist.dz/en/downArticle/275/11/2/140829

Benadla, D., & Hadji, M. (2021). EFL students' affective attitudes towards distance e-learning based on moodle platform during the covid-19the pandemic: Perspectives from Dr. Moulay Tahar University of Saida, Algeria. *Arab World English Journal (AWEJ) Special Issue on Covid, 19*, 55-67. DOI: 10.24093/awej/covid.4

Berestok, O. V. (2021). Synchronous and asynchronous e-learning modes: Strategies, methods, objectives. *Engineering and Educational Technologies*, 9(1), 19–27. DOI: 10.30929/2307-9770.2021.09.01.02

Bernstein, D. (2013). How SoTL-active faculty members can be cosmopolitan assets to an institution. *Teaching & Learning Inquiry*, 1(1), 35–40. DOI: 10.20343/teachlearninqu.1.1.35

Bishop, J., & Verleger, M. A. (2013, June 23-26). *The flipped classroom: A survey of the research.* 2013 ASEE annual conference & exposition (pp. 23-1200). Retrieved from https://aktuelt.osloskolen.no/SysSiteAssets/laringsteknologi/dokumenter/the-flipped-classroom-a-survey-of-the-research.pdf

Blizak, D., Blizak, S., Bouchenak, O., & Yahiaoui, K. (2020). Students' perceptions regarding the abrupt transition to online learning during the COVID-19 pandemic: Case of faculty of chemistry and hydrocarbons at the university of Boumerdes, Algeria. *Journal of Chemical Education*, 97(9), 2466–2471. DOI: 10.1021/acs.jchemed.0c00668

Boyer, E. (1990). *Scholarship reconsidered: Priorities of the professoriate.* The Carnegie Foundation for the Advancement of Teaching.

Brooks, A. W. (2014). Information literacy and the flipped classroom: Examining the impact of a one-shot flipped class on student learning and perceptions. *Communications in Information Literacy*, 8(2), 4. DOI: 10.15760/comminfolit.2014.8.2.168

Chelghoum, A., & Chelghoum, H. (2020). The COVID-19 pandemic and education: big changes ahead for teaching in Algeria. *Altralang Journal, 2*(2), 118-132. Retrieved from: https://www.asjp.cerist.dz/en/downArticle/597/2/2/139887

Chung, J., McKenzie, S., Schweinsberg, A., & Mundy, M. E. (2022). Correlates of academic performance in online higher education: A systematic review. *Frontiers in Education*, 7, 820567. Advance online publication. DOI: 10.3389/feduc.2022.820567

Collado-Valero, J., Rodríguez-Infante, G., Romero-González, M., Gamboa-Ternero, S., Navarro-Soria, I., & Lavigne-Cerván, R. (2021). Flipped classroom: Active methodology for sustainable learning in higher education during social distancing due to COVID-19. *Sustainability (Basel)*, 13(10), 5336. Advance online publication. DOI: 10.3390/su13105336

Davies, R. S., Dean, D. L., & Ball, N. (2013). Flipping the classroom and instructional technology integration in a college-level information systems spreadsheet course. *Educational Technology Research and Development*, 61(4), 563–580. DOI: 10.1007/s11423-013-9305-6

Davis, F. D. (1985). *A Technology Acceptance Model for Empirically Testing New End-User Information Systems*. [Doctoral dissertation, University of Queensland]. Massachusetts Institute of Technology. http://hdl.handle.net/1721.1/15192

DeLozier, S., & Rhodes, M. (2016). Flipped classrooms: A review of key ideas and recommendations for practice. *Educational Psychology Review*, 29(1), 141–151. DOI: 10.1007/s10648-015-9356-9

Denscombe, M. (2014). *The good research guide for small-scale social research projects*. Open University Press.

Dignan, A. (2011). *Game frame: Using games as a strategy for success*. Simon and Schuster.

Efriana, L. (2021). Problems of online learning during COVID-19 pandemic in EFL classroom and the solution. *Journal of English Language Teaching and Literature*, 2(1), 38–47. https://jurnal.stkipmb.ac.id/index.php/jelita/article/view/74

Elkateb, N. (2022). Challenges associated with e-learning on MOODLE platform during COVID 19 Pandemic from Chlef EFL Students' Perspective. *Journal of Languages & Translation*, 2(2), 120–133. DOI: 10.70204/jlt.v2i2.250

Emerick, E., Caldarella, P., & Black, S. (2019). Benefits and distractions of social media as tools for undergraduate student. *College Student Journal*, 53(3), 265–276. https://www.ingentaconnect.com/content/prin/csj/2019/00000053/00000003/art00001

Enfeld, J. (2013). Looking at the impact of the flipped classroom model of instruction on undergraduate multimedia students at CSUN. *TechTrends*, 57(6), 14–27. DOI: 10.1007/s11528-013-0698-1

Felten, P. (2013). Principles of good practice in SoTL. *Teaching & Learning Inquiry*, 1(1), 121–125. DOI: 10.20343/teachlearninqu.1.1.121

Fonseca, D. (2019). *Technology-enhanced learning*. Learning and Teaching in Higher Education., DOI: 10.4337/9781788975087.00031

Ford, N., Bowden, M., & Beard, J. (2011). Learning together: Using social media to foster collaboration in higher education. In Wankel, L. A., & Wankel, C. (Eds.), *Higher education administration with social media* (Vol. 2, pp. 105–126). Emerald Group Publishing Limited., DOI: 10.1108/S2044-9968(2011)0000002009

Fraga, L. M., & Harmon, J. (2014). The flipped classroom model of learning in higher education: An investigation of preservice teachers' perspectives and achievement. *Journal of Digital Learning in Teacher Education*, 31(1), 18–27. DOI: 10.1080/21532974.2014.967420

Ghobrini, R. E., Sarnou, H., & Benaicha, F. (2023). Upgrading Algerian secondary teachers' e-savoir-faire post COVID-19 via MOOC-based continuous professional development. In Boadu, G., Odhiambo, G., & Marandi, P. (Eds.), *Practices and perspectives of teaching and teacher education in Africa* (pp. 1–254). IGI Global., DOI: 10.4018/978-1-6684-7722-9.ch011

Ghobrini, R. E. A. (2020). Synergizing Facebook and YouTube for e-Teaching Grammar during COVID-19 Pandemic. *International Journal of Educational Sciences*, 3(4), 33. DOI: 10.26697/ijes.2020.4.8

Ghobrini, R. E. A. (2021, January 21–22, 2021). *Voicing the unvoiced: Potential of offline MOOCs e-content to cater for non-digitally-fluent students.* Proccedings of the First Workshop on Technology Enhanced Learning Environments for Blended Education (teleXbe2021), Foggia, Italy.https://ceur-ws.org/Vol-2817/paper31.pdf

Ghobrini, R. E. A., Benaicha, F., & Sarnou, H. (2024). Strategies for Tomorrow: Unraveling Algerian university instructors' e-practices in the face of pandemic challenges. *Online Science Education Journal, 9*(1), 1-15. https://dergipark.org.tr/en/download/article-file/3613505

Ghobrini, R. E. A., Benzert, F. Z., & Sarnou, H. (2022). Creative e-pedagogy in massive grammar e-tutoring via the simultaneous use of social media platforms. In Radj, G. R. (Ed.), *Creativity as progressive pedagogy: Examinations into culture, performance, and challenges* (pp. 64–86). IGI Global., DOI: 10.4018/978-1-7998-8287-9.ch004

Ghounane, N. (2020). Moodle or social networks: What alternative refuge is appropriate to Algerian EFL students to learn during COVID-19 pandemic. [AWEJ]. *Arab World English Journal*, 11(3), 21–41. DOI: 10.24093/awej/vol11no3.2

Ghounane, N. (2021). Facebook as a learning platform in Algeria during the COVID-19 pandemic. *Global Journal of Foreign Language Teaching.*, 11(2), 80–93. DOI: 10.18844/gjflt.v11i2.5555

Ghounane, N. (2022). Learning in the Algerian context during the pandemic: Is it online or offline? *AWEJ*, 492-503. DOI: 10.24093/awej/covid2.33

Glazier, R. (2016). Building rapport to improve retention and success in online classes. *Journal of Political Science Education*, 12(4), 437–456. DOI: 10.1080/15512169.2016.1155994

Gopinathan, S., Kaur, A. H., Veeraya, S., & Raman, M. (2022). The role of digital collaboration in student engagement towards enhancing student participation during COVID-19. *Sustainability (Basel)*, 14(11), 6844. DOI: 10.3390/su14116844

Guessabi, F. (2021). Flipped classrooms in higher education in Algeria during period of COVID-19: Challenges and difficulties. *International Journal of Linguistics. Literature and Translation*, 4(2), 196–202. DOI: 10.32996/ijllt.2021.4.2.23

Gupta, N., & Irwin, J. (2016). In-class distractions: The role of Facebook and the primary learning task. *Computers in Human Behavior*, 55, 1165–1178. DOI: 10.1016/j.chb.2014.10.022

Haddad, M. (2020). State of art of the distancial education at the University of Biskra during the COVID-19 : Challenges and prospects? *Elacadimia de Recherche En Sciences Sociales, 1*(2), 561–583. https://asjp.cerist.dz/en/article/122288

Hamari, J., Koivisto, J., & Sarsa, H. (2014, January 6-9, 2014). *Does gamification work?: A literature review of empirical studies on gamification*. Proceedings of the 47th Hawaii International Conference on System Sciences, (pp. 3025-3034), Hawaii, USA. https://creativegames.org.uk/modules/Gamification/Hamari_etal_Does_gamification_work-2014.pdf

Han, S. (2022). Flipped classroom: Challenges and benefits of using social media in English language teaching and learning. *Frontiers in Psychology*, 13, 996294. Advance online publication. DOI: 10.3389/fpsyg.2022.996294 PMID: 36211927

Heitink, M., Voogt, J., Verplanken, L., van Braak, J., & Fisser, P. (2016). Teachers' professional reasoning about their pedagogical use of technology. *Computers & Education*, 101, 70–83. DOI: 10.1016/j.compedu.2016.05.009

Hong, X., Liu, Q., & Zhang, M. (2021). Dual stressors and female pre-school teachers' job satisfaction during the COVID-19: The mediation of work-family conflict. *Frontiers in Psychology*, 12, 691498. DOI: 10.3389/fpsyg.2021.691498 PMID: 34168602

Hwang, G., Lai, C., & Wang, S. (2015). Seamless flipped learning: A mobile technology-enhanced flipped classroom with effective learning strategies. *Journal of Computers in Education*, 2(4), 449–473. DOI: 10.1007/s40692-015-0043-0

Johnson, C., Hill, L., Lock, J., Altowairiki, N., Ostrowski, C., dos Santos, L. da R., & Liu, Y. (2017). Using design-based research to develop meaningful online discussions in undergraduate field experience courses. *International Review of Research in Open and Distance Learning*, 18(6). Advance online publication. DOI: 10.19173/irrodl.v18i6.2901

Koessmeier, C., & Büttner, O. (2021). *Why are we distracted by social media? Distraction situations and strategies, reasons for distraction, and individual differences*. National Library of Medicine., DOI: 10.3389/fpsyg.2021.711416

Kurtz, G., Tsimerman, A., & Steiner-Lavi, O. (2014). The flipped-classroom approach: The answer to future learning? *European Journal of Open, Distance and E-Learning, 17*(2), 172–182. Retrieved from https://www.ceeol.com/search/article-detail?id=848825

Lancaster, K., Rhodes, T., & Rosengarten, M. (2020). Making evidence and policy in public health emergencies: Lessons from COVID-19 for adaptive evidence-making and intervention. *Evidence & Policy*, 16(3), 477–490. DOI: 10.1332/174426420X15913559981103

Long, T., Cummins, J., & Waugh, M. (2016). Use of the flipped classroom instructional model in higher education: Instructors' perspectives. *Journal of Computing in Higher Education*, 29(2), 179–200. DOI: 10.1007/s12528-016-9119-8

Malik, R. (2023). *Impact of technology-based education on student learning outcomes and engagement*. 10th International Conference on Computing for Sustainable Global Development (INDIACom), New Delhi, India. 784-788. https://ieeexplore.ieee.org/abstract/document/10112303

Martinelli, S. M., Chen, F., Mcevoy, M. D., Zvara, D. A., & Schell, R. M. (2018). Utilization of the flipped classroom in anesthesiology graduate medical education: An initial survey of faculty beliefs and practices about active learning. *The Journal of Education in Perioperative Medicine : JEPM*, 20(1). https://pmc.ncbi.nlm.nih.gov/articles/PMC5991778/ PMID: 29928664

Maurer, T. W. (2022). Leveraging SoTL to improve teaching and learning during the COVID-19 pandemic. *International Journal for the Scholarship of Teaching and Learning*, 16(1), 3. DOI: 10.20429/ijsotl.2022.160103

Maurer, T. W., Woolmer, C., Powell, N., Sisson, C., Snelling, C., Stalheim, O., & Turner, I. (2021). Sharing SoTL findings with students: An intentional knowledge mobilization strategy. *Teaching & Learning Inquiry*, 9(1), 333–348. Advance online publication. DOI: 10.20343/teachlearninqu.9.1.22

McKinney, K. (2007). *Enhancing learning through the scholarship of teaching and learning: The challenges and joys of juggling*. Jossey-Bass.

Mellati, M., & Khademi, M. (2019). *Technology-based education*. Advanced Online Education and Training Technologies., DOI: 10.4018/978-1-5225-7010-3.ch003

Moran, M., Seaman, J., & Tinti, H. (2011). *Teaching, learning, and sharing: How today's higher education faculty use social media*. Pearson.

Mortensen, C. J., & Nicholson, A. M. (2015). The flipped classroom stimulates greater learning and is a modern 21st century approach to teaching today's undergraduates. *Journal of Animal Science*, 93(7), 3722–3731. DOI: 10.2527/jas.2015-9087 PMID: 26440038

Munastiwi, E., & Puryono, S. (2021). Unprepared management decreases education performance in kindergartens during COVID-19 pandemic. *Heliyon*, 7(5), e07138. Advance online publication. DOI: 10.1016/j.heliyon.2021.e07138 PMID: 34136697

Navarro, J. M., & McGrath, B. M. (2021). Strategies for effective online teaching and learning: Practices and techniques with a proven track of success in online education. In Ramlall, S., Cross, T., & Love, M. (Eds.), *Handbook of Research on Future of Work and Education: Implications for Curriculum Delivery and Work Design*., DOI: 10.4018/978-1-7998-8275-6.ch029

Nwosisi, C., Ferreira, A., Rosenberg, W., & Walsh, K. (2016). A study of the flipped classroom and its effectiveness in flipping thirty percent of the course content. *International Journal of Information and Education Technology (IJIET)*, 6(5), 348–351. DOI: 10.7763/IJIET.2016.V6.712

Octaberlina, L. R., & Muslimin, A. I. (2020). EFL students perspective towards online learning barriers and alternatives using Moodle/Google Classroom during COVID-19 pandemic. *International Journal of Higher Education*, 9(6), 1–9. DOI: 10.5430/ijhe.v9n6p1

Orifamah, D. (2021). The implication of COVID-19 on educational disparity between the developed and the developing countries, urban and rural dwellers and, on ICT in Nigeria. *Journal of Education and Practice*. Advance online publication. DOI: 10.7176/JEP/12-30-06

Penuel, W. R., Fishman, B. J., Cheng, B., & Sabelli, N. (2011). Organizing research and development at the intersection of learning, implementation, and design. *Educational Researcher*, 40(7), 331–337. Advance online publication. DOI: 10.3102/0013189X11421826

Pierce, R., & Fox, J. (2012). Vodcasts and active-learning exercises in a "flipped classroom" model of a renal pharmacotherapy module. *American Journal of Pharmaceutical Education*, 76(10), 196. DOI: 10.5688/ajpe7610196 PMID: 23275661

Rabiman, R., Nurtanto, M., & Kholifah, N. (2020). Design and development e-learning system by learning management system in vocational education. *International Journal of Scientific & Technology Research*, 9, 1059–1063. https://files.eric.ed.gov/fulltext/ED605316.pdf

Reeves, T. C. (2006). Design research from a technology perspective. In van den Akker, J., Gravemeijer, K., McKenney, S., & Nieveen, N. (Eds.), *Educational design research* (pp. 52–66). Routledge.

Ryan, M. D., & Reid, S. A. (2015). Impact of the flipped classroom on student performance and retention: A parallel controlled study in general chemistry. *Journal of Chemical Education*, 93(1), 13–23. DOI: 10.1021/acs.jchemed.5b00717

Ryu, S. (2020). The role of mixed methods in conducting design-based research. *Educational Psychologist*, 55(4), 232–243. DOI: 10.1080/00461520.2020.1794871

Sadiku, M., Adebo, P., & Musa, S. (2018). Online teaching and learning. *International Journal of Advanced Research in Computer Science and Software Engineering*, 8(2), 73. Advance online publication. DOI: 10.23956/ijarcsse.v8i2.549

Sahraoui, D., & Chaibendraa, W. (2020). The Role of social media in strengthening scientific communication to face the consequences of the corona pandemic on scientific research: A field study on a sample of students and professors of the Algerian university. *Bibliophilia*, 44–71. https://asjp.cerist.dz/en/article/128704

Sarnou, D. (2020). Questioning the significance of technologizing Algerian schools and universities: Did it fail or succeed? *International Journal of Integrating Technology in Education*, 9(1), 1–13. DOI: 10.5121/ijite.2020.9101

Selcuk, H., & Jones, J. (2022). Turkish EFL learner perceptions of using a social network environment for collaborative writing: Creating a trustful affinity space. *International Journal of Smart Education and Urban Society*, 13(1), 1–14. DOI: 10.4018/IJSEUS.297063

Shamsabadi, A., Pashaei, A., Rahmani, N., Mahmoodabadi, A., Norouzi, S., Bahador, F., & Mehraeen, E. (2023). Social media application in education during the COVID-19 pandemic; pros and cons: A systematic review. *Journal of Iranian Medical Council*, 6(3), 389–400. DOI: 10.18502/jimc.v6i3.12841

Shulman, L. (2011). Feature essays: The scholarship of teaching and learning: A personal account and reflection. *International Journal for the Scholarship of Teaching and Learning*, 5(1), 30. DOI: 10.20429/ijsotl.2011.050130

Siemens, G. (2002). Instructional design in e-learning. Retrieved from https://eddl.tru.ca/wp-content/uploads/2018/12/instructional-design-in-e-learning-Siemens.pdf

Social Media Stats Algeria. (2021). Statcounter. Retrieved from https://gs.statcounter.com/social-media-stats/all/algeria

Tadesse, S., & Muluye, W. (2020). The impact of COVID-19 pandemic on education system in developing countries: A review. *Open Journal of Social Sciences*, 8(10), 159–170. DOI: 10.4236/jss.2020.810011

Tallent-Runnels, M., Thomas, J., Lan, W., Cooper, S., Ahern, T., Shaw, S., & Liu, X. (2006). Teaching courses online: A review of the research. *Review of Educational Research*, 76(1), 135–193. DOI: 10.3102/00346543076001093

Tawafak, R., Romli, A., Arshah, R., & Almaroof, R. (2018). Assessing the Impact of technology learning and assessment method on academic performance: Review paper. *Eurasia Journal of Mathematics, Science and Technology Education*, 14(6), 2241–2254. DOI: 10.29333/ejmste/87117

Teo, T. W., Tan, K. C. D., Yan, Y. K., Teo, Y. C., & Yeo, L. W. (2014). How flip teaching supports undergraduate chemistry laboratory learning. *Chemistry Education Research and Practice*, 15(4), 550–567. DOI: 10.1039/C4RP00003J

Tlhoaele, M., Suhre, C., & Hofman, A. (2016). Using technology-enhanced, cooperative, group-project learning for student comprehension and academic performance. *European Journal of Engineering Education*, 41(3), 263–278. DOI: 10.1080/03043797.2015.1056102

Tune, J. D., Sturek, M., & Basile, D. P. (2013). Flipped classroom model improves graduate student performance in cardiovascular, respiratory, and renal physiology. *Advances in Physiology Education*, 37(4), 316–320. DOI: 10.1152/advan.00091.2013 PMID: 24292907

Uçar, H., & Goksel, N. (2020). Enhancing online EFL learners' motivation and engagement through supplementary activities on Facebook. *Asian Journal of Distance Education*, 15, 154–168. https://www.asianjde.com/ojs/index.php/AsianJDE/article/view/445

Ulla, M., & Perales, W. (2021). Facebook as an integrated online learning support application during the COVID-19 pandemic: Thai university students' experiences and perspectives. *Heliyon*, 7(11), e08317. Advance online publication. DOI: 10.1016/j.heliyon.2021.e08317 PMID: 34746477

Vaillancourt, T., McDougall, P., Comeau, J., & Finn, C. (2021). COVID-19 school closures and social isolation in children and youth: Prioritizing relationships in education. *Facets*, 6(1), 1795–1813. DOI: 10.1139/facets-2021-0080

Valeeva, R., & Kalimullin, A. (2021). Adapting or changing: The COVID-19 pandemic and teacher education in Russia. *Education Sciences*, 11(8), 408. DOI: 10.3390/educsci11080408

Van Alten, D. C., Phielix, C., Janssen, J., & Kester, L. (2019). Effects of flipping the classroom on learning outcomes and satisfaction: A meta-analysis. *Educational Research Review*, 28, 100281. DOI: 10.1016/j.edurev.2019.05.003

Vaughan, M. (2014). Flipping the learning: An investigation into the use of the flipped classroom model in an introductory teaching course. *Education Research and Perspectives*, 41, 25–41. https://search.informit.org/doi/epdf/10.3316/informit.135571943100260. DOI: 10.70953/ERPv41.14002

Wilson, S. G. (2013). The flipped class: A method to address the challenges of an undergraduate statistics course. *Teaching of Psychology*, 40(3), 193–199. DOI: 10.1177/0098628313487461

Yu, Z., & Gao, M. (2022). Effects of video length on a flipped English classroom. *SAGE Open*, 12(1), 21582440211068474. Advance online publication. DOI: 10.1177/21582440211068474

Zappe, S., Leicht, R., Messner, J., Litzinger, T., & Lee, H. W. (2009). "Flipping" the classroom to explore active learning in a large undergraduate course. *Proceeding of the American Society for Engineering Education*. Retrieved from https://www.nyu.edu/content/dam/nyu/facultyResources/images/ESMITimages/flippedclass/flipping-the-classroom-to-explore-active-learning-in-a-large-undergraduate-course.pdf

Zermane, H., & Aıtouche, S. (2020). Digital learning with COVID-19 in Algeria. *International Journal of 3D printing technologies and digital industry, 4*(2), 161-170.DOI: 10.46519/ij3dptdi.776978

Zhao, X., & Yang, Y. (2023). Impact of social media-supported flipped classroom on English as a foreign language learners' writing performance and anxiety. *Frontiers*, 13, 1052737. Advance online publication. DOI: 10.3389/fpsyg.2022.1052737 PMID: 36687902

Chapter 11
Connecting Adult Learners:
The Role of Communication Tools in an Adv MPH Online

Jonathan Zaccarini
http://orcid.org/0009-0000-2293-5577
Mailman School of Public Health, Columbia University, USA

Roxanne Russell
https://orcid.org/0009-0001-5037-0734
Mailman School of Public Health, Columbia University, USA

ABSTRACT

Higher education institutions need to adapt to new technology and new student demographics; however, this requires careful consideration of communication tools among adult learners. The main focus of this chapter is to examine the need for communication tools, along with asynchronous and synchronous learning activities, and how they contribute to peer social presence amongst adult learners within an online graduate public health program. Student experiences with using Yellowdig and Zoom will be discussed, using data from a survey focus group. Results show that these adult learners were able to perceive impressions of each other and build a community while completing the first year of their graduate program. This chapter extends the findings on student perceptions of technology facilitated social presence within text-centered environments; however, additional research is needed using larger student samples within online graduate public health programs.

DOI: 10.4018/979-8-3693-7595-2.ch011

INTRODUCTION

Because the growth of distance learning has allowed professionals to advance their knowledge and skills, isolation and limited peer trust persist (Rasheed et al., 2020); social presence is needed. Social presence is defined as the degree to which participants perceive one another as real (Boston et al., 2010). With that said, the purpose of this chapter is to report how communication tools contributed to peer social presence by offering opportunities for students to play an active role in forming impressions of their peers and shaping their online learning community. The program for this research study was the Advanced MPH Online, which is a two-year degree designed for motivated public health professionals. The communication tools chosen for the research study were Yellowdig, a social media-inspired asynchronous platform for interactive discussions, and Zoom, a video platform for real-time communication in synchronous sessions. A study on the integration of communication tools within an Advanced MPH Online serves to fill a gap within the scholarship of teaching and learning (SoTL), which is a set of practices to help faculty answer questions about their student learning (Grise-Owens, et al., 2016). Social presence is an essential component of online learning; thus, online instructors need to understand the significance of students forming impressions of each other while using communication tools, in order to inform their instruction and enhance positive student outcomes.

A REVIEW OF THE LITERATURE

To understand the role of communication tools in facilitating social presence, it is essential to examine the existing body of literature on social presence and tools with asynchronous and synchronous learning activities.

Social Presence

Even though the meaning of social presence has evolved over time, Short et al. (1976) originally defined social presence as the "degree of salience of the other person in the interaction" (p. 65). In their definition, "degree," reflects the focus on the evaluation of communication media and how specific technology influences perceived social interaction between students. Their work centered on the role of technology in conveying visual and vocal cues, which are critical for interpreting non-verbal communications (Whiteside, 2017). Earlier definitions of social presence were focused on helping people ascertain non-verbal cues that were lost in mediated communication.

Contemporary researchers emphasize the connectivity between individual students (McGurty, 2022). Studies have shown that engagement in asynchronous discussions contributes to students' ability to project their personalities through text, perceive impressions of their peers, and build online learning communities (Swan & Shih, 2019). Students intentionally craft their messages to shape how their peers perceive them, highlighting the importance of perceived connections in online learning. These connections are significant predictors of student success in online degree programs (Swan & Shih, 2019). One must identify the factors that foster students' online connections and feelings of closeness to understand social presence.

One factor is relational closeness which can be measured through qualitative methods. Gooch and Watts (2015) required participants to keep daily diaries of their interactions with their peers. Participants were instructed to reflect on their communication with others they felt close to and keep track of them. They identified social presence and closeness as important factors in studying interpersonal communication among students. These diaries provided insight into participants' perceptions of closeness and how social presence developed over time; however, data showed that the type of communication technology did not determine closeness (Gooch and Watts, 2015). The relationship between participants is more important than whether participants used instant messaging, email, or Skype to communicate. Despite these findings, other researchers have argued that the type of communication tool can determine relational closeness. Based on an extensive literature review of past social presence studies, Cui et al, (2013) found that the type of technology can contribute to perceptions of social presence.

Cui et al., (2013) reviewed the origin, major definitions, and historical studies on social presence. Based on empirical evidence, it was found that between 2000 and 2013, students used web tools such as blogs and social media applications to communicate with peers and established social presence. Web tools contribute to social presence because users are communicating in a manner conducive to "networking," which is defined as the system of digitally connected individuals (Cui et al., 2013). In contrast, Gooch and Watts (2015) examined individual acts of communication rather than a broader digital network of people. Social presence studied within the context of the web was not found to be the same as social presence studied within traditional computer-mediated communication (CMC) technology such as text or emails. Since there is disagreement about the role of technology in fostering social presence, it helps to highlight studies that examine the integration of specific tools within an online learning environment.

Technology Facilitated Social Presence

Tools with Asynchronous Learning Activities

Asynchronous discussion boards are a commonly used tool for student bi-weekly communication within an online degree and evidence of their success is supported by numerous studies (Lowenthal et al., 2018; Swan & Shih, 2019; Whiteside et al., 2017). Lowenthal and Dunlap (2018) investigated student perceptions of instructional strategies to improve student perceptions of social presence. Some examples of techniques included digital storytelling, musical activities, and Flickr. Student responses to these techniques were measured by a survey and focus group and included questions adapted from the Community of Inquiry (CoI) Framework (Lowenthal & Dunlap, 2018). Students perceived digital storytelling, prior relationships with peers, and open access to peers' projects as the most impactful in establishing social presence. Students positively responded to opportunities that encourage sharing, creativity, and self-expression. While asynchronous discussions offer valuable opportunities to contribute to social presence, they can also be substituted with other tools.

Google Docs, an online word processor, can replicate the functionality of asynchronous discussions while providing additional features. Morse (2021) compared student participation between a traditional learning management system (LMS) and Google Docs. An analysis of the quantity and quality of posts, particularly those involving shared experiences, uncovered a significant increase in meaningful interactions when students used Google Docs. Specifically, students who used Google Docs shared experiences and teaching strategies 52% more often during a discussion compared to students who used the LMS platform (Morse, 2021). This increased engagement may stem from the collaborative interface of Google Docs, which encouraged students to read and respond to all of their classmates' posts. Despite this finding, Morse (2021) claimed further research is needed to validate this explanation. Even tools categorized asynchronous, such as Google Docs, have additional modalities such as audio and video, which expand the ways students communicate with one another.

Voicethread provides students with options to participate asynchronously through text, audio, or video. Pacansky-Brock (2014) examined student preferences for technologies that allow students to use voice and video features within online learning and what factors contribute to those preferences. Pacansky-Brock (2014) discovered that students have anxiety with certain types of modality and students would prefer to leave a written text-based response instead of making a video. Students in the study (94%) agreed they built a community while using VoiceThread (Pacansky- Brock, 2014). Overall, the students perceived that this asynchronous communication tool contributed to their ability to establish peer social presence.

While this could imply many assumptions about how students prefer to communicate with their peers, it also revealed that students prefer communication that is most convenient for them. This is relative to Lowenthal and Dunlap's (2018) supporting evidence on student centered social presence techniques and how individual students have different needs. While communication tools used with asynchronous learning activities offer flexibility and creativity through various media, communication tools with synchronous learning activities provide real-time interactions.

Tools with Synchronous Learning Activities

Zoom, a video-based communication medium, is commonly used for synchronous learning activities in online degree programs to contribute to peer social presence. Nisa et al. (2021) studied student perceptions of each other during breakout activities. Zoom breakout activities significantly contributed to students' perceptions of their peers. During breakout sessions, 13 out of 17 students reported being more productive, solving problems collaboratively, and practicing negotiation skills. Similarly, Belt and Lowenthal (2023) conducted semi-structured interviews with online instructors to understand their observations of student engagement in Zoom. They found that student-centered activities during synchronous Zoom sessions were more productive because they brought everyone together. Rather than using synchronous time solely for lectures, faculty observed students benefitted from student-led discussions, faculty-to-student feedback, and check-ins. These specific student-led activities enhanced engagement and peer interaction. While these activities may be integrated into asynchronous discussions, it is video-based communication tools that allow students to have real-time connections.

The immediate connection that synchronous video discussions offer students helps overcome challenges, such as the lack of non-verbal cues, often found with asynchronous discussion (Rasheed et al., 2020; Whiteside, 2017). Real-time video interactions in Zoom can address these challenges by enabling richer communication through voice, facial expressions, and body language. While some students prefer text-based responses over video (Pacansky-Brock, 2014), this preference often stems from convenience rather than a desire for meaningful interaction. The assumption that professional students lack time for video-based synchronous activities can be reconsidered, as studies have shown that students can effectively collaborate to create videos when given the opportunity.

DeGagne et al. (2018) focused on nursing students enrolled in an education course who were required to complete video-based assignments (VBA). Students benefitted from creating videos and showcasing work because these student-led activities enabled them to collaborate with each other. Essentially, students want opportunities to see their peers' work and evaluate it rather than feel they are in competition with each other. This can be considered synchronous-based learning because students had the opportunity to create video presentations on a PowerPoint or participate in multimedia group projects either synchronously or asynchronously. A student shared a positive feeling toward seeing their classmates speak in a video presentation rather than reading their work (DeGagne et al., 2018). Students enjoyed their classmate's videos because different modalities contributed to student connection.

Similarly, Ching and Hsu (2013) examined the experiences of graduate students in an online course using VoiceThread. They found that 50% of students felt more connected to their peers through the use of different modalities, such as audio and video, which contributed to building a stronger sense of peer presence. This aligns with the previously mentioned studies because of the importance of multimodal communication in fostering social presence (DeGagne et al., 2018; Lowenthal & Dunlap; Nisa et al., 2021; Pacansky-Brock, 2014) In these previously mentioned studies, students preferred options to to select from communication tools and whether they wanted to use them synchronously or asynchronously.

Given that the type of tool can contribute to social presence and that students want choice, it is evident that communication tools—whether asynchronous discussions on Google Docs, or synchronous breakout activities on Zoom—play a crucial role in establishing peer social presence. This is especially important to an Adv MPH Online, where students are attempting to balance academic and professional responsibilities while building a community with their peers— challenges faced by adult learners.

Adult Learners

Highly motivated students in the Adv MPH Online are adult learners. They are at least 25 years old, employed full-time, and may have additional responsibilities such as raising children or serving as first-generation university students (MacDonald, 2018). Often referred to as non-traditional students or working professionals, adult learners seek online programs that accommodate their busy schedules while providing an academic experience comparable to that of traditional in-person students (MacDonald, 2018; Markle, 2015). Research on adult learners, derived from the andragogy or the practices of teaching adult learners, shows adult learners' academic success is closely linked to their perceived peer support (Shatila, 2024). A key factor in this chapter's exploration of how communication tools can help foster peer social presence.

Past studies have shown that adult learners face challenges distinct from those encountered by traditional in-person students. One of these is technical challenges (Kara et al., 2019), which can greatly affect academic performance. Adult learners often lack the technical skills required to engage fully in online learning activities. This is especially evident in students aged 41 to 51, who may struggle with technical skills that hinder their ability to connect with peers or access information online, whether through the web or learning management software. Students aged 50 and above face even greater difficulties due to limited experience learning online and being used to traditional in-person learning (Kara et al., 2019). Additionally, adult learners may struggle with balancing academic responsibilities with family obligations, which then leads to difficulty establishing connections with their peers (Kara et al., 2019). As such, the use of communication tools to help adult learners form impressions and build relationships is essential.

The integration of technology does not guarantee immediate success because adult learners may lack digital literacy skills. Roumell and Jabarkhail (2023) suggest that degree program design should be tailored to address these technological gaps among adult learners. Technology can be used to address adult online student challenges because it is instrumental to how they communicate with each other. Students communicate, build a community, and become exposed to new ideas. Cherrstrom et al. (2019) thematically coded ten discussion forums and analyzed 239 evaluations of 125 student-selected tools. They discovered students created a community through educational technology and were able to build deep relationships with each other. Although adult learning theories may appear useful to this study, they do not offer a lens for measuring the impact of communication tools alongside asynchronous and synchronous learning activities on student impressions of their peers. Social presence is not rooted in pedagogy and a communication theory is more appropriate for framing this work.

Social Information Processing Theory

Walther's (1996, 2015) social information processing theory provides a framework for this research. Walther's central hypothesis is how impressions and relationships develop through computer-mediated communication (CMC). People are motivated to engage in relationship-building with others as successfully as they could in person if given enough time (Walther, 2015). Time is the key variable here because the rate of disclosure impacts the impressions people create through CMC. Interpersonal communication still occurs when nonverbal cues are absent because of the rate of disclosure of personal information. Information must be shared over a period of time.

Walther's work may appear obsolete given that it originated in 1996; yet, the work focused on computer-mediated communication (CMC) in asynchronous discussion boards and focused on heightened interpersonal communication (Walther, 1996). Yet, its internal structure provides an abstract framework that lends itself to current forms of technology and online environments (Walther, 2015). Walther (2015) even claims that social information processing theory holds up because of its application to experimental studies on different types of CMC. One example is a study that measured response latency and conversational contingency in customer-agent chat room dialogues (Lew et al., 2018). Another study measured how the absence of audiovisual cues during initial conversations impacted perceptions of social and romantic attraction among prospective daters. This study even looked at the effects of switching from online to face-to-face interaction (Antheunis et al., 2020). While these examples are outside an online learning context, they represent the expandability of social information processing theory.

The social information processing theory was relevant to examining perceptions of our Adv MPH Online students who engaged in Yellowdig asynchronous discussions and Zoom synchronous sessions. The aim of this research was to understand students' perceptions of each other within the first year of the program. We needed to consider how much time students had and how much information was disclosed between students. The research built on the work of Gooch and Watts (2015) and Cui et al. (2013) because we examined the communication acts between online students within a digital system, the Adv MPH Online. The following section of the chapter reports a study conducted with a sample of Adv MPH Online students to further examine perceptions of students using communication tools to facilitate peer social presence within the first year of the program.

METHODOLOGY

To measure student perceptions, we employed a mixed methods sequential explanatory design. The first phase involves the collection and analysis of quantitative data, and the second phase involves the collection and analysis of qualitative data (Ivankova et al., 2006). The rationale for this method is that the quantitative phase provides a general understanding of student perceptions of their peers' social presence, while the qualitative phase helps provide a more in-depth view of participant perceptions. Both quantitative and qualitative data were collected on the perceptions of Adv MPH online students over the course of a year. The first quantitative phase included a survey, and the qualitative phase included a focus group. The focus group questions were created based on the results of the survey, which demonstrates the rationale for this methodology and how the qualitative phase can explain the survey results by exploring participants' views in more depth.

Setting

The setting for this study is a public health graduate school within a large, private university. In the course of a calendar year, these students experienced faculty-led live sessions on Zoom and asynchronous discussions on Yellowdig. Students were required to complete four discussions in their Foundations of Public Health course for one semester. Faculty-led course design in the Adv MPH Online is supported by our instructional design team. There was a doctoral student present to help facilitate discussion, but their role was not part of this study. Students were given instructions, and a prompt and instructional template remained the same, though the topic was different for each discussion. Students were given instructions about how to participate by creating posts and responding to at least two of their classmates. Synchronous four-hour live sessions on Zoom were every week for the entire academic calendar year. Students were given opportunities for live discussions, including small group work during Zoom breakout rooms.

Participants

There were 14 students enrolled in the Adv MPH Online. They are working professionals in health care, higher education, and other health-related fields. Some students already hold master's degrees, and most have at least two years of experience in the public health field. This program is designed for working professionals with an age range from 24 to 54. These students were informed about the purpose of this study and were aware that the data would not affect their grades or current status at the university.

Research Questions

To understand how these students perceived their peers' social presence with communication tools to complete asynchronous and synchronous learning activities, this study sought to address these two research questions:

i. What elements of peer social presence are present in asynchronous and synchronous portions of the program?
ii. How and in what ways can Yellowdig and Zoom be used to establish peer social presence amongst students?

Instrument

Survey

Cobb's Social Presence and Satisfaction Scale (2009) was chosen to measure student perceptions of using Yellowdig with asynchronous discussions. This scale was originally used to measure student perceptions of computer-mediated communication within online nursing courses. The scale demonstrated high reliability with a Cronbach's Alpha score exceeding .80, ensuring consistency and validity of the questionnaire items. Questions from the original survey were slightly modified to include Yellowdig (see Appendix A).

Survey participation was anonymous and given the small population of the students in the program; this was a convenience sample. The questionnaire items in Appendix A were organized into three sections: (1) online learning communities, (2) Yellowdig as a communication platform, and (3) online learning and academic progress. The survey contained 20 statements with Likert scale response options (1) strongly agreed, (2) agreed, (3) undecided (4) disagreed, or (5) strongly disagreed. The first email invitation with a Qualtrics link to the survey was sent to all 14 students enrolled in the Adv MPH Online at the end of their second semester.

Focus Group

After survey results were collected and analyzed, a focus group was facilitated after the end of their second semester. Students consented and participated in an hour-long interview. Focus group questions were semi-structured and designed based on the data collected from the survey responses. Participants were asked questions to expand on their experiences using Yellowdig as well as their experiences during the synchronous live session on Zoom.

Data Analysis

Survey data were downloaded from Qualtrics and uploaded to SPSS. Given the small sample of survey responses, only independent-sample t-tests were calculated. We then implemented an inductive approach to the focus group interview transcription, which included open coding to allow for the emergence of patterns. Codes were initially created based on the focus group questions and then modified after analysis of the transcript (see Appendix B). After refining the codes and reviewing the focus group transcript again, patterns were looked for because the goal was to identify themes and patterns in the data to address the two research questions (Maguire and Delahunt, 2017). The first set of codes was created by one of our research team members and then the focus group transcript and codes were uploaded to Dedoose Version 9.0.107. Dedoose is a cloud-based research and analysis tool. Training tests were created in Dedoose and then a co-researcher was invited to be the second coder or, in the case of Dedoose testing, "the trainee."

Results

Research Question 1: What elements of peer social presence are present in asynchronous and synchronous portions of the program?

This section presents the results addressing the first research question. Out of the 14 students enrolled in the program, ten students participated. The response rate was adequate for this limited, localized study resulting in a 71% rate of return; however, generalizations cannot be made about all students in an Adv MPH Online. Appendix C shows the descriptive results of the questionnaire items on the Yellowdig asynchronous discussions.

Table 1 reports the descriptive results and the means and standard deviations on the demographic questionnaire items of participants. Demographic questionnaire items were grouped into variables to measure differences between age (under 34 or over 34), employment (employed or unemployed), and degree status (bachelor's or master's degree). Results show that the survey participants' age, employment, or degree status did not hinder their ability to perceive impressions of their peers while engaging in Yellowdig asynchronous discussions.

Table 1. Participant demographics

		N	%	M	SD
AGE	Under 34	5	50	13	6
	Over 34	4	40	11.25	2.6
EMPLOYMENT	Employed	6	60	7.3	1.96
	Unemployed	4	40	12.25	6.9
DEGREE STATUS	Bachelors	6	60	13.1	5.3
	Masters	4	40	10.7	2.0

Note: n = 10

Questionnaire items 5- 9 were grouped into a variable, Yellowig, in SPSS. An independent-sample t-test was calculated to compare the mean score using Yellowdig to establish student social presence and student age groups. No significant difference was found ($t(11)= .259$, $p > .05$) between students younger than 34 and students older than 34. The mean of the younger than 34 students (M= 13, *sd* = 6) was not significantly different from the mean of the older than 34 students (M= 11.25, *sd* = 2.6). In other words, student age did not affect their ability to perceive impressions of their peers while engaging in Yellowdig.

An independent sample t-test was calculated to compare using Yellowdig to establish student social presence and student employment status. No significant difference was found ($t(11) = .114$, $p > .05$) between students who were employed and students who were unemployed. The mean of the employed students (M= 12.1, *sd* = 2.31) was not significantly different from the mean of the unemployed students (M= 12.25, *sd* = 6.9). In other words, student employment status did not affect their ability to perceive impressions of their peers while engaging in Yellowdig.

An independent-sample t-test was calculated to compare the mean score using Yellowdig to establish social presence present and student degree level. No significant difference was found ($t(11) = .262$, $p > .05$) between students with a bachelor's degree and students with a master's degree. The mean of the students with a bachelor's degree (M= 13.1, *sd* = 5.3) was not significantly different from the mean of the students with a master's degree (M= 10.7, *sd* = 2.0). In other words, students' degree level did not affect their ability to perceive impressions of their peers while engaging in Yellowdig.

The qualitative portion of this study elaborates on the survey results. Participants in the focus group shared how they enjoyed communicating with each other on Yellowdig rather than CourseWorks. Students shared personal information on the asynchronous portions of the program because they believed only their peers and faculty would have access to their discussions, which contributed to their ability to perceive the impressions of their peers. Students stated:

> *I feel like I was more likely to interact genuinely with the other students because it was a closed forum (Student #3).*
>
> *I think sometimes people wrote things on Yellowdig that maybe they wouldn't have felt comfortable saying in person (Student #4).*
>
> *It's like when you're in CourseWorks all you think about is a grades, assignments, submissions test, you know, it's not a conducive ecosystem to natural conversation (Student #5).*

While students found it convenient to find their discussions on Yellowdig and share information with each other, it was the type of information shared that shaped their perceptions of Yellowdig as an effective communication tool. Since students had to make connections to public health issues on Yellowdig, this was an opportunity to share personal information. One student stated, "A lot of people wrote how their childhood or their history connected to some topic and I was like, oh wow" (Student #5). Students learned about each other through the disclosure of their personal information. Additionally, because students had weekly four-hour synchronous Zoom sessions with the same people, this contributed to them feeling comfortable sharing about themselves.

The opportunity for students to use Zoom to communicate and work together greatly contributed to their impressions of each other. One participant said: "I've taken a class before that was online and didn't have any synchronous components to it. This is way nicer. I think it definitely adds to the learning experience of an online program" (Student #3). Another student shared: "I like meeting with everyone. I wish we had more discussion time" (Student #4). This revealed how students benefitted from both Yellowdig asynchronous sessions and Zoom synchronous sessions. While some students benefitted from meeting with everyone on Zoom, some students found it difficult to schedule time with each other to complete group work. One shared, "It was very difficult to bring people all on the same time on a Zoom call and expect work from them" (Student #2). The amount of synchronous and asynchronous opportunities for students, such as a live lecture or even group work, was observed by students.

Students became aware of how often they were engaging in either Yellowdig asynchronous discussions or Zoom synchronous sessions. One participant from the focus group stated, "I think it's a combination. I think like there were some things that people felt comfortable speaking about on Zoom" (Student #4). Another student stated, "I have gone through like four years of school without ever raising my hand in class. Zoom, I think at least, gives me a little leverage and a more likely to engage" (Student #1). Student awareness of how often and how they engage with their peers is an element of peer social presence.

The elements of peer social presence present in the Yellowdig asynchronous portions was that students shared personal information on Yellowdig such as childhood stories. In the Zoom synchronous sessions, students felt more comfortable speaking in Zoom, raised their hands more, and wanted more discussion time with their classmates. While students shared difficulty organizing group work with their peers, difficulties with student collaboration are examples of peer social presence. One can assume that learning how a peer has time management issues is also learning more about peers. Adv MPH Online students perceived Yellowdig asynchronous discussions and Zoom synchronous sessions to contribute to their ability to communicate with their classmates, which leads to our second research question which focuses more on how the specific technology contributed to students' ability to establish social presence with their peers.

Research Question 2: How and in what ways do Yellowdig and Zoom establish peer social presence amongst students?

Yellowdig is similar to most social media applications, such as Instagram, because of its user interface. It is similar because students have the opportunity to react with emoticons, and pictorial-based emotions, and include tags. This study did not focus on these Yellowdig features but focused on how students built perceptions of their peers' social presence while using Yellowdig to engage in asynchronous discussions.

Students discussed public health issues and given the sensitivity around this topic, students liked that Yellowdig was private and inaccessible to the broader internet, which makes it better than other social media applications and even CourseWorks. Students want the appearance and interface of a social media application but without public accessibility. Since the choice of technology does not mean social presence will immediately be established, it is about how individual students use the technology to create social presence. One student shared: "We used the CourseWorks. I think for something else and it was very confusing. It wasn't user-friendly as far as the actual site of Yellowdig. I think Yellowdig was a lot more clear" (Student #3). Students perceived the difference between CourseWorks discussions and Yellowdig discussions. CourseWorks is the learning management software used in the Adv MPH Online and Yellowdig was the chosen external tool as a substitute for its discussion feature.

While students greatly benefitted from interacting with each other on Yellowdig, the technology they used was pivotal to the rate of disclosure and what they disclosed. One student shared, "I think what makes the Yellowdig cool by the way we used it, was people would write what they thought and then they'd often link an article. It was a little more factual than what you see on social media. It was more academic" (Student #5). Students benefitted from using Yellowdig to complete their discussions on public health issues because they perceived it to be easier to make connections to their course material. They successfully made connections with each other while discussing public health issues through Yellowdig asynchronous discussions and Zoom synchronous sessions.

Zoom positively contributed to student perceptions of their peers' social presence. Two main reasons were the ability to create break-out groups and facilitate non-graded student group work that consisted of small group sizes of (three-four). One participant said, "I think that having these opportunities to discuss on Zoom was very helpful" (Student #3). Students need opportunities to break from the lecture and talk about the material with each other. Another participant said, "I like Zoom but only because we're such a small class and I think we have this comfort of being with the same people consistently" (Student #4). Zoom also revealed which students struggled with technology.

The focus group revealed an issue that was not originally part of the second research question. Participants recognized that working with each other was difficult because of their technological skill level and personal lives. If technologies can be used to establish peer social presence, then technological barriers can occur. Focus group participants brought up technology issues that affected their ability to connect with students. This is important because if students are not technologically skillful then they could negatively impact their group's work dynamics ultimately impacting their perception of each other's social presence. Students shared their grievances about working with their peers and what they identified as a hurdle for online learning. Two participants shared:

One thing that I did notice was detrimental to our groups was that only two of us showed up to receive tech support help at the beginning of the year. This was very detrimental to our groups and the learning process. People didn't know how to use even CourseWorks by the end of the year and that was frustrating (Student #3).

It was very difficult to bring people all on the same time on a Zoom call and expect from them that they might have done the same thing that I have done (Student #2).

Even some students found the Yellowdig tool to be inconsistent with the learning management software, CourseWorks. Yellowdig had some issues with its own technological interface. Students shared:

I think sometimes you would get emails, oh you haven't participated in a while, butYellowdig emails were off sync from our weekly assignments and so that was really jarring (Student #4).

I think that one thing that kind of made Yellowdig nice, they had like the grading disabled (Student #3).

Faculty create their own grading criteria in CourseWorks which does not integrate with Yellowdig and has its own grading scheme. Students depend on CourseWorks to understand their academic progress, but they become confused by Yellowdig. This issue appeared in the focus group where students shared their concerns about using the tool. Students said they received emails to participate when they already had. They also didn't understand how their Yellowdig points corresponded to their course grade. Additionally, some students felt indifferent towards Zoom:

I don't feel like I got to know my classmates better because of Zoom. I feel like I got to know some of my classmates well but that was because we took it offline onto like um, you know, like a different messaging platform like WhatsApp (Student #3).

I agree with student #3. At the same time here I will say that Zoom combined with Yellowdig combined with our WhatsApp group is about as good as you can do from a virtual perspective. I thought it worked really well, but nothing's perfect (Student #5).

Adv MPH Online students used additional communication technology, beyond those required by the program. Focus group participants shared there was a WhatsApp group for their cohort. In relation to the technological skill issues expressed by students, problems with Yellowdig grading, and indifference towards Zoom, the size of this program enhanced the opportunity for students to communicate with each other and build relationships over time. One participant said, "I think the size of our cohort definitely contributed to the fact that we know who the other people in our class are, we feel more inclined to speak up during class because it's built a sense of community" (Student #4). Yellowdig asynchronous discussions and Zoom synchronous sessions played an imperative role in helping students form impressions of one another and build a sense of community.

Discussion

The descriptive statistical results on Yellowig, which included multiple t-tests, showed there is no significant difference between student age groups, employment status, and degree level when it comes to building an online community. This is supported by Swan and Shih (2019) because participants intentionally crafted their messages to shape how their peers perceived them. They chose to incorporate childhood stories. These connections are predictors of student success in online degree programs. Thus, students in this program were able to build a community because they felt comfortable using Yellowdig to communicate with each other and felt their points of view were acknowledged by their peers. It took students a year to see how students communicated with each other, which connects to Gooch and Watts's (2015) evidence on relational closeness and how it is about participants knowing each other. If students agreed that their point of view was acknowledged by their peers, then the rate at which students communicated with each other builds over time. Walther's (1996; 2015) social information processing theory reminds us that the rate at which information is exchanged can help students compensate for the missing nonverbal cues. Ideally, student conversations should gradually move from superficial topics to more meaningful dialogue. As seen in the focus group results when students observed how different information was shared in Yellowdig asynchronous discussions than in Zoom synchronous sessions.

Results in this study confirm the Yellowdig asynchronous discussions and Zoom synchronous sessions enhanced interpersonal communication and positively contributed to student perceptions of their peers' social presence. Students expressed that they built an online learning community and perceived impressions of each other after the first year of the program. This finding supports the evidence that asynchronous discussions can be used to establish social presence (Lowenthal & Dunlap, 2018, Morse, 2021, Pacansky-Brock, 2014; Swan & Shih, 2019). The contents of their Yellowdig asynchronous discussions, such as connections between public health issues and their childhood, contributed to their ability to build an online community.

The type of information students share can change depending on the technology. Both students observed how different information was shared on Yellowdig than on Zoom. One assumption can be that Zoom synchronous sessions should be combined with Yellowdig asynchronous discussions to contribute to student perceptions of peer social presence, which is supported by Nisa et al. (2021). While their findings suggest students use Zoom to collaborate and problem-solve, our findings revealed that students benefitted from weekly Zoom synchronous sessions. Belt and Lowenthal (2023) confirmed how student-centered Zoom activities were more productive than traditional lectures. Students need options because some prefer opportunities to break from the lecture and some prefer to have more discussion time.

Specifically, looking at student group work and their experiences together on Zoom, students had both positive and negative experiences. Students may have experienced difficulty meeting their peers on Zoom, but this was due to technological skill level issues. There were negative group experiences because students struggled with technology, could not agree on when to meet, and could not rely on each other to complete work on time. Students expressed difficulty completing group work because some of their classmates did not manage their time well or know how to use technology to complete work. Shatila's (2024) findings showed that the academic success of adult learners is closely linked to their perceived peer support and connection. Kara et al. (2019) found students aged 41 to 51 struggle with technical skills. Past research on adult learners using technology connects to Adv MPH Online students and the challenges they face working together. Adv MPH Online students are within the 41-51 age range. Thus, it can be suggested that student work schedules and skill levels should be considered when facilitating Zoom synchronous sessions. It can be suggested that students need to work with the same people who share similar work schedules, especially in an Adv MPH Online. This was more apparent for group projects that required meeting synchronously, which confirms Roumell and Jabarkhail (2023) that degree program design should be tailored to address technological skill gaps among adult learners.

Adult learners will benefit from a combination of Zoom synchronous sessions and Yellowdig asynchronous discussions because they need exposure to technology. Roumell and Jabarkhail (2023) encourage program designers to tailor course design to technological gaps among adult learners. Focus group participants liked the combination of both types of learning activities. This finding supports evidence from studies on tools with multiple modalities (De Gagne et al., 2018; Pacansky-Brock, 2014; Ching & Hsu, 2013). When students have options for tools with different modalities, this addresses individual needs, enabling students to engage more effectively with both course material and their peers. This approach resonates with students' reflections in the focus group and how their experiences of collaborating and discussing course content with peers were successful or difficult. For an Adv MPH Online to succeed in fostering social presence, it is essential to offer ample opportunities for students to connect both asynchronously and synchronously using communication tools. These combined modalities not only contribute to students' ability to build impressions of each other but enhance the overall learning experience of the Adv MPH Online.

MOVING FORWARD

Of particular importance is that online instructors should consider a combination of communication tools to help adult learners. Through this approach, online instructors are engaging in the scholarship of teaching and learning (SoTL). Our study revealed adult learners need multiple opportunities to communicate with their peers. SoTL emphasizes engaging in effective education in order to make an impact on student learning (Grise-Owens, et al., 2016). In order to make an impact, adult learners need multiple opportunities to use a tool and communicate with each other over extended periods of time. Social presence through computer-mediated communication will occur if there is ample time (Walther, 2015). Students in the Adv MPH Online only participated in four Yellowdig discussions within the first semester of their program. This tool was not integrated into other courses, which may have limited student opportunities to deepen connections with each other in the program. One could assume that Adv MPH Online students could have benefitted from additional Yellowdig asynchronous discussions given how much they learned about each other within their first semester.

Yellowdig asynchronous discussions were only integrated in the Foundations of Public Health course. This course teaches students to develop a critical capacity for thinking broadly and deeply about public health issues. The first-year courses model the in-person core curriculum, which was designed to provide students with an integrated and interdisciplinary learning experience. Thus, Adv MPH Online students could benefit from additional opportunities to engage in Yellowidg asynchronous discussions. This would address technical issues experienced by students using the tool. Yellowdig had a different point system and would track student participation; however, this was not adequately addressed. In order for Yellowdig asynchronous discussion boards to contribute to student social presence, it needs to be integrated into multiple courses to give students time with it. Eventually, students found it helpful to communicate with their peers. They need multiple opportunities to use a new tool rather a limited amount.

Zoom synchronous sessions occurred throughout the entirety of their academic calendar year for four hours weekly. In almost all of their courses, break-out session activities were periodic because most courses incorporated opportunities for students to discuss course material in small groups. Students agreed that they wanted more discussion time on Zoom and benefitted from having a small cohort to engage with.

The program incorporated Zoom breakout rooms to consider the social needs of students while fulfilling the learning objectives of the program through active learning.

The Adv MPH Online specifically chose Yellowdig asynchronous discussion and Zoom synchronous sessions in order to meet the Council on Education and Public Health (CEPH) learning objectives. The selection of communication tools to integrate must meet the learning objectives of a degree program as well as student needs. For example, Yellowdig asynchronous discussions were used as assessments to determine whether students met the CEPH degree competencies, within their Foundations of Public Health course, and whether students understood the connection between health equity and social inequities.

Additionally, online degree programs should even consider non-traditional tools, such as What'sApp, to contribute to students' perception of social presence. As mentioned previously, a student in the focus group shared, "I feel like I got to know some of my classmates well because we took it offline onto a different messaging platform like WhatsApp. Versus having gotten to know them through Zoom" (Student #3). This student's sentiment reveals how students want to socialize with each other through additional communication tools that were not required by the Adv MPH Online. One could assume that students, even adult learners, want to connect with their peers more. The purpose of this chapter was to understand how Adv MPH students perceived impressions of their peers through Yellowdig asynchronous discussions and Zoom synchronous sessions within the first year of their program. Because students mentioned communication tools not originally part of the program, it suggests that students felt comfortable extending the conversation outside the Adv MPH Online. This initiative likely stems from opportunities within the program to establish initial communication with classmates. Without the opportunity to engage in Yellowdig asynchronous discussions or Zoom synchronous sessions, students may not have taken the step to extend communication beyond the program's boundaries.

The Adv MPH Online is supported by the instructional design team who have to make careful decisions about the type of communication tools incorporated into the program. Tools are needed to support both program goals and student needs. The types of tools that students use to learn and communicate with each other are parallel with the future of higher education and its ability to maintain success. The longevity of higher education institutions involves the successful implementation of technology (Horizon Report, 2024). Higher education institutions need flexibility with technology integration. There needs to be careful consideration of technological barriers and digital literacy. Adult learners and other nontraditional students still experience difficulty navigating and responsibly using technology because they lack previous experience using technology in their former schooling. As touched on throughout this chapter, students can experience difficulty working with other students because of technological barriers.

Higher education institutions will need to identify areas where development and investment can benefit from technology-facilitated learning. Students preferred Yellowdig asynchronous discussions versus the course learning management software, CourseWorks. One assumption could be that learning management software (LMS) could benefit from external tools that provide features not available in the LMS. We believe a team responsible for the development of online degree programs and the integration of tools should consider the backgrounds of students enrolled, as well the amount of time students need with new tools, especially a program designed for highly motivated working professionals. Given the diverse backgrounds of Adv MPH Online students, Yellowdig and Zoom were chosen with the goal of a manageable workload and student-centered learning experiences.

CONCLUSION

Instructional design teams should consider how their selection of communication tools can be integrated while preparing faculty and students to effectively use them. This chapter revealed the critical role communication tools play in enhancing the experiences of students in an Adv MPH Online. These students shared their perceptions of using communication tools that can help improve online learning experiences as well as how students learn with communication tools, and what barriers exist, which ultimately contribute to the successful integration of tools. The goal of tool integration should be to elevate the student online learning experience rather than contributing to learning and technical challenges.

Students' preference for using technology to learn is expanding because they want hybrid or completely online modalities (Roberts, 2022). If the future of higher education involves the successful implementation of technology, then instructional design teams need to create opportunities for students to consistently use tools as part of their online learning experience. Specifically, adult learners which are a new demographic for online graduate programs, need more experience using technology to learn (Kara et al., 2019). Our student perceptions of using communication tools within an Adv MPH Online provide insight into how educators can improve the online learning experience of their own students by integrating more communication tools. Adv MPH Online students shared how they took communication outside the program, which reveals additional gaps in communication tool integration and potential future research.

McKinney (2012) encouraged researchers to identify and fill in the gaps where studies are needed in SoTL. Adult learners within an online graduate program have not been studied enough. SoTL can benefit from examining student perceptions within distance learning programs in order to amplify adult learner voices. Future research should focus on larger samples, more diverse student bodies, and how or if communication tools contribute to peer social presence towards the goal of more equitable online learning communities.

While students have access to tools available in their learning management software, there are other communication tools available that can be used. There is a distinction between program-related tools and outside tools. Within the context of this chapter, CourseWorks Discussions includes features that enhance student learning such as allowing students to see threaded replies and liking posts. Options that are not included in CourseWorks discussions are emoticons or email notifications reminding students to participate. Instructional design teams need to create opportunities for students to use tools that provide additional features to further boost engagement.

Since this book chapter focused on a small cohort of students, the conclusions made here cannot be used to make generalizations about students in other online graduate public health programs. As more studies emerge on student perceptions of their peers' social presence within online graduate health programs, a distinct understanding of how adult learners build a community, while using communication tools to discuss and learn, will become more self-evident. In keeping with the scholarship of teaching and learning (SoTL), additional scholarship on this topic will even contribute to an improved and current understanding of the relationship between adult learners, social presence, and communication tools – all needed to inform practice and improve student performance. This research is valuable to faculty and instructional design within online educational spaces.

REFERENCES

Antheunis, M. L., Schouten, A. P., & Walther, J. B. (2020). The hyperpersonal effect in online dating: Effects of text-based CMC vs. videoconferencing before meeting face-to-face. *Media Psychology*, 23(6), 820–839. DOI: 10.1080/15213269.2019.1648217

Belt, E. S., & Lowenthal, P. R. (2023). Synchronous video-based communication and online learning: An exploration of instructors' perceptions and experiences. *Education and Information Technologies*, 28(5), 4941–4964. DOI: 10.1007/s10639-022-11360-6 PMID: 36320822

Boston, D., Gibson, I., & Richardson, S. (2010). An exploration of the relationship between indicators of the Community of Inquiry framework and retention in online programs. *Journal of Asynchronous Learning Networks*, 14(1), 67–83.

Cherrstrom, C. A., Robbins, S. E., Boden, C. J., & Bixby, J. (2019). Need tech? Non-traditional student perceptions of educational technology tools. *The Journal of Continuing Higher Education*, 67(2–3), 109–122. DOI: 10.1080/07377363.2019.1680266

Ching, Y.-H., & Hsu, Y.-C. (2013). Collaborative learning using VoiceThread in an online graduate course. *Knowledge Management and E-Learning*, 5(3), 298–314. DOI: 10.34105/j.kmel.2013.05.021

Cobb, S. C. (•••). Social presence and online learning: A current view from a research perspective. *Journal of Interactive Online Learning*, 8(3), 241–254.

Cui, G., Lockee, B., & Meng, C. (2013). Building modern online social presence: A review of social presence theory and its instructional design implications for future trends. *Education and Information Technologies*, 18(4), 661–685. DOI: 10.1007/s10639-012-9192-1

De Gagne, J. C., Kim, S. S., Schoen, E. R., & Park, H. K. (2018). Assessing the impact of video-based assignments on health professions students' social presence on web: Case study. *JMIR Medical Education*, 4(2), e11390. DOI: 10.2196/11390 PMID: 30478027

EDUCAUSE. (2024). *Horizon report: Teaching and learning edition* (Boulder, CO). https://library.educause.edu/resources/2024/5/2024-educause-horizon-report-teaching-and-learning-edition

Gooch, D., & Watts, L. (2015). The impact of social presence on feelings of closeness in personal relationships. *Interacting with Computers*, 27(6), 661–674. DOI: 10.1093/iwc/iwu020

Grise-Owens, E., Owens, L. W., & Miller, J. J. (2016). Conceptualizing the scholarship of teaching and learning for social work education. *Journal of Social Work Education*, 52(1), 6–17. DOI: 10.1080/10437797.2016.1112628

Lew, Z., Walther, J. B., Pang, A., & Shin, W. (2018). Interactivity in online chat: Conversational contingency and response latency in computer-mediated communication. *Journal of Computer-Mediated Communication*, 23(4), 201–221. DOI: 10.1093/jcmc/zmy009

Lowenthal, P., West, R.E., Archambault, L., Borup, J., & Belt, E. S. (2021). Faculty perceptions of using synchronous video-based communication technology. *Online Learning, 25*(4), 74-103. Htttps:// DOI: 10.24059/olj.v25i4.2890

Lowenthal, P. R., & Dunlap, J. C. (2018). Investigating students' perceptions of instructional strategies to establish social presence. *Distance Education*, 39(3), 281–298. DOI: 10.1080/01587919.2018.1476844

Macdonald, K. (2018). A review of the literature: The needs of nontraditional students in postsecondary education. *Strategic Enrollment Management Quarterly*, 5(4), 159–16. https://doi.org/gf6wh4. DOI: 10.1002/sem3.20115

Maguire, M., & Delahunt, B. (2017). Doing a thematic analysis: A practical, step-by-step guide for learning and teaching scholars. *All Ireland Journal of Teaching and Learning in Higher Education*, 3, 3351–3365.

Markle, G. (2015). Factors influencing persistence among nontraditional university students. *Adult Education Quarterly*, 65(3), 267–285. https://doi.org/f7jfb7. DOI: 10.1177/0741713615583085

McGurty, R. E. (2022). *Student perception of social presence in an asynchronous online doctoral program*. [Doctoral dissertation, Johnson University].

McKinney, K. (2012). Making a difference: Application of SoTL to enhance learning. *The Journal of Scholarship of Teaching and Learning*, 12(1), 1–7.

Morse, M. L. (2021). Increase engaged student learning using google docs as a discussion platform. *Teaching & Learning Inquiry*, 9(2), 1–18. DOI: 10.20343/teachlearninqu.9.2.20

Nisa, L. Z., Prameswari, T. N., & Alawiyah, Y. I. (2021). The effect of using small group discussions through zoom breakout room to increase the frequency of individual speaking participation in the speaking courses. *Journal of Digital Learning and Education*, 1(3), 18–26. DOI: 10.52562/jdle.v1i3.264

Pacansky-Brock, M. (2014). Learning out loud: Increasing voluntary voice comments in online classes. In Lowenthal, P. R., York, C. S., & Richardson, J. C. (Eds.), *Online learning: Common misconceptions, benefits, and challenges* (pp. 99–114). Nova Science Publishers.

Rasheed, R., Kamsin, A., & Abdullah, N. (2020). Challenges in the online component of blended learning: A systematic review. *Computers & Education*, 144, 1–17. DOI: 10.1016/j.compedu.2019.103701

Roberts, J. (2022, October 3). Students and technology report: Rebalancing the student experience. *Educause.*https://www.educause.edu/ecar/research-publications/2022/students-and-technology-report-rebalancing-the-student-experience/modality-preferences

Roumell, E. A., & Jabarkhail, S. (2023). Supporting adult working learners. *New Directions for Adult and Continuing Education*, 2023(179), 5–16. DOI: 10.1002/ace.20498

Shatila, S. (2024). Not alone when i'm feeling stressed: Online adult learner connection and retention. *Adult Education Quarterly*, 74(1), 43–61. DOI: 10.1177/07417136231184570

Short, J., Williams, E., & Christie, B. (1976). *The social psychology of telecommunications*. John Wiley and Sons.

Swan, K., & Shih, L. F. (2019). On the nature and development of social presence in online course discussions. *Online Learning : the Official Journal of the Online Learning Consortium*, 9(3), 115–136. DOI: 10.24059/olj.v9i3.1788

Walther, J. B. (1996). Computer-mediated communication: Impersonal, interpersonal, and hyperpersonal interaction. *Communication Research*, 23(1), 3–43. DOI: 10.1177/009365096023001001

Walther, J. B. (2015). Social information processing theory (CMC). In Berger, C. R., Roloff, M. E., Wilson, S. R., Dillard, J. P., Caughlin, J., & Solomon, D. (Eds.), *The international encyclopedia of interpersonal communication* (pp. 1–13). Wiley., DOI: 10.1002/9781118540190.wbeic192

Whiteside, A. L., Garrett Dikkers, A., Swan, K., & Gunawardena, C. N. (2017). *Social presence in online learning: Multiple perspectives on practice and research.* Stylus Publishing, LLC.

APPENDIX A

Questionnaire Items in the Social Presence Survey

1. I felt comfortable introducing myself in the online courses.
2. The introductions enabled me to form a sense of online community.
3. My peers created a feeling of an online community.
4. The TA(s) created a feeling of an online community.
5. I felt comfortable participating in Yellowdig with my peers.
6. The Discussion Facilitator effectively facilitated Yellowdig Conversations.
7. I was able to form distinct individual impressions of my peers even when we only communicated through Yellowdig Conversations.
8. I felt that my point of view was acknowledged by my peers in Yellowdig Conversations.
9. Yellowdig Conversations tend to be more impersonal than face-to-face discussions.
10. The diversity of topics in the online courses prompted me to participate in Yellowdig Conversations.
11. I put a great deal of effort to learn how to use CourseWorks to participate in the online course.
12. The online courses were a useful learning experience.
13. I would like to participate in other online courses in the future.

APPENDIX B

Table 2. Code Examples

Code	Definition	When to Use	When Not to Use	Example Quote
Discussion platform	Participants described their experience with the asynchronous tool, Yellowdig, to answer prompts and share articles.	Use when a participant is speaking about their experience with Yellowdig.	Do not use it when participants talk about taking conversations outside of class.	"I feel like I was more likely to interact genuinely with the other students because it was a closed forum." - Student #3
Video Conference Platform	Participants described their experience using the synchronous tool, Zoom, during live lecture sessions.	Use when a participant is speaking about their experience using Zoom and communicating with their classmates through it.	Do not use when a participant is talking about the asynchronous tool, Yellowdig.	"For purposes of learning the subject and receiving information it is pretty good. It's as good as it can be for a virtual purpose." - Student #5
Online Learning Community	Participants described their ability to identify with a community.	Use when a participant is speaking about their experience getting to know their classmates. How they felt as group with each other.	Do not use when a participant is speaking about their poor group work experience.	" I like Zoom but only because we're a small class" -Student #4

APPENDIX C

Questionnaire Items on Online Learning Communities and Yellowdig

Statements Strongly Agree Undecided Disagree Strongly Agree Disagree

I felt comfortable introducing myself in the online courses.7 3 0 0 0
The introductions enabled me to form a sense of online community. 2 7 0 1 0
My peers created a feeling of an online community. 3 6 1 0 0
The TA(s) created a feeling of an online community. 2 5 1 2 0
I felt comfortable participating in Yellowdig with my peers. 4 5 0 0 1
The Discussion Facilitator effectively facilitated conversations. 4 5 0 0 1
I was able to form distinct individual impressions of my peers. 3 4 1 1 1
I felt that my point of view was acknowledged by my peers 3 7 0 0 0
Yellowdig tends to be more impersonal than face-to-face discussions. 3 3 1 3 0
The diversity of topics in the online courses prompted me to participate. 3 5 1 1 0

Chapter 12
Revolutionizing Community Engagement and Impact With AI

Margaret S. Sass
Boise State University, USA

Brian Martin
https://orcid.org/0009-0005-7487-3036
Boise State University, USA

ABSTRACT

The evolution of artificial intelligence (AI) has profoundly impacted education, particularly in service-learning (SL) and community-based learning (CBL). This chapter explores how AI enhances these pedagogical approaches by enabling educators to design innovative, community-based assignments and projects. It highlights AI's role in addressing equity and access challenges, encouraging engagement, and supporting personalized learning experiences for diverse student populations. The chapter discusses how AI tools assist in curriculum development, real-world problem-solving, and stakeholder collaboration while emphasizing the importance of ethical considerations in AI integration. Grounded in the Scholarship of Teaching and Learning (SoTL), this work underscores AI's potential to transform experiential education, advancing both student success and meaningful community impact.

DOI: 10.4018/979-8-3693-7595-2.ch012

INTRODUCTION

The rapid evolution of artificial intelligence (AI) has revolutionized numerous fields, including education, where it has enlightened my practice as an educator and scholar. AI's potential offers new opportunities to enhance teaching and learning, enabling me to encourage students to engage with content, communities, and stakeholders. The advancement of AI has not only reshaped my approach to course design but also inspired me to explore the intersection of AI and the Scholarship of Teaching and Learning (SoTL), focusing on how these tools can support experiential, service-learning (SL) and community-based learning (CBL).

Incorporating AI into my practice and courses has allowed me to address diverse student needs more effectively, particularly for those in rural or online settings, by providing access to resources and opportunities that were once limited or unavailable. From integrating AI-driven tools for curriculum development to empowering students to identify and address community issues, AI has become an effective resource for enhancing engagement and fostering meaningful connections in higher education courses.

As an advocate for experiential education, specifically SL and CBL, I see AI as a tool that encourages innovation in service-learning (SL) and community-based education. By leveraging AI's ability to analyze community data, brainstorm possible outcomes, and personalize learning experiences, I believe it will deepen students' understanding of course material while contributing to the public good. At the same time, this research into the connection between AI and SL/CBL has prompted deeper thought on AI's ethical use and its equity for my students

This chapter explores how the revolutionary capabilities of AI have informed my teaching practice, emphasizing its role in advancing SoTL by providing strategies for enhancing student engagement, addressing community needs, and enriching the learning process in dynamic and forward-thinking ways.

WHAT IS SERVICE-LEARNING AND COMMUNITY-BASED LEARNING?

Service-learning emerged in the late 1960s, with the term first introduced in 1967 (Kenny & Gallagher, 2002). It gained momentum during the 1980s and 1990s, emphasizing the integration of community service with academic study (Kenny & Gallagher, 2002). The National Community Service Act of 1990 provided funding and encouraged its adoption in education (Woods & Conderman, 2005). This approach allows students, both in K-12 and higher education, to participate in service activities directly related to their coursework, enabling them to apply and deepen their understanding through active, hands-on learning. The roots of service-learning can be traced back to Dewey's concept of active learning (Kucey & Parsons, 2012), where he believed that students learn by doing. In the 1980s, Kolb built on this idea with his theory of experiential learning, another active form of learning (National Center for Education Statistics, 1999). Today, service-learning is an emerging pedagogical approach gaining traction, with its integration into experiential and community-based learning serving as a focus for Scholarship of Teaching and Learning (SoTL) research on effective educational practices and student engagement.

Service-learning is also referred to as community-based learning (CBL), drawing from Vygotsky's theory of the zone of proximal development (Savin-Baden, 2003), which suggests that students can learn more advanced tasks with guidance. CBL shares similarities with problem-based learning, which encourages students to solve real-world problems (Baturay & Bay, 2010).

Project-based learning (PjBL), a form of CBL, is related but not identical. Early researchers have provided insights. Wolk (1994) noted that PjBL fosters intrinsic motivation and essential skills. Katz and Chard (1992) offered that PjBL also boosts self-esteem and confidence, both important skills. Both service-learning and community-based learning focus on active, experiential education, where students apply their knowledge to real-world scenarios. Through community projects, students work outside the classroom while applying course content, with the core aim of making their learning meaningful and impactful.

These two forms of pedagogy can be strong collaborators with artificial intelligence (AI). The implementation of artificial intelligence (AI) into service-learning (SL) and community-based learning (CBL) introduces transformative opportunities for both educators and students. AI can support the design and execution of SL and CBL projects by providing tools to analyze community needs, identify potential stakeholders, and generate solutions for social challenges. By integrating AI, educators can enhance the experiential learning process. Additionally, AI provides quick access to resources and insights that may be unavailable in traditional learning environments. This integration also encourages reflective learning by offering students AI-driven prompts to critically analyze their projects and community impact. As a result, the implementation of AI into SL and CBL enriches educational practices, encourages meaningful community engagement, and aligns with the goals of the Scholarship of Teaching and Learning (SoTL) by advancing research on effective pedagogical approaches.

THE CONNECTION OF SOTL, AI, AND SL/CBL

The Scholarship of Teaching and Learning (SoTL) plays an important and elemental role in enhancing higher education (Hubbal & Clark, 2010). Through evidence-based practices, SoTL encouraging educators to explore their teaching methods and how to improve the way their students learn (Dickson & Tremi, 2013). SoTL's reflective approach helps educators identify what works for them and their students. AI can help SoTL practitioners learn and understand their research and the growth of their students understanding of content.

Integrating artificial intelligence (AI) into the Scholarship of Teaching and Learning (SoTL) offers significant benefits for educators, students, and the broader academic community, particularly in the context of service-learning (SL) and community-based learning (CBL) pedagogies. AI tools enable data-driven insights into teaching practices, allowing educators to systematically analyze the effectiveness of instructional strategies and their impact on student learning in SL and CBL environments. For example, AI can help identify and address specific community needs, track the progress of student-led projects, and provide personalized feedback that enhances both learning outcomes and community impact. These capabilities align seamlessly with the experiential and reflective format of SL and CBL, where students engage directly with real-world challenges. Additionally, AI enhances the efficiency of SoTL research allowing educators to evaluate the success of SL and CBL initiatives more effectively. By fostering innovation through adaptive learning environments and AI-driven collaborative tools, educators can explore new ways to deepen student engagement and enhance community partnerships. Incorporating AI into SoTL not only enriches research and pedagogy but also ensures that SL and CBL practices remain dynamic, equitable, and impactful in an ever-evolving educational landscape. The chapter delves deeper of how AI enhances SoTL's purpose, particularly within the context of service-learning (SL) and community-based learning (CBL) pedagogies, by demonstrating its ability to further innovation, improve teaching strategies, and strengthen student engagement and community impact.

ANALYZING AND PREDICTING STUDENT NEEDS WITH AI

The use of artificial intelligence (AI) in educational settings has drawn significant attention, particularly for its potential to enhance the Scholarship of Teaching and Learning (SoTL). AI's ability to possibly predict academic outcomes offers valuable insights for advancing student success and improving teaching practices. Parapadakis (2020) highlights how AI can analyze student satisfaction, providing data that administrators and educators can use to refine curricula and co-curricular programs. Additionally, Rincon (2020) demonstrates that AI tools can support faculty in identifying key factors that enhance academic performance, contributing to pedagogical strategies that align with SoTL's focus on improving learning outcomes and fostering innovative educational practices. Additionally, research on AI in Education 4.0 shows that AI can help students succeed by identifying their learning challenges. Parapadakis (2020) argues that AI can assess students' academic performance, predict how they will learn and work, and provide teachers with insights to either intervene or support the student's learning progress (Rincon, 2020). In an intriguing study by Ilic (2024), it was found that AI can track and predict a student's academic actions. Overall, researchers agree that AI offers valuable tools for creating personalized learning experiences, helping students achieve better outcomes in school.

Personalized Learning Pathways

AI can be leveraged to tailor learning experiences to meet the unique needs and abilities of individual students, offering a more personalized educational journey. By analyzing a student's strengths, weaknesses, and learning styles, AI can create customized learning plans that best suit each student. This approach allows for a more flexible and adaptive education that aligns with both academic and professional growth. According to Naseer (2024), deep learning (DL) models enhance this personalization by providing targeted guidance that accounts for students' individual capabilities. Additionally, AI is not only beneficial in education but also in professional training. Morozevich's and Korotkikh's (2022) research on machine learning (ML) shows that ML can recommend specific resources and training programs tailored to employees' needs, making AI a valuable tool for professional development as well.

Identifying At-Risk Students

Another important use of AI in education is identifying at-risk students. Sometimes it can be difficult for educators to discover what students are at-risk until it's too late. AI is allowing educators a more stable path on discovering the students we need to help. AIs can help with early detection, discovering what the warning signs are for certain students. Also, AI can assist educators on finding what resources or tactic to use to help students get back on track. Latif (2021) believed AI algorithms could actually predict a student's grade based on assessing the student through quizzes, assignments and other related measurements.

Equity and Access

Equity and access have been ongoing challenges in education, including higher education. Researchers, educators, and students alike have been affected by the fact that not all schools, resources, and tools are equitably accessible or distributed. The key question now is whether AI exacerbates this gap or holds the potential to help reduce it among students. This dilemma exists across both K-12 and higher education. While AI can be empowering for students and teachers, there remains a pressing concern about its inclusivity. Educators need to be aware that some tools may not be available to all students.

The digital divide now includes AI, raising concerns about how accessible these technologies are to all students, regardless of background. Roshanei (2023) emphasizes the need to break down these barriers to achieve equity, suggesting strategies to make AI more inclusive. Reducing the digital divide among college students involves addressing disparities in access to technology, digital literacy, and online resources. Some strategies are to ensure better access such as provide free or discounted licenses of certain software to students. Many universities also provide free Wi-Fi hotspots on college campuses. However, they should consider expanding that range by partnering with local libraries or other community organizations that provide access as well.

The digital divide is not only about limited access. Barriers can include the ability to access the internet based on knowledge. Colleges could check that course materials are mobile-friendly for those that only access the internet through their phones. Classes could provide asynchronous content so students can access it if their internet connection is unreliable. With financial support, colleges could expand financial aid with laptops or internet services. However, these are possible strategies that may be hard to implement at certain higher education institutions.

There are concerns regarding the negative impact on students. Does this affect their ability to think critically? The answer is yes and no with its own set of pros and cons. AI can help students with problem-solving skills by being a brainstorming partner and discussing possible solutions to problems. Students can use AI to counterargue and provide different perspectives. It can assist with research by collecting data and information and allowing the student to spend more time on analyzing that collected information. However, there can be over-reliance on AI where students use it to create answers without verifying it. Students fail to check on sources and other information, assuming that is correct. AI is not perfect and expecting such can cause a student to check biases and inaccuracies. Students may use AI to create speeches and essay outlines without putting the critical thinking that is needed for organization, processes and analysis.

Being aware of this is the key into managing AI so it supports a student's knowledge base rather than hinder it. Educators can ask students to evaluate the information they receive from generative AI by checking facts and biases. Showing students that AI can be a partner and not a replacement in their thinking can assist students in using it ethically (Darwin et al, 2023).

Even with these barriers, there are notable positive impacts AI can have on students with limited accessibility. AI can expand access to education, particularly in rural communities, tribal areas, and locations without higher education institutions. It can serve as an educational assistant or tutor, providing personalized learning and support to help students with materials they find challenging. However, while AI offers new opportunities, it's crucial to recognize that some students still may not have access to these tools due to lack of Wi-Fi, computers, or smartphones. Further research is needed to ensure that all students can access these valuable resources.

ARTIFICIAL INTELLIGENCE IN THE CLASSROOM

AI in education has been researched since the 2010s, as noted by Zhai et al. (2021). In recent years, its popularity has surged in higher education. Hwang (2020) agrees that with AI's continued development, research on implementing AI into educational practices will only increase. Hwang (2020) highlights AI's ability to support students and improve educational systems by better tracking student progress. However, concerns about the trustworthiness of AI have grown as well. While ethical considerations are important, there are also substantial benefits for both faculty and students. Zhang and Aslan (2021) agree that AI will continue to grow in education, particularly in enhancing learning outcomes and improving accessibility for students.

Despite this growth, concerns remain. Pedro (2019) acknowledges that AI can promote inclusivity and equity, but there are still challenges, such as digital divides and infrastructure or policy limitations. Alam (2021) echoes these concerns, arguing that educators and educational leaders need to be aware of potential consequences when AI is integrated into education. Issues such as privacy and data security, particularly when dealing with minors and their families, are of significant concern. Additionally, as education increasingly operates like a business, there is a risk of hacking and data leaks. Algorithmic bias is another issue, as AI can reinforce existing societal biases, disproportionately affecting marginalized communities.

There are also concerns about teacher and administrator preparedness. Many may not have adequate training to effectively use AI tools, and students may not be taught how to use AI ethically. This could hinder the development of critical thinking, creativity, and social skills, which are essential for well-rounded individuals.

AI is a powerful and exciting tool that has the potential to make education more accessible and beneficial for students and educators. However, careful consideration must be given to policy, ethical guidelines, and strategies to avoid widening the gap between those who have access to AI and those who do not.

ARTIFICIAL INTELLIGENCE AND EDUCATORS

The integration of artificial intelligence (AI) in education has generated both direct and indirect shifts in how educators approach teaching and learning from a Scholarship of Teaching and Learning (SoTL) perspective. Before adopting AI as a supplemental tool, faculty should first develop AI literacy for themselves and their students, ensuring a shared understanding of its capacities and limitations. Rather than replacing authentic and engaged instruction, AI tools should support and enrich pedagogical strategies, reflecting evidence-based practices. Holmes et al. (2019) emphasize the importance of identifying which AI applications effectively foster student learning, aligning with SoTL's emphasis on inquiry into teaching and learning processes. AI should serve to enhance, not supplant, the educator's role in facilitating meaningful educational experiences.

One way for educators to learn about AI is through professional development. Universities and colleges may provide educational courses and resources, but the instructor should be able to seek out educational opportunities that are available and free in different platforms. Some of the content they should be learning about are managing data privacy and AI biases, as this can be a present and future issue. There are also ethical considerations that should be addressed before implementation. This includes informing students how AI can be used ethically in the classroom and in the workplace. This would help students be more responsible when working with AI (Williamson & Eynon, 2020), especially as they progress in their degrees and eventually in the professional arena.

Even with concerns about AI, there are many positive outcomes for both students and educators. Onesi-Ozigagun (2024) notes that AI can transform education by helping individual students learn and by making administrative responsibilities much easier to manage. AI can also be tailored to suit each student's unique learning style (Kanchon, 2024). Additionally, it can serve as an administrative assistant by automating tasks such as assessments, tests, and lesson planning (Sajji, 2023). AI is also known to assist with managing student progress and streamlining responsibilities that educators often lack the time for (Ahmed, 2022). The potential for AI to improve learning outcomes and reduce the administrative burden on teachers presents exciting possibilities for education.

The great possibilities of AI may help students learn more effectively and remove some of the burden of time-consuming administrative duties that teachers face. By alleviating administrative burdens, educators can devote more attention to fostering student engagement and creativity, which are crucial to the development of their students. As AI continues to evolve, its potential to address logistical duties provides a promising outlook for our education system.

THE ROLE OF CHATBOTS IN THE CLASSROOM

The world of chatbots is becoming increasingly embedded in courses and workplaces. Many students use chatbots for various purposes, while others may have never been exposed to AI. Though some educators and students are wary of chatbots, they are useful tools that should be explored further. However, it may be challenging to not use chatbots while other students are using them daily. Teachers and students have the opportunity to learn about chatbots rather than fear it.

One way that educators can utilize chatbots is by treating them as administrative assistants to help with educational tasks (Hwang, 2023). Chatbots can help with developing lesson plans, writing out directions for assignments that are clear and understandable, and creating rubrics. It can also help with emails to parents, letters of recommendation for students, and brainstorming. However, students and teachers may not be aware of these tools due to lack of knowledge or exposure. Bringing awareness is a solid place to start, but the AI that is used should be user-friendly and meet educational outcomes (Ipperciel, 2023). To be more specific, here are some ways to incorporate AI within courses. Chatbots can help answer questions and are available to students outside of the classroom. Chatbots can create examples, grammar checks, and explanations of assignments. They can also carry on discussions with students, helping them prepare for assigned work.

ETHICAL CONSIDERATIONS IN USING AI IN THE CLASSROOM

Ethical considerations regarding AI use in education are continually being discussed and developed. One of the main concerns is data privacy and security. Some AI tools do not inform users how their data is being used (Nazeer, 2024). Though this seems to be the main point of discussion, there can be bias as well. Nazeer (2024) mentions that AI algorithms may also be biased and found so in his research in health care settings. Transparency also needs to be further explored. To address these concerns, some chatbots have shared what they do with the data they collect. However, the question remains if that is enough, or if policies should be in place for all AI apps, sites, and developed algorithms.

Data Privacy and Security for Different Chatbots

AI tools like ChatGPT, Copilot and Google Gemini have policies addressing ethical use, privacy, intellectual property, and data security. Below are general principles based on their practices. It's important to use these tools responsibly and avoid any unethical, illegal, or misleading applications.

OpenAI OpCo, LLC (https://openai.com/safety/) claims to safeguard a user's privacy and protect any personal information that is collected when a person uses its services, which include its website, applications, and other platforms. This Privacy Policy outlines the types of personal information OpenAI gathers, such as account details, user content, and communication information, and how this data is handled. Personal information collected can include data provided directly by users, such as account information, social media interactions, and communications, as well as data automatically gathered during service use, such as device details, log data, and cookies. This information is used for a variety of purposes, including improving services, conducting research, communicating with users, and preventing fraud. OpenAI may aggregate or anonymize personal data for analysis purposes but will never attempt to re-identify it without legal obligations. In some cases, OpenAI may share personal information with third parties.

Copilot, owned by Microsoft (https://github.com/features/security)provides commercial data protection via work or school accounts. Copilot advertises that it does not store prompts or responses for training large language models (LLMs) and has multiple safeguards against harmful content. Microsoft complies with privacy regulations like the General Data Protection Regulation (GDPR) and European Union (EU) Data Boundary requirements.

Gemini's website (https://support.google.com/gemini/answer/13594961?hl=en) provides information on how Gemini uses personal data and addresses common questions related to your privacy when using the tool. Google collects your conversations in Gemini Apps, related usage data, location information, and feedback to enhance and develop its products and services, including machine-learning technologies like Google Cloud, in line with its Privacy Policy. By default, Gemini Apps Activity is only for users 18 and older, while those under 18 can opt to enable it. If this setting is active, Google stores a user's Gemini Apps activity for up to 18 months, with options to adjust this to three or 36 months. Location information from a personal device, IP address, or saved addresses is also stored with a user's activity.

Learning about one's privacy falls mainly on the user of these apps. However, educational institutions should be educating and informing their staff, faculty and students about what student data is being collected and for what purpose prior as well as their privacy rights. Users should be aware of the possibility of a data breach even if data security is in place. There is also the risk of data profiling where AI algorithms could create detailed profiles of students which could result in discrimination and targeted advertising.

Though these educational institutions have a duty to inform information that affects their staff and students, it is still best for the user to go directly to the website and investigate the most up-to-date policies for these tools as policies can change rapidly due to technological advancements. Each platform has different terms of service, privacy policies, and usage restrictions that may significantly affect how users integrate their AI tools into educational or community-based projects. By staying informed, it will ensure compliance and make the most of the AI tools.

ARTIFICIAL INTELLIGENCE TOOLS FOR EDUCATORS

From a Scholarship of Teaching and Learning (SoTL) perspective, educators today have access to an expanding variety of AI tools that can enhance teaching practices, streamline workflows, and foster deeper student engagement. These tools not only serve as resources for educators but also provide opportunities for analysis into how AI impacts teaching effectiveness and learning outcomes. As noted by Sağın et al. (2023), AI tools such as chatbots can support educators by offering feedback, aiding in curriculum development and design, creating lesson plans, and generating course materials. By leveraging these tools, educators can explore evidence-based practices that align with SoTL's goals of improving pedagogy and understanding the relationship between teaching innovations and student success.

Below is an overview of AI tools designed to assist with various teaching tasks, including content creation, personalized learning, and interactive presentations. Price points range from completely free to free trials or subscription-based plans, so it's important to visit each site for specific costs. This can be a key factor when deciding whether to use a tool for a one-time need, on a monthly basis, or making it a student responsibility to purchase.

AI Tools for Classroom Content and Student Engagement

- ChatGPT (https://openai.com/index/chatgpt/): This is a tool that can be a tutor when the instructor doesn't have the time to do direct tutoring, or the student needs a tutor of specific content. It can generate lesson plans and even answer student questions.

- Knewton Alta (https://www.wiley.com/en-us/education/alta): This is a way for educators to personalize their teaching based on each student. By analyzing how students interact with content, it tailors lessons to meet individual needs, focusing on areas where students need improvement and adjusting pacing accordingly.
- Otter.ai (https://otter.ai): An amazing tool that can transcribe lectures, making class content accessible to all students. It can also save time through automated lecture notes. Even more, it can join your virtual meetings. When recording Zoom meetings, it can capture slides and add them to the notes as well.
- Mentimeter (https://www.mentimeter.com): This tool helps create interactive presentations and gather real-time student feedback, making classes more engaging and participatory. With Mentimeter, you can boost participation with a variety of interactive features that everyone can join, no matter their location. Responses are anonymous which can encourage honest comments.

AI Tools for Visual and Slide Creation

In addition to content generation and classroom engagement, several AI tools assist educators in creating visually appealing slides and multimedia content.

- Beautiful.ai (https://www.beautiful.ai): An AI-powered presentation design tool that allows users to create professional-looking slides with minimal effort.
- Visme (https//www.visme.co): An AI-powered design platform for creating presentations, infographics, and other visual content that is helpful for education and professional purposes.
- Lumen5 (https//www.lumen5.com): This video-creation platform transforms written content into engaging video slideshows, which can be used for video-based presentations.
- Google Slides with AI Add-ons (e.g., SlidesAI) (https://workspace.google.com/products/slides/): These add-ons help automate the creation of slide decks based on provided content, saving educators time.
- VistaCreate (https://create.vista.com): Like Canva, this AI-powered tool assists in designing images and visuals for slides and presentations.
- Piktochart (https://piktochart.com): This tool specializes in creating infographics and visual aids for slide presentations with AI-assisted design features.

ARTIFICIAL INTELLIGENCE TOOLS FOR STUDENTS

Students can also leverage AI tools to improve their learning experience, stay organized, and create engaging content. Below is a breakdown of AI-driven tools that support writing, research, presentations, and task management. The descriptions for these AI tools are found on their websites, but I've listed them here as well.

AI Tools for Writing and Research

- Grammarly (https://www.grammarly.com): This can be an essential tool for improving writing by checking grammar, punctuation, and style and even detecting plagiarism, ensuring polished and professional work. This tool has been around for a while and is currently used by many students.
- Wolfram Alpha (https://www.wolframalpha.com): A computational engine that helps students solve complex problems, particularly in math and science, by providing step-by-step solutions and explanations.
- Notion AI (https://www.notion.so): Notion AI enhances notetaking, task management, and organization, helping students manage research, track assignments, and generate content.
- Mendeley (https://www.mendeley.com): Mendeley is an AI-driven research management tool that helps organize papers, create bibliographies, and collaborate on academic projects. It can be a very useful tool when writing essays that involve references.
- Hemingway Editor (https://hemingwayapp.com): Hemingway Editor is another writing tool designed to help users make their writing clearer and more readable. Actually, this tool is inspired by the writing style of Ernest Hemingway. Hemingway Editor encourages clear, direct language by highlighting areas that may be overly complicated or difficult for readers to understand.
- QuillBot (https://quillbot.com): QuillBot is a writing assistant that specializes in paraphrasing, grammar correction, and enhancing sentence structure. It allows users to rewrite or rephrase sentences and entire paragraphs. QuillBot can help improve the readability of content, avoiding plagiarism by rewording existing text, and making writing more polished and professional.

AI Tools for Homework Assistance

- Socratic by Google (https://socratic.org): An AI-powered app that provides step-by-step explanations to help students with homework in subjects like math, science, and more.

- Chegg Study (https://www.chegg.com/study): Offers AI-driven solutions to textbook questions and homework problems, providing explanations and study assistance in various subjects.

AI Tools for Content Creation and Task Management

- Speechify (https://speechify.com): This tool converts text into speech, allowing students to listen to textbooks, notes, or articles while on the go, which is ideal for those who prefer listening to audio or those with busy schedules. Speechify is useful for students on the go and can be listened to anywhere.
- Replika (https://replika.ai): This interesting AI chatbot is designed to help students manage stress and think through ideas by simulating conversations and providing emotional and intellectual support.

AI Tools for Visual Design and Presentations

- Canva (https://www.canva.com): A versatile tool for creating visually appealing presentations, offering AI-powered suggestions and templates for everything from slides to graphics.
- Beautiful.ai (https://www.beautiful.ai): Automates the design process, allowing students to focus on content while the AI handles the layout, ensuring professional-looking presentations with ease. Beautiful.ai also has many templates to choose from.
- Slidebean (https://www.slidebean.com): Though used mainly for sales, this tool can help educators generate professional, creative presentations with optimized layouts, making the design process fast and simple.
- Visme (https://www.visme.co): A tool that offers interactive presentations as well as docs featuring infographics, charts, and multimedia elements, helping to create more engaging and visually rich content.
- Pitch (https//www.pitch.com): A tool mainly used for sales, it can still be used as an educational tool that supports collaborative presentation design, offering beautifully designed templates to streamline the creative process.
- Designs.ai (https://www.design.ai): Provides AI-based tools for designing presentations, logos, and images, helping students create polished and professional visuals and videos quickly. Additionally, it's a useful tool for a social media campaign.
- Powtoon (https://www.powtoon.com): Known for making interesting videos for YouTube, this tool allows students to create animated presentations and videos, adding a creative and dynamic touch to their academic work.

- Haiku Deck (https://www.haikudeck.com): Focusing on simplicity and creativity, this tool suggests visuals and layout designs based on the content provided, making presentations quick and easy to develop specifically for the web, iPad, or iPhone.
- Decktopus (https://www.dectopus.com): This tool helps users create professional, visually appealing slide decks quickly and easily. Decktopus will generate relevant slides, complete with design elements like fonts, colors, images, and icons. This helps students who need to create presentations without spending too much time on design.

Generative AI Media for Students

Generative AI media is revolutionizing the way students create, learn, and engage with content. Generative AI tools can assist students in producing different types of media, from written essays and presentations to digital art and videos.

- DALL-E (https://openai.com/dall-e): DALL-E specializes in generating images from text descriptions. It can produce highly creative, artistic, and sometimes even surreal images by combining elements. It's widely used in various fields, such as marketing, design, and education
- Gamma AI (https://gamma.app): Gamma AI creates presentations, web pages, and documents. The platform integrates interactive elements, embedded media, and real-time collaboration, allowing users to create and share content.
- HeyGen AI (https://www.heygen.com): HeyGen AI is a video generation platform that creates personalized videos. It allows users to produce professional-looking videos without needing extensive video editing skills.
- The Multiverse AI (https://www.themultiverse.ai): Multiverse creates personalized headshots for $29 within two hours that can be used for marketing and resumes.
- Ideogram (https:/ideogram.ai): Ideogram helps users create text-based images. Ideogram's AI capabilities enable users to input text and receive designs that integrate fonts, colors, and layouts automatically, without the need for advanced design skills. This tool is effective for creating logos, social media graphics, advertisements, and other digital content.
- ElevenLabs (https://elevenlabs.io): This is an AI-powered platform that generates high-quality, natural-sounding voiceovers and synthetic speech. It provides a variety of customizable voices, with options for different accents, tones, and speaking styles that work well with audiobooks, podcasts, video narrations, and interactive voice applications.

- Microsoft Copilot Designer (https://www.microsoft.com/en-us/microsoft-365/copilot): Though Microsoft Copilot Designer is a multi-faceted tool, it can also create visually appealing content. As an art generator, Copilot Designer helps users produce high-quality graphics, illustrations, and creative visuals based on text prompts or provided content.
- Mubert (https://mubert.com): Mubert generates royalty-free, customizable music based on user preferences and inputs. It can compose original tracks, allowing users to create background music, soundscapes, and unique audio for various projects.
- Claude (https://www.anthropic.com/index/claude): Named after Claude Shannon, a pioneering figure in information theory, this tool emphasizes safety and ethical use while offering conversational abilities similar to other AI chatbots like ChatGPT. Claude can help with writing, research, coding, and brainstorming, making it a versatile tool for students, professionals, and creators alike. Its focus on safe and responsible AI use means that it's designed to reduce harmful outputs, ensuring interactions are helpful and positive.

AI Research for Student Papers and Presentations

- Mendeley (https://www.mendeley.com): A great tool for students to manage, organize, and annotate their research papers and articles. This tool also helps students organize their research.
- ChatPDF (https//www.chatpdf): As mentioned above for educators, this also helps students summarize articles and answer questions about the content.
- PDF AI (https://www.pdf.ai): Similar to ChatPDF, this tool allows you to interact with your PDF documents by uploading them and then asking questions and getting insights.
- NotebookLM (https://notebooklm.google): This is another tool that focuses on summarizing PDFs, making it easier to analyze several PDFs at once. It has an interesting feature that can create an audio podcast based on any PDF you provide. NotebookLM can also create study notes from your PDFs.
- Elicit (https://elicit.org): An amazing tool for research, Elicit is designed to help users find and organize their research.
- Perplexity (https://perplexity.ai): An AI-powered research and search engine that provides conversational, reliable answers. Students can use the Reading Coach for developing reading skills. It can help create study guides and be used a tool for brainstorming.
- Consensus (https://consensus.app): Consensus is an academic search engine that helps find pertinent research on science. It claims that students and researchers at 500+ universities have already used it.

Student Study/Learning Tools

- ChatPDF (https://www.chatpdf.com): This chatbot can help answer questions about an uploaded PDF that a student saves on their computer.
- Wolfram Alpha (https://www.wolframalpha.com): This is an AI-powered study tool for math and science that provides expert-level answers.
- Natural Readers (https://www.naturalreaders.com): This is a text-to-speech tool mainly for personal use. It converts text, PDFs, images, webpages, and a physical book into natural-sounding audio.
- Doctrina AI (https://doctrina.ai): This AI app generates notes for you on any topic. It can generate essays, quizzes, and exams to help you prepare for actual assessments. It also has an extensive collection of books.
- Tutor AI (https://tutorai.me): Tutor AI personalizes learning. It generates a learning pathway for students to complete on any topic. It even offers free online courses generated by other users.
- Otter AI (https://tutorai.me): Otter AI transcribes and summarizes meetings and takes notes.

AI SUPPORTING A SERVICE-LEARNING OR COMMUNITY-BASED COURSE

Since Artificial Intelligence is a vast and ever-expanding field, a brief overview is provided on how AI is transforming service-learning and community-based courses. There is not much research on implementing AI into community-orientated classes. However, some recent research shows success in utilizing AI to help students. Ahmad et. al. (2024) found that AI within community-oriented projects, can enhance student engagement. Educators have used AI to increase English learners' participation (Chandra et. al, 2024). A series of AI projects called "Hands-On AI Projects for the Classroom" have taught K-12 teachers to teach their own students on how to use AI (Black, 2022). These are just a few examples, but there are several benefits of AI tools intertwined with SL and CBL courses such as real-world problem-solving, collaboration, and student engagement in community-oriented projects.

Listed are only some of the AI tools that could be used in a SL or CBL course. There are many others out there that can assist students in their learning and exploration of many community issues. AI tools also allow for a different type of engagement where students don't need to leave their homes, making these tools extremely powerful for an online course. Since AI technology is rapidly developing and becoming more popular to use, it's likely that there will be even more AI tools available that weren't present when this chapter was written. It's an exciting moment in our lives to know what we can do now and what we will be capable of doing soon.

AI Tools for SL or CBL Courses

- ChatGPT (https://chatgpt.com): ChatGPT is evolving rapidly and serves as a resourceful tool for students, particularly in brainstorming ideas for community projects. It aids in problem-solving by generating potential solutions and stimulating new ideas. Additionally, it helps students create community partner personas and develop strategies for community outreach. For brainstorming, students can investigate their specific community's needs and use ChatGPT to explore different ways to address those challenges.
- Kumu (https://kumu.io): Kumu is a powerful tool that organizes complex data into visually appealing relationship maps. These maps help students understand community relationships, stakeholders, and societal systems. It is particularly useful for creating impact maps that highlight key stakeholders, nonprofit organizations, government agencies, and their connections to the community. The visualizations provided by Kumu allow students to see relationships rather than just read about them, potentially sparking out-of-the-box thinking for solving community issues.
- Zooniverse (https://www.zooniverse.org): Zooniverse is a citizen science platform that connects students with community members for collaborative data analysis and research. It offers a hands-on experience for students learning about data collection and research by allowing them to participate in large-scale community-based projects. In a research assignment, students can use Zooniverse for crowdsourcing and analyzing data, providing them with valuable experiential learning opportunities.
- Character AI (https://character.ai): This tool allows students to create and interact with AI characters. Students can interact with important characters from history, written work, etc. This tool offers a unique and immersive way to engage with important figures from different subject matters that the instructor is teaching. Students can hold conversations with these AI-driven characters, ask questions, learn about different perspectives, and gain insights into historical events, literary themes, or scientific concepts that students may not have been able to explore in the past.

EXPERIENTIAL LEARNING THROUGH AI AND SOTL PERSPECTIVE

Service-learning and community-based learning are recognized as high-impact practices in higher education, providing valuable opportunities for experiential learning that extend beyond traditional classroom instruction. From a Scholarship of Teaching and Learning (SoTL) perspective, these approaches allow educators to investigate how hands-on, real-world activities enhance student engagement and learning outcomes. The integration of AI tools into such practices can further support experiential learning by offering innovative ways to connect course content with community-based applications. As AI expands into teaching and learning, SoTL encourages instructors to critically assess the use of AI by considering 1) how the tool aligns with and supports specific course objectives; 2) how it integrates with existing course materials, such as readings, videos, and podcasts; 3) whether this AI tool can help with real-time feedback; 4) if the AI tool can create prompts for reflective writing; and (5) whether the AI creates interaction between students and the chatbot that encourages deeper thinking, collaboration, and experience with hypothetical community projects.

For purposes of this chapter, four examples of AI assignments in varying subject matter are provided (**see Appendix**). These assignments were created using a chatbot, showing that instructors can create assignments that meet the objectives of the course and can be engaging for the students.

In the first example, students gather and analyse water quality data using AI over the course of a semester. They share their findings and recommend practical solutions to community partners. The second example focuses on social work and designing AI chatbots to provide emotional support. Students collect the data from these chatbots and based on the analysed results, they suggest additional resources and education to help these nonprofit centers meet the demand of those they serve. The third assignment focuses on using AI to understand why and how local bus routes are ineffective. Based on what students discover, they can suggest new routes or schedules that are more efficient. The next example is in the education department, where students design a program or offer a workshop that involves an AI tutor to help elementary students with reading skills or other needed skills. The last example involves public health where students monitor air quality near schools and residential neighborhoods. Students use AI to analyse the data and then work with community organizations to create awareness campaigns or other ways to educate the community.

The examples in the appendices showcase a selection of assignments specifically generated by artificial intelligence (AI) to assist educators in designing projects tailored to their subject matter. These examples highlight how generative AI can be utilized to create creative, community-based assignments that align with course objectives and desired learning outcomes. From a Scholarship of Teaching and Learning (SoTL) perspective, these AI-generated assignments serve as valuable resources for exploring innovative teaching practices and their impact on student engagement and learning. By leveraging AI to design assignments, educators can integrate community-based learning into their courses, fostering experiential education while contributing to the study of effective teaching strategies.

CONCLUSION

As AI use within the classroom is increasing, it may be important to learn whether students like AI being utilized more and more by their instructors. In the last few years, studies have shown that students have a positive attitude toward AI being used in education. Students report enjoying AI-enhanced learning experiences and find AI tools helpful for writing tasks (Sumakul et al., 2022). However, students have some concerns about possible drawbacks of AI in education (Idroes et al., 2023). This may be due to a lack of knowledge about what AI is. Whether this is considered a negative or a positive, students feel that AI does not replace human creativity (Marrone et al., 2022). It is suggested that teachers and instructors teach students what AI is, how it can be used to benefit them, and also possible ethical issues. However, the best idea may be to pilot it in your next class and see if students embrace it or find it an unnecessary tool that hinders their learning. That may be the evidence to continue including AI within your curriculum, stop using it altogether, or find a middle ground.

As artificial intelligence (AI) continues to evolve rapidly, the integration of AI into educational practices presents opportunities for advancing the Scholarship of Teaching and Learning (SoTL). For educators, the next step involves actively engaging with the latest AI research and trends to better understand how these technologies can enhance teaching and learning. This ongoing learning process allows educators to incorporate tools and techniques that align with evidence-based pedagogical strategies.

A SoTL perspective emphasizes the importance of critically evaluating the rapid pace of AI development, as tools available today may become obsolete in months. Additionally, educators must examine the financial implications of adopting AI tools, ensuring accessibility and equity by considering whether costs are borne by the institution or passed on to students. By addressing these factors, educators can contribute to SoTL by systematically studying the effectiveness of AI in fostering student engagement, improving learning outcomes, and supporting innovative teaching practices.

In addition to researching these AI tools, taking advantage of formal training programs in AI can help educators understand the value and significance of these tools so they're a right fit for their teaching. These programs may also cover technical aspects of AI that educators may need help with. Additionally, staying abreast of state and district-level policies related to AI integration in education is critical to aligning course content with legal and educational guidelines.

Equally important is teaching students how to interact with AI responsibly and ethically. Educators should emphasize ethical standards, such as data privacy, bias mitigation, and transparency in AI. Lastly, educators should create excitement about AI's potential, encouraging students to embrace AI as a tool for innovation and problem-solving rather than something to fear. Educators have an opportunity not only to educate students on the ethical and practical use of AI tools, but also to create professional skills for businesses that utilize AI.

REFERENCES

Ahmad, A. (2024). Pendampingan Pengembangan Bahan Ajar berbasis Artificial Intelligence. AJAD: Jurnal Pengabdian kepada Masyarakat, 4(1), 210-217.

Ahmad, S. F., Khan, I., & Patel, M. (2022). Academic and administrative role of artificial intelligence in education. *Journal of Educational Technology & Society*, 25(3), 75–89.

Ait Baha, T., El Hajji, M., Es-Saady, Y., & Fadili, H. (2024). The impact of educational chatbot on student learning experience. *Education and Information Technologies*, 29(8), 10153–10176. DOI: 10.1007/s10639-023-12166-w

Alam, A. (2021). Possibilities and apprehensions in the landscape of artificial intelligence in education. *Journal of Educational Technology & Society*, 24(3), 12–25.

Aleedy, M., Atwell, E., & Meshoul, S. (2022). Using AI chatbots in education: Recent advances challenges and use case. Artificial Intelligence and Sustainable Computing. *Proceedings of ICSISCET*, 2021, 661–675.

Baturay, M. H., & Bay, O. F. (2010). The effects of problem-based learning on the classroom community perceptions and achievement of web-based education students. *Computers & Education*, 55(1), 43–52. DOI: 10.1016/j.compedu.2009.12.001

Bayly-Castaneda, K., Ramirez-Montoya, M.-S., & Morita-Alexander, A. (2024). Crafting personalized learning paths with AI for lifelong learning: A systematic literature review. *Frontiers in Education*, 9, 1–12. DOI: 10.3389/feduc.2024.1424386

Black, N. B. (2022, June). Teaching AI with the hands-on AI projects for the classroom series. *Proceedings of the AAAI Conference on Artificial Intelligence*, 36(11), 12859–12859. DOI: 10.1609/aaai.v36i11.21566

Castillo, A. G. R., Rivera, H. V. H., Teves, R. M. V., Lopez, H. R. P., Reyes, G. Y., Rodriguez, M. A. M., & Arias-Gonzáles, J. L. (2023). Effect of Chat GPT on the digitized learning process of university students. *Journal of Namibian Studies: History Politics Culture*, 33, 1–15.

Cheddadi, S., & Bouache, M. (2021). Improving equity and access to higher education using artificial intelligence. *International Journal of Education and Development Using Information and Communication Technology*, 17(2), 112–125. DOI: 10.1109/ICCSE51940.2021.9569548

Chen, Y., Jensen, S., Albert, L. J., Gupta, S., & Lee, T. (2023). Artificial intelligence (AI) student assistants in the classroom: Designing chatbots to support student success. *Information Systems Frontiers*, 25(1), 161–182. DOI: 10.1007/s10796-022-10291-4

Chen, Z., Zhang, Y., Li, P., & Wang, X. (2020). Education 4.0 using artificial intelligence for students' performance analysis. *Journal of Educational Technology Systems*, 48(4), 1–15.

Chiu, T. K., Moorhouse, B. L., Chai, C. S., & Ismailov, M. (2023). Teacher support and student motivation to learn with Artificial Intelligence (AI) based chatbot. *Interactive Learning Environments*, •••, 1–17. DOI: 10.1080/10494820.2023.2172044

Corey, J. F. (1972). A brief history of service-learning internship programs. *Higher Education in North Carolina*, 7(4), 1–7.

Darwin, R., Rusdin, D., Mukminatien, N., Suryati, N., Laksmi, E. D., & Marzuki, . (2023). Critical thinking in the AI era: An exploration of EFL students' perceptions, benefits, and limitations. *Cogent Education*, 11(1), 2290342. Advance online publication. DOI: 10.1080/2331186X.2023.2290342

Dickson, K. L., & Treml, M. M. (2013). Using assessment and SoTL to enhance student learning. *New Directions for Teaching and Learning*, 2013(136), 7–16. DOI: 10.1002/tl.20072

Eka Chandra, N., Mariani, N., Rosalina, E., Elyani, E. P., Asrimawati, I. F., Anwar, M. N., & Nazmi, Y. F. (2024). The use of artificial intelligence technology in enhancing student participation in classroom activities at the English Subject Teacher's Association. *Bubungan Tinggi: Jurnal Pengabdian Masyarakat*, 6(2), 441–448. DOI: 10.20527/btjpm.v6i2.10261

Firat, M. (2023). What ChatGPT means for universities: Perceptions of scholars and students. *Journal of Applied Learning and Teaching*, 6(1), 57–63.

Harland, T. (2003). Vygotsky's zone of proximal development and problem-based learning: Linking a theoretical concept with practice through action research. *Teaching in Higher Education*, 8(2), 263–272. DOI: 10.1080/13562510320000052483

Holmes, W., Bialik, M., & Fadel, C. (2019). *Artificial intelligence in education promises and implications for teaching and learning*. Center for Curriculum Redesign.

Hubball, H., & Clarke, A. (2010). Diverse methodological approaches and considerations for SoTL in higher education. *The Canadian Journal for the Scholarship of Teaching and Learning*, 1(1), 2. DOI: 10.5206/cjsotl-rcacea.2010.1.2

Hwang, G. J., Xie, H., Wah, B. W., & Gašević, D. (2020). Intelligence in education. *Journal of Educational Technology & Society*, 23(4), 1–5.

Idroes, G. M., Noviandy, T. R., Maulana, A., Irvanizam, I., Jalil, Z., Lensoni, L., Lala, A., Abas, A. H., Tallei, T. E., & Idroes, R. (2023). Student perspectives on the role of artificial intelligence in education: A survey-based analysis. *Journal of Educational Management and Learning*, 1(1), 8–15. DOI: 10.60084/jeml.v1i1.58

Ilic, M., Petrović, J., & Stanković, M. (2024). Predicting student performance in a programming tutoring system using AI and filtering techniques. *Educational Data Mining Journal*, 10(1), 45–60.

Ipperciel, D., Thibaudeau, P., & Kalive, V. (2023). AI in the classroom: An evaluation and design framework for educational chatbots. In T. Bastiaens (Ed.), *Proceedings of edMedia + innovate learning* (pp. 924-929). Vienna, Austria: Association for the Advancement of Computing in Education (AACE).

Kanchon, M. K. H., Lee, Y., & Choi, J. (2024). Enhancing personalized learning: AI-driven identification of learning styles and content modification strategies. *Journal of Learning Analytics*, 10(2), 35–56.

Kenny, L. A. K. Simon, K. Kiley-Brabeck, & R. M. Lerner (Eds.). *Learning to serve: Promoting civil society through service learning* (pp. 15-29), Springer.

Kenny, M. E., & Gallagher, L. A. (2002). Service-learning: A history of systems. In M. E. DOI: 10.1007/978-1-4615-0885-4_2

Kucey, S., & Parsons, J. (2012). Linking past and present: John Dewey and assessment for learning. *Journal of Teaching and Learning*, 8(1), 107–116. DOI: 10.22329/jtl.v8i1.3077

Latif, G., Alghazo, R., & Pilotti, M. A. E. (2021). Identifying "at-risk" students: An AI-based prediction approach. *International Journal of Computing and Digital Systems*, 10(4), 231–240.

Marrone, R., Taddeo, V., & Hill, G. (2022). Creativity and artificial intelligence—A student perspective. *Journal of Intelligence*, 10(3), 65. DOI: 10.3390/jintelligence10030065 PMID: 36135606

Merelo, J. J., Castillo, P. A., Mora, A. M., Barranco, F., Abbas, N., Guillén, A., & Tsivitanidou, O. (2024). Chatbots and messaging platforms in the classroom: An analysis from the teacher's perspective. *Education and Information Technologies*, 29(2), 1903–1938. DOI: 10.1007/s10639-023-11703-x PMID: 37361787

Morozevich, E. S., Korotkikh, V. S., & Kuznetsova, Y. (2022). The development of a model for a personalized learning path using machine learning methods. *Business Info*, 16(2), 54–65. DOI: 10.17323/2587-814X.2022.2.21.35

Naseer, F., Khan, M. N., Tahir, M., Addas, A., & Aejaz, S. M. H. (2024). Integrating deep learning techniques for personalized learning pathways in higher education. *Heliyon*, 10(11), e32628. DOI: 10.1016/j.heliyon.2024.e32628 PMID: 38961899

National Center for Education Statistics. (1999). *Teacher quality: A report on the preparation and qualifications of public school teachers*. U.S. Department of Education.

Nazeer, Y. N. (2024). Algorithmic conscience: An in-depth inquiry into ethical dilemmas in artificial intelligence. *International Journal of Research and Innovation in Social Science*, 8(5), 725–732. DOI: 10.47772/IJRISS.2024.805052

Onesi-Ozigagun, O., Adeyemi, A., & Okeke, C. (2024). Revolutionizing education through AI: A comprehensive review of enhancing learning experiences. *Journal of Artificial Intelligence in Education*, 12(1), 23–45. DOI: 10.51594/ijarss.v6i4.1011

Parapadakis, D. (2020). Can artificial intelligence help predict a learner's needs? Lessons from predicting student satisfaction. *London Review of Education*, 18(2), 178–195. DOI: 10.14324/LRE.18.2.03

Pedro, F., Subosa, M., Rivas, A., & Valverde, P. (2019). *Artificial intelligence in education: Challenges and opportunities for sustainable development*. UNESCO Publishing.

Rincón-Flores, E. G., Guerrero-Rodriguez, J., & Rodríguez-Reséndiz, J. (2020). Predicting academic performance with artificial intelligence (AI), a new tool for teachers and students. *International Journal of Emerging Technologies in Learning*, 15(2), 23–34.

Roshanaei, M., Smith, J., & Li, X. (2023). Harnessing AI to foster equity in education: Opportunities, challenges, and emerging strategies. *Journal of Educational Technology & Society*, 26(3), 45–60.

Sağın, F. G., Özkaya, A. B., Tengiz, F., Geyik, Ö. G., & Geyik, C. (2024). Current evaluation and recommendations for the use of artificial intelligence tools in education. *Türk Biyokimya Dergisi*, 48(6), 620–625. DOI: 10.1515/tjb-2023-0254

Sajja, R., Krishnan, P., & Nair, S. (2023). Artificial intelligence-enabled intelligent assistant for personalized and adaptive learning in higher education. *Journal of Educational Technology Systems*, 52(1), 67–85.

Sumakul, D. T. Y., Hamied, F. A., & Sukyadi, D. (2022, February). Students' perceptions of the use of AI in a writing class. In 67th TEFLIN International Virtual Conference & the 9th ICOELT 2021 (TEFLIN ICOELT 2021) (pp. 52-57). Atlantis Press.

Tamim, S. R., & Grant, M. M. (2013). Definitions and uses: Case study of teachers implementing project-based learning. *The Interdisciplinary Journal of Problem-Based Learning*, 7(2). Advance online publication. DOI: 10.7771/1541-5015.1323

Williamson, B., & Eynon, R. (2020). Historical threads, missing links, and future directions in AI in education. *Learning, Media and Technology*, 45(3), 223–235. DOI: 10.1080/17439884.2020.1798995

Woods, C. S., & Conderman, G. (2005). Service learning and teacher education. *Academic Exchange Quarterly*, 9, 155–160.

Zhai, X., Chu, X., Chai, C. S., Jong, M. S. Y., Istenic, A., Spector, M., Liu, J.-B., Yuan, J., & Li, Y. (2021). A review of artificial intelligence (AI) in education from 2010 to 2020. *Complexity*, 2021(1), 1–18. DOI: 10.1155/2021/8812542

Zhang, K., & Aslan, A. B. (2021). AI technologies for education: Recent research & future directions. *Journal of Educational Technology Development and Exchange*, 14(1), 1–17.

APPENDIX

A. Environmental Science and Local Ecosystems Assignment

Project Focus: Using AI to monitor and improve local water quality.

- AI Tools Used:
  - AI Sensors and Data Analysis Platforms: AI-driven sensors deployed in local rivers or lakes can collect real-time data on water quality (e.g., pH levels, pollutants, temperature). AI algorithms analyze the data to identify patterns and potential pollution sources.
  - Zooniverse: A citizen science platform where students and local community members collaborate to track wildlife and environmental changes, using AI to categorize images and analyze trends.
- How AI is Implemented:
  - Students work with community partners (local environmental groups or city water departments) to install AI-powered sensors in nearby bodies of water.
  - AI tools analyze data, and students use the insights to present recommendations to local authorities for improving water quality.
- Realistic Example:
  - Students gather and analyze water quality data using AI over the course of a semester. They collaborate with community organizations to share their findings and recommend practical solutions, such as adding filtration systems or addressing potential agricultural runoff.

B. Social Work and Mental Health Services Assignment

Project Focus: Using AI chatbots to provide mental health resources to underserved communities.

- AI Tools Used:
  - Replika: An AI chatbot that can offer emotional support and simulate conversations, which helps community members in need of mental health assistance.
  - Natural Language Processing (NLP) AI: Used to analyze trends in chatbot interactions and assess common concerns or needs within the community.
- How AI is Implemented:

- Students work with local mental health organizations to deploy AI chatbots like Replika. The AI assists individuals by providing mental health resources or emotional support while also gathering anonymized data to understand broader mental health issues in the community.
- Students analyze the interactions to develop community-focused programs, identifying common stressors or mental health concerns that could benefit from additional local resources.

- Realistic Example:
  - AI chatbots are introduced in community centers to offer emotional support and refer users to real-life mental health services. Students analyze the data gathered from the interactions to find gaps in service availability and recommend additional resources or interventions to local mental health providers.

C. Urban Planning and Community Development Assignment

Project Focus: Using AI to map and improve transportation systems.

- AI Tools Used:
  - Kumu: Analyzes the relationships between community stakeholders, such as transit authorities, businesses, and residents.
  - AI-Powered Transportation Models: Simulate traffic patterns and analyze the efficiency of current public transportation options.
- How AI is Implemented:
  - Students collect data on current transportation use in their community and utilize AI to model traffic flow and predict future demand for public transit options.
  - Using AI analysis, students develop proposals to improve public transit routes or introduce biking and walking infrastructure to reduce traffic congestion and environmental impact.
- Realistic Example:
  - Students use AI to identify inefficiencies in local bus routes. Based on their findings, they propose new routes or schedules to reduce congestion and improve accessibility for residents in underserved areas. AI-powered traffic simulations help demonstrate the potential impact of the proposed changes.

D. Education and Technology Integration Assignment

Project Focus: Using AI to improve literacy rates in underserved communities.

- AI Tools Used:

    a. ChatGPT or other AI Tutors: Provides one-on-one tutoring for students in low-income neighborhoods, helping improve reading comprehension and writing skills.
    b. AI-Powered Learning Platforms (e.g., Knewton): Personalized learning paths help students progress at their own pace.

- How AI is Implemented:

    a. College students partner with local schools or after-school programs to introduce AI-powered tutoring platforms to support reading and writing development.
    b. AI tools track students' progress, identify areas of difficulty, and adapt learning materials accordingly.

- Realistic Example:

    a. Students design a program where elementary students use AI tutors like ChatGPT to improve reading skills. Over the semester, AI tracks the students' progress, and the college students help the local school district analyze the data to inform future literacy interventions.

E. Public Health and Community Engagement Assignment

Project Focus: Using AI to track and improve local air quality.

- AI Tools Used:
    - Kumu: Helps students map and analyze the stakeholders and systems affecting local air quality (e.g., businesses, government, residential areas).
    - AI-Powered Sensors: Installed throughout the city to track real-time air pollution levels.
    - Zooniverse: Engages the local community to participate in data collection and categorization of air quality levels.
- How AI is Implemented:
    - Students collaborate with local health departments and environmental groups to set up sensors in different areas. AI models analyze air quality data, identifying high-risk zones and potential pollution sources.

    - Based on the data, students propose interventions, such as increased green spaces or policies for reducing vehicular emissions.
- Realistic Example:
    - The students monitor air quality near schools and residential neighborhoods. After analyzing the data with AI, they work with community leaders to create awareness campaigns or advocate for local regulations to improve air quality. AI visualizations are used in public meetings to demonstrate the impact on public health.

Chapter 13
Nurturing a Socio-Emotionally Engaged Learner in Higher Education Online Setting:
Rapid Literature Review

Nymisha Yadati
https://orcid.org/0000-0002-4913-1656
Christ University, India

Benny Thomas
https://orcid.org/0000-0002-8270-2553
Christ University, India

Santhosh Kareepadath Rajan
https://orcid.org/0000-0003-1423-5428
Christ University, India

ABSTRACT

Given the growth of online learning courses in higher education, there is a need to understand the role of Social-Emotional Learning (SEL) in online learning spaces to ensure holistic development. This rapid literature review aims to identify factors influencing SEL among higher education students in online space. PRISMA method of screening was adopted to conduct this review. Four databases were systematically searched and, 23 studies were selected. The findings highlighted the importance of five factors contributing to nurturing a socio-emotionally engaged learner in an online higher education setting: student-centric pedagogy, online instructional tools, online instructors' proficiency, ensuring a safe learning environment, and online

DOI: 10.4018/979-8-3693-7595-2.ch013

SEL workshops. Research on online SEL is developing and needs a clearer structure. Integration of scholarship of teaching-learning with online SEL can provide directions for further exploration into content knowledge, pedagogical knowledge and building a mutually engaged online learning space focusing on students' social-emotional well-being.

INTRODUCTION

Stakeholders of higher educational institutions foresee growth in the hybrid/blended forms of learning in the post-COVID-19 context. The future of higher education lies in the meaningful integration of face-to-face and online mediums of education (Guppy et al., 2022). Given this transition, it is important to understand the factors impacting student learning engagement and satisfaction in an online context. Gray and DiLoreto (2016) found that interaction among students and the course structure statistically impact students' perceived learning in an online context. The instructors' presence in the form of interaction and guidance also impacts the students' perceived learning and satisfaction with learning in an online context. Ma'arif et al. (2024) found that the hybrid learning method was significant in improving learners' understanding of material concepts. This learning method is gaining popularity and significance in the post-COVID-19 education context. However, there are many challenges and tensions involved in ensuring effective learning.

The difference in students' and instructors' learning and teaching objectives impedes students' engagement in learning. Also, instructors' pedagogical skills in conducting a class on videoconferencing platforms determine how effectively students are engaged in online learning (Maimaiti et al., 2021). Yet another challenge of the online learning medium in higher education is the increasing attrition rates. The poor course quality, challenges to stay motivated to learn, technology-related challenges, and poor support systems available to the learner impact their persistence in the online course and contribute to the drop-out rates (Rahmani et al., 2024).

With the growth of online learning courses in higher education, there is a need to understand the role of social-emotional dimensions in online learning spaces to ensure holistic development. Social-emotional dimensions of learning help understand student engagement levels. Emotions influence students' learning experiences, cognitive load, and academic performance. Positive emotions can enhance creativity and problem-solving, whereas negative emotions like anxiety hinder learning efficiency (Ren,2023). Dagher et al. (2024) stressed that higher education students need to be engaged in social-emotional learning as it positively impacts their academic performance, lifelong learning, and also in their work life. It is highlighted that given the complex emotional characteristics experienced by college students, engaging in social-emotional learning would support their mental health and academic success (Ngan et al., 2024). Elmi (2020) found that integrating social-emotional learning with higher education courses improves students' interest in the academic course they are pursuing, improves resilience to stress, and contributes to positive engagement. It also improves their sense of community and makes them more confident as learners. Along with improving academic performance, engaging higher education students in social-emotional learning contributes to their positive interpersonal relationships and work success and improves their overall well-being (Conley, 2015). It is to be noted that not all programs on SEL contribute in an equal manner; few of them are better than others based on the nature of the practices adopted. It was found that in higher education institutions, mindfulness informed programs, relaxation programs, social skill interventions, and cognitive behavioral programs impact students' social-emotional well-being (Conley, 2015). This signifies the necessity to systematically explore the nature of SEL programs in higher educational institutions. The growth of hybrid/blended/online forms of learning in the post-COVID-19 context necessitates the need for effective integration of social and emotional learning programs into the higher education system to keep the learners engaged and motivated and curb the attrition rates.

In this regard, Scholarship of Teaching and Learning (SoTL) social-emotional skills through online medium would determine the experiences and engagement levels of students. SoTL is an evidence-based approach backed by research to improve the learning experiences of students (Prosser, 2008). Lee Shulman (1987) stressed that the teaching practice should be informed by knowledge on content and pedagogical reasoning. The bodies of knowledge an instructor needs to be well equipped with include content knowledge, pedagogical knowledge, curriculum knowledge, pedagogical content knowledge, knowledge on learners' characteristics, knowledge on educational context and knowledge on need and purpose of education. The aspects of pedagogical reasoning instructors need to be equipped with include understanding the content they are teaching (comprehension), tailoring the content for the students (transformation), understanding methods in which they can engage students in learning (instruction), grasping if students have learnt the concepts (evaluation), reflecting on their own practice and considering if anything could have been changed (reflection). In this process, the instructor creates a new and refined understanding on the content as well as their pedagogical practice (new comprehension) (Shulman, 1987). This model proposed by Lee Shulman can be applied to teaching and learning of social-emotional skills in online platforms. The online instructor needs to build their knowledge base and pedagogical reasoning on social emotional learning related concepts to facilitate SEL among students. They need to be aware of various teaching methods, age and culturally appropriate skills to be developed among students, evaluation procedures and suitability of SEL programs in diverse educational contexts. Although there is a need for such in-depth training on SEL among instructors in pre-service period, it has received minimal attention. This study is a rapid literature review on few important aspects of teaching and learning social-emotional skills through an online medium.

METHODS

A rapid literature review was conducted to synthesize literature on online SEL among higher education students. The rapid review method was preferred over systematic review due to the specific nature of the question, as well as time and resource constraints. Although conducted in a limited time, rapid reviews involve systematically searching academic databases and gathering evidence in an organized manner. King et al. (2022) identify the rapid review steps. The following steps were followed in this review process - protocol development, literature search, screening and study selection, data extraction, synthesis, and reporting. Each of these steps is discussed.

The objective of this review is to identify teaching-learning factors that influence social and emotional engagement in the context of online learning among higher education students.

Eligibility Criteria

The eligibility criteria were defined based on the Population Concept Context framework. This study focuses on the literature on online social-emotional learning among higher education students.

- Population – Higher education students.
- Concept – Social-emotional learning.
- Context – Online medium (Both synchronous or asynchronous were considered)
- Time Frame - Articles need to be published between 2019-2024 (Last five years).
- Grey literature was not considered in this review.

Database and Search Strategy

Four databases (Scopus, Sage, Taylor and Francis, Springer) were systematically searched using a defined search string. The search string used was - ("synchronous" OR "asynchronous") AND ("online") AND ("social-emotional learning" OR "social and emotional learning" OR "Socio-emotional learning") AND ("higher education students" OR "University students" OR "college students" OR "undergraduate students" OR "Postgraduate students"). A total of 109 results were found.

Screening and Study Selection

After obtaining the results, the RIS files for each of these results were downloaded and exported to Zotero, a referencing software (Roy Rosenzweig Center for History and New Media, 2016). All 109 studies were exported to Rayyan, an AI-driven tool that helps screen studies collaboratively. Through Rayyan, 14 duplicate results were identified and excluded (Ouzzani et al., 2016). Preferred Reporting Items for Systematic Reviews and Meta-Analyses (PRISMA) guidelines were used to screen the literature (Page et al., 2021). The screening was conducted in two phases - abstract screening and full-text screening. After the abstract screening, 34 studies qualified for full-text screening. All 34 studies were obtained, and the full text was read to determine the study's eligibility. Eleven studies were excluded, and 23 were retained for the review. The reasons for excluding studies at each stage are presented in Figure 1 PRISMA chart.

Figure 1. PRISMA chart

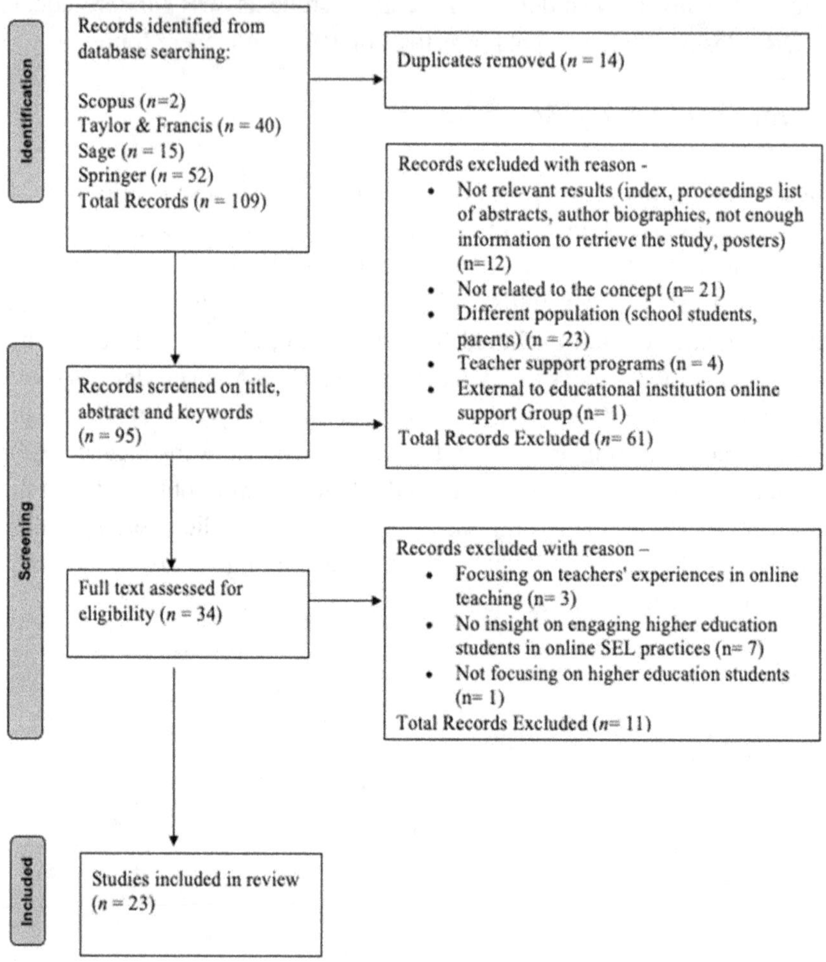

Data Extraction, Data Synthesis, and Reporting

Data were extracted from the selected studies. The extraction items were – author details, year of publication, title of the study, journal name and insights from the study. The data were extracted from conceptual and empirical studies **(seeAppendix)**. The data were synthesized using qualitative deductive coding techniques and three themes emerged: methods/pedagogies, instructional tools, and concerns about expressing online.

FINDINGS AND DISCUSSION

Most of the studies in the review discuss the need for a transition to online learning felt during the COVID-19 pandemic. The pandemic led to the sudden closure of in-person classes and a shift to online instruction. It is reported that in such a scenario, students faced several challenges concerning anxiety, health, productivity, and financial instability during the transition (Kim et al., 2021). Also, the instructors had to rapidly adapt to the new normal and transition to Emergency Remote Teaching (ERT) (Brzezinska & Cromarty, 2022). The lack of preparation and the limited content available to deliver online classes caused an increased workload among online instructors. Instructors had to undergo rapid training and acquire skills to teach online. This scenario became the catalyst for the evolving online education system in the post-COVID period.

The lack of access to stable internet connection, devices, equipment, gadgets' affordability, and power outages have made it extremely challenging for students from underprivileged communities to engage in quality online learning (Sum & Oancea, 2022). On the other hand, students who could participate in online education have reported facing challenges of social isolation, low motivation, and mental health issues (Ren, 2023). A few fundamental aspects that would determine the quality of online education are ensuring access to technology and resources, professional development of instructors and institutions, engaging students in interactive student-centric pedagogies, strengthening students and online instructors' connection, and integrating trauma-informed and culturally responsive social-emotional support to students (Brzezinska & Cromarty, 2022; Martin et al., 2022).

Phaire (2022) highlights that higher educational institutions need to provide resources and assist students in developing socially and emotionally to increase their preparedness in both online and in-person contexts. Pandya (2023) examined the impact of online spiritual lessons among college students and found that they improved their self-regulation, emotional regulation, peer relations, and well-being. Hence, exclusive well-being programs or SEL strategies integrated with academic content are needed for successful student engagement in online learning spaces. Scholarship of teaching and learning social-emotional skills is still evolving and it is important to identify the existing literature on pedagogies, insights into content and tools that can be used by instructors to engage learners in SEL. Through this literature review, it is identified that along with explicit well-being programs, implicit methods of integrating SEL practices through pedagogies, academic content, and improving the social-emotional environment of the college itself can contribute to students' and instructors' well-being.

Pedagogies and Teaching Methods

SoTL points out that understanding of instructional pedagogy helps bridge the gap between learning theory and classroom practice (Sperling, 2003). One of the major challenges of online learning is ensuring that students are engaged in learning socially, cognitively, and emotionally and are motivated to learn (Akar, 2024). Hence, there is a need to identify instructional strategies/teaching methods to engage students in social-emotional learning and also nurture a socially and emotionally engaged learner. This review identified five online teaching methods to improve student engagement and create a socially and emotionally supportive space in online learning: contemplative pedagogy, formative education, the community of practice method, emotional scaffolding, and increasing social presence.

Contemplative Pedagogy

Students might experience higher levels of distraction and disconnect while engaging in online education. Ren (2023) discusses the need and importance of incorporating contemplative pedagogy in designing, developing, and delivering online courses to improve student engagement in learning. Contemplative pedagogy is a mindfulness-informed teaching practice. It integrates exercises, meditation, and reflective practices into the teaching practice. Online instructors can incorporate strategies like intentional reading, mindful writing, and deep listening to enhance students' understanding of the course material. These practices develop self-awareness, empathy, and emotional balance. This further contributes to learner engagement in online classrooms. It also helps create a learner-centered environment where learners become attentive to the present context.

Formative Education

Kim et al. (2021) discuss the importance of formative education in supporting the holistic development of students in online learning during the COVID-19 pandemic. They empirically explored online instructors' experiences integrating empathetic, reflective, and adaptive approaches in their classes. The empathetic approach was implemented by regular check-ins, modelling vulnerability, and creating an empathetic classroom environment. Online instructors also used the breakout room function in ZOOM to facilitate discussions in smaller groups on sensitive matters. Online instructors encouraged students to reflect on the course content in relation to their personal experiences during the pandemic to enhance a deeper understanding of the concepts. They designed assignments such as journaling or composing poetry where students could freely express their real-world experiences in connection with the course content. Online instructors realized that the sudden transition necessitated adapting existing learning to suit the online medium. Also, online instructors were flexible in revising the syllabus and deadlines concerning the student tasks to align with the unpredictable events. They asked for student feedback to improve the course experience.

Community of Practice Method

Mavri et al. (2023) explored the effectiveness of the cross-organizational Communities of Practice (COP) approach in a higher education setting to encourage university-industry collaboration. The approach of COP considers learning to happen through participation in a community that provides diverse learning opportunities. The study focused on developing guidelines on three components to successfully integrate the COP into the virtual medium: Set, Social, and Epistemic. The Set component focused on technological configurations, software setup, and installing online interaction platforms for the participants to interact with each other. The social component focused on developing power-sharing guidelines by promoting trust to ensure equitable participation. The Epistemic component focused on bringing industry experts and mentors who can provide authentic learning opportunities for students. This component focused on the guidelines specific to the co-evolution of knowledge in the community, transforming learners' identities to pre-professional identities, building healthy relations between students and experts, and creating guidelines regarding receiving and working on the feedback given by the experts. Supportive social-emotional context needed to be created in all forms of COPs to facilitate healthy interaction.

Emotional Scaffolding

Emotional scaffolding (ES) can be used by online instructors to improve students' learning and motivation to engage in learning. Scaffolding involves dividing the learning outcome into smaller units integrated with the online instructor's support. In the initial stages, the level of support is higher; in later stages, it is gradually withdrawn to make the learner independent. Creating positive emotional experiences for the learner in the scaffolding process is called emotional scaffolding. Rafidi and Wagner (2023) studied incorporating this method in an online learning context among higher education students to enhance students' motivation to attend online classes. Online instructors practiced careful listening, tried to gain responses through questioning, and tried to respond to student's needs, which helped students persist in the online classes. Sharing and reflecting on personal experiences and analogies helped students learn to connect with the instructor and amongst themselves, creating a positive emotional learning experience. The emotional scaffolding approach to learning made students feel comfortable, safe, and less socially anxious.

Social Presence Method

Social presence is yet another method that instructors can use to enhance effective student engagement in online learning. Fensie et al. (2023) studied the experience of working mother students during the pandemic. Social presence refers to enhancing the bonds of participants amongst each other and developing a feeling of belongingness. In an online platform, instructors can improve social presence by using personalized communications through sharing personal stories and experiences. It can also be enhanced by creating online platforms for peer interactions and designing collaborative assignments. Other strategies include organizing live office hours for students to clarify their doubts, creating individual instructor-student interaction time online, and organizing smaller groups to provide space for all students to express themselves (Fensie et al., 2023).

There are two common elements inferred from the teaching methods discussed above. Firstly, all these methods aim to create an empathetic and socio-emotionally supportive learning environment for students and enhance their sense of belongingness. Secondly, they allow students to actively reflect on their learning and express themselves in class. Both these elements contribute to improved student engagement while highlighting the importance of online instructors' role in creating socially and emotionally informed spaces in an online medium via adopting suitable pedagogies.

Online Instructional Aids/Tools

The review identified four online instructional aids/ tools to improve student engagement and create a socially and emotionally supportive space in online learning - Nearpod, Perusall, Google Slides integrated with Voice Thread, and adaptive live chat activities through Reddit.

Caroy (2023) points out the use of a digital tool, "Nearpod." It assists online instructors in sharing multimedia learning content with students, supports different ways of learning, and improves collaboration among students. It helps online instructors create interactive content and assess and monitor the student's progress. However, the major challenge of using Nearpod is the requirement for high-speed internet connectivity, which hinders the equitable engagement of learners. Kerrigan and Andres (2022) explored the effectiveness of a social annotation platform called "Perusall," an interactive collaboration and sharing tool called "VoiceThread" and a co-authoring tool "Google Slides." These tools can contribute to creating a social experience in an online setting. Through Perusall, students can annotate the texts, share their views, ask questions, seek clarification, respond to peers, and upvote annotations. This tool helped students and the instructor to understand different perspectives and created a sense of community in class. To collaborate for group assignments, students used Google Slides to prepare content for presentation. Then, they uploaded the same on VoiceThread and added their voice annotations to share their understanding. These tools make collaboration possible via an asynchronous medium.

Tilak et al. (2022) discuss how adaptive live chat activities through "Reddit" can contribute to egalitarian participation and collaborative interactions in lecture-based classrooms. The chat activities provided a space for students to discuss critically the concepts they dealt with in class. This tool helped the instructor create an active learning environment in and beyond the classroom. The students pointed out that the anonymity, synchronous live chatting feature, and the possibility of interaction regarding the class content made the platform important for sharing their views. While other participants found it challenging as the live chats were fast, and participants would find it difficult to enter the conversation. Also, the setting up logistics could be complicated for a few participants, and the voluntary nature of the discussions on the platform may not engage all the students.

The major challenge of engaging in online learning is the feeling of social and emotional disconnect between the content being learned and a lack of connection with peers and the online instructor. This may lead to a feeling of isolation, disconnect, and lack of motivation. These challenges can be managed by adopting educational and technological tools such as Nearpod, Perusall, Google Slides, and Reddit that make content-sharing possible and have mechanisms through which students can interact to develop a shared understanding of the concepts. By adopting effective online instructional tools to enhance content-sharing and meaning-making experiences, online instructors can create a socially supportive space for online learners.

Expressing Online

It is important to note that expressing one's views on an online platform can be agentic for a few, and it can feel vulnerable for others. One of the major aspects of improving connection among online learners is to provide a socially, emotionally, and psychologically safe space for them to express and reflect on their experiences. The quality of interactions among students in group depends on the learner's feeling of psychological safety concerning the interactional space (Beigpourian et al., 2020). Participants who feel vulnerable prefer to hide in online spaces. Knickerbocker and Tawfik (2024) found that students welcomed the feature of anonymously posting questions to the online instructor as they feared appearing ignorant and incompetent in front of their peers otherwise. While engaging in conversation on controversial issues/topics, students feared being misunderstood. The lack of social cues regarding facial expressions or tone of voice in response to students' views created a sense of unsafety.

Additionally, the permanent and public nature of the written content shared made students self-censor their views and use hedging and neutral language. Students expressed that a negative assessment could appear offensive in assignments where peer feedback was necessary. Hence, they often framed formulaic feedback. This leads to questioning the authenticity of such feedback. However, it was found that group cohesion plays a vital role in making students feel psychologically safe in online spaces. Familiarity with peers and creating shared experiences impact psychological safety and can shape authentic interactions in online spaces (Knickerbocker & Tawfik, 2024)).

Similarly, switching on the camera in synchronous online spaces comes with a social expectation. It may make students more accountable for engaging in classroom discussions (Novotny et al., 2022). Pham and Phan (2022) found that it may also make them self-conscious and add to their concerns about appearance and privacy. From the instructor's perspective, students keeping their cameras switched off adds to their feelings of loneliness and disconnect. To address the problem of emotional disconnect, online instructors have encouraged students to customize their profiles by using pictures and establishing ground rules concerning turning the camera on while they are speaking and turning it off while instructors or peers are engaging. It is observed that students confidently and willingly express themselves while they are anonymous. This tendency can result from feelings of psychological safety or unsafety while expressing via online learning spaces.

In this regard SoTL points out that mutual engagement in all spaces of learning is key to creating a safe space for students to learn (Kiener, 2009). Mutual engagement is a practice through which students and the instructor co-create a space for learning, this theory stresses on group dynamics as foundational to learning. A safe environment encourages students to express and voice their opinions and it improves their ownership towards learning (Kiener, 2009). The possibilities of creating a mutual engagement in online learning spaces needs further exploration.

CONCLUSION

Online learning in higher education contexts is seen as more of an individualized experience dependent on resources, access, family dynamics, learning styles, perception of technology, and off-screen experiences (Damast et al., 2021). However, it is identified that social and affective experiences impact learning in digital environments. Students' social-emotional experiences determine their engagement in learning. In an online platform, connecting with the online instructor, relation with peers, and relatable content determine students' social-emotional experiences (Novotny et al., 2022). Limited opportunities for social-emotional interactions for students and online instructors negatively impact engagement levels, causing online fatigue and a lack of motivation to learn/teach (Maloney et al., 2023). Given the challenges, adopting active learner-centered pedagogies, organizing SEL workshops, improving online instructor proficiency, and creating psychologically safe spaces for learners to interact are crucial for efficient online learner engagement.

This review emphasizes the role of social-emotional learning in online higher education settings. Five factors contribute to socially and emotionally engaged learners in an online environment: student-centric pedagogy, online instructional tools, online instructor proficiency, ensuring a safe learning environment, and online social-emotional learning workshops. A visual representation of the same is presented in Figure 2.

Figure 2. Factors contributing to socially and emotionally engaged learners

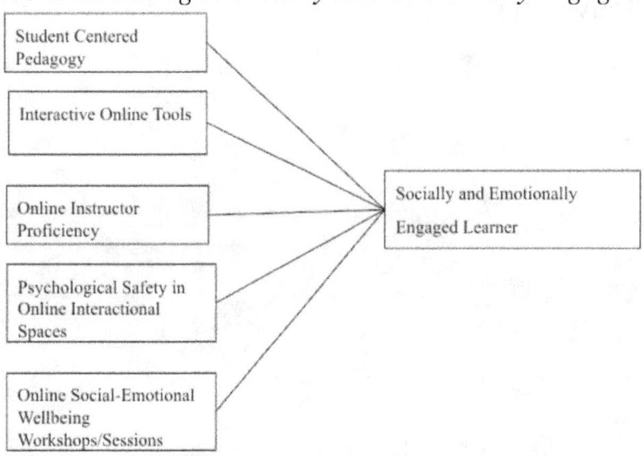

Through this review, it can also be inferred that the literature in the domain of online SEL is nascent and lacks a structure. Integration of scholarship of teaching-learning with online SEL domain can provide directions to researchers for future exploration -

- Content Knowledge - organizing the course structure by situating the needs of the students engaged in online learning.
- Instructional/ Pedagogical Knowledge - equipping instructors to use online learning platforms and teaching strategies while engaging students in online

learning. Also training instructors to adopt technological tools that facilitate effective content sharing and online interaction among students.
- Mutually Engaged Space of Learning - creating a psychologically safe space for students to encourage them to share their views.

A few limitations to this rapid review need to be acknowledged. We have searched four databases to identify the literature. Systematically searching more databases can result in more insights. Additionally, grey literature was not included in this review. Also, only studies reported in the English language were included.

DECLARATION

The findings and abstract of this study were presented at the National e-Conference on National Education Policy- A Paradigm Shift & Implications on Online Education. 27th-28th September 2024, organized by Dr. D. Y. Patil Vidyapeeth, Pune (Deemed to be University).

REFERENCES

Akar, S. G. M. (2024). Students' disengagement in online courses: Validity and reliability of an instrument. [EduLearn]. *Journal of Education and Learning*, 19(1), 506–514. DOI: 10.11591/edulearn.v19i1.21733

Beigpourian, B., Ohland, M., & Ferguson, D. (2020). Effect of psychological safety on the interaction of students in teams. *2020 ASEE Virtual Annual Conference Content Access Proceedings*. DOI: 10.18260/1-2--34497

Brzezinska, M., & Cromarty, E. (2022). Emergency remote teaching in the university context: Responding to social and emotional needs during a sudden transition online. In *Lecture notes in computer science*, 30–47. https://doi.org/DOI: 10.1007/978-3-031-05064-0_3

Caroy, A. A. (2023). A technology report on Nearpod. *RELC Journal*, 54(2), 551–560. DOI: 10.1177/00336882231153669

Conley, C. S. (2015). SEL in higher education. In Durlak, J. A., Domitrovich, C. E., Weissberg, R. P., & Gullotta, T. P. (Eds.), *Handbook of social and emotional learning: Research and practice* (pp. 197–212). The Guilford Press.

Dagher, S., Hilal-Alnaqbi, A., & Akozaheya, B. (2024). Needs assessment study for social-emotional learning in higher education. In *Advances in Science* (pp. 1–5). Technology & Innovation/Advances in Science, Technology & Innovation., DOI: 10.1007/978-3-031-49393-5_1

Damast, D., Cohen, P., & Martinez, D. L. (2021). "Hey students, how was that first semester of remote instruction?": Graduate students' reflections on remote learning during COVID-19. *Dance Education in Practice*, 7(2), 15–24. DOI: 10.1080/23734833.2021.1916288

Elmi, C. (2020). Integrating social emotional learning strategies in higher education. *European Journal of Investigation in Health, Psychology and Education*, 10(3), 848–858. DOI: 10.3390/ejihpe10030061 PMID: 34542515

Fensie, A., St Pierre, T., Jain, J., & Sezen-Barrie, A. (2023). Engaged learning during distraction: A case study of successful working moms in distance education. *Journal of Computing in Higher Education*, 36(2), 389–434. DOI: 10.1007/s12528-023-09359-0 PMID: 37359045

Fisher, M. E., Dorner, M. A., Maghzi, K. S., Achieng-Evensen, C., Whitaker, L. C., Hansell, F., St Amant, J., & Gapinski, S. M. (2021). Liminality, disruption, and change: A prismatic look at pandemic education. *Prospects*, 51(1–3), 523–540. DOI: 10.1007/s11125-021-09563-9 PMID: 34219814

Gray, J. A., & DiLoreto, M. (2016). The effects of student engagement, Student satisfaction, and perceived learning in online learning environments. *The International Journal of Educational Leadership Preparation*, 11(1), 98–119. https://files.eric.ed.gov/fulltext/EJ1103654.pdf

Guppy, N., Verpoorten, D., Boud, D., Lin, L., Tai, J., & Bartolic, S. (2022). The post-COVID-19 future of digital learning in higher education: Views from educators, students, and other professionals in six countries. *British Journal of Educational Technology*, 53(6), 1750–1765. DOI: 10.1111/bjet.13212

Kara, A., Ergulec, F., & Eren, E. (2024). The mediating role of self-regulated online learning behaviors: Exploring the impact of personality traits on student engagement. *Education and Information Technologies*, 29(17), 1–30. DOI: 10.1007/s10639-024-12755-3

Kerrigan, J., & Andres, D. (2022). Technology-enhanced communities of practice in an asynchronous graduate course. *Journal of Educational Technology Systems*, 50(4), 473–487. DOI: 10.1177/00472395221079288

Kidron, A., & Kali, Y. (2023). Promoting interdisciplinary understanding in asynchronous online higher education courses: A learning communities approach. *Instructional Science*, 52(1), 139–169. DOI: 10.1007/s11251-023-09635-7

Kiener, M. (2009). Applying the scholarship of teaching and learning: Pursuing a deeper understanding of how students learn. *InSight a Journal of Scholarly Teaching*, 4, 21–27. DOI: 10.46504/05201002ki

Kim, D., Wortham, S., Borowiec, K., Yatsu, D. K., Ha, S., Carroll, S., Wang, L., & Kim, J. (2021). Formative education online: Teaching the whole person during the global COVID-19 pandemic. *AERA Open*, 7(233285842110152), 1–12. DOI: 10.1177/23328584211015229

King, V. J., Stevens, A., Nussbaumer-Streit, B., Kamel, C., & Garritty, C. (2022). Paper 2: Performing rapid reviews. *Systematic Reviews*, 11(1), 151. Advance online publication. DOI: 10.1186/s13643-022-02011-5 PMID: 35906677

Knickerbocker, J., & Tawfik, A. A. (2024). Perceptions of psychological safety in healthcare professionals' online learner-learner interactions. 1-27. *Journal of Computing in Higher Education*. Advance online publication. DOI: 10.1007/s12528-024-09401-9

Levenberg, A. (2023). Lecturer responsiveness in online learning – availability, accessibility, and flexibility: A matter of kindness. *Journal of Further and Higher Education*, 47(6), 740–753. DOI: 10.1080/0309877X.2023.2226073

Ma'arif, M., Santoso, R., Arif, D. B., & Nuryana, Z. (2024). The battle of learning modes: Hybrid vs online learning in higher education. [EduLearn]. *Journal of Education and Learning*, 19(2), 963–970. DOI: 10.11591/edulearn.v19i2.20870

Maimaiti, G., Jia, C., & Hew, K. F. (2021). Student disengagement in web-based videoconferencing supported online learning: An activity theory perspective. *Interactive Learning Environments*, 31(8), 4883–4902. DOI: 10.1080/10494820.2021.1984949

Maloney, S., Axelsen, M., Stone, C., Galligan, L., Redmond, P., Brown, A., Turner, J., & Lawrence, J. (2023). Defining and exploring online engagement fatigue in a university context. *Computers and Education Open*, 4, 100139. DOI: 10.1016/j.caeo.2023.100139

Martin, F., Xie, K., & Bolliger, D. U. (2022). Engaging learners in the emergency transition to online learning during the COVID-19 pandemic. *Journal of Research on Technology in Education, 54*(sup1), S1–S13. https://doi.org/DOI: 10.1080/15391523.2021.1991703

Mavri, A., Ioannou, A., & Loizides, F. (2023). A model for enhancing creativity, collaboration and pre-professional identities in technology-supported cross-organizational communities of practice. *Education and Information Technologies*, 29(11), 13325–13366. DOI: 10.1007/s10639-023-12295-2

Ngan, M. D. H., Nguyen, T. H., Phan, T., & Rong, L. H., DO, Tran, V. P., & Dang, T. S. (2024). A technology-driven approach to fostering social and emotional skills in first-year students at the University of Danang - University of Technology and Education. In *9th International Conference on Applying New Technology in Green Buildings (ATiGB),Danang, Vietnam*, 224-228. https://doi.org/DOI: 10.1109/ATiGB63471.2024.10717832

Nguyen, V. T. T., & Chen, H. L. (2023). Examining impacts of information system success and perceived stress on students' self-regulated learning mediated by intrinsic motivation in online learning environments: Second-order structural equation modelling analyses. *Education and Information Technologies*, 28(10), 12945–12968. DOI: 10.1007/s10639-023-11685-w PMID: 37361765

Novotny, B., Ko, K., & Garris, B. R. (2022). Lights, camera, action: A focus group study exploring university students' experiences of learning via zoom. *The Journal of Educators Online*, 19(1). Advance online publication. DOI: 10.9743/JEO.2022.19.1.2

Ouzzani, M., Hammady, H., Fedorowicz, Z., & Elmagarmid, A. (2016). Rayyan—A web and mobile app for systematic reviews. *Systematic Reviews*, 5(1), 210. Advance online publication. DOI: 10.1186/s13643-016-0384-4 PMID: 27919275

Page, M. J., McKenzie, J. E., Bossuyt, P. M., Boutron, I., Hoffmann, T. C., Mulrow, C. D., Shamseer, L., Tetzlaff, J. M., Akl, E. A., Brennan, S. E., Chou, R., Glanville, J., Grimshaw, J. M., Hróbjartsson, A., Lalu, M. M., Li, T., Loder, E. W., Mayo-Wilson, E., McDonald, S., & Moher, D. (2021). The PRISMA 2020 statement: An updated guideline for reporting systematic reviews. *BMJ (Clinical Research Ed.)*, (71), n71. Advance online publication. DOI: 10.1136/bmj.n71 PMID: 33782057

Pandya, S. P. (2023). College students with high abilities in liberal arts disciplines: Examining the effect of spirituality in bolstering self-regulated learning, affect balance, peer relationships, and well-being. *High Ability Studies*, •••, 1–27. DOI: 10.1080/13598139.2023.2278811

Phaire, C. B. (2022). In the zoom Where it happens: From overwhelmed to overcome, collegiate students' experiences during the COVID-19 pandemic. *the Clearing House/the Clearing House, 95*(5), 220–229. https://doi.org/DOI: 10.1080/00098655.2022.2105782

Pham, L. T. T., & Phan, A. N. Q. (2022). Whilst COVID-19: The educational migration to online platforms and lessons learned. *the Clearing House/the Clearing House, 95*(4), 159–165. https://doi.org/DOI: 10.108000098655.2022.2065230

Prosser, M. (2008). The scholarship of teaching and learning: What is it? A personal view. *International Journal for the Scholarship of Teaching and Learning*, 2(2). Advance online publication. DOI: 10.20429/ijsotl.2008.020202

Rafidi, T. J., & Wagner, B. (2023). The impact of emotional scaffolding on online teaching and learning in Palestinian English language classrooms during COVID-19. *Innovation in Language Learning and Teaching*, 18(2), 155–168. DOI: 10.1080/17501229.2023.2245810

Rahmani, A. M., Groot, W., & Rahmani, H. (2024). Dropout in online higher education: A systematic literature review. *International Journal of Educational Technology in Higher Education*, 21(1), 19. DOI: 10.1186/s41239-024-00450-9

Ren, X. (2023). Contemplative pedagogy for positive engagement in online teaching and learning in higher education. *Teaching in Higher Education*, 29(1), 334–347. DOI: 10.1080/13562517.2023.2280254

Roy Rosenzweig Center for History and New Media. (2016) Zotero [Computer software]. Retrieved from_www.zotero.org/download

Scianna, J., & Kaliisa, R. (2023). 'SSEEN': A networked approach to uncover connections between sentiment, social, and epistemic elements of student online forum discourse. *Educational Technology Research and Development*, 72(5), 2817–2839. DOI: 10.1007/s11423-023-10310-4

Shulman, L. S. (1987). Knowledge and teaching: Foundations of the new reform. *Harvard Educational Review*, 57(1), 1–22. DOI: 10.17763/haer.57.1.j463w79r56455411

Slakmon, B., Keynan, O., & Shapira, O. (2022). Emotion expression and recognition in written digital discussions on civic issues. *International Journal of Computer-Supported Collaborative Learning*, 17(4), 519–537. DOI: 10.1007/s11412-022-09379-5

Sperling, C. B. (2003). How community colleges understand the scholarship of teaching And learning. *Community College Journal of Research and Practice*, 27(7), 593–601. DOI: 10.1080/713838214

Sum, M., & Oancea, A. (2022). The use of technology in higher education teaching by academics during the COVID-19 emergency remote teaching period: A systematic review. *International Journal of Educational Technology in Higher Education*, 19(1), 59. Advance online publication. DOI: 10.1186/s41239-022-00364-4 PMID: 36531306

Tilak, S., Evans, M., Wen, Z., & Glassman, M. (2022). Social network analysis as a cybernetic modelling facility for participatory design in technology-supported college curricula. *Systemic Practice and Action Research*, 36(5), 691–724. DOI: 10.1007/s11213-022-09625-9 PMID: 36466296

APPENDIX

Table 1. Data Extracted from Conceptual Studies

Citation	Insights
(Martin et al., 2022)	The study reviews 14 articles on learner engagement during the COVID-19 pandemic. It identifies theories and frameworks to engage learners in online learning and strategies and support students require during the transition from in-person to online medium of learning.
(Caroy, 2023)	The study focuses on the effectiveness of a digital presentation tool called Nearpod in engaging students in collaborative learning.
(Ren, 2023)	The study discusses contemplative pedagogy as a mindfulness-informed teaching practice, effectively improving student engagement by improving self-awareness and concentration in an online education setting.

Table 2. Data Extracted from Empirical Studies

Citation	Insights
(Kim et al., 2021)	This study discusses formative education integrated with reflective, empathetic, and adaptive approaches to engage students in effective online learning.
(Fisher et al., 2021)	The study used prismatic inquiry to explore experiences across educational levels during the COVID-19 Pandemic and the adaptability process of education systems. The analysis highlighted the importance of connections, voice, social-emotional skills, and academic knowledge for students supported by school leaders, teachers, parents, and students.
(Damast et al., 2021)	The study offers insights into the need for integrating approaches to wellness and self-care among participants, encouraging healthy communication, and organizing the course in response to the needs of the students in online education.
(Tilak et al., 2022)	The study emphasizes the role of second-order cybernetics in participatory learning. It shows that adaptive live chat functions like Reddit can support egalitarian student participation and collaborative interaction.
(Kerrigan & Andres, 2022)	The study focuses on two tools, Perusall and Google Slides/voice thread, that assist asynchronous collaborative activities.
(Slakmon et al., 2022)	The study explores students' emotion regulation strategies while engaged in written digital communication, especially on controversial content.
(Brzezinska & Cromarty, 2022)	The study explains the experiences of two educators adopting emergency remote teaching during the pandemic. It explains strategies they used to improve student engagement in online learning.
(Phaire, 2022)	The study discusses the experience of college students who stayed off-campus with limited access to social interaction. These students depended on online synchronous class interaction for social-emotional support.
(Pham & Phan, 2022)	With the COVID-19 pandemic, universities have been forced to conduct classes online. This study offers insights into Vietnamese university teachers' strategies to maintain an emotional connection with students in and after class.

continued on following page

Table 2. Continued

Citation	Insights
(Novotny et al., 2022)	The study explains the challenges and benefits of videotelephony software such as ZOOM. It stresses teachers' proficiency in using such software and how students' social and emotional experiences impact learning.
(Rafidi & Wagner, 2023)	The study delves into emotional scaffolding to engage students in learning. It was used to motivate students to attend and engage in online classes.
(Mavri et al., 2023)	The study focused on integrating technology into a cross-organizational community of practice (COP) to improve university and industry collaboration. This can bridge the gap between actual and expected skills among participants.
(Fensie et al., 2023)	The study explores working student mothers' experience in learning during the pandemic and stresses reducing cognitive load by leveraging prior knowledge, scaffolding instruction, and promoting social presence.
(Scianna & Kaliisa, 2023)	The study presents a case analysis of SSEEN (social sentiment embedded epistemic networks), exploring social networks, course content, and student sentiment in online learning settings.
(Levenberg, 2023)	The study elaborates on kindness as an approach to engaging with students, and this is linked to improved student satisfaction, perseverance, and learning outcomes.
(Nguyen & Chen, 2023)	The study revealed a positive direct and indirect relation between information system success, intrinsic learning motivation, and online self-regulated learning. The relation between stress, intrinsic learning motivation, and online self-regulated learning was insignificant.
(Pandya, 2023)	The study explores the impact of online spiritual lessons to improve self-regulation, emotion regulation, affect balance, peer relations, and well-being of high-ability college students.
(Kidron & Kali, 2023)	The study explores how an asynchronous online learning community learning approach can help students in interdisciplinary learning.
(Knickerbocker & Tawfik, 2024)	This study explains the feeling of psychological safety being important in online classrooms to express freely and engage in learning on an online platform.
(Kara et al., 2024)	This study explores the relationship between five-factor personality traits, self-regulated online learning, and student engagement among university students.

Compilation of References

Abbot, S. (2024). SoTL citizen: A memoir of home and exile in the scholarship of teaching and learning. In Miller-Young, J., & Chick, N. L. (Eds.), *Becoming a SoTL scholar* (pp. 36–51)., DOI: 10.36284/celelon.oa6.3

Abd Halim, H., Hamzah, M. I., & Zulkifli, H. (2024). A systematic review on the formative assessment practice in teaching and learning in secondary school. *International Journal of Evaluation & Research in Education*, 13(2), 1173–1183. DOI: 10.11591/ijere.v13i2.26187

Abodunrin, O., Olagunju, M. T., Alade, O. T., & Foláyan, M. O. (2023). Relationships between oral health and the sustainable development goals: A scoping review. *Biomed*, 3(4), 460–470. DOI: 10.3390/biomed3040037

Adnan, M., & Anwar, K. (2020). Online learning amid the COVID-19 pandemic: Students' perspectives. *Journal of Pedagogical Sociology and Psychology,* 2(1), 45-51. https://www.doi.org/10.33902/JPSP. 2020261309

Aguilar, J. M., & Rütti-Joy, O. (2023). Language teaching in the 'third space': Identity trajectories and professional development needs. *Language Teaching Research Quarterly*, 33, 99–114. DOI: 10.32038/ltrq.2023.33.05

Ahmad, A. (2024). Pendampingan Pengembangan Bahan Ajar berbasis Artificial Intelligence. AJAD: Jurnal Pengabdian kepada Masyarakat, 4(1), 210-217.

Ahmad, S. F., Khan, I., & Patel, M. (2022). Academic and administrative role of artificial intelligence in education. *Journal of Educational Technology & Society*, 25(3), 75–89.

Ahmed, N., Adam, S. M. A., & Mohamed, R. M. H. (2023). Effect of emotional intelligence training program on critical thinking skills and self-esteem of nurse students. *JPTCP*, 30(5), 548–561. DOI: 10.47750/jptcp.2023.30.05.055

Ahmed, S., Mohammed, H., Ayed, M., El-Ghadban, F., & Amin, F. (2022). Effect of simulation-based education on nurses' performance and satisfaction regarding peripherally inserted central catheters at neonatal intensive care unit. *Tanta Scientific Nursing Journal*, 26(3), 252–269. DOI: 10.21608/tsnj.2022.254429

Ainiyah, N., Zahroh, C., Khamida, K., Budury, S., Nurjanah, S., Hasina, S., & Wardhany, S. E. (2021). Emotional intelligence and self-efficacy as predictor factors of student resilience in online learning during pandemic era. *Open Access Macedonian Journal of Medical Sciences*, 9(T5), 40–43. DOI: 10.3889/oamjms.2021.7854

Ait Baha, T., El Hajji, M., Es-Saady, Y., & Fadili, H. (2024). The impact of educational chatbot on student learning experience. *Education and Information Technologies*, 29(8), 10153–10176. DOI: 10.1007/s10639-023-12166-w

Akar, S. G. M. (2024). Students' disengagement in online courses: Validity and reliability of an instrument. [EduLearn]. *Journal of Education and Learning*, 19(1), 506–514. DOI: 10.11591/edulearn.v19i1.21733

Alali, H., Salim, J., Zwayda, Y., & Alsewi, S. M. (2016). Knowledge sharing success model of virtual communities of practice in healthcare sector. In Lee, I. (Ed.), *Encyclopedia of e-commerce development, implementation, and management* (pp. 272–284). IGI Global., DOI: 10.4018/978-1-4666-9787-4.ch021

Alam, A. (2021). Possibilities and apprehensions in the landscape of artificial intelligence in education. *Journal of Educational Technology & Society*, 24(3), 12–25.

Alamri, H. A., Watson, S., & Watson, W. (2021). Learning technology models that support personalization within blended learning environments in higher education. *TechTrends*, 65(1), 62–78. DOI: 10.1007/s11528-020-00530-3

Al-Bashabsheh, M. W. T. F., & Pradhan, P. (2023). The importance of social media in education during COVID-19. [JARSSC]. *Journal of Advance Research in Science and Social Science*, 5(2), 1–13. DOI: 10.46523/jarssc.05.02.07

Aleedy, M., Atwell, E., & Meshoul, S. (2022). Using AI chatbots in education: Recent advances challenges and use case. Artificial Intelligence and Sustainable Computing. *Proceedings of ICSISCET*, 2021, 661–675.

Aljarboa, B., An, E., Dator, W., Alshammari, S., Mostoles, R., Uy, M., & Gonzales, A. (2022). Resilience and emotional intelligence of staff nurses during the covid-19 pandemic. *Health Care*, 10(11), 2120. DOI: 10.3390/healthcare10112120 PMID: 36360460

Americans with Disabilities Act of 1990, Pub. L. 101-336, 104 Stat. 327 (1990).

Amresh, A., Carberry, A. R., & Femiani, J. (2013, October). *Evaluating the effectiveness of flipped classrooms for teaching CS1. In 2013 IEEE Frontiers in Education Conference*. FIE., DOI: 10.1109/FIE.2013.6684923

Ananyina, A. (2022). Anonimity of learners in virtual learning environment. *Studia Humanitatis / Northern Humanitarian Studies, 3*, 71-76. .DOI: 10.15393/j12.art.2022.3881

Anderson, O. (2024). *Professional learning communities as transformative spaces for the advancement of social and emotional learning in schools* (Doctoral dissertation, California State University, Stanislaus https://scholarworks.calstate.edu/concern/theses/ng451r36t,)

Anderson, J. R. (1988). A spreading activation theory of memory. In Collins, A., & Smith, E. E. (Eds.), *Readings in cognitive science: A perspective from psychology and artificial intelligence* (pp. 137–154). Morgan Kaufmann Publishers, Inc., DOI: 10.1016/B978-1-4832-1446-7.50016-9

Anderson, J. R., & Reder, L. M. (1979). An elaborative processing explanation of depth of processing. In Cermak, L. S., & Craik, F. I. M. (Eds.), *Levels of processing in human memory* (pp. 385–403). Lawrence Erlbaum Associates., DOI: 10.4324/9781315796192

Anderson, T. (2011). The MOOC revolution: The promise and the problem. *Educational Researcher*, 40(4), 16–24.

Anderson, T., Liam, R., Garrison, D. R., & Archer, W. (2001). Assessing teaching presence in a computer conferencing context. *Online Learning : the Official Journal of the Online Learning Consortium*, 5(2), 1–17. DOI: 10.24059/olj.v5i2.1875

Anderson, T., & Rivera Vargas, P. (2020). A critical look at educational technology from a distance education perspective. *Digital Education Review*, 2020(37), 208–229. DOI: 10.1344/der.2020.37.208-229

Andrews, S. (2021c). A knowledge-based risk-driven model supporting collaborative online course creation. In L. M. Fraga, S. Hall, & K. Bottaro's (Eds.), *Shifting to online learning through faculty collaborative support* (pp. 142-162). IGI-Global. DOI: 10.4018/978-1-7998-6944-3.ch008

Andrews, S. (2021a). Innovation process for problem conceptualization. *International Journal of Software Innovation*, 9(3), 91–103. DOI: 10.4018/IJSI.2021070107

Andrews, S. (2021b). The evolution of elearning within a software engineering graduate program. In Crawford, C. M., & Simons, M. A. (Eds.), *Learning engagement in a transformative social learning environment* (pp. 244–262). IGI Global. DOI: 10.4018/978-1-7998-6956-6.ch012

Andrews, S. K., & Crawford, C. M. (2022). Synthesizing anti-human trafficking efforts: the paths already taken, amplifiers of risk, and the paths forward. In Andrews, S. K., & Crawford, C. M. (Eds.), *Paths to the prevention and detection of human trafficking* (pp. 1–23). IGI Global. DOI: 10.4018/978-1-6684-3926-5.ch001

Andrews, S. K., Lacher, L., & Dunnavant, T. (2021a). Additional elearning considerations around the instructor's philosophical belief systems: potential transformative impacts. In Crawford, C. M., & Simons, M. A. (Eds.), *eLearning engagement in a transformative social learning environment* (pp. 114–134). IGI Global. DOI: 10.4018/978-1-7998-6956-6.ch006

Andrews, S., Bradbury, R., & Crawford, C. (2020, January-March). Fiero and flow in online competitive gaming: The gaming engagement framework. *International Journal of Gaming and Computer-Mediated Simulations*, 12(1), 28–42. DOI: 10.4018/IJGCMS.2020010102

Andrews, S., & Crawford, C. (2021). Barriers, issues and similarities among women in esports and similar mixed gender sports: ascertaining common ground. In Andrews, S., & Crawford, C. M. (Eds.), *Handbook of research on pathways and opportunities into the business of esports* (pp. 25–46). IGI-Global., DOI: 10.4018/978-1-7998-7300-6.ch002

Andrews, S., Newsum, J., Crawford, C. M., & Moffett, N. L. (2021c). Sisyphus leans into the professoriate: faculty discuss career considerations and the academic landscape. In Moffett, N. L. (Ed.), *Navigating post-doctoral career placement, research, and professionalism* (pp. 185–226). IGI-Global., DOI: 10.4018/978-1-7998-5065-6.ch009

Andrews, S., & Sheppard, M. (2020). Architecture erosion: Impacts, causes, and management of issues. *International Journal of Computer Science and Security*, 14(2), 82–93.

Ansari, J., & Khan, N. (2020). Exploring the role of social media in collaborative learning the new domain of learning. *Smart Learning Environments*, 7(1), 9. Advance online publication. DOI: 10.1186/s40561-020-00118-7

Anselmo, L., Wright, A., & Stepanchuk, A. (2022). Advancing the scholarship of teaching and learning in large enrolment courses: Lessons learned from an online community of practice. *Imagining SoTL*, 2(2), 52–62. DOI: 10.29173/isotl613

Antheunis, M. L., Schouten, A. P., & Walther, J. B. (2020). The hyperpersonal effect in online dating: Effects of text-based CMC vs. videoconferencing before meeting face-to-face. *Media Psychology*, 23(6), 820–839. DOI: 10.1080/15213269.2019.1648217

Archer, E. (2019). Design research: Developing effective feedback interventions for school-based monitoring. *Research Methods in the Social Sciences*, 317, 317–336. Advance online publication. DOI: 10.18772/22019032750.25

Aslan, İ. (2021). Evaluating wellbeing and worries of university students during COVİD-19 pandemic. *Atatürk Üniversitesi Iktisadi Ve Idari Bilimler Dergisi, 35*(1), 245-261. https://dergipark.org.tr/en/download/article-file/1226893

Atkinson, R. K., Renkl, A., & Merrill, M. M. (2003). Transitioning from studying examples to solving problems: Effects of self-explanation prompts and fading worked-out steps. *Journal of Educational Psychology*, 95(4), 774–783. DOI: 10.1037/0022-0663.95.4.774

Ayto, J. (2020). The Oxford dictionary of idioms (4th ed.). Oxford University Press eBooks. https://doi.org/DOI: 10.1093/acref/9780198845621.001.0001

Babu, G. S., & Sridevi, K. (2018). Importance of e-learning in higher education: A study. *International Journal of Research Culture Society*, 2(5), 84–88. https://www.academia.edu/36868903/IMPORTANCE_OF_E_LEARNING_IN_HIGHER_EDUCATION_A_STUDY

Bagheri, M. S., & Fazel, I. (2010). Effects of etymological elaboration on the EFL students' comprehension and retention of idioms. *Journal of Pan-Pacific Association of Applied Linguistics*, 14(1), 45–55. https://files.eric.ed.gov/fulltext/EJ920503.pdf

Baker, N., Hornsby, D. J., & Turner, N. K. (n.d.). The importance of online, open, and equitable education during the global pandemic. *Online, Open, and Equitable Education, 1.*

Baleghizadeh, S., & Bagheri, M. I. M. (2012). The effect of etymology elaboration on EFL students' comprehension and retention of idioms. *3L: Language, linguistics, literature, 18*(1), 23-32. http://journalarticle.ukm.my/4061/

Bangert, D., Blakeslee, T., & Burns, J. (2000). Evaluating online learning: The need to go beyond student satisfaction. *American Journal of Distance Education*, 14(3), 10–25.

Barbosa, A. (2023). Graduating nurses in the time of covid-19. *Open Journal of Nursing*, 13(10), 641–663. DOI: 10.4236/ojn.2023.1310042

Barnett, S., Jones, S. C., Caton, T., Iverson, D., Bennett, S., & Robinson, L. (2014). Implementing a virtual community of practice for family physician training: A mixed-methods case study. *Journal of Medical Internet Research*, 16(3), e83–e83. DOI: 10.2196/jmir.3083 PMID: 24622292

Bates, A. W. (2020, December 16). A review of online learning in 2020. *Online Learning and Distance Education Resources*. https://www.tonybates.ca/2020/12/16/a-review-of-online-learning-in-2020

Bates, T. (2019). Teaching in a digital age: Guidelines for designing teaching and learning. BCcampus Open Education.

Bates, T. (2023). Teaching in a digital age: Guidelines for designing teaching and learning. BCcampus Open Education.

Baturay, M. H., & Bay, O. F. (2010). The effects of problem-based learning on the classroom community perceptions and achievement of web-based education students. *Computers & Education*, 55(1), 43–52. DOI: 10.1016/j.compedu.2009.12.001

Bayly-Castaneda, K., Ramirez-Montoya, M.-S., & Morita-Alexander, A. (2024). Crafting personalized learning paths with AI for lifelong learning: A systematic literature review. *Frontiers in Education*, 9, 1–12. DOI: 10.3389/feduc.2024.1424386

Beaty, R. E., Kenett, Y. N., & Hass, R. W. (2019). Fanning creative thought: Semantic richness impacts divergent thinking. *Proceedings of the Annual Meeting of the Cognitive Science Society, 41*, 126–131. https://escholarship.org/uc/item/40p1s98s

Beaty, R. E., Kenett, Y. N., Hass, R. W., & Schacter, D. L. (2023). Semantic memory and creativity: The costs and benefits of semantic memory structure in generating original ideas. *Thinking & Reasoning*, 29(2), 305–339. DOI: 10.1080/13546783.2022.2076742 PMID: 37113618

Beers, K. (2015). *When kids can't read-what teachers can do: A guide for teachers*. Pearson Education.

Beetham, H., & Sharpe, R. (Eds.). (2019). *Rethinking pedagogy for a digital age: Principles and practices of design* (3rd ed.). Routledge., DOI: 10.4324/9781351252805

Beigpourian, B., Ohland, M., & Ferguson, D. (2020). Effect of psychological safety on the interaction of students in teams. *2020 ASEE Virtual Annual Conference Content Access Proceedings*. DOI: 10.18260/1-2--34497

Bellatreche, R., & Alloti, L. (2020). E-learning challenges in higher education institutions: Algeria case study. , *11*(2), 264-276. Retrieved from https://www.asjp.cerist.dz/en/downArticle/275/11/2/140829

Belt, E. S., & Lowenthal, P. R. (2023). Synchronous video-based communication and online learning: An exploration of instructors' perceptions and experiences. *Education and Information Technologies*, 28(5), 4941–4964. DOI: 10.1007/s10639-022-11360-6 PMID: 36320822

Benadla, D., & Hadji, M. (2021). EFL students' affective attitudes towards distance e-learning based on moodle platform during the covid-19the pandemic: Perspectives from Dr. Moulay Tahar University of Saida, Algeria. *Arab World English Journal (AWEJ) Special Issue on Covid, 19*, 55-67. DOI: 10.24093/awej/covid.4

Bendelier, S., Bond, M., Buntins, K., Zawacki-Richter, O., & Kerres, M. (2020). Facilitating student engagement through educational technology in higher education: A systematic review in the field of arts and humanities. *Australasian Journal of Educational Technology*, 36(4), 126–150. DOI: 10.14742/ajet.5477

Berestok, O. V. (2021). Synchronous and asynchronous e-learning modes: Strategies, methods, objectives. *Engineering and Educational Technologies*, 9(1), 19–27. DOI: 10.30929/2307-9770.2021.09.01.02

Bergmann, J., & Sams, A. (2012). *Flip Your Classroom: Reach Every Student in Every Class Every Day*. International Society for Technology in Education.

Bernard, R., Abrami, P. C., Lou, Y., Borokhovski, E., Wade, A., Wozney, L., Wallet, P. A., Fiset, M., & Huang, B. (2009). How does distance education compare with classroom instruction? A meta-analysis of the empirical literature. *Review of Educational Research*, 74(3), 379–439. DOI: 10.3102/00346543074003379

Bernstein, D. (2013). How SoTL-active faculty members can be cosmopolitan assets to an institution. *Teaching & Learning Inquiry*, 1(1), 35–40. DOI: 10.20343/teachlearninqu.1.1.35

Berry, D. C. (1983). Metacognitive experience and transfer of logical reasoning. *The Quarterly Journal of Experimental Psychology. A, Human Experimental Psychology*, 35(1), 39–49. DOI: 10.1080/14640748308402115

Bicchi, F. (2024). Cultivating communities of practice: From institutions to practices. *Global Studies Quarterly*, 4(1), 1–10. DOI: 10.1093/isagsq/ksad076

Birgin, O., & Yılmaz, M. (2023). Development and validation of a scale to assess the frequency of using classroom assessment tools and methods for mathematics teachers. *IJERI: International Journal of Educational Research and Innovation*, (20), 1–20. DOI: 10.46661/ijeri.8075

Bishop, J., & Verleger, M. A. (2013, June 23-26). *The flipped classroom: A survey of the research.* 2013 ASEE annual conference & exposition (pp. 23-1200). Retrieved from https://aktuelt.osloskolen.no/SysSiteAssets/laringsteknologi/dokumenter/the-flipped-classroom-a-survey-of-the-research.pdf

Bishop-Clark, C., & Dietz-Uhler, B. (2012). *Engaging in the scholarship of teaching and learning: A guide to the process, and how to develop a project from start to finish*. Routledge.

Bisra, K., Liu, Q., Nesbit, J. C., Salimi, F., & Winne, P. H. (2018). Inducing self-explanation: A meta-analysis. *Educational Psychology Review*, 30(3), 703–725. DOI: 10.1007/s10648-018-9434-x

Black, N. B. (2022, June). Teaching AI with the hands-on AI projects for the classroom series. *Proceedings of the AAAI Conference on Artificial Intelligence*, 36(11), 12859–12859. DOI: 10.1609/aaai.v36i11.21566

Blizak, D., Blizak, S., Bouchenak, O., & Yahiaoui, K. (2020). Students' perceptions regarding the abrupt transition to online learning during the COVID-19 pandemic: Case of faculty of chemistry and hydrocarbons at the university of Boumerdes, Algeria. *Journal of Chemical Education*, 97(9), 2466–2471. DOI: 10.1021/acs.jchemed.0c00668

Bochner, A. P., & Ellis, C. (2022). Why autoethnography? *Social Work & Social Sciences Review*, 23(2), 8–18. DOI: 10.1921/swssr.v23i2.2027

Boers, F. (2000). Metaphor awareness and vocabulary retention. *Applied Linguistics*, 21(4), 553–571. DOI: 10.1093/applin/21.4.553

Boers, F., Demecheleer, M., & Eyckmans, J. (2004). Etymological elaboration as a strategy for learning idioms. In *Language learning and language teaching* (pp. 53–78). John Benjamins Publishing Co., DOI: 10.1075/lllt.10.07boe

Boers, F., Eyckmans, J., & Stengers, H. (2007). Presenting figurative idioms with a touch of etymology: More than mere mnemonics? *Language Teaching Research*, 11(1), 43–62. DOI: 10.1177/1362168806072460

Bonwell, C. C., & Eison, J. A. (1991). ASHE-ERIC Higher Education Report: Vol. 1. *Active Learning: Creating Excitement in the Classroom*. George Washington University.

Borko, H. (2004). Professional Development and Teacher Learning: Mapping the Terrain. *Educational Researcher*, 33(8), 3–15. DOI: 10.3102/0013189X033008003

Boston, D., Gibson, I., & Richardson, S. (2010). An exploration of the relationship between indicators of the Community of Inquiry framework and retention in online programs. *Journal of Asynchronous Learning Networks*, 14(1), 67–83.

Botes, K., & Botha, A. J. (2021). Experiential e-learning: A creative prospect for education in the built environment? In advances in web-based learning–ICWL 2021: 20th International Conference, ICWL 2021, Macau, China, November 13–14, 2021, Proceedings (pp. 102-114). *Springer International Publishing*. DOI: 10.1007/978-3-030-90785-3_9

Botnaru, D., Maurer, T. W., & Langdon, J. (2022). SoTL at Georgia Southern: Perceptions, engagement and impact. *International Journal for the Scholarship of Teaching and Learning*, 16(1), 1–15. DOI: 10.20429/ijsotl.2022.160104

Bourhis, A., & Duba, L. (2005). The success of virtual communities of practice: The leadership factor. *Electronic Journal of Knowledge Management*, 3(1), 23–34. https://academic-publishing.org/index.php/ejkm/article/view/719

Boyer, E. L. (1990). *Scholarship reconsidered: Priorities of the professoriate*. Carnegie Foundation for the Advancement of Teaching. https://eric.ed.gov/?id=ed326149

Boyer, E. L. (1990). *Scholarship reconsidered: Priorities of the professoriate*. Princeton University Press.

Brady, A. C., Botnaru, D., Alt, K., Carroll, G. D., Moldavan, A. M., Mesenbrink-Sainz, J., Nafziger, B., Reagan, K. J., & Rich, L. E. (2024). Understanding the influence of intelligent agents on students' sense of classroom belonging, engagement, and academic performance in online classes. *American Journal of Distance Education*, 1–17. Advance online publication. DOI: 10.1080/08923647.2024.2430766

Brod, G. (2021). Prediction as a learning strategy. *Psychonomic Bulletin & Review*, 28(6), 1839–1847. DOI: 10.3758/s13423-021-01904-1 PMID: 33768503

Brookfield, S. D. (1995). *Becoming a critically reflective teacher*. JosseyBass.

Brooks, A. W. (2014). Information literacy and the flipped classroom: Examining the impact of a one-shot flipped class on student learning and perceptions. *Communications in Information Literacy*, 8(2), 4. DOI: 10.15760/comminfolit.2014.8.2.168

Brzezinska, M., & Cromarty, E. (2022). Emergency remote teaching in the university context: Responding to social and emotional needs during a sudden transition online. In *Lecture notes in computer science*, 30–47. https://doi.org/DOI: 10.1007/978-3-031-05064-0_3

Bunnell, S. L., Chick, N., Hamilton, M., Leoni, A. S., & Woolmer, C. (2024). Generations of SoTL scholars: Transferable lessons and new possibilities. *Transformative Dialogues: Teaching and Learning Journal*, 17(1), 24–40.

Bunnell, S. L., Chick, N., Hamilton, M., Leoni, A. S., & Woolmer, C. (2024). Generations of SoTL scholars: Transferable lessons and new possibilities. *Transformative Dialogues: Teaching and Learning Journal, 17*(1), 25–40. DOI: 10.26209/td2024vol17iss11801

Burnham, B., & Walden, B. (1997). Interactions in distance education: A report from the other side. In *Proceedings of the Adult Education Research Conference*. Oklahoma State University. http:// www.edst.educ.ubc.ca/aerc/1997/97burnham.html

Bush, V. (1945). *As we may think. The Atlantic*. Tribune Content Agency.

Bush, V. (2021). As we may think. In Lewis, H. R. (Ed.), *Ideas that created the future: Classic papers of computer science* (pp. 107–120). The MIT Press., DOI: 10.7551/mitpress/12274.003.0013

Callender, A. A., & McDaniel, M. A. (2007). The benefits of embedded question adjuncts for low and high structure builders. *Journal of Educational Psychology*, 99(2), 339–348. DOI: 10.1037/0022-0663.99.2.339

Callen, J. C. (2012). Impossible things: An investigation of madness as resistance in Tim Burton's *Alice in Wonderland.Administrative Theory & Praxis*, 34(1), 120–124. DOI: 10.2753/ATP1084-1806340108

Çam, O., & Büyükbayram, A. (2015). The results of nurses' increasing emotional intelligence and resilience. *Journal of Psychiatric Nursing/Psikiyatri Hemsireleri Dernegi, 6*(3) 130-136 DOI: 10.5505/phd.2015.96729

Camarao, J., & Din, C. (2023). "A group of people to lean on and learn from": Graduate teaching assistant experiences in a pedagogy-focused community of practice. *Teaching & Learning Inquiry*, 11. Advance online publication. DOI: 10.20343/teachlearninqu.11.11

Cant, R., Ryan, C., & Kelly, M. (2022). Use and effectiveness of virtual simulations in nursing student education. *Computers, Informatics, Nursing*, 41(1), 31–38. DOI: 10.1097/CIN.0000000000000932 PMID: 35926237

Carless, D., & Boud, D. (2018). The development of student feedback literacy: Enabling uptake of feedback. *Assessment & Evaluation in Higher Education*, 43(8), 1315–1325. DOI: 10.1080/02602938.2018.1463354

Caroy, A. A. (2023). A technology report on Nearpod. *RELC Journal*, 54(2), 551–560. DOI: 10.1177/00336882231153669

Carroll, L. (1897). *Alice's adventures in wonderland.* Macmillan.

CAST. (2024). *Universal design for learning guidelines version 3.0.* https://udlguidelines.cast.org

Castillo, A. G. R., Rivera, H. V. H., Teves, R. M. V., Lopez, H. R. P., Reyes, G. Y., Rodriguez, M. A. M., & Arias-Gonzáles, J. L. (2023). Effect of Chat GPT on the digitized learning process of university students. *Journal of Namibian Studies: History Politics Culture*, 33, 1–15.

Cavanaugh, C., Dawson, K., & Bali, M. (2020). Teacher professional development and online learning during COVID-19: Emergency response and lasting change. *Educational Researcher*, 49(8), 650–658.

Çelik, M. Y., Öztürk, E., Karasu, F., & Elmaoğlu, E. The Stress Dimension of Online Education in Nursing Students During The Covid-19 Process: A University Example. Sağlık Akademisi Kastamonu, 7(Covid-19 Ek Sayısı), 65-77.

Centre for Applied Special Technology. ([CAST], 2021). Universal design for learning guidelines version 2.2. https://www.cast.org/impact/universal-design-for-learning-udl

Chandra, Y. (2021). Online education during COVID-19: perception of academic stress and emotional intelligence coping strategies among college students. *Asian education and development studies, 10*(2), 229-238.

Chang, H. (2008). *Autoethnography as method.* Left Coast Press.

Cheddadi, S., & Bouache, M. (2021). Improving equity and access to higher education using artificial intelligence. *International Journal of Education and Development Using Information and Communication Technology*, 17(2), 112–125. DOI: 10.1109/ICCSE51940.2021.9569548

Chelghoum, A., & Chelghoum, H. (2020). The COVID-19 pandemic and education: big changes ahead for teaching in Algeria. *Altralang Journal, 2*(2), 118-132. Retrieved from: https://www.asjp.cerist.dz/en/downArticle/597/2/2/139887

Chen, S., Binning, K. R., Manke, K. J., Brady, S. T., McGreevy, E. M., Betancur, L., & Kaufmann, N. (2021). Am I a science person? A strong science identity bolsters minority students' sense of belonging and performance in college. *Personality and Social Psychology Bulletin*, 47(4), 593–606.

Chen, Y., Jensen, S., Albert, L. J., Gupta, S., & Lee, T. (2023). Artificial intelligence (AI) student assistants in the classroom: Designing chatbots to support student success. *Information Systems Frontiers*, 25(1), 161–182. DOI: 10.1007/s10796-022-10291-4

Chen, Z., Zhang, Y., Li, P., & Wang, X. (2020). Education 4.0 using artificial intelligence for students' performance analysis. *Journal of Educational Technology Systems*, 48(4), 1–15.

Cherrstrom, C. A., Robbins, S. E., Boden, C. J., & Bixby, J. (2019). Need tech? Non-traditional student perceptions of educational technology tools. *The Journal of Continuing Higher Education*, 67(2–3), 109–122. DOI: 10.1080/07377363.2019.1680266

Chick, N. L. (2014). 'Methodologically sound' under the 'big tent': An ongoing conversation. *International Journal for the Scholarship of Teaching and Learning*, 8(2), 1–15. DOI: 10.20429/ijsotl.2014.080201

Chick, N. L. (2015). Holding it up to the light: Looking at learning through the lenses of the arts and humanities. *The Canadian Journal for the Scholarship of Teaching and Learning*, 6(2), 1–7. DOI: 10.5206/cjsotl-rcacea.2015.2.3

Chick, N. L., Cruz, L., Friberg, J. C., & Steiner, H. H. (2023). Making space for failure in the scholarship of teaching and learning: A blueprint. *Teaching & Learning Inquiry*, 11. Advance online publication. DOI: 10.20343/teachlearninqu.11.36

Chick, N., Nowell, L., & Lenart, B. (2019). The scholarship of teaching and learning: A scoping review protocol. *Teaching & Learning Inquiry*, 7(2), 186–19. DOI: 10.20343/teachlearninqu.7.2.12

Chikobvu, P., & Harunavamwe, M. (2022). The role of emotional intelligence and work engagement on nurses' resilience in public hospitals. *SA Journal of Human Resource Management*, 20, 259–268. DOI: 10.4102/sajhrm.v20i0.1690

Chi, M. T., Bassok, M., Lewis, M. W., Reimann, P., & Glaser, R. (1989). Self-explanations: How students study and use examples in learning to solve problems. *Cognitive Science*, 13(2), 145–182. DOI: 10.1016/0364-0213(89)90002-5

Chi, M. T., De Leeuw, N., Chiu, M., & Lavancher, C. (1994). Eliciting self-explanations improves understanding. *Cognitive Science*, 18(3), 439–477. DOI: 10.1207/s15516709cog1803_3

Ching, Y.-H., & Hsu, Y.-C. (2013). Collaborative learning using VoiceThread in an online graduate course. *Knowledge Management and E-Learning*, 5(3), 298–314. DOI: 10.34105/j.kmel.2013.05.021

Chiu, T. K., Moorhouse, B. L., Chai, C. S., & Ismailov, M. (2023). Teacher support and student motivation to learn with Artificial Intelligence (AI) based chatbot. *Interactive Learning Environments*, •••, 1–17. DOI: 10.1080/10494820.2023.2172044

Cho, D., Lee, W., Kim, S., & Choi, S. (2022). Effect of online education on the knowledge on, attitudes towards, and skills in patient safety for nursing students in Korea: A mixed-methods study. *Journal of Educational Evaluation for Health Professions*, 19, 14. DOI: 10.3352/jeehp.2022.19.14 PMID: 35918141

Chung, J., McKenzie, S., Schweinsberg, A., & Mundy, M. E. (2022). Correlates of academic performance in online higher education: A systematic review. *Frontiers in Education*, 7, 820567. Advance online publication. DOI: 10.3389/feduc.2022.820567

Clark, J. M., & Paivio, A. (1991). Dual coding theory and education. *Educational Psychology Review*, 3(3), 149–210. DOI: 10.1007/BF01320076

Cleary, K., Loton, D., & Samarawickrema, G. (2022). Activating SoTL partnerships and ethical processes: A model to capture pedagogical innovation. In *Ethics and the Scholarship of Teaching and Learning* (pp. 79–94). Springer International Publishing., DOI: 10.1007/978-3-031-11810-4_6

Cleaver, E., Mclinden, M., Lintern, M., & Birch, A. (2020). The enquiring university: The scholarship of teaching and learning as a foundation for strategic educational transformation. In *Evidence-Based Faculty Development Through the Scholarship of Teaching and Learning (SoTL)* (pp. 20–41). IGI Global., DOI: 10.4018/978-1-7998-2212-7.ch002

Cobb, S. C. (•••). Social presence and online learning: A current view from a research perspective. *Journal of Interactive Online Learning*, 8(3), 241–254.

Collado-Valero, J., Rodríguez-Infante, G., Romero-González, M., Gamboa-Ternero, S., Navarro-Soria, I., & Lavigne-Cerván, R. (2021). Flipped classroom: Active methodology for sustainable learning in higher education during social distancing due to COVID-19. *Sustainability (Basel)*, 13(10), 5336. Advance online publication. DOI: 10.3390/su13105336

Collins, A. (2023). *Examining teachers' perceptions of preparedness to teach in low-income schools upon completing a Master of Arts in teaching degree*. [Doctoral dissertation, National Louis University https://digitalcommons.nl.edu/diss/723/,]

Collins, A. M., & Loftus, E. F. (1975). A spreading-activation theory of semantic processing. *Psychological Review*, 82(6), 407–428. DOI: 10.1037/0033-295X.82.6.407

Conley, C. S. (2015). SEL in higher education. In Durlak, J. A., Domitrovich, C. E., Weissberg, R. P., & Gullotta, T. P. (Eds.), *Handbook of social and emotional learning: Research and practice* (pp. 197–212). The Guilford Press.

Cook, S. C. (2020). Emerging response-abilities: A reflection on the 2019 SoTL in the South conference. *Scholarship of Teaching and Learning in the South*, 4(1), 69–85. DOI: 10.36615/sotls.v4i1.135

Copland, S. (2023). A case study on the value of humanities-based analysis, modes of presentation, and study designs for SoTL: Close reading students' pre-surveys on gender-inclusive language. *Teaching & Learning Inquiry*, 11. Advance online publication. DOI: 10.20343/teachlearninqu.11.34

Corcoran, N., & Duane, A. (2017). Using enterprise social networks as a knowledge management tool in higher education. *VINE Journal of Information and Knowledge Management Systems*, 47(4), 555–570. DOI: 10.1108/VJIKMS-12-2016-0073

Corey, J. F. (1972). A brief history of service-learning internship programs. *Higher Education in North Carolina*, 7(4), 1–7.

Cowley, S. A., Tzouvara, V., & Horta Reis da Silva, T. (2023). Public Health: healthy ageing and well-being. In *Redfern's Nursing Older People*. Fifth edition. Editors: Ross, Harris, Fitzpatrick and Abley. Elsevier.

Cox, M. (2004). Introduction to faculty learning communities. *New Directions for Teaching and Learning*, 97(97), 5–23. DOI: 10.1002/tl.129

Craik, F. I. M., & Tulving, E. (1975). Depth of processing and the retention of words in episodic memory. *Journal of Experimental Psychology. General*, 104(3), 268–294. DOI: 10.1037/0096-3445.104.3.268

Craik, F. I., & Lockhart, R. S. (1972). Levels of processing: A framework for memory research. *Journal of Verbal Learning and Verbal Behavior*, 11(6), 671–684. DOI: 10.1016/S0022-5371(72)80001-X

Cranton, P. (2011). A transformative perspective on the Scholarship of Teaching and Learning. *Higher Education Research & Development*, 30(1), 75–86. DOI: 10.1080/07294360.2011.536974

Crawford, C. M. (2001). Developing webs of significance through communications: Appropriate interactive activities for distributed learning environments. *Campus-Wide Information Systems*, 18(2), 68–72. DOI: 10.1108/10650740110386675

Crawford, C. M. (2003). Emerging learning environments: Enhancing the online community. *Academic Exchange Quarterly*, 7(4), 131–135.

Crawford, C. M. (2023). Now what?: A case study on the impact of nefarious Queen Bees. In Clarke, K. L., & Moffett, N. L. (Eds.), *Addressing the Queen Bee Syndrome in academia* (pp. 1–25). IGI Global., DOI: 10.4018/978-1-6684-7717-5.ch001

Crawford, C. M., Andrews, S., & Wallace, J. K. Y. (2021). Co-creative collegial communities of instructional engagement. *International Journal of Hyperconnectivity and the Internet of Things*, 5(2), 38–56. DOI: 10.4018/IJHIoT.2021070103

Cruz, L. (2023). *Finding your audience: A workshop on publishing your SoTL project* [Workshop]. SoTL Commons Conference, Savannah, Georgia.

Cruz, L. (2024). Converging spaces? Re-imagining the scholarship of teaching and learning (SoTL) as the subject of transdisciplinary research. *Transformative Dialogues: Teaching and Learning Journal, 17*(1). DOI: 10.26209/td2024vol17iss11823

Cruz, L. E., & Grodziak, E. M. (2021). SoTL under stress: Rethinking teaching and learning scholarship during a global pandemic. *Teaching & Learning Inquiry*, 9(1), 3–13. DOI: 10.20343/teachlearninqu.9.1.2

Cruz, L., Grodziak, E., Botnaru, D., Walker, D., Maurer, T., Altany, A., Abraham-Settles, B., Amos, M., Bunch-Crump, K., Cook, A., Eisenreich, H., Gregory, D., Howell, M., James, I., Landge, S., Lynes, J., Pompey, J., Shapiro, B., Smith, A., & Zhang, Y. (2023). The hospitality of the Commons: A collaborative reflection on a SOTL conference. *International Journal for the Scholarship of Teaching and Learning*, 17(2), 1–10. DOI: 10.20429/ijsotl.2023.17207

Cruz, L., Leoni, A. S., & Mojarad, S. N. (2024). Meaning and manifesto: Embracing transdisciplinarity in SoTL. *Transformative Dialogues: Teaching and Learning Journal*, 17(1), 1–13.

Cruz, L., Santucci Leoni, A., & Nasrollahian Mojarad, S. (2024). Meaning and manifesto: Embracing transdisciplinarity in SoTL. *Transformative Dialogues: Teaching and Learning Journal, 17*(1), 1–13. https://doi.org/DOI: 10.26209/TD2024VOL17ISS11836

Cui, G., Lockee, B., & Meng, C. (2013). Building modern online social presence: A review of social presence theory and its instructional design implications for future trends. *Education and Information Technologies*, 18(4), 661–685. DOI: 10.1007/s10639-012-9192-1

da Silva, T. H. R. (2022). Emotional awareness and emotional intelligence. *British Journal of Community Nursing*, 27(12), 573–574. DOI: 10.12968/bjcn.2022.27.12.573 PMID: 36519463 da Silva, T. H. R., & Rodrigues, E. C. P. (2023). Body Image Related Discrimination. In Leal Filho, W., Azul, A. M., Brandli, L., Lange Salvia, A., Özuyar, P. G., & Wall, T. (Eds.), *Reduced Inequalities. Encyclopedia of the UN Sustainable Development Goals*. Springer., DOI: 10.1007/978-3-319-71060-0_61-1

Dagher, S., Hilal-Alnaqbi, A., & Akozaheya, B. (2024). Needs assessment study for social-emotional learning in higher education. In *Advances in Science* (pp. 1–5). Technology & Innovation/Advances in Science, Technology & Innovation., DOI: 10.1007/978-3-031-49393-5_1

Damast, D., Cohen, P., & Martinez, D. L. (2021). "Hey students, how was that first semester of remote instruction?": Graduate students' reflections on remote learning during COVID-19. *Dance Education in Practice*, 7(2), 15–24. DOI: 10.1080/23734833.2021.1916288

Darby, F., & Lang, J. (2019). *Small teaching online: Applying learning science to online classes*. Jossey-Bass.

Darling-Hammond, L., Hyler, M. E., & Gardner, M. (2017). *Effective Teacher Professional Development*. Learning Policy Institute. DOI: 10.54300/122.311

Darwin, R., Rusdin, D., Mukminatien, N., Suryati, N., Laksmi, E. D., & Marzuki, . (2023). Critical thinking in the AI era: An exploration of EFL students' perceptions, benefits, and limitations. *Cogent Education*, 11(1), 2290342. Advance online publication. DOI: 10.1080/2331186X.2023.2290342

Davies, R. S., Dean, D. L., & Ball, N. (2013). Flipping the classroom and instructional technology integration in a college-level information systems spreadsheet course. *Educational Technology Research and Development*, 61(4), 563–580. DOI: 10.1007/s11423-013-9305-6

Davis, F. D. (1985). *A Technology Acceptance Model for Empirically Testing New End-User Information Systems*. [Doctoral dissertation, University of Queensland]. Massachusetts Institute of Technology. http://hdl.handle.net/1721.1/15192

De Gagne, J. C., Kim, S. S., Schoen, E. R., & Park, H. K. (2018). Assessing the impact of video-based assignments on health professions students' social presence on web: Case study. *JMIR Medical Education*, 4(2), e11390. DOI: 10.2196/11390 PMID: 30478027

DeLozier, S., & Rhodes, M. (2016). Flipped classrooms: A review of key ideas and recommendations for practice. *Educational Psychology Review*, 29(1), 141–151. DOI: 10.1007/s10648-015-9356-9

Denscombe, M. (2014). *The good research guide for small-scale social research projects*. Open University Press.

Deterding, S., Dixon, D., Khaled, R., & Nacke, L. (2011). From game design elements to gamefulness: Defining "gamification." *Proceedings of the 15th International Academic MindTrek Conference: Envisioning Future Media Environments*, 9–15. DOI: 10.1145/2181037.2181040

Dewey, J. (1933). *How we think: A restatement of the relation of reflective thinking to the educative process*. Heath.

Dickson, K. L., & Treml, M. M. (2013). Using assessment and SoTL to enhance student learning. *New Directions for Teaching and Learning*, 2013(136), 7–16. DOI: 10.1002/tl.20072

Dignan, A. (2011). *Game frame: Using games as a strategy for success*. Simon and Schuster.

Donnelly, R., & Kennelly, I. (2024). A framework-based cross-institutional CPD for academic staff in Gen-AI literacy, critical inquiry, and authentic assessment. In *Effective Practices in AI Literacy Education: Case Studies and Reflections* (pp. 51-59). Emerald Publishing Limited. DOI: 10.1108/978-1-83608-852-320241006

Donnelly, C. M., & McDaniel, M. A. (1993). Use of analogy in learning scientific concepts. *Journal of Experimental Psychology. Learning, Memory, and Cognition*, 19(4), 975–987. DOI: 10.1037/0278-7393.19.4.975 PMID: 8345330

Dufflemeyer, F. (1994). Effective anticipation guide statements for learning from ex. *Journal of Reading*, 37(6), 452.

Dunlosky, J., Rawson, K. A., Marsh, E. J., Nathan, M. J., & Willingham, D. T. (2013). Improving students' learning with effective learning techniques: Promising directions from cognitive and educational psychology. *Psychological Science in the Public Interest*, 14(1), 4–58. DOI: 10.1177/1529100612453266 PMID: 26173288

Dweck, C. S. (2006). *Mindset: The New Psychology of Success*. Random House.

Dziuban, C., Graham, C. R., Moskal, P. D., Norberg, A., & Sicilia, N. (2018). Blended learning: The new normal and emerging technologies. *International Journal of Educational Technology in Higher Education*, 15(1), 1–16. DOI: 10.1186/s41239-017-0087-5

Eady, M. J., Abrahamson, E., Green, C. A., Arcellana-Panlilio, M., Hatfield, L., & Namaste, N. (2021). Re-positioning SoTL toward the T-shaped community. *Teaching & Learning Inquiry*, 9(1), 262–278. DOI: 10.20343/teachlearninqu.9.1.18

EDUCAUSE. (2024). *Horizon report: Teaching and learning edition* (Boulder, CO). https://library.educause.edu/resources/2024/5/2024-educause-horizon-report-teaching-and-learning-edition

Efriana, L. (2021). Problems of online learning during COVID-19 pandemic in EFL classroom and the solution. *Journal of English Language Teaching and Literature*, 2(1), 38–47. https://jurnal.stkipmb.ac.id/index.php/jelita/article/view/74

Eka Chandra, N., Mariani, N., Rosalina, E., Elyani, E. P., Asrimawati, I. F., Anwar, M. N., & Nazmi, Y. F. (2024). The use of artificial intelligence technology in enhancing student participation in classroom activities at the English Subject Teacher's Association. *Bubungan Tinggi: Jurnal Pengabdian Masyarakat*, 6(2), 441–448. DOI: 10.20527/btjpm.v6i2.10261

Elkateb, N. (2022). Challenges associated with e-learning on MOODLE platform during COVID 19 Pandemic from Chlef EFL Students' Perspective. *Journal of Languages & Translation*, 2(2), 120–133. DOI: 10.70204/jlt.v2i2.250

Elmi, C. (2020). Integrating social emotional learning strategies in higher education. *European Journal of Investigation in Health, Psychology and Education*, 10(3), 848–858. DOI: 10.3390/ejihpe10030061 PMID: 34542515

Emerick, E., Caldarella, P., & Black, S. (2019). Benefits and distractions of social media as tools for undergraduate student. *College Student Journal*, 53(3), 265–276. https://www.ingentaconnect.com/content/prin/csj/2019/00000053/00000003/art00001

Enfeld, J. (2013). Looking at the impact of the flipped classroom model of instruction on undergraduate multimedia students at CSUN. *TechTrends*, 57(6), 14–27. DOI: 10.1007/s11528-013-0698-1

Ertmer, P. A. (2005). Teacher Pedagogical Beliefs: The Final Frontier in Our Quest for Technology Integration? *Educational Technology Research and Development*, 53(4), 25–39. DOI: 10.1007/BF02504683

Fanghanel, J. (2013). Going public with pedagogical inquiries: SoTL as a methodology for faculty professional development. *Teaching & Learning Inquiry*, 1(1), 59–70. DOI: 10.20343/teachlearninqu.1.1.59

Fanghanel, J., Pritchard, J., Potter, J., & Wisker, G. (2016). *Defining and supporting the scholarship of teaching and learning (SoTL): A sector-wide study*. Higher Education Academy.

Felten, P. (2013). Principles of good practice in SoTL. *Teaching & Learning Inquiry*, 1(1), 121–125. DOI: 10.20343/teachlearninqu.1.1.121

Felton, P., & Chick, N. (2018). Is SoTL a signature pedagogy of educational development? *To Improve the Academy*, 37(1), 4–16. DOI: 10.1002/tia2.20077

Fensie, A., St Pierre, T., Jain, J., & Sezen-Barrie, A. (2023). Engaged learning during distraction: A case study of successful working moms in distance education. *Journal of Computing in Higher Education*, 36(2), 389–434. DOI: 10.1007/s12528-023-09359-0 PMID: 37359045

Fields, L., Perkiss, S., Dean, B., & Moroney, T. (2021). Nursing and the sustainable development goals: A scoping review. *Journal of Nursing Scholarship*, 53(5), 568–577. DOI: 10.1111/jnu.12675 PMID: 34056841

Fiorella, L., & Mayer, R. E. (2021). The generative activity principle in multimedia learning. In Mayer, R. E., & Fiorella, L. (Eds.), *The Cambridge handbook of multimedia learning* (pp. 339–350). Cambridge University Press., DOI: 10.1017/9781108894333.036

Firat, M. (2023). What ChatGPT means for universities: Perceptions of scholars and students. *Journal of Applied Learning and Teaching*, 6(1), 57–63.

Fisher, M. E., Dorner, M. A., Maghzi, K. S., Achieng-Evensen, C., Whitaker, L. C., Hansell, F., St Amant, J., & Gapinski, S. M. (2021). Liminality, disruption, and change: A prismatic look at pandemic education. *Prospects*, 51(1–3), 523–540. DOI: 10.1007/s11125-021-09563-9 PMID: 34219814

Fitzpatrick, J. M., Bianchi, L. A., Hayes, N., Da Silva, T., & Harris, R. (2023). Professional development and career planning for nurses working in care homes for older people: A scoping review. *International Journal of Older People Nursing*, 18(1), e12519. DOI: 10.1111/opn.12519 PMID: 36441621

Fonseca, D. (2019). *Technology-enhanced learning*. Learning and Teaching in Higher Education., DOI: 10.4337/9781788975087.00031

Ford, N., Bowden, M., & Beard, J. (2011). Learning together: Using social media to foster collaboration in higher education. In Wankel, L. A., & Wankel, C. (Eds.), *Higher education administration with social media* (Vol. 2, pp. 105–126). Emerald Group Publishing Limited., DOI: 10.1108/S2044-9968(2011)0000002009

Fraga, L. M., & Harmon, J. (2014). The flipped classroom model of learning in higher education: An investigation of preservice teachers' perspectives and achievement. *Journal of Digital Learning in Teacher Education*, 31(1), 18–27. DOI: 10.1080/21532974.2014.967420

Frake-Mistak, M., Friberg, J., & Hamilton, M. (2023). Reimagining the 4M framework in educational development for SoTL. *Teaching & Learning Inquiry*, 1. Advance online publication. DOI: 10.20343/teachlearninqu.11.14

Freeman, S., Eddy, S. L., McDonough, M., Smith, M. K., Okoroafor, N., Jordt, H., & Wenderoth, M. P. (2014). Active learning increases student performance in science, engineering, and mathematics. *Proceedings of the National Academy of Sciences of the United States of America*, 111(23), 8410–8415. DOI: 10.1073/pnas.1319030111 PMID: 24821756

Friesen, S. (2020). The Flipped Classroom with Digital Whiteboards [TechTrends]. *Enhancing Student Engagement and Learning.*, 64(2), 182–192.

Fullan, M. (1993). *Change Forces: Probing the Depths of Educational Reform*. Falmer Press.

Galanis, P., Katsiroumpa, A., Moisoglou, I., Nikiforou, A., Kothonas, K., Athanasopoulou, K., & Panagiotopoulos, E. (2024). Effectiveness of an e-learning activity regarding research methodology and fragility fractures in a sample of nurses: Evidence from Greece. https://doi.org/DOI: 10.21203/rs.3.rs-3975218/v1

Gansemer-Topf, A., Webb, A., Kensington-Miller, B., Maheux-Pelletier, G., Lewis, H., Luu, J., & Hofmann, A. (2021). Navigating the chaos: The value of SoTL during times of uncertainty. *Transformative Dialogues: Teaching and Learning Journal, 14*(2).

García-Monge, A., González-Calvo, G., & Bores-García, D. (2019). "I like the idea but...": The gap in participation in a virtual community of practice for analysing physical education. *Open Learning*, 34(3), 257–272. DOI: 10.1080/02680513.2018.1505486

Gardner, A., & Willey, K. (2016). Academic identity reconstruction: The transition of engineering academics to engineering education researchers. *Studies in Higher Education*. Advance online publication. DOI: 10.1080/03075079.2016.1162779

Gardner, H. (1983). *Frames of mind: The theory of multiple intelligences*. Basic Books.

Garrison, D. R. (2016). E-learning in the 21st century: A community of inquiry approach. Routledge.

Garrison, D. R. (1997). *Distance education and critical theory*. Falmer Press.

Garrison, D. R., & Anderson, T. (2006). E-learning in the 21st century: A framework for the research agenda. *The Internet and Higher Education*, 9(2), 1–17. DOI: 10.1016/j.iheduc.2005.11.001

Garrison, D. R., Anderson, T., & Archer, W. (2000). Critical inquiry in a text-based environment: Computer conferencing in higher education. *The Internet and Higher Education*, 2(2), 87–105.

Garrison, D. R., Anderson, T., & Archer, W. (2000). Critical Inquiry in a Text-Based Environment: Computer Conferencing in Higher Education. *The Internet and Higher Education*, 2(2-3), 87–105. DOI: 10.1016/S1096-7516(00)00016-6

Garrison, D. R., & Vaughan, N. D. (2008). *Blended Learning in Higher Education: Framework, Principles, and Guidelines*. Jossey-Bass.

Gearing, R. E., Mian, I. A., Barber, J., & Ickowicz, A. (2006). A methodology for conducting retrospective chart review research in child and adolescent psychiatry. *Journal of the Canadian Academy of Child and Adolescent Psychiatry = Journal de l'Académie Canadienne de Psychiatrie de l'Enfant et de l'Adolescent*, 15(3), 126–134. https://psycnet.apa.org/record/2006-12856-002 PMID: 18392182

Gentner, D., & Jeziorski, M. (2012). Historical shifts in the use of analogy in science. In Gholson, B., Shadish, W. R.Jr, Neimeyer, R. A., & Houts, A. C. (Eds.), *Psychology of science: Contributions to metascience* (pp. 296–325). Cambridge University Press., DOI: 10.1017/CBO9781139173667.016

Georgia Southern Faculty Center. (n.d.). *SoTL learning community*. Georgia Southern University. https://www.georgiasouthern.edu/academics/sotlgsu/

Ghobrini, R. E. A. (2021, January 21–22, 2021). *Voicing the unvoiced: Potential of offline MOOCs e-content to cater for non-digitally-fluent students*. Proccedings of the First Workshop on Technology Enhanced Learning Environments for Blended Education (teleXbe2021), Foggia, Italy.https://ceur-ws.org/Vol-2817/paper31.pdf

Ghobrini, R. E. A., Benaicha, F., & Sarnou, H. (2024). Strategies for Tomorrow: Unraveling Algerian university instructors' e-practices in the face of pandemic challenges. *Online Science Education Journal, 9*(1), 1-15. https://dergipark.org.tr/en/download/article-file/3613505

Ghobrini, R. E. A. (2020). Synergizing Facebook and YouTube for e-Teaching Grammar during COVID-19 Pandemic. *International Journal of Educational Sciences*, 3(4), 33. DOI: 10.26697/ijes.2020.4.8

Ghobrini, R. E. A., Benzert, F. Z., & Sarnou, H. (2022). Creative e-pedagogy in massive grammar e-tutoring via the simultaneous use of social media platforms. In Radj, G. R. (Ed.), *Creativity as progressive pedagogy: Examinations into culture, performance, and challenges* (pp. 64–86). IGI Global., DOI: 10.4018/978-1-7998-8287-9.ch004

Ghobrini, R. E., Sarnou, H., & Benaicha, F. (2023). Upgrading Algerian secondary teachers' e-savoir-faire post COVID-19 via MOOC-based continuous professional development. In Boadu, G., Odhiambo, G., & Marandi, P. (Eds.), *Practices and perspectives of teaching and teacher education in Africa* (pp. 1–254). IGI Global., DOI: 10.4018/978-1-6684-7722-9.ch011

Ghorbani, M. R. (2017). The synergistic effect of funny pictures and etymological elaboration on promoting EFL students' idiom retention and recall. *Journal of Language and Linguistic Studies*, 13(1), 146–155. https://files.eric.ed.gov/fulltext/EJ1140674.pdf

Ghounane, N. (2022). Learning in the Algerian context during the pandemic: Is it online or offline? *AWEJ*, 492-503. DOI: 10.24093/awej/covid2.33

Ghounane, N. (2020). Moodle or social networks: What alternative refuge is appropriate to Algerian EFL students to learn during COVID-19 pandemic. [AWEJ]. *Arab World English Journal*, 11(3), 21–41. DOI: 10.24093/awej/vol11no3.2

Ghounane, N. (2021). Facebook as a learning platform in Algeria during the COVID-19 pandemic. *Global Journal of Foreign Language Teaching.*, 11(2), 80–93. DOI: 10.18844/gjflt.v11i2.5555

Gick, M. L., & Holyoak, K. J. (1980). Analogical problem solving. *Cognitive Psychology*, 12(3), 306–355. DOI: 10.1016/0010-0285(80)90013-4

Gick, M. L., & Holyoak, K. J. (1983). Schema induction and analogical transfer. *Cognitive Psychology*, 15(1), 1–38. DOI: 10.1016/0010-0285(83)90002-6

Gjerde, V., Paulsen, V. H., Holst, B., & Kolstø, S. D. (2022). Problem solving in basic physics: Effective self-explanations based on four elements with support from retrieval practice. *Physical Review. Physics Education Research*, 18(1), 010136. Advance online publication. DOI: 10.1103/PhysRevPhysEducRes.18.010136

Glazier, R. (2016). Building rapport to improve retention and success in online classes. *Journal of Political Science Education*, 12(4), 437–456. DOI: 10.1080/15512169.2016.1155994

Golaghaei, N., & Kakolian, S. (2015). The effect of visual and etymological treatments on learning decomposable idioms among EFL students. *International Journal of Applied Linguistics and English Literature*, 4(5), 72–81. DOI: 10.7575/aiac.ijalel.v.4n.5p.72

Golke, S., Steininger, T., & Wittwer, J. (2022). What makes students overestimate their text comprehension? The impact of student characteristics on judgment bias. *Educational Psychology Review*, 34(4), 2405–2450. DOI: 10.1007/s10648-022-09687-0

Gómez-García, G., Ramos-Navas-Parejo, M., de la Cruz-Campos, J. C., & Rodríguez-Jiménez, C. (2022). Impact of COVID-19 on university students: An analysis of its influence on psychological and academic factors. *International Journal of Environmental Research and Public Health*, 19(16), 10433. DOI: 10.3390/ijerph191610433 PMID: 36012067

González, G., Azucena, M., Mandeville, C., Edwards, F., & Rice, P. (2024). Innovating interdisciplinarity in higher education: Exploring the impact of a grassroots community of practice. *Teaching & Learning Inquiry*, 12, 1–17. DOI: 10.20343/teachlearninqu.12.11

Gooch, D., & Watts, L. (2015). The impact of social presence on feelings of closeness in personal relationships. *Interacting with Computers*, 27(6), 661–674. DOI: 10.1093/iwc/iwu020

Goodyear, V. A., Casey, A., & Kirk, D. (2014). Tweet me, message me, like me: Using social media to facilitate pedagogical change within an emerging community of practice. *Sport Education and Society*, 19(7), 927–943. DOI: 10.1080/13573322.2013.858624

Gopinathan, S., Kaur, A. H., Veeraya, S., & Raman, M. (2022). The role of digital collaboration in student engagement towards enhancing student participation during COVID-19. *Sustainability (Basel)*, 14(11), 6844. DOI: 10.3390/su14116844

Graham, C. R., Manheim, J. B., & McLaughlin, M. W. (2001). Teachers' professional development in a blended learning environment. *Journal of Technology and Teacher Education*, 9(1), 49–65.

Gray, J. A., & DiLoreto, M. (2016). The effects of student engagement, Student satisfaction, and perceived learning in online learning environments. *The International Journal of Educational Leadership Preparation*, 11(1), 98–119. https://files.eric.ed.gov/fulltext/EJ1103654.pdf

Grise-Owens, E., Owens, L. W., & Miller, J. J. (2016). Conceptualizing the scholarship of teaching and learning for social work education. *Journal of Social Work Education*, 52(1), 6–17. DOI: 10.1080/10437797.2016.1112628

Guessabi, F. (2021). Flipped classrooms in higher education in Algeria during period of COVID-19: Challenges and difficulties. *International Journal of Linguistics. Literature and Translation*, 4(2), 196–202. DOI: 10.32996/ijllt.2021.4.2.23

Guppy, N., Verpoorten, D., Boud, D., Lin, L., Tai, J., & Bartolic, S. (2022). The post-COVID-19 future of digital learning in higher education: Views from educators, students, and other professionals in six countries. *British Journal of Educational Technology*, 53(6), 1750–1765. DOI: 10.1111/bjet.13212

Gupta, N., & Irwin, J. (2016). In-class distractions: The role of Facebook and the primary learning task. *Computers in Human Behavior*, 55, 1165–1178. DOI: 10.1016/j.chb.2014.10.022

Guskey, T. R. (2002). Professional Development and Teacher Change. *Teachers and Teaching*, 8(3), 381–391. DOI: 10.1080/135406002100000512

Haddad, M. (2020). State of art of the distancial education at the University of Biskra during the COVID-19 : Challenges and prospects? *Elacadimia de Recherche En Sciences Sociales, 1*(2), 561–583. https://asjp.cerist.dz/en/article/122288

Halpern, D. F., Hansen, C., & Riefer, D. (1990). Analogies as an aid to understanding and memory. *Journal of Educational Psychology*, 82(2), 298–305. DOI: 10.1037/0022-0663.82.2.298

Hamari, J., Koivisto, J., & Sarsa, H. (2014, January 6-9, 2014). *Does gamification work?: A literature review of empirical studies on gamification*. Proceedings of the 47th Hawaii International Conference on System Sciences, (pp. 3025-3034), Hawaii, USA. https://creativegames.org.uk/modules/Gamification/Hamari_etal_Does_gamification_work-2014.pdf

Hamid, F. (2024). Effect of massive online courses on improving nurses' performance regarding infection prevention measures. *Zagazig Nursing Journal*, 20(1), 40–60. DOI: 10.21608/znj.2024.335085

Han, S. (2022). Flipped classroom: Challenges and benefits of using social media in English language teaching and learning. *Frontiers in Psychology*, 13, 996294. Advance online publication. DOI: 10.3389/fpsyg.2022.996294 PMID: 36211927

Harland, T. (2003). Vygotsky's zone of proximal development and problem-based learning: Linking a theoretical concept with practice through action research. *Teaching in Higher Education*, 8(2), 263–272. DOI: 10.1080/1356251032000052483

Harvey, M., & Jones, S. (2021). Enabling leadership capacity for higher education scholarship in learning and teaching (SoTL) through action research. *Educational Action Research*, 29(2), 173–190. DOI: 10.1080/09650792.2020.1803941

Hassan, L. (2024). Gamification. A conceptual critique to move forwards. *Gamevironments*, (20), 88–113.

Hathaway, T. (2018). Negotiating transitions in academic identity: Teacher or researcher? In Hosein, A., Rao, N., Yeh, C. S.-H., & Kinchin, I. M. (Eds.), *Academics' international teaching journeys: Personal narratives of transitions in higher education* (pp. 93–108). Bloomsbury Academic.

Hattie, J., & Timperley, H. (2007). The Power of Feedback. *Review of Educational Research*, 77(1), 81–112. DOI: 10.3102/003465430298487

Hawkins, J. E., Chiu, P., Mumba, M. N., Gray, S. E., & Hawkins, R. J. (2024). Nurses' Knowledge and Attitudes Regarding the Sustainable Development Goals: A Global Study. *The American Journal of Nursing*, 124(7), 18–27. DOI: 10.1097/01.NAJ.0001025184.93381.68 PMID: 38837235

Hayes, D. A., & Henk, W. A. (1986). Understanding and remembering complex prose augmented by analogic and pictorial illustration. *Journal of Reading Behavior*, 18(1), 63–78. DOI: 10.1080/10862968609547556

Head, M. H., & Readence, J. E. (1986). Anticipation guides: Meaning through prediction. In Dishner, E. R., Bean, T. W., Readence, J. E., & Moore, D. W. (Eds.), *Reading in the content areas* (2nd ed., pp. 229–234). Kendall/Hunt.

Healey, M., Flint, A., & Harrington, K. (2016). Students as partners: Reflections on a conceptual model. *Teaching & Learning Inquiry*, 4(2), 1–13. DOI: 10.20343/teachlearninqu.4.2.3

Healey, M., Matthews, K. E., & Cook-Sather, A. (2019). Writing scholarship of teaching and learning articles for peer-reviewed journals. *Teaching & Learning Inquiry*, 7(2), 28–50. DOI: 10.20343/teachlearninqu.7.2.3

Heitink, M., Voogt, J., Verplanken, L., van Braak, J., & Fisser, P. (2016). Teachers' professional reasoning about their pedagogical use of technology. *Computers & Education*, 101, 70–83. DOI: 10.1016/j.compedu.2016.05.009

Henrikson, R. (2020). Using online lectures to promote engagement: Recognizing the self-directed learner as critical for practical inquiry. *Journal of Open, Flexible &. Distance Learning : for Educators, Trainers, and Leaders*, 24(1), 17–32.

Hernández-Soto, R., Gutiérrez-Ortega, M., & Rubia-Avi, B. (2021). Key factors in knowledge sharing behavior in virtual communities of practice: A systematic review. *Education in the Knowledge Society*, 22, 1–14. DOI: 10.14201/eks.22715

Hillman, D., Willis, D. J., & Gunawardena, C. (1994). Learner-interface interaction in distance education: An extension of contemporary models and strategies for practitioners. *American Journal of Distance Education*, 8(2), 30–42. DOI: 10.1080/08923649409526853

Holmes, W., Bialik, M., & Fadel, C. (2019). *Artificial intelligence in education promises and implications for teaching and learning*. Center for Curriculum Redesign.

Holyoak, K. J., Ichien, N., & Lu, H. (2024). Analogy and the generation of ideas. *Creativity Research Journal*, 36(3), 1–12. DOI: 10.1080/10400419.2023.2232673

Holyoak, K. J., & Koh, K. (1987). Surface and structural similarity in analogical transfer. *Memory & Cognition*, 15(4), 332–340. DOI: 10.3758/BF03197035 PMID: 3670053

Hong, X., Liu, Q., & Zhang, M. (2021). Dual stressors and female pre-school teachers' job satisfaction during the COVID-19: The mediation of work-family conflict. *Frontiers in Psychology*, 12, 691498. DOI: 10.3389/fpsyg.2021.691498 PMID: 34168602

Horta Reis Da Silva, T. (2022). Falls - prevention, assessment and management. In Curr, S., & Fordham-Clarke, C. (Eds.), *Clinical Skills at Glance* (pp. 130–131). Wiley. [56]

Howard, S., & McKeown, J. (2011) Online practice & offline roles: A cultural view of teachers' low engagement in online communities. American Educational Research Association. https://hdl.handle.net/10779/uow.27697410.v1

Howard, B., Ilyashenko, N., & Jacobs, L. (2023). Cross-cultural collaboration through virtual teaming in higher education. *Perspectives in Education*, 41(1), 74–87. DOI: 10.38140/pie.v41i1.6319

How, Z. J. (2020). A systematic review of scholarship of teaching and learning research in higher education institutes from 2014–2019. In *Transforming teaching and learning in higher education: A chronicle of research and development in a Singaporean Context* (pp. 11–43). Springer Singapore., DOI: 10.1007/978-981-15-4980-9_2

Hrastinski, S. (2008). Asynchronous and Synchronous E-Learning. *EDUCAUSE Quarterly*, 31(4), 51–55.

Huang, H., & Fang, Y. (2023). Stress and coping strategies of online nursing practicum courses for Taiwanese nursing students during the covid-19 pandemic: A qualitative study. *Health Care*, 11(14), 2053. DOI: 10.3390/healthcare11142053 PMID: 37510494

Hubball, H., & Clarke, A. (2010). Diverse methodological approaches and considerations for SoTL in higher education. *The Canadian Journal for the Scholarship of Teaching and Learning*, 1(1), 2. DOI: 10.5206/cjsotl-rcacea.2010.1.2

Huber, M. T., & Hutchings, P. (2005). *The advancement of learning: Building the teaching commons*. Jossey-Bass.

Hueske, A., Pontoppidan, C., & Iosif-Lazar, L. (2021). Sustainable development in higher education in Nordic countries: Exploring e-learning mechanisms and SDG coverage in MOOCS. *International Journal of Sustainability in Higher Education*, 23(1), 196–211. DOI: 10.1108/IJSHE-07-2020-0276

Hutchings, P., Huber, M. T., & Ciccone, A. (2011). *Scholarship of teaching and learning re-considered: Institutional integration and impact*. Jossey-Bass.

Hutchings, P., Huber, M. T., & Ciccone, A. (2011). *The scholarship of teaching and learning reconsidered: Institutional integration and impact*. Jossey-Bass/Wiley.

Hwang, G. J., Xie, H., Wah, B. W., & Gašević, D. (2020). Intelligence in education. *Journal of Educational Technology & Society*, 23(4), 1–5.

Hwang, G., Lai, C., & Wang, S. (2015). Seamless flipped learning: A mobile technology-enhanced flipped classroom with effective learning strategies. *Journal of Computers in Education*, 2(4), 449–473. DOI: 10.1007/s40692-015-0043-0

Idroes, G. M., Noviandy, T. R., Maulana, A., Irvanizam, I., Jalil, Z., Lensoni, L., Lala, A., Abas, A. H., Tallei, T. E., & Idroes, R. (2023). Student perspectives on the role of artificial intelligence in education: A survey-based analysis. *Journal of Educational Management and Learning*, 1(1), 8–15. DOI: 10.60084/jeml.v1i1.58

Ilic, M., Petrović, J., & Stanković, M. (2024). Predicting student performance in a programming tutoring system using AI and filtering techniques. *Educational Data Mining Journal*, 10(1), 45–60.

İnangil, D., Dinçer, B., & Kabuk, A. (2022). Effectiveness of the use of animation and gamification in online distance education during pandemic. *Computers, Informatics, Nursing*, 40(5), 335–340. DOI: 10.1097/CIN.0000000000000902 PMID: 35266898

Ipperciel, D., Thibaudeau, P., & Kalive, V. (2023). AI in the classroom: An evaluation and design framework for educational chatbots. In T. Bastiaens (Ed.), *Proceedings of edMedia + innovate learning* (pp. 924-929). Vienna, Austria: Association for the Advancement of Computing in Education (AACE).

Isangula, K., Pallangyo, E., & Ndirangu-Mugo, E. (2023). Improving nursing education curriculum as a tool for strengthening the nurse–client relationships in maternal and child healthcare: Insights from a human-centered design study in rural Tanzania. *Frontiers in Public Health*, 11, 1072721. Advance online publication. DOI: 10.3389/fpubh.2023.1072721 PMID: 36817890

Jaber, L., Stirbys, C., & Saint-Cyr, C. (2024). Decolonizing the higher education curriculum: An evaluation of incorporating indigenous ways of knowing and pedagogy. *The Canadian Journal for the Scholarship of Teaching and Learning*, 15(1), 6. Advance online publication. DOI: 10.5206/cjsotlrcacea.2024.1.14796

Jan, N. (2023). A literature review of simulation-based training for nurses in India. *International Journal of Advance Research in Nursing*, 6(2), 46–48. DOI: 10.33545/nursing.2023.v6.i2.A.340

Jeon, H. (2024). The impact of virtual simulation in capstone design: Enhancing communication, critical thinking, and team efficacy. *Asia-Pacific Journal of Convergent Research Interchange*, 10(2), 709–719. DOI: 10.47116/apjcri.2024.02.54

Ji, Y., Lee, H., Lee, T., Choi, M., Lee, H., Kim, S., Do, H. K., Kim, S., Chu, S. H., Park, J., Kim, Y. M., & Park, T. (2021). Developing an integrated curriculum for patient safety in an undergraduate nursing program: A case study. *BMC Nursing*, 20(1), 172. Advance online publication. DOI: 10.1186/s12912-021-00694-0 PMID: 34535121

Johnson, C., Hill, L., Lock, J., Altowairiki, N., Ostrowski, C., dos Santos, L. da R., & Liu, Y. (2017). Using design-based research to develop meaningful online discussions in undergraduate field experience courses. *International Review of Research in Open and Distance Learning*, 18(6). Advance online publication. DOI: 10.19173/irrodl.v18i6.2901

Kalenzaga, S., Sperduti, M., Anssens, A., Martinelli, P., Devauchelle, A., Gallarda, T., Delhommeau, M., Lion, S., Amado, I., Krebs, M., Oppenheim, C., & Piolino, P. (2015). Episodic memory and self-reference via semantic autobiographical memory: Insights from an fMRI study in younger and older adults. *Frontiers in Behavioral Neuroscience*, 8. Advance online publication. DOI: 10.3389/fnbeh.2014.00449 PMID: 25628546

Kamler, B., & Thomson, P. (2014). *Helping doctoral students write: Pedagogies for supervision* (2nd ed.). Taylor & Francis Group., DOI: 10.4324/9781315813639

Kamya, M., & Otim, S. (2019). Integration of technology-enabled learning at higher education in developing countries: A case of Uganda Management Institute (UMI) [Paper presentation]. Pan-Commonwealth Forum, Scotland.

Kanchon, M. K. H., Lee, Y., & Choi, J. (2024). Enhancing personalized learning: AI-driven identification of learning styles and content modification strategies. *Journal of Learning Analytics*, 10(2), 35–56.

Kang, Y., Yang, I., Lee, E., & Bang, C. (2022). Development of international nursing standard–based curriculum for north Korean nurses. *International Nursing Review*, 69(4), 503–513. DOI: 10.1111/inr.12761 PMID: 35775835

Kapp, K. M. (2012). *The gamification of learning and instruction: Game-based methods for improving performance*. Pfeiffer Publishing.

Kara, A., Ergulec, F., & Eren, E. (2024). The mediating role of self-regulated online learning behaviors: Exploring the impact of personality traits on student engagement. *Education and Information Technologies*, 29(17), 1–30. DOI: 10.1007/s10639-024-12755-3

Karpicke, J. D., & Smith, M. A. (2012). Separate mnemonic effects of retrieval practice and elaborative encoding. *Journal of Memory and Language*, 67(1), 17–29. DOI: 10.1016/j.jml.2012.02.004

Keefer, L. A., & Landau, M. J. (2016). Metaphor and analogy in everyday problem solving. *Wiley Interdisciplinary Reviews: Cognitive Science*, 7(6), 394–405. DOI: 10.1002/wcs.1407 PMID: 27582354

Kellam, H., Cook, C., Smith, D. L., & Haight, P. (2023). The virtual community of practice facilitation model: A conceptual framework for healthcare professional education. *International Journal of Technology and Human Interaction*, 19(1), 1–14. DOI: 10.4018/IJTHI.328578

Kennedy, A. (2005). Models of continuing professional development: A framework for analysis. *Journal of In-service Education*, 31(2), 235–250. DOI: 10.1080/13674580500200277

Kenney, J., Kumar, S., & Hart, M. (2013). More than a social network: Facebook as a catalyst for an online educational community of practice. *International Journal of Social Media and Interactive Learning Environments*, 1(4), 355–369. DOI: 10.1504/IJSMILE.2013.057467

Kenny, L. A. K. Simon, K. Kiley-Brabeck, & R. M. Lerner (Eds.). *Learning to serve: Promoting civil society through service learning* (pp. 15-29), Springer.

Kenny, M. E., & Gallagher, L. A. (2002). Service-learning: A history of systems. In M. E. DOI: 10.1007/978-1-4615-0885-4_2

Kerman, N. T., Banihashem, S. K., Karami, M., Er, E., Van Ginkel, S., & Noroozi, O. (2024). Online peer feedback in higher education: A synthesis of the literature. *Education and Information Technologies*, 29(1), 763–813. DOI: 10.1007/s10639-023-12273-8

Kern, B., Mettetal, G., Dixson, M., & Morgan, R. K. (2015). The role of SoTL in the academy: Upon the 25th anniversary of Boyer's scholarship reconsidered. *The Journal of Scholarship of Teaching and Learning*, 15(3), 1–14. DOI: 10.14434/josotl.v15i3.13623

Kerrigan, J., & Andres, D. (2022). Technology-enhanced communities of practice in an asynchronous graduate course. *Journal of Educational Technology Systems*, 50(4), 473–487. DOI: 10.1177/00472395221079288

Kesebir, S., & Oishi, S. (2010). A spontaneous self-reference effect in memory: Why some birthdays are harder to remember than others. *Psychological Science*, 21(10), 1525–1531. DOI: 10.1177/0956797610383436 PMID: 20855903

Khoo, S. (2010). Academic mobbing: Hidden health hazard at workplace. *Malaysian Family Physician : the Official Journal of the Academy of Family Physicians of Malaysia*, 5(2), 61–67. PMID: 25606190

Khosa, N. G. (2022). A review of literature on the effective pedagogy strategies for online teaching and learning in higher education institutions: Lessons from the COVID-19 pandemic. *European Journal of Education*, 5(1), 43–55. DOI: 10.26417/738tqq65

Khumalo, N. (2024). Online learning changed the learning motivation: Challenges of the higher education students. In *Accessibility of Digital Higher Education in the Global South* (pp. 20–38). IGI Global.

Kidron, A., & Kali, Y. (2023). Promoting interdisciplinary understanding in asynchronous online higher education courses: A learning communities approach. *Instructional Science*, 52(1), 139–169. DOI: 10.1007/s11251-023-09635-7

Kiener, M. (2009). Applying the scholarship of teaching and learning: Pursuing a deeper understanding of how students learn. *InSight a Journal of Scholarly Teaching*, 4, 21–27. DOI: 10.46504/05201002ki

Kim, D., Wortham, S., Borowiec, K., Yatsu, D. K., Ha, S., Carroll, S., Wang, L., & Kim, J. (2021). Formative education online: Teaching the whole person during the global COVID-19 pandemic. *AERA Open*, 7(233285842110152), 1–12. DOI: 10.1177/23328584211015229

Kim-Godwin, Y., Matthias, A., & Dieckman, L. (2022). Graduate nurse educator students' perceptions of the use of narrative pedagogy in online learning: A pilot study. *Nursing Education Perspectives*, 44(4), 241–243. DOI: 10.1097/01.NEP.0000000000001053 PMID: 36731071

Kim, S. (2024). The effect of metacognition and self-directed learning readiness on learning performance of nursing students in online practice classes during the covid-19 pandemic period. *Nursing Open*, 11(1), e2093. Advance online publication. DOI: 10.1002/nop2.2093 PMID: 38268284

King, V. J., Stevens, A., Nussbaumer-Streit, B., Kamel, C., & Garritty, C. (2022). Paper 2: Performing rapid reviews. *Systematic Reviews*, 11(1), 151. Advance online publication. DOI: 10.1186/s13643-022-02011-5 PMID: 35906677

Kintsch, W. (1988). The role of knowledge in discourse comprehension: A construction-integration model. *Psychological Review*, 95(2), 163–182. DOI: 10.1037/0033-295X.95.2.163 PMID: 3375398

Klein, S. B. (2012). Self, memory, and the self-reference effect: An examination of conceptual and methodological issues. *Personality and Social Psychology Review*, 16(3), 283–300. DOI: 10.1177/1088868311434214 PMID: 22291045

Klein, S. B., Loftus, J., & Burton, H. A. (1989). Two self-reference effects: The importance of distinguishing between self-descriptiveness judgments and autobiographical retrieval in self-referent encoding. *Journal of Personality and Social Psychology*, 56(6), 853–865. DOI: 10.1037/0022-3514.56.6.853

Knickerbocker, J., & Tawfik, A. A. (2024). Perceptions of psychological safety in healthcare professionals' online learner-learner interactions. 1-27. *Journal of Computing in Higher Education*. Advance online publication. DOI: 10.1007/s12528-024-09401-9

Koehler, M. J., Mishra, P., & Cain, W. (2013). What is technological pedagogical content knowledge (TPACK)? *Journal of Education*, 193(3), 13–19. DOI: 10.1177/002205741319300303

Koessmeier, C., & Büttner, O. (2021). *Why are we distracted by social media? Distraction situations and strategies, reasons for distraction, and individual differences*. National Library of Medicine., DOI: 10.3389/fpsyg.2021.711416

Kolomitro, K., Laverty, C., & Stockley, D. (2017). Sparking SoTL: Triggers and stories from one institution. *The Canadian Journal for the Scholarship of Teaching and Learning*, 9(1). Advance online publication. DOI: 10.5206/cjsotl-rcacea.2018.1.10

Kosteniuk, J., Stewart, N., Wilson, E., Penz, K., Martin-Misener, R., Morgan, D., Karunanayake, C., & MacLeod, M. (2019). Communication tools and sources of education and information: A national survey of rural and remote nurses. *Journal of the Medical Library Association: JMLA*, 107(4). Advance online publication. DOI: 10.5195/jmla.2019.632 PMID: 31607811

Kreber, C. (2006). Developing the scholarship of teaching through transformative learning. *The Journal of Scholarship of Teaching and Learning*, 6(1), 88–109.

Kruger, J., & Dunning, D. (1999). Unskilled and unaware of it: How difficulties in recognizing one's own incompetence lead to inflated self-assessments. *Journal of Personality and Social Psychology*, 77(6), 1121–1134. DOI: 10.1037/0022-3514.77.6.1121 PMID: 10626367

Kucey, S., & Parsons, J. (2012). Linking past and present: John Dewey and assessment for learning. *Journal of Teaching and Learning*, 8(1), 107–116. DOI: 10.22329/jtl.v8i1.3077

Kuh, G. D. (2009). What student affairs professionals need to know about student engagement. *Journal of College Student Development*, 50(6), 683–706. DOI: 10.1353/csd.0.0099

Kumar, A. A. (2021). Semantic memory: A review of methods, models, and current challenges. *Psychonomic Bulletin & Review*, 28(1), 40–80. DOI: 10.3758/s13423-020-01792-x PMID: 32885404

Kurtz, G., Tsimerman, A., & Steiner-Lavi, O. (2014). The flipped-classroom approach: The answer to future learning? *European Journal of Open, Distance and E-Learning, 17*(2), 172–182. Retrieved from https://www.ceeol.com/search/article-detail?id=848825

Kuzminykh, I., Ghita, B., & Xiao, H. (2021, August). The relationship between student engagement and academic performance in online education. In *2021 5th International Conference on E-Society, E-Education and E-Technology* (pp. 97-101). DOI: 10.1145/3485768.3485796

Kwon, K., Park, S. J., Shin, S., & Chang, C. Y. (2019). Effects of different types of instructor comments in online discussions. *Distance Education*, 40(2), 226–242. DOI: 10.1080/01587919.2019.1602469

Lancaster, K., Rhodes, T., & Rosengarten, M. (2020). Making evidence and policy in public health emergencies: Lessons from COVID-19 for adaptive evidence-making and intervention. *Evidence & Policy*, 16(3), 477–490. DOI: 10.1332/174426420X15913559981103

Landrum, R. E., Brakke, K., & McCarthy, M. A. (2019). The pedagogical power of storytelling. *Scholarship of Teaching and Learning in Psychology*, 5(3), 247–253. DOI: 10.1037/stl0000152

Langan, L., Halligan, P., Frazer, K., Darley, A., Goodman, L., & Redmond, C. (2022). Inclusive pedagogy in online simulation-based learning in undergraduate nursing education: A scoping review protocol. *HRB Open Research*, 5(39), 538–554. DOI: 10.12688/hrbopenres.13557.2 PMID: 37224309

Lang, J. M. (2016). *Small teaching: Everyday lessons from the science of learning*. Jossey-Bass.

Latif, G., Alghazo, R., & Pilotti, M. A. E. (2021). Identifying "at-risk" students: An AI-based prediction approach. *International Journal of Computing and Digital Systems*, 10(4), 231–240.

Lave, J., & Wenger, E. (1991). *Situated learning: Legitimate peripheral participation*. Cambridge University Press., DOI: 10.1017/CBO9780511815355

Lawrence, R., & Chai, X. J. (2021). Self-referential encoding of source information in recollection memory. *PLoS One*, 16(4), e0248044. DOI: 10.1371/journal.pone.0248044 PMID: 33857141

LearnDash Collaborator. (2020). *How is AI being used in e-learning in 2020?*https://www.learndash.com/how-is-ai-being-used-in-e-learning-in-2020/

Lee, C., Nguyen, H., & Seel, N. M. (Eds.). (2021). *Equity and Quality in Digital Learning: Realizing the Promise in Remote and Hybrid Environments*. Routledge.

Lee, J. S., Srinivasan, S., Trail, T., Lewis, D., & Lopez, S. (2021). Examining the impact of professional development on early childhood educators' self-efficacy and practices. *Journal of Research in Childhood Education*, 35(1), 124–139.

Lee, J., Bae, S. J., & Lee, K. M. (2021). The role of online platforms in professional development for teachers: A systematic review. *Computers & Education*, 166, 104181.

Lei, S., & Yin, D. (2020). Curricular and departmental characteristics influencing satisfaction, retention and success of undergraduate students: A review of literature. *College Student Journal*, 54(3), 357–363.

Levenberg, A. (2023). Lecturer responsiveness in online learning – availability, accessibility, and flexibility: A matter of kindness. *Journal of Further and Higher Education*, 47(6), 740–753. DOI: 10.1080/0309877X.2023.2226073

Lew, Z., Walther, J. B., Pang, A., & Shin, W. (2018). Interactivity in online chat: Conversational contingency and response latency in computer-mediated communication. *Journal of Computer-Mediated Communication*, 23(4), 201–221. DOI: 10.1093/jcmc/zmy009

Lhbibani, A., Daaif, J., Lotfi, S., Tridane, M., & Belaaouad, S. (2022). Effect of online training in the continuing education of nurses in hospitals in the casablanca-settat region. *The Open Nursing Journal*, 16(1), e187443462208100. Advance online publication. DOI: 10.2174/18744346-v16-e2208100

Liao, C., & Masters, R. S. (2001). Analogy learning: A means to implicit motor learning. *Journal of Sports Sciences*, 19(5), 307–319. DOI: 10.1080/02640410152006081 PMID: 11354610

Li, E., Xiao, F., Zou, T., & Guo, J. (2021). Positive emotion of self-referential contexts could facilitate adult's novel word learning: An fNIRS study. *Brain and Language*, 221, 104994. DOI: 10.1016/j.bandl.2021.104994 PMID: 34303109

Lin, L., & Atkinson, R. K. (2013). Enhancing learning from different visualizations by self-explanation prompts. *Journal of Educational Computing Research*, 49(1), 83–110. DOI: 10.2190/EC.49.1.d

Liston, D. D., & Rahimi, R. (2017a). Introduction: Unlocking SoTL's potential for transformative education. In Liston, D. D., & Rahimi, R. (Eds.), *Promoting social justice through the scholarship of teaching and learning* (pp. xi–xxx). Indiana University Press., DOI: 10.2307/j.ctt2005zc2.3

Liu, Z., Wen, J., Liu, Y., & Hu, C. (2024). The effectiveness of self: A meta-analysis of using self-referential encoding techniques in education. *The British Journal of Educational Psychology*, 94(1), 112–137. DOI: 10.1111/bjep.12636 PMID: 37722845

Li, Y., Li, X., Su, Y., Peng, Y., & Hu, H. (2020). Exploring the role of EFL learners' online self-regulation profiles in their social regulation of learning in wiki-supported collaborative reading activities. *Journal of Computers in Education*, 7(4), 575–595. DOI: 10.1007/s40692-020-00168-3

Long, T., Cummins, J., & Waugh, M. (2016). Use of the flipped classroom instructional model in higher education: Instructors' perspectives. *Journal of Computing in Higher Education*, 29(2), 179–200. DOI: 10.1007/s12528-016-9119-8

Lowenthal, P., West, R.E., Archambault, L., Borup, J., & Belt, E. S. (2021). Faculty perceptions of using synchronous video-based communication technology. *Online Learning, 25*(4), 74-103. Htttps:// DOI: 10.24059/olj.v25i4.2890

Lowenthal, P. R., & Dunlap, J. C. (2018). Investigating students' perceptions of instructional strategies to establish social presence. *Distance Education*, 39(3), 281–298. DOI: 10.1080/01587919.2018.1476844

Luo, N., Li, H., Zhao, L., Wu, Z., & Zhang, J. (2022). Promoting student engagement in online learning through harmonious classroom environment. *The Asia-Pacific Education Researcher*, 31(5), 541–551. DOI: 10.1007/s40299-021-00606-5

Lyman, F. (1981). The responsive classroom discussion: The inclusion of all students. In A. Anderson (Ed.), *Mainstreaming digest* (pp. 109-113), University of Maryland College of Education.

Ma'arif, M., Santoso, R., Arif, D. B., & Nuryana, Z. (2024). The battle of learning modes: Hybrid vs online learning in higher education. [EduLearn]. *Journal of Education and Learning*, 19(2), 963–970. DOI: 10.11591/edulearn.v19i2.20870

Macdonald, K. (2018). A review of the literature: The needs of nontraditional students in postsecondary education. *Strategic Enrollment Management Quarterly*, 5(4), 159–16. https://doi.org/gf6wh4. DOI: 10.1002/sem3.20115

Maguire, M., & Delahunt, B. (2017). Doing a thematic analysis: A practical, step-by-step guide for learning and teaching scholars. *All Ireland Journal of Teaching and Learning in Higher Education*, 3, 3351–3365.

Maimaiti, G., Jia, C., & Hew, K. F. (2021). Student disengagement in web-based videoconferencing supported online learning: An activity theory perspective. *Interactive Learning Environments*, 31(8), 4883–4902. DOI: 10.1080/10494820.2021.1984949

Makinde, S. O. (2023). Effects of a developed flipped classroom package on senior secondary school students' performance in mathematics in Lagos, Nigeria. *The Journal of Educational Research*, 13(2), 115–116. DOI: 10.51474/jer.v13i2.718

Malik, R. (2023). *Impact of technology-based education on student learning outcomes and engagement*. 10th International Conference on Computing for Sustainable Global Development (INDIACom), New Delhi, India. 784-788. https://ieeexplore.ieee.org/abstract/document/10112303

Malmberg, K. J., Raaijmakers, J. G. W., & Shiffrin, R. M. (2019). 50 years of research sparked by Atkinson and Shiffrin (1968). *Memory & Cognition*, 47(4), 561–574. DOI: 10.3758/s13421-019-00896-7 PMID: 30689198

Maloney, S., Axelsen, M., Stone, C., Galligan, L., Redmond, P., Brown, A., Turner, J., & Lawrence, J. (2023). Defining and exploring online engagement fatigue in a university context. *Computers and Education Open*, 4, 100139. DOI: 10.1016/j.caeo.2023.100139

Manarin, K., Adams, C., Fendler, R., Marsh, H., Pohl, E., Porath, S., & Thomas, A. (2021). Examining the focus of SoTL literature—Teaching and learning? *Teaching & Learning Inquiry*, 9(1), 349–364. DOI: 10.20343/teachlearninqu.9.1.23

Manokore, V., & McRae, D. (2021). Revolutionizing learning environments with guerrilla pedagogy in large classes. *Journal of Practical Nurse Education and Practice*, 1(1). Advance online publication. DOI: 10.29173/jpnep7

Marg, O., & Theiler, L. (2023). Effects of transdisciplinary research on scientific knowledge and reflexivity. *Research Evaluation*, 32(4), 635–647. DOI: 10.1093/reseval/rvad033

Markle, G. (2015). Factors influencing persistence among nontraditional university students. *Adult Education Quarterly*, 65(3), 267–285. https://doi.org/f7jfb7. DOI: 10.1177/0741713615583085

Marrone, R., Taddeo, V., & Hill, G. (2022). Creativity and artificial intelligence—A student perspective. *Journal of Intelligence*, 10(3), 65. DOI: 10.3390/jintelligence10030065 PMID: 36135606

Martin, F., Xie, K., & Bolliger, D. U. (2022). Engaging learners in the emergency transition to online learning during the COVID-19 pandemic. *Journal of Research on Technology in Education, 54*(sup1), S1–S13. https://doi.org/DOI: 10.1080/15391523.2021.1991703

Martinelli, S. M., Chen, F., Mcevoy, M. D., Zvara, D. A., & Schell, R. M. (2018). Utilization of the flipped classroom in anesthesiology graduate medical education: An initial survey of faculty beliefs and practices about active learning. *The Journal of Education in Perioperative Medicine : JEPM*, 20(1). https://pmc.ncbi.nlm.nih.gov/articles/PMC5991778/ PMID: 29928664

Mason, C., Castleman, T., & Parker, C. M. (2008). Socio-technical factors influencing channel use for knowledge-sharing in regional SME networks. *International Journal of Knowledge Management Studies*, 2(3), 303–319. DOI: 10.1504/IJKMS.2008.018794

Maurer, T. W. (2022). Leveraging SoTL to improve teaching and learning during the COVID-19 pandemic. *International Journal for the Scholarship of Teaching and Learning*, 16(1), 3. DOI: 10.20429/ijsotl.2022.160103

Maurer, T. W., Woolmer, C., Powell, N., Sisson, C., Snelling, C., Stalheim, O., & Turner, I. (2021). Sharing SoTL findings with students: An intentional knowledge mobilization strategy. *Teaching & Learning Inquiry*, 9(1), 333–348. Advance online publication. DOI: 10.20343/teachlearninqu.9.1.22

Maurer, T., Sturges, D., Shankar, P., Allen, D., & Akbarova, S. (2010). A faculty learning community on the scholarship of teaching & learning: A case study. *International Journal for the Scholarship of Teaching and Learning*, 4(2), 1–7. DOI: 10.20429/ijsotl.2010.040208

Mavri, A., Ioannou, A., & Loizides, F. (2023). A model for enhancing creativity, collaboration and pre-professional identities in technology-supported cross-organizational communities of practice. *Education and Information Technologies*, 29(11), 13325–13366. DOI: 10.1007/s10639-023-12295-2

Mayer, R. E. (2009). *Multimedia Learning* (2nd ed.). Cambridge University Press. DOI: 10.1017/CBO9780511811678

Mayer, R. E. (2020). Designing multimedia instruction in anatomy: An evidence-based approach. *Clinical Anatomy (New York, N.Y.)*, 33(1), 2–11. DOI: 10.1002/ca.23265 PMID: 30144175

Mayer, R. E. (2024). The past, present, and future of the cognitive theory of multimedia learning. *Educational Psychology Review*, 36(1), 8. Advance online publication. DOI: 10.1007/s10648-023-09842-1

McBrien, J. L., Jones, P., & Cheng, R. (2009). Virtual Spaces: Employing a Synchronous Online Classroom to Facilitate Student Engagement in Online Learning. *International Review of Research in Open and Distance Learning*, 10(3). Advance online publication. DOI: 10.19173/irrodl.v10i3.605

McCarthy, M. (2024). Building transdisciplinary SoTL: Creating a culture and language of listening and learning for understanding. *Transformative Dialogues: Teaching and Learning Journal, 17*(1), 101–113. DOI: 10.26209/td2024vol17iss11810

McClurg, C., MacMillan, M., & Chick, N. (2019). Visions of the possible: Engaging with librarians in SoTL. *Teaching & Learning Inquiry*, 7(2), 3–13. DOI: 10.20343/teachlearninqu.7.2.1

McDaniel, M. A. (2023). Combining retrieval practice with elaborative encoding: Complementary or redundant? *Educational Psychology Review*, 35(3), 75. Advance online publication. DOI: 10.1007/s10648-023-09784-8

McDaniel, M. A., & Donnelly, C. M. (1996). Learning with analogy and elaborative interrogation. *Journal of Educational Psychology*, 88(3), 508–519. DOI: 10.1037/0022-0663.88.3.508

McDonald, B. D.III, Hatcher, W., Bacot, H., Evans, M. D., McCandless, S. A., McDougle, L. M., Young, S. L., Elliott, I. C., Emas, R., Lu, E. Y., Abbott, M. E., Bearfield, D. A., Berry-James, R. M., Blessett, B., Borry, E. L., Diamond, J., Franklin, A. L., Gaynor, T. S., Gong, T., & Zhang, Y. (2024). The scholarship of teaching and learning in public administration: An agenda for future research. *Journal of Public Affairs Education*, 30(1), 11–27. DOI: 10.1080/15236803.2023.2294654

McGurty, R. E. (2022). *Student perception of social presence in an asynchronous online doctoral program.* [Doctoral dissertation, Johnson University].

McKinney, K. (2007). *Enhancing learning through the scholarship of teaching and learning: The challenges and joys of juggling*. Anker Publishing.

McKinney, K. (2012). Making a difference: Application of SoTL to enhance learning. *The Journal of Scholarship of Teaching and Learning*, 12(1), 1–7.

McNamara, D. S. (2004). SERT: Self-explanation reading training. *Discourse Processes*, 38(1), 1–30. DOI: 10.1207/s15326950dp3801_1

McSweeney, J., & Schnurr, M. (2023). Can SoTL generate high quality research while maintaining its commitment to inclusivity? *International Journal for the Scholarship of Teaching and Learning*, 17(1), 1–15. DOI: 10.20429/ijsotl.2023.17104

Means, B., Toyama, Y., Murphy, R., Bakia, M., & Jones, K. (2010). *Evaluation of Evidence-based practices in online learning: A meta-analysis and review of online learning studies*. U.S. Department of Education.

Mehdizadeh, M., Pourhaji, M., & Derakhshan, A. (2024). Evolution of communities of practice, realignment of possible selves, and repositionings in EFL teacher professional identity development: A longitudinal case study. *Language Learning Journal*, 52(3), 336–348. DOI: 10.1080/09571736.2022.2163685

Meijerman, I., Kirschner, F., & Prins, F. (2023). Experiences with supporting teachers with scholarship of teaching and learning at a research-intensive university: Lessons learned. *Teaching & Learning Inquiry*, 11. Advance online publication. DOI: 10.20343/teachlearninqu.11.27

Mellati, M., & Khademi, M. (2019). *Technology-based education*. Advanced Online Education and Training Technologies., DOI: 10.4018/978-1-5225-7010-3.ch003

Mera, Y., Rodriguez, G., & Marin-Garcia, E. (2022). Unraveling the benefits of experiencing errors during learning: Definition, modulating factors, and explanatory theories. *Psychonomic Bulletin & Review*, 29(3), 753–765. DOI: 10.3758/s13423-021-02022-8 PMID: 34820785

Merelo, J. J., Castillo, P. A., Mora, A. M., Barranco, F., Abbas, N., Guillén, A., & Tsivitanidou, O. (2024). Chatbots and messaging platforms in the classroom: An analysis from the teacher's perspective. *Education and Information Technologies*, 29(2), 1903–1938. DOI: 10.1007/s10639-023-11703-x PMID: 37361787

Merkley, D. J. (1997). Modified anticipation guide. *The Reading Teacher*, 50(4), 365–368.

Miller, G. A. (1994). The magical number seven, plus or minus two: Some limits on our capacity for processing information. *Psychological Review*, 101(2), 343–352. DOI: 10.1037/0033-295X.101.2.343 PMID: 8022966

Millet, A., Turcotte, N., & Yan, S. (2021). Retrieval practice and online learning. In Hoffman, J., & Blessinger, P. (Eds.), *International perspectives in online instruction: Innovations in higher education teaching and learning* (Vol. 40, pp. 95–112). Emerald Publishing Limited., DOI: 10.1108/S2055-364120210000040007

Mishra, P., & Koehler, M. J. (2006). Technological pedagogical content knowledge: A framework for teacher knowledge. *Teachers College Record*, 108(6), 1017–1054. DOI: 10.1111/j.1467-9620.2006.00684.x

Mishra, P., & Koehler, M. J. (2006). Technological pedagogical content knowledge: Learning to teach with technology. *Journal of Research on Technology in Education*, 38(4), 375–400.

Miyatsu, T., & McDaniel, M. A. (2019). Adding the keyword mnemonic to retrieval practice: A potent combination for foreign language vocabulary learning? *Memory & Cognition*, 47(7), 1328–1343. DOI: 10.3758/s13421-019-00936-2 PMID: 31077068

Molato, B., & Sehularo, L. (2022). Recommendations for online learning challenges in nursing education during the covid-19 pandemic. *Curationis*, 45(1). Advance online publication. DOI: 10.4102/curationis.v45i1.2360 PMID: 36331216

Moore, M. (1989). Three types of interaction. *American Journal of Distance Education*, 3(2), 1–7. DOI: 10.1080/08923648909526659

Moore, M. G. (1997). *Distance education: Theory and practice*. Wadsworth Publishing Company.

Moore, M. G., & Kearsley, G. (2011). *Distance Education: A Systems View of Online Learning* (3rd ed.). Wadsworth.

Moran, E., & Misra, D. (2018). Professional doctorates: A pathway to legitimacy for non-academic HE professionals? *London Review of Education*, 16(1), 75–89. DOI: 10.18546/LRE.16.1.08

Moran, M., Seaman, J., & Tinti, H. (2011). *Teaching, learning, and sharing: How today's higher education faculty use social media*. Pearson.

Morozevich, E. S., Korotkikh, V. S., & Kuznetsova, Y. (2022). The development of a model for a personalized learning path using machine learning methods. *Business Info*, 16(2), 54–65. DOI: 10.17323/2587-814X.2022.2.21.35

Morse, M. L. (2021). Increase engaged student learning using google docs as a discussion platform. *Teaching & Learning Inquiry*, 9(2), 1–18. DOI: 10.20343/teachlearninqu.9.2.20

Mortensen, C. J., & Nicholson, A. M. (2015). The flipped classroom stimulates greater learning and is a modern 21st century approach to teaching today's undergraduates. *Journal of Animal Science*, 93(7), 3722–3731. DOI: 10.2527/jas.2015-9087 PMID: 26440038

Müggenburg, H. (2021). Beyond the limits of memory? The reliability of retrospective data in travel research. *Transportation Research Part A, Policy and Practice*, 145, 302–318. DOI: 10.1016/j.tra.2021.01.010

Mukattil, N., & Pangandaman, H. (2024). Barriers and strategies in the implementation of virtual learning modalities amid covid-19 among students in nursing schools at Sulu province, Philippines. *Critical Medical and Surgical Nursing Journal*, 13(1), 20–25. DOI: 10.20473/cmsnj.v13i1.51366

Munastiwi, E., & Puryono, S. (2021). Unprepared management decreases education performance in kindergartens during COVID-19 pandemic. *Heliyon*, 7(5), e07138. Advance online publication. DOI: 10.1016/j.heliyon.2021.e07138 PMID: 34136697

Munna, A. S., & Kalam, M. A. (2021). Impact of active learning strategy on the student engagement. *GNOSI: An Interdisciplinary Journal of Human and Theory Praxis*, 4, 96–114.

Naseer, F., Khan, M. N., Tahir, M., Addas, A., & Aejaz, S. M. H. (2024). Integrating deep learning techniques for personalized learning pathways in higher education. *Heliyon*, 10(11), e32628. DOI: 10.1016/j.heliyon.2024.e32628 PMID: 38961899

Nasrollahian Mojarad, S., & Cruz, L., (2022). MegaSoTL: Supporting pedagogical research across multiple institutions. *To Improve the Academy: A Journal of Educational Development, 41*(1), 78–95. DOI: 10.3998/tia.470

National Center for Education Statistics. (1999). *Teacher quality: A report on the preparation and qualifications of public school teachers*. U.S. Department of Education.

Navarro, J. M., & McGrath, B. M. (2021). Strategies for effective online teaching and learning: Practices and techniques with a proven track of success in online education. In Ramlall, S., Cross, T., & Love, M. (Eds.), *Handbook of Research on Future of Work and Education: Implications for Curriculum Delivery and Work Design*., DOI: 10.4018/978-1-7998-8275-6.ch029

Nazeer, Y. N. (2024). Algorithmic conscience: An in-depth inquiry into ethical dilemmas in artificial intelligence. *International Journal of Research and Innovation in Social Science*, 8(5), 725–732. DOI: 10.47772/IJRISS.2024.805052

Nelson, D. L., Kitto, K., Galea, D., McEvoy, C. L., & Bruza, P. D. (2013). How activation, entanglement, and searching a semantic network contribute to event memory. *Memory & Cognition*, 41(6), 797–819. DOI: 10.3758/s13421-013-0312-y PMID: 23645391

Nelson, D. L., McEvoy, C. L., & Pointer, L. (2003). Spreading activation or spooky action at a distance? *Journal of Experimental Psychology. Learning, Memory, and Cognition*, 29(1), 42–52. DOI: 10.1037/0278-7393.29.1.42 PMID: 12549582

Newby, T. J., Ertmer, P. A., & Stepich, D. A. (1995). Instructional analogies and the learning of concepts. *Educational Technology Research and Development*, 43(1), 5–18. DOI: 10.1007/BF02300478

Ngan, M. D. H., Nguyen, T. H., Phan, T., & Rong, L. H., DO, Tran, V. P., & Dang, T. S. (2024). A technology-driven approach to fostering social and emotional skills in first-year students at the University of Danang - University of Technology and Education. In *9th International Conference on Applying New Technology in Green Buildings (ATiGB),Danang, Vietnam*, 224-228. https://doi.org/DOI: 10.1109/ATiGB63471.2024.10717832

Nguyen, V. T. T., & Chen, H. L. (2023). Examining impacts of information system success and perceived stress on students' self-regulated learning mediated by intrinsic motivation in online learning environments: Second-order structural equation modelling analyses. *Education and Information Technologies*, 28(10), 12945–12968. DOI: 10.1007/s10639-023-11685-w PMID: 37361765

Niebert, K., Marsch, S., & Treagust, D. F. (2012). Understanding needs embodiment: A theory-guided reanalysis of the role of metaphors and analogies in understanding science. *Science Education*, 96(5), 849–877. DOI: 10.1002/sce.21026

Nilson, L. B., & Goodson, L. A. (2021). *Online teaching at its best: Merging instructional design with teaching and learning research.* John Wiley & Sons.

Nisa, L. Z., Prameswari, T. N., & Alawiyah, Y. I. (2021). The effect of using small group discussions through zoom breakout room to increase the frequency of individual speaking participation in the speaking courses. *Journal of Digital Learning and Education*, 1(3), 18–26. DOI: 10.52562/jdle.v1i3.264

Novak, R. T., Bailey, E. G., Blinsky, B. D., Soffe, B. W., Patterson, D., Ockey, J., & Jensen, J. L. (2022). Verbalized studying and elaborative interrogation in the virtual classroom: Students with social anxiety prefer working alone, but working with a peer does not hurt their learning. *Journal of Microbiology & Biology Education*, 23(1), e00232–e21. DOI: 10.1128/jmbe.00232-21 PMID: 35496708

Novotny, B., Ko, K., & Garris, B. R. (2022). Lights, camera, action: A focus group study exploring university students' experiences of learning via zoom. *The Journal of Educators Online*, 19(1). Advance online publication. DOI: 10.9743/JEO.2022.19.1.2

Nurse-Clarke, N., & Sockol, L. (2022). An exploration of resiliency among nurse educators during the covid-19 pandemic. *Nursing Education Perspectives*, 43(5), 283–286. DOI: 10.1097/01.NEP.0000000000001014 PMID: 35947139

Nwosisi, C., Ferreira, A., Rosenberg, W., & Walsh, K. (2016). A study of the flipped classroom and its effectiveness in flipping thirty percent of the course content. *International Journal of Information and Education Technology (IJIET)*, 6(5), 348–351. DOI: 10.7763/IJIET.2016.V6.712

Octaberlina, L. R., & Muslimin, A. I. (2020). EFL students perspective towards online learning barriers and alternatives using Moodle/Google Classroom during COVID-19 pandemic. *International Journal of Higher Education*, 9(6), 1–9. DOI: 10.5430/ijhe.v9n6p1

Ogle, D. (1986). K-W-L: A teaching model that develops active reading of expository text. *The Reading Teacher*, 39(6), 564–570. DOI: 10.1598/RT.39.6.11

Omidvar, O., & Kislov, R. (2014). The evolution of the communities of practice approach: Toward knowledgeability in a landscape of practice—An interview with Etienne Wenger-Trayner. *Journal of Management Inquiry*, 23(3), 266–275. DOI: 10.1177/1056492613505908

Onesi-Ozigagun, O., Adeyemi, A., & Okeke, C. (2024). Revolutionizing education through AI: A comprehensive review of enhancing learning experiences. *Journal of Artificial Intelligence in Education*, 12(1), 23–45. DOI: 10.51594/ijarss.v6i4.1011

Online Education. (n.d.). *Artificial intelligence innovations in online learning*. https://www.onlineeducation.com/features/ai-in-distance-learning

Openo, J. (2024). The right relationship between teaching and educational technology: How Ursula Franklin's technology as practice can guide SoTL. *The Canadian Journal for the Scholarship of Teaching and Learning*, 15(1). Advance online publication. DOI: 10.5206/cjsotlrcacea.2024.1.15640

Orifamah, D. (2021). The implication of COVID-19 on educational disparity between the developed and the developing countries, urban and rural dwellers and, on ICT in Nigeria. *Journal of Education and Practice*. Advance online publication. DOI: 10.7176/JEP/12-30-06

Osingada, C., & Porta, C. (2020). Nursing and sustainable development goals (SDGS) in a covid-19 world: The state of the science and a call for nursing to lead. *Public Health Nursing (Boston, Mass.)*, 37(5), 799–805. DOI: 10.1111/phn.12776 PMID: 32716089

Ossiannilsson, E. (2023). Open educational resources (OER) and some of the United Nations Sustainable Development Goals. *International Journal of Information and Learning Technology*, 40(5), 548–561. DOI: 10.1108/IJILT-01-2023-0002

Ouzzani, M., Hammady, H., Fedorowicz, Z., & Elmagarmid, A. (2016). Rayyan—A web and mobile app for systematic reviews. *Systematic Reviews*, 5(1), 210. Advance online publication. DOI: 10.1186/s13643-016-0384-4 PMID: 27919275

Pacansky-Brock, M. (2014). Learning out loud: Increasing voluntary voice comments in online classes. In Lowenthal, P. R., York, C. S., & Richardson, J. C. (Eds.), *Online learning: Common misconceptions, benefits, and challenges* (pp. 99–114). Nova Science Publishers.

Padilla, B. (2023). Using the community of inquiry as a framework to promote online teaching and learning in advanced practice nursing education. *Journal of the American Association of Nurse Practitioners*, 35(9), 575–581. DOI: 10.1097/JXX.0000000000000909 PMID: 37410024

Page, M. J., McKenzie, J. E., Bossuyt, P. M., Boutron, I., Hoffmann, T. C., Mulrow, C. D., Shamseer, L., Tetzlaff, J. M., Akl, E. A., Brennan, S. E., Chou, R., Glanville, J., Grimshaw, J. M., Hróbjartsson, A., Lalu, M. M., Li, T., Loder, E. W., Mayo-Wilson, E., McDonald, S., & Moher, D. (2021). The PRISMA 2020 statement: An updated guideline for reporting systematic reviews. *BMJ (Clinical Research Ed.)*, (71), n71. Advance online publication. DOI: 10.1136/bmj.n71 PMID: 33782057

Palmerola, E. D. (2024). Clarification evaluation of e-learning implementation: A developmental research design. *American Journal of Education and Technology*, 3(2), 119–127. DOI: 10.54536/ajet.v3i2.2890

Pandya, S. P. (2023). College students with high abilities in liberal arts disciplines: Examining the effect of spirituality in bolstering self-regulated learning, affect balance, peer relationships, and well-being. *High Ability Studies*, •••, 1–27. DOI: 10.1080/13598139.2023.2278811

Pan, Y., Xu, Y., Wang, X., Zhang, C., Ling, H., & Lin, J. (2015). Integrating social networking support for dyadic knowledge exchange: A study in a virtual community of practice. *Information & Management*, 52(1), 61–70. DOI: 10.1016/j.im.2014.10.001

Parapadakis, D. (2020). Can artificial intelligence help predict a learner's needs? Lessons from predicting student satisfaction. *London Review of Education*, 18(2), 178–195. DOI: 10.14324/LRE.18.2.03

Paris, N. A., & Glynn, S. M. (2003). Elaborate analogies in science text: Tools for enhancing preservice teachers' knowledge and attitudes. *Contemporary Educational Psychology*, 29(3), 230–247. DOI: 10.1016/S0361-476X(03)00033-X

Pechenkina, E. (2020). Chasing impact: The tale of three SoTL studies. *Teaching & Learning Inquiry*, 8(1), 91–107. DOI: 10.20343/teachlearninqu.8.1.7

Pedro, F., Subosa, M., Rivas, A., & Valverde, P. (2019). *Artificial intelligence in education: Challenges and opportunities for sustainable development*. UNESCO Publishing.

Peeters, W., & Pretorius, M. (2020). Facebook or fail-book: Exploring "community" in a virtual community of practice. *ReCALL*, 32(3), 291–306. DOI: 10.1017/S0958344020000099

Penuel, W. R., Fishman, B. J., Cheng, B., & Sabelli, N. (2011). Organizing research and development at the intersection of learning, implementation, and design. *Educational Researcher*, 40(7), 331–337. Advance online publication. DOI: 10.3102/0013189X11421826

Phaire, C. B. (2022). In the zoom Where it happens: From overwhelmed to overcome, collegiate students' experiences during the COVID-19 pandemic. *the Clearing House/the Clearing House, 95*(5), 220–229. https://doi.org/DOI: 10.1080/00098655.2022.2105782

Pham, L. T. T., & Phan, A. N. Q. (2022). Whilst COVID-19: The educational migration to online platforms and lessons learned. *the Clearing House/the Clearing House, 95*(4), 159–165. https://doi.org/DOI: 10.108000098655.2022.2065230

Phipps, R., & Merrill, M. D. (2000). What makes learning technologies effective? *Journal of Interactive Learning Research*, 11(2), 117–144.

Piaget, J. (1936). *Origins of intelligence in the child*. Routledge & Kegan Paul.

Pierce, R., & Fox, J. (2012). Vodcasts and active-learning exercises in a "flipped classroom" model of a renal pharmacotherapy module. *American Journal of Pharmaceutical Education*, 76(10), 196. DOI: 10.5688/ajpe7610196 PMID: 23275661

Pierson, H. D. (1989). Using etymology in the classroom. *ELT Journal*, 43(1), 57–63. DOI: 10.1093/elt/43.1.57

Pintrich, P. R. (1999). The role of motivation in promoting and sustaining self-regulated learning. *International Journal of Educational Research*, 31(6), 459–470. DOI: 10.1016/S0883-0355(99)00015-4

Pi, Z., Zhang, Y., Shi, D., Guo, X., & Yang, J. (2022). Is self-explanation better than explaining to a fictitious student when learning from video lectures? *British Journal of Educational Technology*, 53(6), 2012–2028. DOI: 10.1111/bjet.13230

Plata, M. R. (2020). *Applying the universal design for learning in higher education; A guide for increased learning in the classroom.* [Thesis, University of Oklahoma, https://shareok.org/items/381c2efa-8538-4594-b7eb-ddb20a5fe824].

Pleschová, G., Roxå, T., Thomson, K. E., & Felten, P. (2021). Conversations that make meaningful change in teaching, teachers, and academic development. *The International Journal for Academic Development*, 26(3), 201–209. https://doi.org/https://doi.org/10.1080/1360144X.2021.1958446. DOI: 10.1080/1360144X.2021.1958446

Poole, G., & Chick, N. L. (2016). On the nature of expertise in SoTL. *Teaching & Learning Inquiry*, 4(2). Advance online publication. https://doi.org/https://doi.org/10.20343/teachlearninqu.4.2.1. DOI: 10.20343/teachlearninqu.4.2.1

Potter, M. K., & Wuetherick, B. (2015). Who is represented in the teaching commons?: SoTL through the lenses of the arts and humanities. *The Canadian Journal for the Scholarship of Teaching and Learning*, 6(2), 2. Advance online publication. DOI: 10.5206/cjsotl-rcacea.2015.2.2

Prosser, M. (2008). The scholarship of teaching and learning: What is it? A personal view. *International Journal for the Scholarship of Teaching and Learning*, 2(2). Advance online publication. DOI: 10.20429/ijsotl.2008.020202

Rabiman, R., Nurtanto, M., & Kholifah, N. (2020). Design and development e-learning system by learning management system in vocational education. *International Journal of Scientific & Technology Research*, 9, 1059–1063. https://files.eric.ed.gov/fulltext/ED605316.pdf

Rafidi, T. J., & Wagner, B. (2023). The impact of emotional scaffolding on online teaching and learning in Palestinian English language classrooms during COVID-19. *Innovation in Language Learning and Teaching*, 18(2), 155–168. DOI: 10.1080/17501229.2023.2245810

Rahmani, A. M., Groot, W., & Rahmani, H. (2024). Dropout in online higher education: A systematic literature review. *International Journal of Educational Technology in Higher Education*, 21(1), 19. DOI: 10.1186/s41239-024-00450-9

Rajabalee, B. Y., Santally, M. I., & Rennie, F. (2020). A study of the relationship between students' engagement and their academic performances in an eLearning environment. *E-Learning and Digital Media*, 17(1), 1–20. DOI: 10.1177/2042753019882567

Rao, K. (2021). Inclusive instructional design: Applying UDL to online learning. *The Journal of Applied Instructional Design*, 10(1), 1–10.

Rapanta, C., Botturi, L., Goodyear, P., Guàrdia, L., & Koole, M. (2021). Balancing technology, pedagogy and the new normal: Post-pandemic challenges for higher education. *Postdigital Science and Education*, 3(3), 715–742. DOI: 10.1007/s42438-021-00249-1

Rasheed, R., Kamsin, A., & Abdullah, N. (2020). Challenges in the online component of blended learning: A systematic review. *Computers & Education*, 144, 1–17. DOI: 10.1016/j.compedu.2019.103701

Rau, M. A., Aleven, V., & Rummel, N. (2014). Successful learning with multiple graphical representations and self-explanation prompts. *Journal of Educational Psychology*, 107(1), 30–46. DOI: 10.1037/a0037211

Recht, D. R., & Leslie, L. (1988). Effect of prior knowledge on good and poor readers' memory of text. *Journal of Educational Psychology*, 80(1), 16–20. DOI: 10.1037/0022-0663.80.1.16

Reeves, T. C. (2006). Design research from a technology perspective. In van den Akker, J., Gravemeijer, K., McKenney, S., & Nieveen, N. (Eds.), *Educational design research* (pp. 52–66). Routledge.

Reis da Silva, T. H (2024e). Oncology and Cancer Medicine: Understanding the complexities in Older Patients. *Biomed J Sci & Tech Res 55*(3)-2024. DOI: DOI: 10.26717/BJSTR.2024.55.008720

Reis da Silva, T. H. (2024a). Chapter 7 – Emotional Intelligence in Higher Education: Humanising Technology for Holistic Student Development. In Tikadar, S.; Liu, H.; Bhattacharya, P.; Bhattacharya, S. *Humanizing Technology With Emotional Intelligence*. Pp. 145-168. IGI Global. DOI: 10.4018/979-8-3693-7011-7.ch007

Reis da Silva, T. H. (2024b). The Value of Emotional Intelligence in Midwifery: Enhancing Care and Outcomes for Mothers and Infants through Sustainable Development Goals and Leadership. *Journal of Womens Healthcare & Midwifery Research, 3*(4), 1-6. SRC/JWHMR-133. Link: https://www.onlinescientificresearch.com/articles/the-value-of-emotional-intelligence-in-midwifery-enhancing-care-and-outcomes-for-mothers-and-infants-through-sustainable-developme.pdf

Reis da Silva, T. H. (2024c). Chapter 8 – Emotional Intelligence in Teaching Geriatric Nursing: Humanising Technology for Compassionate Care in Higher Education. In Tikadar, S.; Liu, H.; Bhattacharya, P.; Bhattacharya, S. *Humanizing Technology With Emotional Intelligence*. Pp. 145-168. IGI Global. DOI: 10.4018/979-8-3693-7011-7.ch008

Reis da Silva, T. H. (2024d). Chapter 12 – Emotional Intelligence in Integrative Medicine: Enhancing Patient-Centred Care Through Humanised Technology. In Tikadar, S.; Liu, H.; Bhattacharya, P.; Bhattacharya, S. *Humanizing Technology With Emotional Intelligence*. Pp. 145-168. IGI Global. DOI: 10.4018/979-8-3693-7011-7.ch012

Reis da Silva, T. H. (2024f). Chapter 11 - Integrating business essentials into Gerontological Nursing: Enhancing Care for Older Adults in Diverse Settings. In Sedky, A. *Resiliency Strategies for Long-Term Business Success*. Pp. 283-316. IGI Global. DOI: DOI: 10.4018/979-8-3693-9168-6.ch011

Reis da Silva, T. H. (2024g). Chapter 6 – Navigating Healthcare Complexity: Integrating Business Fundamentals into Nursing Leadership. In Sedky, A. *Resiliency Strategies for Long-Term Business Success*. Pp. 145-168. IGI Global. DOI: 10.4018/979-8-3693-9168-6.ch006

Reis da Silva, T. H. (2024i). The Evolution of Nursing for Older Adult: A Historical Perspective. *Associative J Health Sci*. 3(3). AJHS. 000561. 2024. DOI: . Link: https://crimsonpublishers.com/ajhs/pdf/AJHS.000561.pdfDOI: 10.31031/AJHS.2024.03.000561

Reis da Silva, , T. H. (2024q). Prevalence of elder abuse: A narrative review. *British Journal of Community Nursing*, 29(9), 442–446. DOI: 10.12968/bjcn.2024.0004 PMID: 39240800

Reis da Silva, T. (2024n). Advancing Gender Equity In Nursing Care For Older Adults: A Pathway To Achieving The United Nations Sustainable Development Goals. *J Comm Med and Pub Health Rep*, 5(12). Advance online publication. DOI: 10.38207/JCMPHR/2024/JUL051201105

Reis da Silva, T. (2024o). Gender Equity In Healthcare: Integrating Emotional Intelligence To Achieve The United Nations Sustainable Development Goals. *J Comm Med and Pub Health Rep*, 5(12). Advance online publication. DOI: 10.38207/JCMPHR/2024/JUL051202106

Reis da Silva, T. H. (2023a). Falls assessment and prevention in the nursing home and community. *British Journal of Community Nursing*, 28(2), 68–72. DOI: 10.12968/bjcn.2023.28.2.68 PMID: 36735363

Reis da Silva, T. H. (2023b). Ageing in place: Ageing at home and in the community. *British Journal of Community Nursing*, 28(5), 213–214. DOI: 10.12968/bjcn.2023.28.5.213 PMID: 37130715

Reis da Silva, T. H. (2024h). Chronic kidney disease in older adults: Nursing implications for community nurses. *Journal of Kidney Care*, 9(4), 174–179. DOI: 10.12968/jokc.2024.9.4.174

Reis da Silva, T. H. (2024j). Death and its significance in Nursing Practice. *Palliative Medicine & Care International Journal*, 4(3), 1–7.

Reis da Silva, T. H. (2024k). Falls prevention in older people and the role of nursing. *British Journal of Community Nursing*, 29(7), 335–339. DOI: 10.12968/bjcn.2024.0005 PMID: 38963269

Reis da Silva, T. H. (2024l) Understanding body fluid balance, dehydration and intravenous fluid therapy. *Emergency Nurse*. *32*(4) doi:DOI: 10.7748/en.2024.e2201

Reis da Silva, T. H. (2024m). Can supplementing vitamin B12 improve mental health outcomes?: a literature review. *British Journal of Community Nursing, 29*(3), 137–146. https://doi.org/DOI: 10.12968/bjcn.2024.29.3.137

Reis da Silva, T. H. (2024p). Loneliness in older adults. *British Journal of Community Nursing*, 29(2), 60–66. DOI: 10.12968/bjcn.2024.29.2.60 PMID: 38300245

Reis da Silva, T. H. (2024r). Pharmacokinetics in older people: An overview of prescribing practice. *Journal of Prescribing Practice*, 6(9), 374–381. DOI: 10.12968/jprp.2024.6.9.374

Reis da Silva, T. H., & Mitchell, A. (2024a). Integrating Digital Transformation in Nursing Education: Best Practices and Challenges in Curriculum Development. In Lytras, M., Serban, A. C., Alkhaldi, A., Malik, S., & Aldosemani, T. (Eds.), *Digital Transformation in Higher Education, Part B Cases, Examples and Good Practices*. Emerald Publishing Limited.

Reis Da Silva, T. H., & Mitchell, A. (2024b). Simulation in nursing: The importance of involving service users. *British Journal of Nursing (Mark Allen Publishing)*, 33(5), 262–265. DOI: 10.12968/bjon.2024.33.5.262 PMID: 38446515

Rembish, M., Snyder, M., Sarage, D., Spadafora, N., & Alexander, I. (2022). Transforming clinical education during a global pandemic: Building new approaches to clinical education. *Nursing Education Perspectives*, 43(5), 325–327. DOI: 10.1097/01.NEP.0000000000001018 PMID: 35947103

Ren, X. (2023). Contemplative pedagogy for positive engagement in online teaching and learning in higher education. *Teaching in Higher Education*, 29(1), 334–347. DOI: 10.1080/13562517.2023.2280254

Retna, K. S., & Tee Ng, P. (2011). Communities of practice: Dynamics and success factors. *Leadership and Organization Development Journal*, 32(1), 41–59. DOI: 10.1108/01437731111099274

Rincón-Flores, E. G., Guerrero-Rodriguez, J., & Rodríguez-Reséndiz, J. (2020). Predicting academic performance with artificial intelligence (AI), a new tool for teachers and students. *International Journal of Emerging Technologies in Learning*, 15(2), 23–34.

Roberts, J. (2022, October 3). Students and technology report: Rebalancing the student experience. *Educause*. https://www.educause.edu/ecar/research-publications/2022/students-and-technology-report-rebalancing-the-student-experience/modality-preferences

Roediger, H. L.III, & Karpicke, J. D. (2006a). The power of testing memory: Basic research and implications for educational practice. *Perspectives on Psychological Science*, 1(3), 181–210. DOI: 10.1111/j.1745-6916.2006.00012.x PMID: 26151629

Roediger, H. L.III, & Karpicke, J. D. (2006b). Test-enhanced learning. *Psychological Science*, 17(3), 249–255. DOI: 10.1111/j.1467-9280.2006.01693.x PMID: 16507066

Roediger, H. L.III, & Tekin, E. (2020). Recognition memory: Tulving's contributions and some new findings. *Neuropsychologia*, 139, 107350. DOI: 10.1016/j.neuropsychologia.2020.107350 PMID: 31978402

Rogers, T. B., Kuiper, N. A., & Kirker, W. S. (1977). Self-reference and the encoding of personal information. *Journal of Personality and Social Psychology*, 35(9), 677–688. DOI: 10.1037/0022-3514.35.9.677 PMID: 909043

Rolfe, G., Jasper, M., & Freshwater, D. (2010). *Critical reflection in practice: Generating knowledge for practice*. Palgrave Macmillian.

Rosa, W., Burnett, C., Butler, C., Rolle, P., Salvage, J., Wignall, A., & Mason, D. (2021). The ICN global nursing leadership institute: Integrating the SDGs into leadership and policy development. *The American Journal of Nursing*, 121(12), 54–58. DOI: 10.1097/01.NAJ.0000803204.19511.8a PMID: 34792506

Rosenberg, M. B. (2001). *E-learning: Strategies for delivering knowledge in the digital age*. Macmillan Publishers Limited.

Roshanaei, M., Smith, J., & Li, X. (2023). Harnessing AI to foster equity in education: Opportunities, challenges, and emerging strategies. *Journal of Educational Technology & Society*, 26(3), 45–60.

Rossler, K., Sankaranarayanan, G., & Duvall, A. (2019). Acquisition of fire safety knowledge and skills with virtual reality simulation. *Nurse Educator*, 44(2), 88–92. DOI: 10.1097/NNE.0000000000000551 PMID: 29847356

Roumell, E. A., & Jabarkhail, S. (2023). Supporting adult working learners. *New Directions for Adult and Continuing Education*, 2023(179), 5–16. DOI: 10.1002/ace.20498

Rovai, A. P. (2004). Building learning communities in online classrooms: A conversation map approach. [JETDE]. *Journal of Educational Technology Development and Exchange*, 1(1), 1–16.

Roy Rosenzweig Center for History and New Media. (2016) Zotero [Computer software]. Retrieved from_www.zotero.org/download

Rubio, A., Vidal-Abarca, E., & Serrano-Mendizábal, M. (2022). How to assist the students while learning from text? Effects of inserting adjunct questions on text processing. *Instructional Science*, 50(5), 749–770. DOI: 10.1007/s11251-022-09592-7

Ryan, M. D., & Reid, S. A. (2015). Impact of the flipped classroom on student performance and retention: A parallel controlled study in general chemistry. *Journal of Chemical Education*, 93(1), 13–23. DOI: 10.1021/acs.jchemed.5b00717

Ryttberg, M. (2022). Legitimacy dynamics of professional support staff at higher education institutions. *Higher Education Policy*, 35(1), 218–233. DOI: 10.1057/s41307-020-00206-w

Ryu, S. (2020). The role of mixed methods in conducting design-based research. *Educational Psychologist*, 55(4), 232–243. DOI: 10.1080/00461520.2020.1794871

Sadiku, M., Adebo, P., & Musa, S. (2018). Online teaching and learning. *International Journal of Advanced Research in Computer Science and Software Engineering*, 8(2), 73. Advance online publication. DOI: 10.23956/ijarcsse.v8i2.549

Sağın, F. G., Özkaya, A. B., Tengiz, F., Geyik, Ö. G., & Geyik, C. (2024). Current evaluation and recommendations for the use of artificial intelligence tools in education. *Türk Biyokimya Dergisi*, 48(6), 620–625. DOI: 10.1515/tjb-2023-0254

Sahraoui, D., & Chaibendraa, W. (2020). The Role of social media in strengthening scientific communication to face the consequences of the corona pandemic on scientific research: A field study on a sample of students and professors of the Algerian university. *Bibliophilia*, 44–71. https://asjp.cerist.dz/en/article/128704

Sajja, R., Krishnan, P., & Nair, S. (2023). Artificial intelligence-enabled intelligent assistant for personalized and adaptive learning in higher education. *Journal of Educational Technology Systems*, 52(1), 67–85.

Salmon, G. (2009). *E-moderating: The Key to Teaching and Learning Online* (2nd ed.). Routledge.

Sarnou, D. (2020). Questioning the significance of technologizing Algerian schools and universities: Did it fail or succeed? *International Journal of Integrating Technology in Education*, 9(1), 1–13. DOI: 10.5121/ijite.2020.9101

Savarimuthu, A., & Ponniah, R. J. (2024). Receive, retain and retrieve: Psychological and neurobiological perspectives on memory retrieval. *Integrative Psychological & Behavioral Science*, 58(1), 303–318. DOI: 10.1007/s12124-023-09752-5 PMID: 36738400

Schacter, D. L. (1999). The seven sins of memory: Insights from psychology and cognitive neuroscience. *The American Psychologist*, 54(3), 182–203. DOI: 10.1037/0003-066X.54.3.182 PMID: 10199218

Scharff, L., Capocchiano, H., Chick, N., Eady, M., Friberg, J., Gregory, D., Loy, K., & Maurer, T. (2023). Grand challenges for SoTL. *International Society for the Scholarship of Teaching and Learning*. https://issotl.com/grand-challenges-for-sotl/

Schunk, D. H., & DiBenedetto, M. K. (2016). Self-efficacy theory in education. In Wentzel, K. R., & Miele, D. B. (Eds.), *Handbook of motivation at school* (pp. 34–54). Routledge.

Schunk, D. H., & DiBenedetto, M. K. (2021). Self-efficacy and human motivation. In Elliot, A. J. (Ed.), (pp. 153–179). Advances in motivation science. Elsevier Academic Press., DOI: 10.1016/bs.adms.2020.10.001

Schunk, D. H., & Usher, E. L. (2011). Assessing self-efficacy for self-regulated learning. In Zimmerman, B. J., & Schunk, D. H. (Eds.), *Handbook of self-regulation of learning and performance* (pp. 282–297). Taylor & Francis. DOI: 10.4324/9780203839010

Schunk, D. H., & Zimmerman, B. J. (Eds.). (2008). *Motivation and self-regulated learning: Theory, research, and applications*. Routledge.

Scianna, J., & Kaliisa, R. (2023). 'SSEEN': A networked approach to uncover connections between sentiment, social, and epistemic elements of student online forum discourse. *Educational Technology Research and Development*, 72(5), 2817–2839. DOI: 10.1007/s11423-023-10310-4

Selcuk, H., & Jones, J. (2022). Turkish EFL learner perceptions of using a social network environment for collaborative writing: Creating a trustful affinity space. *International Journal of Smart Education and Urban Society*, 13(1), 1–14. DOI: 10.4018/IJSEUS.297063

Serbun, S. J., Shih, J. Y., & Gutchess, A. H. (2011). Memory for details with self-referencing. *Memory (Hove, England)*, 19(8), 1004–1014. DOI: 10.1080/09658211.2011.626429 PMID: 22092106

Shamsabadi, A., Pashaei, A., Rahmani, N., Mahmoodabadi, A., Norouzi, S., Bahador, F., & Mehraeen, E. (2023). Social media application in education during the COVID-19 pandemic; pros and cons: A systematic review. *Journal of Iranian Medical Council*, 6(3), 389–400. DOI: 10.18502/jimc.v6i3.12841

Sharma, R. (2017). Computer-assisted learning – A study. *International Journal of Advanced Research in Education & Technology*, 4(3), 102–105.

Shatila, S. (2024). Not alone when i'm feeling stressed: Online adult learner connection and retention. *Adult Education Quarterly*, 74(1), 43–61. DOI: 10.1177/07417136231184570

Shea, P., & Bidjerano, T. (2010). Learning presence: Towards a theory of self-efficacy, self-regulation, and the development of a communities of inquiry in online and blended learning environments. *Computers & Education*, 55(4), 1721–1731. DOI: 10.1016/j.compedu.2010.07.017

Shea, P., Hayes, S., Smith, S. U., Vickers, J., Bidjerano, T., Pickett, A., Gozza-Cohen, M., Wilde, J., & Jian, S. (2012). Learning presence: Additional research on a new conceptual element within the Community of Inquiry (CoI) framework. *The Internet and Higher Education*, 15(2), 89–95. DOI: 10.1016/j.iheduc.2011.08.002

Shea, P., Hayes, S., Uzuner Smith, S., Vickers, J., Bidjerano, T., Gozza-Cohen, M., Jian, S.-B., Pickett, A., Wilde, J., & Tseng, C. H. (2013). Online learner self-regulation: Learning presence viewed through quantitative content-and social network analysis. *International Review of Research in Open and Distance Learning*, 14(3), 427–461. DOI: 10.19173/irrodl.v14i3.1466

Shepard, K. (2024, April 15-16). *Support online student engagement using intelligent agents* [session presentation]. University Systems of Georgia Teaching and Learning Conference, Athens, Georgia. https://virtual.oxfordabstracts.com/#/event/5034/submission/205

Short, J., Williams, E., & Christie, B. (1976). *The social psychology of telecommunications*. John Wiley and Sons.

Shulman, L. (2011). Feature essays: The scholarship of teaching and learning: A personal account and reflection. *International Journal for the Scholarship of Teaching and Learning*, 5(1), 30. Advance online publication. DOI: 10.20429/ijsotl.2011.050130

Shulman, L. S. (1986). Those who understand: Knowledge growth in teaching. *Educational Researcher*, 15(2), 4–14. DOI: 10.3102/0013189X015002004

Shulman, L. S. (1987). Knowledge and teaching: Foundations of the new reform. *Harvard Educational Review*, 57(1), 1–23. DOI: 10.17763/haer.57.1.j463w79r56455411

Shulman, L. S. (1998). *Teaching and teacher education among the professions. 38th Charles W. Hunt Memorial Lecture*. AACTE Publications.

Shulman, L. S. (2002, May/June). Truth and consequences? Inquiry and policy in research on teacher education. *Journal of Teacher Education*, 53(3), 248–253. DOI: 10.1177/0022487102053003009

Shulman, L. S. (2004). *The wisdom of practice: Essays on teaching, learning, and learning to teach*. Jossey-Bass.

Shulman, L. S. (2023). Foreword. In Huber, M. T., & Morreale, S. P. (Eds.), *Disciplinary styles in the scholarship of teaching and learning: Exploring common ground* (pp. v–ix). Taylor & Francis.

Shulman, L. S. (2023). Reprint: Truth and consequences? Inquiry and policy in research on teacher education. *Journal of Teacher Education*, 74(2), 144–148. DOI: 10.1177/00224871231161457

Shulman, L. S. (2023). Truth and consequences in teacher education. *Journal of Teacher Education*, 74(2), 149–150. DOI: 10.1177/00224871231160386

Siah, C., Lim, F., Lau, S., & Tam, W. (2020). The use of the community of inquiry survey in blended learning pedagogy for a clinical skill-based module. *Journal of Clinical Nursing*, 30(3-4), 454–465. DOI: 10.1111/jocn.15556 PMID: 33174239

Siemens, G. (2002). Instructional design in e-learning. Retrieved from https://eddl.tru.ca/wp-content/uploads/2018/12/instructional-design-in-e-learning-Siemens.pdf

Sienkewicz, J. A. (2021). Guest editor introduction: Cultivating our field through SoTL practice: Teaching and learning the art history of the United States. *Art History Pedagogy & Practice*, 6(1), 1.

Silva, S., Gates, M., & Waczek, A. (2021). Utilization of an online education module and standardized patient simulation experience to improve nursing student learning outcomes with heart failure patients. *Nursing Education Perspectives*, 43(3), 178–180. DOI: 10.1097/01.NEP.0000000000000782 PMID: 33660684

Simmons, N., Abrahamson, E., Deshler, J., Kensington-Miller, B., Manarin, K., Morón-García, S., Oliver, C., & Renc-Roe, J. (2013). Conflicts and configurations in a liminal space: SoTL scholars' identity development. *Teaching & Learning Inquiry*, 1(2), 9–21. DOI: 10.20343/teachlearninqu.1.2.9

Simmons, N., Scharff, L., Eady, M., & Gregory, D. (2021). SoTL in the margins: Teaching-focused role case studies. *Teaching & Learning Inquiry*, 9(1), 61–78. DOI: 10.20343/teachlearninqu.9.1.6

Singh, P. (2018). Learning Management Systems: Benefits and Challenges. [Journal of Educational Technology Development and Exchange (JETDE)], 11(2), 121-132.

Slakmon, B., Keynan, O., & Shapira, O. (2022). Emotion expression and recognition in written digital discussions on civic issues. *International Journal of Computer-Supported Collaborative Learning*, 17(4), 519–537. DOI: 10.1007/s11412-022-09379-5

Smith, B. L., Holliday, W. G., & Austin, H. W. (2010). Students' comprehension of science textbooks using a question-based reading strategy. *Journal of Research in Science Teaching*, 47(4), 363–379. DOI: 10.1002/tea.20378

Smith, C., Holden, M., Yu, E., & Hanlon, P. (2021). 'So what do you do?': Third space professionals navigating a Canadian university context. *Journal of Higher Education Policy and Management*, 43(5), 505–519. DOI: 10.1080/1360080X.2021.1884513

Smith, S., & Walker, D. (2021). Scholarship and academic capitals: The boundaried nature of education-focused career tracks. *Teaching in Higher Education*. Advance online publication. DOI: 10.1080/13562517.2021.1965570

Smith, S., & Walker, D. (2024). Scholarship and teaching-focused roles: An exploratory study of academics' experiences and perceptions of support. *Innovations in Education and Teaching International*, 61(1), 193–204. DOI: 10.1080/14703297.2022.2132981

Social Media Stats Algeria. (2021). Statcounter. Retrieved from https://gs.statcounter.com/social-media-stats/all/algeria

Spake, E., & Salem, A. (2005). Setting the stage: The scholarship of teaching and learning. *Journal, Physical Therapy Education*, 19(3), 5–13. DOI: 10.1097/00001416-200510000-00003

Specht, J. A., Wood, E. J., Willoughby, T., & Boudreau, R. L. (1999). Evaluating the efficacy of elaborative strategies for remembering expository text. *The Alberta Journal of Educational Research*, 45(2), 170–183. https://www.proquest.com/scholarly-journals/evaluating-efficacy-elaborative-strategies/docview/228617178/se-2

Sperling, C. B. (2003). How community colleges understand the scholarship of teaching And learning. *Community College Journal of Research and Practice*, 27(7), 593–601. DOI: 10.1080/713838214

Stanley, M., & Martin, C. (2019). Training model for online nurse educators. *Journal of Nursing Education and Practice*, 9(6), 82. DOI: 10.5430/jnep.v9n6p82

Stein, B. S., & Bransford, J. D. (1979). Constraints on effective elaboration: Effects of precision and subject generation. *Journal of Verbal Learning and Verbal Behavior*, 18(6), 769–777. DOI: 10.1016/S0022-5371(79)90481-X

Straub, S., & Rummel, N. (2020). Promoting interaction in online distance education: Designing, implementing and supporting collaborative learning. *Information and Learning Science*, 121(5/6), 251–260. DOI: 10.1108/ILS-04-2020-0090

Sumakul, D. T. Y., Hamied, F. A., & Sukyadi, D. (2022, February). Students' perceptions of the use of AI in a writing class. In 67th TEFLIN International Virtual Conference & the 9th ICOELT 2021 (TEFLIN ICOELT 2021) (pp. 52-57). Atlantis Press.

Sum, M., & Oancea, A. (2022). The use of technology in higher education teaching by academics during the COVID-19 emergency remote teaching period: A systematic review. *International Journal of Educational Technology in Higher Education*, 19(1), 59. Advance online publication. DOI: 10.1186/s41239-022-00364-4 PMID: 36531306

Supple, B., Fennell, C., & McCarthy, M. (n.d.). Reviewing reflective teaching portfolios about online learning: What are they telling us? *Transforming Patterns through the Scholarship of Teaching and Learning, 13*, 245.

Supple, B., & Cronin, J. G. (2023). A pedagogy of slow: Integrating experiences of physical and virtual gallery spaces to foster critical engagement in SoTL. *Teaching & Learning Inquiry*, 11, 11. DOI: 10.20343/teachlearninqu.11.2

Supramaniam, K., Razak, M. I. M., & Arumugam, N. (2020). Changing identities in community of practice: Expert teachers to novice researchers. *Asian Journal of University Education*, 16(2), 59–68. DOI: 10.24191/ajue.v16i2.10297

Swaminathan, R., & Mulvihill, T. (2022). Synergistic pedagogies in virtual spaces: Preparing social justice educational researchers through SoTL. In *Teaching and Learning for Social Justice and Equity in Higher Education: Virtual Settings* (pp. 85-105). Springer International Publishing. https://doi.org/DOI: 10.1007/978-3-030-86683-6_5

Swan, K., & Shih, L. F. (2019). On the nature and development of social presence in online course discussions. *Online Learning : the Official Journal of the Online Learning Consortium*, 9(3), 115–136. DOI: 10.24059/olj.v9i3.1788

Sweller, J. (1988). Cognitive load during problem solving: Effects on learning. *Cognitive Science*, 12(2), 257–285. DOI: 10.1207/s15516709cog1202_4

Symons, C. S., & Johnson, B. T. (1997). The self-reference effect in memory: A meta-analysis. *Psychological Bulletin*, 121(3), 371–394. DOI: 10.1037/0033-2909.121.3.371 PMID: 9136641

Tadesse, S., & Muluye, W. (2020). The impact of COVID-19 pandemic on education system in developing countries: A review. *Open Journal of Social Sciences*, 8(10), 159–170. DOI: 10.4236/jss.2020.810011

Tallent-Runnels, M., Thomas, J., Lan, W., Cooper, S., Ahern, T., Shaw, S., & Liu, X. (2006). Teaching courses online: A review of the research. *Review of Educational Research*, 76(1), 135–193. DOI: 10.3102/00346543076001093

Tamim, S. R., & Grant, M. M. (2013). Definitions and uses: Case study of teachers implementing project-based learning. *The Interdisciplinary Journal of Problem-Based Learning*, 7(2). Advance online publication. DOI: 10.7771/1541-5015.1323

Tan, S. C., & Chen, S. H. A. (2020). *Transforming teaching and learning in higher education*. Springer Singapore., DOI: 10.1007/978-981-15-4980-9

Tariq, M. U. (2024b). Harnessing persuasive technologies for enhanced learner engagement and motivation. In M. Sanmugam, D. Lim, N. Mohd Barkhaya, W. Wan Yahaya, & Z. Khlaif (Eds.), *Power of persuasive educational technologies in enhancing learning* (pp. 30-62). IGI Global. https://doi.org/DOI: 10.4018/979-8-3693-6397-3.ch002

Tariq, M. U. (2024a). Generative AI in curriculum development in higher education. In Fields, Z. (Ed.), *Impacts of generative AI on creativity in higher education* (pp. 227–258). IGI Global., DOI: 10.4018/979-8-3693-2418-9.ch009

Tariq, M. U. (2024c). Navigating the personalization pathway: Implementing adaptive learning technologies in higher education. In Minh Tung, T. (Ed.), *Adaptive learning technologies for higher education* (pp. 265–291). IGI Global., DOI: 10.4018/979-8-3693-3641-0.ch012

Tariq, M. U. (2024d). AI-powered language translation for multilingual classrooms. In Doshi, R., Dadhich, M., Poddar, S., & Hiran, K. (Eds.), *Integrating generative AI in education to achieve sustainable development goals* (pp. 29–46). IGI Global., DOI: 10.4018/979-8-3693-2440-0.ch002

Tariq, M. U. (2025a). *AI-driven learning and engagement in higher education*. IGI Global., DOI: 10.4018/979-8-3693-4074-5

Tariq, M. U. (2025b). Navigating bias and fairness in digital AI systems. In Bhattacharya, P., Hassan, A., Liu, H., & Bhushan, B. (Eds.), *Ethical dimensions of AI development* (pp. 127–156). IGI Global., DOI: 10.4018/979-8-3693-4147-6.ch006

Tariq, M. U., & Sergio, R. P. (2025c). Innovative assessment techniques in physical education: Exploring technology-enhanced and student-centered models for holistic student development. In Garcia, M. (Ed.), *Global innovations in physical education and health* (pp. 85–112). IGI Global., DOI: 10.4018/979-8-3693-3952-7.ch004

Tawafak, R., Romli, A., Arshah, R., & Almaroof, R. (2018). Assessing the Impact of technology learning and assessment method on academic performance: Review paper. *Eurasia Journal of Mathematics, Science and Technology Education*, 14(6), 2241–2254. DOI: 10.29333/ejmste/87117

Teo, T. W., Tan, K. C. D., Yan, Y. K., Teo, Y. C., & Yeo, L. W. (2014). How flip teaching supports undergraduate chemistry laboratory learning. *Chemistry Education Research and Practice*, 15(4), 550–567. DOI: 10.1039/C4RP00003J

Tertiary Education Quality and Standards Agency (TEQSA). (2022). *Guidance Note: Scholarship* (Version 3.0). https://www.teqsa.gov.au/guides-resources/resources/guidance-notes/guidance-note-scholarship

Thibodeau, P. H., & Boroditsky, L. (2011). Metaphors we think with: The role of metaphor in reasoning. *PLoS One*, 6(2), e16782. DOI: 10.1371/journal.pone.0016782 PMID: 21373643

Tierney, A. M., Aidulis, D., Park, J., & Clark, K. (2020). Supporting SoTL development through communities of practice. *Teaching & Learning Inquiry*, 8(2), 32–52. DOI: 10.20343/teachlearninqu.8.2.4

Tilak, S., Evans, M., Wen, Z., & Glassman, M. (2022). Social network analysis as a cybernetic modelling facility for participatory design in technology-supported college curricula. *Systemic Practice and Action Research*, 36(5), 691–724. DOI: 10.1007/s11213-022-09625-9 PMID: 36466296

Tlhoaele, M., Suhre, C., & Hofman, A. (2016). Using technology-enhanced, cooperative, group-project learning for student comprehension and academic performance. *European Journal of Engineering Education*, 41(3), 263–278. DOI: 10.1080/03043797.2015.1056102

Trigwell, K., Martin, E., Benjamin, J., & Prosser, M. (2000). Scholarship of teaching: A model. *Higher Education Research & Development*, 19(2), 155–168. DOI: 10.1080/072943600445628

Tulving, E. (1974). Cue-dependent forgetting. *American Scientist*, 62(1), 74–82. https://psycnet.apa.org/record/1974-20253-001

Tulving, E., & Thomson, D. M. (1973). Encoding specificity and retrieval processes in episodic memory. *Psychological Review*, 80(5), 352–373. DOI: 10.1037/h0020071

Tune, J. D., Sturek, M., & Basile, D. P. (2013). Flipped classroom model improves graduate student performance in cardiovascular, respiratory, and renal physiology. *Advances in Physiology Education*, 37(4), 316–320. DOI: 10.1152/advan.00091.2013 PMID: 24292907

Turk, D. J., Cunningham, S. J., & Macrae, C. N. (2008). Self-memory biases in explicit and incidental encoding of trait adjectives. *Consciousness and Cognition*, 17(3), 1040–1045. DOI: 10.1016/j.concog.2008.02.004 PMID: 18395467

Uçar, H., & Goksel, N. (2020). Enhancing online EFL learners' motivation and engagement through supplementary activities on Facebook. *Asian Journal of Distance Education*, 15, 154–168. https://www.asianjde.com/ojs/index.php/AsianJDE/article/view/445

Ulla, M., & Perales, W. (2021). Facebook as an integrated online learning support application during the COVID-19 pandemic: Thai university students' experiences and perspectives. *Heliyon*, 7(11), e08317. Advance online publication. DOI: 10.1016/j.heliyon.2021.e08317 PMID: 34746477

Vaillancourt, T., McDougall, P., Comeau, J., & Finn, C. (2021). COVID-19 school closures and social isolation in children and youth: Prioritizing relationships in education. *Facets*, 6(1), 1795–1813. DOI: 10.1139/facets-2021-0080

Valeeva, R., & Kalimullin, A. (2021). Adapting or changing: The COVID-19 pandemic and teacher education in Russia. *Education Sciences*, 11(8), 408. DOI: 10.3390/educsci11080408

Van Alten, D. C., Phielix, C., Janssen, J., & Kester, L. (2019). Effects of flipping the classroom on learning outcomes and satisfaction: A meta-analysis. *Educational Research Review*, 28, 100281. DOI: 10.1016/j.edurev.2019.05.003

Van Popta, E., Kral, M., Camp, G., Martens, R. L., & Simons, P. R. J. (2017). Exploring the value of peer feedback in online learning for the provider. *Educational Research Review*, 20, 24–34. DOI: 10.1016/j.edurev.2016.10.003

VanLehn, K., Jones, R. M., & Chi, M. T. (1992). A model of the self-explanation effect. *Journal of the Learning Sciences*, 2(1), 1–59. DOI: 10.1207/s15327809jls0201_1

Vaughan, M. (2014). Flipping the learning: An investigation into the use of the flipped classroom model in an introductory teaching course. *Education Research and Perspectives*, 41, 25–41. https://search.informit.org/doi/epdf/10.3316/informit.135571943100260. DOI: 10.70953/ERPv41.14002

Veles, N., & Carter, M.-A. (2016). Imagining a future: Changing the landscape for third space professionals in Australian higher education institutions. *Journal of Higher Education Policy and Management*, 38(5), 519–533. DOI: 10.1080/1360080X.2016.1196938

Vendetti, M. S., Wu, A., & Holyoak, K. J. (2014). Far-out thinking. *Psychological Science*, 25(4), 928–933. DOI: 10.1177/0956797613518079 PMID: 24463552

Vosniadou, S., & Schommer, M. (1988). Explanatory analogies can help children acquire information from expository text. *Journal of Educational Psychology*, 80(4), 524–536. DOI: 10.1037/0022-0663.80.4.524

Vygotsky, L. S. (1962). *Thought and language*. MIT Press. DOI: 10.1037/11193-000

Vygotsky, L. S. (1978). *Mind in society: The development of higher psychological processes*. Harvard University Press.

Vygotsky, L. S. (1978). *Mind in Society: The Development of Higher Psychological Processes*. Harvard University Press.

Vygotsky, L. S., & Cole, M. (1978). *Mind in society: Development of higher psychological processes*. Harvard University Press.

Wade, S., & Kidd, C. (2019). The role of prior knowledge and curiosity in learning. *Psychonomic Bulletin & Review*, 26(4), 1377–1387. DOI: 10.3758/s13423-019-01598-6

Wade, S., & Kidd, C. (2019). The role of prior knowledge and curiosity in learning. *Psychonomic Bulletin & Review*, 26, 1377–1387.

Wald, N., & Harland, T. (2024). Students as scholars and the scholarship of student learning. *Teaching in Higher Education*, 29(2), 442–453. DOI: 10.1080/13562517.2021.1989583

Waller, K. L., & Prosser, M. (2023). The rapidly changing teaching and research landscape: The future of SoTL and the teaching-research nexus. In *The educational turn: Rethinking the scholarship of teaching and learning in higher education* (pp. 27–41). Springer Nature Singapore., DOI: 10.1007/978-981-19-8951-3_3

Walther, J. B. (1996). Computer-mediated communication: Impersonal, interpersonal, and hyperpersonal interaction. *Communication Research*, 23(1), 3–43. DOI: 10.1177/009365096023001001

Walther, J. B. (2015). Social information processing theory (CMC). In Berger, C. R., Roloff, M. E., Wilson, S. R., Dillard, J. P., Caughlin, J., & Solomon, D. (Eds.), *The international encyclopedia of interpersonal communication* (pp. 1–13). Wiley., DOI: 10.1002/9781118540190.wbeic192

Watts, L. (2015). An autoethnographic exploration of learning and teaching reflective practice. *Social Work Education*, 34(4), 363–376. DOI: 10.1080/02615479.2015.1016903

Wea, L. (2022). Effect of the standard operating procedure box method to increase self-confidence and basic nursing skills of nursing students during the covid-19 pandemic. *Gaceta Medica de Caracas*, 130(Supl. 5), S1101–S1107. DOI: 10.47307/GMC.2022.130.s5.33

Weaver, M., Jenkins, R., Wichman, C., Robinson, J., Potthoff, M., Menicucci, T., & Vail, C. (2019). Sowing across a state: Development and delivery of a grassroots pediatric palliative care nursing curriculum. *Journal of Palliative Care*, 36(1), 22–28. DOI: 10.1177/0825859719889700 PMID: 31771423

Weinstein, Y., Sumeracki, M., & Caviglioli, O. (2019). *Understanding how we learn: A visual guide*. Routledge. https://eric.ed.gov/?id=ED591769

Weller, M. (2010). *The Digital Scholar: How Technology Is Transforming Scholarly Practice*. Bloomsbury Academic.

Wenger, E. (1998). *Communities of Practice: Learning, Meaning, and Identity*. Cambridge University Press. Wenger's work emphasizes the role of communities of practice in facilitating learning and knowledge sharing among professionals. DOI: 10.1017/CBO9780511803932

Wenger, E., McDermott, R., & Snyder, W. (2002). *Cultivating communities of practice: A guide to managing knowledge*. Harvard Business School Press.

Wenger-Trayner, B. (2015). *Communities of practice: A brief overview of the concept and its uses.* 08 Brief introduction to communities of practice (wenger-trayner.com)

Wenger-Trayner, E., & Wenger-Trayner, B. (2015). Communities of practice: A brief introduction. https://wenger-trayner.com/introduction-to-communities-of-practice/

Wenger-Trayner, E., Fenton-O'Creevy, M., Hutchison, S., Kubiak, C., & Wenger-Trayner, B. (2014). *Learning in landscapes of practice: Boundaries, identity, and knowledgeability in practice-based learning*. Routledge., DOI: 10.4324/9781315777122

Wenger-Trayner, E., & Wenger-Trayner, B. (2020). *Learning to make a difference: Value creation in social learning spaces*. Cambridge University Press., DOI: 10.1017/9781108677431

Whiteside, A. L., Garrett Dikkers, A., Swan, K., & Gunawardena, C. N. (2017). *Social presence in online learning: Multiple perspectives on practice and research*. Stylus Publishing, LLC.

Wiggins, G., & McTighe, J. (2005). *Understanding by design* (2nd ed.). Association for Supervision and Curriculum Development ASCD.

Wiliam, D., & Black, P. (1998). Meaningful assessment in classroom education. *Schooling for Tomorrow*, 1(1), 31–52.

Williams, J. J., Lombrozo, T., & Rehder, B. (2013b). The hazards of explanation: Overgeneralization in the face of exceptions. *Journal of Experimental Psychology. General*, 142(4), 1006–1014. DOI: 10.1037/a0030996 PMID: 23294346

Williamson, B., & Eynon, R. (2020). Historical threads, missing links, and future directions in AI in education. *Learning, Media and Technology*, 45(3), 223–235. DOI: 10.1080/17439884.2020.1798995

Wilson, S. G. (2013). The flipped class: A method to address the challenges of an undergraduate statistics course. *Teaching of Psychology*, 40(3), 193–199. DOI: 10.1177/0098628313487461

Woloshyn, V. E., Pressley, M., & Schneider, W. (1992). Elaborative-interrogation and prior-knowledge effects on learning of facts. *Journal of Educational Psychology*, 84(1), 115–124. DOI: 10.1037/0022-0663.84.1.115

Wong, R. M., Lawson, M. J., & Keeves, J. (2002). The effects of self-explanation training on students' problem solving in high-school mathematics. *Learning and Instruction*, 12(2), 233–262. DOI: 10.1016/S0959-4752(01)00027-5

Woods, C. S., & Conderman, G. (2005). Service learning and teacher education. *Academic Exchange Quarterly*, 9, 155–160.

Wu, Y., & Schunn, C. D. (2023). Passive, active, and constructive engagement with peer feedback: A revised model of learning from peer feedback. *Contemporary Educational Psychology*, 73, 102160. DOI: 10.1016/j.cedpsych.2023.102160

Wylie, R., & Chi, M. T. H. (2014). The self-explanation principle in multimedia learning. In Meyer, R. E. (Ed.), *The Cambridge Handbook of Multimedia Learning* (pp. 413–432)., DOI: 10.1017/CBO9781139547369.021

Xing, W., Ao, L., Xiao, H., Cheng, L., Liang, Y., & Wang, J. (2018). Nurses' attitudes toward, and needs for online learning: Differences between rural and urban hospitals in shanghai, east China. *International Journal of Environmental Research and Public Health*, 15(7), 1495. DOI: 10.3390/ijerph15071495 PMID: 30011965

Yang, C. C., Wu, J. Y., & Ogata, H. (2024). Learning analytics dashboard-based self-regulated learning approach for enhancing students' e-book-based blended learning. *Education and Information Technologies*, •••, 1–22. DOI: 10.1007/s10639-024-12913-7

Yildirim, S., & Chandra, Y. (2013). University students' perceptions of online interactive activities in web-based learning environments: A case study. [JETDE]. *Journal of Educational Technology Development and Exchange*, 6(2), 111–129.

Yılmaz, Ö., & Malone, K. L. (2020). Preservice teacher's perceptions about the use of blended learning in a science education methods course. *Smart Learning Environments*, 7(1), 18. DOI: 10.1186/s40561-020-00126-7

Yin, R. K. (2015). *Qualitative research from start to finish*. Guilford Publications.

Yunus, M., Setyosari, P., Utaya, S., & Kuswandi, D. (2021). The influence of online project collaborative learning and achievement motivation on problem-solving ability. *European Journal of Educational Research*, 10(2), 813–823. DOI: 10.12973/eu-jer.10.2.813

Yu, Z., & Gao, M. (2022). Effects of video length on a flipped English classroom. *SAGE Open*, 12(1), 21582440211068474. Advance online publication. DOI: 10.1177/21582440211068474

Zappe, S., Leicht, R., Messner, J., Litzinger, T., & Lee, H. W. (2009). "Flipping" the classroom to explore active learning in a large undergraduate course. *Proceeding of the American Society for Engineering Education.* Retrieved from https://www.nyu.edu/content/dam/nyu/facultyResources/images/ESMITimages/flippedclass/flipping-the-classroom-to-explore-active-learning-in-a-large-undergraduate-course.pdf

Zermane, H., & Aıtouche, S. (2020). Digital learning with COVID-19 in Algeria. *International Journal of 3D printing technologies and digital industry, 4*(2), 161-170.DOI: 10.46519/ij3dptdi.776978

Zhai, X., Chu, X., Chai, C. S., Jong, M. S. Y., Istenic, A., Spector, M., Liu, J.-B., Yuan, J., & Li, Y. (2021). A review of artificial intelligence (AI) in education from 2010 to 2020. *Complexity*, 2021(1), 1–18. DOI: 10.1155/2021/8812542

Zhang, K., & Aslan, A. B. (2021). AI technologies for education: Recent research & future directions. *Journal of Educational Technology Development and Exchange*, 14(1), 1–17.

Zhan, Y., Sun, D., Kong, H. M., & Zeng, Y. (2024). Primary school teachers' classroom-based e-assessment practices: Insights from the theory of planned behaviour. *British Journal of Educational Technology*, 55(6), 2740–2759. DOI: 10.1111/bjet.13478

Zhao, X., & Yang, Y. (2023). Impact of social media-supported flipped classroom on English as a foreign language learners' writing performance and anxiety. *Frontiers*, 13, 1052737. Advance online publication. DOI: 10.3389/fpsyg.2022.1052737 PMID: 36687902

Zheng, L., Long, M., Chen, B., & Fan, Y. (2023). Promoting knowledge elaboration, socially shared regulation, and group performance in collaborative learning: An automated assessment and feedback approach based on knowledge graphs. *International Journal of Educational Technology in Higher Education*, 20(1), 46. Advance online publication. DOI: 10.1186/s41239-023-00415-4

Zheng, M., Bender, D., & Lyon, C. (2021). Online elarning during COVID-19 produced equivalent or better student course performance as compared with pre-pandemic: Empirical evidence from a school-wide comparative study. *BMC Medical Education*, 21(1), 495. DOI: 10.1186/s12909-021-02909-z PMID: 34530828

Zhu, W., Wang, F., Mayer, R. E., & Liu, T. (2024). Effects of explaining a science lesson to others or to oneself: A cognitive neuroscience approach. *Learning and Instruction*, 91, 101897. DOI: 10.1016/j.learninstruc.2024.101897

Zizka, L. (2020). Reflections and SoTL: Putting reflection (back) on faculty radar. In Plews, R., & Amos, M. (Eds.), *Evidence-based faculty development through the scholarship of teaching and learning (SoTL)* (pp. 96–120). IGI Global., DOI: 10.4018/978-1-7998-2212-7.ch006

Zolfagharkhani, M., & Ghorbani Moghadam, R. (2011). The effect of etymology instruction on vocabulary learning of upper-intermediate EFL Iranian students. *Canadian Social Science*, 7(6), 1–9. DOI: 10.3968/j.css.1923669720110706.180

About the Contributors

Regina Rahimi earned an Ed.D. from Georgia Southern University. She is a full professor in the Department of Middle and Secondary Education at Georgia Southern University. In addition to numerous publications in academic journals, she has published the following books: Rahimi, R., & Liston, D. Eds (2023). Exploring social emotional learning in diverse academic settings. IG Global. Liston, D. & R. Rahimi (2019) Promoting Social Justice through the Scholarship of Teaching and Learning. Indiana University Press. Rahimi, R. & Liston, D. (2012): Pervasive Vulnerabilities: Sexual Harassment in School. Peter Lang: New York

Lina Soares is a Professor in the College of Education's Department of Middle Grades and Secondary Education at Georgia Southern University and currently serves as the Program Director of the Education Specialist Program in Teaching and Learning and the Gifted In-field Endorsement. Dr. Soares has published over 30 research and practitioner-oriented articles and conducted numerous research presentations from international to national and state settings, focusing on effective pedagogical practices for content area teachers, critical literacy, gifted education, and teacher leadership.

***

Sharon Andrews is Professor of Software Engineering at the University of Houston-Clear Lake in Houston, Texas, United States of America. She holds a PhD in Computer Science from the University of Louisiana, Lafayette Louisiana. She has served as committee member, reviewer, and editorial board member for numerous international refereed journals and international and national professional conferences. She is Chair of the Software Engineering MS program as well as the founding creator and Chair of the Software Engineering Online MS program. Dr. Andrews's areas of research include software architecture design, software knowledge reuse, problem conceptualization, as well as learning engagement and curriculum design, human trafficking prevention, and Esports in academia. Dr. Andrews's scholarly works include numerous publications within international, national, and regional refereed journals, edited referred research books and conference proceedings. She has been the recipient of funding in the area of domain specification and knowledge-reuse for research and graduate student projects with Honeywell, Boeing, IBM, Lockheed as well as a grant reviewer for the National Science Foundation and NASA.

Faiza Benaicha is a PhD student in Applied Linguistics and a full-time secondary school English teacher. Her research areas include language learning and teaching adjustments, language assessment, and educational technology.

Deb Clarke is an Adjunct Associate Professor Charles Sturt University Australia. She has a passion for and extensive experience in mentoring those new to the higher education academy. Her research focuses on communities of practice, the scholarship of teaching and learning and school-university partnerships. Deb has been the Vice President of the Higher Education Research and Development Society of Australasia (HERDSA) and a long standing HERDSA executive member. She is both a HERDSA Fellow and an Advance Higher Education Senior Fellow, and recipient of multiple Australian teaching awards.

Caroline M. Crawford, Ed.D., is a Professor of Instructional Design and Technology at the University of Houston-Clear Lake in Houston, Texas, United States of America. She earned her doctoral degree from the University of Houston in Houston, Texas, United States of America, in 1998, with specialization areas in Instructional Technology and Curriculum Theory, and began her tenure at the University of Houston-Clear Lake (UHCL) the same year. At this point in Dr. Crawford's professional career, her main areas of interest focus upon communities of learning and the appropriate and successful integration of technologies into the learning environment; the learning environment may be envisioned as face-to-face, blended and online (virtual or text-driven) environments, as well as microlearning and micro-assist deliverables. Dr. Crawford may be contacted through her e-mail address, crawford@uhcl.edu.

Phuc Diem Le serves as the Teaching and Learning Specialist at RMIT Vietnam, actively engaging in the development, implementation, and assessment of strategies, programs, projects, and services to enhance, assure, recognise, and reward individual and institutional learning and teaching innovation and quality. Her research focuses on educational assessment, language assessment and testing, and professional development."

Alyson Froehlich is a teacher and scholar interested in how people learn about and perceive the world around them. She received her PhD in Cognitive Neuroscience Psychology at the University of Utah. She spent 8 years researching cognition and neural development in autism. She is currently an Assistant Professor (Lecturer) in the department of Psychology at the University of Utah and a Higher Education Instructional Consultant for the university's Martha Bradley Evans Center for Teaching Excellence. She is also an Adjunct Assistant Professor in the department of Psychology at the University of Maryland Global Campus.

Rafik El Amine Ghobrini is an associate professor at the University of Abdelhamid Ibn Badis, Mostaganem. His research areas include applied linguistics, shadow education, educational technology, particularly social media-based learning, and digital literacy. He has participated in numerous conferences worldwide and published articles related to these fields.

Tiago Horta Reis da Silva is a Lecturer in Nursing Education (AEP) at King's College London, with a range of qualifications including BSc in Nursing, BSc in Traditional Chinese Medicine, MSc in Emotional Intelligence, Counselling and NLP, a Master of Business Administration, and MSc in Traditional Chinese Medicine. He has experience in other Higher Education Institutions and NHS and is a member of the Adult Nursing department, assisting with the running, development, and administration of BSc and MSc programmes. He also assists with teaching other modules' content and assists with interviews and assessment matters for other courses. Tiago is a Senior Fellow in Higher Education, a Fellow of the Royal Society of Medicine, and a Fellow for Faculty Nursing and Midwifery at the Royal College of Southern Ireland.

J.Sudarvel working as an Assistant Professor of Management at Karpagam Academy of Higher Education. He produced five Ph.D. Scholars and four Ph.D. Scholars are under his guidance. Further, to his credit he published more than five articles in Scopus indexed journals and published more than 50 articles in international journals. He is acting as a Subject Experts in Board of studies of various autonomous colleges.

Santhosh Kareepadath Rajan is an Associate Professor in the Department of Psychology at CHRIST University, where he has been a faculty member since 2016. He completed his Ph.D. at Bharathiar University, Coimbatore. Dr. Santhosh has commendable expertise in behavioral research methods and statistics, psychometrics, and structural equation modeling.

Semiu Olawale Makinde is an experienced educator and researcher with a focus on online learning and instructional design. With more than 10 years of experience in digital education, he has contributed to various academic publications and led numerous initiatives to improve teaching and learning in online environments. Dr. Makinde currently serves as the Director of the Institute of Education, Al-Hikmah University Ilorin, Nigeria where he continues to explore innovative approaches to online education and professional development for educators.

Brian Martin is an Instructional Design Consultant at Boise State University's eCampus Center. Since receiving his Master of Science in Instructional Design and Technology at California State University-Chico in 2007, he has helped design online learning experiences for both University of Phoenix and Boise State. Brian specializes in the creation of digital media and is currently researching how AI tools can be used effectively in online teaching and learning.

Alesia Moldavan is an Assistant Professor of Elementary Mathematics and Science Education in the College of Education at Georgia Southern University. Her research interests include equity and asset-based teaching practices that promote cultural awareness, inclusion, and justice-oriented advocacy. Her work in teacher preparation and in-service professional development leverages culturally responsive pedagogy to cultivate STEM identities and agency while challenging social injustices.

Janice Moore Newsum received a bachelor's degree from Rhodes College in Memphis, Tennessee. She earned a master's degree in early childhood education from the University of St. Thomas, Houston, Texas. Janice has an MLIS and her PhD in Library and Information Studies from Florida State University. Dr. Newsum served the students of the Houston Independent School District (HISD) in the Department of Library Services as a school librarian, a Library Services Specialist, and as Manager of the Department of Library Services. She is currently employed as an Associate Professor at the University of Houston Clear Lake. Dr. Newsum has served as the Representative at Large on the Texas Library Association (TLA) Executive Board, as Co-chair of the TLA Diversity and Inclusion Committee, as a member of the AASL/CAEP Coordinating Committee, and as a Counselor for the TLA Library Instruction Round Table. She is the Chair of the Coretta Scott King Book Awards Round Table, and a member of the Florida State University School Advocacy Board. Her research interests include school librarian leadership and administration, library advocacy, diversity in literature, and technology applications.

Trisha Poole (SFHEA) is an inspiring Academic Developer at the University of Southern Queensland, Australia. She has worked in higher education institutions for over 20 years, both nationally and internationally. Through her work and research, she supports educators in enhancing their learning and teaching practice. Her research interests include teacher professional development, online pedagogies, learning design, academic development, educational technologies, higher education, and the scholarship of teaching and learning. Trisha's career objectives are to be innovative in presenting materials that inspire learning and encourage professional development and growth within the higher education realm; to be a leader, an innovator, and an inspiration in education and knowledge acquisition; and to coach, mentor, and support academics in achieving success in their teaching and learning. Trisha most recently won the 2023 ASCILITE Innovation Award for her innovative work in supporting students to provide immediate feedback on their online learning content, activities, and experiences.

R. Bhuvaneswari working as an Assistant Professor of English at Dr. Mahalingam College of Engineering and Technology, Pollachi. To her credit she completed 10 NPTEL / SWAYAM and published few articles in Scopus indexed journals.

Roxanne Russell is a teacher and instructional designer with 20+ years of university-level teaching experience and 15+ years of professional experience with designing, developing, integrating, and evaluating online learning environments in a global context. She now brings her teaching, instructional design, and web development background to helping schools navigate the complexities of technology integration for learning. Roxanne received her M.A. in English from Auburn University and Ph.D. in Instructional Technology and Design from Georgia State University. Her groundbreaking work on the cultural dynamics of the instructional design process is cited in the 2020 edition of the Handbook of Research on Educational Communications and Technology.

Melissa Saligari is an Education-focussed Lecturer in the School of BioSciences at The University of Melbourne, Australia, where she specialises in genetics and foundational biology education. Mel completed her doctoral degree in developmental genetics before undertaking further graduate studies in education and university teaching. Mel is passionate about designing and delivering highly engaging student-focussed learning experiences, and leverages evidence-based pedagogy in combination with discipline-specific knowledge to drive assessment reform and curriculum innovation across undergraduate biology and genetics, particularly in large-cohort contexts. These contributions to teaching have been recognised in Mel's appointment as the Deputy Director of Teaching and Learning for her School, and as a Student Success lead at Faculty level.

Margaret Sass began her academic career earning a bachelor's degree in criminal justice and a master's degree in communication from the University of Nevada, Las Vegas. After graduating, Sass moved to Los Angeles to pursue a career in marketing and public relations in the nonprofit sector. Sass returned to academia in 2004 by entering and graduating from a Southern California law school. After she completed her J.D., she moved to Boise to complete her educational specialist degree and her doctorate in education, curriculum and instruction. She began her teaching career in California in 2004 and has continually taught courses in wills and trusts, hospitality law, business law, communication and multidisciplinary studies. Her main interest is implementing and researching service-learning in higher education curriculum.

Sue Sharpe is an Education Designer at the Australian National University, with a Graduate Certificate in Tertiary Teaching, a Master of Exercise Science (Strength and Conditioning) and 15 years' experience in higher education across professional, academic and management roles. She publishes and presents on communities of practice, third space roles, assessment, and accessibility and inclusion, informed by an extensive history of cross-institutional and transdisciplinary collaboration. Sue is committed to mentoring and supporting others and co-facilitates the Higher Education Research and Development Society of Australasia (HERDSA) Scholarship of Teaching and Learning special interest group. Previously an occupational therapist and associate discipline lead in undergraduate health sciences, Sue has frequently drawn on this background in designing and delivering curriculum for students from equity cohorts and those with non-traditional pathways to study.

Jennifer Z. Sun (FHEA) is a Lecturer in Finance at the University of Sydney, focusing her research on assessment and feedback design that fosters sustainable learning practices to encourage student growth and development. With a dozen years of teaching experience, she is highly innovative in curriculum design and improvement. She is passionate about building meaningful student-staff partnerships, believing these collaborations are essential for creating transformative learning experiences.

Muhammad Usman Tariq has more than 16+ year's experience in industry and academia. He has authored more than 200+ research articles, 110+ case studies, 100+ book chapters and several books other than 4 patents. He is founder and CEO of The Case HQ, a unique repository for courses, narrative and video case studies. He has been working as a consultant and trainer for industries representing six sigma, quality, health and safety, environmental systems, project management, and information security standards. His work has encompassed sectors in aviation, manufacturing, food, hospitality, education, finance, research, software and transportation. He has diverse and significant experience working with accreditation agencies of ABET, ACBSP, AACSB, WASC, CAA, EFQM and NCEAC. Additionally, Dr. Tariq has operational experience in incubators, research labs, government research projects, private sector startups, program creation and management at various industrial and academic levels. He is Certified Higher Education Teacher from Harvard University, USA, Certified Online Educator from HMBSU, Certified Six Sigma Master Black Belt and has been awarded PFHEA, SMIEEE, and CMBE.

Ravi Thirumalaisamy working as an Assistant Professor, Department of Business and Economics, Modern College of Business and Science. To his credit, he published more than 10 articles in Scopus indexed journals.

Benny Thomas is a Professor of Computer Science at CHRIST University. He has a doctoral degree in Education from CHRIST University. His interest areas include whole-person education, educational leadership, and educational administration.

Nymisha Yadati is a doctoral scholar in the School of Education at CHRIST University. She has an MA in Education from Tata Institute of Social Sciences. Her research interests include social-emotional learning and educational psychology.

Jonathan Zaccarini is a Digital Learning Support Specialist at the Mailman School of Public Health. Jonathan's research interest focuses on how students use communication technology to perceive the presence of their peers in online degree programs, which was shaped by his experience as a doctoral student in education and technology at Central Michigan University. Jonathan is an experienced remote educator and is responsible for the formatting, editing, and preparation of online learning content for the Advanced Online MPH at the Mailman School of Public Health.

Index

A

artificial intelligence 36, 37, 41, 51, 59, 178, 182, 183, 192, 210, 211, 216, 217, 218, 223, 253, 323, 324, 325, 326, 329, 330, 333, 335, 339, 341, 342, 344, 345, 346, 347, 348
asynchronous activities 35, 100, 102
autoethnography 119, 120, 127, 140, 144, 149

C

capacity building 135, 137, 140
communication tools 172, 188, 280, 295, 296, 299, 300, 301, 302, 303, 311, 312, 313, 314, 315
community-based learning 323, 324, 325, 326, 341, 342
Community Building 100, 101
community of practice 9, 12, 23, 42, 112, 113, 119, 120, 121, 125, 126, 132, 133, 144, 145, 146, 147, 148, 149, 150, 360, 361, 373
Course Design 3, 7, 11, 23, 26, 33, 40, 75, 76, 178, 184, 185, 191, 192, 195, 198, 199, 200, 201, 206, 208, 212, 213, 214, 225, 240, 303, 311, 324

D

digital classrooms 1, 2, 3, 4, 5, 6, 9, 14, 15
digital pedagogy 101
Digital Tools 1, 2, 3, 5, 6, 8, 11, 12, 15, 35, 56, 67, 69, 99, 100, 101, 103, 104, 106, 107, 108, 113, 278
Distance Education 16, 42, 70, 115, 116, 117, 171, 177, 178, 179, 180, 181, 182, 183, 184, 186, 187, 188, 194, 195, 196, 197, 198, 203, 204, 205, 206, 207, 208, 209, 211, 212, 213, 214, 215, 216, 217, 218, 219, 221, 222, 224, 225, 257, 293, 317, 367

E

Educational Technology 12, 16, 17, 19, 32, 44, 53, 90, 96, 108, 114, 115, 117, 118, 258, 259, 261, 269, 287, 301, 316, 344, 345, 346, 347, 348, 368, 370, 371
elaborative interrogation 227, 234, 235, 236, 237, 240, 251, 258, 262
Emotional Intelligence 16, 151, 153, 154, 155, 156, 157, 165, 166, 167, 169, 170, 173, 174
etymological elaboration 227, 249, 250, 253, 254, 255, 262
evidence-based teaching 3
experiential education 323, 324, 325, 342

F

Facebook 9, 146, 147, 263, 264, 265, 267, 268, 270, 271, 272, 274, 275, 276, 277, 278, 279, 280, 281, 288, 289, 293, 294
Facilitation 102, 138, 146, 167, 177, 178, 179, 180, 182, 183, 199, 203, 217, 218, 224
flipped learning 289

H

Higher Education 12, 16, 17, 18, 24, 43, 44, 45, 53, 54, 67, 71, 72, 73, 76, 90, 92, 95, 115, 116, 119, 120, 121, 122, 123, 125, 128, 130, 132, 136, 145, 146, 148, 149, 150, 171, 173, 175, 178, 182, 183, 185, 209, 219, 221, 224, 258, 261, 285, 286, 287, 288, 289, 290, 291, 295, 303, 313, 314, 316, 317, 324, 326, 328, 329, 341, 344, 345, 347, 353, 354, 355, 356, 357, 361, 364, 365, 367, 368, 369, 370, 371
Higher Education Students 18, 353, 354, 355, 356, 357, 361
Holistic Care 151

I

Inclusivity 5, 23, 47, 48, 50, 52, 53, 54, 69, 72, 97, 328, 329

instructional design 12, 13, 31, 37, 39, 53, 79, 80, 100, 178, 187, 218, 222, 223, 225, 241, 293, 303, 313, 314, 315, 316
Intelligent Agents 51, 70, 73
Interactive Activity 177, 181, 182, 183, 198, 218, 219, 224

L

Learning Communities 2, 16, 21, 29, 31, 39, 40, 47, 48, 71, 75, 88, 99, 107, 117, 125, 297, 304, 315, 321, 368
Learning Engagement 158, 179, 180, 181, 182, 183, 184, 197, 207, 217, 218, 220, 225, 354
Learning Outcomes 1, 2, 4, 5, 6, 10, 14, 15, 21, 22, 25, 27, 29, 30, 31, 37, 38, 39, 41, 47, 48, 52, 57, 96, 107, 108, 109, 110, 111, 113, 114, 152, 153, 158, 160, 165, 175, 179, 240, 265, 272, 290, 294, 326, 327, 329, 330, 333, 341, 342, 373

N

new scholars 122, 126
Nursing Curriculum 154, 156, 176
Nursing Education 151, 152, 153, 154, 155, 156, 157, 158, 159, 160, 161, 162, 163, 164, 165, 166, 167, 168, 171, 172, 173, 175

O

Older People 170, 174, 175
online learning 3, 5, 7, 8, 9, 10, 12, 13, 15, 16, 18, 21, 22, 23, 24, 25, 26, 28, 29, 31, 32, 33, 35, 36, 37, 38, 39, 40, 44, 45, 51, 79, 80, 81, 84, 88, 90, 91, 92, 96, 97, 98, 99, 100, 101, 103, 106, 107, 113, 115, 117, 152, 153, 154, 155, 156, 158, 161, 163, 164, 165, 167, 168, 169, 172, 176, 186, 187, 205, 213, 217, 220, 223, 227, 229, 234, 236, 237, 243, 244, 247, 251, 252, 258, 263, 264, 265, 266, 268, 271, 272, 273, 277, 278, 280, 281, 282, 285, 286, 287, 291, 294, 296, 297, 298, 300, 302, 304, 309, 310, 314, 315, 316, 317, 318, 320, 321, 353, 354, 356, 359, 360, 361, 362, 363, 364, 365, 368, 369, 372, 373
online learning community 33, 80, 164, 296, 310, 320, 373
Online Nursing Education 151, 152, 153, 154, 155, 156, 158, 160, 161, 162, 163, 164, 165, 166, 167, 168
Online Teaching 3, 5, 12, 14, 21, 22, 26, 27, 28, 29, 30, 31, 34, 39, 40, 43, 95, 96, 97, 98, 99, 100, 104, 105, 107, 109, 112, 113, 114, 151, 153, 166, 168, 173, 222, 266, 282, 291, 292, 360, 370, 371

P

pedagogical excellence 1, 3, 6, 14, 15, 48
professional connections 131
professional development 1, 3, 12, 13, 15, 17, 21, 25, 27, 28, 29, 30, 39, 45, 47, 48, 50, 55, 67, 68, 71, 77, 84, 95, 96, 97, 98, 99, 100, 102, 104, 105, 106, 107, 108, 109, 110, 111, 112, 113, 114, 115, 116, 124, 125, 134, 141, 143, 144, 150, 153, 161, 166, 168, 170, 185, 186, 222, 272, 282, 288, 327, 330, 359

S

scholarly identity 120, 124, 150
Scholarship of Teaching and Learning (SoTL) 1, 2, 3, 14, 17, 21, 24, 28, 29, 39, 42, 43, 44, 45, 47, 48, 49, 50, 56, 70, 71, 72, 73, 75, 76, 88, 92, 119, 120, 130, 144, 146, 147, 150, 178, 180, 219, 221, 222, 223, 257, 265, 269, 290, 291, 293, 296, 312, 315, 317, 323, 324, 325, 326, 330, 333, 341, 342, 345, 355, 359, 368, 370, 371
self-explanation 227, 234, 235, 236, 237, 240, 241, 251, 253, 257, 258, 259, 260, 261, 262
self-reference effect 227, 242, 243, 244,

245, 256, 260, 262
Sense of Belonging 51, 52, 54, 59, 60, 62, 67, 70, 101, 127, 129, 132, 135, 136, 139, 141, 142, 153, 155, 159
service-learning 23, 323, 324, 325, 326, 339, 341, 345, 346
Small Teaching Practices 75, 76, 77, 85, 86, 88
Social-emotional Learning 353, 354, 355, 356, 360, 365, 367
social media 9, 145, 146, 153, 159, 265, 267, 268, 270, 271, 272, 273, 276, 278, 279, 285, 287, 288, 289, 290, 291, 292, 293, 294, 296, 297, 307, 308, 332, 336, 337
social presence 80, 84, 153, 295, 296, 297, 298, 299, 300, 301, 302, 303, 305, 306, 307, 308, 309, 310, 311, 312, 313, 315, 316, 317, 318, 319, 360, 362, 373
student engagement 1, 2, 3, 5, 6, 8, 9, 12, 13, 14, 21, 24, 25, 27, 28, 34, 36, 39, 45, 59, 62, 73, 78, 79, 80, 81, 82, 84, 90, 91, 97, 98, 102, 106, 107, 113, 115, 117, 152, 155, 159, 160, 163, 164, 165, 167, 168, 280, 289, 299, 324, 325, 326, 331, 333, 339, 341, 342, 354, 359, 360, 362, 368, 372, 373
Sustainable Development Goals 45, 151, 154, 160, 167, 169, 170, 172, 173, 174
synchronous activities 299

T

Teaching Skills 13, 28
teaching strategies 2, 5, 7, 22, 25, 27, 28, 30, 32, 33, 47, 48, 103, 152, 154, 166, 167, 298, 326, 342, 365
Transdisciplinary Approach 52

V

virtual classrooms 22, 46, 98, 99, 154, 267

Y

Yellowdig 295, 296, 302, 303, 304, 305, 306, 307, 308, 309, 310, 311, 312, 313, 314, 319, 320, 321

Z

Zoom 14, 30, 50, 55, 56, 58, 62, 63, 67, 82, 84, 99, 100, 102, 188, 189, 191, 193, 201, 208, 241, 267, 280, 281, 295, 296, 299, 300, 302, 303, 304, 306, 307, 308, 309, 310, 311, 312, 313, 314, 317, 320, 334, 360, 370, 373

www.ingramcontent.com/pod-product-compliance
Lightning Source LLC
LaVergne TN
LVHW080347011026
849161LV00009B/2218
* 9 7 9 8 3 6 9 3 7 5 9 5 2 *